COMPLETE

Home
Improvement
and Repair

LOWE'S®
Home Improvement Warehouse

Visit our
web site at
www.lowes.com

Editor: Don Vandervort
Project Director: René Klein

Art Director: Harry Kerker
Coordinating Editor: Louise Damberg
Contributing Editors: Jeff Beneke, Carol Crotta,
   Dan Newberry, Marylee MacDonald, Joe Truini
Copy Editor: Patricia Connell
Cover Design: Vasken Guiragossian
Production/Design Coordinator: Dan Nadeau
Page Makeup: John Miller, Marsha Russell, Grace Chang
Illustration: Bill Oetinger, Ng Sun Hong, Jagger Gonzales
Photo Coordinator: Stephen O'Hara
Editorial Assistants: Gabriel Vandervort, Mindy Hokama
Proofreaders: Lisa Black, Lorna Sullivan
Indexer: Rick Hurd

Special thanks to Lisa Anderson, Bridget Biscotti Bradley, Marianne Lipanovich,
   Patricia S. Williams, Applied Graphics Technologies, and Anawalt Lumber

Lowe's Companies, Inc.
Bob Tillman, Chairman/CEO/President

Harry Baldwin, Merchandise Manager
Melissa Birdsong, Director, Trend Design and Forecasting
Gregg Bridgeford, Senior VP, Business Development
Robin Gelly, Marketing Manager
Bob Gfeller, Senior VP, Marketing
Joy Hinson, Merchandising Assistant
Ben Mauceri, VP, Merchandising
Mike Menser, Senior VP, General Merchandise Manager
Angie Milstead, Merchandising Assistant
Gregg Plott, Director, Marketing
Dale Pond, Executive VP, Merchandising
Tim Rains, Merchandiser
Jack Reeves, Director, Creative Services
John Saunders, Merchandise Manager
Terry Shaw, Marketing Administrator

Be sure to visit our web site at www.lowes.com

Cover and Title Page Photography:
Top left: Photo by Noel Barnhurst; styling by Jean Warboy. **Top right:** Photo by Philip Harvey.
Architect: Luther M. Hintz, AIA. Interior Designer: Pamela Pearce Design. **Bottom left:** Photo
by Noel Barnhurst; styling by Vasken Guiragossian; set construction by Peter Gaxham.
Middle right: Photography by Emily Minton, Southern Progress Photo Collection. Residential
Designers: Jeff Blake and Frank Vagnone. **Bottom right:** Steven Mays Photography. Painted
by Justina Jorrin Barnard/Peinture Decorative, New York City.

*Readers note: Almost any do-it-yourself project involves risk of some sort. Your tools, materials, and skills
will vary, as will conditions at your project site. Lowe's Companies, Inc., and the editors of this book
have made every effort to be complete and accurate in the instructions. We will, however, assume no
responsibility or liability for injuries, damages, or losses incurred in the course of your home improvement
or repair projects. Always follow manufacturers' operating instructions in the use of tools, check and
follow your local building codes, and observe all standard safety precautions.*

Foreword

In 1950, Korean War veterans returned to the United States and purchased houses through the Federal Housing Administration (FHA) loan program. These houses were often small, but roomy compared to the cramped apartment living in the city. Additionally these mass-produced homes could be easily tailored to suit the owner's needs, giving homeowners the opportunity to add a significant touch to their homes without going bankrupt. This was the beginning of the do-it-yourself (DIY) trend.

By 1950, two-thirds of all wallpapering and three-fourths of household painting projects in the U.S. were completed by DIYers. Now, nearly 50 years after the first mass flight to the suburbs, learning the skills needed to accomplish do-it-yourself projects has become as common for many home-owners as learning to cook new recipes.

Lowe's, which opened its first store in 1946, has been a part of the do-it-yourself industry since the beginning. Lowe's maintains a level of success because Lowe's cares about its customers and is continually striving to make home improvement easier and more affordable. To ensure that our customers can always find what they need—from saws, to carpet, to advice—every Lowe's store has industry professionals on staff and stocks tens of thousands of products to meet every home care need or desire at everyday low prices.

This book contains instructions on how to complete many of the projects that you ask our associates about everyday and it covers projects for every area of your home, from installing new lighting fixtures to building a new deck. In addition, these how-to projects provide tips and directions for improving your home's décor and design. Lowe's hopes to prepare you for each step of every project—from dreams to reality.

Since joining Lowe's in 1962, I have enjoyed working with thousands of home improvement specialists and I am proud to say their knowledge is found within the covers of this book. It will provide you with the comfort and confidence to tackle many do-it-yourself projects. We have designed this book as a guide; I hope you find it both useful and informative.

Thanks,

Bob Tillman
Lowe's Chairman and CEO

Contents

Contents

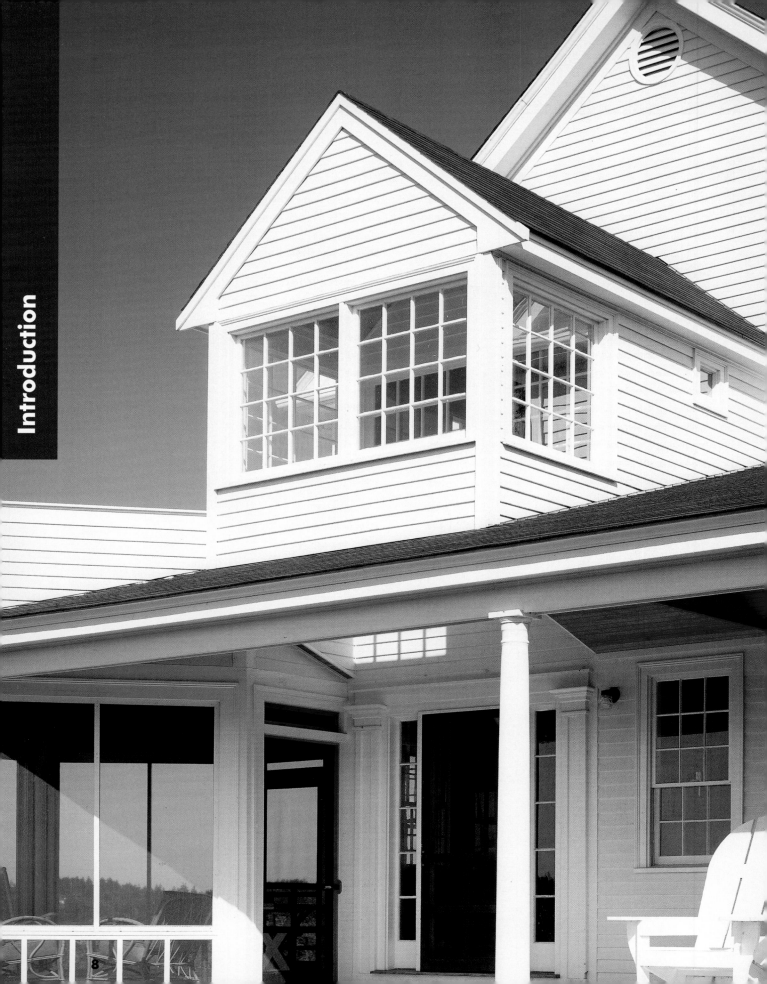

Welcome

Since the dawn of time, people have sought comfort and shelter within the walls of one sort of house or another, from primitive huts to modern marvels. But in contemporary life, a house is far more than simple shelter. It is the heart of family life, the place where we spend time that matters—building family memories, enjoying friends, and recharging our batteries. A house also makes a statement to others about who we are and what's important to us. It can be a point of pride or—if it's in poor repair—a source of embarrassment. For these reasons, and because a house is such an important financial investment, it only makes sense to provide some tender loving care.

Sometimes this is easier said than done, because houses are as complex as the roles they play. A house isn't a single construction, but the sum of many parts. It has structural elements—roof, walls, ceilings, floors, stairs—and essential comfort systems—electrical, plumbing, heating, and cooling. Windows and doors mark the boundary between inside and out, and control passage from one to the other. The yard and garage complete the picture, adding functional spaces to the whole.

When all of a house's parts work smoothly, you hardly notice they exist. On the other hand, when something is out of whack, the problem usually becomes clear in a hurry. A crisis can occur—a burst pipe or leaking roof. Or you may simply grow tired of the lack of light, storage, or living space in certain areas.

With a little know-how and the right tools, you can usually take on repair projects yourself. Major improvements are a little trickier because they require a greater range of skills and knowledge. In some cases, you can break down a major project into manageable parts; in other situations, you may be better off hiring a professional. Understanding where to draw the line between handling a project yourself and getting it done by a pro is key.

This book offers an inside look at your home, examining the anatomy of how its components are crafted and providing a compendium of the tools you'll need to work on them. It takes you step by step through typical projects, from minor fixes to elaborate improvements. The goal is to give you enough information so you can tackle projects yourself or make informed decisions about hiring professionals to do the work for you.

After paging through this book, you may feel ready to build that extra closet you've been needing, or to lay the hardwood flooring you've always wanted in the living room. If you're a do-it-yourself novice, you may be emboldened to stop by Lowe's and get the things you need to try a simple plumbing repair. Or you may just use the information as inspiration to get the job done for you. At the very least, you will understand and maybe have newfound respect for how your house is put together. Ultimately, you'll gain an ability to converse knowledgeably with the professionals you hire and better evaluate the work they do.

Enjoy this journey through your home and the opportunity to give it the care it deserves.

About Improving Your Home

Home improvements accomplish a variety of things. Beyond keeping your home running smoothly, safely, and efficiently, improvements such as wallpapering, tiling a counter, or changing a bathroom fixture can better reflect your family's tastes and lifestyle. Change can be wonderful—the prospect of a new addition or creating the kitchen or master suite of your dreams is infinitely exciting. Such an improvement can also increase the value of your house.

How much are home improvements worth? That depends on a number of factors. In the short term, not all improvements will return your full investment, so you need to do your homework if you're thinking in terms of improving for profit. If you are living in your potential dream house and intend to stay there for a significant period of time—10 years or more—improving your home makes sense.

Avoid "overbuilding" your neighborhood. If your improvements result in a house of far greater value than others in the neighborhood, you may not be able to recoup your costs when you sell. If you love your location and intend to stay put, this factor may not matter to you.

Certain improvements—to landscaping, kitchens, and baths, in particular—show a strong payoff when it comes time to sell your home. Others—that hot tub or billiard room, for instance—do not. Of course, there are benefits to home improvements that have nothing to do with profit. A major one is getting the house you want without having to move.

Be advised that major improvements often mean major, temporary hassles. It can be distressing to have your back wall ripped out, your roof removed, your interior covered with dust, and a slew of workers on your doorstep promptly at 7 every morning (if you are lucky!). Extensive improvements may necessitate moving out for a time—a factor to work into the budget.

Whether or not to improve is a question for the whole family to consider. The more thought, research, and planning you put into it upfront, the more prepared you will be to make the important decisions and guide the project to a happy conclusion.

Factory-made, wood-framed windows were ganged to brighten and visually expand this once-dark kitchen (see insert) with garden views. Fixed panes align above and below tall casement windows in the 8-foot-square window wall. The shapes repeat in an adjacent 3-foot-wide French door.

The Lowe's story began in North Carolina more than 54 years ago, when H. Carl Buchan, part owner of the North Wilkesboro Hardware Company, envisioned creating a chain of hardware stores. At the time, Lowe's was a typical small town hardware store, selling everything from overalls and snuff to wash tubs and work boots. Lowe's even sold horse collars at its first store in downtown North Wilkesboro.

Carl Buchan later bought out his brother-in-law and partner, James Lowe, and—foreseeing the post-World War II building boom—concentrated on selling only hardware, appliances, and hard-to-find building materials. By dealing directly with manufacturers, Lowe's established a lasting reputation for low prices. Sales grew, and additional Lowe's stores opened in neighboring towns throughout western North Carolina.

The company went public in 1961, and began trading on the New York Stock Exchange in 1979 (NYSE: LOW). During this time U.S. housing starts soared, and professional builders became Lowe's loyal customers, accounting for the majority of our business.

In 1982, Lowe's had its first billion-dollar sales year. Our stores then reported serving a new type of customer—do-it-yourself homeowners seeking to improve the value of their properties. Anticipating their needs, Lowe's began to enlarge its stores and expand its merchandise offerings. Today, Lowe's stores average 150,000 square feet—compared with the typical 11,000-square-foot Lowe's stores of the 1980s—and stock practically everything you need to build, improve, repair, beautify, and enjoy your home. Lowe's uses the latest technology to order and maintain stock on the vast array of products to better help you create solutions for your home improvement needs. In over 576 stores in 37 states, record numbers of consumers are turning to Lowe's and, with the help of more than 80,000 employee-owners, are solving their home improvement and repair challenges.

Although times have changed since Lowe's first opened its doors in 1946, our values have not. We remain committed to offering quality home improvement products at the lowest prices while delivering superior customer service.

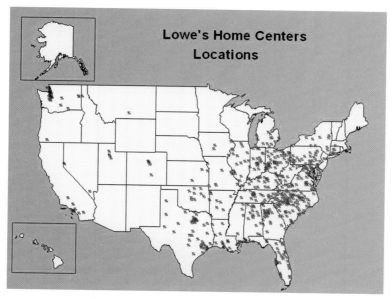

Lowe's: More than 576 stores in 37 states

Planning & Strategy

Although simple repairs are, of necessity, often handled on the spur of the moment, when you contemplate major repairs or improvements, you need to develop a plan of attack. The more carefully researched and considered the plan, the better its chances of success.

A well-mapped plan will serve you, whether you opt to do the work yourself or hire someone to do it for you. It takes a bit of organization, some phoning and legwork, and some quiet study time, but in the end, you and your project will profit from the preparation.

First, clearly delineate your goal, define the extent of the work you want, and establish a budget. Use this figure as the standard against which you'll weigh any bids or cost estimates you receive or independently put together. Consider also the time line you want, from project start to finish date. It may be helpful to collect all this data in a notebook, including prices for materials and services.

Beware of the "while we're at it" syndrome, which can destroy the best intentions for budget and schedule. Remodeling projects can open the floodgate to other improvements and repairs. Unless you have unlimited funds, if you're planning to update the bath, stick to this goal and avoid expanding the project to include other areas or improvements. Likewise, think twice before turning a simple roof repair into a complete reroofing, unless that becomes clearly indicated.

Take some time to research your project. This book is designed to facilitate the process. Carefully read through the appropriate sections, making sure you understand each step. Also look for any other material on the subject and, by all means, seek the advice of the store personnel at Lowe's. Such background study is critical, since one of the most important parts of your planning is determining whether you will do the work yourself or hire a professional.

Should You Do It Yourself?

Once you understand what will be involved in getting the job done, give honest thought to your time, your tools, and your talents.

YOUR TIME When it comes to home repairs or improvements, most people tend to undervalue their time enormously. You may enjoy the hands-on experience and developing some new skills that come with it, as well as the sense of pride and accomplishment from a job well done. But your time has value, too. Consider carefully whether your investment in time is worth the cost savings. Remember that you probably will be doing the work nights and weekends, which also means it will take longer to complete than if you have a professional do it.

YOUR TOOLS Even if you have the time and talent to do a particular job, do you have all the necessary tools? At the beginning of most chapters in this book, you'll find information on the tools necessary to complete the various step-by-step repairs and improvements outlined in the chapter. Certain jobs, such as laying tile, call for many specialized tools that aren't commonly needed for other household tasks. Others, particularly the carpentry jobs, call for basic tools that are discussed on pages 18–27.

If you lack the necessary tools for your project, everything from a hammer to a jackhammer is usually available for rental. If there are tools you think you may need in the future, it's probably worth the investment to buy them. Make a list of the tools you need and head over to Lowe's, where you know you can get quality tools at the best prices. Whether you decide to buy or rent, factor these costs into your budget, because they can raise the

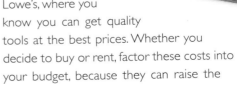

price tag significantly. A professional's bid might not end up looking so high after all.

If the tools are unfamiliar to you, be sure to have someone instruct you carefully in their safe use. Spend some time practicing on scrap pieces before you put them to use on actual materials. If your results aren't what you expected—your mitered corners are looking like boomerangs, or your tile turns into mosaic when you try to cut it—either practice until you achieve the desired result or reconsider having a professional do the work.

YOUR TALENT Beyond the issues of your time and your tools, be realistic about your talent—your experience and skill level—when considering doing the job yourself. Taking on a project you haven't tried before is an exciting challenge and an opportunity for growth. If you have an aptitude for this type of work, you may be able to step up to the plate easily. Only you can judge whether a project is the next logical step in your construction education or too big a leap for your abilities.

Another factor to consider is how visible the results of your work will be. The more visible, the greater the stakes. Refinishing a hardwood floor, for example, can be tricky, and mistakes caused by problems operating a power sander can be expensive to remedy. Painting a room, on the other hand, is virtually risk-free. If the paint comes out streaky or blotchy, or the absolute worst shade of green, you can simply repaint—and paint is relatively cheap. The more permanent and important the appearance of a repair or improvement, the more important it may be to consider a professional doing the job.

Also think about how strenuous the job may be. Concrete work, or anything involving digging foundations or lifting heavy beams, is physically very demanding. Professionals who deal in these materials every day have built up the strength and stamina to accomplish the work. Even if you are in good health and reasonably fit, keep in mind that heavy work does take a physical toll.

In addition, evaluate potential hazards and risks of doing a project yourself. You may be capable of patching the roof, but think twice about it if your roof pitch is so steep that scaling it poses a danger.

Doing Part of the Work

Sometimes a project may just seem too intriguing to pass up, but you realize that doing all of it is either too time-consuming or beyond your skill level. What parts of the job can you do yourself and which can you hand off to a professional? You could, for example, install bathroom cabinetry yourself but have a plumber hook up the pipes and drains. An electrician could do the rough wiring, but you could put in the switches and fixtures. Have a carpenter build your new closet while you construct the closet organizer. Just observing a professional contribute to a job you're working on is a good way to learn some new techniques.

Putting together an effective plan in this manner is the best way to keep control of your project, save on costs, and guarantee a satisfying result.

TIPS FOR DO-IT-YOURSELFERS

If you decide to do a repair project yourself, consider these helpful tips.

■ Take some close-up and detail photographs (digital or instant cameras are ideal) of anything you decide to take apart, for reference.

■ Label parts, either numerically or alphabetically, in the order of removal, so re-assembly will be easy.

■ If you know which part is defective, be sure to take it with you when you go to your home improvement center so you can buy the correct replacement.

Working with Pros

Even if you've determined that you want to hire a professional to accomplish your project, your work isn't over—which is one of the purposes of this book. Knowing how to choose your professional well—someone experienced, licensed, and bonded—will reward you with a solid and safely completed job.

Finding the Right Pro for the Job

For reliable repair people and general contractors, nothing is better than referrals from people you know and trust. In addition to asking about the quality of the work itself, ask about the person's responsiveness and punctuality, the accuracy of the cost and time estimates, and how clean the area was left each day. A wide variety of installation and remodeling services are available through your Lowe's store, and these will line you up with some of the best subcontractors in your area. However, real estate brokers and

your insurance company can also offer referrals, and careful scrutiny of the telephone directory can help steer you in the right direction. Once you have found someone you like, be sure to keep a careful log of the contact numbers. Establishing a relationship with a plumber, an electrician, and other tradespeople can pay dividends when pipes burst or power fails on a Sunday morning.

Depending on the size of the job, you may want to solicit several bids. Have candidates tender their bids in writing, and request a breakdown of time, hourly rates, materials costs, and start and finish dates. Ask how much experience they've had with similar projects and how long they've been in the business.

Also ask what type of guarantee they provide for their work—specifically, if the same problem occurs within a reasonable time after the repair or construction, will they return without charge to correct it? Educate yourself through this book and other reference material about your project so that you will understand what they propose to do and why. When they arrive for the job, don't be shy about occasionally looking over their shoulders and asking any questions, but don't become a pest or hindrance. Respect the skills and expertise of the people you choose unless you find reason to take issue with their work.

Hiring Contractors for Major Work

If you are planning a major improvement such as an addition, kitchen remodel, or any other job that requires multiple technical skills, you may want to hire a general contractor. A general contractor negotiates a contract with you and then uses his or her own crew and/or hires subcontractors—individual specialists such as plumbers, concrete workers, carpenters, electricians, and painters—to get the work done. Considering what's at stake with any major improvement, solicit more than three bids, and spend some time interviewing each contractor in person. Compatibility is as important as skills and experience, since you will have a close relationship with this person for the life of your project.

The key facts to find out are:

▦ Do they have experience with jobs such as yours, and can they provide you with a list of references?

▦ Do they have their own crew or do they rely solely on subcontractors?

▦ How many other jobs will they be working on simultaneous with yours, and how available are their various subcontractors?

▦ When are they available to start your project, and how long do they estimate it will take?

▦ Are they licensed and insured, and what amount of liability insurance do they carry (obtain a copy of the insurance policy)?

▦ Will they be working or supervising on-site during the work, and for how much time each day?

Be sure to give all of your contractor candidates identical sets of plans. Review the plans with them and be honest about your expectations. They, in turn, should be honest with you about the realities of budget, time, and potential disruption to your homestead. Encourage each candidate to suggest cost-saving ideas and point out the plans' high-cost elements, such as custom doors or windows, and cabinetry. Request a bid broken out by task or technical expertise, such as plumbing, framing, and electrical, and agree on a date for the bid's submission. Find out how long the bid will be valid, which should be at least 30 days.

When the bids come in, don't make price your only criterion for selection. Reliability, quality of work, and on-time performance are not only critical but valuable. These factors are best determined by interviews with the contractor's references, so do not shortchange this process. If possible, visit their other projects, examine the workmanship, and ask questions about work practices, punctuality, and cleanliness—these may seem minor before the project begins, but they will become big issues when you are in the throes of construction.

A contractor may propose a "time and materials" contract instead of a fixed-price contract. "Time and materials" means that the contractor charges in fees a percentage of the cost of materials and labor. While this sounds enticing, it can become a budget booby trap. Under this form of contract, the homeowner bears the risk of changing costs in materials such as lumber, drywall, doors, and windows, and is playing roulette with the amount of time a particular job will take. If, for example, something unforeseen comes up, such as unusual drainage problems or a large granite slab where the foundation should go, the homeowner bears the cost of the additional time and labor. Generally, a fixed-price contract protects you from these cost increases.

(continued on page 16)

(continued from page 15)

GET IT IN WRITING When you choose your general contractor, get everything in writing. Before signing the contract, be sure that it includes start and completion dates, and if there are any amendments, have both of you initial them. Make sure the contract includes a payment schedule that is tied to completion of work at varying stages. Do not agree to pay more than one-third up front, and provide in the contract that the final payment is tendered only upon satisfactory completion of the work. Make the final payment a substantial one, since a thousand dollars or two may not be enough to compel a contractor to finalize small details. You may want to consider including a penalty clause for delayed completion and a bonus clause for early completion, if time is a factor.

Provide for a warranty of at least one year on the work. Most important, make sure that all subcontractor liens are waived, since, in some states, subcontractors can place a lien on your property if they are not paid by the general contractor. Check with your local building department, or a qualified real estate attorney, if you have questions about this or any other provision of the proposed contract.

IF PROBLEMS ARISE After the contract is signed and some or all of the work has taken place, you can lodge a formal complaint with your local or state licensing board and request a hearing or arbitration if problems arise. If the professional is found liable, his or her license can be revoked. You can also sue, either in small claims or a higher court depending on the amount of money at stake. Unless there is a lawyer in the family, a lawsuit can be expensive, so consider including an arbitration clause in your contract.

 FREE IN-STORE SERVICES

Lowe's home improvement centers have Installed Sales programs for everything from carpet and flooring to kitchen cabinets, plumbing fixtures, appliances, and garage doors. The knowledgeable people who staff these departments can assist you with planning for many types of home improvement projects. Be sure to look into these services—they can save you a great deal of time and expense.

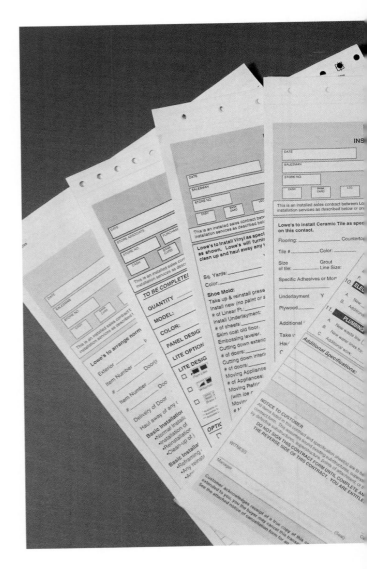

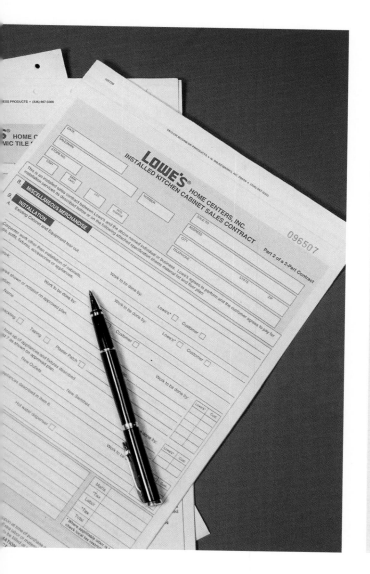

If you are planning a major remodel, you'll need to consider whether an architect or designer is in order, or if a contractor alone will do.

Generally, if you are planning to do any structural work that involves building or removing walls, you'll want to call on an architect. Architects are generally the most pricey of the three, but they can draw plans acceptable to building department officials, send out bids, help you select a contractor, and supervise the contractor's work to ensure that your plans and time schedule are met. Architects must be licensed, and some even double as contractors.

Designers can do much of the above, but if stress calculations need to be made, designers need to engage state-licensed engineers to design the structure and sign the working drawings. Most states do not require designers to be licensed.

Contractors can also be skilled draftspeople, able to draw working plans acceptable to building department officials, however they are limited in the same way that designers are.

Many architects are members of the American Institute of Architects (AIA), and many designers belong to the American Institute of Building Designers (AIBD). Certain home areas, such as kitchens and baths, have their own associations. Each association has a code of ethics and sponsors continuing programs to inform their members about the latest building materials and techniques.

Architects and designers may charge for time spent in an exploratory interview, while a contractor may simply charge a fee or percentage of the project. For plans, you'll probably be charged on an hourly basis. Architects and designers also often will agree to actively supervise construction, usually for either an hourly or a set fee based on a percentage of the project. Take advantage of this offer. With any of these professionals, make sure they describe the scope of their services in writing before any work is performed.

Using Basic Tools

If you intend to tackle some or all of your own home improvements and repairs, you'll need a fairly complete assortment of tools—and the know-how to use them properly. Having the right tool makes a big difference in the relative difficulty of a task, and often affects the quality of the final result.

As you investigate this book's chapters, you'll discover each offers a glimpse of the tools needed for repairs and improvements. Here, and on the next few pages, you'll find helpful information about how to properly use conventional—and a few somewhat specialized—tools.

Working Safely

Here are a few important rules and practices to ensure the safe use of tools and materials:

SAFE WORKPLACE Work in a well-lit, uncluttered area. Keep tools and materials organized. Plan your set-up carefully before you begin work. Whenever possible, avoid working with a partner in cramped quarters; you can too easily be injured by the swing of another's hammer, or by a wrecking bar dropped from above. Clean up as you go, preventing an accumulation of bent nails or wood scraps, or spills that might cause uncertain footing.

TOXIC MATERIALS Some of the materials you encounter in improvements and repairs can be dangerous to your health: wood preservatives; oil-based enamel, varnish, and lacquer—and their solvents; adhesives (especially resorcinol, epoxy, and contact cement); insulation (asbestos fibers and urea formaldehyde); and even sawdust or the dust particles from wallboard joint compound. Read all the precautions on product labels and follow them exactly. Ventilate the workplace adequately when needed, and clean up the area frequently.

CLOTHING & GEAR Wear sturdy clothing and the appropriate safety gear to avoid contact with dangerous materials (see illustration on this page). Always wear safety glasses when using power tools or tools that involve striking an object—such as when using a hammer and chisel.

POWER TOOL SAFETY Although power tools offer the potential for injury, these tools can be quite safe if they are handled with respect, and if you adopt some basic safety habits. Read the owner's manual carefully before using the tool to understand its capabilities and limitations. Be absolutely certain to unplug any tool before servicing or adjusting it, and after you've finished using it. Check that any safety devices, such as guards on the tool, are in good working order. Follow the manufacturer's specifications to clean and lubricate power tools, and make sure all blades and bits are sharp and undamaged.

 HELPFUL SAFETY GEAR

Safety glasses will protect your eyes when operating power tools and high-impact hand tools. A hard hat is important when working with others in tight quarters or where something could fall on you. Earmuff protectors or earplugs will protect your ears from permanent damage that can be caused by loud tools. A respirator is important when you're in danger of breathing harmful vapors, dust, or fibers; be sure to get one that is approved for the hazardous material. All-leather or leather-reinforced gloves will protect your hands; wear rubber gloves when handling caustic materials.

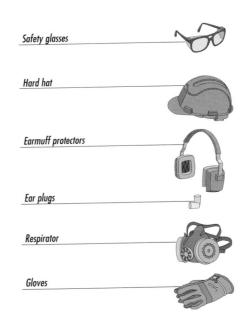

Safety glasses

Hard hat

Earmuff protectors

Ear plugs

Respirator

Gloves

SAFETY WITH ELECTRICITY Unless it's double-insulated, a power tool should be properly grounded. Power tools that are neither grounded nor double-insulated can give a serious—and even fatal—shock. Double-insulated tools are the best defense against a questionable electrical source. These tools contain a built-in second barrier of protective insulation; they are clearly marked and should not be grounded (they'll have two-prong plugs only). If you are working in a damp area or outdoors, a ground-fault circuit interrupter (GFCI or GFI)—either the portable type or built into the outlet—is an essential piece of equipment.

Use the shortest extension cord you can for the job. A very long cord can overheat, creating a fire hazard. Furthermore, the longer the cord, the less amperage it will deliver, which translates into less power for the tool's motor. The most important factor to consider is the maximum amp load your extension cord will need to carry. Look for the nameplate on the tool, which contains its amperage requirement. Add up the requirements of all the tools you plan to plug into the cord at the same time and make sure it has an amp capacity that equals or exceeds this sum.

Measuring & Marking

The ability to accurately measure, lay out, and mark are skills that are critical to the start of any home project. While you can buy many tools for these vital preliminary steps, you only need a few for basic repairs and improvements. A tape measure, a combination square, and a pencil will see you through many tasks; buy more specialized tools, such as a reel tape, carpenter's square, or chalk line as you need them.

Buying high-quality tools will pay off in the long run, since the ultimate quality of nearly every project depends on precise dimensions. Keep in mind the old rule "Measure twice, cut once." Develop careful work habits right from the start and you'll be satisfied with the results.

 MEASURING TOOLS

A 16- or 25-foot tape measure is sufficient for most jobs, but for laying out distances beyond 25 feet, choose a reel tape. The tape measure's end hook should be loosely riveted to adjust for precise "inside" and "outside" readings.

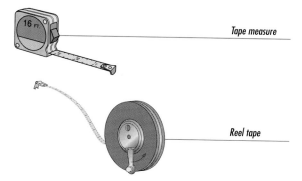

Tape measure

Reel tape

MEASURING TOOLS To measure distances of a foot or less, you can get by with a combination square, but for accurate gauging of greater distances, a tape measure is generally the answer; in fact, the flexible steel tape measure is critically important to many jobs.

(continued on page 20)

 MEASURING ACCURATELY

To make an accurate measurement, your tape measure must be parallel to the material you're measuring. To make an inside measurement, press the end hook against the vertical inside surface. To avoid possible inaccuracies from including the length of the case, measure partway (to an even inch mark), then make a second measurement and add it to the first.

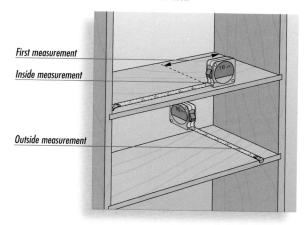

First measurement

Inside measurement

Outside measurement

Using Basic Tools

(continued from page 19)

LAYOUT TOOLS The main tools for laying out cutting or installation lines are squares. Most indicate 90-degree angles; some, in addition, indicate 45-degree miter angles.

To lay out a curve, your best tool is a French or flexible curve; both are available at woodworking or drafting supply stores.

Any layout tool must be true, or your most careful work will be wasted. To test a square, hold the body tight against the edge of a perfectly straight board and draw a line along the blade. Then flop the square over and draw another line; both lines should match exactly.

 LAYOUT TOOLS

Shown here are typical squares and a French curve used for laying out various types of projects.

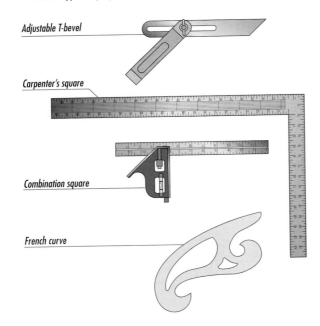

Adjustable T-bevel

Carpenter's square

Combination square

French curve

 USING A CARPENTER'S SQUARE

To mark a straight line across a board, panel, or surface, hold the square's tongue against one edge and mark along the body as shown. Lay out accurate 45-degree angles by matching the inch marks on both body and tongue. Many squares are also embossed with formulas for laying out roof rafters and stairs.

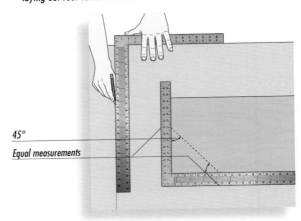

45°
Equal measurements

 USING A COMBINATION SQUARE

A combination square is wonderfully versatile. Depending upon how you adjust the body on the blade, it can handle any of many tasks, as shown here.

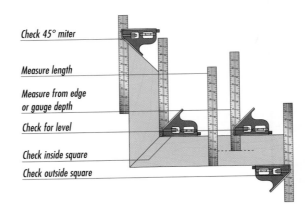

Check 45° miter

Measure length

Measure from edge or gauge depth

Check for level

Check inside square

Check outside square

MARKING TOOLS Not surprisingly, the trusty pencil serves as your basic marking tool. But don't use a lead so soft that it needs constant resharpening. Flat-sided carpenter's pencils are also handy, although some people may find they're awkward for scribing irregular lines or curves.

Mark off distances with a sharp pencil, then carefully recheck each one. Many carpenters find that a V mark or "caret" is more effective than a straight line to mark a point on the edge of a board. When you draw a cutting line, tilt the pencil so that the lead lies flush against the layout tool.

A chalk line is a long cord wound onto a spool within a case that's filled with colored chalk. It's ideal for both marking long cutting lines on sheet materials and for laying out reference lines on a wall, ceiling, or floor. Its end hook allows you to work alone.

 MARKING TOOLS

For various marking jobs, you'll need a good pencil, a compass, and a chalk line. The type of chalk line with a pointed case can do double-duty as a plumb bob.

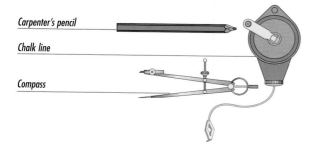

Carpenter's pencil

Chalk line

Compass

To mark a line with a chalk line, pull the chalk-covered cord from the case and stretch it taut between two points. Then, toward one end, lift the cord and release quickly, so that it snaps down sharply, leaving a long, straight line of chalk. For long lines over uneven surfaces, fasten the cord at one end, have a helper hold down the center of the string, and snap from both sides of the center.

Gauging Level & Plumb

An ongoing concern in many improvement projects is keeping all horizontal surfaces level and all vertical surfaces plumb. Problems with ill-fitting windows, doors, and finish work can often be traced back to inaccurate leveling at an earlier stage.

 HELPFUL LEVELING TOOLS

A carpenter's level accurately indicates both level and plumb. Standard length is 24 inches, but you can get other sizes. A short torpedo level, typically 9 inches long, is handy for tight spots. A line level hooks onto a taut string; level the string, then use it for reference when laying out decking or other large jobs. A plumb bob hangs from a string to gauge plumb by gravity.

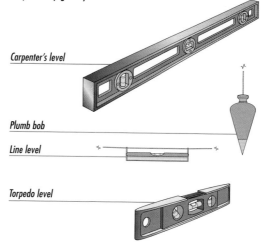

Carpenter's level

Plumb bob

Line level

Torpedo level

As a rule, the longer the level, the more accurate the reading. You can increase the accuracy of a carpenter's level for long spans by placing it on a long, straight board. Test a level before using it by placing it on a surface that you've determined to be perfectly flat, then turning the instrument around and rechecking it on the other edge. The readings in each case should be identical.

To test a horizontal surface for level, place the tool on the surface; when the air bubble in the liquid enclosed in the center glass tubing lines up exactly between the two marks, you know the surface is level. When the level is held vertically, the tubes near each end indicate plumb.

(continued on page 22)

Using Basic Tools

(continued from page 21)

To use a plumb bob, maneuver the weight from above as close to the floor as possible without touching it. Use either your overhead or floor point as a reference. You'll find it helps to have a partner at the other end. Once the weight stops swinging, line up and mark the other point.

Cutting with Handsaws

In any carpentry-related repair or improvement, you'll need to start with accurate, consistent sawing, which is essential to strong, square joints and assembly. Along with precise measuring, careful cutting is the key to success.

Power saws aren't necessary; you could build an entire house with a crosscut saw, perhaps supplemented by a compass saw. And there are times when only the handsaw will do—spots without electricity or where a power saw might be dangerous. As a rule, though, power saws perform much faster and more accurately, once you've had some practice using one.

Saws differ in shape, blade size, and the position and number of teeth along the blade. Both tooth size and number of teeth per inch (tpi) are indicated by the term "point." An 8-point saw has only 7 teeth per inch, since the points at both ends of that inch are included. In general, you'll get a rougher but faster cut with fewer teeth; many teeth means a smooth but slower cut.

The degree to which the teeth are set, or bent outward, determines the thickness of the cut. Saw teeth are set to produce a cut wider than the blade; otherwise, the saw would bind in the kerf, or saw cut. The wider the set, the faster and rougher the cut will be; a smaller tooth set gives a fine kerf.

A basic collection of handsaws is illustrated on this page.

 HANDSAWS

A crosscut saw is designed to cut across wood grain and makes a good all-purpose tool. A backsaw, with its straight, rigid backbone, is used with a miter box for fine cuts—such as when trimming moldings. A compass saw makes cutouts and general curves. A coping saw makes fine, accurate cuts and will cut very tight curves, though it's limited to small stock because of the reach of its frame. The hacksaw and mini-hacksaw are used for cutting metal.

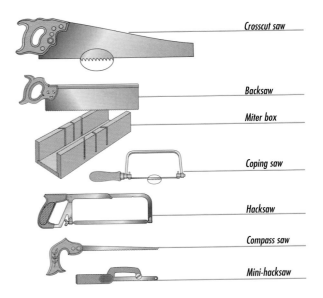

Crosscut saw

Backsaw

Miter box

Coping saw

Hacksaw

Compass saw

Mini-hacksaw

CROSSCUT SAW A good multi-purpose handsaw is the crosscut saw with a 26-inch blade. When you choose a crosscut saw, be sure the handle feels comfortable in your hand. Sight down the back of the saw blade to make sure it's straight. Flex the tip; it should bounce back to the center position. Look for a "taper ground" saw; the blade's thickness tapers toward the back and the tip, preventing the saw from binding in the kerf and allowing a narrower set to the teeth. Premium saws are also "skew-backed," meaning the back is slightly cut away to improve balance and minimize weight, although this makes the saw impractical for heavy-duty work. High-quality steel, though more costly, will flex better and stay sharp much longer than lower grades. When saw teeth go dull, they must be leveled and filed and (after long, hard use) reset. You can do this yourself or take the saw to a professional sharpener.

COPING SAW This saw, with its thin, wiry blade strung taut within a small, rectangular frame, is very handy for cutting curves or making cutouts near an edge. Clamp the material to a sawhorse or vise for better control. For a cutout, first drill a pilot hole the size of the blade width, slip the blade through this hole and then reattach it to the frame. You can install the blade with the teeth pointed away from the handle to cut on the push stroke, or toward the handle to cut on the pull stroke.

BACKSAW & MITER BOX Unlike the blade of the crosscut saw, the backsaw's blade is held parallel to the stock. Commonly used with a miter box, backsaws are primarily for precise cutting—the miter box holds the blade at a 90-degree or 45-degree angle.

Cutting with Power Saws

The circular saw and saber saw, or jigsaw, are the basic power saws. The circular saw makes straight cuts, while the saber saw's specialty is curves and cutouts. Wear eye protection when working with either tool.

PORTABLE CIRCULAR SAW This saw allows you to make straight crosscuts much faster than with a handsaw, and is unparalleled for ripping along the lengths of boards. Common sizes are from 5½ to 8¼ inches; this refers to the largest diameter of blade that fits the saw's arbor (axle). The most common 7¼-inch model will go through surfaced 2-by framing lumber at any angle between 45 degrees and 90 degrees. Look for a model rated at between 8 and 12 amps.

(continued on page 24)

USING A CROSSCUT SAW

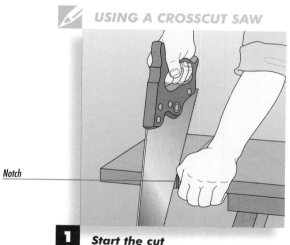

Notch

1 Start the cut
Hold the saw upright and slowly draw the blade up several times to cut a notch on the board's edge. At first, guide the blade with your thumb knuckle. Be sure to allow for the width of the saw blade.

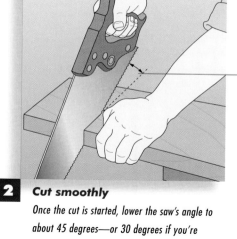

45°

2 Cut smoothly
Once the cut is started, lower the saw's angle to about 45 degrees—or 30 degrees if you're cutting plywood—and make smooth, full strokes. Sight down the back of the saw from overhead to align it; your forearm and shoulder must remain lined up with the blade. Whenever the blade veers from the line, twist the handle slightly to the opposite side to bring it back.

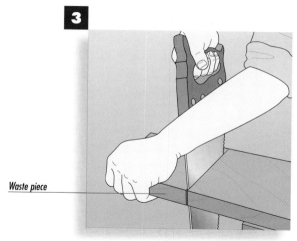

Waste piece

Finish the cut
Toward the end of the cut, reach around the saw and support the waste piece with your free hand. Bring the saw to a vertical position once more and make the last strokes slowly to avoid breaking off—and splintering—the board.

Using Basic Tools

 CUTTING STRAIGHT

Ripping fence

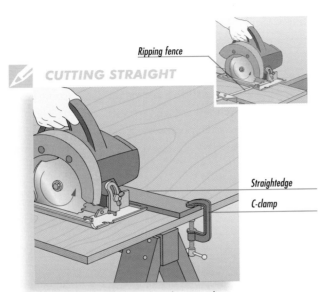

Straightedge

C-clamp

To cut straight with a power circular saw, either use the ripping fence that comes with the saw, as shown in the detail, or fasten a straightedge to the surface you're cutting. For the latter approach, measure from the saw's base plate to the blade and secure the guide that distance from your cutting line.

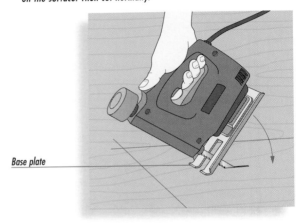 **MAKING A CUTOUT**

Either drill a hole for the saber saw's blade in the waste area, or, in a thin, soft material, start by "plunge cutting" with a rough-cutting blade. Rock the saw forward onto the front edge of the base plate until the blade is free at its full extension. Turn on the saw and, with the nose of its base planted solidly, lower it slowly until the base sits flat on the surface. Then cut normally.

Base plate

Shaping Wood

Once sawn, the stock for many projects still needs to be cut, shaped, or smoothed before being fastened; this is where the shaping tools come into play.

(continued from page 23)

SABER SAW The saber saw's high-speed motor drives one of many types of blades in an up-and-down (reciprocating) motion; the blade on an orbital model goes forward and up, then back on the downstroke, for faster cuts. The tool excels at cutting curves, circles, and cutouts in a variety of materials, but you can also use it for straight cutting or beveling. Consider a variable-speed model for greater control on tight curves or different materials.

Choose the right blade for the job. Blades with 4 to 7 teeth per inch (tpi) are designed for rough, rapid cuts in wood. Fine finish work, tight curves, and scrollwork require blades in the 10 to 20 tpi range. For thick metals, use 14 to 18 tpi blades; thin metals demand even finer teeth (24 to 32 tpi). Specialty blades also are available to cut other materials.

PLANES Turn to planes—either bench or block type—to smooth surfaces, square boards, and make fine joint adjustments. Bench planes smooth and square in line with the grain. Three main types are the jointer plane (about 22 inches long), the versatile and popular jack plane (14 inches long), and the smoothing plane ($9\,^3/_4$ inches long). The shorter block plane—typically 6 inches long—smooths end grain and cuts bevels. To get the most from planes, keep them sharp and adjusted.

CHISELS If kept sharp, chisels perform a variety of tasks—rough shaping of framing members, paring notches and grooves, and cutting mortises for door hinges and hardware.

RASPS & FILES These should only be used when planes or sanding tools aren't suitable, such as on contours or cutouts. Files can handle metal as well, and perforated rasps will shape several materials. Tooth pattern, tooth coarseness, length (a longer tool has larger teeth), and shape determine performance. Common shapes include flat, half-round, and round. For general-purpose work, choose the half-round style.

 WOOD SHAPING TOOLS

Planes, chisels, rasps, and files are used to help shape wood; certain types of files can also be used on metals.

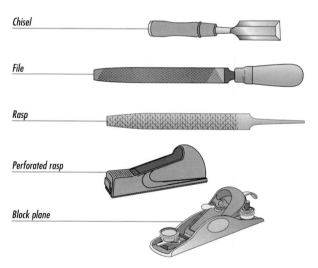

Chisel

File

Rasp

Perforated rasp

Block plane

Drilling Holes

Drilling holes is a necessary task in many different types of repairs and improvements. You need to drill holes for screws, bolts, dowels, locksets, hinges, masonry fasteners, wires, pipes, and more. Electric drills are used for driving screws and other jobs.

An electric drill is classified by the biggest bit shank that can be accommodated in its chuck (jaws), most commonly $^1/_4$-inch, $^3/_8$-inch, and $^1/_2$-inch. The bigger the chuck size, the higher the power output, or torque. Electric drills are rated light, medium, and heavy-duty. A heavy-duty model is only needed if you'll be using it daily or for long, uninterrupted sessions. In addition to single-speed drills, there are vari-

 POWER DRILL

The portable electric drill has virtually replaced its manual counterparts. Plug-in drills are both powerful and reliable; a cordless model, with its rechargeable battery, is handy when you're working far from electrical power.

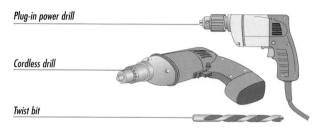

Plug-in power drill

Cordless drill

Twist bit

Combination bit

able-speed models that allow you to use the appropriate speed for the job—very handy when starting holes, drilling metals, or driving screws. Reversible gears are good for removing screws and stuck bits. For most jobs, the $^3/_8$-inch variable-speed drill is your best bet; it can handle a wide range of bits and accessories. If you're drilling large holes in masonry, you'll need a $^1/_2$-inch drill or a hammer drill; both can be rented.

Tool catalogs and hardware stores are brimming with special drill bits, guides, and accessories for electric drills.

When operating an electric drill, clamp down the materials whenever possible beforehand, particularly when using a $^3/_8$- or $^1/_2$-inch drill. Wear safety goggles, especially when drilling masonry or metal. If your drill allows, match the speed to the job, using the highest speeds for small bits or soft woods, and slower speeds for large bits when drilling hard woods or metals.

Don't apply much pressure when you're drilling, and don't turn off the motor until you've removed the bit from the material. If you're boring large holes in hard woods or metal—especially with oversize twist bits—first make a smaller pilot hole. Back the bit out occasionally to cool it and clear out the waste.

(continued on page 26)

Using Basic Tools

(continued from page 25)

When drilling tough metal, lubricate it with cutting oil as you go. If you want to stop at a certain depth, buy a stop collar designed for the purpose, use a pilot bit, or wrap tape around the bit at the correct depth to serve as a visual guide.

Fastening

The art of fastening, like measuring and cutting, is fundamental to repair and improvement work. You should become familiar with the tools that make it possible; hammers and screwdrivers are the most basic. You'll also need wrenches and pliers for bolts and lag screws.

HAMMERS Everyone knows what the claw hammer looks like, but not all are aware that differences in the tool's shape, weight, and head determine the one to pick for any specific project. Carpenters occasionally turn to other tools for driving nails or pounding stubborn joints together; the roofer's hatchet and the mallet are two examples.

Hammer faces may be either flat or slightly convex. The convex, or bell-faced, type allows you to drive a nail flush without marring the wood's surface. Mesh-type faces are available for rough framing work—the mesh pattern keeps the face from glancing off large nail heads, and can help guide the nails. Don't use this face for finish work, since the pattern will imprint the surface.

Head weights range from 7 to 28 ounces. Pick a weight that's comfortable but not too light: Your arm may actually tire sooner swinging a light hammer for heavy work than it would wielding a heavier hammer.

Nearly all home projects call for some type of fastening—so you'll need a variety of fastening tools for improvements and repairs. Be sure to have a claw hammer, a variety of screwdrivers—including screw tips that fit into a drill—a pair of pliers, and an adjustable wrench at the very minimum. A nailset is helpful for recessing nails from view when woodworking.

FASTENING TOOLS

Nearly all home projects call for some type of fastening—so you'll need a variety of fastening tools for improvements and repairs. Be sure to have a claw hammer, a variety of screwdrivers—including screw tips that fit into a drill—a pair of pliers, and an adjustable wrench at the very minimum. A nailset is helpful for recessing finishing nails from view.

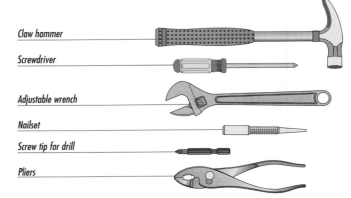

Claw hammer
Screwdriver
Adjustable wrench
Nailset
Screw tip for drill
Pliers

HAMMERING A NAIL

To start a nail, hold it just below the head between your thumb and forefinger, and give it a few light taps with the hammer. Once the nail is started, remove your fingers and swing more fully, with a fluid stroke that combines wrist, arm, and shoulder action as shown here. When the hammer's face strikes the nail, the handle should be perpendicular to the nail's shank.

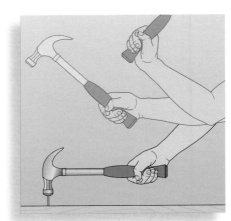

TOENAILING

When you can't nail through the face of one board into the end of another, you must drive nails at an angle—called toenailing—as shown. Drive the nails from both sides at about a 30-degree angle from the vertical; stagger the nails so they won't hit one another.

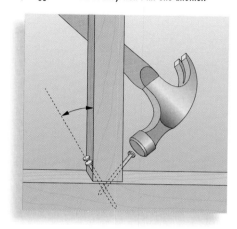

WRENCHES You may be surprised how often you'll reach for a wrench on a repair job—to drive lag screws, tighten bolts and nuts, or remove existing structures such as cabinets and built-ins. An adjustable wrench is a good multi-purpose choice.

SCREWDRIVERS The screwdriver vies with the hammer as the most frequently employed tool in a do-it-yourselfer's collection. When you're choosing a screwdriver, keep in mind the three main types: standard, Phillips, and square drive. The screwdriver tip must fit the screw exactly; an ill-fitting tip may lead to a burred screw head or gouged work surface. A long screwdriver lets you apply more torque than does a shorter one, but the long shank may not leave you room to maneuver. When buying a large, all-purpose screwdriver, choose one with a square shank; you can fit a wrench onto it to apply extra leverage to stubborn screws. Don't forget that you can also install a screwdriver bit in a variable-speed electric drill.

PULLING NAILS

Cat's paw

Nail

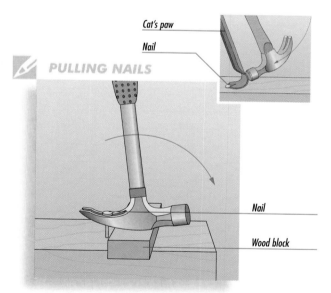

Nail

Wood block

To pull a tough nail, place your hammer on top of a scrap block for more leverage. Note: Wooden-handled hammers may not be strong enough for this technique. To start the process of pulling a nail, you can drive a cat's paw or prybar underneath the nail head as shown in the detail, then pry it up. Because this will damage the wood's surface, it's only recommended during rough construction or demolition.

DRILLING A PILOT HOLE

Screws require pilot holes in all but the softest materials. (Pilot holes are unnecessary if you're driving drywall screws into soft wood with a power drill.) To counterbore a screw, it takes three separate holes, as shown, unless you buy a pilot bit that drills all three at once.

Counterbore

Wood plug

Countersink

Hole same size as screw shank

Hole same diameter as core between threads

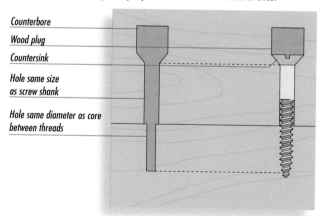

Painting

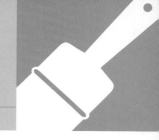

Paint is the ultimate interior and exterior decorator. It sets the mood, the tone, and even the period of your home's exterior and rooms. There is no quicker or more economical way to transform a house, inside and out, than with paint, especially if colors are well-chosen, complement one another, and are creatively applied. Once you learn some tricks of the trade, you will be amazed at the possibilities paint offers—to warm up and cool down rooms, expand a space visually or create coziness. Don't be afraid to experiment with techniques such as sponging, stippling, and stenciling that create depth and texture to a wall's surface. Paint is enormously forgiving—if you don't like the result, buy a new can and start over again. On the next several pages you will learn all you need to know about paint and painting techniques to get you started.

Choosing Paints

The most common types of paint for interior and exterior surfaces are water-base, or latex, and oil-base, or alkyd. Primers, wood stains, and clear finishes also are generally available in both latex and alkyd formulations. The chief advantage of high-quality, more expensive products is better "hiding," meaning fewer coats, and better washability.

Interior Paints

Interior-use paints are available in a range of finishes, from flat to gloss. Their formulations differ slightly among manufacturers, but generally semigloss is halfway between flat and gloss, while eggshell is halfway between flat and semigloss.

Higher-gloss finishes are more washable and durable, but they will show more imperfections on the surface. High-gloss paint generally is reserved for trim. Semigloss is also excellent on trim, as well as on kitchen, bathroom, and other surfaces exposed to grease, moisture, and heavy wear. A flat or eggshell finish is best for surfaces that receive less wear, such as living room and bedroom walls and ceilings.

LATEX PAINTS Latex accounts for the vast majority of house paints sold today, and for good reason: It cleans up with soap and water, dries quickly, is practically odorless, and poses the least threat to the environment. It also has excellent resistance to yellowing with age.

The type of resin used in the formula determines the quality of latex paint. The highest quality and most durable paints contain 100 percent acrylic resin, which offers excellent adhesion over alkyds. Vinyl acrylic and other blends are next in quality. Paint containing solely vinyl resin is the least durable and lowest quality of the available latex formulations.

ALKYD PAINTS Alkyds, or solvent-base paints, level out better than latexes, drying virtually free of brush marks for a smoother, harder finish. They are a wise choice for glossy surfaces since they offer better adhesion. However, alkyds are harder to apply, tend to sag more, and take longer to dry than latexes. They also require cleanup with paint thinner. When painting large areas with alkyd paint, you should ventilate the room or wear a respirator.

 To test if existing paint is alkyd or latex, apply nail polish remover to a small section. Latex will dissolve; alkyd won't.

SPECIAL-USE PAINTS The word enamel usually refers to high-gloss paints—either alkyd or latex—that dry to a hard finish. These paints are typically used on interior trim. Polyurethane enamel, sometimes called liquid-plastic paint, is used for floors because of its high abrasion resistance. Pigmented, or dye-colored, wiping stain is commonly applied to bare wood. You simply apply the stain, wait awhile, and wipe it off. If the surface feels rough, apply a clear, quick-drying sanding sealer, then sand smooth.

Clear Finishes

If you want to display the grain of wood that is bare or has been stained, choose polyurethane, varnish, shellac, or one of several clear, nonyellowing water-base coatings. Most come in a range of finishes from flat to gloss.

(continued on page 32)

 HOW PAINT IS CHANGING

Paint contains thinners, or solvents, which release volatile organic compounds as they evaporate. These contribute to smog and can pose health risks. Modern oil-base paints, made with synthetic resins called alkyds, have less thinner and give off less odor and toxic fumes than their oil-based predecessors. Still, thinner is an essential component of alkyd paint.

Because the thinner content of latex paint has always been much less than that of alkyd, there has been a dramatic shift over the years toward latex. In fact, some oil-base paints are now restricted or illegal in certain areas of the country. More recently, the already low solvent content of latex paints (maximum 8 percent) has been reduced to zero in some cases. These paints are marked "0 VOC" (short for "zero volatile organic compounds") on the label. While this is good news for the environment, 0 VOC paint is harder to work with because it dries very quickly.

SURFACE	PRIME OR FIRST COAT	FINISH COAT(S)	COMMENTS
New wallboard	Prime with latex sealer and let dry at least 4 hours.	Apply two coats of latex or alkyd paint in finish of choice. Sand lightly between coats of eggshell, semigloss, or gloss alkyd paint.	Don't use alkyd primer—it will raise nap in paper.
New plaster	Prime with latex sealer and let dry at least 4 hours.	Apply two coats of latex or alkyd paint in finish of choice. Sand lightly between coats of eggshell, semigloss, or gloss alkyd paint.	
Existing wallboard or plaster	When painting over existing latex paint, scuff sand to remove surface imperfections. If surface is dirty, wash and rinse thoroughly first.	Apply two coats of latex or alkyd paint in finish of choice. Sand lightly between coats of eggshell, semigloss, or gloss alkyd paint.	
Bare wood to be painted	Use an alkyd enamel undercoat.	Lightly sand enamel undercoat and apply two coats of finish paint.	Minimum sheen for woodwork is eggshell. Semigloss is preferable on doors and trim.
Painted wood to be repainted	Remove loose, flaking paint and sand smooth. Spot-prime bare wood with alkyd enamel under-coat.	Apply a first coat of latex or alkyd enamel paint; let dry thoroughly. Sand lightly, then apply a second coat and allow to dry overnight.	Minimum sheen for woodwork is eggshell. Semigloss is preferable on doors and trim.
Bare wood to be stained	Sand wood smooth. Apply a single coat of interior wiping stain and allow to dry overnight. For open-grain woods such as oak and mahogany, stain can be mixed 1:1 with paste wood filler to stain and fill grain in one application.	Apply one coat of varnish and allow to dry overnight. Sand lightly with steel wool or fine sandpaper. Apply at least three more coats, with overnight drying and sanding between coats.	Don't apply polyurethane over shellac or sanding sealers since adhesion problems can result.
Bare wood to be coated with a clear finish	Apply varnish, polyurethane, or other clear finish in desired sheen.	Apply two or three additional coats of clear finish, sanding between coats.	Don't apply polyurethane over shellac or sanding sealers since adhesion problems can result.
Masonry	On new block, use latex block filler. On poured concrete or brick, prime with latex sealer.	Apply two coats of latex finish.	White, powdery residue (efflorescence) is a sign of moisture in masonry. Check exterior walls for drainage problems and make needed repairs.
Metal	Remove rust with wire brush. Prime steel with rust-inhibitive primer. Prime aluminum or galvanized metal with galvanized metal primer.	Apply two coats of finish paint.	Use of flat finish paint is not recommended.

Choosing Paints

(continued from page 30)

POLYURETHANE Polyurethane is favored for cabinets, wood paneling, and other surfaces where maximum durability is important.

VARNISH While durable, varnishes aren't as tough as polyurethane. Ask your paint dealer for the best type for your job. Thin and clean up with paint thinner.

SHELLAC Apply shellac, which comes in orange or white, only over bare or stained wood. It isn't suggested for areas exposed to moisture, since water can cause spotting on the finish. Most brush marks disappear when shellac dries. Use denatured alcohol for thinning and cleanup.

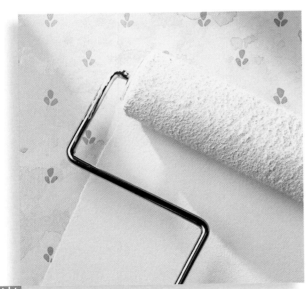

Wallcovering primer permits painting over the top of flat, sound wallpaper.

WATER-BASE TRANSPARENT COATINGS Some transparent coatings, including nonyellowing types, can be used on bare or stained wood as well as on painted surfaces, specifically to protect decorative latexes. For more information about decorative finishes, see page 58.

Primers

You need a primer when the surface to be painted is porous or the paints are incompatible (such as when you apply latex over alkyd).

An existing painted surface in good condition and compatible with the finish coat may not need an additional primer. Consult the chart on the facing page to determine if a primer is required.

Exterior Paints

The main difference between exterior alkyd and latex paints is how they cure. Alkyd paints usually are dry to the touch in 4 to 6 hours and are dry to recoat in 8 to 12 hours. They will continue to harden for several months after application to endure moisture. Latex paint usually is dry to the touch in half an hour and in warm, dry weather is resistant to light showers or dew after about 4 hours.

ALKYD PAINTS Alkyd paints are available in enamel and so-called house paint. Enamel paint is typically found in a range of ready-to-mix colors suitable for general use and particularly good for trim. Alkyd enamel dries to a hard, nonporous finish.

Alkyd house paint is more flexible than enamel but is not available in some states because of air-quality regulations. In others, it is available only in quart cans, making it expensive to use as a coating for exterior siding.

Alkyd paints tend to adhere better than latex to problematic and glossy surfaces, and because they dry more slowly, brush and roller marks have time to flow out, leaving a smoother surface finish.

This chart does not recommend the use of primers in most cases—for a number of reasons. Wood doesn't need primer if it will be stained or painted with enamel. Vinyl or aluminum siding is sufficiently covered with two coats of acrylic latex. With brick, stucco, and concrete, the first latex finish coat performs the function of a primer.

SURFACE	PRIMER	FINISH
Wood or plywood siding	Alkyd	2 coats alkyd paint, flat/semigloss/gloss
	Latex	2 coats latex paint, flat/semigloss/gloss
	None	2 coats latex stain, solid hide
	None	2 coats alkyd stain, solid hide/semi-transparent
Hardboard siding	Alkyd	2 coats latex paint, semigloss/gloss
Wood trim	Latex	2 coats latex paint, semigloss/gloss
	Alkyd	2 coats alkyd paint, flat/semigloss/gloss
Wood deck	None	2 coats semi-transparent stain
Vinyl or aluminum siding	None	2 coats acrylic latex paint, flat/semigloss/gloss
Brick	None	2 coats latex paint, flat
Block	Latex block filler	2 coats latex paint, flat
Stucco	None	2 coats latex paint, flat
Concrete	None	2 coats latex paint, flat
Ferrous metal	Metal primer	2 coats alkyd paint, gloss
Galvanized metal	Galvanized metal primer	2 coats alkyd paint, gloss

LATEX PAINTS The best exterior latex paint is made with all-acrylic resin. Lower-quality varieties are made with vinyl acrylic and other additives. While all-acrylic paints are more expensive, they offer better adhesion, gloss, and color retention. The water-based formulation of latex paints also makes them easier to clean up, less expensive, and faster drying than alkyds. In addition, latex paint dries to a porous finish, allowing moisture in wood to evaporate through the paint film, which prevents peeling.

Whether you choose alkyd or latex, flat paint is best on siding for resisting moisture, while semigloss or gloss paint is best for trim and doors because of its durability and contrast.

STAINS Stains come in transparent, semi-transparent, and solid-hide formulations. Solid-hide stains are used on wood siding and fences. Semi-transparent stains are used on wood siding and fences, as well as on decks. Transparent formulations are used only on cedar and redwood, which are naturally rot-resistant woods.

Estimating Paint Needs

To figure out how much paint you'll need, you must know the square footage of the area to be painted and the spread rate of the paint (usually about 400 square feet to the gallon, but check the can to be sure).

(continued on page 34)

Choosing Paints

(continued from page 33)

To determine square footage, measure the width of each wall, add the figures together, and multiply the total by the height of the surface to be painted. Next, estimate how much of this area contains surfaces that won't be painted, such as a fireplace, windows, wallpaper, and areas you'll paint separately, such as trim. If these surfaces account for 10 percent or more of the room, deduct the amount from the total.

Finally, to figure out how many gallons of paint you'll need, divide the square footage by the spread rate of the paint. Calculate the amount of trim paint separately, or, like professional painters, figure on about a quarter as much trim paint as wall paint.

Decorative Paints

Conventional unthinned paints are not normally used for decorative finishes because they don't offer the subtle variations and transparency needed for layered effects. Quick-drying washes work best for decorative techniques such as sponging. Techniques that require a buildup of color, such as marbling, are best accomplished with glazes, which stay wet longer, allowing more time to manipulate them.

Oil glazes, the traditional medium of decorative painters, stay wet and workable longer than washes and acrylic glazes, and produce a wonderfully translucent finish. Also, mistakes are easy to correct—you can just wipe off the paint with thinner.

Acrylic glazes and latex washes are easy to use—they're mixed and cleaned up with water. Although water-base finishes aren't as durable as oil-base ones, you can always apply a clear coating over the top to protect the finish.

 PAINTING SAFETY

Although paint is fairly user-friendly, exercise caution when working with it nonetheless. Following are some basic guidelines for painting safely:

☐ Always work in a well-ventilated area. Open doors and windows, and use exhaust fans. Excessive inhalation of fumes from paints and solvents can cause dizziness, headache, fatigue, and nausea. Also keep pets out of freshly painted rooms. Paint fumes are especially dangerous to birds.

☐ If you can't ventilate the area well enough to get rid of the fumes, wear a respirator approved for such use, available at paint and hardware stores.

☐ Wear a dust mask and safety goggles when sanding to keep from breathing in dust particles and to protect your eyes.

☐ Wear safety goggles when using chemical strippers or caustic cleaning compounds, or when painting overhead.

☐ Use canvas dropcloths on the floor. Cloth stays in place and isn't as slippery as plastic.

☐ Don't use or store paint products near a flame or heat source. Avoid smoking while painting or using thinner.

☐ Many paints and solvents are harmful to the skin and eyes. Be especially careful when handling or applying products that contain strong solvents. Wear gloves and a respirator when called for by label directions. Also wear gloves when applying paint with a sponge or rag.

☐ Inspect ladders for sturdiness. Make sure that all four legs rest squarely on the floor and that both cross braces are locked in place. Never stand on the top step or the utility shelf. Never lean away from a ladder; get off and move it if you can't reach a spot easily.

☐ For scaffolding planks, use 2 by 10s no more than 12 feet long. If you place the planks between two ladders, position the ladders so their steps are facing each other. If you run planks between ladders or a ladder and sawhorse or stairway step, be sure the planks are level and secure.

☐ Clean up promptly after painting and properly dispose of soiled rags: To eliminate any chance of spontaneous combustion, spread rags soaked with alkyd paint or thinner outdoors and let them dry all day before disposing of them at a toxic waste dump. Don't leave rags to dry in areas accessible to children or pets.

Washes are simple to make—you just mix ordinary latex paint with water. Adding commercial acrylic glaze may extend the drying time.

To make a glaze, start with a transparent commercial glaze (which is basically paint without any pigment). Then add regular paint—alkyd or acrylic, depending on the recipe. The intensity of the color will be thinned by the commercial glaze, producing a translucent paint.

Next, add the appropriate diluent (paint thinner for an oil glaze; water for an acrylic glaze). The diluent further thins the paint, allowing it to be applied in very thin coats. To extend the drying time of an acrylic glaze slightly, add a retarding agent.

The following recipes are just a starting point. Decorative painting (see page 58) isn't an exact science, so don't be afraid to experiment a little.

LATEX WASH

The percentage of water in this formula can be increased if you wish. The higher the paint content the more durable the finish, but also the more opaque it becomes. Commercial glaze is added to this recipe simply to extend the drying time.

1 part latex paint
1 part water
1 part commercial acrylic glaze

OIL GLAZE

This is a good general recipe for beginners. It stays wet even if you take a long time to get the job done. Make a faster-drying, harder finish by reducing the quantity of oil glaze and increasing the amount of paint thinner.

1 part commercial oil glaze
1 part alkyd paint
1 part paint thinner

ACRYLIC GLAZE #1

This glaze recipe is suitable for ragging, sponging, and simple marbling. To adapt the recipe for decorative techniques requiring greater translucency (such as dragging, wood graining, and intricate marbling), change the proportions to 5 parts commercial acrylic glaze, 1 part paint, and 1 part water.

1 part commercial acrylic glaze
2 parts acrylic paint
1 part water
2 to 4 oz. retarder per gallon (optional)

ACRYLIC GLAZE #2

Use this recipe if you don't have access to a commercial acrylic glaze. Acrylic gel medium is carried in most art supply stores.

1 part acrylic gel medium
1 part acrylic paint
2 parts water
2 to 4 oz. retarder per gallon (optional)

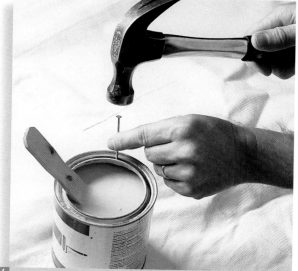

Use a hammer and nail to puncture the paint can's rim in two or three places. That way, paint won't pool and spill over.

Paint Failure

Daily exposure to various elements takes its toll on all painted surfaces. Other factors, including poor surface preparation, incompatible paints, or sloppy application, can hasten the process.

Depending on the symptoms, some surfaces may need to be stripped bare while others may require no more than a light sanding or scraping.

1) Mildew

Mildew is a fungus that grows on cool, damp surfaces, showing up as black spots. To treat, wash the area with a solution of $2/3$ cup TSP (trisodium phosphate), $1/3$ cup detergent, 1 quart household bleach, and 3 quarts warm water. Wear rubber gloves and eye protection when preparing and applying the solution.

2) Inter-coat peeling

Applying latex finish coats over surfaces previously painted with gloss alkyd often results in poor adhesion. To treat, sand off the latex paint, prime the surface with an alkyd primer, then apply latex finish coats. Some top-of-the-line acrylic paints can be applied over old alkyd paint without the need for priming, but thorough sanding is required first to give the surface "bite."

3) Chalking

Chalking is the normal breakdown of a paint finish after long exposure to sunlight. To treat, wash off the loose, powdery material and repaint.

4) Lap marks

Lap marks are caused by a wet edge not being maintained during staining or painting. To treat, sand down, then restain or repaint only two to three boards at a time, from top to bottom on vertical siding, from side to side on horizontal siding.

5) Wrinkling

Wrinkling is caused by a coat of paint being applied over another that isn't thoroughly dry, or by a coat that is applied too heavily. To treat, allow the paint to dry thoroughly, sand off the wrinkles, and repaint.

6) Peeling varnish

Even the best exterior-grade varnishes do not last more than a few years when exposed to direct sunlight. To treat, sand down, then apply a minimum of 5 coats, followed by a light sanding. Recoat every year or two.

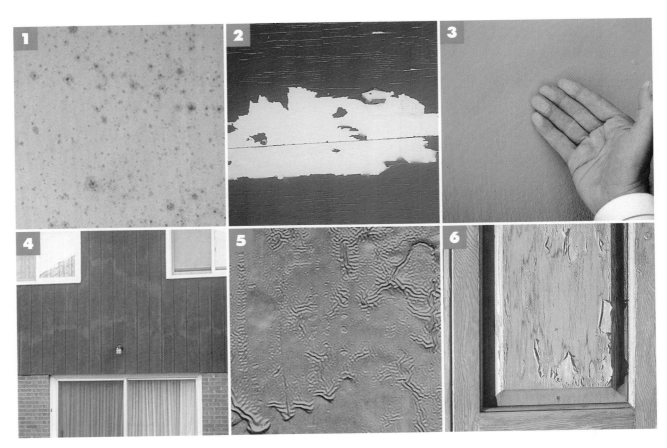

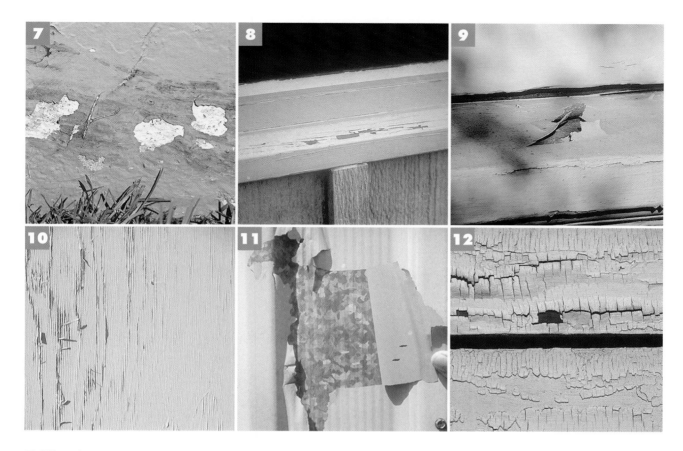

7) Blistering

Blistering can be caused by moisture invading the subsurface of paint through lack of a vapor barrier, cracked boards, or poor caulking. Blistering also can be caused by the use of oil-based paints in hot weather, which can trap solvents. In either case, scrape and sand the blistered paint and repair any sources of moisture, then repaint in cool weather.

8) Peeling on windowsills

Properly designed sills slope away from the window to prevent water from pooling on the surface. Still, heavy rains or exposure to water from sprinklers can allow moisture to find its way into the wood, causing peeling and cracks. To treat, sand down to the bare wood, prime with alkyd primer, fill all cracks with paintable caulk, and apply two coats of finish paint.

9) Multiple-coat peeling

Structures that have been painted over many times, especially with oil-based paints, sometimes will show paint failure down to the bare wood. This is caused by the paint layers becoming brittle, then cracking as the wood below expands and contracts with temperature changes. These cracks allow moisture to enter through the cracks and cause peeling. To treat, strip the surface down to bare wood and prepare as you would new wood before repainting.

10) Grain cracking on plywood

When plywood is exposed to repeated moisture, the surface develops cracks as the wood expands and contracts. Once cracked, repair is not possible. Treat by replacing the plywood, priming it with an exterior-grade primer, then painting with at least two coats of alkyd or latex finish.

11) Peeling from galvanized metal

If an alkyd paint has been applied to a galvanized surface without a galvanized-metal primer being applied beforehand, loss of adhesion will eventually occur. To treat, remove all the alkyd paint, prime, and apply new finish coats, or, ask your paint dealer about acrylic latex paints that can be applied without the need for priming.

12) Alligatoring

Alligatoring can be caused by applying a hard finish coat over a soft primer, or by the loss of flexibility caused by thick layers of paint being applied on wood surfaces. To treat, remove all the old paint by scraping and sanding, then repaint with a primer and two finish coats.

Painting Tools

A variety of tools are helpful for completing a successful paint job. Some tools are necessary regardless of whether you're working on an interior, an exterior, or a decorative painting job. Others are more specialized for specific tasks. On the next few pages, we'll take a closer look at the primary tools you'll want to have on hand before you begin to paint. High-quality tools will go a long way toward achieving a professional-looking paint job.

PAINTBRUSHES Natural-bristle brushes are traditionally used to apply alkyd paint and other finishes that require paint thinner for cleanup. Avoid using these brushes for applying latex paint and other water-base products because the bristles become limp when they soak up water. For latex, choose synthetic bristles; polyester brushes stay stiff in water, humidity, and heat, keeping their shape for detail work. Nylon is more abrasion resistant but can lose stiffness on hot days.

You can get by nicely with three brushes for most projects: a 2-inch trim brush, a 1½-inch sash brush, and a 4-inch straight-edged brush. Good-quality brushes perform very differently than cheap ones. They have long, tapered bristles set firmly into a wooden handle with epoxy cement, not glue. The bristles are flagged, or split at the ends, enabling them to hold more paint. Look for multiple lengths of split flagged bristles packed tightly through a ¾- to 1-inch thickness for a standard 4-inch brush.

Always test a brush before purchase by holding it as if you were painting. It should feel comfortable in your hand, not awkward or heavy. Test it for springiness, little fanning, and no bristle gaps.

GENERAL EQUIPMENT

For nearly all jobs, you'll need a stepladder (see more about ladders and scaffolding on pages 42–43). Protect your hands with work gloves, rubber gloves, or disposable latex gloves. Wear safety glasses or goggles and, when needed, a dust mask or respirator. An edge guide helps to protect adjacent surfaces while you paint.

Edge guide

Rubber gloves

Dust mask

Safety goggles

Work gloves

Stepladder

PAINTBRUSHES

These three brushes will get you through most conventional paint jobs. Choose synthetic bristles for latex paint, and natural bristles for alkyd paint.

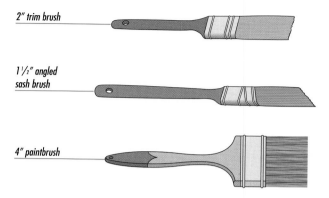

2" trim brush

1½" angled
sash brush

4" paintbrush

PAINT ROLLERS Look for the type of roller with a heavy-gauge steel frame and a comfortable handle threaded with a metal sleeve to accommodate an extension pole. Nine-inch rollers will handle nearly all jobs, but for some work you may prefer a special roller: a trim roller for painting trim and window sashes; a beveled corner roller for corners, ceiling borders, and grooves in paneling; and a roller made of grooved foam for acoustical surfaces.

Choose the right nap for the paint you're using. With latex, use a nylon nap. Nylon and wool blend, lambskin, and mohair covers are recommended for alkyd paint. Nap thickness varies from ¹/₁₆ inch to 1¼ inches. The smoother the surface you're painting or the higher the gloss of paint you're applying, the shorter the nap you will need.

A 3- to 4-foot extension pole lets you reach high walls and ceilings, in many cases eliminating the need for a ladder. Use the extension pole for painting low areas, too, to prevent the need for stooping.

For big jobs, rolling from a 5-gallon bucket equipped with a roller grid is faster and neater than using a roller tray.

OTHER PAINT APPLICATORS Disposable foam brushes come in handy for small jobs and quick touch-ups. A pad applicator with a replaceable pad is useful for painting corners and edges. As with roller covers, nylon pads are used with latex paints; nylon and wool blend, lambskin, and mohair pads are recommended for alkyds. Finally, a painter's mitt is ideal for coating irregular or contoured surfaces, such as pipes, grilles, and radiators.

(continued on page 40)

ROLLER EQUIPMENT

Though a tray suffices for small jobs, rolling from a grid in a 5-gallon bucket insures a quicker, neater job. Add an extension pole to your supplies to lengthen your reach and give you more leverage.

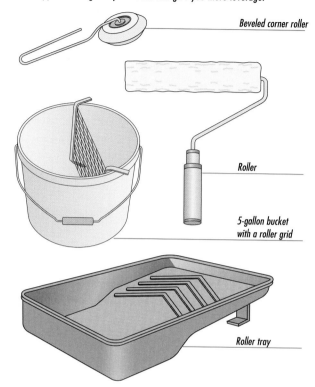

Beveled corner roller

Roller

5-gallon bucket
with a roller grid

Roller tray

PAINT APPLICATORS

Disposable foam brushes are convenient for small jobs and apply paint in a very smooth coat. A pad applicator works well for painting corners and edges. If you have metalwork or highly irregular surfaces, use a painter's mitt.

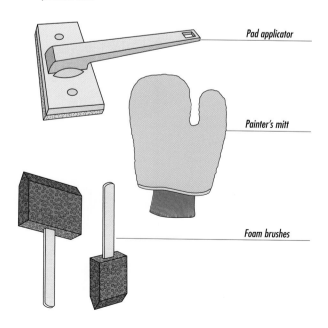

Pad applicator

Painter's mitt

Foam brushes

39

Painting Tools

(continued from page 39)

SCRAPERS AND SANDERS Both of these are essential for removing loose paint or, when necessary, an entire finish. A disk sander, which you may choose to rent, is useful for big sanding jobs, such as those required on exterior surfaces. To smooth the rough edges of small scraped areas, use an electric drill with a rotary sander attachment.

(continued on page 42)

PREPARATION TOOLS

For wall preparation, you may need a sanding block, putty knife or broad knife, and caulking gun. For exterior work, a molding scraper, wire brush, power sander, and heat gun can be helpful. Be sure you have plenty of new masking tape and dropcloths—canvas types stay in place and are absorbent.

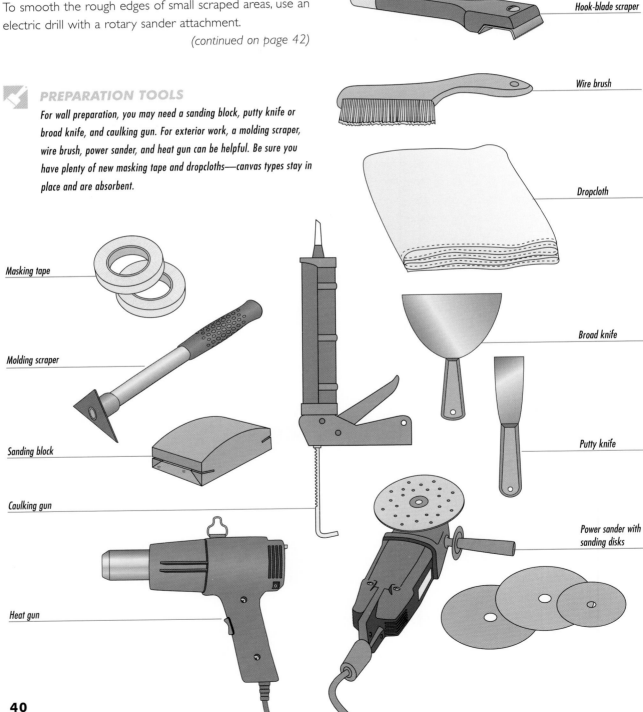

Hook-blade scraper

Wire brush

Dropcloth

Masking tape

Molding scraper

Sanding block

Caulking gun

Heat gun

Broad knife

Putty knife

Power sander with sanding disks

DECORATIVE PAINTING TOOLS

You can create a variety of decorative techniques with such common household items as rags and tissue paper, though some techniques call for specific sponges and brushes. The information on creating decorative effects with these tools begins on page 58.

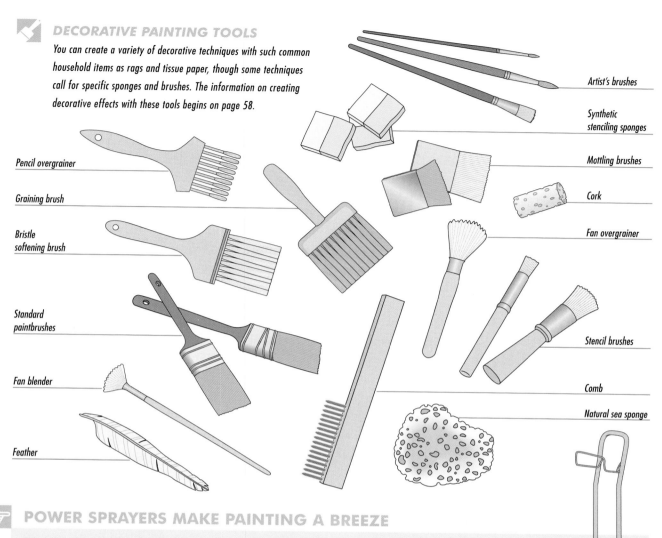

Artist's brushes

Synthetic stenciling sponges

Mottling brushes

Cork

Fan overgrainer

Stencil brushes

Comb

Natural sea sponge

Pencil overgrainer

Graining brush

Bristle softening brush

Standard paintbrushes

Fan blender

Feather

POWER SPRAYERS MAKE PAINTING A BREEZE

Power sprayers can save you considerable time, and while there is some disagreement among professionals whether sprayed surfaces are as durable as brushed surfaces, most agree that if the sprayer is used properly the finish will last just as long as one created with a brush or roller.

The most common paint sprayers are known as airless sprayers and are made in a variety of sizes. In general, sprayers are particularly useful for painting deeply textured, hard-to-reach, or multipiece surfaces with many nooks and crannies, like eaves, lattices, or even rough stucco. They require careful masking and dropcloth placement.

When using a power sprayer, follow these tips:

■ Test the sprayer on a large piece of cardboard, adjusting the unit to get a uniform spray pattern with minimum pressure.

■ To achieve a smooth, even coat, keep the gun about 10 inches from the surface and spray a succession of overlapping strips. Move the sprayer smoothly, at a consistent pace— about 3 inches per second. Release the trigger at the end of each stroke, then pull it again as you begin to reverse direction.

■ Spray straight at the surface and avoid swinging your arm back and forth.

■ Once you have begun to work, do not leave the sprayer idle for more than 20 minutes or the paint will begin to harden.

■ When you have finished painting for the day or are taking an extended break, clean the paint from the unit according to the manufacturer's instructions.

■ To avoid mishaps or injury, always wear protective clothing and gloves, as well as goggles. Never point the sprayer head at your body. The jet of paint from a sprayer can be powerful enough to force paint through your skin (if that happens, get immediate medical attention).

■ Before you clean a power sprayer, turn off and unplug the unit, then pull the spray-gun trigger to release the remaining pressure in the hose.

■ Make sure to set the safety lock on the spray gun when you're not spraying.

Painting Tools

(continued from page 40)

LADDERS & SCAFFOLDING Most exterior painting projects require at least one ladder and a scaffolding unit. The stepladder (see page 38) is the standard for most interior jobs, and will provide good service for exterior jobs if the walls are not too high.

Aluminum ladders are stronger than wooden ones, and are particularly recommended when you require an extension ladder because they are much lighter in weight. There are three grades of aluminum extension ladders, measured by how much weight they can hold: residential, commercial, and industrial. A commercial-grade ladder provides a good balance between strength and light weight. Though they are more costly than residential ladders, if you are painting your house yourself, you should think seriously about buying a commercial-grade model for ease of use and safety.

With two extension ladders, doubled 2-by-10 wooden planks, and two ladder jacks set at the same level on opposite ladder rungs, you can make a simple scaffold. However, because these units have no safety rails, only use them if you have experience working at heights and feel confident that you can work safely on them.

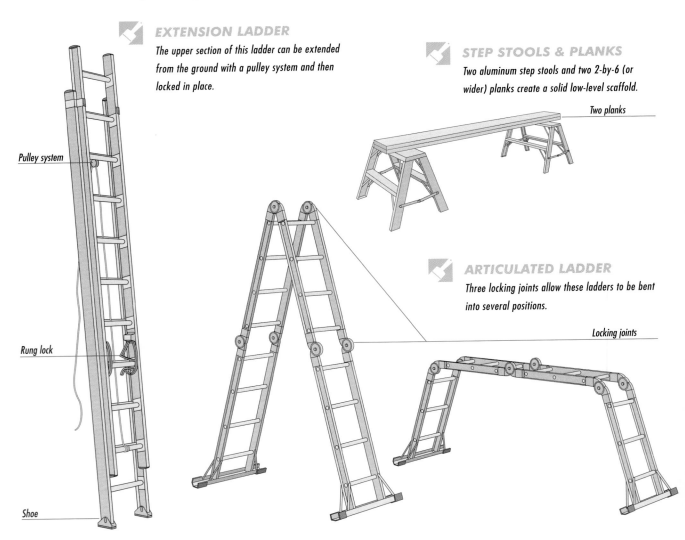

EXTENSION LADDER
The upper section of this ladder can be extended from the ground with a pulley system and then locked in place.

Pulley system

Rung lock

Shoe

STEP STOOLS & PLANKS
Two aluminum step stools and two 2-by-6 (or wider) planks create a solid low-level scaffold.

Two planks

ARTICULATED LADDER
Three locking joints allow these ladders to be bent into several positions.

Locking joints

For some large painting jobs, it pays to rent one or more sections of scaffolding. When set up properly, scaffolding is sturdier and safer than a ladder for working at heights, and it minimizes the need to climb up and down.

SCAFFOLDING

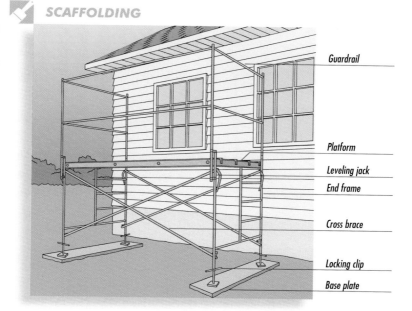

- Guardrail
- Platform
- Leveling jack
- End frame
- Cross brace
- Locking clip
- Base plate

LADDER LEVELER

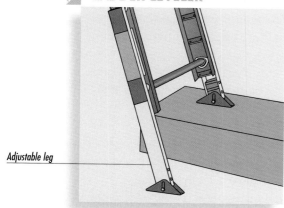

Adjustable leg

Ladder levelers adjust for uneven surfaces.

CLEANUP TOOLS

A utility knife is useful for removing masking tape around freshly painted window fames, and a window scraper for removing paint around muntins. A paintbrush spinner will remove excess paint from rollers.

- Utility knife
- Paintbrush spinner
- Window scraper

LADDER & SCAFFOLDING SAFETY

Ladders and scaffolding should always be used with great care. Keep the following safety tips in mind:

■ Position ladders on solid ground, and avoid wet or slippery surfaces. If the ground is not level, equip the ladder with levelers (see above).

■ To steady a ladder—especially when you are working close to a corner of the house—secure it with a rope to a tree or other immovable anchor.

■ Keep ladders away from power lines; aluminum ones can conduct electricity.

■ Keep at least one hand on the ladder as you paint.

■ Never stand higher than the third-highest rung of an extension ladder or the second-highest step of a stepladder.

■ On an extension ladder, hang the paint can from a rung with a hook; on a stepladder, place the paint can on the utility shelf.

■ Never overreach to one side.

■ On an extension ladder, make sure the hooks that support the top section are securely fastened and face away from you as you climb.

■ If you can't position an extension ladder without leaning the top of it against a gutter, insert a piece of 2 by 4 into the gutter to prevent it from buckling under your weight.

Preparing a Room

Proper preparation not only makes painting easier, it reduces the possibility of making messes and mistakes that can cost hours of tedious cleanup and helps ensure a quality job that will last. Here are a few key steps you should take when painting a room:

CLEAR THE ROOM Move light furniture and decorative objects out of the room. Remove everything you can from the walls, including heating register covers and electrical faceplates (turn off the power first). Put a piece of masking tape over switches and receptacles. Ideally, remove knobs, handles, and locks from doors and windows (mark them so you can replace them correctly later) or else mask them.

Push heavy furniture into the middle of the room and cover with dropcloths. Cover the floor with plastic sheeting, then a canvas dropcloth. If you can't take down a light fixture, tie a plastic garbage bag around it.

Dropcloths are made of plastic, paper, or canvas. Plastic works well for draping furniture. Disposable paper is fine for small jobs, but a sturdy canvas dropcloth is preferred by painters for most work because it absorbs spatters and doesn't become slippery.

REMOVE WALLPAPER Although you can sometimes paint over wallpaper, it's usually a good idea to remove it, especially if it's tearing or flaking. (For information on removing wallpaper, see page 78.) After all the adhesive is removed, wash the wall with an abrasive cleaner, rinse well, and let dry for 24 hours. If the wallpaper is sound and secure, you may be able to apply a special wallcovering primer over the top, then paint. Ask your paint dealer about the primer and whether it's appropriate in your situation.

SCRAPE OR STRIP (IF NECESSARY) Chipped or peeling paint must be scraped off before new paint is applied. The trick is to scrape hard enough to remove the paint, but not so hard that you dig into the surface. The best scrapers have edges that can be sharpened with a metal file. A broad knife does a fast job on large areas; a hook-blade scraper is more convenient for small areas. A wire brush is effective for removing light flaking.

Sometimes the old finish on woodwork is in such bad condition that the paint must be removed entirely. The easiest way to strip old paint from woodwork is with a commercial liquid paint stripper; carefully follow the instructions on the container.

SAND (IF NECESSARY) One reason to sand a surface is to smooth it, so surfaces that have been scraped should be sanded lightly before painting. You also need to sand newly patched areas and bare wood before beginning to paint. Use fine-grade sandpaper.

Another reason to sand is to rough up glossy surfaces before painting so the new paint will adhere better. You can use fine-grade sandpaper or, for alkyd paints, liquid deglosser. Trisodium phosphate (TSP) or a phosphate-free substitute will work as a light-duty deglosser. Always wear rubber gloves when using liquid deglosser or TSP. Rinse the wall thoroughly afterward and allow to dry thoroughly (about 24 hours).

PROTECTING THE AREA

1) Drape & cover

Put garbage bags over hanging fixtures and fasten them to their cords with twist ties or masking tape. Drape furniture at the center of the room.

2) Protect the floor

Run 2-inch-wide masking tape along the floor's edge and then tape the dropcloth to the band of tape. A disposable paper dropcloth works fine where you're painting only a wall or trim.

3) Mask adjacent surfaces

Cover trim with masking tape. Tape plastic sheeting to larger wall surfaces, such as wainscoting.

4) Mask or remove hardware

Cover hard-to-remove hardware with masking tape. Take off easily removed hardware, put each piece in a separate plastic bag with its screws, and make notes of their sequence.

CLEAN After vacuuming the room, use a tack cloth to dust all the surfaces that will be painted. Then wash walls that have a grease film (kitchens) or a soap film (bathrooms) with TSP or a phosphate-free substitute. Greasy or mildewed surfaces should be washed both before and after you sand. For very greasy spots, sponge on paint thinner, blot dry, and wash with the cleaner. Wearing rubber gloves and safety glasses, scrub mildewed areas with a mixture of 3 ounces TSP or a nonphosphate substitute, 1 ounce dry detergent, 1 quart chlorine bleach, and 3 quarts water. Allow to dry thoroughly (about 24 hours).

MASK If you have a steady hand, you may not need masking tape to protect hardware and surfaces next to those being painted. However, most people find tape helpful for keeping surfaces from being splattered and for keeping a crisp edge between two types or colors of paint.

If you're using a brush against the tape, use tape with good adhesion rather than all-purpose tape to prevent paint from seeping in. There is a type of tape (often called painter's tape) that can be fastened to delicate surfaces such as wallpaper without causing damage when it is pulled away. For more about masking, see above and right.

5 Mask glass

Before painting windows, unless you have a very steady hand, mask the glass. Press masking tape in place with a putty knife to seal the edge. Remove the tape while paint is still tacky—about half an hour after painting with latex paint, 2 hours after applying alkyd paint.

Ceilings & Walls

The best way to avoid painting yourself into a corner, splattering paint onto newly painted surfaces, or inadvertently touching a just-painted edge is to follow a painting sequence. If you are using stains or clear finishes on woodwork, apply them first. Next, paint the ceiling. Then paint the walls, starting from the top and working your way down. Finally, brush paint on trim—first the moldings and then the windows, doors, and cabinets.

When you apply two coats of glossy paint on trim, ensure a good bond by sanding lightly between coats with very fine-grade sandpaper and wiping with a tack cloth. Rollers cover walls much faster and more easily than brushes, but use a brush to "cut in" borders around areas that will be rolled (see facing page) and to paint trim. You may want to "box" the paint—that is, mix paint from two or more cans in a larger bucket—to eliminate slight color differences among cans.

When you're working overhead, carry less paint on your brush or roller to avoid splatters.

Cutting In

Cutting in is the technique of painting with a brush along the edges and corners of a surface and around any fixtures or trim. The rest of the surface is filled in later (usually with a paint roller, but a brush may be preferable in some cases).

With latex paint, you can cut in the entire room before painting the open spaces. With alkyd paints or deep colors, however, cut in one section at a time and then complete an area before moving on to the next. This is done because the cut-in area has a working time of only about 20 minutes; after that, the overlapped areas will look inconsistent when they have dried. *(continued on page 48)*

 DEALING WITH LEAD-BASED PAINT

Long known as a health hazard, lead-based paint was phased out of use in the United States by 1978. If your house predates the late 1970s, however, layers of lead-based paint may be hiding under your current finish. While lead-based paint isn't known to pose a threat when covered and left untouched, once you start sanding to prepare a surface for painting, lead dust will be released into the air, posing significant health risks, especially for young children and pregnant women.

If you suspect your house may contain lead-based paint, call the National Lead Clearinghouse (NLC) at 1-800-424-5323. Experts there can tell you where to send a paint chip for analysis. In cases where the lead level is low, you can remove the paint yourself as long as you take the recommended precautions. Otherwise, you will be advised to hire professionals to deal with the problem. The NLC does not recommend the use of lead-paint test kits.

Spread a brush's bristles to check for flagging and springiness.

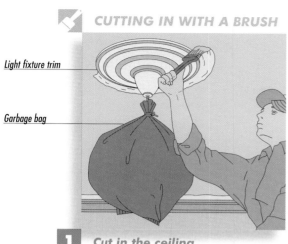

Light fixture trim

Garbage bag

Door frame

1 **Cut in the ceiling**

Paint above the molding or at the ceiling line and around any light fixtures or, even better, turn off the power and lower the fixture's ceiling trim.

2 **Cut in the walls**

Brush paint below the molding or at the ceiling line, above the baseboard, and around door and window frames.

Ceiling

2" strip

Corner

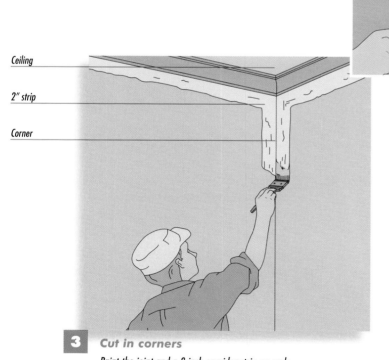

3 **Cut in corners**

Paint the joint and a 2-inch or wider strip on each side of it. As shown in the detail illustration, you can also use a special corner roller for cutting in corners quickly and easily.

Ceilings & Walls

(continued from page 46)
Cut in first where the ceiling meets the wall. If you're using the same color and type of paint for the ceiling and wall, you can paint the joint and several inches out on both sides. If you're using a different color or type of paint on the ceiling, cut in and roll the ceiling before you paint the walls.

Painting Surfaces

When it comes to painting most ceiling and wall surfaces, nothing works more quickly and easily than a roller. Once you've cut in with a brush, move on to the roller work.

PAINTING TRICKS & SHORTCUTS

The following tips from professional painters can help you achieve a top-quality job yourself:

■ For best adhesion when using alkyd enamels and polyurethane varnishes, apply all coats within 72 hours of each other.

■ To avoid having to clean your paint tray, line the inside with aluminum foil or plastic. When the job is done, simply remove the liner.

■ To remove bristles that come off as you apply paint, touch them with the tip of your wet brush; the bristles should stick to it. Wipe the stray bristles off the brush with a cloth.

■ If insects get trapped in the wet paint, let the paint dry before brushing them off.

■ When applying an enamel finish coat, brush paint on generously and use a light touch. Avoid overbrushing when you use enamel since it can produce an irregular finish. Work quickly and avoid touching up areas already painted.

■ If you're sensitive to the odor of paint, mix in a few drops of vanilla extract or add a commercial paint fragrance additive. Still, always wear a respirator if you can't properly ventilate a room.

PAINTING WITH A ROLLER

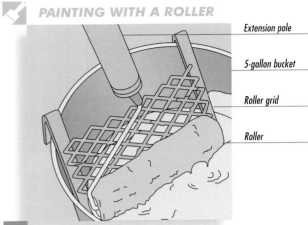

Extension pole

5-gallon bucket

Roller grid

Roller

1 Load the roller

For larger jobs, use a 5-gallon bucket, filling it with 1 to 2 gallons of paint at a time. Roll back and forth on a grid positioned in the bucket. For smaller jobs, paint from a roller tray, pouring just enough paint at a time to fill the reservoir. Roll up and down the textured part of the tray to saturate the nap. In both cases, the roller should be full but not dripping.

Work diagonally

Corner

2 Roll the ceiling

Paint the ceiling first. Do a small section (about 2 feet by 3 feet) at a time, starting in a corner and applying paint diagonally until you reach the opposite corner. Reload the roller often, distribute the paint evenly, and roll slowly.

Painting Interior

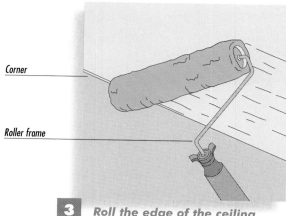

Corner

Roller frame

W pattern

3 **Roll the edge of the ceiling**

Roll as close to the edges of the ceiling as possible to cover the differences between brush marks made when cutting in and roller marks. Finish by lightly running the roller, unloaded, across each section in one direction only.

4 **Roll the walls**

Start in an upper corner of one wall and apply paint thickly in a series of big Ws. Then go back over the area, rolling in different directions to fill in the Ws. Roll slowly to avoid splattering.

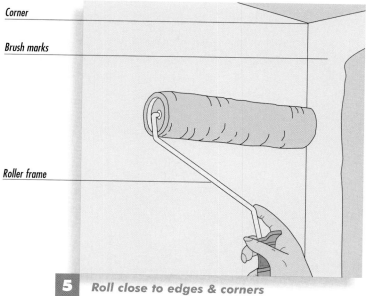

Corner

Brush marks

Roller frame

5 **Roll close to edges & corners**

As with the ceiling, roll walls as close to the edges and corners as possible, then finish by running the roller, unloaded, from top to bottom.

Painting Woodwork

Painting Interior

Painting woodwork—doors, windows, and trim—is a more intricate job than painting ceilings and walls, so it calls for slightly more exacting skills. Be sure to refer to page 31 for more about the appropriate paints, tools, and preparation for painting woodwork. Prime any bare wood or spackled and sanded surfaces. Paint the ceiling, then the walls, and finally the trim.

Painting Doors

You can paint a door on its hinges if you tarp the floor beneath it with a dropcloth. Or you can remove it from its hinges. To do this, slip the hinge pins out but don't unscrew the hinges. Lean the door against a wall with two small blocks under the bottom edge and a third wedge between the top edge and the wall. You can also lay the door across a pair of sawhorses; don't apply too much paint, though, or it may puddle.

Whether you paint a door on or off its hinges, the painting sequence is exactly the same. Work from top to bottom. For flush doors, roll on the paint with a lint-free cover, and then brush it out in the direction of the grain. For doors with inset panels, follow the sequence shown below left. Match the color of the latch edge to the room the door opens into and the color of the hinge edge to the room the door opens away from.

When painting the door casing, begin with the head casing and work down the side casings. If the door opens away from the room, paint the jamb and the two surfaces of the door stop visible from the room. If the door opens into the room, paint the jamb and the door side of the doorstop. Don't rehang or close the door until all the paint is completely dry.

Painting Windows

When painting windows, choose an angled sash brush, which will reach into corners. Load the brush lightly.

(continued on page 52)

▸ PAINTING A DOOR

Stile
Stile
Recess
Raised panel
Rail

Painting inset panels
Paint sections of a door in the following order: panel moldings, recesses, panels, horizontal rails, vertical stiles.

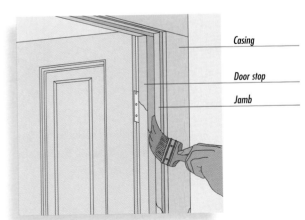

Casing
Door stop
Jamb

Painting door jamb & stops
If the door opens away from a room, paint the jamb and two surfaces of the stop as shown. If the door opens into a room, paint the jamb, then the door side of the stop.

PAINTING A WINDOW

Painting along glass
With a steady hand, draw a lightly loaded tapered sash brush along the window frame; let the paint lap slightly onto the glass.

Removing wet paint from glass
Wrap a rag around the end of a putty knife and, holding it at an angle, pull along the joint between frame and glass to remove wet paint from the glass. After the paint dries (but before it hardens), remove leftover paint with a razor blade or window scraper.

 PAINTING A DOUBLE-HUNG WINDOW

Paint double-hung window sections in the order shown. Start with the outer sash, move on to the inner sash, then finish with the frame trim elements.

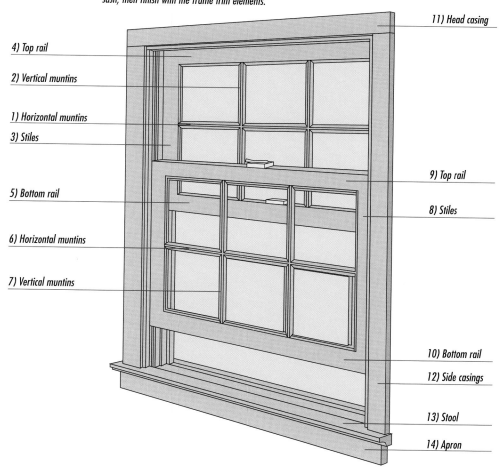

4) Top rail

2) Vertical muntins

1) Horizontal muntins

3) Stiles

5) Bottom rail

6) Horizontal muntins

7) Vertical muntins

11) Head casing

9) Top rail

8) Stiles

10) Bottom rail

12) Side casings

13) Stool

14) Apron

Painting Woodwork

(continued from page 50)

If you don't have a steady hand, cover the edges of the glass with masking tape (see page 45 for information on masking and page 51 for techniques on removing paint from windowpanes.) But if you feel you can guide a paintbrush straight and smoothly, try painting without masking—and save yourself time and hassle. Use a tapered sash brush, lightly loaded, on the frames. Let the paint slightly overlap the glass; this will seal the finish to the glass so that condensation cannot get under the paint and cause it to peel. Then wipe off the excess with a rag wrapped around a putty knife blade.

DOUBLE-HUNG WINDOWS If the sashes are removable, lift them out, lay them on a table, and paint them. Be prepared to leave the sashes out long enough to dry thoroughly (at least 24 hours). If the sashes aren't removable, you'll need to raise and lower them as needed to reach all of the window parts..

For a professional-looking job, after priming but before painting new trim, run a light bead of latex caulk along all seams and smooth the caulk with a wet finger.

Paint the outer, or upper, sash first. If the window has small glass panes, begin with the horizontal muntins and then work on the vertical ones. Next, paint the exposed parts of the stiles, the top rail, and the bottom rail, in that order. Then paint the inner, or lower, sash, starting with the muntins and finishing with the rails.

To paint the trim of a double-hung window, begin with the head casing, then paint down the sides. Next paint the stool, and finish with the apron.

CASEMENT WINDOWS First paint any vertical muntins, then any horizontal ones. Next, paint the top rails, the bottom rails, and the stiles, in that order. Finish the job by painting the casing.

No matter what type of window you have, don't paint the jamb. This may cause the window to stick. Once the window is painted, wax the jamb with floor wax if it is made of wood. This is unnecessary for a metal jamb.

As soon as you've finished any painting project, clean your tools; delay can make a later cleanup extremely difficult.

Tools used with latex paint wash up easily with soap and water. Be sure to remove excess paint before washing instead of letting it go down the drain.

Use paint thinner to clean tools used with alkyd paint, and always wear rubber gloves. Do not pour paint thinner down the drain. Keep it in an old paint can or other container that won't be dissolved by the chemicals in the thinner. Then dispose of it properly at a toxic waste disposal site.

It's not necessary to clean brushes and rollers if you plan to return to your project shortly. Brushes will keep for a few days if you soak them in an appropriate solvent; or wrap them in foil, then in plastic and put those used with alkyd paint in the freezer and those used with latex paint in the refrigerator. Rollers or applicators will keep overnight wrapped tightly in a plastic bag.

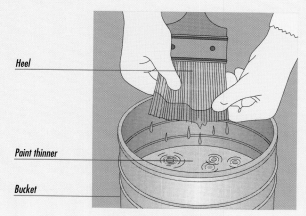

Heel

Paint thinner

Bucket

Cleaning alkyd paint
Wearing rubber gloves, work paint thinner into the brush's bristles until you've removed the paint all the way up to the heel.

CLEANING BRUSHES

Remove excess paint from brushes by brushing them out onto cardboard or newspaper. To clean a synthetic brush used with latex paint, hold the brush under running water until the water runs clear. Wash the brush with soap and lukewarm water, forcing water into the bristles and heel until the water drains clear. Rinse well.

To clean a natural-bristle or synthetic brush used with alkyd paint, work paint thinner into the bristles, especially at the

heel. Then use a wire brush to get out more paint. Once the brush is clean, remove excess thinner by shaking the brush vigorously and lightly tapping the handle against a hard edge, or use a brush spinner. When you've finished cleaning any brush, straighten the bristles with a bristle comb. Once the brush dries, wrap it in its original cover or in stiff paper. Store the brush flat or hang it to keep pressure off the bristles.

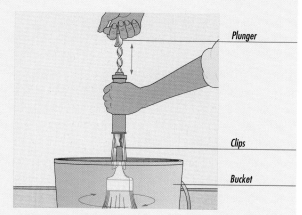

Plunger

Clips

Bucket

Using a brush spinner
After cleaning a brush, you can clip it into a brush spinner, hold it in a bucket, and push the handle in and out of the cylinder to clear the brush of water or solvent.

CLEANING ROLLERS

Squeeze out paint by pressing the roller against the lip of the bucket or roller tray. Scrape off caked-on paint with a putty knife, then remove the roller cover.

If the cover was used with latex paint, hold it under running water until the water runs clear. Wash with soap and lukewarm water, forcing water into the nap. Rinse, squeeze out excess water, blot lightly, and let dry. Wash the frame in soap and water.

To clean a cover used with alkyd paint, wash it in paint thinner, forcing the thinner into the nap. After it's clean, squeeze out any excess thinner. (Since covers are inexpensive, you may prefer to dispose of those used with alkyd paint after each use.) Wash the roller frame in thinner.

Store clean roller covers in plastic bags. Place on end to prevent the nap from becoming flattened.

Preparing Siding

When painting your home's exterior walls, preparation is critically important to a successful and lasting job. In many cases, simply washing the surface to be painted is not enough. Paint that has begun to fail usually must be completely removed to ensure that the new coat will adhere properly. While this is a significant job, the reward is a better-looking, durable finish.

SCRAPING To scrape small areas of peeling paint, a paint scraper, putty knife, or molding scraper is sufficient. Even where a sander is needed to remove an entire finish, you still will need to scrape areas where the sanding wheel won't reach, such as corners and other tight spots.

To be sure you loosen as much paint as possible, scrape areas of loose paint from every direction; sometimes old paint scraped from left to right seems solid but comes off easily when scraped from the opposite direction. Use two hands on the scraper, keeping it flat to avoid gouging the wood. If you do create gouge marks, sand them down or

fill them with a vinyl exterior spackling compound so they won't show through the new paint job. If the paint that remains after scraping has high or rough edges, sand, or "feather," them down with coarse sandpaper to make them less noticeable when painted over.

POWER SANDING Power sanders can be used to smooth the edges of scraped areas or to clear an entire surface of paint. For big jobs, an industrial 7-inch sander works best. This is something you can rent at an equipment rental firm.

Sanding is accomplished in two stages: First the paint cover is completely removed with coarse sandpaper—60-grit paper is recommended. It will leave cuts in the wood, so the same area must then be smoothed with medium sandpaper (100-grit).

Sanding is a meticulous process that requires the following precautions:
- Make sure the sander is running at full speed before touching the wheel to the surface.
- As you bring the sander into contact with the wall, lean on it slightly until you hear the motor slow, and keep moving it along the surface so you don't gouge the wood.
- Keep the sanding wheel at a very slight angle (5 to 10 degrees) to the wall; otherwise, the wheel will spin out of control across the surface.
- Discard sanding disks as they become clogged with paint or they will begin to burn the surface.
- Protect yourself from flying paint chips, dust, noise, and the spinning disk of the sander with the proper safety equipment—earplugs, a dust mask, safety goggles, gloves, and heavy work clothes.
- Be sure the sander is turned off when you plug it in.
- Keep the sanding wheel well away from your body.
- Do not use a power sander in the rain.
- Never use a power sander near flammable liquids.

PAINT-REMOVAL ALTERNATIVES

Although scraping and sanding are the most commonly used methods for preparing surfaces, other options make more sense in certain circumstances.

■ LIQUID PAINT REMOVER Ornate woodwork can be damaged by scraping and sanding. Liquid paint remover breaks down the bond between the paint and the surface, causing the paint to bubble and soften, allowing it to be removed from the surface with a putty knife or paint scraper. Liquid paint removers are caustic, so use them only in the open air, and always wear protective gloves and safety goggles.

■ HEAT GUNS To remove especially tenacious areas of paint, a heat gun is an option (see page 40). Heat guns, though, can be dangerous, since they function at extremely high temperatures and can easily ignite any surrounding flammable material. When using a heat gun, wear protective gloves and hold it several inches from the surface. As the paint begins to bubble and melt, turn off the heat gun and scrape off the paint with a putty knife or paint scraper.

Lip

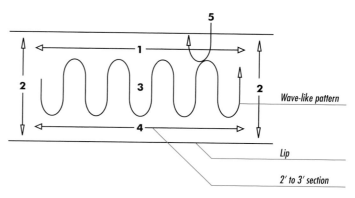

5

1

2   3   2

4

Wave-like pattern

Lip

2' to 3' section

1 **Sand clapboard in sequence**

Starting with coarse paper, sand successive 2- or 3-foot sections, starting along the lip, then sanding both ends of the section. To sand the middle of the section, move the sander in a wave-like pattern (see detail). Finally, sand the bottom of the section and along the underside of the lip.

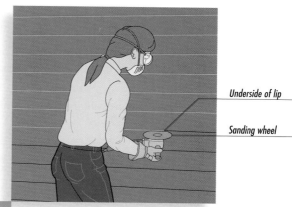

Underside of lip

Sanding wheel

2 **Sanding the lip's underside**

Hold the sander on its side with the wheel facing upward. Once the surface is finished, sand it again with fine sandpaper to eliminate sander marks.

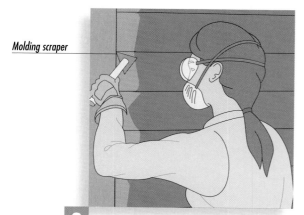

Molding scraper

3 **Feather & scrape corners**

Corners and edges cannot be fully reached by the sander. Feather the edges, using the sander fitted with coarse sandpaper. Then scrape any loose paint out of the corners with a molding scraper.

Painting Siding & Trim

Once you have made all the necessary repairs and prepared the surfaces, it's time to paint—almost. Before you begin any exterior project, protect the surrounding area with thick cotton dropcloths. Use 3-inch tape to mask roofing or other surfaces that will not be coated but can become splattered with paint. Carry a scraper with you in case you come across small areas of loose paint you missed during surface preparation.

Let a wall dry fully before deciding whether touch-ups are needed. A paint finish often will look patchy or uneven until it has fully dried.

Most people paint the trim a different color than the siding. If that is your plan, wait until the siding is completely dry before beginning on the trim, then apply masking tape to protect the siding from the trim paint and remove the tape immediately after finishing.

For the best possible finish, paint the overhangs and gutters, then the main surfaces, then the trim. Last, do shutters, railings, the porch (if applicable), and the foundation.

PAINTING SIDING

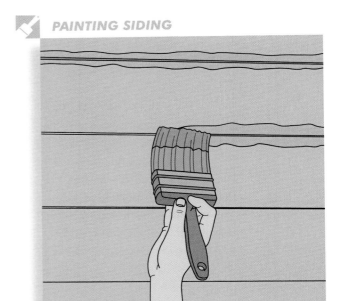

1 **Paint the edges**

Working in 3- or 4-foot-square sections, paint against the bristles along the bottom edges of horizontal boards. To prevent drips and lap marks, paint all the way across three or four boards. Dip the brush no more than 1 inch into the paint.

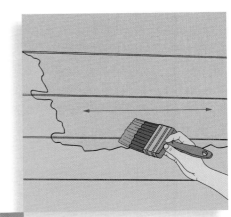

2 **Paint the surface**

Dip the brush about 2 inches into the paint and tap it against the side of the bucket to clear paint from one side, then turn the brush parallel to the ground as you lift it. Quickly press the paint-heavy side of the brush against the surface, spreading the paint in a side-to-side motion on horizontal siding or up and down on vertical siding.

STAINING SIDING

Exterior staining requires no primer and is easier to apply than paint. Stain can be applied to new wood, wood sanded clear of paint, and surfaces previously stained.

A disadvantage of stain is that it fades more quickly than paint, and so requires more frequent recoating; however, if you apply two or more coats at one application, you can extend the life of the finish considerably. Also, lap marks are more difficult to eliminate because stain dries more quickly than paint; an added frustration is that you cannot see lap marks until the surface has dried, and the only way to eliminate them is to add another coat.

As you work, be sure to mix the stain at regular intervals, as the pigment settles quite quickly. Use a stain brush, which is wider and has shorter bristles than a paintbrush, to control dripping.

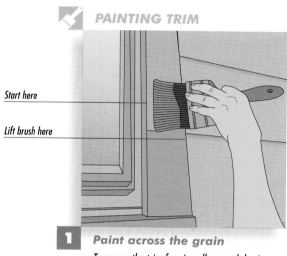

Start here

Lift brush here

Brush in line
with grain

1 **Paint across the grain**

To ensure the trim face is well covered, begin
applying the paint by brushing perpendicular to
the direction of the wood grain. Start at the inside
edge and paint toward the siding, lifting the brush
off the board just as you reach the other edge.

2 **Paint with grain**

To smooth out the paint and create an even cover,
finish painting the trim by brushing with the grain.
Turn the brush diagonally to the trim if it is too
wide to avoid getting paint on the siding.

PAINTING TIPS

■ Hold the brush comfortably, with a grip that gives you
good control.

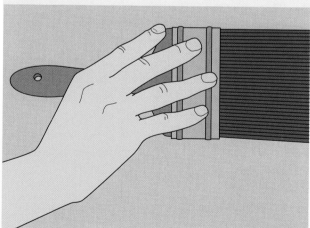

Paint exterior doors and windows using the sequence outlined for interior surfaces (see pages 50–51). Shutters are
easier to paint if you remove them and use a power
sprayer (see page 41). If you decide to paint shutters with
a brush, begin with the joints where the louvers meet the
frame, then paint the louvers and finish with the frame.
Paint against the grain, then smooth out the finish by painting with the grain.

Paint in fair (above 50-degree), dry weather; cooler temperatures mean poor adherence. Apply paint after the
morning dew dries, and stop at least 2 hours before
evening damp. Avoid painting in direct sun; if possible, follow the sun around the house. Don't apply solvent-thinned
paints to cool surfaces that will be heated by the sun in a
few hours or they may blister.

■ After painting for a while, the bristles next to a brush's
metal band will become thick with paint and start to drip.
Clean them by dragging each side of the brush over the
rim of the paint can a few times.

■ As you paint, check for drips and streaks every 15 minutes or so and smooth them out immediately. Once the
paint has dried, these imperfections will be much harder to
hide. If you find a drip after the paint has dried, cut it off
with a putty knife, slicing carefully from bottom to top,
then touch up.

Decorative Painting

Decorative finishes, frequently called faux or false finishes, often fool you into thinking that you're looking at wood, marble, or stone. In a larger sense, decorative painting is simply a means to creating a colorful, eye-catching finish with depth and vitality. Before undertaking your choice of decorative technique, organize the room, prepare surfaces, and follow basic painting guidelines as you would for any interior painting project (see pages 44-45).

CHOOSING A TECHNIQUE Most decorative painting techniques use tinted washes and glazes to achieve textural layers of color. A wash is watered-down latex paint, and a glaze is thinned, translucent oil-base or acrylic color.

Techniques fall into two categories: applicative and subtractive. Applicative techniques—sponging, ragging, and colorwashing—involve applying color with the appropriate tool, gradually building up layers until the desired effect is achieved. Subtractive techniques—dragging, marbling, and wood graining—involve applying color and removing some of it to get the desired effect. In both cases, the background color, or base coat, is intended to be partly visible.

To give walls added dimension and warmth, try colorwashing. To create an abstract pattern, consider sponging or ragging. If you'd like to tie together several decorative elements of a room, a floor-to-ceiling stencil copied from a design on the curtains or rug may be the answer. Marbling is an obvious choice to lend richness to a fireplace mantel and surround.

Some techniques, such as dragging, look best on a smooth surface since they make flaws more noticeable. Sponging and ragging are the techniques most appropriate for bumpy, irregular walls since they camouflage imperfections.

If you don't have much painting experience, try one of the easier techniques, such as sponging, ragging, colorwashing, or stenciling with a precut pattern. Sponging off, ragging off, and dragging are more difficult and require a little practice. Marbling and wood graining are the most challenging. Before you take on any of these, do a test on a white piece of cardboard or an area of wall that you don't mind repainting to see if the colors you've chosen are appealing.

Be aware that if you work with fast-drying latex washes, the edges of the paint will dry quickly, creating lap marks; mixing some commercial glaze into the recipe will lengthen the drying time. Working with a partner also helps: one can apply the base coat while the other does the technique work.

BASE COAT Examine the base coat on your walls carefully before beginning. If the existing paint is in good shape and the color is compatible with the finish you want, you won't need to repaint. But if the walls are dingy, damaged, or the wrong color, you will need to apply a new base coat.

The water-base mediums—latex washes and acrylic glazes—adhere best to latex base coats with an eggshell, satin, or semigloss finish. They don't stick well to a gloss finish, even if it has been deglossed (see page 44 for deglossing techniques). Oil glazes adhere well to an eggshell, satin, or semigloss latex or alkyd base. You can even use oil glazes over a high-gloss finish if you sand first. For applicative techniques, an eggshell base coat is recommended; for subtractive techniques, a semigloss base coat is best.

CORNERS If you have a steady hand, you can paint corners as shown on the following pages, working carefully and finishing with a brush. An alternative approach is to decorate one wall at a time after masking adjacent surfaces (with a slow-drying glaze, let the painted surfaces dry overnight before masking them to paint adjacent walls).

TRANSPARENT COATINGS A clear coating applied to the painted surface protects it, makes it washable, and can give it a glossier finish. To cover the project with a clear coating, use a nonyellowing water-base product that can be applied over any finish. Most of these coatings are classified as waterborne liquid plastics, varnishes, or urethanes and are available in satin, semigloss, and gloss. Apply these products with a brush, since a roller will create air bubbles.

Sponging

Sponging creates a mottled finish suitable for walls, ceilings, doors, and furniture. Since sponging hides flaws, the surface does not have to be perfectly smooth. Apply the paint to an eggshell base coat (page 30), using a large, flat sea sponge with medium-size pores.

Note: A more subtle, subtractive variation—sponging off—is to apply paint over the base with a brush or roller, then to dab the surface with a moistened sponge to remove some of the paint.

1) Moisten the sponge
One hour before starting to paint, moisten the sponge with water and wring it dry. (For oil-base glaze, use solvent instead of water.) Dip sponge lightly into wash or glaze, loading only about one quarter of the surface. Squeeze so sponge is wet but not dripping.

2) Dab the surface
Dab the wall lightly, rotating the sponge as you lift it to vary the pattern.

3) Sponge corners
Tear off a small piece of sponge and gently dab into corner. You may wish to mask the adjacent surface as described on page 45.

4) Finish corners
On spots in corners where the sponge will not reach, use a fine artist's brush to make dots that mimic the mottled impressions of the sponge.

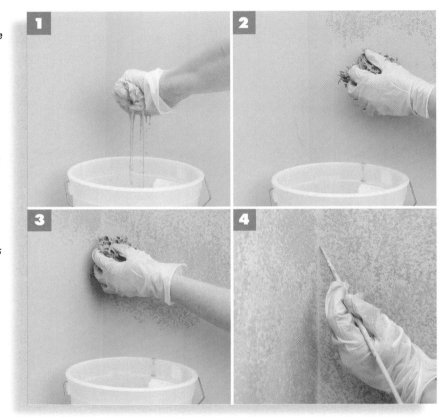

ADD COLORS
If you wish, you may apply a second and even a third color, following these steps. Be sure to allow each coat to dry completely before applying the next one.

The color you apply last will be the most dominant. Experiment with your base coat and top coats to decide which color should be applied first.

Dragging

1 **Apply the glaze**
Over the top of a dry base coat (page 58), brush or roll on glaze or wash from ceiling to floor in strips no more than 18 inches wide.

2 **Drag with a dry brush**
Place a wide, dry paintbrush at the top of a strip and press so that the bristles bend back to the heel of the brush. Drag the brush down the length of the strip. Wipe the brush after each pass.

Dragging creates a pattern of thin stripes on a surface. The best candidates for this technique are smooth and regular walls, doors, and furniture. The traditional dragging tool is a brush, but you can also use cheesecloth or a comb sold for decorative painting.

It's best to drag over a semigloss base coat. Drag a complete section before it dries, and try to keep stripes parallel unless you want to achieve a rough, irregular effect.

ALTERNATIVE METHOD

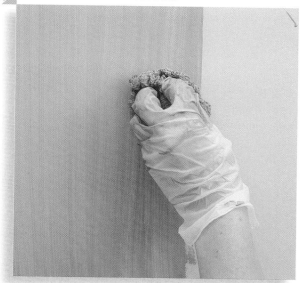

Instead of brushing or rolling, then dragging with a dry paintbrush, you can achieve the same effect by simply dipping wadded cheesecloth into the glaze or wash and dragging downward in narrow passes.

Ragging On

Suitable for walls, ceilings, doors, and furniture, ragging creates a larger mottled effect than sponging and is the simplest of all decorative painting techniques. Clean, lint-free soft cotton cloths work best, as do old cotton napkins or new T-shirts. To create a dramatic effect, select bold, contrasting colors; for a more subtle look, use soft or pastel colors; to achieve a sense of depth, try variations of the same color. No matter how many colors you apply, always let some background show through.

1) Moisten the rag
Soak a clean, dry, lint-free rag in the wash or glaze and wring it out well.

2) Rag the surface
Loosely bunch up the rag and lightly dab the surface. To vary the pattern, rebunch and rotate the rag as you work.

3) Dab the corners
Gently dab the rag as far as you can into the corner. Protect the adjacent wall with masking tape if you don't intend to continue the treatment onto it.

4) Finish the corners
In corner areas the rag will not reach, use an artist's brush to mimic the impressions made by the rag.

5) Add colors
You may apply a second and even a third color, following these steps. Allow each coat to dry.

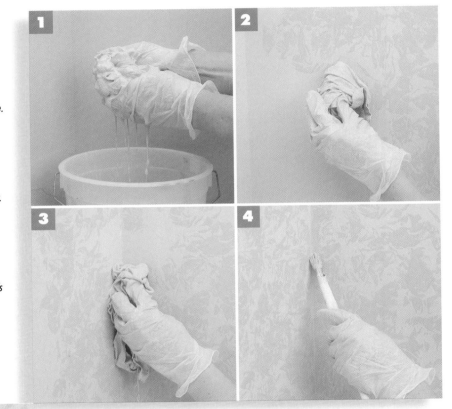

Painting Decorative

Ragging off is just another method of ragging. Instead of ragging on color, apply a wash or glaze (page 35) with a brush or roller, then rag it off to achieve a mottled effect similar to ragging on. Using an alkyd glaze is easiest since it remains wet longer.

1 *Cut in with a brush*

Begin by cutting in at a corner, brushing on wash or glaze in sections no more than 15 inches long.

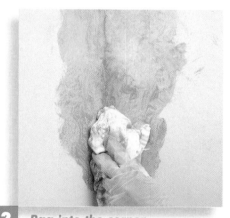

2 *Rag into the corner*

Press a clean, dry, bunched-up rag as far into the corner as possible. Don't be concerned if the color in the corners ends up a little darker than the walls. Of course, if you don't want to continue onto the adjacent wall, mask it off (page 45).

3 *Glaze & rag*

Moving out from the corners, continue applying wash or glaze with a paintbrush or roller to areas no more than 6 feet square. Blot the wet surfaces with a dry, bunched-up rag, working back into previous sections to blur lap lines. To vary the pattern, rebunch and rotate the rag occasionally. When the rag becomes saturated, switch to a clean one. Ragging off is a perfect project for two people, one to brush or roll, the other to rag.

Colorwashing

◤ COLORWASHING WITH GLAZE

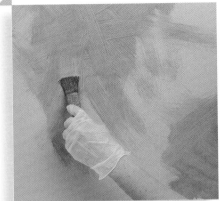

1 *Brush on glaze*
Brush on a thin layer of glaze made with 70 to 90 percent solvent in small, irregular patches of different sizes and shapes.

Colorwashing is a particularly good choice when you're seeking to create a rustic or informal appearance on rough, flawed walls because it emphasizes any surface imperfections. It also makes a perfect backdrop to stenciling. It can be achieved with a glaze as shown in the three-step process below or with latex wash or paint, using one of the three methods shown on the facing page.

Generally, the thinner the coat you apply, the richer the result will be. You can use variations of a single color or different but related colors. Applying a light-colored glaze over a darker one produces a chalky, antique effect. A darker glaze over a light one will create a translucent quality.

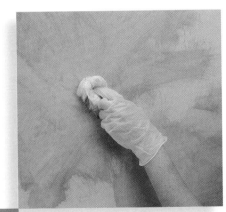

2 *Blend with a rag*
While glaze is wet, blend out with a clean, dry cotton rag or cheesecloth, or a large, dry paintbrush. Wipe off the glaze until you achieve the desired effect.

3 *Add colors*
If you wish, you may apply a second and even a third color, following these steps. Be sure to allow each coat to dry completely before applying the next one.

 Glazes produce a richer, more dramatic finish than latex washes or paint, and they're easier to work with because they dry more slowly.

Building up thin layers
Brush on three or four layers of very thin washes (9 parts water to 1 part paint), allowing each layer to dry thoroughly before applying the next one. Slap on each wash quickly and haphazardly.

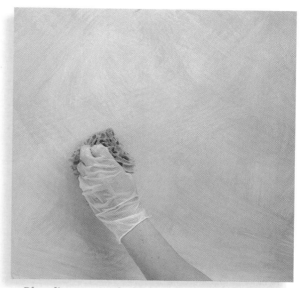

Blending a single layer
Brush on a thin wash (4 parts water to 1 part paint) in small irregular patches of not more than 6 square feet. Blur wet brush marks with a clean, damp sponge or paintbrush.

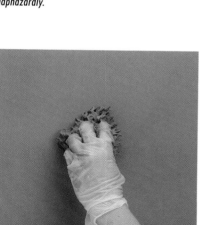

Smearing an undiluted paint layer
On a background with the same color value as the paint to be applied, smear on and push around undiluted latex paint with a natural sea sponge.

Marbling

Marbling, a somewhat advanced technique, uses a glaze or latex wash to simulate the delicate, veined look of marble. As such, it is a perfect choice for accenting surfaces such as fireplace surrounds, moldings, and doors (but ornate surfaces are very difficult to marble).

Working with glaze, the traditional method, requires a lot of practice and a good sense of timing (the surfaces can't be too wet or too dry when you work the glaze). Latex washes are more forgiving—each layer dries quickly, making the process easier.

1) Brush on the background
On an area no more than 6 square feet, brush on a background glaze to match the surface color. Using glazes in other colors, paint irregular shapes, or drifts, on the wet surface and blot each with a dry, bunched-up rag.

2) Paint lines
Put a dab of paint (artist's oils for oil glaze, artist's acrylics for acrylic glaze) on one side of a small brush tip. Holding the side of the brush without paint against the surface, paint lines, or veins, with a light, shaky motion (paint from the other side of the brush will bleed through). Blot the veins with a dry rag.

3) Soften lines
Wait several seconds for the glaze to dry slightly, then soften and blur the veins with a blending brush held at a right angle to the surface, or with crumpled tissue paper.

MARBLING WITH GLAZE

4) Scrape to create lines
Make additional veins by scraping away glaze with the edge of a cork, using a shaky, squiggly motion. Blot the veins with a dry rag or crumpled tissue paper, or soften them with a blending brush.

5) Apply fine lines
Apply a small amount of thinned paint in a color that will stand out from the others to a fine liner brush or the tip of a feather. While supporting the opposite elbow with your free hand, make final veins with a light, shaky touch.

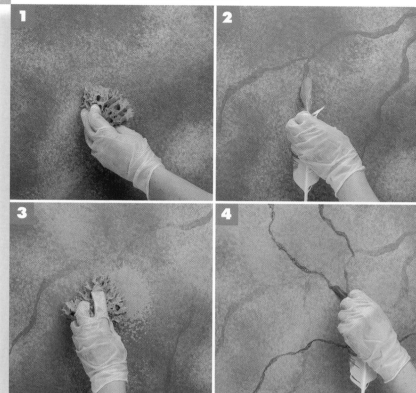

1) Apply the background wash

Use a natural sea sponge to dab on latex wash in irregular shapes, or drifts, to small sections. Immediately after applying the wash, blot the wet surface with a clean, damp sponge to spread drifts and soften them.

2) Paint lines

With a light, shaky touch, paint lines, or veins, over the entire surface with a feather dipped into thinned latex paint or artist's acrylics. Use the same color as the background to create the appearance of fissures.

3) Apply the second wash

Using another color, sponge on a second wash in drifts, blotting each drift before it dries. Cover some areas not coated by the first wash.

4) Add lines

Make additional veins with thinned latex paint or artist's acrylics in a harmonizing color, using a feather (see Step 2). Sponge on a third wash of the background color in drifts, blotting as you go. Cover areas not covered by first and second washes.

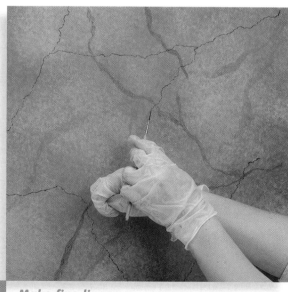

5) Make fine lines

Using a color that will stand out from the others, make veins over the surface with a fine liner brush or the tip of a feather. Use a light, shaky touch.

Wood Graining

Fool-the-eye authentic wood graining is a difficult art to master, but you can employ basic wood graining techniques—both fantasy and authentic—to imitate the warmth and feel of wood. Fantasy treatments, as shown on this page, are the easiest. To create an authentic look, using the methods for mahogany graining on the facing page, experiment on a practice surface before you tackle your walls or woodwork.

With fantasy finishes, applying a dark brown glaze over a background color or canary yellow will give a very realistic look; you can also use reds, blues, or other colors. Varying values of similar colors work well together; apply the darker shade over the lighter one. Protect finished graining with a transparent coating.

SIMPLE WOOD GRAINING

1 **Drag the surface**

After applying glaze to a panel or other area no more than 6 feet square, drag the wet surface with an ordinary paintbrush or cheesecloth, or pat the wet surface with the flat of a brush, using a quick, bouncing motion.

2 **Create wood graining**

Create wood grain using a pencil overgrainer, an artist's brush, a fan overgrainer (shown), or a homemade tool such as a squeegee cut with notches. Experiment on a trial surface.

MOTTLED GRAINING

1 **Apply glaze**

Apply glaze with a paintbrush to a panel or area no larger than 6 feet square using a scumbling, or sideways scratching, motion.

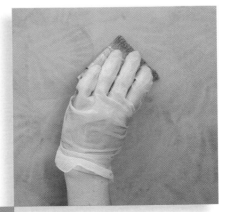

2 **Brush the surface**

Holding the mottling brush in the palm of your hand, press your fingertips into the bristles and push the wet glaze around in irregular curves or swirls.

1) Flog the surface
After brushing glaze on a panel or small area, pat the wet surface with the flat of a brush, using a quick bouncing motion.

2) Create arched graining
Make a series of arches by dipping a fan overgrainer brush into paint, dabbing off the excess, then spreading the bristles with your fingertips. Hold the brush nearly parallel to the surface and at a right angle to the arches you're creating.

3) Soften the graining
Soften the grain by brushing it lightly with a softening brush held at a right angle to the surface.

4) Create straight graining
With a fan overgrainer, make straight grains at a slight angle on both sides of arches.

 For mahogany graining, ask your paint store to mix the rich, warm mahogany hue or do it yourself by mixing equal parts of burnt sienna, alizarin crimson, and raw umber. Use artist's oils in an oil glaze or artist's acrylics in an acrylic glaze. Some professionals paint over a dirty-pink base coat; others prefer to paint over a reddish-yellow background.

5 Grain the rails & stiles
If your project includes rails, brush glaze above and below the completed panel, then flog at a slight angle away from the panel. Use a fan overgrainer to make horizontal arches—those on the upper rail should go in the opposite direction to those on the lower rail. Then brush the rails lightly with a softening brush. Repeat this method for the stiles.

Stenciling

Stenciling is a great way to create personal, handcrafted accents or repeating patterns on walls, ceilings, floors, cabinetry, and furniture. Stenciled designs can be a single color, two colors, or more. Artist's acrylics are easiest to use because they're water-soluble yet provide intense, quick-drying color (oils and slow-drying paints can smudge easily).

Plan your layout before actually painting stencils. When stenciling across the top of a wall, for example, start at the center and work toward the corners; adjust the spacing between designs as needed to ensure that the last designs at the corners will be complete.

For information on making stencils, see facing page. To apply the paint, use either a small-celled synthetic sponge or a short, blunt-bristled stencil brush; you may find the sponge easier to manipulate.

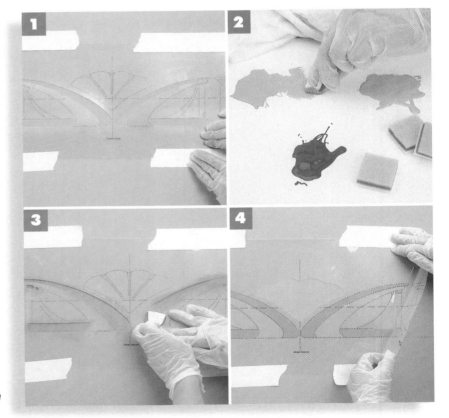

1) Tape up the stencil
Measure and mark stencil placement guidelines with a steel tape measure and a pencil. Secure the stencil to the surface with tape that won't leave marks.

2) Mix the paint
Mix the paint to a thick, pasty consistency. Dip a sponge or stencil brush into it, then tap the applicator on a piece of scrap paper to get rid of excess (otherwise paint may seep under the stencil).

3) Apply paint to the stencil
Apply paint to the surface with a sponge or brush by tapping it directly against the surface or using a circular motion. Work from the outside of each shape toward the shape's center.

4) Touch up
After all shapes are filled in with paint, carefully remove the stencil and touch up any smudges at the image's edges. Allow to dry. Repeat with another stencil if you wish to add another color; carefully align the designs. Each color should have a separate stencil unless the sections to be painted in different colors are spaced far apart. You'll need separate stencils if the design has many small pieces or lines that run close together, even if they're in the same color.

MAKING YOUR OWN STENCIL

While commercial stencils are available in a wide variety of styles, you can greatly increase your design options by making your own. This is particularly useful when you want to match an existing decorative element in your home or create a motif with a favorite design. Copying an existing design is easy. If the example is not the right size, simply reduce or enlarge it on a photocopier.

SUPPLIES Clear acetate (.0075 gauge) works best for stencils because it's transparent and allows you to layer as many sheets as you need and still see the design clearly. Stencil board is another option, but it is opaque.

You'll also need colored pencils, a utility or craft knife and a supply of sharp blades, a ruler, masking tape, and a good cutting surface. If you have not been able to photocopy the design to make a cutting guide, use drawing supplies and graph paper to transfer the design onto the stencil material.

TRANSFERRING THE DESIGN Draw the design to the desired size on graph paper. If you're copying from a stencil book, the design will already have bridges—narrow strips that link the different parts of the design and prevent the stencil from falling apart. Otherwise, you must put in bridges yourself by breaking the design into logical segments and

Graph paper for registration

placing bridges between them. Color the completed design with the appropriate colors so you'll know which shapes to cut out for each stencil.

Trim the stencil material, leaving a 1-inch margin around the design. Tape the first stencil layer over the entire design

and trace the areas that will be painted with the first color. If you are using more than one layer, leave the first one in place and tape successive stencils on top.

To align succeeding stencils, trace a section of the next stencil with a dotted line. Also number the top front side of each stencil in its order of application.

CUTTING THE STENCILS Place each stencil on a flat, firm cutting surface. Using a utility or craft knife, cut out the stencil design, drawing the blade slowly toward you in a smooth, continuous movement. When you are cutting curves, turn the

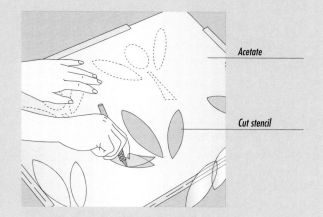

Acetate

Cut stencil

design rather than the knife. Trim any jagged edges after the original cut is made. Don't worry if the cut edges of the stencil aren't perfect; slight flaws won't be noticeable in the finished work.

USING PHOTOCOPIES If you have a clear photocopy of the design in the exact size you need, you don't have to draw the design onto stencil material (however, you will have to draw in bridges if there aren't any in the design). You can simply attach the photocopy to the stencil material and use it as a cutting guide. Remember that you will need a separate photocopy for each color in the design.

To cut from a photocopied design, coat the back of each copy with removable spray adhesive and press it firmly to the stencil material. To make sure it is securely attached, also tape down the edges. On each stencil, cut registration marks, then all the areas that will be painted the same color. After each stencil is cut, remove the photocopy.

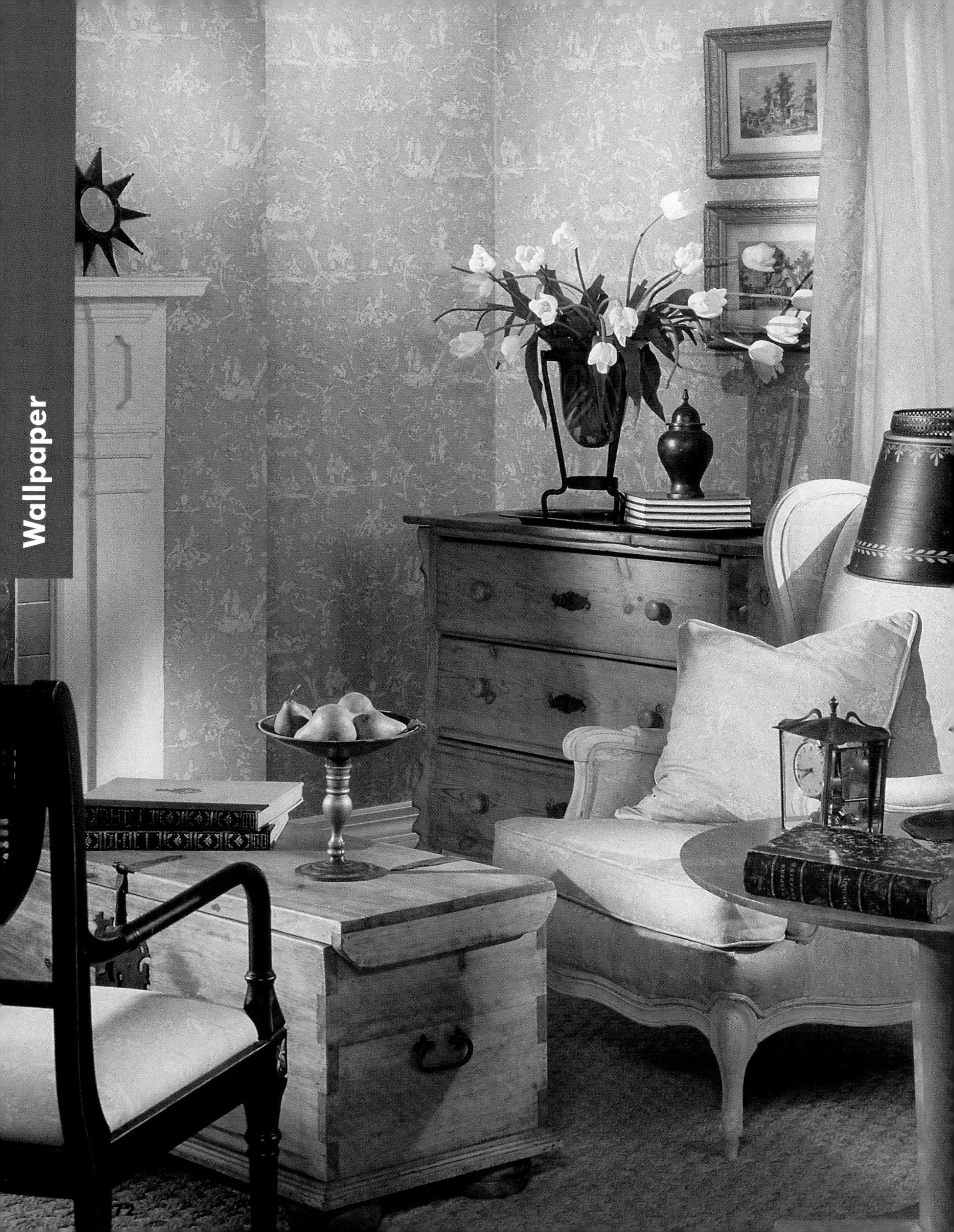

Wallpaper

If you think of wallpaper as clothing for your walls, you will begin to get a sense of the tremendous possibilities this versatile decorating material offers. An amazing array of colors, patterns, textures, and embellishments—priced from downright cheap to extraordinarily expensive—exists today.

Originally designed to give the middle class the look of hand-painted wall treatments at a fraction of the price, wallpaper, together with coordinating accent borders, opens up a world of design possibilities impossible to duplicate with paint. If you've been traumatized by wallpaper installation attempts in your past, fear not. Gone are the days of gluepots and messy disasters. Most do-it-yourself wallpapers today are easier and more forgiving to install than ever before. Study the techniques offered on the next few pages, then get creative!

Buying Wallpaper

Wallpaper stores and home centers have dozens of sample books with hundreds of colors, patterns, and textures. Before you go to choose a wallcovering, know the effect you want to achieve and the location where you will hang it. If possible, take along samples of your upholstery fabric and carpet, as well as a list of textures and colors that feature prominently in the room to be papered. Bring along a photo and scale drawing of the room to help you visualize different wallpapers in the space. Then, before you buy, bring home samples to see how they look in the room—by day and night.

Don't necessarily think in terms of papering an entire room. Perhaps you can get the look you want by papering just one wall or the ceiling. You may decide to use two coordinating papers (if they are both hung on one wall, the darker pattern should be on the bottom), separated by a border. At the ceiling line, a border can accentuate a crown molding or compensate for the lack of one; chair rail borders lend a traditional feel to a room.

Choosing Materials

A wallcovering's material content determines its durability, cleanability, cost, and ease of installation and removal. Before purchasing any wallpaper, ask about these qualities, as well as the manufacturer's guarantees.

VINYL The most popular wallcoverings are made of a continuous, flexible vinyl film applied to a backing. They are durable, strong, and easy to maintain. Backings may be fabric or paper. Fabric-backed vinyl, the sturdiest wallpaper, is washable (often scrubbable), moisture resistant, and usually strippable (it can be removed from the wall by hand without leaving any residue). Fabric-backed vinyl usually comes unpasted.

Paper-backed vinyl is lightweight, so it often comes prepasted. Expanded vinyl, a paper-backed type, produces a three-dimensional effect on the wall and is especially well suited to walls that aren't perfectly smooth. It frequently comes in styles that mimic the look of such surfaces as rough plaster, granite, textured paint, or grass cloth.

Vinyl-coated paper is paper coated with a vinyl layer so thin that it looks like paper. It lends a finished look to a wall but is best for light-use areas because it stains and tears more easily than papers that have greater vinyl content.

TEXTILES These wallcoverings come in many colors and textures, in styles ranging from very casual to formally elegant. They're usually made of natural fibers such as cotton or linen, or polyester, bonded to a paper backing. A traditional favorite is grass cloth, which can be hung horizontally, vertically, or in a combination of the two. Hemp, similar to grass cloth but with thinner fibers, is easier to install.

HAND-SCREENED PAPER This vividly colorful paper is more expensive than most machine-printed wallpapers because each color is applied with a separate handmade and hand-placed silk screen. Some newer machine-printed papers have the look of hand-screened ones and are less expensive. Hanging these types of papers can be tricky. Patterns may match less evenly than many other wallcoverings, and edges often need to be trimmed and double-cut at seams. Also, because water-soluble dyes are often used in their manufacture, great care must be taken to ensure that the printed side is kept free of paste and water.

SOLID PAPER Paper wallcoverings with no vinyl content tear easily, and should only be considered for extremely light-use areas.

FOILS AND FLOCKS Foils and flocks (paper resembling damask or cut velvet) can brighten up any small, dark space. They require an absolutely smooth wall surface, and can wrinkle easily.

Estimating Needs

Once you've chosen your wallpaper, be sure to order enough so you don't have to go back for more—that way you're much more likely to get all of the rolls from the same lot so they don't vary in color.

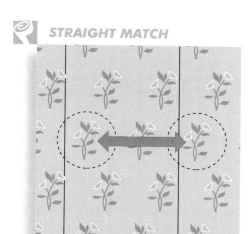

The design is continuous across strips. This type is easier to hang.

The design alternates between strips; pattern at strip's left edge is half a repeat lower than right edge.

THE REPEAT LENGTH You'll need to determine the repeat length (the distance between one design element on a pattern and the next occurrence of that element) and whether it is a straight match or drop match pattern (see illustrations above). The repeat length is usually printed on the back of the wallpaper sample, but you can measure it, too.

 The following estimates will help you determine the wallpaper's usable yield. For a single roll, the usable yield for a repeat length of:

0 to 6 inches = 25 square feet

7 to 12 inches = 22 square feet

13 to 18 inches = 20 square feet

19 to 23 inches = 18 square feet

Divide the calculated total square footage of the room by the usable yield of the wallpaper to get the number of rolls needed. Wallpaper rolls are sold in doubles, so always consider this when estimating.

WALL MEASUREMENTS To calculate the area to be covered, start by measuring the walls from floor to ceiling (excluding baseboards and/or moldings). Take your measurements in feet, rounding off to the next highest half or full foot. Then measure the width of the walls again, rounding to the next highest half or full foot. Multiply the height by the width to obtain the total square footage. Add 15 percent to this total for wastage. If the wall has several—or large—windows and doors, deduct their total square footage.

MULTIPLE PAPERS AND BORDERS When hanging different papers above and below a chair rail, use the same methods to figure the square footage of the separate spaces. For borders, measure the lengths you'll need, then divide by 3 to get the number of yards—most border material is sold in 5-yard lengths. If you're planning to border around doors or windows, add a little extra for mitering the corners (cutting them at 45-degree angles).

ESTIMATING WALLPAPER ROLLS

This chart will help you estimate the number of single rolls (remember, wallpaper only comes in double rolls, so round up) for walls of specific heights and widths. A rule of thumb is to subtract one-half roll for each standard door or window opening. Adjust for pattern-repeat length.

WALL'S WIDTH (FEET)	WALL'S HEIGHT (FEET)				
	8	9	10	11	12
6	3	3	3	4	5
8	3	4	4	5	6
10	5	5	5	6	7
12	5	5	5	7	8
14	5	5	7	7	8
16	7	7	8	8	9
18	7	8	8	8	10
20	8	8	9	10	11
22	9	9	10	11	12
24	9	9	10	12	13
26	10	10	12	13	14
28	10	12	13	14	16
30	10	12	13	15	16
32	12	13	14	16	18
34	13	14	15	16	18
36	14	14	16	18	20

First Steps & Wallpaper Tools

Before you start, gather together the tools, equipment, and supplies you'll need so everything will be on hand when you're ready for it. And, because wallpapering can be messy, you'll want to prepare the room for your work. Here are the steps to take and the equipment to gather:

Protect the Room

Remove all light furnishings and decorative objects. Cover the floor and any remaining furniture with dropcloths. For extra floor protection, use masking tape to fasten towels to the top of the baseboards under the dropcloths. Never use newspapers for protection because any moisture may cause the newsprint to bleed onto wall or floor coverings.

Remove everything from the walls, including drapery rods. Turn off the power to the room before removing wall sconces or electrical faceplates.

If you are painting woodwork or adjoining walls before wallpapering, allow the paint to dry completely. You can safely install any new flooring—except carpeting—before wallpapering.

Gather Equipment & Supplies

You'll need a ladder to reach the tops of walls; a sander or sanding block and 50-grit sandpaper for smoothing the walls; and a bucket, sponges, and trisodium phosphate (TSP), ammonia, or household bleach, which kill mildew, to clean the walls. You also may need a primer-sealer if walls are new.

CUTTING TOOLS

You will need a razor or utility knife to cut the paper. Buy plenty of blades, because dull ones will cause tears. Also have on hand a metal straightedge and large utility shears or scissors.

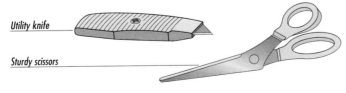

Utility knife

Sturdy scissors

Metal straightedge

Set up a pasting table—a long table, boards on sawhorses, or a table rented from your wallpaper dealer—and keep a large plastic bag handy for booking strips (see page 81).

Walls, seams, and borders may each require a different adhesive. The type depends on the kind of paper, so check the manufacturer's recommendations. Premixed adhesive is generally easier to work with than dry adhesive. Clay-base products hold to the wall better than cellulose or wheat-base paste, but they are messier and harder to handle. Mix dry paste with distilled water only.

If your wallcovering contains vinyl, buy a tube of vinyl-to-vinyl seam adhesive. To hang borders—even prepasted borders—over vinyl paper, you may need vinyl-to-vinyl adhesive in tub form formulated specifically for use on vinyl and not on paint.

LAYOUT TOOLS

You'll need a measuring tape and, depending on your project, a plumb bob or a long carpenter's level for aligning vertical lines. A short level is handy for use in small spaces and to check the straightness of the paper as you work.

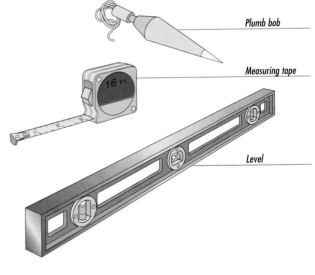

Plumb bob

Measuring tape

Level

REMOVAL TOOLS

To remove existing wallpaper, depending on its type, you'll need a broad knife, a sanding block (or scarifying tool), and a tool for helping release the old wallpaper—either a steamer, a canister-style garden sprayer (available for rent), or a sponge. Enzyme-based gel wallpaper remover goes on with a roller; it is the least messy alternative.

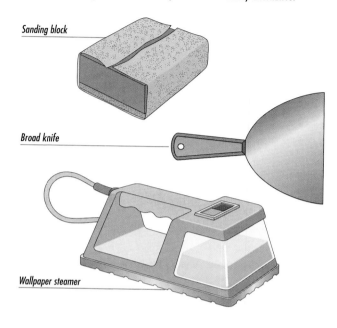

Sanding block

Broad knife

Wallpaper steamer

 SMOOTHING TOOLS

For smoothing, work with a wallpaper smoother, a rag, a sponge, or a high-quality smoothing brush. Whichever tool you choose, it should allow you to apply pressure evenly yet feel whether the wallpaper is smooth or uneven. With textured or embossed paper, always use a smoothing brush. After paper has dried for about 15 minutes, smooth with a smoother or sponge; using a seam roller (on conventional wallpapers only) helps flatten seams and make them unnoticeable.

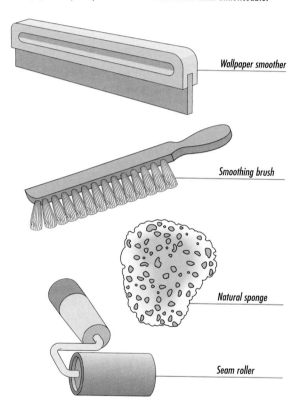

Wallpaper smoother

Smoothing brush

Natural sponge

Seam roller

 PASTING TOOLS

For pasting, use a short-napped paint roller with a paint tray, or a pasting brush with a bucket. A whisk works well for mixing dry paste. For prepasted paper, you'll need only a water tray.

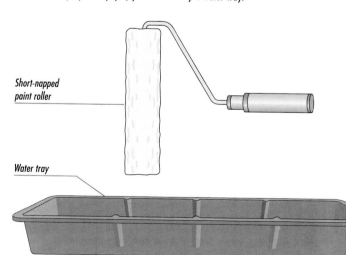

Short-napped paint roller

Water tray

Preparing a Surface

Making sure your walls are clean, smooth, and free of surface treatments that might cause problems beneath your new wallpaper is the first step toward a successful job. Proper wall preparation also will make the project go faster and easier.

Preparing a Papered Wall

You can hang new wallpaper over old under some conditions, but it's usually best to remove old paper before applying the new. Moisture from the pasting process can loosen the old paper, spoiling the smoothness of the new layer. And the ink from old paper can bleed through new paper unless you seal it with a special primer-sealer formulated to seal stains. Vinyl paper can also reject the adhesive used to apply new wallpaper.

Only consider applying new over old if the old paper is in good condition, smooth, and only one layer thick, and the new paper is a porous type. To prepare a papered surface to receive the new wallcovering, repaste and roll any loose seams, then spackle and sand all nicks, rough spots, or overlapping seams. Starting at the bottom, wash the wall with a solution of TSP (or a nonphosphate substitute) or ammonia and water, then let it dry completely.

To check if your old paper will bleed ink through the new wallcovering, moisten a small piece of the old paper with a clean sponge. If any ink comes off on the sponge, apply stain-sealing primer. If the existing paper is nonporous, use vinyl-to-vinyl primer to ensure proper drying of the adhesive and prevent mildew.

With strippable wallpaper, start at a seam and gently pull off both the vinyl coating and the backing. With peelable paper, the top layer will peel off easily but leave a thin residue of paper and adhesive. Remove this backing and adhesive with a wet sponge or with enzyme-based wallpaper remover, according to label directions.

Once paper and adhesive are removed, repair any wall damage (see page 122), then wash from the bottom up with a solution of TSP (or a nonphosphate substitute) or ammonia and water. When dry, apply primer-sealer.

Preparing Other Surfaces

Most surfaces are easier to prepare than previously papered walls, but any uneven or irregular surface needs special attention.

PAINTED WALLS Scrape and sand painted walls until they're smooth, then dust. Degloss by using sandpaper or an extra-strong solution of TSP (or nonphosphate substitute) or ammonia and water. Repair and wash the walls as previously described. Once the surface is dry, apply primer-sealer unless you know the paint is alkyd.

MILDEW Wearing eye protection and rubber gloves, scrub the area with a solution of half bleach and half water. If you are not sure whether the stains are mildew-caused, try washing them with a solution of detergent and water, which is ineffective on mildew. Next, sponge on straight liquid bleach to kill the spores, then a solution of TSP (or a nonphosphate substitute) and water, and finally rinse well. Let the surface dry completely—at least 24 hours. Then apply a coat of alkyd primer-sealer mixed with a fungicide additive.

NEW PLASTER WALLS Before papering, you'll have to wait until the new plaster has cured thoroughly—anywhere between one and four months. Consult with your contractor for the recommended time. Wash the new plaster with vinegar to neutralize it, then apply two coats of high-quality primer-sealer.

NEW WALLBOARD All wallboard joints should be taped, spackled, and sanded, then dusted with a short-napped soft brush. Remove the last particles of dust with a damp sponge. Finally, apply primer-sealer.

UNEVEN SURFACES Cinder block, concrete, wood paneling, textured plaster, and textured paint can be uneven enough surfaces that you'll have to smooth them before wallpapering. To check whether a wall's roughness will be a problem, apply adhesive to a piece of the wallpaper, smooth it on the wall, and examine it. If surface roughness shows through the paper, you'll have to smooth the wall.

Sanding block

Coarse sandpaper

Scoring

1 **Score the old wallpaper**

If your wallpaper has a vinyl or foil covering, abrade the surface so moisture or remover can penetrate and help break down the adhesive. Score the surface with coarse sandpaper or an inexpensive wallpaper scarifying tool (see photo at top of facing page).

For light to moderate unevenness or a small area, you can apply nonshrinking spackle or wallboard taping compound. When it's completely dry, sand and apply primer-sealer. You can also smooth such a surface by hanging liner paper, available where you buy the wallpaper. If a surface is severely uneven, it should be plastered or replastered.

Priming & Sizing

Primers and sizing are formulated to ease application and make wallpaper adhere well.

PRIMING In most cases, wallpaper adheres more easily if primer-sealer is applied to the wall. This compound keeps the wall surface from absorbing moisture from the adhesive and also protects the wall from damage if the covering is later removed. Walls painted with a high-quality flat alkyd paint may not need a primer.

Choose a primer-sealer designed as a wallcovering undercoat. Apply it with a roller at least 24 hours before hanging the wallcovering to allow it to dry thoroughly.

When you're hanging a light-colored paper over existing wallpaper or a colored wall, use pigmented primer-sealer matched to the paper's background color.

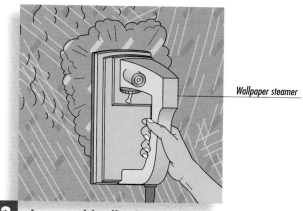

Wallpaper steamer

2 **Loosen old adhesive**

To loosen adhesive, move a steamer slowly along the walls or apply a fine mist of hot water with a canister-style garden sprayer. Or, you can use a liquid or gel enzyme-based remover; be sure to follow label directions.

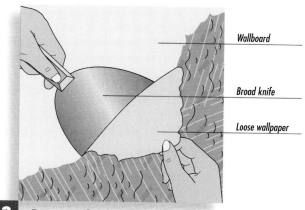

Wallboard

Broad knife

Loose wallpaper

3 **Remove the paper**

Working from the top of the wall down, remove all paper and adhesive thoroughly, using a broad knife or wide putty knife (be careful not to damage wallboard). If there are multiple layers of paper, remove one layer at a time, following the previous two steps.

SIZING A liquid coating designed to make wallpaper apply and adhere better and go on more easily, sizing is thought unnecessary in most cases due to advanced technology in primer-sealers. You may want to consider sizing if you're hanging a porous or heavy paper, if the wall is textured or alkyd-painted, if the paper isn't sticking well, or if the wallcovering manufacturer specifically recommends it.

Apply sizing with a roller or brush. It dries quickly, so you can begin hanging the wallcovering immediately unless the manufacturer recommends otherwise.

Basic Techniques

With proper preparation and the right tools, you can master the basic techniques of cutting, pasting, and hanging wallpaper. Always thoroughly review the manufacturer's instructions that come with your wallpaper, and try to work during the day—you'll match patterns better and see seams more clearly. When you're done for the day, cover wet wallpaper rolls and tools with plastic (if possible, put them in a refrigerator).

PLANNING PROPER LAYOUT

The three main options for choosing start and end points are: starting and ending above a door (see gold line), starting and ending in a corner behind a door (see pink line), and centering the first strip at a focal point in the room (see blue line). To determine which option is best, hold a wallpaper roll at the start point and mark with a pencil where the seams will fall, working your way around the room. Ideally, keep seams at least 4 inches away from corners, as well as the edges of windows and doors. In addition, try to plan seams so they fall near the center of windows and doors.

The first step in any wallpapering project is deciding where to hang the first and last strips. Since the pattern on the last strip you hang probably won't match that of the strip it meets, you may want to choose your end point first. The layout (below) shows several possible start and end points.

Because most house walls are not plumb—that is, at perfect right angles—you'll need to establish a plumb line on each wall to properly align the first strips, and thus all succeeding strips. To draw a plumb line, use a plumb bob and a carpenter's level. Once you've determined your layout strategy and established plumb lines, you're ready to start papering the walls.

CUTTING THE PAPER For the most visually appealing results, a wallpaper's design should be perfectly even at the ceiling line.

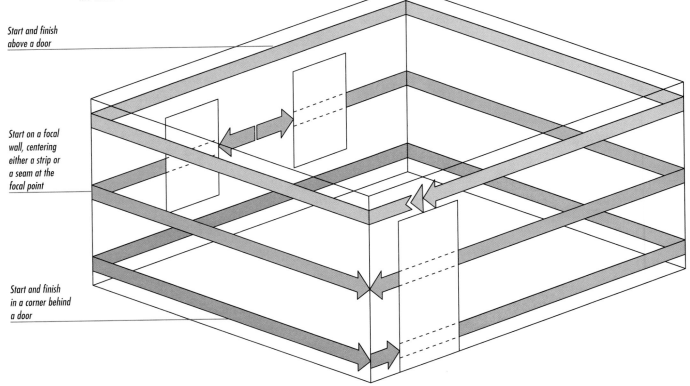

Start and finish
above a door

Start on a focal
wall, centering
either a strip or
a seam at the
focal point

Start and finish
in a corner behind
a door

To determine where to cut a strip, first measure the height of the wall. On the wallpaper roll, locate the design element you want at the top edge, measure 2 inches above that, and cut across the paper with a straightedge and a razor or utility knife (alternatively, you can lightly crease the paper and cut with utility shears or scissors). Add 2 inches to the wall-height measurement and cut a piece to that length (add 4 inches instead of 2 for a "drop match" pattern to achieve the proper pattern match). Roll the strip with the pattern side in to straighten it out.

(continued on page 82)

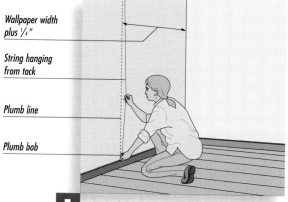

Wallpaper width
plus ¼"

String hanging
from tack

Plumb line

Plumb bob

1   **Establish a plumb starting point**
From your start point, make a mark at the ceiling (or molding) line equal to the width of your wallpaper plus ¼ inch (this is to prevent the plumb line from bleeding through the seam).

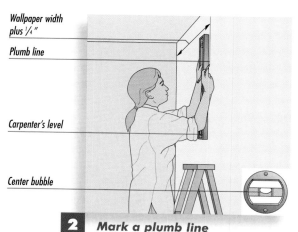

Wallpaper width
plus ¼"

Plumb line

Carpenter's level

Center bubble

2   **Mark a plumb line**
Starting at the ceiling, hold a carpenter's level against the mark you've just made and adjust until the bubble that designates plumb is perfectly centered. Draw a faint line with pencil along the level's edge. Move the level down, repeating the process and connecting the plumb lines down to the baseboard.

BOOKING A STRIP

To promote even adhesion, some wallpapers need time before being hung to absorb the paste, or "relax." To allow for this, use a technique called "booking."

1) Fold the bottom third of the strip over the middle.

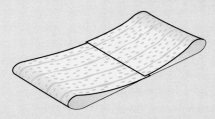

2) Then fold over the remaining portion until it slightly overlaps the end of the first portion. Take care to align the edges, and do not crease. (If the strip is untrimmed, cut it at this point with a razor or utility knife along the trim marks.)

3) After waiting the time recommended by the manufacturer—usually 5 to 15 minutes—loosely roll the strip to prepare it for hanging and enclose it in a large plastic bag so it can relax without drying out.

Basic Techniques

(continued from page 81)
At first, cut and hang only one strip at a time, to ensure that the lengths are adequate for a random or straight match. You then can cut several strips at one time, but cut only enough strips to reach the next obstacle, such as a window, fireplace, or door.

PASTING AND SOAKING THE PAPER Some wallcoverings require applying adhesive to the backing before hanging the strips. Prepasted papers simply need to be soaked to activate the paste, so they're considerably easier to use. Both methods usually require the papers to be booked (see Booking a Strip, page 81), a special folding technique that allows the paper to "relax" as it absorbs the adhesive.

The instructions that come with the paper are the best guide to choosing the proper adhesive. Both premixed and dry adhesives are available. Premixed adhesives are more convenient; if you use a dry adhesive, mix it with distilled water according to the manufacturer's directions until it's the consistency of gravy.

SOAKING PREPASTED PAPER

Front of paper

Towel

Water tray

Place a long tray, filled two-thirds with lukewarm water on the floor next to your worktable. Loosely roll up a strip, pattern side out, and immerse the roll in the water for 10 to 15 seconds. Then pull it up slowly, about a foot per second. Place the strip pattern side down on the table, then book it (see page 81), unless the manufacturer recommends against it.

Place the strip, pattern side down, on the pasting table. Apply the adhesive with a short-napped roller, working from the center of the strip to the edges. Or, use a pasting brush, working in a figure-eight pattern. Cover the paper completely, thinly, and smoothly, especially at the edges. On a hot, dry day, use a bit more paste to keep the paper from drying quickly.

PASTING WALLPAPER

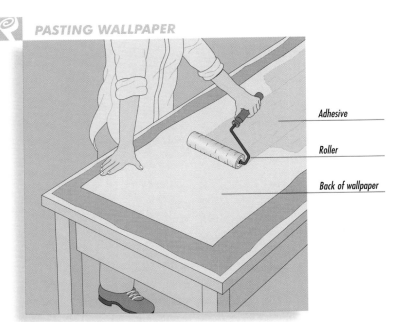

Adhesive

Roller

Back of wallpaper

Before hanging the first strip, make sure the wall is well prepared and you have drawn your plumb line, as discussed on page 81. When you've finished hanging it, wipe any excess paste off the surface of the strip according to manufacturer's instructions.

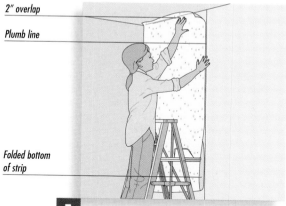

2" overlap

Plumb line

Folded bottom of strip

1 Position the strip

Unroll the first booked strip. Hold the strip by its upper corners and slowly unfold just the top portion. Allow the rest of the strip to drop down. Place the strip against the wall so that the top overlaps the ceiling line by about 2 inches and the edge is close to but not on the plumb line. Then press the strip to the wall at the ceiling line so it won't fall.

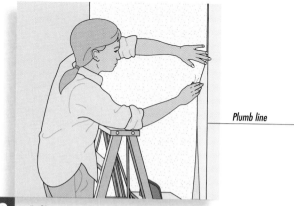

Plumb line

2 Adjust to the plumb line

Adjust the side edge so that it is perfectly parallel to the plumb line, taking care not to stretch the paper. If necessary, adjust the top corners so the paper hangs without wrinkles.

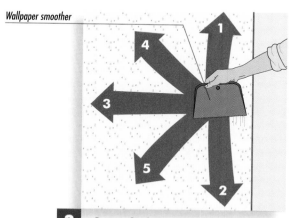

Wallpaper smoother

3 Smooth the paper

Smooth the top portion of the strip with a wallpaper smoother in the sequence shown.

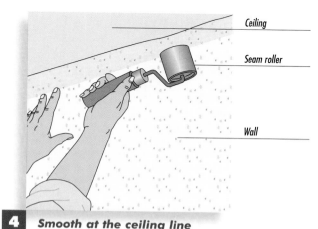

Ceiling

Seam roller

Wall

4 Smooth at the ceiling line

Smooth the paper tightly where the wall and ceiling meet with a wallpaper smoother, sponge, or seam roller. If you use the latter, apply only gentle pressure; too firm a touch will squeeze adhesive from the seam.

(continued on page 84)

Hanging the First Strip

(continued from page 83)

Wallpaper Improvements

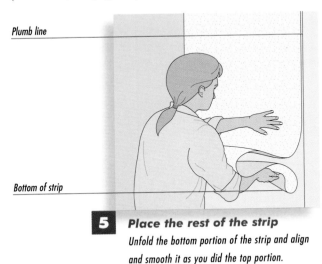

Plumb line

Bottom of strip

5 **Place the rest of the strip**
Unfold the bottom portion of the strip and align and smooth it as you did the top portion.

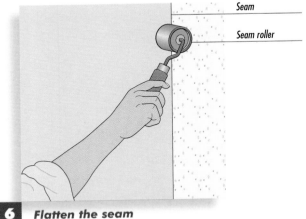

Seam

Seam roller

6 **Flatten the seam**
When the entire seam is straight and smooth, run a smoother, sponge, or seam roller along any edge that will not meet another strip.

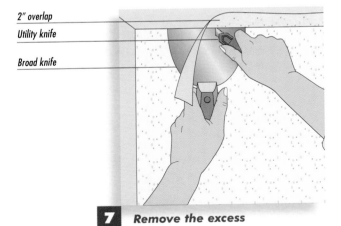

2" overlap
Utility knife
Broad knife

7 **Remove the excess**
Trim the ceiling and baseboard edges with a razor or utility knife, keeping a broad knife between the blade and the wallpaper to ensure a straight cut and protect the paper. For smooth cuts, don't pick up the knife blade; leave it in contact with the paper as you move the broad knife. Never move both tools at the same time. Be sure to change blades frequently.

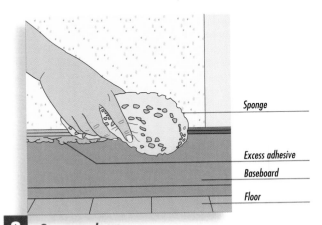

Sponge

Excess adhesive
Baseboard
Floor

8 **Sponge clean**
Wipe excess adhesive off the wallpaper, ceiling, and baseboard with a clean, damp sponge. Rinse the sponge often, and clean it thoroughly after hanging each strip.

Hanging the Next Strips

The second strip creates a seam where it meets the first one (and the second, the third, and so on). In most situations, a butt seam (below) is the best way to join two wallpaper strips because it's the least noticeable. Some wallcoverings, such as hand-screened papers and certain textiles, require double-cut seams (bottom).

Place the strip against the wall as you did the first one. Working from the top down, align the second strip with the first one, using one hand and spreading your fingers broadly to create even pressure; with the other hand, hold the strip away from the wall so you can align the edge without stretching the wallpaper. When the strip's top portion butts tightly to the adjoining strip, unfold the rest of the strip and finish aligning. Smooth and trim. Finally, wipe the strip clean with a damp sponge.

MAKING A BUTT SEAM

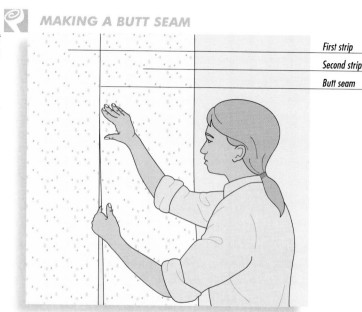

First strip
Second strip
Butt seam

MAKING A DOUBLE-CUT SEAM

First strip
Second strip

Overlap

Metal straightedge
Razor knife

1 Set the second strip
Place the strip against the wall as you did for a butt seam, but allow it to overlap the first slightly. Using a razor or utility knife and a straightedge, cut through both strips in the area of overlap, taking care not to cut the wall surface.

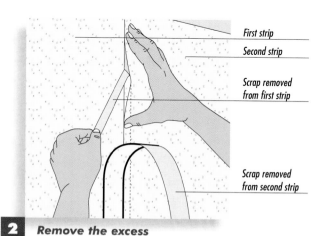

First strip
Second strip

Scrap removed
from first strip

Scrap removed
from second strip

2 Remove the excess
Carefully lift off the scrap from the second strip. Then lift the second strip slightly and remove the scrap underneath. Press the seam back into place and smooth it. After trimming the strip at the top and bottom edges, lightly roll the seam.

Papering Corners

Applying wallpaper around corners requires special attention, especially since most walls are not plumb.

Simply pushing a strip of wallpaper into an inside corner and continuing the strip on the next wall can result in puckered, crooked paper. It's best to split the strip and hang some on each side of the corner, as shown on the facing page.

Depending on how plumb an outside corner's adjacent walls are, you can use two different techniques. With walls only slightly out of plumb, slit the second strip halfway and overlap it on itself so its uncut edge aligns with a plumb line (see below). Alternatively, simply hang the second strip parallel to the plumb line and use a lap seam where the two strips overlap.

If a strip ends at an outside corner, cut it back 1/8 to 1/4 inch to prevent the paper from fraying and peeling at the corner.

COVERING OUTSIDE CORNERS

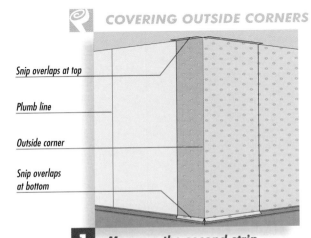

Snip overlaps at top

Plumb line

Outside corner

Snip overlaps at bottom

1 **Measure the second strip**
Smooth the first strip tightly to the wall. Draw a plumb line on the second wall from the edge of the first strip equal to the width of a strip plus 1/2 inch. Measure the distance between the edge of the plumb line and the edge of the corner strip at three different heights.

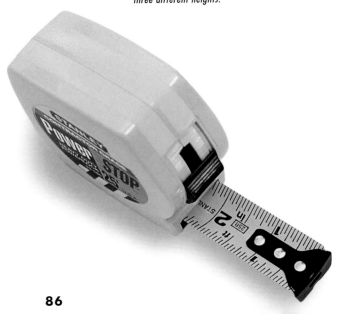

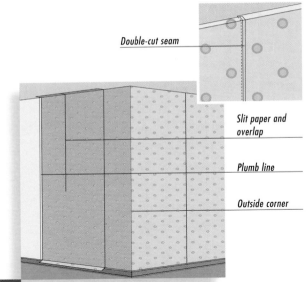

Double-cut seam

Slit paper and overlap

Plumb line

Outside corner

2 **Set the second strip**
If the distance from the plumb line to the previous strip is greater at the top of the wall than at the bottom, slit the next strip halfway from the bottom in a background area (if it's greater at the bottom, make the slit at the top). Make the length of the cut as long as necessary to overlap the edges of the slit until the strip is plumb. Then double-cut the overlap (see detail above).

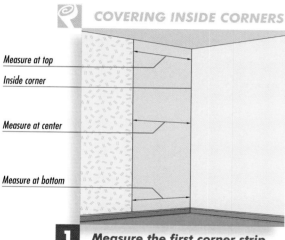

Measure at top

Inside corner

Measure at center

Measure at bottom

1 **Measure the first corner strip**

Measure from the preceding strip to the corner at three different heights. Cut the strip ¼ inch wider than the largest measurement. Do not discard the leftover paper.

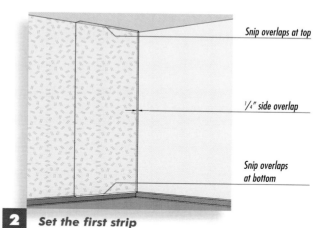

Snip overlaps at top

¼″ side overlap

Snip overlaps at bottom

2 **Set the first strip**

After preparing the strip, butt it to the previous one and smooth it firmly into and around the corner. Trim at the ceiling line and baseboard.

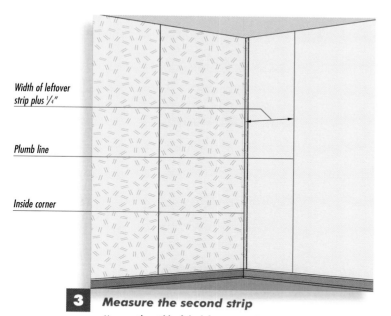

Width of leftover strip plus ¼″

Plumb line

Inside corner

3 **Measure the second strip**

Measure the width of the leftover strip. Draw a plumb line on the adjacent wall at that measurement plus ¼ inch from the corner. Position the strip's uncut edge next to but not on the plumb line, allowing the edge to overlap the previous one. Cover the overlapping section with a nonporous, vinyl-to-vinyl adhesive. Pattern misalignment generally is not noticeable in corners.

Papering Around Openings

The methods for hanging paper around openings really are just variations on those for papering a solid wall.

PAPERING AROUND WINDOWS & DOORS

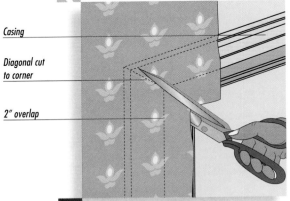

Casing

Diagonal cut to corner

2" overlap

1 **Fit the paper**
Hang the paper around the opening and trim the excess to within 2 inches of the final trim. Using utility shears or scissors, cut diagonal slits to the corners of the opening.

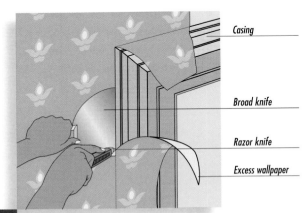

Casing

Broad knife

Razor knife

Excess wallpaper

2 **Smooth & trim**
With a smoother or sponge, press the wallpaper down along all edges of the opening. Then trim the excess using a razor or utility knife, protecting the wallpaper with a broad knife. If the frame is intricate, use shears or scissors instead.

PAPERING AROUND RECESSED WINDOWS

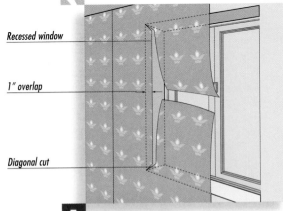

Recessed window

1" overlap

Diagonal cut

1 **Fit the paper**
Hang the paper around the opening and trim the excess to within 2 inches of the final trim. Using utility shears or scissors, cut diagonal slits to the corners of the opening.

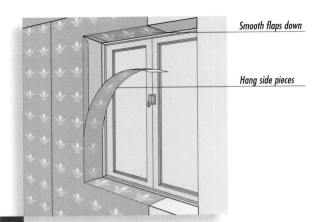

Smooth flaps down

Hang side pieces

2 **Apply matched side pieces**
Smooth the top, bottom, and side flaps. Next, install a matched piece to fit each side, cutting it $1/4$ inch narrower than the width of the space.

Using a carpenter's level aligned with a design element in strip 1, mark a horizontal line above and below the window. Hang strips according to this sequence: 2A, 2B, 3A, 3B, strip 4. If necessary, make adjustments in strip 4 to match the pattern.

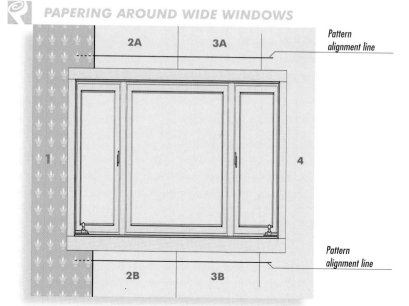

Pattern alignment line

Pattern alignment line

Before papering around an outlet or switch, shut off the power to the circuit and remove the faceplate. Paper right over the box. Then, with a utility knife, make an X-shaped cut over the opening from corner to corner. Trim the excess along the edges and reinstall the faceplate.

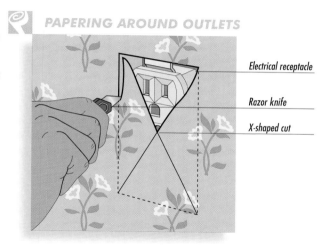

Electrical receptacle

Razor knife

X-shaped cut

Before reinstalling the faceplate, sand and prime it and cut a scrap of wallpaper the size of the faceplate with a 1-inch border. Apply vinyl-to-vinyl adhesive to the front of the plate and back of the paper. Set the faceplate up to the wall, cover it with the scrap to match the pattern, and stick the paper to the plate. Set the plate face down on a table, then trim the excess to within $1/2$ inch of the edges and cut off the corners. Wrap the paper around the plate, pressing the edges firmly to the back. Cut the plug openings with a utility knife and reinstall the faceplate.

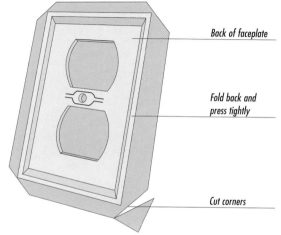

Back of faceplate

Fold back and press tightly

Cut corners

Special Papering Situations

Wallpapering around bulky, immovable objects or curved shapes can be tricky, but if you know the right techniques to use, you can make these hard-to-paper areas look just as good as the rest of the walls—or even better. Here is how to wallpaper around archways, light fixtures, thermostats, and more:

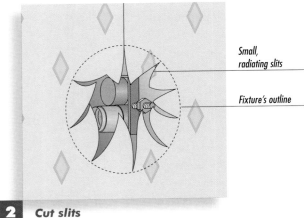

Small, radiating slits

Fixture's outline

2 Cut slits

Cut a series of slits from the fixture's center to its outer edges until you can smooth down the paper around it.

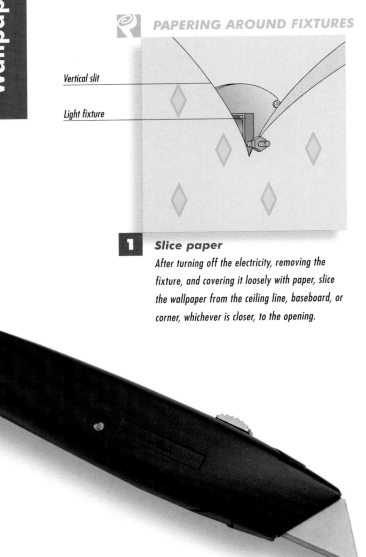

PAPERING AROUND FIXTURES

Vertical slit

Light fixture

1 Slice paper

After turning off the electricity, removing the fixture, and covering it loosely with paper, slice the wallpaper from the ceiling line, baseboard, or corner, whichever is closer, to the opening.

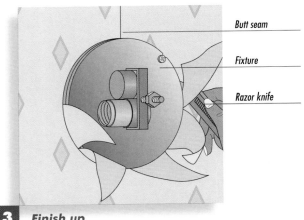

Butt seam

Fixture

Razor knife

3 Finish up

Crease the edges of the slits against the wall tightly, then carefully trim them with a razor or utility knife.

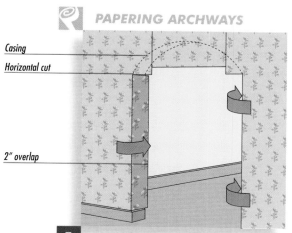

Casing

Horizontal cut

2" overlap

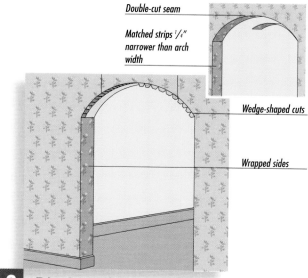

Double-cut seam

Matched strips ¹/₄"
narrower than arch
width

Wedge-shaped cuts

Wrapped sides

1 **Hang archway strips**

Cut two strips of matching paper, equal to the
height of the archway and as wide as the jamb's
depth, and hang them. Just below the curve, make
a horizontal cut in each side strip from the inner
edge to within 1 inch of the wall. Wrap the lower
portions of each side strip around the arch's edge
and smooth.

2 **Trim & match**

Using utility shears or scissors, trim the
unsmoothed paper on the archway to within 1 inch
of the edge, then make small, wedge-shaped cuts
in it to within ¹/₄ inch of the edge. Measure the
length of the arch, then divide that length in two.
Cut two matched strips for the arch ¹/₄ inch
narrower than the arch depth (to prevent fraying)
and ¹/₄ inch longer than each divided length.
Apply the strips from side to top, then double-cut
the seam.

Hang the strip from the ceiling line as you would
for any wall. When you reach the thermostat,
smooth the paper down as close to it as you can
without tacking it onto the thermostat. Make an X-
shaped cut over the thermostat large enough for
the paper around it to lie flat, but not so large
that the paper will show cut marks. Trim the
excess, then smooth the paper.

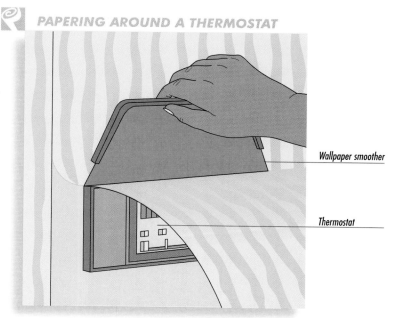

Wallpaper smoother

Thermostat

Wallpaper Borders

Bordering with wallpaper can add flair to any room in the home. Popular as accents to paint or to divide coordinating papers or wall treatments, borders are especially effective along the ceiling line or at chair rail height.

If you're bordering over a painted wall, prepare the wall according to the instructions on page 78. If you're placing a border between two wallpapers, use a primer-sealer just on the area the border will cover, and only after any new wallcovering has dried thoroughly.

BORDERING AT A CEILING

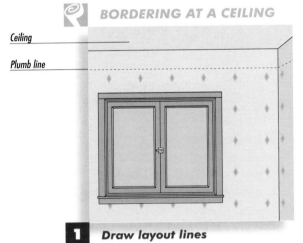

Ceiling

Plumb line

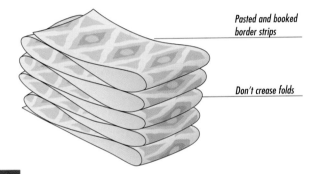

Pasted and booked border strips

Don't crease folds

1 **Draw layout lines**

If the border is to be applied over paper with a straight or drop match and the wall is not plumb, determine the shortest wall height, subtract the width of the border from that measurement, and then, using a carpenter's level, mark a plumb line around the room.

2 **Prepare border strips**

Paste the strip with adhesive or soak it if it is prepasted. Use vinyl-to-vinyl adhesive when hanging over vinyl wallpaper. Book the border accordion-style without creasing folds.

3 **Hang strips**

Unfold and tack up an arm's length of paper at a time. Smooth the strip and wipe off excess adhesive. If the design at the end of the first strip matches the beginning of the second, simply butt strips together and continue. Otherwise, overlap the paper to achieve a match, then double-cut the seams. At inside corners, use lap seams (page 87).

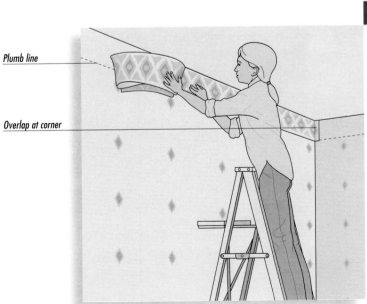

Plumb line

Overlap at corner

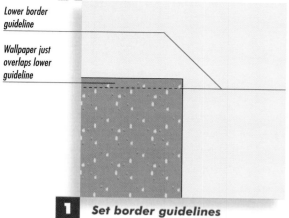

Lower border
guideline

Wallpaper just
overlaps lower
guideline

1 Set border guidelines

Using a carpenter's level, draw border guidelines
for the top and bottom edges of the border,
allowing the lower guideline to overlap the
existing wallpaper.

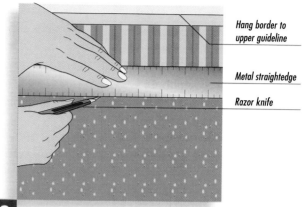

Hang border to
upper guideline

Metal straightedge

Razor knife

2 Hang the border

Hang the border according to the top guideline.
Using a straightedge or broad knife at the bottom
edge of the border, cut the existing wallpaper with
a razor or utility knife and remove the excess
carefully. Then smooth down the border and roll
the seam.

BORDERING WITH WALLPAPER ABOVE & BELOW

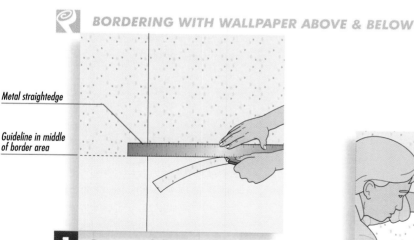

Metal straightedge

Guideline in middle
of border area

1 Draw guidelines

Draw a line on the wall midway between where
you want the border to go. Hang the top
wallpaper to just below the line and trim.

Align border with
design element in
wallpaper

2 Finish the job

Hang the bottom wallpaper to butt with the
wallpaper above. Then hang the border, aligning
it with a design element of the wallpaper above
and below.

Wallpaper Repairs

As wallpaper ages, it can loosen, tear, bubble, and be damaged in other ways. Fortunately, most repairs are easy to make with the help of lap-and-seam adhesive (but don't use too much—it can soak through and stain the wallpaper). When you apply new wallpaper, it's smart to store away a couple of large leftover pieces for future repairs.

Bubbles are a common problem. To remove them, first moisten the area with a clean sponge. Then, using a utility knife, slit the bubble in the direction of the wallpaper pattern. Force adhesive through the slit with a putty knife and spread it underneath the area with a wet sponge. Then press the wallpaper smoothly to the wall, wipe off excess glue, and allow to dry.

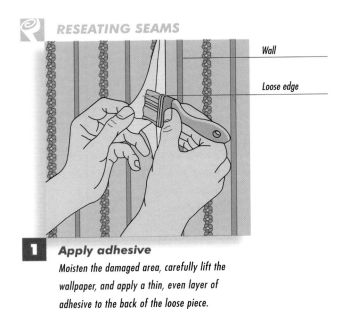

RESEATING SEAMS

Wall

Loose edge

1 **Apply adhesive**
Moisten the damaged area, carefully lift the wallpaper, and apply a thin, even layer of adhesive to the back of the loose piece.

2

Reseat the wallpaper
Press the wallpaper back in place. Sponge off any excess adhesive, but don't soak the paper so much that the adhesive loosens.

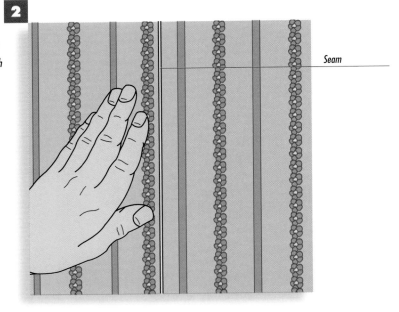

Seam

 To remove dirt, grease, and stains from a washable wallpaper, thoroughly sponge the soiled area with a solution of mild soap and cold water. Rinse with clear, cold water; wipe dry with a clean, absorbent cloth. Note: Test wallpaper before washing it.

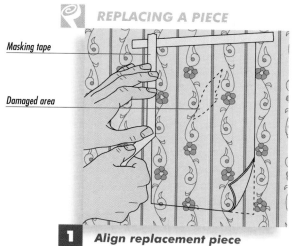

Masking tape

Damaged area

1 Align replacement piece

Use masking tape to affix an identical
replacement piece over the damaged area so that
the pattern matches perfectly.

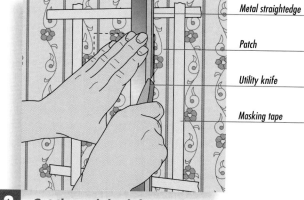

Metal straightedge

Patch

Utility knife

Masking tape

2 Cut through both layers

Using a straightedge and a utility knife, make a
rectangular cutout around the damaged area, cutting
through both the new and damaged material.

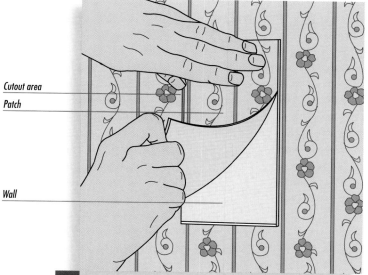

Cutout area

Patch

Wall

3 Replace the section

Untape the patch, then dampen and peel away the
damaged section. Apply a thin layer of adhesive to
the back of the patch, position it carefully, and
press it in place (ideally with a seam roller). Wipe
off excess adhesive.

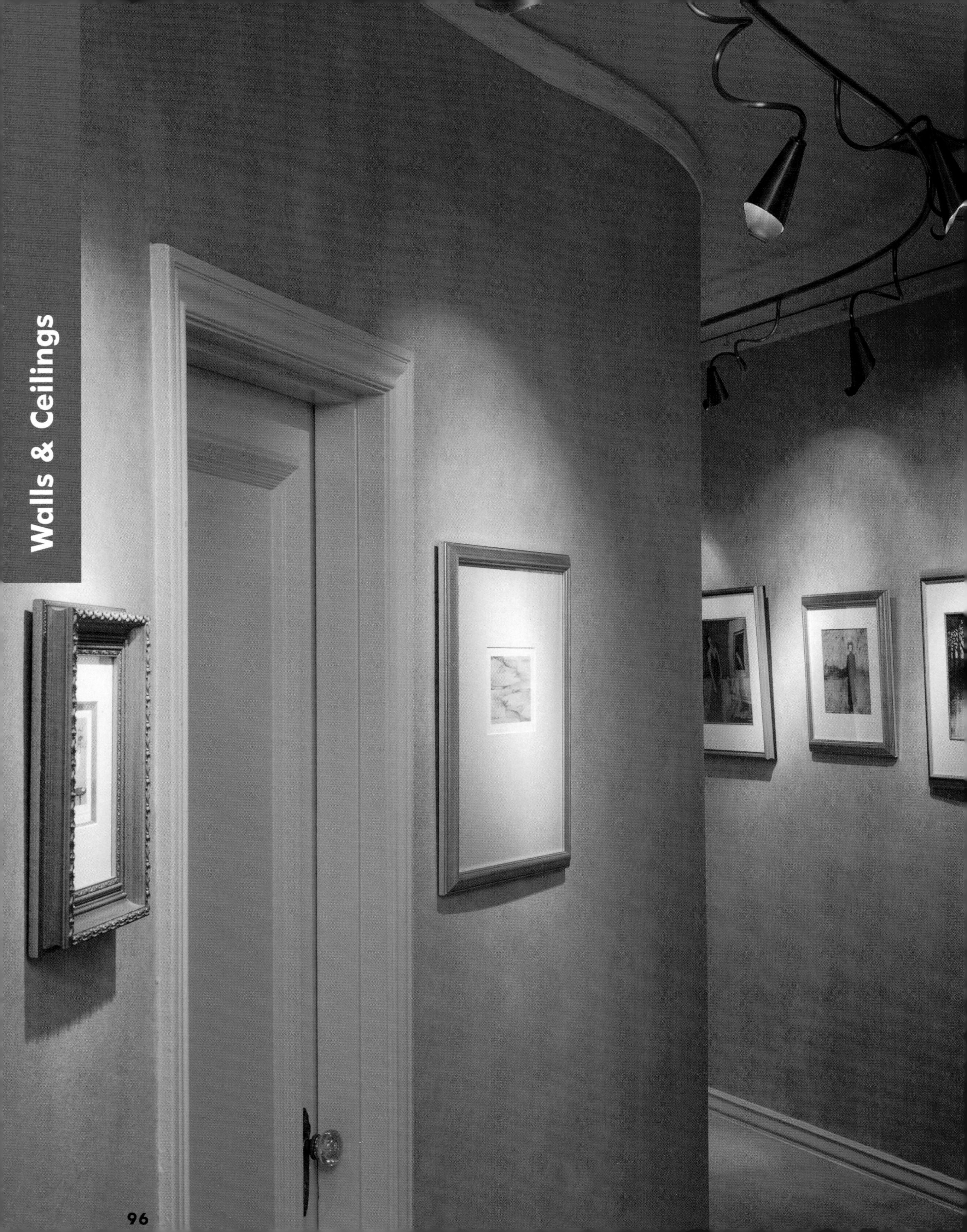

Walls & Ceilings

Walls and ceilings carve up open space, give our homes their structure, and can be very effective in establishing a decorating style. Easily installed wood or composition moldings—for example, a crown where walls and ceiling meet, a base where walls and floor meet, trim, chair rails, and picture rails—provide a distinctive finishing touch to any space. Victorian-style pressed-metal ceiling panels, available in a wide variety of patterns and designs, are also a creative and unique way to give a ceiling panache.

This chapter begins with a look at wall and ceiling construction, including how to open up or build a wall, how to fasten items to walls properly, and how to install suspended and pressed-metal ceilings. Finally, we offer tips on simple wall and ceiling repairs.

Wall & Ceiling Anatomy

Walls & Ceilings

Inside a home, walls and ceilings form the layout, creating individual rooms and passageways. Walls are classified as either bearing or nonbearing. Bearing walls help carry the weight of the house, providing support to floors above and keeping the building rigid. While all exterior walls are bearing, many interior walls are also bearing, especially in multi-level homes. Normally, at least one main interior wall, situated over a girder or interior foundation wall, is also bearing.

Traditionally, walls were built from 2-by-4 studs and plates, with studs placed on 16-inch centers. In recent years, 2-by-6 studs have been used increasingly, often placed on 24-inch centers, to allow for more insulation in the walls. Basic wall construction is the same with both types.

Nonbearing walls (also called "partitions"), while not essential from a construction standpoint, help shape the interior by defining rooms within the house and serving as conduits for essential plumbing and electrical systems. The framing for an opening (such as a door) in a nonbearing wall may be built from lighter materials than those needed for an opening in a bearing wall.

The standard ceiling height for interior spaces is 8 feet. But you'll have trouble installing 4-by-8-foot gypsum wallboard or sheet paneling on walls unless you frame the walls slightly higher to allow for the ceiling material's thickness: 8 feet, $3/4$ inch is the standard overall height of wall framing. When you subtract the thickness of the sole plate and doubled top plates, this leaves a length of 7 feet, 8 $1/4$ inches (92 $1/4$ inches) for the wall studs. Lumberyards frequently stock precut studs in this length.

TYPES OF CONSTRUCTION Three basic types of construction make up most typical homes. The most common by far, shown on the facing page, is called platform framing (also known as "western"). The simplest and safest house-building method in practice today, platform framing starts with the foundation and floor structure; the walls are built up from the subfloor with 2-by dimension lumber (in some regions, steel studs are used in place of dimension lumber). If the house is taller than one story, additional platforms and walls are stacked on top of the first floor walls. The structure is completed with ceiling and roof framing.

Balloon framing, where wall studs extend in one piece from the mudsill on top of the foundation wall to the doubled top plate two stories above, was standard practice until about 1930 and is still used in some two-story houses, especially those with stucco, brick, or other masonry exteriors. A third, less-common construction method called post-and-beam utilizes heavy structural members at greater intervals instead of smaller, closely spaced lumber.

Though some homes are now built from metal wall studs, most do-it-yourself construction calls for wooden studs and framing members, nailed together and reinforced by metal framing connectors as required by local codes.

BEHIND WALLS & CEILINGS Most of a home's mechanical, electrical, and plumbing systems are contained inside the walls and ceilings. Plumbing supply and waste pipes, electrical wires and telephone lines, and heating, ventilation, and air-conditioning systems are all installed once a house has been framed. These systems (as well as insulation and the other parts that are added once the floors, walls, and ceilings are framed) are discussed in their respective chapters in this book.

STRUCTURAL INSULATED PANELS

Structural insulated panels (SIPs) are gaining in popularity as a fast and economical method of constructing interior and exterior walls. SIPs are typically constructed of oriented strand board, expanded polystyrene foam insulation, and sometimes gypsum wallboard laminated together under pressure to produce panels having both structural and insulating properties. Channels for electrical wires are precut at the factory or can be made on site. Window and door openings are cut out, and the panels are set into place and secured as an entire unit.

Platform framing utilizes a series of vertical wall studs, horizontal ceiling and floor joists, and roof rafters. Extra framing members help bear the loads where walls or ceilings have openings.

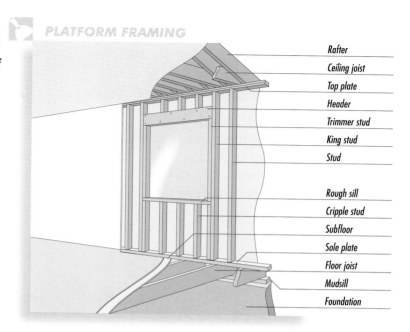

- Rafter
- Ceiling joist
- Top plate
- Header
- Trimmer stud
- King stud
- Stud
- Rough sill
- Cripple stud
- Subfloor
- Sole plate
- Floor joist
- Mudsill
- Foundation

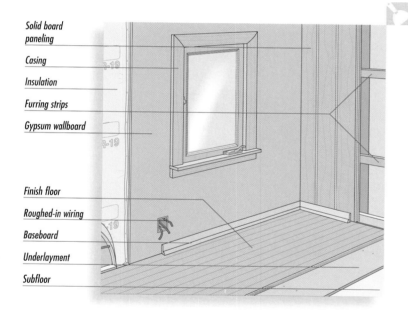

- Solid board paneling
- Casing
- Insulation
- Furring strips
- Gypsum wallboard
- Finish floor
- Roughed-in wiring
- Baseboard
- Underlayment
- Subfloor

In a typical room, vertical studs fasten to a sole plate that is secured to the subfloor. Wiring, ductwork, pipes, and insulation run between the studs. Here, one wall is finished with gypsum wallboard, and an interior wall has been finished with solid board paneling attached to furring strips (lumber run horizontally between wall studs). Floor trim and interior window casings complete the room.

WALL & CEILING FINISHES Once a house's frame has been built and all of the necessary systems have been roughed in, wall and ceiling finishes can be completed. Windows and exterior doors can be installed. Ceiling materials are fastened directly to the ceiling joists or to a metal or wooden grid suspended from the joists.

Gypsum wallboard or sheet paneling is applied directly to wall studs; solid board paneling may first require a wallboard backing or furring strips as a nailing base. Plaster walls need a gypsum, fiberboard, or metal lath backing. If you choose gypsum wallboard as a final covering for either ceilings or walls, you'll need to tape, fill, and then sand the joints between the panels.

After the finish floor is put in place, doors and windows are installed in their openings. Then interior trim, including baseboards, moldings, and window or door casings as needed, completes the basic job.

Tools for Walls & Ceilings

The tools and materials used to construct and repair walls and ceilings are basic carpentry tools with a few task-specific items thrown in for good measure. In addition to common tools like hammers, tape measure, utility knife, and screwdrivers, many specialty tools, such as combination squares, taping knives, and corner knives, can reduce the time needed to complete tasks and can also improve the final result.

MEASURING & MARKING TOOLS

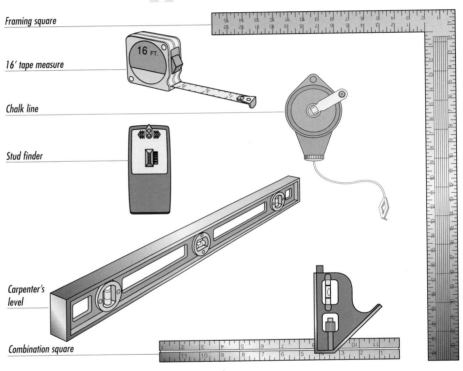

Framing square

16' tape measure

Chalk line

Stud finder

Carpenter's level

Combination square

For measuring, purchase a 16-foot tape measure marked with 16- and 24-inch stud layouts. For marking straight and square lines, you'll want a combination square, a chalk line, and a framing square. A carpenter's level is essential for checking plumb and level. A stud finder will make locating studs easy.

 CUTTING INTO A WALL

To safely and easily open walls covered with gypsum wallboard, use a saber saw fitted with an old blade broken off so that it extends only about 1/2 inch beyond the saw's base plate on the downstroke. As it cuts, the blade will retract above the base plate on the upstroke, then punch through the wallboard on each downstroke. But because wallboard is relatively soft, this isn't difficult. By barely cutting through the surface, you minimize the risk of cutting into hidden wires or pipes. (Regardless, always shut off power to the receptacles and switches in the wall you're opening before cutting.) Be sure to wear safety glasses.

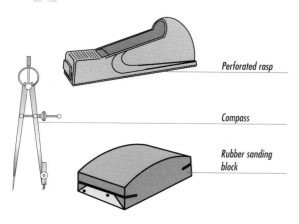

Perforated rasp

Compass

Rubber sanding block

In addition to the various carpentry, measuring, and cutting tools, you'll want a simple compass and pencil to transfer the profile of uneven surfaces to materials that will butt against them. A perforated rasp removes material quickly, and a rubber sanding block eases sanding.

CUTTING TOOLS

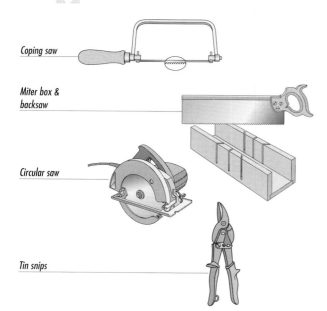

Coping saw

Miter box & backsaw

Circular saw

Tin snips

Used with a common backsaw, a miter box eases the task of cutting angles. A power circular saw is the tool of choice for cutting framing members (though a handsaw will work). A coping saw has a thin, fine-toothed blade for precise cuts by hand on molding and trim. Tin, or aviation, snips cut aluminum and sheet metal.

DRYWALL FINISHING TOOLS

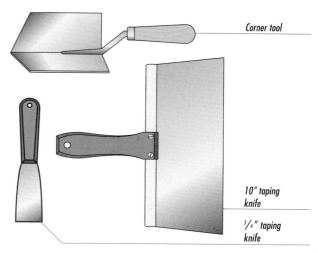

Corner tool

10" taping knife

³/₄" taping knife

Taping, or putty, knives have a thin metal blade in a variety of widths, ranging from ³/₄ inch to 10 inches. Use them in varying widths to feather out layers of joint compound when finishing drywall seams. Companions to taping knives, corner tools have 90-degree blades to shape and smooth plaster and joint compound on corners.

DEMOLITION TOOLS

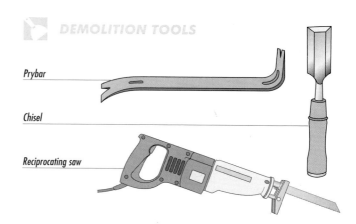

Prybar

Chisel

Reciprocating saw

For demolition work, a reciprocating saw is a real labor saver—as is a saber saw. A prybar's sharp, tapered blades are excellent for prying, scraping, and nail pulling. Woodworking chisels are handy for a variety of prying and cutting jobs.

Fastening to Walls & Ceilings

Hanging heavy objects such as picture frames, plant hangers, and shelves on gypsum wallboard, paneling, or masonry walls can be accomplished in several ways. The simplest solution for nonmasonry walls is to hang items where a nail or screw can be driven into a stud or joist behind the finished wall or ceiling. (See facing page for information on locating hidden studs and joists.)

You can use conventional nails to hang light objects from these walls (drill pilot holes to avoid creating cracks), though picture hooks may be a better option. Picture hooks are rated in pounds. Determine the weight of the item to be hung, and purchase the appropriate hook. For example, a 35-pound picture frame should be secured by a 50-pound picture hook.

To secure shelf brackets and other heavy items, use wood screws driven into studs.

When you can't drive into a stud, choose anchors or toggle bolts; once in the holes, they expand to distribute weight more widely than do screws. Be sure to buy the proper size fastener for the thickness of the wall and the weight of the object you're hanging.

To install anchors, drill a hole, install the anchor, and insert the screw; then tighten it to spread the anchor.

With a toggle bolt, slide the bolt through the hook or object to be mounted before inserting the toggle in a hole drilled into the wall; if you remove the bolt when the fastener is in place, you'll lose the toggle. Don't fasten the bolt or screw too tightly. This pulls the anchor or toggle into the wall material and weakens its grip.

MASONRY ANCHORS For masonry walls, hang light objects from special tempered-steel masonry nails. For heavier objects, use anchors that have a resilient sleeve that expands to hold a screw or bolt in place. Drive in nails with a hammer (be sure to wear safety glasses).

The key to successful installation of masonry anchors is proper drilling of the hole to receive the sleeve and screw. Use an electric drill with a carbide-tipped masonry bit to drill the hole. Then push in the sleeve, insert the screw through whatever you are fastening, and drive it into the sleeve.

MASONRY FASTENERS

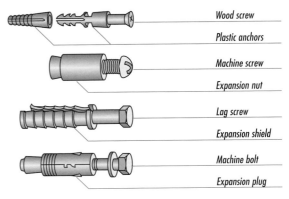

Wood screw

Plastic anchors

Machine screw

Expansion nut

Lag screw

Expansion shield

Machine bolt

Expansion plug

When fastening items to masonry walls, you'll need special two-part fasteners: an anchor that expands in a hole drilled in the wall, and a screw or bolt that you drive into the anchor.

NAILS & SCREWS

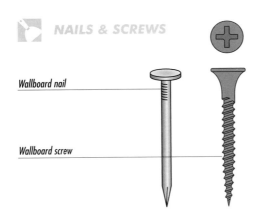

Wallboard nail

Wallboard screw

Conventional nails and screws will secure items to walls when driven directly into wall studs.

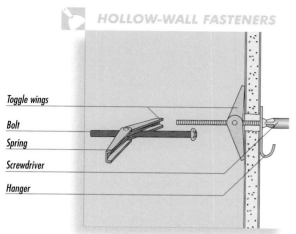

Toggle wings
Bolt
Spring
Screwdriver
Hanger

Split-wing toggle bolt

Drill a hole, then insert the bolt through the hanger and toggle. Pinch the toggle wings together, insert the bolt with the toggle, and pull it toward you. Tighten the bolt.

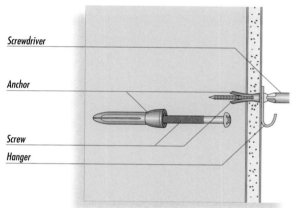

Screwdriver

Anchor

Screw
Hanger

Plastic anchor

Drill a pilot hole slightly smaller than the anchor. Tap the anchor into the hole. Add the hanger, then insert and tighten the screw.

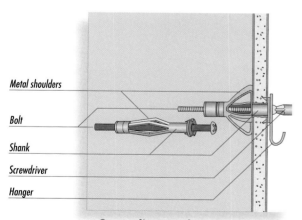

Metal shoulders

Bolt

Shank

Screwdriver

Hanger

Spreading anchor

Drill a hole, then insert the anchor. Tighten the bolt until you feel resistance. Remove the bolt, add the hanger, then reinsert and tighten the bolt.

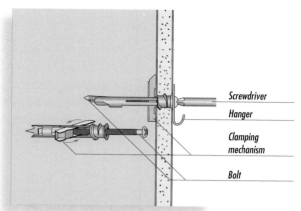

Screwdriver

Hanger

Clamping mechanism

Bolt

Clamping toggle bolt

Drill a hole. Press in the bolt and turn with a screwdriver until the bolt is flush with the wall and the arrows on the head are parallel to the wall stud. Add the hanger and tighten the screw to engage the clamp.

FINDING HIDDEN STUDS & JOISTS

Hidden studs and joists can be located in several ways. With most construction, walls and studs are spaced 16 inches or 24 inches apart, from center to center. To locate a stud or ceiling joist, measure out from a corner in multiples of 16 or 24 inches (depending on how the structure was built). Then lightly tap the area to find a section of wall with a solid backing (a stud or joist).

If you're not sure about the locations, you can buy a small, handheld electronic device called a stud finder (see page 100) at hardware stores and home centers. This device will beep or flash when it passes over a solid framing member; simply slide the finder along the surface until it signals the location of a wall stud or joist, then find others by measuring (one will usually be located 16 or 24 inches from there). Find studs behind plaster walls by driving a small test nail just above the baseboard.

The easiest way to find studs is often to look for visible signs of the nails that hold wallboard to the studs—small dents or nail heads. Hold a strong flashlight at a sharp angle to the wall or ceiling to highlight them.

Opening Up a Wall

Opening up a wall, whether to install a doorway or to completely remove an interior partition, is simple yet messy work. Before you remove any wall studs, you must find out whether or not the wall is a bearing wall, as discussed on page 98. If it is, you must engineer the opening with the proper beams or headers to carry the loads that will no longer be supported by the studs. If you are unsure whether an interior wall is a bearing wall or not, consult a local building professional before doing any demolition work. For more about headers, see pages 188–189.

Next, check for obstructions before opening the wall (see page 211); for instance, extensive plumbing may cause you to rethink installing a doorway or pass-through at that location. Then mask off the area with plastic sheeting to prevent the dust from permeating your home, and protect the floor with dropcloths. Wear work gloves, protective goggles, and a dust mask during your demolition work.

SURFACE REMOVAL Most walls are surfaced with gypsum wallboard. No matter how it is attached to the studs—with nails, screws, or adhesive—the removal procedure is exactly the same. Use a utility knife to slit through the taped joints. Then punch through the center of the panel with a

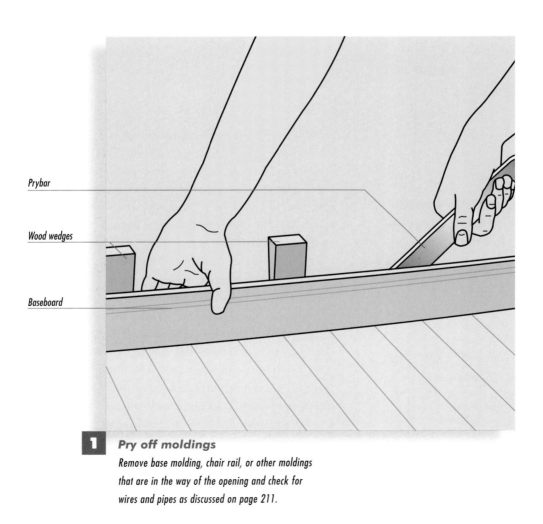

Prybar

Wood wedges

Baseboard

1 **Pry off moldings**
Remove base molding, chair rail, or other moldings that are in the way of the opening and check for wires and pipes as discussed on page 211.

hammer or prybar and pull off pieces. To remove plaster and lath, chisel through the plaster, then cut the lath and pry it loose.

Working from the center, use a prybar to pry the panel off the studs. When the panel is removed, pull out any remaining nails with a hammer or unscrew the screws. If you are removing the entire partition (nonbearing walls only), remove any studs by cutting them either with a circular or reciprocating saw, and pull with a prybar any nails securing the top and bottom plates to the subfloor.

STRUCTURE REMOVAL If you are removing material for a new opening (such as a doorway) but leaving the majority of the partition intact, plan an opening large enough to accommodate the necessary rough framing—an extra 1 1/2 inches on top and sides. Often it's simplest to remove the wall covering from floor to ceiling between the two bordering studs (the new king studs) that will remain in place. On taller walls—a 10-foot wall, for example—cutting your opening slightly larger than the intended doorway may save extra drywall work later.

Try to use at least one existing stud as part of the rough framing. Locate the studs in the area. Then, using a carpenter's level as a straightedge, draw plumb lines to mark the outline of the opening on the wall.

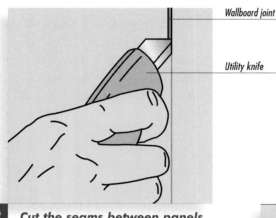

Wallboard joint

Utility knife

2 ***Cut the seams between panels***
Slit through taped joints between the panel you intend to remove and adjacent panels, using a sharp utility knife.

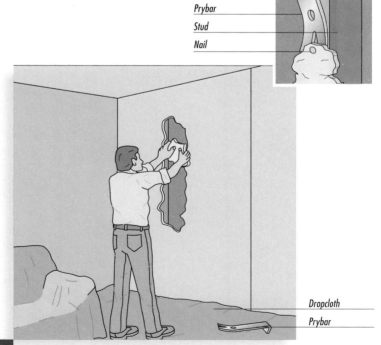

Prybar

Stud

Nail

Dropcloth

Prybar

3 ***Break away unwanted material***
Punch through the center with a hammer or prybar and pull off pieces. Working from the center, pry the panel edges off the studs with a prybar.

Building a New Interior Wall

During the course of a remodeling project, it often becomes necessary to construct additional walls to create new spaces. New interior walls must be built where they will be installed, so expect a fair amount of disruption in the work area while the job is in progress. Depending on the finish flooring and ceiling material in the room, it may be necessary to do additional demolition work to uncover the subfloor and ceiling joists to provide secure attachment points for the new wall. Typical components of an interior wall are shown below.

ANCHORING THE PLATES The new wall should be anchored securely to the floor, to the ceiling joists, and to wall framing on at least one side. For information on finding hidden wall studs and ceiling joists, see page 103. If you are unsure of joist locations, you can go into the attic above and drive small nails down through the ceiling on both sides of a joist to serve as reference points.

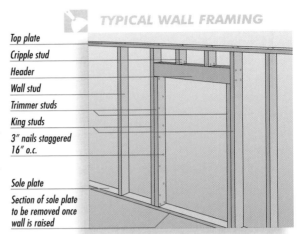

TYPICAL WALL FRAMING

Top plate
Cripple stud
Header
Wall stud
Trimmer studs
King studs
3" nails staggered 16" o.c.
Sole plate
Section of sole plate to be removed once wall is raised

A wall is framed with evenly spaced wall studs sandwiched between a top plate and a sole plate (horizontal fire blocks are sometimes placed between studs midway up the wall). Doorway openings are reinforced with extra studs and a header across the top.

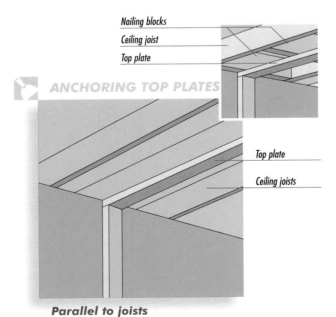

ANCHORING TOP PLATES

Nailing blocks
Ceiling joist
Top plate

Top plate
Ceiling joists

Parallel to joists
When walls and joists will run parallel, center the wall under a single joist. If securing the wall to a single joist is not possible, install nailing blocks every 2 feet between two parallel joists.

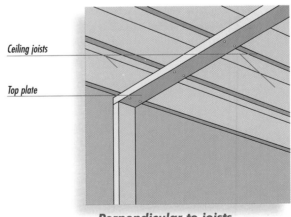

Ceiling joists
Top plate

Perpendicular to joists
If the top plate runs perpendicular to ceiling joists, simply nail it to each joist.

Three methods of anchoring top plates are shown on the facing page. The right one to use depends upon the conditions where the new wall will fall in relation to the joists (the ceiling surface material is not shown).

On the ceiling, mark both ends of the centerline of the new wall. Measure 1¾ inches (half the width of a 2-by-4 top plate) on both sides of each mark; snap parallel chalk lines between the marks.

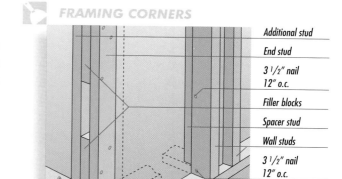

Additional stud
End stud
3 ½" nail
12" o.c.
Filler blocks
Spacer stud
Wall studs
3 ½" nail
12" o.c.
3" nails
Sole plate

Where two new interior walls meet, you need extra studs for structure and wallboard backing. After the first wall is assembled, add an extra stud inside the end stud to provide a solid anchoring spot for an adjoining wall. Nail the end stud of the adjoining wall to the corner assembly.

MARKING THE PLATES

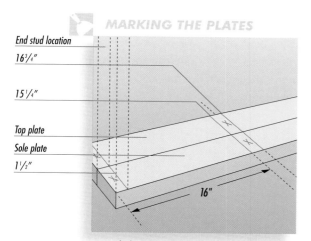

End stud location
16¾"
15¼"
Top plate
Sole plate
1½"
16"

Mark the sole plate and top plate side by side. Measure in 1½ inches from one end and draw a line on the plates with pencil and a combination square for the end stud. For studs on 16-inch centers, start once more from that end, measure and draw lines at 15¼ inches and 16¾ inches, and continue marking at 16-inch intervals.

Cut both sole plate and top plate to the desired lengths. If you need more than one piece for each, locate the joints at stud centers; offset any joints between top and sole plates at least 4 feet.

Lay the sole plate between the chalk lines on the floor and nail it in place with 3-inch nails spaced every 16 inches. (If you're planning a doorway, don't nail through that section of the plate.) With masonry floors, use a masonry bit to drill holes through the sole plate and into the floor every 2 or 3 feet, then insert expanding anchors.

Lift the top plate into position between the chalk lines marked on the ceiling and nail it either to the joists or to the nailing blocks.

INSTALL WALL STUDS Measure and cut each stud to the exact length. Attach one end stud (or both) to existing studs or to nailing blocks between studs. It's best to cut and install one stud before starting on the next one. To install each stud, lift the stud into place, line it up on the marks, and check plumb using a carpenter's level. Toenail the stud to both the top plate and the sole plate with 2½-inch nails. Some building codes require horizontal fire blocks between the studs.

To position the sole plate, hang a plumb bob from each end of the lines you just marked and mark these points on the floor. Snap two more chalk lines to connect the two pairs of floor points.

If the side of the new wall falls between existing studs, remove wall materials and install additional nailing blocks.

Hanging & Finishing Drywall

The most common finish material for walls and ceilings is gypsum wallboard, or "drywall." Available in $1/2$- and $5/16$-inch-thick panels measuring 4 by 8 feet, drywall is straightforward to install, but the weight of full panels can be awkward to work with. The job will go much more smoothly with a helper or two.

Concealing the joints with drywall tape and compound between panels and in the corners demands patience and care. You'll need to finish the wallboard if the wall will be painted or wallpapered, but you may not need to hide joints and corners on installations that serve as a backing for paneling, ceramic tile, or cabinets. Buy pre-creased wallboard tape and premixed joint compound.

If you're installing drywall on both ceilings and walls, apply the ceiling first—wall panels should support the edges of the ceiling panels. When handling wallboard, take care not to bend or break the corners or tear the paper covering; this will make finishing much easier.

CUTTING DRYWALL Mark the cutting line on the front paper layer with a pencil and straightedge, or snap a chalk line. Cut through the front paper with a utility knife. Next, turn the wallboard over and break the gypsum core by bending it toward the back. Finish by cutting the back paper along the crease.

When fitting wallboard around obstructions such as doorways, windows, or outlets, carefully measure from the edge of an adjacent wallboard panel or reference point and up from the floor to the obstruction. Transfer the measurements to a new panel and make the necessary cuts with a wallboard or compass saw or a saber saw. For small cuts such as outlets, cut the opening about $1/8$ inch to $3/16$ inch bigger than needed. If the fit is too tight, then trim with a perforated rasp.

End centered on stud

Double-nailing every 8" along ends and edges

Wallboard

Double-nailing every 12" in the field

Wall studs

2 Install the walls

Before installing panels on walls, mark the stud locations on the floor and ceiling. Starting from one corner, push the first panel up tight against the ceiling. Stagger the end joints of the bottom row so that they don't line up with those of the top row.

INSTALLATION TECHNIQUES

Joists

Double-nailing

1 Install the ceiling

With a helper, install panels perpendicular to joists. The attachment method shown here (and described in the text above) is called "double-nailing."

FASTENING DRYWALL On ceilings, fasten drywall panels perpendicular to joists with annular ring nails or drywall screws. Driving screws with a screw gun is the easiest and fastest method (screw guns can be rented). Screw spacing is governed by local codes, but typical spacing is every 8 inches along panel ends and at intermediate joists (called "in the field").

Another fastening method for ceilings is "double-nailing." With this technique, you space a first set of nails every 7 inches along the ends and every 12 inches in the field. Then you place a second nail about 2 inches away from each nail in the first set. Nails should be spaced at least $^3/_8$ inch in from the edges around the perimeter.

On walls, nail or screw panels to studs, spacing nails according to code. Normally, screw or nail spacing is every 8 inches along panel ends and edges and along intermediate supports. Fasteners must be at least $^3/_8$ inch from edges.

Use a bell-faced hammer, since your goal is to dimple the wallboard surface without puncturing the paper.

APPLICATION TECHNIQUES For the ceiling, position a pair of stepladders, or set up a couple of sturdy sawhorses, laying a few planks across them to serve as a short scaffold to stand on. Then you and a helper can hold your ends of each panel in place with your heads. Put in fasteners at the center of each panel. Then place the next few fasteners at the edges to take the weight off your heads. When working alone, construct one or two T-braces. The length of the braces should equal the height from the floor to the ceiling joists. When the panel is positioned, the extra thickness will help wedge the brace in place.

On walls, panels may be positioned either vertically or horizontally. Install the panels horizontally if possible, which helps bridge irregularities between studs, results in a stronger wall, and makes finishing easier. If you choose the this method, panel ends should be centered over studs (otherwise you'll have to back them with 2-by-4 blocking).

FINISHING DRYWALL Apply drywall tape to joints as shown in the sequence below. Sand the final coat with fine sandpaper to remove all imperfections.

TAPING TECHNIQUES

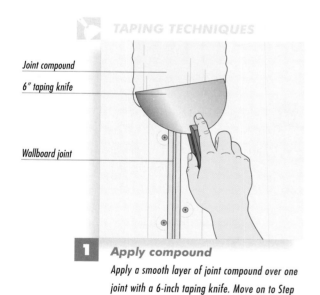

Joint compound

6" taping knife

Wallboard joint

1 Apply compound

Apply a smooth layer of joint compound over one joint with a 6-inch taping knife. Move on to Step 2, then repeat Steps 1 and 2 for each joint.

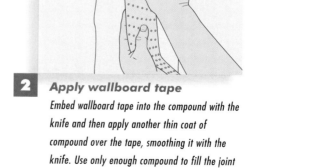

Joint compound

Perforated tape

2 Apply wallboard tape

Embed wallboard tape into the compound with the knife and then apply another thin coat of compound over the tape, smoothing it with the knife. Use only enough compound to fill the joint and cover the tape evenly.

(continued on page 110)

Walls & Ceilings Improvements

(continued from page 109)

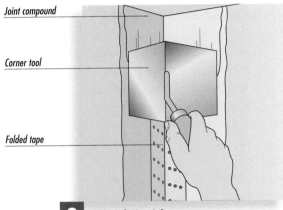

Joint compound

Corner tool

Folded tape

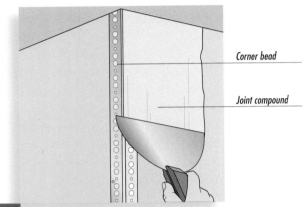

Corner bead

Joint compound

3 **Finish inside corners**

On inside corners, apply a layer of compound to
the wallboard on each side of the corner. Press
pre-creased drywall tape into the corner with a
corner tool or putty knife. Apply a thin layer of
compound over the tape and smooth it out.

4 **Finish outside corners**

To finish outside corners, cover corners with a
protective metal corner bead cut to length and
nailed through its perforations every 12 inches.
Run your knife down the metal edge to fill the
spaces with compound.

5 **Apply joint compound**

When all the joints and corners are taped, use smooth,
even strokes with a 6-inch drywall knife to cover the nail
dimples with compound. Once dry, apply two more coats
(allow to dry in between) with a 10-inch knife,
feathering out edges and sanding between coats. Sand
lightly with fine sandpaper to finish.

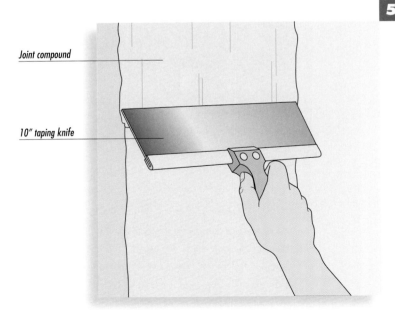

Joint compound

10" taping knife

Installing Interior Trim

Trim and moldings are available in a large variety of profiles, ranging from standard lumber trim to custom one-of-a-kind creations. No matter what style you choose, trim and moldings accomplish two basic tasks: concealing gaps between the wall covering and floor, windows, and door; and adding architectural interest to a room.

Many styles and profiles, milled from both softwood and hardwood, are available at lumberyards, home improvement centers, and millwork shops. Some of the more intricate styles of moldings used in a room are actually made by combining two or more profiles.

It's easiest and best to stain or paint molding before installation, then fill nail holes, lightly sand, and touch up with stain or paint after installation.

(continued on page 112)

TYPICAL MOLDINGS

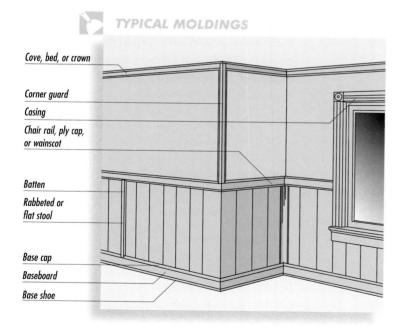

Cove, bed, or crown

Corner guard

Casing

Chair rail, ply cap, or wainscot

Batten

Rabbeted or flat stool

Base cap

Baseboard

Base shoe

MOLDING PROFILES

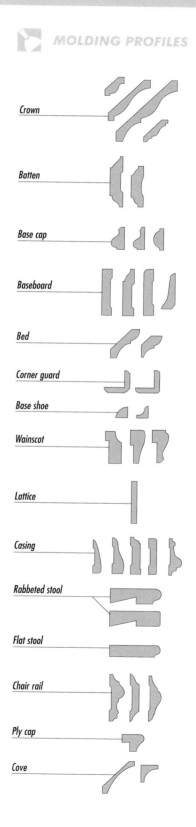

Crown

Batten

Base cap

Baseboard

Bed

Corner guard

Base shoe

Wainscot

Lattice

Casing

Rabbeted stool

Flat stool

Chair rail

Ply cap

Cove

Installing Interior Trim

(continued from page 111)

CUTTING MOLDING

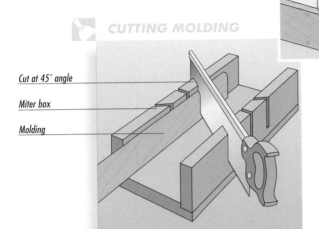

Cut at 45° angle

Miter box

Molding

Cutting a miter

A miter box and backsaw are the most commonly used tools for neatly cutting trim. With these you can cut the precise 45-degree and 90-degree angles necessary for most joints. If you are going to do a lot of cutting or are working with unusual angles, it may be worthwhile to rent or borrow a power miter saw.

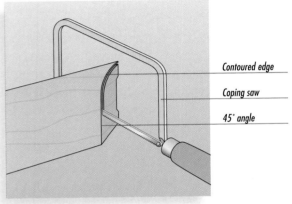

Contoured edge

Coping saw

45° angle

Coping a joint

When two contoured moldings—such as lengths of decorative crown molding—meet at an inside corner, making a coped joint is usually easiest. Cut the first piece of molding square and butt it into the corner. Then cut back the second piece at a 45-degree angle. Using a coping saw, follow the curvature of the molding's front edge while cutting a 90-degree angle. It pays to first practice on scrap material.

TYPES OF JOINTS

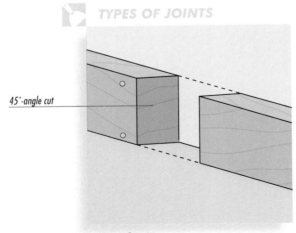

45°-angle cut

Scarf joint

Where two lengths of molding join along a wall, miter the ends at 45 degrees to create a scarf joint. Nail through the joint to secure the pieces.

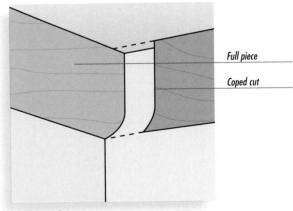

Full piece

Coped cut

Coped joint

With a coped joint, you butt and nail one piece into place, then cut the second piece to match the molding's curvature, butt it to the first piece, and nail into framing behind the finished wall.

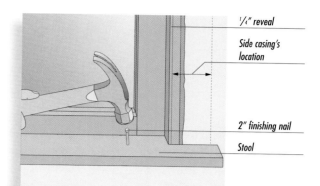

Jamb

Reveal

Sash

Stool

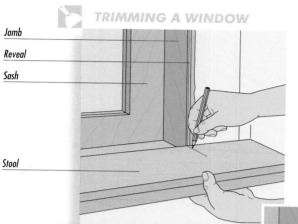

1 **Measure & cut the stool**

Center the stool in the opening. Mark the inside edge of each side jamb on the stool's back edge. Angle one end of the stool against a jamb, as shown in the detail, and mark the front edge of the jamb on the stool. Repeat at the other end. Extend the marks with a square, then cut the notches with a handsaw.

¹/₄" reveal

Side casing's location

2" finishing nail

Stool

2 **Fasten the stool to the sill**

Use either a flat piece of lumber or a preformed rabbeted or flat stool and nail with 2-inch finishing nails. Then, along the jambs, mark a "reveal," or setback line, ¹/₄ inch in from each jamb's inside edge.

45° angle

Top reveal mark

Side casing

Jamb

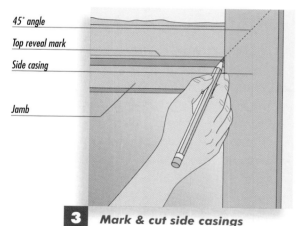

3 **Mark & cut side casings**

Align one length of side casing along your marks for a ¹/₄-inch reveal. Mark the inside edge of the casing where the head jamb's reveal crosses it. Then, using the 45-degree angle on a combination square, carry the mark across the piece. Repeat for the other side casing. Then cut both miters.

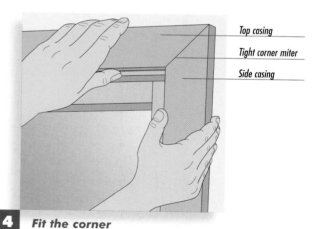

Top casing

Tight corner miter

Side casing

4 **Fit the corner**

Tack the two side casings in place with two nails each. Measure the distance between the inside edges of the side casings and cut the top casing to length with miters at both ends. Test fit to make sure corners are tight, then nail casings to the jambs and wall. Finally, cut and nail on the apron beneath the stool.

Paneling a Wall

There is a style of paneling to suit almost any decor. Choices include rustic boards, frame and panel designs with or without molding, and elaborate raised panels. You can cover an entire wall or choose waist- or shoulder-high wainscoting. Paneling can be made of fine hardwoods or inexpensive pine. Finishes run the gamut as well: Panels can be painted, stained, given a clear finish, or coated with any number of decorative finishes.

Paneling is sold in two main forms: sheets and boards. Sheets are typically 4 feet by 8 feet. Solid boards range from $^3/_8$- to $^7/_8$-inch thick, but the most common thicknesses are $^1/_2$ and $^3/_4$ inch. Boards fall between 3 and 10 inches wide and may have either square, tongue-and-groove, or shiplap edges.

Before installing paneling, move the materials into the room where they will be installed for two to five days to allow the wood to adjust to the home's humidity level. This will help eliminate any excess shrinkage or expansion once the panels are secured to the wall.

ATTACHING A PANEL

Panel tacked in place
Nails along top
Adhesive
Furring strips 24" o.c.
Panel blocked out from wall
Nails along bottom
$^1/_4$" space

It's easiest to glue sheets to horizontal furring strips spaced on 24-inch centers. Start in the corner that is adjacent to the most irregular wall and work clockwise. Nail and glue the panels in place as described in the text.

PREPARING A WALL When applying sheet or board panels over a finished wood-frame wall, you may be able to attach the material through the wallboard or plaster to the wall studs; otherwise, attach furring strips—1-by-3s or 1-by-4s—to the studs as a base for securing the panels. If the wall is new, without wallboard or plaster, you can attach sheets or boards directly to the studs or to 2-by-4 blocks nailed between the studs. Attach furring strips to wall studs with nails long enough to penetrate the studs by at least 1 inch. Fasten them to masonry walls with concrete nails or screws and shield-type masonry anchors.

Furring strips should be plumb and flat; you can make small adjustments with cedar shingle shims wedged behind the strips. If the existing wall is severely out of plumb, shim out furring strips as needed. Leave a $^1/_4$-inch space at both the top and bottom of the wall when applying the strips to allow for unevenness in the floor or ceiling.

Note that furring strips and paneling will add to the thickness of the wall. Window and door jambs must be built out in order to compensate for this added dimension. It's likely that you'll have to add extensions to electrical switches and receptacle boxes as well.

INSTALLING SHEET PANELING Before installing each sheet, cut it $^1/_4$ inch shorter than the distance from floor to ceiling. Apply adhesive to the framing in wavy lines. Drive four finishing nails through the top edge of the panel. Position the panel on the wall, leaving a $^1/_4$-inch space at the bottom; drive nails partway into the wall to act as hinge pins. Pull the bottom edge of the panel out about 6 inches from the wall and push a block behind it; wait for the adhesive to become tacky. Remove the block and press the panel firmly into place. Knock on the panel with a rubber mallet or hammer against a padded block. Drive the top-edge nails all the way in, then nail the panels at the bottom. Cover the nail heads and the $^1/_4$-inch gap with molding.

Fitting a panel around any opening requires careful measuring, marking, and cutting. Keep track of all the measurements by sketching them on a piece of paper.

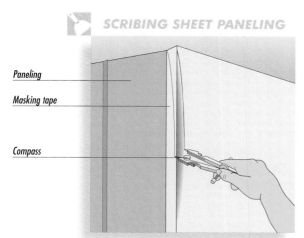

Paneling

Masking tape

Compass

To mark a wall's irregularities on the panel's edge, prop the panel into place about 1 inch from the uneven surface and shim it so that its long edge is plumb. Draw the points of a compass (open to the greatest gap) along the irregular surface so the pencil leg duplicates the unevenness onto a strip of masking tape on the paneling. Cut the paneling along the scribed line.

Starting from the corner of the wall or the edge of the nearest panel, measure to the edge of the opening or electrical box; then, from the same point, measure to the opening's opposite edge. Next, measure the distance from the floor to the opening's bottom edge and from the floor to the opening's top edge. (Remember that you'll install the paneling $1/4$ inch above the floor.) Transfer these measurements to the panel, marking the side of the panel that will face you as you cut (face-up for a handsaw, face-down for a power saw).

INSTALLING VERTICAL BOARD PANELING Before installing vertical solid-board paneling, install horizontal furring strips. Measure the width of the paneling boards and then the width of the wall. Calculate the width of the final board. To avoid a sliver-size board, split the difference so the first and last boards are the same. Cut boards $1/4$ inch shorter than the height from floor to ceiling. When you place the first board into the corner, check the outer edge with a carpenter's level. If the board isn't plumb or doesn't fit exactly, scribe and trim the edge facing the corner.

Attach the first board, leaving a $1/4$-inch space above the floor (use a prybar as a lever), then butt the second board against its edge and check for plumb. Repeat with all subsequent boards, then nail 24 inches on center. To make the last board fit easily into place, cut its edge at a slight angle (about 5 degrees) toward the board's back edge. At the inside corners, simply butt adjacent board edges together, scribing if necessary. At the outside corners, you can either bevel the joints for a neat fit (cut the bevels at an angle slightly greater than 45 degrees so they'll fit snugly) or you can butt boards and then conceal the joints with trim.

INSTALLING HORIZONTAL BOARD PANELING To avoid ending up with a very narrow board at the ceiling, measure the distance from floor to ceiling, figure the number of full-width boards, then split the difference between the top and bottom boards so they will be the same. Start at the bottom of the wall and work toward the ceiling. Nail the first board temporarily at one end, $1/4$ inch above the floor; use $1 1/2$- or 2-inch finishing nails. Level that board, then complete the nailing and set the nail heads. If you need to scribe and trim a board at its ends, follow the instructions for scribing sheet paneling, on this page. Working toward the ceiling, attach each board in the same way, nailing every stud. Rip the last board to width as required. If you have trouble fitting the last board, bevel its back edge slightly and pivot it into place. Set all nail heads and fill the holes with matching wood putty.

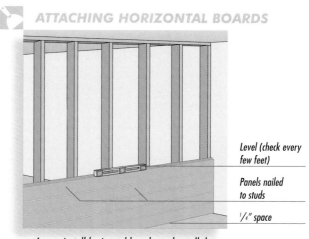

Level (check every few feet)

Panels nailed to studs

$1/4$" space

As you install horizontal boards up the wall, keep checking for level and make slight adjustments as necessary. Nail as described in the text.

Installing a Suspended Ceiling

Easy-to-install suspended ceilings consist of a metal grid supported from above by wire or spring-type hangers. The grid holds acoustic or decorative fiberboard panels. If you don't like the conventional look of the types sold in home improvement centers, look at some of the commercial offerings in manufacturers' catalogs.

The most common panel dimension is 2 feet by 4 feet. Transparent and translucent plastic panels and egg-crate grills are made to fit the supporting grid and admit light from above. Recessed lighting panels that exactly replace one panel are available from some manufacturers.

All components are replaceable, and panels can be raised for access to wiring, ducts, and pipes. Tiles are usually sold in packages containing a certain number of square feet of material. Measure the length and width of the room, eliminating areas not to be covered (a skylight, for example). Multiply these figures for the square footage, and add 10 percent for waste.

For a professional-looking job, plan equal-size borders on opposite sides of the room. To determine the nonstandard width of tiles or panels needed for perimeter rows, measure the extra space from the last full row of pieces to one wall and divide by two. This final figure will be the dimension of border pieces against that wall and the opposite wall. When purchasing, add 5 percent for waste. To complete your plan, repeat this procedure for the other room dimensions.

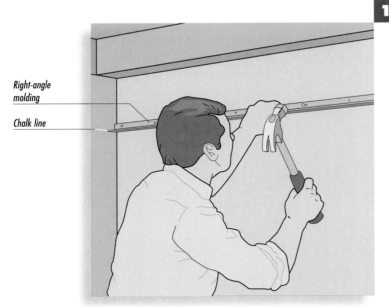

Right-angle molding

Chalk line

1 ***Install molding***

First, figure the ceiling height—at least 3 inches below plumbing, 5 inches below lights; minimum ceiling height is 7 feet, 6 inches. Snap a chalk line around the room at your chosen level and install right-angle molding just covering the chalk line.

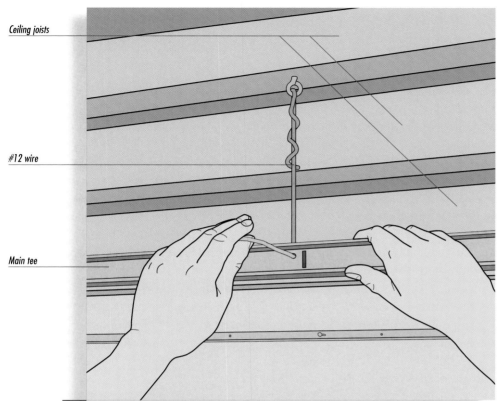

Ceiling joists

#12 wire

Main tee

2 **Hang the main runners**

Cut the main tees to length with tin snips or a
hacksaw. Setting them on the right-angle molding
at each end, support them every 4 feet with #12
wire attached to small eye screws fastened into
joists above.

4 **Install panels**

Slide the panels up diagonally through the grid
openings and lower them into place. Install any
recessed lighting panels. Cut border panels as
necessary with a sharp utility knife. Be sure your
hands are clean when handling panels—smudges
and fingerprints are hard to remove.

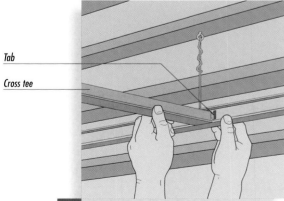

Tab

Cross tee

3 **Add the cross tees**

Lock 4-foot cross tees to the main tees by
inserting the tabs into the slots in the main tees
and snapping them in place.

Installing a Metal Ceiling

A pressed-metal ceiling (usually tin) can add a beautiful, traditional accent to a room. Because these ceilings offer no sound-deadening qualities, they are best suited to small, relatively quiet rooms.

Installation can be broken down into three major steps (with many smaller steps in between). First, hang a plywood base for the metal panels. Then figure and mark the layout of the metal panels (cornice, field panels, and filler panels) to determine the exact location of each. Last, cut and attach each panel. Once the parts are installed, cover gaps between panels and apply a finish such as clear polyurethane or paint. Although no particular step is difficult, each must be carefully executed to ensure that the finished ceiling has a uniform appearance.

On average, a metal ceiling will cost about $4 per square foot. Panels are typically available in 4- and 8-foot lengths.

A wide range of patterns is available; choose one that suits the style and size of the room. Use subtle patterns with a lower relief in smaller rooms or rooms with low ceilings.

Use tin snips to cut the material; you'll need straight-cutting snips, and you may also need right- or left-cutting types. Always wear sturdy leather gloves when handling the metal—it is as sharp as a knife. Also, wear protective glasses when working overhead. When nailing, it's a good idea to pre-punch nail holes with an awl or large nail.

PLANNING & ORDERING The single most important step is planning. Make a sketch of the ceiling and mark off the areas to be converted to determine how much material to purchase. Calculate the number of lineal feet of cornice pieces you will need to cover the room's perimeter. Also determine the number of 4-by-4- and 4-by-8-foot panels that will be needed to cover the center of the room. Finally, measure the number of square feet needed to fill the gaps between the cornice and the field panels with filler panels (a panel with a "neutral" pattern that will not conflict with the cornice and field patterns). Be sure to make accommodations for any electrical or ceiling-hung fixtures.

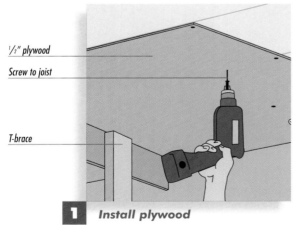

1/2" plywood

Screw to joist

T-brace

1 Install plywood

Use ¹/₂-inch plywood to cover the existing ceiling. In new construction, the plywood can be attached directly to the ceiling joist. In either case, run the plywood sheets perpendicular to the ceiling joists, fastening each sheet to the joist above. Leave a ¹/₈-inch gap between panels to allow the wood to expand.

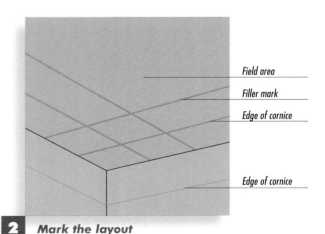

Field area

Filler mark

Edge of cornice

Edge of cornice

2 Mark the layout

Proper layout is the key to a successful installation. Mark the edges of the cornice, the field and filler panels and snap chalk lines for each. Also mark and snap lines for each individual field panel.

Once you have determined the amount of materials that will be needed, figure an extra 10 percent for waste. When estimating the number of panels to purchase, remember that panels cannot be cut exactly in half (doing so disrupts the pattern's repeat). Instead, add a full panel for any panel that will have to be trimmed.

Nail

Flat block of wood with hole

3 **Attach the field panels**

Place each nail so that it will be overlapped by the adjoining panel. Do not completely secure the nails around the perimeter. Later, you will need to slip the filler pieces underneath. Drill a hole through a flat block, as shown, to protect the panels from hammer dents.

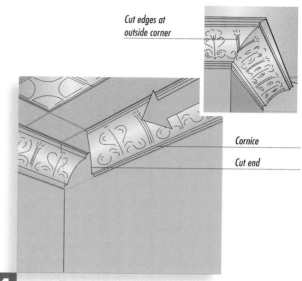

Cut edges at outside corner

Cornice

Cut end

4 **Install the cornice**

With the field panels installed, begin the cornice installation. At each corner, butt one cornice piece against the wall. Miter the second cornice piece at a 45-degree angle and test the fit; trim as necessary. Miter outside corners and test the fit. Once they join snugly, file any sharp edges until smooth.

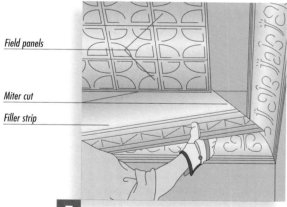

Field panels

Miter cut

Filler strip

5 **Finish with filler strips**

Slide the filler strips under the field panels and over the lip of the cornice pieces. Miter the corners. To determine the correct miter angles, cut a filler panel to the correct length and slide it in place without securing it. Mark the corner of the cornice and the field. Draw a line and cut the angle. Repeat for the adjoining corner. Tighten seams with a hammer and fill gaps with caulk.

PAINTING METAL PANELS

You must finish a metal ceiling with some type of protective coating or it will eventually rust. A coat of polyurethane can be applied if you wish to keep the metal finish, but be aware that it will not hide caulk and imperfections. Here are more finishing tips:

▪ Before using any finish, wipe the panels with mineral spirits to remove grease and factory coatings.

▪ Use an oil-based primer; the water in latex primers can rust the panels.

▪ Use a metallic paint if you want to keep the look of the metal.

▪ An oil-based finish coat is less likely to show brush and roller strokes.

Repairing Drywall

Drywall repairs typically involve repairing dents and popped nails, filling nail holes, and patching holes punched through the wall. These problems can usually be fixed with simple techniques and tools—joint compound or spackling compound, a putty knife, and a few basic carpentry tools. After the repair, you must paint the repaired area to match the rest of the wall. If you don't have paint that matches, you will have to completely repaint the wall.

MINOR REPAIRS For minor repairs like dents and small nail holes, sand the damaged area clean and fill it with one or more layers of all-purpose joint compound, using a flexible, narrow-bladed putty knife. Allow each layer to dry before applying the next. Fix popped nails by recessing the nail below the finished surface of the wall and driving another nail just beside it to hold it in. Cover the dimples with joint compound. When the repairs are dry, you'll need to sand and prime the area, and paint it to match.

REPAIRING A LARGE HOLE To repair a large hole, the damaged section of wallboard must be cut out and replaced with a new piece of gypsum wallboard that is the same thickness. The key to a quality job is blending the repair with the surrounding surface. This is often done in stages over a period of days. The tools and supplies you'll need include ready-mixed all-purpose joint compound; 2-inch perforated or mesh wallboard tape; 4-, 6-, and 10-inch taping knives; and 400-grit silicon-carbide sandpaper.

Make the repair as shown in the illustrations on these pages. To apply compound, dip the edge of a clean taping knife blade into the compound, loading about half the blade. Apply the compound across the joint, then, holding the knife at a 45-degree angle to the wall, draw the blade along the joint. Using increasingly wider knives for each layer makes the joint smoother. Let each layer dry for at least 24 hours before applying the next. When dry, remove minor imperfections by wetting the compound with a sponge and sanding along the joints with sandpaper wrapped around a sanding block. Never sand the wallboard itself—scratches in the paper may show through the finish.

REPAIRING DRYWALL

Studs 16" o.c.

4" minimum

1 Make a rectangular cutout

After making sure there are no hidden wires or obstacles (see pages 210–211), use a keyhole saw and utility knife to cut the damaged wallboard between the studs. Remove the piece with a prybar; pull out any remaining nails.

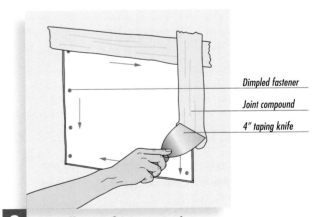

Dimpled fastener

Joint compound

4" taping knife

2 Install a replacement piece

Cut the replacement piece and smooth the edges with a perforated rasp; then nail or screw the new piece in place. Apply a large daub of joint compound across a joint with a 4-inch taping knife, drawing the knife along the joint at a 45-degree angle to the wall.

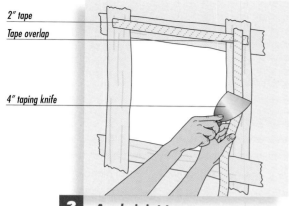

2" tape
Tape overlap
4" taping knife

3 *Apply joint tape*

Center tape over each joint; press down. Remove excess compound with a knife, feathering the edges. Thinly apply compound over the tape. When dry, wet-sand the compound (see text on facing page).

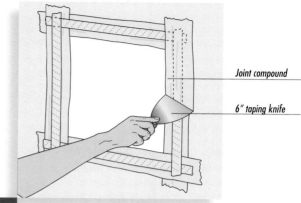

Joint compound
6" taping knife

4 *Apply a second coat*

Using a 6-inch taping knife, apply a second layer of compound and feather the edges. When the compound is dry, wet-sand the edges to remove minor imperfections.

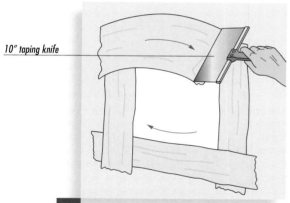

10" taping knife

5 *Apply a third coat*

Apply as much compound as necessary to cover the previous layer, using a 10-inch taping knife held at a 45-degree angle to the wall. Feather the edges 12 to 18 inches out. Allow the compound to dry before doing the final sanding.

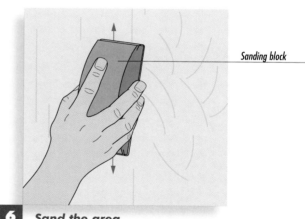

Sanding block

6 *Sand the area*

With a sponge and sanding block, wet-sand the compound to remove imperfections. Wipe off sanding residue, prime, then paint.

 QUICK DRYWALL PATCHES

Look for precut wallboard patches designed with adhesive fins or metal braces that hold them in place. Available at home improvement centers in a range of sizes, they provide a convenient alternative to traditional wallboard patches. You typically make a rectangular cutout around the damaged area, adhere the patch in place, smooth the fin to the wall, cover the patch with joint compound, then sand and finish it.

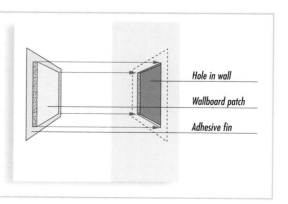

Hole in wall
Wallboard patch
Adhesive fin

Repairing Plaster

Before gypsum wallboard became the interior surface finish material of choice in the 1950s, plaster was very commonly used for finishing interior walls and ceilings. Plaster is a very hard and durable material, but—because it isn't a resilient material—it has a tendency to crack as a home moves with earthquakes or naturally settles over the years. Once cracks form, plaster may eventually work loose.

A mixture of portland cement, sand, and water, plaster may be applied over wood lath, metal mesh, special gypsum wallboard, or masonry. During application, a scratch coat is applied onto the backing material. Next, a thick undercoat is troweled onto the surface, then a finish coat is applied.

Here you'll find instructions for patching cracks and holes in plaster. If a large area is damaged or the base needs repair, consult a professional.

SMALL CRACKS & HOLES Fine cracks, nail holes, and small gouges in plaster usually can be repaired with spackling compound. Widen the hairline cracks to about $1/8$ inch with the tip of a lever-type can opener; blow out dust and debris. With your finger or a putty knife, fill the crack with spackling compound. Sand the compound in a circular motion when dry, using a block wrapped with fine-grade sandpaper. Prime the patch with sealer before painting.

LARGE CRACKS For larger cracks, undercut the crack with a lever-type can opener or a putty knife to help bond the new plaster; blow out dust and debris. Dampen the crack with a sponge, then use a putty knife to fill just over half the depth of the crack with patching plaster. Score the plaster with a nail when firm but not hard to provide "bite" for the next layer. Dampen the dry patch again and use a broad knife to apply the next layer to within $1/8$ and $1/4$ inch of the surface. Let the patch dry before applying the finish coat. Fill with finishing plaster and strike off with a straightedge to remove excess.

FINISHING TIPS Matching an existing texture requires skillful treatment of the still-wet finishing plaster. You'll have to experiment to achieve a good match. For a smooth surface, pull a metal float or wide putty knife dipped in water across the plaster. When dry, sand to remove minor imperfections, prime, and paint. For a textured surface, use a paintbrush, stippling brush, household sponge, sponge float, whisk broom, or wire brush—whatever will give you the desired finish. Daub or swirl the plaster in a uniform, random, or overlapping pattern. To create peaks in the plaster, use a brush or a tool with bristles; when the peaks start to stiffen, gently draw a clean metal float over the surface to smooth them. Let the plaster dry, then prime and paint.

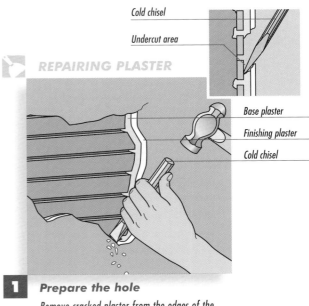

Cold chisel

Undercut area

REPAIRING PLASTER

Base plaster

Finishing plaster

Cold chisel

1 **Prepare the hole**
Remove cracked plaster from the edges of the hole with a cold chisel and hammer. Undercut the edges to ensure a good bond; blow away debris. Dampen the edges with a sponge.

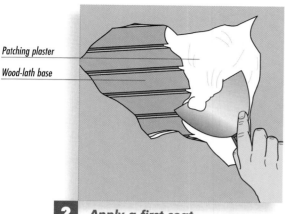

Patching plaster
Wood-lath base

2 **Apply a first coat**

Using a broad knife, fill a little more than half the hole's depth with patching plaster; force it through gaps in the lath. Score the plaster with a nail when firm and let it dry.

Scored plaster
Patching plaster

3 **Apply a second coat**

Dampen the patch again; use a broad knife to apply a second layer of plaster to within $^1/_8$ and $^1/_4$ inch of the surface. When firm, score the plaster with a nail to provide "bite" for the next layer; allow to dry.

4 **Apply the finish coat**

Use a broad knife or a 10-inch taping knife to apply finishing plaster; feather the edges an inch or more beyond the edges of the patch. Remove excess wet plaster with a straightedge. For a smooth finish, dip a metal float in water and, holding the float at a slight angle to the wall, draw it down from top to bottom. When dry, sand and prime.

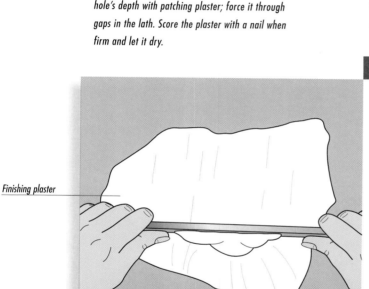

Finishing plaster

 IF THE HOLE HAS NO BACKING

If there isn't any lath or backing to support a new coat of plaster, your patching material will just fall down into the wall—so you need to provide backing. After preparing the hole, loop a wire through a piece of rust-resistant metal mesh. Roll the edges, insert the mesh into the hole, flatten it out by pulling the wire, then wind it up with a stick. After you've patched the hole, remove the stick and snip off the wire.

Before attempting to repair wooden wall paneling, see the paneling installation information on pages 114–115. You'll see that paneling comes in a variety of types and forms; you'll want to take your particular type into consideration when making repairs. Boards may have square edges, but most are milled to overlap or interlock. Paneling is attached to studs, furring strips, or wallboard.

REPLACING SOLID PANELING

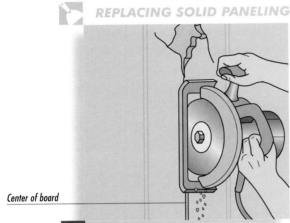

Center of board

1 Cut out damaged panel

After removing the baseboard, adjust the blade depth of a circular saw to the board's thickness and saw up the damaged board's center, then split the board with a chisel.

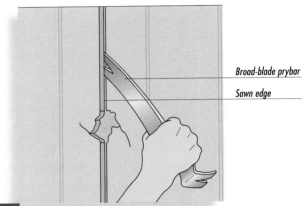

Broad-blade prybar

Sawn edge

2 Pry off sections

Wedge a broad-blade prybar or wide chisel between the sawn edges. Pry the sections away from the wall, one at a time. (The tongue section may be blind-nailed.)

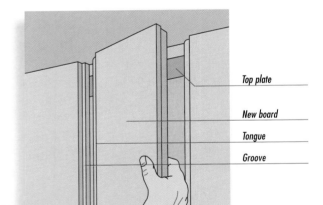

Top plate

New board

Tongue

Groove

4 Install the replacement

Align the replacement board with the adjacent one, starting at the ceiling. Fit the tongue of the new board into the groove of the adjacent board and slip it into place. Tap the board into place with a padded block. Drive finishing nails at top and bottom, sinking heads with a nailset; fill holes with wood putty and finish. Replace baseboard.

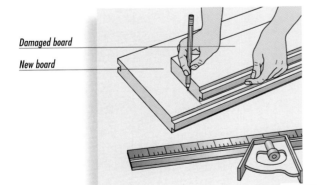

Damaged board

New board

Back of groove

Front of board

Wood block

3 Cut a replacement

Place the damaged board over the new board; mark the correct length using a pencil and combination square. Use a crosscut saw to cut the replacement board to length. Remove the back of the new board's groove with a wood chisel (inset).

Damaged solid board paneling responds well to techniques for repairing minor scratches, dents, and gouges. If the damage is more serious, you may want to replace one or more boards, carefully matching the new paneling to the existing surface.

MINOR SCRATCHES & GOUGES On solid board paneling, it's common to conceal shallow scratches and gouges by filling them with a putty stick, then wiping away excess putty with a clean cloth. You can also conceal minor scratches as you would those on furniture—with furniture polish or an almond stick, a compressed fabric stick impregnated with oil.

When sheet paneling is damaged, the simplest way to conceal flaws is to use a putty stick to "draw" over the mar; wipe away any excess putty with a clean cloth. (Putty sticks come in a variety of colors to match finished wood paneling.) You can also hide scratches and nicks with shoe polish (test first), floor wax, or an almond stick.

DENTS & DEEP GOUGES Restore dented solid panels by removing the finish from the dent area, then placing a damp cloth and hot iron over the dent until the wood fibers rise to the level of the surrounding surface. Let the wood dry thoroughly before sanding it smooth and refinishing the area. To repair a deep gouge or a nail hole, apply matching wood putty with a flexible putty knife. Let it dry, then sand smooth with fine-grade sandpaper wrapped around a sanding block. Finish to match the surrounding area.

For badly damaged sheet panels, use a putty knife to fill deep gouges and cracks with wood putty. When the putty is dry, sand it smooth. Use a small brush to stain or paint the putty so it matches the finish of the panel, or use colored putty that matches the finish.

REPAIRING SHEET PANELING

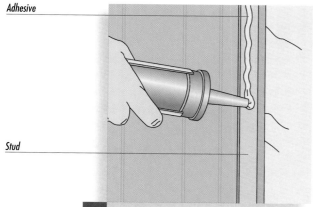

Stud

Damaged panel

1 Remove the damaged panel
After removing the baseboard, split the panel near one edge (not on a stud), using a hammer and chisel; pry the panel off the studs with a prybar, being careful not to damage adjacent panels. Wedge a prybar between the panel and studs to break any adhesive bond.

Adhesive

Stud

2 Apply paneling adhesive
After pulling off the old paneling and scraping off any adhesive (or removing nails), apply a bead of adhesive along the length of the studs to hold the new panel.

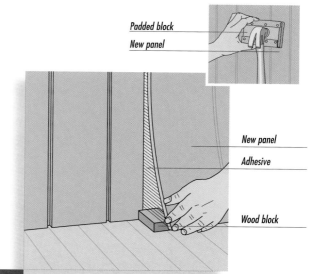

Padded block

New panel

New panel

Adhesive

Wood block

3 Install the new panel
Position the new panel; drive 4 finishing nails near the top of the panel to secure it. Then pull out the base, holding it with a wood block until the adhesive becomes tacky. Remove the block and press the panel in place. With a padded block, hammer along edges and over studs. Remove finishing nails if not needed. Replace baseboard.

Replacing Ceiling Tiles

Square ceiling tiles are available in a variety of decorative and acoustic styles. These tiles, most commonly 1 foot square, are applied with special adhesive or staples to existing flat ceilings or to 1-by-3 furring strips fastened across joists or an irregular ceiling.

Stains from water damage are a common problem with these tiles. To conceal stains or streaks, apply a primer or clear sealer. When the tiles are completely dry, paint them with latex paint.

Because the tiles are made from a soft, compressed cellulose material, another common problem is that they can dent, chip, or break. When this happens, the best thing to do is to replace the damaged tiles. Illustrated below are the steps for removing and replacing a standard tile (the type that has tongue-and-groove edges).

REPLACING A TILE The process of replacing a tile is simple. Cut through all four joints and pry the tile off its backing. Then pry out the cut-off tongues from the grooves in the adjacent tiles. Use pliers to remove any remaining staples or nails; scrape off the adhesive.

After cutting the tongue off one side of the replacement tile, apply adhesive to the back of the tile or to the ceiling (follow the tile manufacturer's directions). Position the tile over the opening, slip the remaining tongue into the groove of an adjacent tile, and press it in place until the adhesive holds; or use a floor-to-ceiling brace to hold the tile until the adhesive is dry.

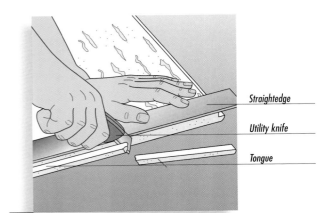

Straightedge

Utility knife

Tongue

2 Prepare the replacement
Cut the tongue from one edge of the new tile using a utility knife and a straightedge.

REPLACING A CEILING TILE

Damaged area

Joints

1 Remove the damaged tile
Cut through all 4 joints of the damaged tile. Use a prybar to remove it.

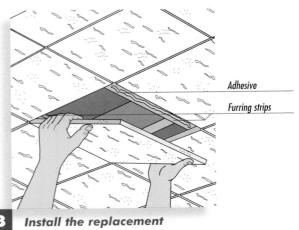

Adhesive

Furring strips

3 Install the replacement
Apply adhesive. Slip the tongue into an adjacent tile's groove and brace it until the adhesive holds.

REPAIRING A LARGE AREA In areas where major damage has occurred (such as extensive water damage), it may be necessary to replace multiple tiles or an entire ceiling. Tiles are usually sold in packages of a certain number of square feet. Measure the length and width of the room, eliminating areas not to be covered (a skylight, for example). Multiply these figures for the square footage, and buy enough material to cover this area plus another 10 percent for waste.

For a professional-looking job, plan equal borders on opposite sides of the room. To determine the nonstandard width of tiles or panels needed for perimeter rows, measure the extra space from the last full row of pieces to one wall, and divide by two. This final figure will be the dimension of border pieces against that wall and the opposite wall. To complete your plan, repeat this procedure for the other room dimensions. If you're replacing tiles over an existing ceiling, first mark your layout across the ceiling by snapping a chalk line for each row. Install the tiles by daubing special adhesive on each corner and the center of the back of each tile.

REPAIRING A LARGE AREA

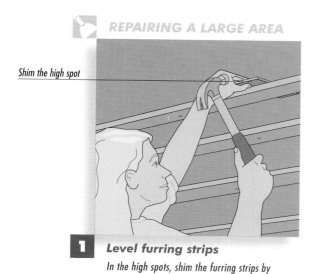

Shim the high spot

1 Level furring strips

In the high spots, shim the furring strips by driving shingles between them and the joists. Also level the strips with each other, checking the evenness with a straightedge.

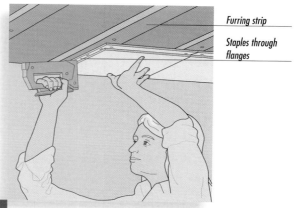

Furring strip

Staples through flanges

2 Cut border tiles to size

Place the cut edges against the wall and face-nail where the molding will cover the nail heads. Staple the other sides to the furring strips through the flanges.

3 Install the remaining tiles

Work outward from the border tiles across the room. Center each tile on the furring strips and staple in place.

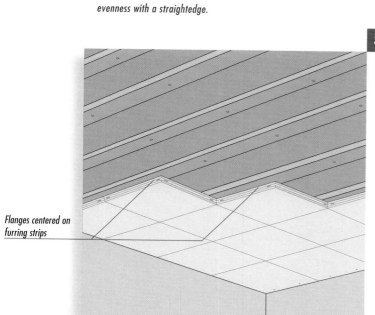

Flanges centered on furring strips

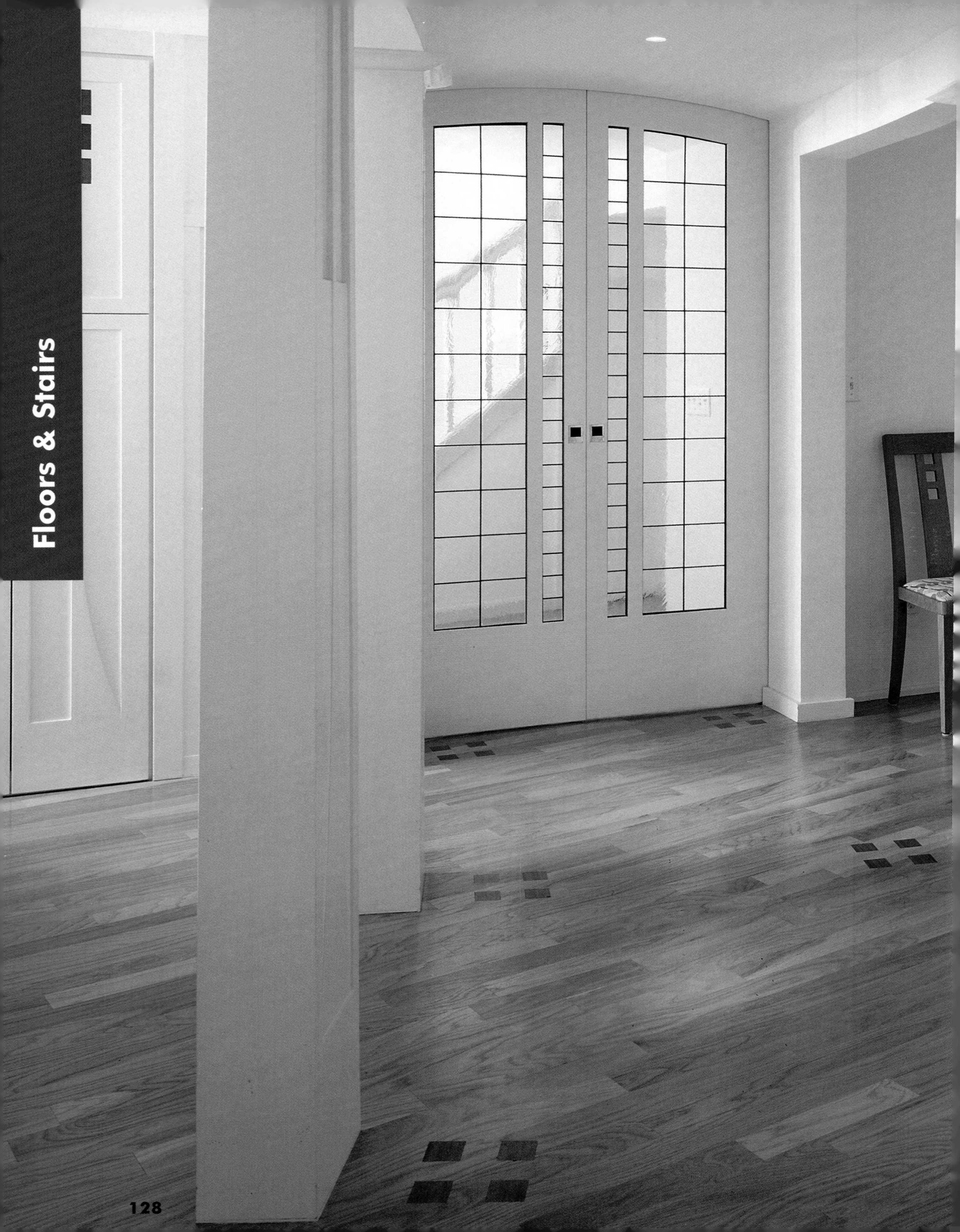

Floors & Stairs

Floors and stairs are often focal points in a home, for good reason. Both are design elements that are meant to catch our eye, especially since they occupy a large and prominent amount of space in any home. A beautifully finished hardwood floor, or cleverly done tile or laminate floor is an asset, as is an elegant sweep of stairs.

Nothing save the roof is subjected to the continual daily wear and tear that floors and stairs take, so these elements often need repairs or improvements. Floor improvements can seem to be intimidating projects for even ardent do-it-yourselfers, but they needn't be. While certain tasks, particularly installation, demand at least a certain amount of skill and self-confidence, others are easier than you might imagine. In this chapter, we focus on installations—of wood, laminate, and tile flooring—and floor and stair repairs, including a cure for the common squeak.

Floor & Stair Construction

Have you ever wondered what is underneath the vinyl, wood, or tile floor in your home? Or have you ever had a chance to see how a staircase is constructed? If you're going to be making repairs or improvements to your floors and stairs, it's important to know how they're built. Here we look at typical floor and stair construction. (For more about stair construction, see "Building Stairs" on page 162.)

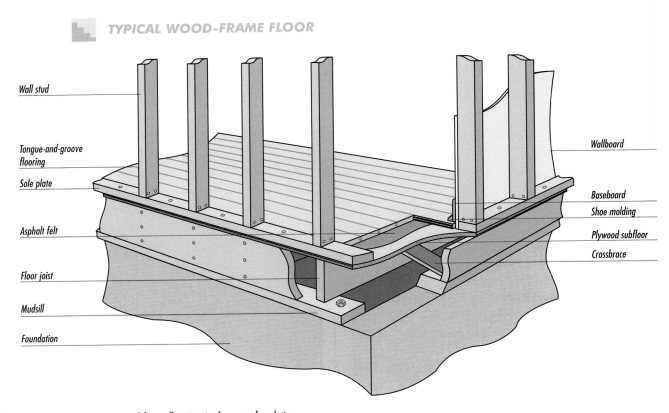

TYPICAL WOOD-FRAME FLOOR

Wall stud

Tongue-and-groove flooring

Sole plate

Asphalt felt

Floor joist

Mudsill

Foundation

Wallboard

Baseboard

Shoe molding

Plywood subfloor

Crossbrace

A wood-frame floor is raised up on a foundation. Joists provide the primary support. Here the subfloor is made from plywood, and the finished flooring is wood. An underlayment of asphalt felt is positioned between the two.

The subfloor is typically constructed from 1-by-4 or 1-by-6 lumber, or plywood panels. In a lumber subfloor, boards are laid diagonally across joists. A plywood subfloor has panels laid in a staggered fashion, with the ends butted together; panels are nailed (and sometimes glued with construction adhesive) to the joists.

The thickness and stiffness of the subfloor determine the types of finished flooring that can be put on top. If your house is built on a concrete slab, the slab can serve as a base for almost any type of flooring. But if your home has a plywood or lumber subfloor, it's important to check out the type and thickness of material to determine its limitations.

A floor that is slightly flexible or springy is not suitable for rigid materials such as ceramic tile and masonry (the grout or materials will crack with movement). Be especially cautious if the floor already has a noticeable bounce.

If your home has a crawl space or basement, you can go underneath to check out the underside of the subfloor. If you can tell that it's plywood, look for a grade stamp that designates the thickness.

A few minor dips in floors are common. Some settling results from stresses and fatigue. But if floors sag, the house could have a serious structural problem. Also look for evidence of rot. Discolored areas on the joists or subfloor usually indicate a plumbing leak. If you're faced with these kinds of problems, call a contractor.

STAIR CONSTRUCTION

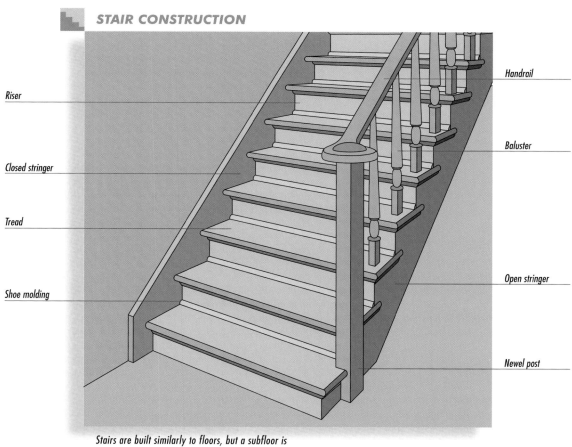

Riser

Closed stringer

Tread

Shoe molding

Handrail

Baluster

Open stringer

Newel post

Stairs are built similarly to floors, but a subfloor is supported with joists, while a stair's treads are supported by stringers. Shown here are the typical components of a staircase.

Buying Flooring Materials

Flooring is an important aesthetic choice in determining the character of a room, but beyond its looks, it must work hard. It gets walked on, spilled on, rolled across, and washed repeatedly. Luckily, there are plenty of great-looking options that create different effects, solve different problems, and suit many budgets.

If you plan to install a floor yourself, read the installation instructions before you buy the material. Often the preparation and physical labor may be more than you want to tackle. In that case, you'll want to allow for installation costs in your budget and obtain bids for the work.

Good-quality flooring will last for years, so avoid designs, colors, and patterns that will date quickly. Determine the kind and amount of traffic the flooring will have to bear. For high-traffic areas, such as hallways, entryways, kitchens, and bathrooms, select the most durable materials you can find. Use less rugged material for areas that receive less wear.

Cost is another factor. All the standard flooring materials come in various grades, their cost directly related to quality. Because floors last a long time, consider installing the best flooring you can afford.

If noise concerns you, realize that soft flooring, such as vinyl and carpeting, deadens sound. Wood, ceramic tile, and stone can magnify sound. And don't forget to consider safety. In baths, marble and glazed tile work well for walls but become slippery when wet. For flooring, it's best to ask if there is a color-compatible, nonslip alternative.

Understanding the basic characteristics of the various materials and how they can be used will help you make these kinds of decisions.

A COMPARATIVE GUIDE TO FLOORING

FLOORING TYPE	ADVANTAGES	DISADVANTAGES
Wood 	A hardwood floor creates a warm decor, feels good underfoot, and can be refinished. Oak is most common; maple, birch, cherry, and beech are also available. Wood tile, often patterned in parquet fashion, is the easiest to install. Strip flooring consists of random-length, narrow, tongue-and-groove boards. Planks hearken back to America's historic houses and consist of tongue-and-groove boards in random widths and lengths. "Floating" floor systems have several veneered strips atop each tongue-and-groove backing board. Wood flooring can generally be refinished, and the kinds of finish available today have improved its resistance to moisture.	Softwood (pine) is appropriate for some country or reproduction homes; but it dents and scratches easily. "Floating" floor systems cannot be refinished. Moisture and inadequate floor systems, especially a sagging subfloor or a damp slab, can create problems. Some finishes scratch easily. Bleaching and some staining processes may wear unevenly and are difficult to repair.
Resilient Flooring 	The variety of colors, textures, patterns, and styles makes it possible to simulate more expensive materials. Comfortable underfoot, resilient flooring is relatively soft. Tiles can be mixed to form custom patterns. Resilient tile is easier to install than sheet goods. Both can be repaired. Sheets are more impervious to water. Available in widths up to 12 feet, sheets allow seamless floors in small rooms. Resilient tile is an economical choice.	Sheet flooring has a top layer of vinyl bonded to a backing (either felt or vinyl). When a soft layer is pressed between the top layer and the backing, it produces cushioned vinyl, which is vulnerable to dents and tears; sometimes such damage can be repaired. If they are improperly installed, resilient floor tiles or sheet goods may collect moisture between seams, causing the edges to curl.

FLOORING TYPE	ADVANTAGES	DISADVANTAGES
Ceramic Tile 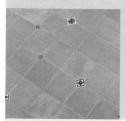	Ceramic tile is durable and easy to maintain; its resistance to water and stains makes it ideal for the kitchen or bath. Made from hard-fired clay, tile comes in dozens of patterns, sizes, and thicknesses. Tiles are classified as quarry tile, unglazed red-clay tile that is rough and water-resistant; pavers, rugged unglazed tile in earth tones; and glazed tile, available in glossy, matte, nonslip, and textured finishes.	Ceramic tile is rigid underfoot, reflects noise, and is susceptible to cracking if the floor shifts or if hard objects are dropped on it. Glazed tile can be slippery and cold. Grout can be tough to keep clean. For outdoor use, consider porcelain tile.
Stone 	Natural stone, such as slate, flagstone, marble, granite, and limestone, has been used as a flooring material for centuries. Today it's even more practical, thanks to sealers. Easy to maintain, it's virtually indestructible. Natural stone includes rough-hewn shapes and uniform tiles. Generally, uniform pieces are butted tightly together; irregular flagstone requires grouted joints. Both marble and slate are typically available as tiles that are relatively easy to install. Slate varies in color from dark blue to gray and green. Marble has a more traditional, formal look. For small areas, such as hearths, stone can be a practical alternative.	Stone can be slippery, and cleaning the grout can be difficult, as with tile. Because of its weight, natural stone can be expensive if it has to be shipped any distance; stone also has the disadvantages of being noisy, as well as cold underfoot. For more expensive stone—marble or granite—budget may be a consideration.
Brick & Concrete 	Manufactured masonry products, such as brick and concrete, were once considered outdoor materials but are becoming increasingly popular for interior flooring. Brick is attractive and relatively inexpensive. Bricks are made in full thicknesses and in splits (half as thick). Because it retains heat, brick is suitable for use in passive-solar heating designs. Concrete is used for slabs and is a perfect subfloor for almost any type of flooring. But concrete can also serve as a permanent floor because it is durable and waterproof. Exposed aggregate relieves the monotony of plain concrete and adds texture and traction. Other special treatments can give concrete character and color.	The weight of masonry materials is such that a very strong, well-supported subfloor is required. Concrete slabs can take the weight of full-thickness bricks, but wooden subfloors require the lighter-weight splits. If you're considering a masonry floor, check your local building code for subfloor requirements. A concrete floor requires building forms and casting concrete, techniques that do not fall within the scope of this book; consult a professional.
Carpeting 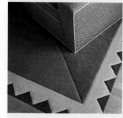	Carpeting cushions feet, provides firm traction, and helps deaden sound. It's especially useful to define areas in master suites. Tightly woven commercial carpet provides the greatest durability. Of all the flooring materials, it's the quickest and least disruptive to install. With padding, carpet can disguise an uneven subfloor. Although natural fibers are still popular, synthetics dominate the market because of their lower prices and easier maintenance. Carpeting is available in wool, nylon, polypropylene (olefin), polyester, and acrylic, as well as combinations of these materials. Olefin is used in the manufacture of Berber carpets. Half a dozen basic manufacturing processes are used to produce carpeting. Among the styles that result are plush, level loop, and sculptured pile. The variety of colors and textures is compatible with a wide range of decorative schemes.	The more elaborate the material and weave, the greater the problems from moisture absorption, staining, and mildew. Carpeting in bathrooms and below-grade rooms should be short pile and unsculptured. Woven or loop-pile wool should be confined to dressing areas. Nylon and other synthetic carpets are a better choice for splash zones; these are washable and hold up well in moist conditions.

Choosing Wood Floors

Despite the development of far less expensive synthetics, wood flooring today is as popular as ever—no doubt because it is a practical surface; has a handsome, natural warmth; and is comfortable underfoot. Wood floors may shrink in heat or swell in dampness, and they require a very carefully prepared subfloor and a moisture-free environment. For a brief look at the advantages and disadvantages of wood flooring, see page 132.

Types of Wood Flooring

The term "wood floor" is used to describe a wide gamut of products and materials, from rustic pine planks to contemporary laminated wood floors. Included in the groups that we look at here are laminate "floating floors," a type that looks much like wood but is not.

STRIP FLOORING Strip flooring is composed of narrow tongue-and-groove boards; the widths don't vary. Strip flooring is generally $3/4$ inch thick with a face width of $2 1/4$ inches and is blind-nailed (through the tongue, where you can't see the nails) to a subfloor. Strip flooring is graded according to color, grain, and knots: Clear, followed by Select, No. 1 Common, and No. 2 Common.

Stacking strips & planks
Untie the bundles and stack the individual boards loosely so air circulates. Wrapped flooring should be unwrapped to allow it to adjust to the room before installation.

PLANK FLOORING A holdover from Colonial days, plank flooring was originally made from maple planks more than a foot wide. Today it differs little from strip flooring, except that it comes in random widths of 3 inches and up. Plank flooring may be $3/4$ or $3/8$ inch thick, and either solid wood or laminated, meaning that it is manufactured from glued-together, thin layers of wood, usually applied over a reconstituted-wood base. The latter holds up better in slightly moist conditions. In both types, length usually ranges from 2 to 8 feet. Because plank flooring can be nailed like strip flooring or screwed down at the ends, the boards may have holes already countersunk; wood plugs come with the boards, which can be prefinished or not. Plank flooring is graded just like strip flooring.

PARQUET FLOORING Produced in dozens of patterns, textures, and thicknesses, parquet is made from solid pieces of wood, laminates, or individual pieces of wood held together by a backing. A parquet floor is easy to install yet has the look of a custom-designed floor. Some parquet tiles have an adhesive backing; others require you to spread adhesive. Both types will require a clean, dry, and smooth surface to adhere properly.

FLOATING FLOOR A floating floor resembles a wood floor but is actually a plastic laminate material, similar to the type used on countertops. It's called a "floating floor" because you do not fasten it down to the subfloor; instead, it is interlocked and placed on top of a thin foam pad over a plywood or concrete subfloor.

Laminate is extremely durable and scratch-resistant and may be used where it occasionally gets wet—such as in a bathroom. Some manufacturers offer a 15-year guarantee against stains, wear, and fading. Many different contemporary colors, patterns, and styles are available, from the look of travertine stone to colored checkerboards. Laminate flooring, sold at home improvement centers, is relatively easy to install yourself with limited tools. This is a prefinished material that need not be—and cannot be—sanded and finished.

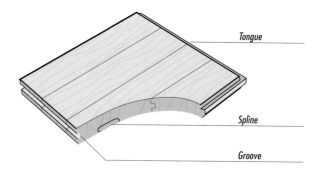

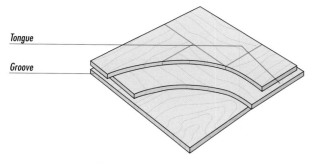

Tongue
Groove

Laminated

The best choice for below-grade floors, the squares of laminated parquet are surfaced with hardwood veneer and may be backed with mesh. Most are 5/16-inch thick.

Solid parquet

Short lengths of wood are held together with splines of metal, wood, or plastic. It comes in thicknesses of 5/16 inch and up.

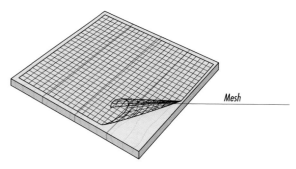

Mesh

Mesh-back

Also known as mosaic, mesh-back parquet is made up of small pieces of wood held together with cotton mesh. Some types are held together with paper on the face; the paper is removed after installation.

Ordering & Storing Wood Flooring

A flooring materials supplier will help you calculate the quantity of material to order. Allow for waste and future repairs. Your flooring should be delivered properly dried. Never allow it to be delivered in snow or rain, or you'll risk the possibility of it warping. If you're redoing your walls at the same time, make sure the drywall is completely dry.

New, unwrapped strip or plank flooring should be delivered at least four days before installation. If possible, store it in the room where it will be installed, or a similar environment. The temperature and humidity should be close to normal levels.

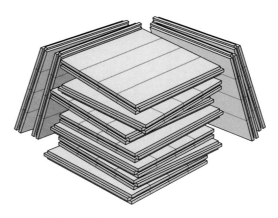

Unpacking parquet

Unpack and store parquet according to the manufacturer's directions—normally in the area where it's to be installed, at least 72 hours before the job begins, stacked loosely so that air can circulate around the material.

HOW THICK IS YOUR FLOORING?

The thickness of the flooring you choose can raise the room's floor level. Take this into account when deciding which flooring to install, because it may create some problems in the way appliances fit under the cabinets or at transitions between rooms.

Tools for Floors & Stairs

Because floors and stairs are essentially wooden structural elements in a home, working on them usually calls for a selection of conventional carpentry tools. Special sanders and other equipment are needed for finishing and refinishing wood floors; these are discussed and shown on pages 146–149. Safety equipment is important to have on hand, too, especially when sanding; you'll need goggles, a dust mask, and gloves. Tools needed for repairing carpets are discussed on pages 172–173.

HELPFUL BUILDING TOOLS

In addition to basic tools such as a claw hammer, saw, and screwdrivers, you'll want to have a carpenter's square, chalk line, combination square, compass, contour gauge, level, straightedge, and measuring tape for layout and marking. For cutting and drilling, you'll probably need a utility knife, chisels, a power circular saw, a saber saw, and a power drill with bits (a table saw or power miter saw can also be very helpful). For miscellaneous jobs, a putty knife, prybar, and caulking gun will come in handy.

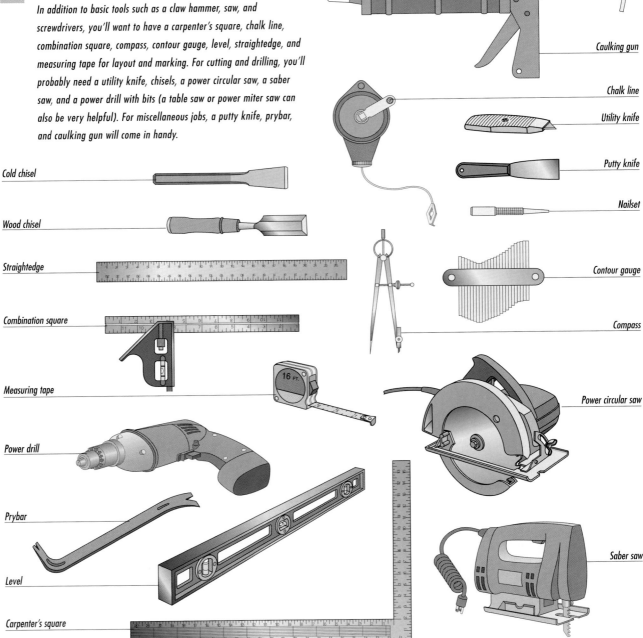

Cold chisel

Wood chisel

Straightedge

Combination square

Measuring tape

Power drill

Prybar

Level

Carpenter's square

Caulking gun

Chalk line

Utility knife

Putty knife

Nailset

Contour gauge

Compass

Power circular saw

Saber saw

TILE & MASONRY TOOLS

If you'll be working with tile or masonry floors, plan to have a cold chisel (and, ideally, a ball-peen hammer for striking it). For working with mortar and grout, you'll need a steel trowel and rubber-backed trowel. For cutting tile, use a wet saw or snap tile cutter (see page 159).

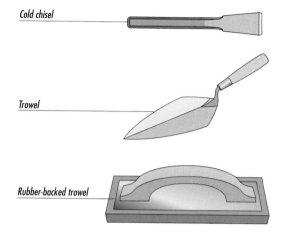

Cold chisel

Trowel

Rubber-backed trowel

RESILIENT-FLOORING TOOLS

Working with vinyl and other resilient-flooring materials calls for a notched trowel and notched spreader for applying adhesive. For cutting, you'll need tin snips (or heavy-duty scissors) and a linoleum knife (you can also use a utility knife fitted with special hooked blades designed for cutting resilient flooring). To seat the flooring firmly in mastic, you'll want to rent a floor roller (you can use a rolling pin for small jobs).

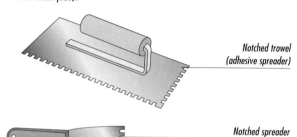

Notched trowel
(adhesive spreader)

Notched spreader

WOOD-FLOORING TOOLS

In addition to the various helpful building tools shown on the facing page, a pneumatic flooring stapler or nailer and a mallet, available through tool supply stores, are almost essential for flooring installation.

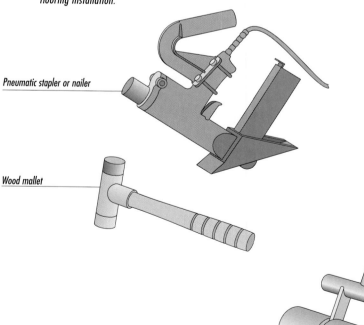

Pneumatic stapler or nailer

Wood mallet

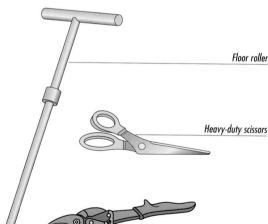

Floor roller

Heavy-duty scissors

Tin snips

Linoleum knife

Preparing for a New Floor

Floor Improvements

As with nearly every type of home improvement project, preparation is key to the success of installing a new floor. Whether you are putting your new floor over the top of an older, existing floor or starting from scratch, be sure to provide the type of base that is suggested by your material's manufacturer.

Choosing the Proper Base

New flooring should be installed on a clean, smooth, level, structurally sound base. Depending upon the situation and type of new flooring, this base may be an earlier floor covering, a new subfloor, a concrete slab, or any of several other possibilities. Following are a few basics you'll need to know to prepare a proper base.

FOR WOOD An existing wood floor in good condition can serve as a base for new strip, plank, or parquet flooring; in fact, parquet flooring can even be installed over old resilient sheet or tile floor covering. The advantages of laying new flooring over old are that you bypass the messy job of removing the old flooring and you gain some soundproofing and insulation from the old floor.

One disadvantage in leaving old flooring in place is that you'll be unable to inspect the subfloor and correct irregularities. Another is that there may not be enough space above appliances (a dishwasher, particularly) after the new

floor is installed. And if you don't put new flooring under the appliances, you may even find it impossible to remove them in the future.

In the long run, removing the finished flooring to expose the subfloor usually provides the most reliable base for your new floor.

In some cases, wood flooring may be installed over a moisture-proofed concrete slab, but in most cases, it should go over a subfloor of plywood fastened to floor joists or sleepers over a concrete floor, as discussed on page 140.

FOR RESILIENT & LAMINATE FLOORS Resilient sheet and tile flooring and laminate "floating floors" can be laid over almost any properly prepared surface. Generally, the base must be structurally sound, dry, and free from foreign matter such as grease, wax, dirt, and old finish. And it must be smooth; if resilient flooring is placed over a material that has separations, such as an old wood floor with wide joints, the separations will show through. Instead, a new underlayment of plywood or hardboard should be placed over the old floor first.

Never place resilient flooring over old ceramic tile floors. The original flooring will show through. Many laminate floors, on the other hand, can go over the top of mildly irregular surfaces without showing irregularities.

Vinyl and similar resilient flooring materials can be installed over dry concrete; follow the manufacturer's directions regarding the proper preparation and adhesive to use.

It is okay to install resilient flooring over old sheet flooring if the flooring is smooth, solid (not cushioned), and firmly attached. Before installing new flooring over the old, clean the surface to remove wax or finish. Refasten any loose pieces or sections. Do not sand because of the danger of asbestos (see "Asbestos Alert" at left).

ASBESTOS ALERT

If your resilient flooring was installed before 1986, it may contain asbestos. Asbestos poses a health hazard if the fibers are released into the air. The only way to find out for sure whether or not your old flooring contains asbestos is to send a sample to a private lab for testing. If you don't know whether your floor contains asbestos, DO NOT sand it. If you want to remove it, follow safety precautions available from the Resilient Floor Covering Institute in Rockville, MD (see "Resources"). The safest alternative is to cover the old floor with plywood underlayment, then install your new flooring on top.

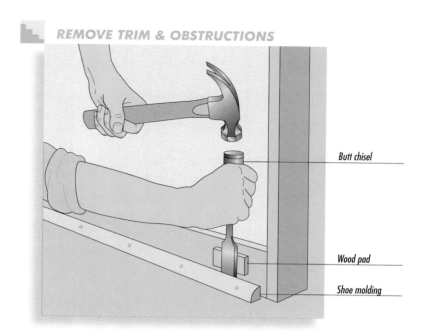

Carefully pry off base moldings and shoe moldings. If the trim looks as if it might split, find the nails and drive them through to the backside of the trim with a narrow nailset, then pry off the trim.

Butt chisel

Wood pad

Shoe molding

FOR CERAMIC TILE & MASONRY Ceramic tile should be laid over a flat, stable, smooth, nonspringy surface. A concrete slab floor is ideal. Tile can be applied over old ceramic tile if the old tile is clean and well bonded. Tile can be laid on a clean plywood subfloor, but it is best to lay it on concrete backer board, which sufficiently stiffens the floor and is not prone to seasonal contraction and expansion.

You can install 1/2-inch concrete backer board on top of the plywood subfloor (be aware that the thickness of backer board may create height problems). Follow the instructions sold with the type of backer board you purchase.

The surface should be flat within 1/8 inch over 10 feet. To check a floor for dips, run a long straightedge over the floor and look at it against the light for gaps under the straightedge. Mark the outer edges of the dips with a pencil and then fill by troweling in a thin-set adhesive. After the adhesive has dried, use an abrasive stone to smooth out the filler along the edges.

FOR CARPET In most cases, carpet may be installed over a carpet cushion on nearly any flat, smooth surface. It may be installed over plywood subflooring, wood flooring, or even a resilient floor. Certain types of carpet and cushion may be installed over concrete slab floors, too, but before installing a particular carpet and cushion over a concrete slab, talk with your carpet dealer about whether or not this is an acceptable base for the products you've chosen.

Preparing an Existing Floor

The type of preparation necessary to place new flooring over an existing floor will depend upon the old floor's type and condition and the type of new flooring you intend to install.

Begin by removing all doors, grates, shoe molding, and baseboards. Number the pieces so you can easily replace them when you're finished.

RESILIENT FLOORING PREPARATION Before removing old flooring, see the "Asbestos Alert" on facing page. If old resilient flooring that you know is free of asbestos is not in good condition, remove it by cutting the flooring into 6-inch-wide strips with a sharp utility knife or linoleum knife and scraping with a wide putty knife.

To remove floor tile, use a long-handled floor scraper (available from a tool rental supply) as shown on page 140. Be careful not to damage the subfloor. Then remove the felt backing and adhesive. Soften old adhesive with a solvent-based adhesive remover or hot water. Or you can carefully heat it with an iron (to prevent the adhesive from sticking to the iron, cover the area with a piece of paper first). If the old covering is extremely hard to remove, you'll find it is much easier to cover the floor with a new underlayment of plywood or untempered hardboard at least 1/4 inch thick. Just be aware that the latter method will raise the height of the floor.

(continued on page 140)

Preparing for a New Floor

(continued from page 139)

INSTALLING UNDERLAYMENT To provide a flat, secure base for some types of flooring, cover old flooring or the newly exposed subfloor with underlayment-grade plywood. Use 1¼-inch ring-shank nails, spaced 3 inches apart along the edges and 6 inches apart in the field (panel center). Start nailing in the center and work out toward the edges. Set nail heads flush with the surface. Fill nail dimples and seams between panels with wood putty. Sand smooth.

PREPARING A CONCRETE SLAB When planning to lay new flooring over a concrete slab, you'll need to determine whether moisture may be a problem. Test for moisture by taping a small piece of plastic sheeting to the floor, as discussed on page 350.

If you find only slight condensation, you can install certain types of flooring directly on the slab with a moisture-resistant adhesive; ceramic tile and laminated flooring approved for this type of installation will work. For damp concrete, take care of the moisture problem as discussed on page 350, then choose ceramic tile or a similar material that is unlikely to be damaged by future moisture and/or build a subfloor over the slab.

Chip off high spots on the slab with a cold chisel; fill minor dips with a concrete leveling compound. Clean grease and oil with a chemical degreaser, available at auto supply stores. Avoid cleaning with water.

For strip or plank flooring, you'll need a plywood subfloor. You can lay a plywood subfloor directly on a (permanently) dry, clean, and level concrete slab. To prevent future moisture problems, it's best to use a two-membrane moisture barrier, as shown on facing page. Another option is to install a subfloor on top of sleepers, also as discussed on facing page, then to install flooring on the subfloor.

For a plywood subfloor, use ¾-inch exterior grade plywood with a tongue-and-groove edge, and leave ¼ to ½ inch between panels. Next to walls, where molding will cover the gap, leave a ¾-inch space; around doors and between panels, leave only ⅛ inch for expansion. Use the type of plywood and nailing pattern shown on facing page.

When nailing directly to a concrete slab, start at the center of each panel and use concrete nails to fasten the plywood to the slab. Nailing is easier with a powder-actuated nailer, available from a tool rental supplier. Make sure to wear earplugs and eye protection, and follow safety precautions.

Using a scraper
Use a long-handled floor scraper to remove resilient floor tile (asbestos-free tile only). Be careful not to damage the surface underneath.

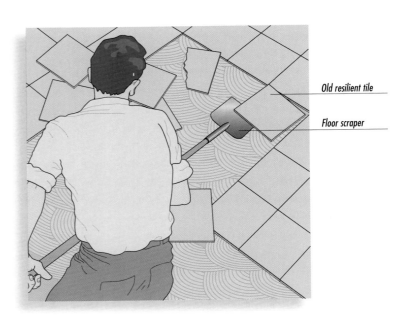

Old resilient tile

Floor scraper

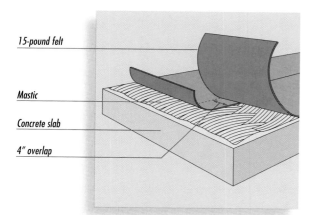

15-pound felt

Mastic

Concrete slab

4" overlap

Installing a moisture barrier

With a notched trowel, spread asphalt mastic over the entire floor and allow it to dry. Unroll 15-pound asphalt felt, overlapping the edges 4 inches and butting the ends. Trowel on a second coat of mastic and then roll out a second layer of asphalt with the seams parallel to, but between, the first layer's seams.

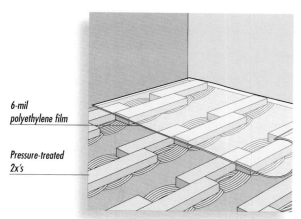

6-mil polyethylene film

Pressure-treated 2x's

Installing sleepers

Lay pressure-treated sleepers in moisture-resistant mastic, spaced 12 to 16 inches apart on center (at a right angle to strip or plank finished flooring). Level across the tops, shimming low spots or planing down high spots. Pour loose-fill insulation between the sleepers and lay polyethylene film over the top, overlapping the edges 6 inches.

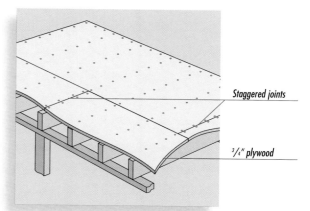

Staggered joints

³/₄" plywood

Laying a subfloor over joists

Center the long edges of ³/₄-inch plywood sheets on joists or sleepers. With 2-inch cement-coated or ring-shank nails, nail every 6 inches along the long edges and every 12 inches along center supports. Stagger panel ends as shown and leave ¹/₈ inch between panels for expansion.

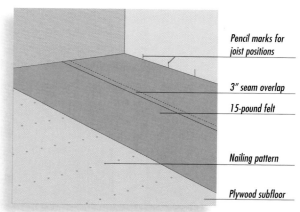

Pencil marks for joist positions

3" seam overlap

15-pound felt

Nailing pattern

Plywood subfloor

Laying asphalt felt

For strip flooring, cover the subfloor with a layer of 15-pound asphalt felt (overlapping the seams about 3 inches). The felt will help prevent squeaks. If the floor is directly above the furnace, use 30-pound felt.

 ## INSULATING FLOORS

For a warmer floor over a crawl space, insulate. It's easiest to insulate under a floor before the subflooring is put in place. Precut 4-foot batts and staple them in place with the vapor barrier facing up. It's best to also support batts with 18-gauge baling wire, crisscrossed between nails. Or cut 13-gauge wire braces 1 inch longer than the space between joists and bow them slightly between the joists. Place wires every 1¹/₂ feet.

Laying Wood Strips or Planks

Before installing wood flooring, give the wood time to adjust to the room's humidity level. Conventional tongue-and-groove strip flooring and plank flooring are attached by blind nailing. With tongue-and-groove plank flooring, screws and plugs can be added for decoration. Install the flooring perpendicular to joists or sleepers, following the subfloor planning and preparations discussed on pages 140–141. Note: The instructions given here are for nailing a new floor to joists or sleepers, not for gluing down a floor.

The first row must be parallel to the centerline of the room. Take several measurements of the width of the room and locate the centerline. Snap a chalk line to establish a centerline that is parallel to your starting wall.

With base moldings removed as discussed on page 139, mark the positions of floor joists or sleepers along the wall near the floor for reference once you start installing the new flooring.

Work with one bundle of flooring at a time. It's usually helpful to lay out several rows of boards to plan a pattern, staggering end joints so that no joint is closer than 6 inches to a joint in the next row. As you actually install the strips, find or cut pieces to fit at the end of each row, leaving a ½-inch gap between each end piece and the wall. No end piece should be shorter than 8 inches. With planks, match widths of boards butted end to end. Work from the widest board to the next widest. Although you can nail a floor by hand, you'll find that renting a pneumatic nailer will greatly ease and accelerate your work.

LAYING WOOD STRIPS OR PLANKS

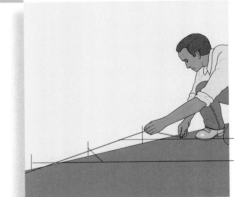

Chalk line for first row

Joist marks

1 **Lay out the first row**
Snap another chalk line about ¾ inch from the wall, measured to be exactly parallel to your centerline. This is where you'll place the first row of flooring, leaving a ¾-inch gap for the wood's expansion in moist conditions. If the room is seriously out of square, position the flooring's tongue parallel to the centerline, and rip the groove side at an angle that will align with the wall.

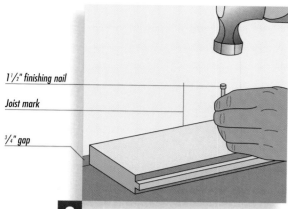

1¹/₂" finishing nail

Joist mark

³/₄" gap

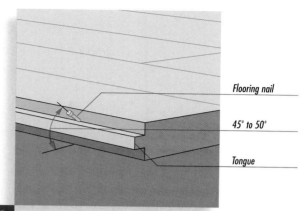

Flooring nail

45° to 50°

Tongue

2 **Fasten the first row**

Choosing the longest boards or widest planks for the first row, predrill pilot holes for 1¹/₂-inch finishing nails, then face-nail the first row to joists or sleepers where the nailheads will be covered by a base shoe.

3 **Blind-nail by hand**

Along the first row of flooring, and on the next six or seven rows, drill pilot holes at a 45- to 50-degree angle through the tongue, centered on each joist or sleeper at the ends and every 10 inches along the lengths. See Step 4 for proper technique. After the first few lengths, you can use a pneumatic nailer for fastening.

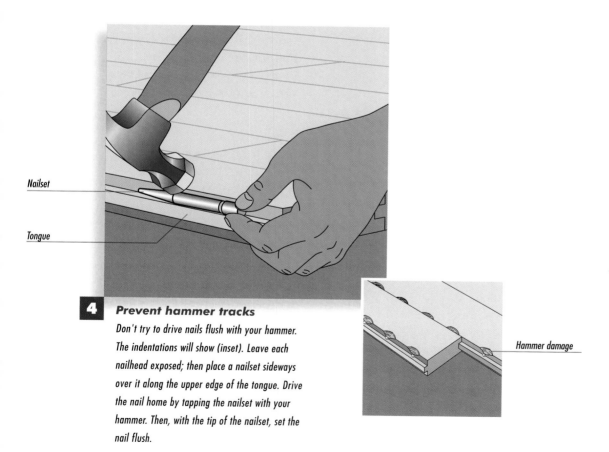

Nailset

Tongue

Hammer damage

4 **Prevent hammer tracks**

Don't try to drive nails flush with your hammer. The indentations will show (inset). Leave each nailhead exposed; then place a nailset sideways over it along the upper edge of the tongue. Drive the nail home by tapping the nailset with your hammer. Then, with the tip of the nailset, set the nail flush.

(continued on page 144)

Laying Wood Strips or Planks

(continued from page 143)

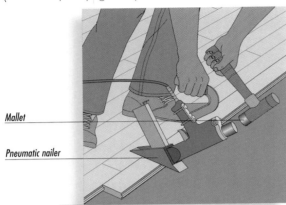

Mallet

Pneumatic nailer

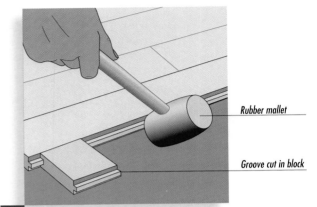

Rubber mallet

Groove cut in block

5 **Fasten the floorboards**

Position a pneumatic nailer at a 45- to 50-degree angle and brace the board with your foot. Use 2-inch nails or staples (1½-inch if you're nailing into plywood over a concrete slab). Fasten the flooring at each end and every 10 inches along the edge. Only the first and last rows (which are face-nailed) should be nailed into the joists.

6 **Tighten the rows**

Move a short piece of flooring along the groove edge and give it a sharp rap with a mallet to tighten loose rows before nailing. Avoid having two adjacent joints fall between the same two sleepers or over joints in the subfloor. If you're installing a plank floor where humidity is high, some manufacturers recommend leaving a crack the width of a putty knife blade between planks.

Install the final rows

Large obstacles such as fireplaces should be framed. Rip floorboards to fit between the flooring and masonry. Leave a ¼-inch gap and fill it with strips of cork, available at the flooring dealer. Floor openings covered with grates don't need to be framed. When you're close to a wall, drill holes and face-nail boards, using the reference lines along the wall to locate joists.

7

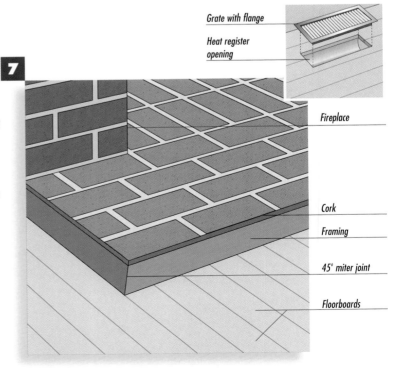

Grate with flange

Heat register opening

Fireplace

Cork

Framing

45° miter joint

Floorboards

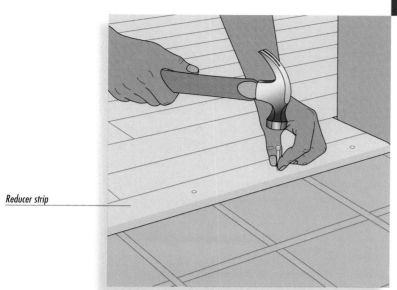

Reducer strip

8 Install a reducer strip

If your new floor will create a change of level from one room to the next, use a reducer strip for a smooth transition. A reducer strip is milled with a rounded or beveled top (see detail below). It will fit onto the tongue of an adjacent board or, if laid perpendicular to the flooring pattern, onto the tongues at the board ends. It can also be butted against grooves' edges or ends. Face-nail the reducer strip at the floor's edge.

SIDE SECTION VIEW

Electric drill

Forstner bit

Counterbored hole

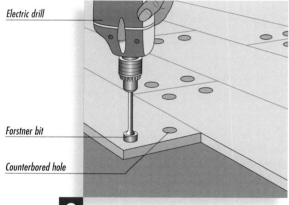

9 Insert screws & plugs

If the boards of a plugged plank floor aren't predrilled, mark where you want to drill, punch starter holes, and use a drill with a Forstner or brad-point bit to counterbore a hole 1/4-inch deep. Then drill a pilot hole, clearance hole, and countersink, using a combination bit. Drive screws, blow dust out of each hole, and glue wood plugs into the holes. Set the plugs flush with the surface of the floor or allow them to protrude slightly so the floor sander will flatten them. Last, reinstall the base trim.

TWO HELPFUL TIPS

■ Longer boards may warp because of humidity. If they do, you can use a block of wood and a wrecking bar to hold the board straight until you nail it. Nail a block to the subfloor, apply pressure with the wrecking bar, and drive in a nail to hold the bar in place while you fasten the floorboard to the subfloor.

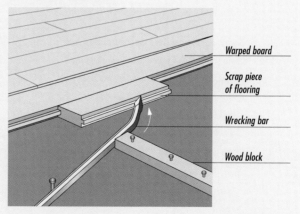

Warped board

Scrap piece of flooring

Wrecking bar

Wood block

■ To compensate for an irregular room, establish a centerline as close as possible to the room's center and snap a chalk line along it. Lay the first row of flooring from the centerline, with the grooves in the boards toward the center. Then work toward the wall. When you return to the center, you'll need a special wood strip, or spline, to join two back-to-back grooved boards along the centerline. If the walls are out of square, you may also have to rip the last rows of boards.

Refinishing a Wood Floor

When wood floors become marred and scratched—or when you want to resurrect an old wood floor that has been buried beneath a carpet—the answer is to refinish. Of course, if you can avoid this messy and disruptive task, do so (in cases where a floor is in good condition but looks dingy or has a few confined problems, for example). For more about this, see "Repairing Wood Floors," pages 166–167.

Also be aware that you can do a lot of damage to your floors if you refinish them improperly. In the hands of amateurs, drum sanders can permanently leave visible ridges and marks. Be sure to get a couple of estimates from professional floor finishing companies so you have a clear idea of your savings if you intend to do the work yourself. You may find that it isn't worth the risk or the effort to refinish the floors yourself.

In scheduling your project, remember that the first coat of the new finish should be applied the same day the sanding is completed. This prevents moisture in the air from raising the grain in the sanded wood.

Standard ³/₄-inch strip flooring can be refinished several times before the erosion from sanding grows too deep (eating into the tongue-and-groove section of the material). If your flooring is thinner than this or is a laminated wood, it may only accept one resanding (any more might dig through the surface layer). Remove a section of base shoe or heating grate to check the flooring's type and thickness.

Sanding the Floor

Some old houses have tongue-and-groove flooring that is only ³/₈ inch thick. It's best to recondition the finish or strip it chemically, spot sanding with an electric orbital sander. Don't use a belt sander. Talk with your flooring dealer about the appropriate product for stripping the finish.

When sanding, be sure you wear ear protection and work in soft-soled shoes that won't leave scuff marks on a newly sanded floor. During the initial sanding, painted floors or very rough floors may require very coarse (20- to 30-grit) sandpaper; otherwise use 30- to 40-grit coarse sandpaper. Before sanding a painted floor, be sure it does not contain lead (see page 517).

Remove grates and base shoe, numbering each piece so you know where to replace them. Nail loose boards and replace any that are damaged. Check for protruding nails and set the heads with a nailset. Empty the room, sweep and vacuum the floor thoroughly, take down draperies, and seal doors and heating registers with plastic sheeting.

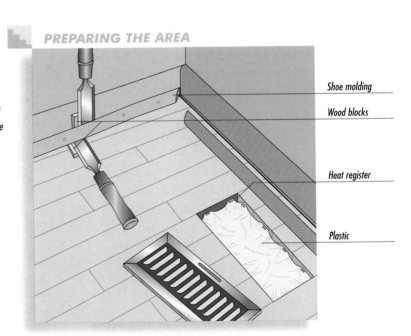

PREPARING THE AREA

Shoe molding

Wood blocks

Heat register

Plastic

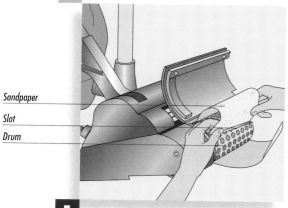

Sandpaper
Slot
Drum

1 Load the sandpaper

Unplug the sander and load the drum with coarse-grit sandpaper. (Make sure the rental store shows you how to do this.) Tuck the ends into the slot so the paper is tight.

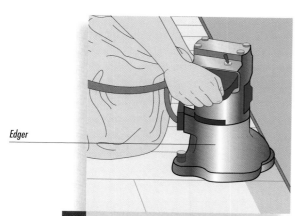

Edger

3 Sand around the borders

When you've finished sanding as much of the floor as you can with the drum sander, load the disc sander with coarse-grit sandpaper and sand the areas the drum sander did not reach. Remove the same amount of material as the drum sander removed.

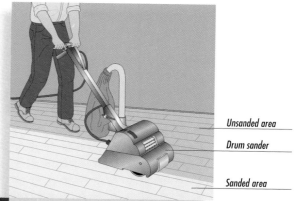

Unsanded area
Drum sander
Sanded area

2 Do the first sanding

First sand in line with the wood grain, always moving forward when the drum is in contact with the floor. After the first pass, shift to overlap the last cut by 2 to 3 inches and pull the sander backwards across the floor. Sand two-thirds of the room's width, then start from the other side of the room and work toward the center to finish.

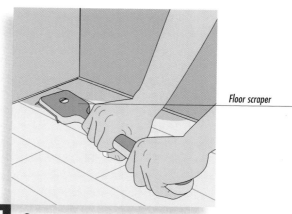

Floor scraper

4 Scrape & sand again

Before the final sanding, clean out tight spots, such as corners and areas around radiator pipes. Pull the blade of a sharp floor scraper toward you, pressing down. Then use a sanding block with medium-grit paper, and finish off with fine sandpaper. Make a second pass as described in the text on page 148.

When using a drum sander, never allow the drum to touch the floor unless the sander is moving. The drum's forward rotation will pull the machine forward; keep it in hand and move forward at a steady pace. When you near the end of the run, raise the drum before stopping—otherwise, it will gouge the floor.

(continued on page 148)

Refinishing a Wood Floor

(continued from page 147)
On the first pass, take off the minimum amount of wood that still allows you to remove all the old finish. Work in line with the wood grain except on a very rough or irregular floor—in that case, make a first pass on the diagonal and then sand again in line with the grain.

After completing the four steps shown on page 147, set exposed nailheads and fill holes with wood putty, then make a second pass with 50- to 60-grit medium sandpaper on the drum sander. Then, with medium-grit paper on the disc sander, go over the edges once again. Again, set and putty any exposed nail heads, then use 80- to 100-grit fine sandpaper to do a final sanding with both the drum sander and the edger.

Vacuum up dust. Wipe down the floor with a rag that's moistened with mineral spirits or, for a water-based finish, a dry cloth. Fill nail holes with putty matching the final finish color, and sand lightly with fine-grit sandpaper. After the floor is sanded, keep foot traffic to a minimum.

SANDING A PARQUET FLOOR

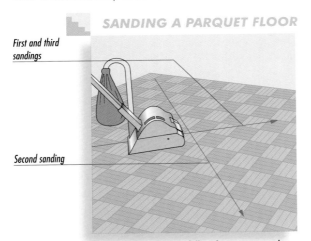

First and third sandings

Second sanding

For parquet flooring, follow the instructions above, but do all three sandings on the diagonal. This compensates for the fact that the grain in these floors runs in several directions. Also, check thickness before sanding, as some parquet floors are only ³⁄₈ inch thick and should not be sanded. Use only coarse, medium, and fine-grit papers (ideally, use medium grit for the first two sandings and fine for the last pass).

Applying the Finish

Be prepared to apply a finish the same day you complete the sanding. Test the finish on a test strip of flooring or in an inconspicuous place. Many prefinished parquet squares are made with rounded or beveled edges, making it impossible to remove the old finish between tiles by machine sanding. If you're refinishing this type, choose a finish that will match or blend with the old one. Consult the floor's manufacturer for color selection. Allow the floor plenty of time to dry before you walk on it. Plan on about 72 hours; then replace the shoe molding and grates. If you've used a penetrating sealer, the floor will require waxing. Choose a floor wax compatible with the sealer.

Choosing a Finish

Floor finishes include stains, penetrating sealers, and surface finishes. Even clear finishes can impart some color to the floor, so it's important to always do a test strip, using the same species of wood that is on your floor. Bring a strip of wood flooring to the paint store and ask them to prepare a test strip for you. If you plan to use stain, apply it first; then apply a penetrating sealer or a surface finish. Products are available that combine stain and sealer. For some surface finishes, you'll first need to apply a sealer. When applying any finish, follow the label directions precisely.

STAIN If you want a color other than natural wood, the first step is to apply stain. A sanding sealer keeps the wood from absorbing the stain unevenly and creating a blotchy appearance. Stain without sealer needs eight hours or less to dry, while one combined with sealer may take 48 hours. For softwood floors, such as pine, poplar, or Douglas fir, always use a sealer if you're applying stain.

PENETRATING SEALER These products actually penetrate the pores and become an integral part of the wood. The finish wears only as the wood wears. The floor can be retouched in heavy-traffic areas without creating a patched appearance. Penetrating sealers are clear or tinted, and some are combined with stains. Normally, two coats are applied. If you buff a penetrating sealer while it's still wet, the dry floor will have a satin sheen. A final coat of paste or liquid wax—but not a water-based wax—is recommended.

SURFACE FINISHES These provide a clear coating over stained or sealed wood. In general, polyurethanes have replaced the more traditional finishes, such as varnish and shellac. Polyurethane and water-based polyurethane finishes are blends of synthetic resins, plastic compounds, and other film-forming ingredients that produce an extremely durable, moisture-resistant surface. They are a good choice for areas subject to spilled water. High-gloss finishes are the most durable. If you object to the reflectance of a high-gloss floor, apply a second coat of satin to tone down the highlights. Polyurethane finishes amber slightly with age; water-based polyurethanes do not change color. Choose stains and finishes made by the same manufacturer; otherwise, you may have problems with adhesion and drying.

APPLYING STAIN To keep the stain color uniform, choose cans with the same batch number. Calculate how many cans you'll need, based on the coverage information on the label, and mix the cans together in a bucket. Dip a lint-free, dry rag into the stain and spread it. Near walls, use a paintbrush. After 5 or 10 minutes, wipe off excess stain with another rag. Work from one corner of the room toward the door, and only apply as much stain as you can comfortably reach. Time the application. If you leave the stain on too long, one section of the floor may absorb more stain than you want. After staining, some manufacturers recommend buffing. When the stain has dried, buff with a buffing pad or No. 2 steel wool. Note: Never use steel wool if you're applying a water-based finish. Follow with a thorough vacuuming. Now the floor is ready for a coat of penetrating sealer or surface finish.

Applying a Penetrating Sealer

Penetrating sealers can be applied with a clean rag, brush, or long-handled lamb's-wool applicator. Apply sealer liberally, letting it flow into the pores of the wood. Start in a corner or next to a wall, and avoid walking over wet sealer. After the sealer has had time to penetrate (check the label) wipe up excess with dry rags. Drying time may be affected by humidity and temperature. If you're not applying a surface finish, apply a second coat of penetrating sealer. (You may need to buff after the second coat.) Finally, apply a coat of liquid nonwater-based floor wax.

Applying a Surface Finish

To apply polyurethane, use a clean brush to put down a coat of finish around the perimeter of the room. Then use a long-handled lamb's-wool applicator to apply the finish evenly over the rest of the floor. With a water-based polyurethane, use a foam painting pad. Apply the finish across the grain, then smooth the brushstrokes in the direction of the grain. Typically, two or three coats are required. Allow the first coat to dry; then use a floor buffer with a No. 2 steel wool or buffing pad to smooth the surface. (Note: Don't use steel wool with water-based polyurethane.) Corners must be done by hand. To pick up fragments of steel wool and dust, first vacuum, then go over the floor with a push broom wrapped in a damp towel. Work the broom back and forth across the floor without picking it up. Then clean up the debris that has accumulated in front of the broom. Be thorough—anything remaining on the surface will be sealed in when you apply the second coat of polyurethane. When the floor is clean and dry, apply a second coat of finish, working across the grain whenever possible.

Reinstalling Trim

When the floor is dry, replace shoe molding and grates. Install the shoe molding, using a piece of thin cardboard as a spacer. To allow the floor to expand and contract, nail the shoe molding to the baseboard, not the floor. The shoe molding will hide the $3/4$-inch gap between the last floorboard and the wall.

 DANGER: Spontaneous combustion occurs when materials burst into flame through chemical reaction, even without a match. In disposing of the debris from the dust bag of the drum sander, do not dump the dust into a closed garbage can. The dust, which contains wax and varnish residue, could catch fire. Put the bag outside to cool and then transfer it to a closed metal container. Never store the container inside, even in a garage, and do not place it near the wall of the garage. Immerse the rags used with the finish in water.

Installing Laminate Floors

Laminate flooring, a European import now widely popular in the United States, can mimic the appearance of traditional wood floors as well as feature decorative and designer patterns. The "wood" in laminate floorings is not wood at all but a highly detailed photographic image overlaid with transparent, extremely durable laminate. The base material is a wood-composite product, often medium-density fiberboard (MDF). A backing layer is added to prevent moisture seepage, which can damage the planks.

Laminate floors are installed as floating floors, which means they are not secured to the subfloor below. Instead, the individual tongue and groove planks—typically about ³/₈ inch thick—are fastened to each other with an adhesive. Some types are installed over a thin foam pad. They can be

installed almost anywhere in a home, even in below-grade applications that can be damaging to traditional wood floors. Special care must be taken when installing laminate floors in kitchens and baths to prevent moisture from seeping between or below the planks. Routine care and maintenance call for vacuuming or using a damp mop. Tough stains, like nail polish, oil, and tar, can be removed with acetone.

Proper preparation is the key to a successful installation. Allow the planks to sit in the area they will be installed for at least two days before beginning. Laminates can be installed over existing flooring materials, including wood, tile, and vinyl; carpet must be removed. When installing laminate over floors with a concrete base, a vapor barrier must be installed. Remove any baseboard trim before you begin installation.

INSTALLING A LAMINATE FLOOR

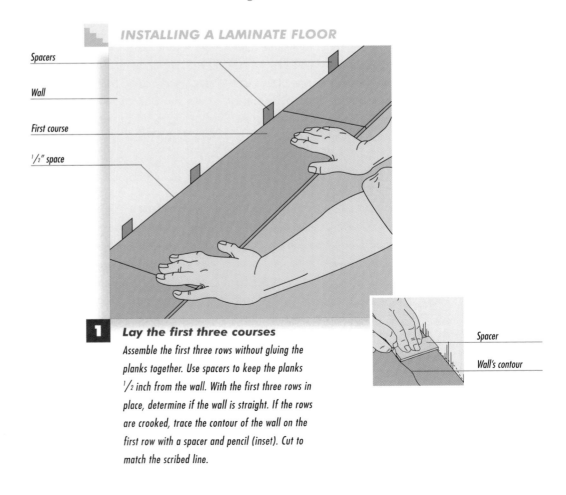

Spacers

Wall

First course

¹/₂″ space

Spacer

Wall's contour

1 Lay the first three courses
Assemble the first three rows without gluing the planks together. Use spacers to keep the planks ¹/₂ inch from the wall. With the first three rows in place, determine if the wall is straight. If the rows are crooked, trace the contour of the wall on the first row with a spacer and pencil (inset). Cut to match the scribed line.

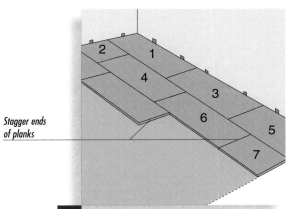

Stagger ends
of planks

2 Install the planks

Glue the planks together as shown above. Make
sure the entire groove of each plank is filled with
adhesive. Stagger the planks so that the ends are
6 to 8 inches apart.

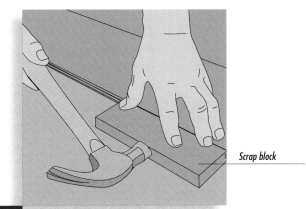

Scrap block

3 Secure the joints

To ensure a tight fit between the joints, use a
piece of scrap wood as a tapping block (never
hammer on the plank itself). Wipe off any glue
that squeezes out of the joint.

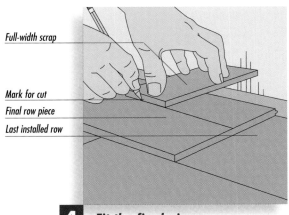

Full-width scrap

Mark for cut

Final row piece

Last installed row

4 Fit the final pieces

Fit the final row of planks by placing a plank on
top of the last installed row. Using a full-width
piece of scrap, scribe a line that follows the
contour of the wall on the planks in the final
row and cut.

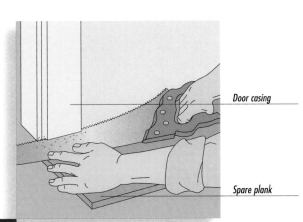

Door casing

Spare plank

5 Work around door casings

Lay a spare plank on the floor, butting it up
against the door casing (make sure any
underlayment materials are in place). Using a
handsaw or backsaw, cut the bottom of the door
casing material and remove, allowing the planks
to slip underneath the existing casing.

Installing Resilient Tile

Resilient tile should be installed on a clean, smooth, flat, and properly prepared surface. This may be a plywood subfloor, a concrete slab, or even an older vinyl floor that is in good shape (the latter is the preferred option if you suspect that the old material may contain asbestos—see page 138). Some types have self-sticking adhesive backs; other types are set with adhesive. You can lay tile from the centerlines of the room, in which case you'll need to cut all tiles along the walls. Or you can lay tile from a corner of the room. In this case, you should verify that the room is perfectly square. Measure from corner to corner of the baseboard. If the dimensions match, the room is square. If not, see page 158 for instructions on how to establish working lines. If you can't see the working lines through the adhesive, don't cover them.

Be sure to follow both the tile and adhesive manufacturers' directions, and be aware of the adhesive's open time—the time it takes to dry. Until you have a feel for how many tiles you can lay before the adhesive sets, work in a small area. Apply it sparingly with a notched trowel—you don't need much. Make sure the adhesive is tacky before laying the tile. If glue squeezes out between the tiles, you haven't left enough time for it to set. Kneel on a piece of plywood so you don't disturb freshly laid tile. Use soapy water or mineral spirits (depending on the type of adhesive) to clean up excess adhesive.

Floor Improvements

TWO SEQUENCES FOR PLACING TILES

Method A

Use Method A when working with an adhesive with sufficient open time or if you're using self-stick tile. Working lines are shown in red.

Method B

Method B is a better choice when you have to work quickly. Start from where the working lines (red) intersect.

INSTALLING RESILIENT TILE

Working line

Working line

1 **Place the tile**

Line up the first tile where the working lines cross. For self-stick tiles with arrows on the back, follow the instructions to point arrows in the same or alternating directions. Align the tile's edge with a working line or an adjacent tile, and let it fall into place. Never slide a tile into position, or you'll force adhesive up between the tiles. Press the tile down firmly. When you've finished laying a workable section, bed the tiles in the adhesive with a floor roller or rolling pin.

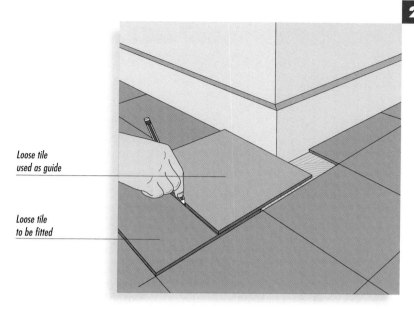

Loose tile
used as guide

Loose tile
to be fitted

2 Mark border tiles

To mark border tiles for straight cuts, place a loose tile squarely on top of the last full tile nearest the wall; then place another tile on top of it so it butts against the wall. With a pencil, draw a line on the lower tile along the edge of the upper tile. When the lower tile is cut, it will fit in the border. To make straight cuts in brittle resilient tile, score the tile with a knife; snap the tile at this line. Irregular cuts can be made with scissors or tin snips if the tile is pliable or warmed (use a hair dryer).

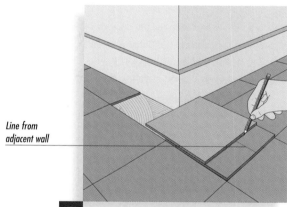

Line from
adjacent wall

3 Mark L-shaped tiles

Mark L-shaped tiles for outside corners in the same way. For the first line, proceed as for border cuts. Next, place the tile to be cut on top of the last full tile closest to the adjoining wall. Place a loose tile on top and draw another line.

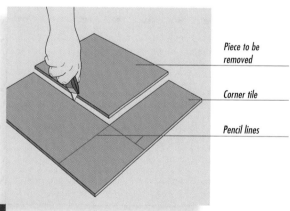

Piece to be
removed

Corner tile

Pencil lines

4 Cut L-shaped tiles

Cut along the lines to remove the border piece. To fit tile around doorjambs, cut a pattern from cardboard and trace it onto a tile. Use a contour gauge or compass to transfer the pattern onto a tile; align the tile with its row before placing the other tile.

Installing Resilient Sheet

Resilient sheet flooring, like resilient tile, may be installed over a clean, flat, smooth, and properly prepared surface such as a plywood subfloor, a concrete slab, or an older vinyl floor in good repair (see information on asbestos flooring, page 138, if you suspect that your old floor contains this hazardous substance). It's wise to get estimates from flooring installers before installing your resilient sheet flooring yourself—the difference in price between having it done and doing it yourself, especially if you must rent equipment, may not be worth the hassle or risk of doing a less-than-professional job.

This job calls for careful measuring and planning; draw an accurate floor plan, using graph paper. Include dimensions of alcoves, counters, closets, and doorways. Try to plan the job so it can be done without seams. Sheet flooring comes in widths up to 12 feet; for wider floors, seams will be necessary. Looking at your floor plan, determine how to combine sheets so you can cover the floor with the least material and fewest seams. Plan any seams so that they do not follow the seams in existing resilient flooring or joints in the subfloor. Be aware that you'll also need to match the pattern at seams. If your flooring has a simulated mortar joint or any other straight line, follow the manufacturer's directions for cutting it. You can either cut the seam along the midpoint of the printed joint on both sheets, or cut the joint off one sheet and leave it on the other.

In addition to purchasing the flooring, adhesive, seam sealer, and possibly double-sided tape, you may need to rent a floor roller. This heavy tool presses out air bubbles and redistributes lumps of adhesive so the floor has an even appearance. Be sure to follow the label directions on both the adhesive and the flooring.

INSTALLING SHEET FLOORING

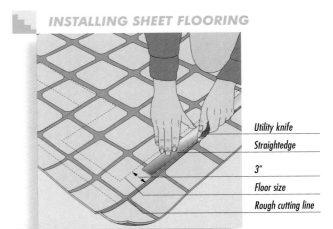

Utility knife
Straightedge
3"
Floor size
Rough cutting line

1 **Cut the sheet**

Unroll the flooring in a large, clean area. Transfer your floor plan to the flooring, marking with chalk or a water-soluble felt-tip pen. On patterned flooring, leave enough margin so you can match the pattern on adjoining sheets. Cut the piece that requires the most intricate fitting roughly 3 inches oversize on all sides, using a utility knife, a straightedge, and heavy-duty scissors or tin snips.

Cutting

Mark your cutting lines with chalk or a water-soluble felt-tip pen, making straight lines with a carpenter's square or straightedge. Then, to cut the material, guide a utility knife with a sharp blade along a straightedge. For curved or intricate cuts, use heavy-duty scissors or tin snips. Before you begin trimming (after basic installation), put a sharp blade in your utility knife. Keep cardboard handy in case you need to make patterns around doorjambs. If you haven't already done so, prepare jambs by undercutting the door casing with a handsaw (see Step 4, page 157). This is best done before installation.

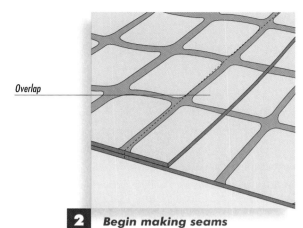

Overlap

2 **Begin making seams**

Place the longest edge of the sheet against the
longest wall, allowing the 3-inch excess to curl up
that wall and the two adjacent walls. For a
seamless job, just trim and finish. If the material
must be seamed, cut the second sheet and position
it to overlap the first at least 2 inches. Roll up the
sheet and spread the adhesive over the remainder
of the floor, stopping a few inches from the edge
of the first sheet. Match up the designs and set it
in the adhesive.

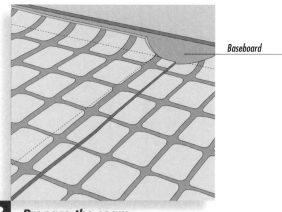

Baseboard

3 **Prepare the seam**

For fully adhered and loose-laid flooring, trim
away excess material at each end of the seam in a
half-moon shape, so the ends butt against the wall
and the seam lies flat. Cut off the excess material.

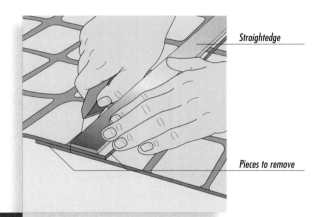

Straightedge

Pieces to remove

4 **Double-cut the seam**

Cut off the excess material using a long
straightedge. Cut through both layers of flooring
on the same pass with the utility knife. See
information in the text on page 156 for
information about how to make this seam, which
depends upon the fastening technique you're using.

Fastening

Some floors are fastened down entirely, others just around
the periphery; still others are loose-laid. For fully adhered
flooring, use a notched trowel to apply the adhesive to the
floor—over the entire floor or in stages as the flooring is
unrolled. Be aware of the "open time" (the time it takes for
the adhesive to dry). Place the longest edge of the sheet
against the longest wall, allowing the 3-inch excess to curl
up that wall and the two adjacent walls. If you can cover
the room with just one sheet, trim the excess and finish the
job. For rooms that require a seam, cut the second sheet
and position it to overlap the first by at least 2 inches (see
Step 2 above). Then, keeping the overlapped seams in
place, roll up the sheet and spread the adhesive over the
remainder of the floor, stopping a few inches from the edge
of the first sheet. Align the designs to match, roll out the
second sheet, and set it in the adhesive.

(continued on page 156)

Installing Resilient Sheet

(continued from page 155)
For peripherally fastened flooring, lay the sheet in the room, aligning the pattern squarely, and allowing the excess to curl up the walls. For a single piece, weight the sheet, trim, and attach. When the room is large enough to require a second sheet, position it so the pattern matches at the seam line. Don't leave excess at the seam line. Cut the seam accurately and trim the excess; then fasten the edges. Use flooring staples if the underlying surface is wood, making sure they're close enough to the wall to be covered by molding. Use adhesive if the subfloor is concrete, spreading it in a 3-inch band around walls.

For loose-laid flooring, lay a single sheet in place, align the pattern squarely in the room, weight the corners, and trim. If you need a second sheet, cut and position it to overlap the first by about 2 inches. Next, lift it up carefully and secure it to the floor with two or three pieces of double-sided tape so it won't move while you cut.

Installation Tips

When double-cutting fully adhered flooring (see Step 4, page 155), roll back the edges of the flooring and lay a strip of double-sided tape on the floor where the seam will be. Spread adhesive on the floor, covering the tape. Peel the backing off the tape and roll the sheets into position one side at a time, lining up the pattern. Roll the seam with a hand roller or rolling pin. When the seam is dry and dirt-free, use a compatible seam sealer to fuse the two pieces.

For peripherally attached flooring, with the seam lines cut, roll back the edges of the flooring and spread adhesive below the seam. Roll the flooring back into position, one side at a time, carefully aligning the pattern. You may need to stretch or compress the material. Use masking tape to hold the seam in position; roll the seam, then wipe up excess adhesive. After trimming the sheet, fasten the perimeter. When the adhesive is dry, remove the tape, clean any adhesive out of the seam with a utility knife, and apply seam sealer. Adhesive in the seam may keep the seam sealer from working properly.

For loose-laid flooring, roll the flooring away from the seam; then stick double-sided tape to the floor, removing one side of the backing paper as you go. Stop 5 inches from the wall. Peel off the remaining backing paper and press the flooring down firmly, keeping the edges close. Following installation, roll the floor one more time with a floor roller, starting in the center of the room and working toward the edges. Then wipe up any adhesive, depending upon the type, with soap and water or mineral spirits.

TRIMMING THE FLOORING

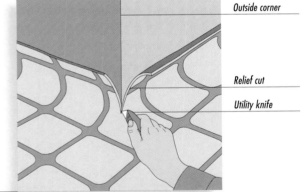

Outside corner

Relief cut

Utility knife

1 **Trim the outside corners**
Make a series of relief cuts at all corners so the flooring will lie flat on the floor. At outside corners, start at the top of the excess flooring and cut straight down to the point where wall and floor meet.

Floor Improvements

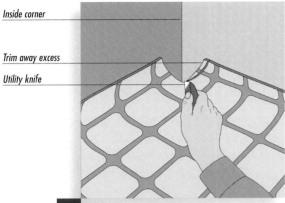

Inside corner

Trim away excess

Utility knife

2 **Trim inside corners**

Cut the excess away with diagonal cuts from top to bottom, gradually trimming it until the flooring lies flat.

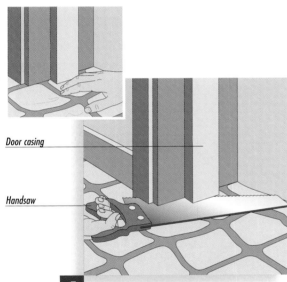

Door casing

Handsaw

4 **Trim around doorways**

The most effective way to hide an exposed edge is to cut away just enough of the door casing to slide the flooring underneath. It's best to cut the door casing when you're preparing the room, before laying your flooring. Otherwise, trim the flooring so it fits against the door casing (make a cardboard pattern and transfer the contours to the flooring).

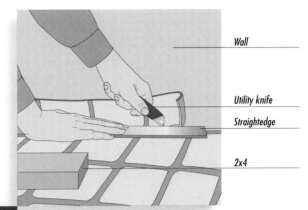

Wall

Utility knife

Straightedge

2x4

3 **Trim near walls & cabinets**

Using a 19- to 24-inch piece of 2 by 4, press the flooring into a right angle where the floor and wall join. Lay a straightedge along the wall and trim the flooring there, leaving a gap of about $1/8$ inch between the edge of the flooring and the wall so the material can expand without buckling. If you're planning to attach cove base molding, be sure it will overlap the edge of the flooring by at least $1/4$ inch.

VINYL CARE TIPS

■ To keep vinyl sparkling clean, sweep or vacuum often and occasionally mop with clean, warm water (avoid soap because it leaves a dull film). For more rigorous cleaning, add clear ammonia to your water. As you mop, keep a second mop and bucket of clear, warm water nearby for rinsing. Follow the manufacturer's advice for general care and scuff removal.

■ Protect vinyl from permanent dents by positioning heavy stationary furniture on wide-bearing, hard plastic floor protectors. Before moving a refrigerator or other heavy appliances across a vinyl floor, lay hardboard or plywood runways on the floor for protection.

■ Minimize foot traffic on the floor for about 24 hours (the time it takes for the flooring's adhesives to cure) and don't move furniture or appliances across the floor. The day after installation, sweep, damp mop with warm water, and rinse.

Laying Ceramic Tile Floors

Floor Improvements

Laying a ceramic tile flooring can be both satisfying and challenging. Of the various types of flooring materials, ceramic tile is usually the most difficult for do-it-yourselfers to install. But when the job is done, the result is often one of the most pride-inspiring. The methods shown on these pages are for laying tile in an adhesive base, the easiest method by far. If you would like to have your tile installed in a mortar base—a method recommended by many tile professionals because of its sturdiness—contact a tile installer.

Subfloor Preparation

For a tile floor, you'll need a very firm, solid, flat subfloor. Many existing floors will work as a backing for ceramic tile, including concrete slab or plywood. If you intend to lay tile over concrete, remove grease and oil stains with a chemical garage floor cleaner, available at auto supply stores. Fill any holes, cracks, or recesses with a concrete patching compound. Then scour the slab with a stiff bristle brush and sweep or vacuum up loose debris.

An existing wood or plywood subfloor must be securely fastened, flat, and sound. Then it should be covered with plywood underlayment. The combined thickness of subfloor and underlayment should be at least 1¼ inches (the underlayment should be at least ³⁄₈-inch exterior-grade plywood).

When putting down underlayment, be sure the joints don't fall directly over those in the layer below. Stagger joints and leave a ¹⁄₈-inch space between the panels; fasten with ring-shank nails that are twice as long as the new plywood is thick, and space them 6 inches apart along the edges and 8 inches apart in the field (center areas). Nail directly into the joists where possible.

An alternative to plywood for flooring underlayment is cement backerboard. This is a moisture-resistant material that will not curl. Follow the manufacturer's directions for installation.

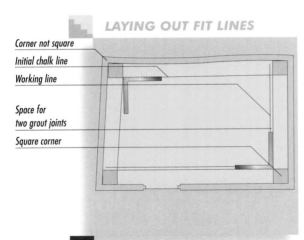

LAYING OUT FIT LINES

Corner not square
Initial chalk line
Working line
Space for two grout joints
Square corner

1 Establish the lines

You can start at any straight wall adjoining a square corner. Snap a new chalk line parallel to the first and about two grout joint widths away from it. Lay a similar line along an adjoining wall. Next, nail a 1 by 2 or 1 by 3 along each of the new working lines so they form a right angle; if they don't, adjust the working lines accordingly. If you're working over a concrete slab, rely on the chalk lines.

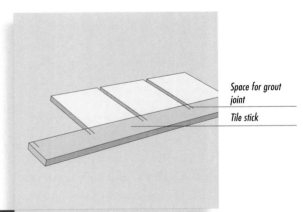

Space for grout joint
Tile stick

2 Make a dry run

Make a dry run before you begin setting tiles in adhesive. The dry run will keep the number of cut tiles to a minimum. Lay the tiles out, allowing the proper spacing for grout joints. Using a tile stick (a batten marked with tile positions) will help you achieve uniform spacing. Mark a board with the tile and grout width. You can also use plastic or wooden spacers. A slight reduction or enlargement of grout joint widths may allow you to set a row of tiles without any cutting.

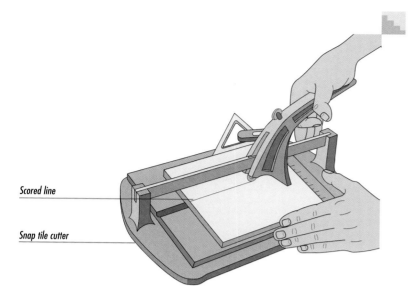

Scored line

Snap tile cutter

MAKING CLEAN CUTS

To make straight cuts near the middle of the tile, use a snap tile cutter, which can be rented at tile stores and equipment rental outlets. First mark the cut with a pencil. Score the finished surface along the pencil line with the cutter; then press down on the handle to break the tile. To make irregular cuts, score the tile with a glass cutter, and then use tile nippers to nibble up to the scored line. For interior cuts, first drill a hole using a masonry bit; then enlarge the hole with a rod saw. Smooth the cut edges with a special abrasive stone or a whetstone.

Removing old flooring before installing new ceramic tile makes it easier to examine the subfloor and make any necessary repairs; it also means there's a better chance that the new floor will be level with the floors in adjacent rooms. However, you can lay the new tile directly over certain old floor surfaces.

You'll have to take up the shoe molding before putting in the new floor. Gently pry the molding away from the wall, using a thin-blade prybar or a butt chisel. Baseboards do not need to be removed unless there is no shoe molding. As you remove the molding, number the pieces with a pencil so you can easily replace them.

WOOD FLOORS Wood strip and plank flooring are not smooth enough to serve as backings for ceramic tile. They should be covered with 1/4-inch exterior plywood, fastened as described above for plywood underlayment.

RESILIENT FLOORS If it's level and in good repair, well-bonded resilient flooring can be covered with tile. To make minor repairs to resilient flooring, see pages 168–169. Cushioned resilient flooring is too springy to be used as a base for ceramic tile and must be removed or covered over. Other resilient flooring that is badly damaged should also be removed or covered over. To cover an old resilient floor, use 1/4-inch exterior-grade plywood panels. Fasten them as described above for plywood underlayment. Note: Your old resilient floor may contain asbestos; refer to the safety information on page 138.

OLD CERAMIC TILE Tile can be applied over old ceramic tile if the old tile is in good condition, clean, and well bonded. Pry up any loose tiles and check the backing. If there is evidence of water damage, the tiles and backing may have to be removed and the moisture problem corrected; consult a professional. If there is no problem with the backing, replace the loose tiles (see pages 170–171).

To prepare the old tile, clean it with a commercial degreasing agent. Apply the adhesive to a small area and examine it the next day. If it hasn't bonded well, roughen the surface of the tile with an abrasive disk mounted on an electric drill (wear a dust mask).

Layout Tips

The key to laying a floor with straight rows of tile is to lay out proper working lines, independent of the walls. You can begin either at the center of the room or at one wall. If you're tiling from the center, begin by laying out working lines that intersect at a right angle at the approximate center of the room. This is the best method to use if the room is badly out of square or if you've chosen tile with a pattern or design. You'll have to cut tiles on all four walls, but the cut tiles will balance out. Start at the wall only if two adjoining straight walls meet at an exact 90-degree angle. Then you'll only have to cut tile on two walls. If you're tiling over firmly attached existing tile, you can simply repeat the layout of the previous tile job, using the grout joints to keep your tile straight.

(continued on page 160)

Laying Ceramic Tile Floors

(continued from page 159)
To check for square corners, place a tile tightly into each corner. Stretch a chalk line between the corners and snap a line. Variations in the distance between the chalk lines and the walls will show any irregularities. You can ignore small variations—the width of a grout joint. With a carpenter's square, check for square where the lines intersect (see Step 1, page 158). Tack battens along the chalk lines to help guide placement.

Cutting Tips

Open all tile boxes to make sure the color is uniform. If the tile is dusty, wash and dry it before beginning. Even a little dust prevents the adhesive from forming a strong bond. Mark 90-degree cuts on tile using a combination square. Angles can be transferred from a wall to a tile with an adjustable T-bevel, and irregular shapes can be transferred with a contour gauge. Always wear eye protection when cutting. If you have a lot of cutting to do, consider renting a "wet saw" with a diamond blade—you'll find it is well worth the relatively small expense.

Installation Tips

Add water sparingly to dry powdered grout. For areas that will be exposed to water, mix in a liquid grout sealer. All dry particles should be thoroughly moistened. Mix a small quantity at a time until there are no visible lumps. Always wear rubber gloves, as the lime in grout is caustic. When you begin, pay attention to the adhesive's open time. (Open time is the amount of time before the adhesive begins to set.) Don't spread too much adhesive, or you'll find yourself racing to set the tile before the adhesive dries.

To establish the proper width for the grout joint, use spacers (available from your tile dealer); take them out when the adhesive begins to set. If you need to work over the newly set tiles, kneel on a sheet of plywood to distribute your weight.

When you're ready to install the border tiles, remove the battens. Mark the tile and snap it. Or, if you have trouble with breakage, mark it, number the tile piece on the back

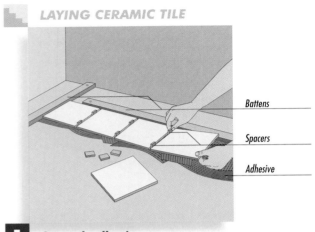

LAYING CERAMIC TILE

Battens

Spacers

Adhesive

1 *Spread adhesive*
Using the smooth edge of the notched trowel, spread a strip of adhesive on the floor, next to a batten; then go back over the area with the notched edge. Distribute the adhesive in a crosshatch pattern, using the trowel recommended by the adhesive manufacturer.

with a grease pencil, and take it to the tile dealer for cutting. After grouting (see facing page), let the grout cure for two weeks. Then, if you've used a cement-based grout and the floor is likely to be subjected to standing water, seal the grout. Except for porcelain tile, unglazed tile should also be sealed. Follow the manufacturer's instructions for applying grout or tile sealer. If you're sealing the grout only, wipe any sealer off the tiles before the sealer hardens.

 If you're not sure how much adhesive to apply, bed a tile, then pull it up. If less than 95 percent of the back is covered with adhesive, you're not applying enough. If adhesive squeezes up around the edges, you're applying too much.

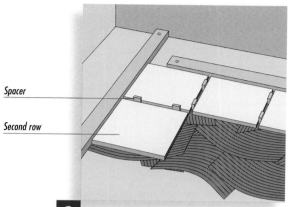

Spacer

Second row

▓2 Set the tiles

Using a gentle twisting motion, place the first tile in the corner formed by the two battens. (For large tiles, such as 10-by-10 inch Mexican tile, spread some adhesive on the back first.) Set the tiles in continuous rows, beginning each row at the same end of the room. Clean off excess adhesive immediately. Periodically use a carpenter's square to check your work.

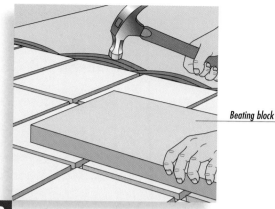

Beating block

▓3 Bed the tiles & finish

When you finish a section of floor, bed the tiles by tapping each one with a rubber mallet or by tapping a beating block—a piece of wood that spans more than one tile—with a hammer. After installing the border tiles, remove spacers, clean up excess adhesive, and allow the adhesive to dry completely. Don't walk on the floor until the tile has been grouted.

GROUTING & FINISHING

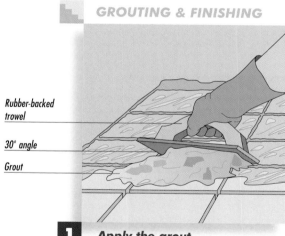

Rubber-backed trowel

30° angle

Grout

▓1 Apply the grout

Pour about 1 cup of grout onto the floor at a time. Spread it using a rubber-backed trowel held at an angle. Force grout into the joints so they're completely filled; make sure that there are no air pockets.

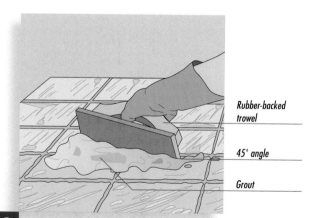

Rubber-backed trowel

45° angle

Grout

▓2 Remove the excess

Scrape away the excess grout, holding the trowel at a 45-degree angle. Work diagonally to avoid disturbing the grout joints. Clean off the trowel frequently. Before the grout dries, wipe the tiles with a damp sponge (rinse frequently), using a circular motion. Smooth and level the grout joints with the tiles. Let the grout dry until a haze appears on the tiles, then polish the tiles with a soft cloth.

Building Stairs

Improvement projects such as converting an attic or loft, finishing a basement, or adding a deck usually require building new stairs—or having them installed or built by a finish carpenter, cabinetmaker, or stair builder.

Here we look at how to build a simple, "rough" stairway, the type that is suitable for outdoor, basement, and attic applications. Primary stairways serving interior living spaces are far more complicated and require a high level of craftsmanship; talk to a professional to have these built.

For information on the basic components of stairs, see page 131. The following information assumes the rough construction at both floors has already been done.

CODE CONCERNS The location of railings and balusters, width and depth of treads, and height of risers affect both the safety and ease of using a stair. These dimensions are regulated by building codes, so you must be sure that any stair you install will meet your local codes. Ask your building department for requirements.

FIGURING YOUR LAYOUT To determine the number of steps you'll need, measure the vertical distance—in inches—from floor to floor. Divide by 7 inches, the ideal riser height (many building codes specify a maximum of 7 1/2 inches). If the answer ends in a decimal, drop the decimal and divide that number into the vertical distance; the resulting figure will give you the exact measurement for each of your risers. For example, a total rise of 89 inches ÷ 7 inches = 12.7 steps. By dividing 89 inches by 12, you'll arrive at a riser height of 7.4 inches.

Now take the exact riser height and subtract it from the ideal sum for both risers and treads—17 1/2 inches—to find the exact depth of each tread. For safety, treads must be at least 10 inches wide.

Determine the total run (horizontal distance between top and bottom risers) to see if your plan will fit the space. Multiply your exact tread depth by the number of risers—minus one—to get the total run. If this run won't fit the space, adjust the riser/tread relationship, increasing the rise and decreasing the run—or vice versa—until you achieve a total run that will work.

CUTTING THE STRINGERS For stringers, choose clear 2 by 12s. First, mark the height of the risers on the tongue of a carpenter's square; then mark the depth of the treads on the square's body (or use square gauges). Line up the marks with the top edge of one stringer and trace the outline of the risers and treads onto it, as shown in Step 1.

With a circular saw, cut out the notches. Finish inside corners with a handsaw; don't weaken the stringers by sawing beyond your marks. Because the tread thickness will add to the first step's height, measure the exact thickness of a tread and cut this amount off the bottom of the stringer. Check the alignment by holding the stringer up in place, then use this stringer as a pattern to mark the second one.

BUILDING THE STAIRWAY

Carpenter's square

Riser

Clear 2x12 stringer

Tread

Subtract tread thickness

1 **Cut stringers**

Use a carpenter's square to mark the treads on one stringer, as discussed at right. Using a circular saw, cut out the notches, carefully finishing the cuts with a handsaw. Also cut the thickness of one tread off the bottom of the stringer. Use this stringer as a pattern for the next one.

 As a general rule, the wider the stair and more subtle the climb, the more inviting the staircase— and the more floor space it will consume.

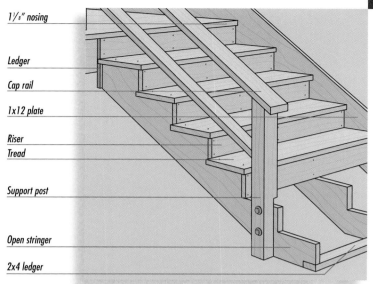

1⅛" nosing

Ledger

Cap rail

1x12 plate

Riser

Tread

Support post

Open stringer

2x4 ledger

 2 **_Assemble components_**

At the top of the stair, nail the stringer to an extra header board, metal joist hangers, or a plywood ledger. Notch and fasten them to a 2-by-4 ledger at the base, fastened to the floor. Nail parts with galvanized finishing nails as shown, set the heads, and fill with wood putty.

If your stairway is 36 inches or wider, space a third stringer midway between the two, outside stringers.

CUTTING & NAILING THE ASSEMBLY Generally, nailing the top of the stringer to the supporting joist, trimmers, or headers is sufficient; but you can increase strength by adding a header board, ledger, or metal joist hangers.

At the bottom, either toenail the stringers to the floor or notch them for a 2-by-4 ledger, which can be glued with construction adhesive to clean, dry concrete. If one or both end stringers will be attached to a wall, first nail an additional 1-by-12 plate to the wall studs: This acts both as trim and as a nailing surface for the main stair stringer.

The bottom edge of the riser overlaps the back of the tread, and the forward edge of the tread should overlap the riser below by 1⅛ inches, the width of the nosing. Nail risers to the stringers, using 2½-inch nails. Then nail treads to the stringers with 3½-inch nails. Gluing treads and risers to the stringer as you nail them will minimize squeaks.

Fasten the handrail to an inside wall by screwing commercial brackets to wall studs (every third stud). For the open sides of stairways, begin with sturdy posts not less than 2 inches square; bolt them directly to the stringer. Cap rails for outdoor and rough stairs are usually 2 by 4s or 2 by 6s nailed to each supporting post. Use galvanized nails.

PRE-MADE STAIRS

Today you can choose from a wide variety of high-quality pre-built and ready-to-assemble stairs that are relatively affordable to buy and easy to install. They come in spiral, circular, straight, and other configurations.

SPIRAL STAIRS Spiral stairs are available in pre-built, one-piece units that can be installed in less than an hour, and as knock-down kits. They are relatively economical in cost and space usage. They're ideal for reaching new attic or basement rooms and for two-story additions. Spiral stairs are also popular for secondary access to rooms. Manufacturers make them from steel, aluminum, hardwoods, and combinations of these materials in a few basic designs that you can customize.

When ordering a spiral stair, specify the diameter and, with some types, the direction of twist (right hand railing up or left hand railing up).

STRAIGHT & CIRCULAR STAIRS Some manufacturers also build conventional straight and sweeping, circular hardwood stairs in unassembled, unfinished sections, ready to connect end to end or at landings. These can be put into a pre-framed opening in a couple of hours by factory installers.

ORDERING TIPS When ordering stairs that turn, such as spiral stairs, pay special attention to where measurements must be taken for code acceptance. Many codes restrict head-height clearance and railing construction, and demand a 9- to 10-inch tread depth (minimum) at a point 12 to 14 inches from the narrow side.

Eliminating Squeaks

Floors and stairs squeak when one piece of wood rubs another. With floors, this friction occurs when flooring pulls away from the joists or subfloor. With stairs, the nails and glue holding treads to the stringers can gradually loosen, allowing the same type of movement. Before you go to a lot of work, try dusting the cracks between floorboards with talcum powder or graphite. Or apply a few drops of floor oil between boards; when the wood expands, the squeaks may stop.

RESEATING LOOSE BOARDS

2x4

Carpet or padding

TOP VIEW

Place a carpeted 2 by 4 at right angles to the flooring and move it over the area, tapping sharply to reseat loose boards.

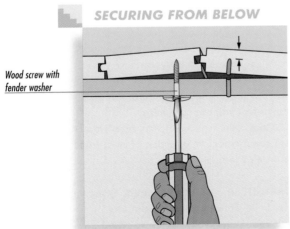

SECURING FROM BELOW

Wood screw with fender washer

For warped or loose flooring, pull the boards tight with a wood screw driven in from below. Drill a pilot hole slightly smaller than the screw's threads. You can also use drywall screws.

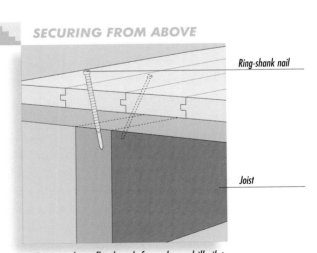

SECURING FROM ABOVE

Ring-shank nail

Joist

To secure loose floorboards from above, drill pilot holes and drive ring-shank nails into the joists. Use a nailset to set the heads. Then fill with wood putty, lightly sand the dry putty with fine sandpaper, and finish to match.

Place a cleat—a 1 by 4 or 1 by 6—against the subfloor and joist. Make a prop to hold the cleat in place. Nail the cleat to the joist with 2-inch nails. If two panels of subfloor rub against each other, cut a cleat to fit under the joint and attach it to the plywood with screws. If the subfloor moves, screw a bracket to the subfloor and joist. Tighten the nut until the subfloor meets the joist. If you can't locate a bracket, use L-braces as shown below.

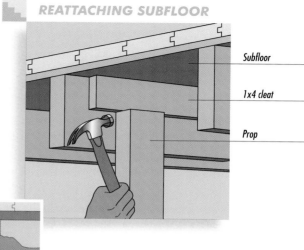

Subfloor

1x4 cleat

Prop

Bracket

USING BRACKETS, BRACES, & BLOCKS

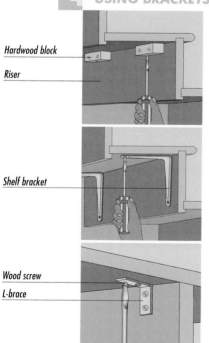

Hardwood block

Riser

Shelf bracket

Wood screw

L-brace

Shelf brackets or L-braces should be installed $\frac{1}{4}$ inch below the top of the riser. When screwed in, the bracket or brace will pull down the tread. Make sure the screw is $\frac{1}{4}$ inch shorter than the thickness of the tread. Hardwood blocks are better than brackets and wedges. Glue 1-by-1 hardwood blocks tightly to the underside of risers and treads. Drill pilot holes and insert wood screws.

Wedges can be used to prevent friction under loose subfloors or between treads and risers. Tap a wood shim between the joist and subfloor, but don't force it or you may lift the subfloor. For stairs, use small (1- to 2-inch) glue-coated shims or wedges. While a helper puts weight on the squeaky step, look for movement. It's best to install them from below, but if you install them from above, be careful not to pry apart the stair and riser. Cut off protruding ends.

USING WEDGES

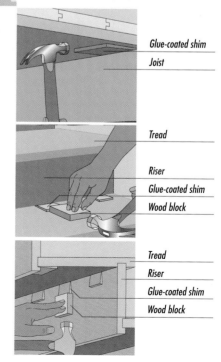

Glue-coated shim

Joist

Tread

Riser

Glue-coated shim

Wood block

Tread

Riser

Glue-coated shim

Wood block

Repairing Wood Floors

You can repair blemishes in the floor's finish without resanding. First remove wax and finish from the surface; then rub the marks with fine steel wool and a little paste wax or a solvent-based liquid floor wax. If the marks don't disappear, wipe the wax with a soft cloth and rub again with fine steel wool and odorless mineral spirits. Wipe clean and finish.

For burn marks that just darken the wood's surface, lightly sand; wipe up sanding residue with a damp cloth. For burns that go deeper, carefully scrape out the burned wood with a sharp knife. Apply one or more coats of a commercial scratch hider, putty stick, or stick shellac; then finish. You can conceal a shallow scratch with a commercial scratch hider or crayon. To repair deep scratches and gouges, remove wax or oil from the damaged area. Fill the scratch or gouge with matching wood putty, putty stick, or stick shellac. Let dry; then sand smooth with fine-grade sandpaper and finish.

Split or warped boards can be secured. Drill pilot holes at a 45-degree angle; then drive ring-shank nails into the sub-floor. Set the heads with a nailset; fill with putty, and finish. If you want to recondition the entire floor, first determine the finish—penetrating or surface. Remove wax. For a penetrating finish, use a commercial reconditioning product to clean and reseal the wood. For a surface finish, dull the surface with sandpaper or steel wool, patch damaged boards, and apply a new coat of finish.

Badly damaged boards will need to be removed and replaced, using one of two methods. One approach, good for areas covered by a rug, is to cut out a rectangle, remove the damaged boards, and replace them. Another approach is to remove the damaged boards in a staggered pattern. This produces a less noticeable repair. If you can't find replacement boards that are a perfect match, consider cutting them from an inconspicuous section of flooring—such as in a closet—and then replacing that section with new boards that are a close but imperfect match.

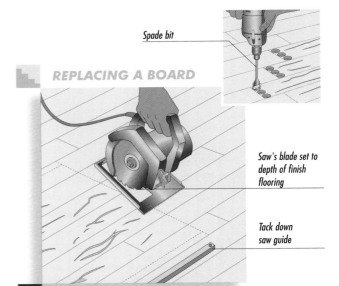

REPLACING A BOARD

Spade bit

Saw's blade set to depth of finish flooring

Tack down saw guide

1 **Cut out damaged boards**
Mark the cutout with a framing square. To avoid hitting nails, keep the lines 1/4 inch away from the joints between boards. Adjust the saw blade's base plate so it won't cut into the subfloor. Place the edge of the base plate against a tacked-down wood guide to keep the saw properly aligned. To replace boards in a staggered pattern, use a spade bit to drill holes across each board's width, then connect the holes with chisel cuts.

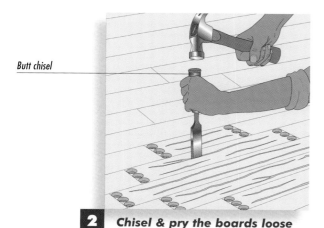

Butt chisel

2 Chisel & pry the boards loose

For square cuts, finish the corner cuts with a chisel. For staggered boards, use the chisel to break up damaged boards. When planks are face-nailed, use a small nailset and hammer to drive nails through into the subfloor and remove boards with a prybar.

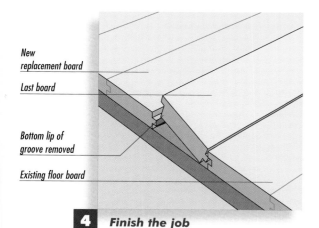

New replacement board

Last board

Bottom lip of groove removed

Existing floor board

4 Finish the job

Remove the bottom lip of the grooved edge with a hammer and chisel or table saw. Face-nail the board into place. For plank floors, daub glue in the plug holes and seat the plugs, removing excess glue. Fill nail holes and any mismatched end joints with wood putty. Sand and finish to match the surrounding floor.

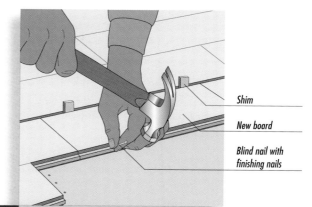

Shim

New board

Blind nail with finishing nails

3 Nail & patch

Cut replacement pieces at 90 degrees, using a miter box and backsaw. Use a scrap of flooring and a rubber mallet to tap the new piece in place. If nearby boards have separated, use thin shims to align the edges of the new boards. Blind nail the new pieces. For plank floors, mark and cut replacement pieces. Using the plugs in the existing planks as guides, fasten as shown in Step 9 on page 145.

REPLACING PARQUET

Mark and cut a rectangle near the perimeter of a square with a circular saw, taking care not to cut any adjacent squares. Remove the damaged square in pieces with a hammer and chisel. Using a cold chisel or butt chisel, chip out as much adhesive as possible so that the replacement parquet will sit level. If you're installing tongue-and-groove parquet, remove the bottom grooved edge. Spread adhesive on the back of the tile or floor and tap lightly into place with a rubber mallet.

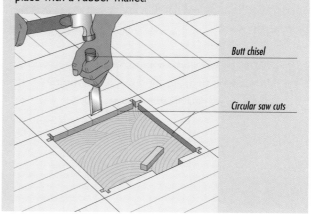

Butt chisel

Circular saw cuts

Repairing Resilient Flooring

Problems with flooring can result from wear and tear, or from structural or plumbing problems. A regular pattern of indentations, running for several feet or forming Ts, may be caused by separations in the subfloor due to shrinkage of the wood or settling of the structure. If you see signs of this type of damage, you'll have to remove the floor covering before repairing the subfloor.

Small bumps that appear in the surface of the floor may be caused by nails that have worked loose. Over a period of time, movement in the structure can cause the subfloor to separate from the joists, forcing the nails up into the resilient flooring. Place a wood block over the bumps and tap it lightly with a hammer to sink the nail heads. If this doesn't work, you may have to remove the floor covering and replace nails with flooring screws to fix the problem.

If flooring curls at the edge, you may have a plumbing leak. Stop the leak before you fix the flooring. Moisture can also cause sheet vinyl to work loose around the perimeter of a room. If the floor is at or below grade, poor drainage outside may be causing the problem.

You can patch badly damaged flooring, but it may be difficult to find a replacement piece that matches your existing flooring. Some flooring dealers carry remnants—you may be able to take a small piece of your flooring and look through the "bone pile" for matches. Or you may be able to cut a small piece from an inconspicuous area in your home, such as under a cabinet or inside a closet, and switch that piece with the damaged one. When installing new or replacement flooring, use an appropriate flooring adhesive (be sure to read the label directions).

 CAUTION: Before removing, chipping, or cutting old resilient flooring, find out if it contains asbestos, as discussed on page 138.

FLATTENING A BUBBLE

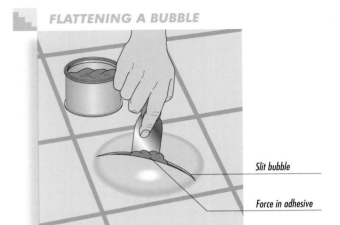

Slit bubble

Force in adhesive

Place an ice pack on the bubble. If this doesn't work, try heat: either a hot, damp cloth or an iron set on medium heat (protect the flooring with a piece of aluminum foil). With a utility knife, cut into the bubble in a straight line. Force new adhesive under the cut, press down, and clean off the edges of the slit. Weight down the bubble overnight. Then apply seam sealer.

REPLACING DAMAGED TILE

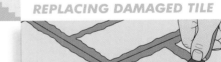
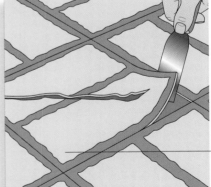

Damaged tile

Soften the adhesive with a propane torch (be careful not to set it on fire!). Pry up the tile with a putty knife. With an old chisel, scrape off old adhesive. Apply new adhesive to the underlayment with a notched trowel. If the flooring's surface is too low, lift it up and apply more adhesive. If it's too high, press it down to squeeze out excess adhesive. Wipe off excess and weight the tile overnight.

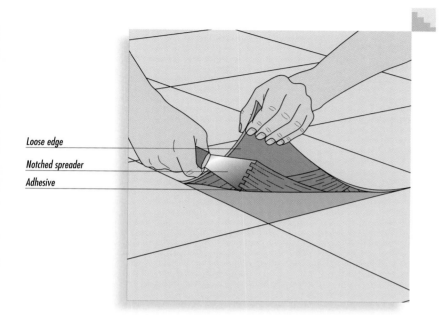

Loose edge

Notched spreader

Adhesive

Cover the affected flooring with a piece of aluminum foil, then use a warm iron to soften the adhesive. Scrape off the adhesive with a putty knife. Using a notched spreader, add new adhesive. Press the material back in place and weight it overnight.

PATCHING AN AREA

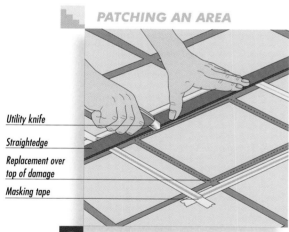

Utility knife

Straightedge

Replacement over top of damage

Masking tape

1 **Cut the patch**

Cut out a replacement piece. Match the pattern and tape the new piece in place over the damaged area. With a utility knife and straightedge, cut out a patch, making sure the blade goes down and through the old flooring underneath. This double-cutting technique is the key to making an inconspicuous patch.

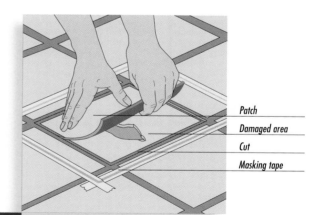

Patch

Damaged area

Cut

Masking tape

2 **Remove the damaged piece**

Lift out the newly cut replacement piece, then pry up the damaged piece as shown on facing page in "Replacing Damaged Tile." With a notched trowel, spread adhesive on the back of the patch, drop it in place, and press. Clean the seams with a utility knife, weight overnight, and apply seam sealer.

169

Replacing Ceramic Tile

Floor Repairs

Ceramic tile is durable and rigid, but when the subfloor or slab beneath it shifts or deflects, cracks may show up in the tile. Replacing ceramic tile isn't difficult, but finding a match between replacement tiles and an old floor can be a problem. If you don't have matching tile left over from the original installation, check several flooring or specialty tile stores for remnants. If you can't find a match, consider using a complementary color.

REPLACING A TILE

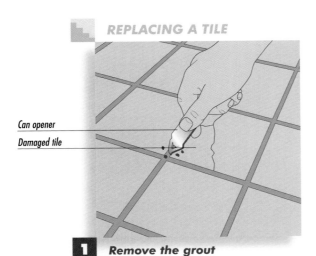

Can opener

Damaged tile

1 Remove the grout
Using a lever-type can opener or an inexpensive grout saw made for this purpose, scrape out the old grout from the joints around the tile.

Nailset

Tile's center

2 Punch a center hole
With a nailset and hammer, punch a hole through the center of the damaged tile (wear safety glasses). Pound gently so as not to crack other tiles or damage the subfloor.

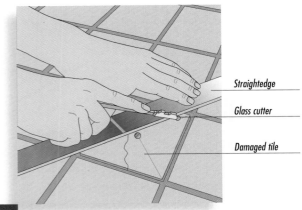

Straightedge

Glass cutter

Damaged tile

3 Score the tile
Use a glass cutter and straightedge to score a deep X across the face of the damaged tile, from corner to corner.

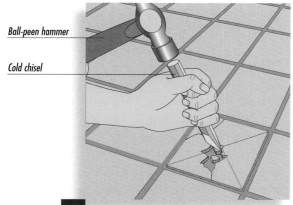

Ball-peen hammer

Cold chisel

4 **Remove the tile**

Starting at the center, chop out the old tile and grout, using a cold chisel and ball-peen hammer (wear safety glasses). Remove any remaining adhesive or grout with a scraper or cold chisel and smooth any irregularities with rough sandpaper.

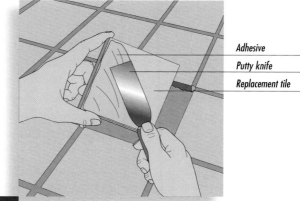

Adhesive

Putty knife

Replacement tile

5 **Seat the tile**

Apply quick-setting ceramic tile adhesive to the back of the tile and the subfloor. Wiggle the tile into place and then, protecting it with a wood block, seat the tile by tapping the block gently with a hammer. Allow the adhesive to set 24 hours (or according to label directions) before grouting. Keep foot traffic off the tile.

CAUTION: Always wear eye protection when removing damaged tile.

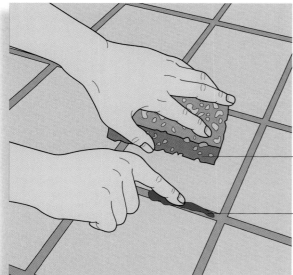

Damp sponge

New grout

6 **Regrout**

Apply new grout using a rubber-backed trowel, a rubber squeegee, or a putty knife, according to the directions on the grout package. Use your finger to smooth the grout joint. Clean off excess with a damp sponge. When the grout is dry, polish tile with a soft cloth.

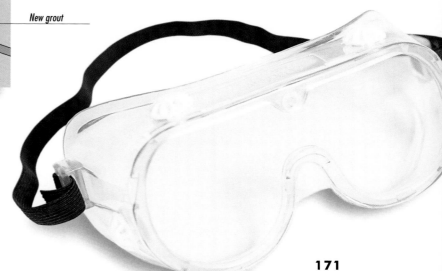

Repairing Carpets

Like a torn suit or dress, carpets can often be repaired by stitching (or taping) the pieces together. For large burns, stains, and tears—or tears far from a corner—replace the damaged carpet with a patch. Wall-to-wall carpeting is installed under tension, which you'll have to release (otherwise, you'll be fighting the tension as you attempt to insert a patch). The trick is to find a replacement piece that will match the surrounding carpet. The ideal replacement is leftover material from the original installation. Otherwise, consider taking a section of original carpet from a closet. Here we show you how to make these repairs, but in many cases, it's better to have a professional carpet installer do the work—that way, you're more likely to get the best possible results. Normally, having this type of work done is relatively affordable. If you decide to do the work yourself, you will need to rent a carpet installer's knee kicker (from a carpet dealer or tool rental company) to reduce tension in the carpet in the corner of the room closest to the tear. Use an awl to free the carpet from the tackless strips along the edges.

You can repair a tear as shown below. Ask a carpet dealer whether it's best to use coated or uncoated tape for your particular type of carpet. For uncoated, you'll need latex seam adhesive. You can also stitch the tear with carpet thread reinforced with latex seam adhesive.

Pull back the carpet to expose the underside of the tear. Repair with seam tape or sew up the seam. Before stitching or seaming, trim the edges. If you sew, use a heavy needle and carpet thread to sew the tear together; make the stitches about 1 inch long and $1/4$ inch apart. Run the needle up through the carpet backing and not the pile (inset). Cover the bottom of the seam with latex carpet adhesive. Place a piece of absorbent tissue (such as toilet paper) over the adhesive, and reattach the carpeting to the tackless strips.

REPAIRING A TEAR

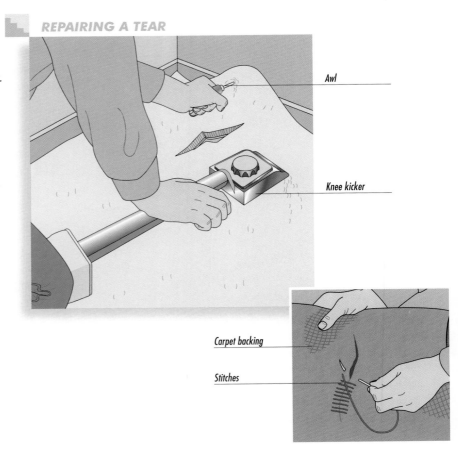

Awl

Knee kicker

Carpet backing

Stitches

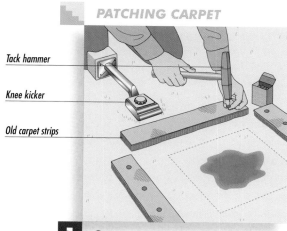

Tack hammer

Knee kicker

Old carpet strips

1 Set up

Set a knee kicker about 1 inch from the area, and nudge it forward until any tension in the area is released. To keep the area loose, tack down the carpet. Use strips of old carpet 2 inches wide and about 2 inches longer than the cuts you plan to make to the damaged area. Place the first strip upside down in front of the knee kicker, and tack it in place. Repeat this process to surround the damaged area.

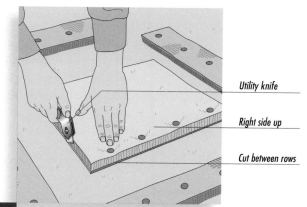

Utility knife

Right side up

Cut between rows

2 Cut the patch

Cut a piece of replacement carpet slightly larger than the damaged section, matching the pattern and direction of the pile. Place it over the damaged area. If your carpet is laid over wood, drive nails or long carpet tacks along one edge of the new piece, into the floor. Otherwise, cut one side of the old carpet and pry it up with your fingers. Secure it with double-sided tape to the new piece. Using the new piece as a guide, cut out the damaged area, then pry out the nails or tacks from the replacement square.

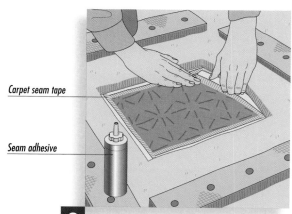

Carpet seam tape

Seam adhesive

3 Fasten the patch

Remove the damaged square and cut lengths of carpet seam tape to fit along the edges of the original carpet. If you're using uncoated tape, cover half of each strip with latex seam adhesive. Place the edge of each strip, sticky side up, under the edge of the original carpet and press the new piece of carpeting into place. When the adhesive is dry, remove carpet tacks from the carpet strips.

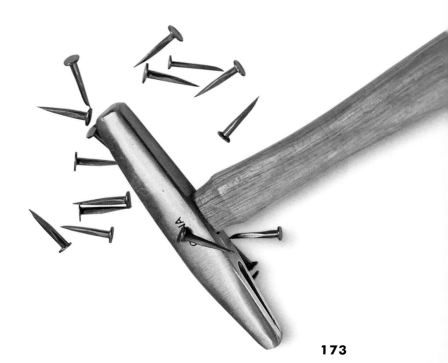

Repairing Stairs

Stair Repairs

Constant use combined with the number of interlocking parts in a stairway make it almost inevitable that some components will need periodic repair. To keep the handrail steady, repair loose balusters—they can be tightened and newel posts secured. Check all balusters to see if the tops are secure. If they rattle or move, it's time to repair them.

Newel posts are sometimes difficult to repair. When bodies or furniture bump the newel post, the thrust acts like a lever, loosening the bottom. Of the two methods shown on the facing page, adding wood screws or adding a lag screw, the second makes the most durable repair. To repair squeaky treads, see page 165.

TIGHTENING A BALUSTER

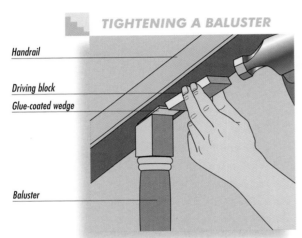

- Handrail
- Driving block
- Glue-coated wedge
- Baluster

Driving in a wedge

Tap a glue-coated wedge between the handrail and the baluster. Don't pry up the handrail. Using a utility knife, trim the wedge flush with the baluster and wipe off excess glue.

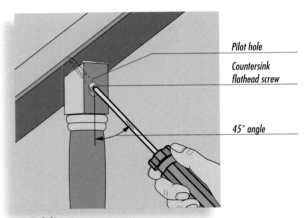

- Pilot hole
- Countersink flathead screw
- 45° angle

Adding a screw

Drill an angled pilot hole through the baluster and into the handrail and countersink for a long screw. Inject wood glue, insert the screw, and tighten. Fill with wood putty, sand, and finish.

Repairing bottom joints

The bottom of the baluster can also become loose. Pry off the molding with a putty knife or chisel. Drill a pilot hole through the tenon into the tread and countersink it for a long screw's head. Apply epoxy around the notch and tenon. Insert a screw and tighten. Replace the molding.

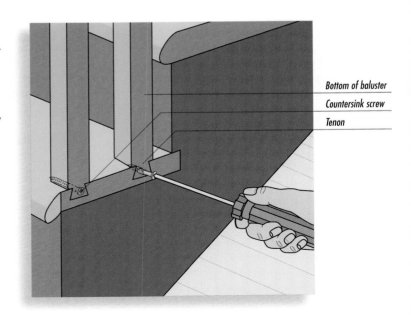

- Bottom of baluster
- Countersink screw
- Tenon

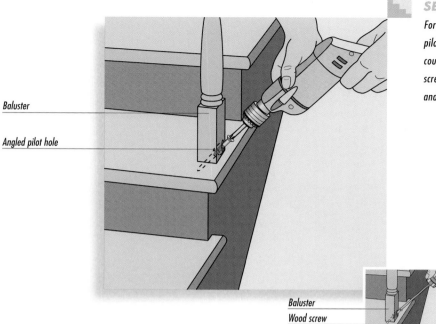

Baluster

Angled pilot hole

For a loose surface-mounted baluster, drill an angled pilot hole through the baluster and into the tread and countersink the hole for the screw head. Insert a wood screw and tighten. Fill the hole with wood putty, sand, and finish.

Baluster
Wood screw

STABILIZING A LOOSE POST

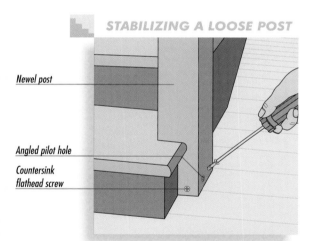

Newel post

Angled pilot hole

Countersink
flathead screw

Securing a post with screws

Drill angled pilot holes near the base of the newel post through the post into the floor; countersink the holes. Then apply wood glue between the post and the floor. Insert flathead wood screws and tighten. Fill the holes with wood putty, sand, and finish to match.

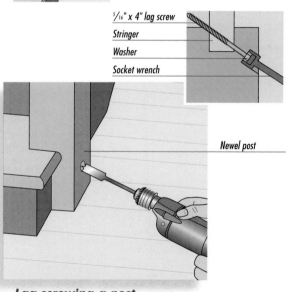

$5/16$" x 4" lag screw
Stringer
Washer
Socket wrench

Newel post

Lag screwing a post

Use a $3/4$-inch spade bit to drill a $3/4$-inch-deep hole into the newel post. With a $7/32$-inch bit, extend the hole back into the rough framing— the stringer and carriage. Enlarge the hole, just through the newel post, with a $5/16$-inch bit. Don't drill all the way back into the framing. Now screw in a $5/16$-inch-by-4-inch-long lag screw (through a washer). Glue in a dowel plug, sand, and finish.

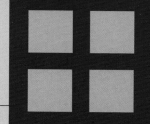

Windows & Doors

Windows and doors play a dramatic role in how a house performs. Ideally, they achieve a delicate balance between providing shelter and offering light, warmth, ventilation, access, or views to the outside world and between rooms. And they can enhance your home's architecture—or fight against it. For these reasons, it's important to have windows and doors that are both practical and integral.

Buying Windows

Windows have a tremendous environmental influence on a house, affecting the light, ventilation, and temperature of the interior—and the comfort of the occupants. In addition, windows are part of a home's architectural identity, immediately conveying period and style. When you are choosing new windows, be sure the styles you select will suit your home both practically and aesthetically.

Window Styles

Windows come in many shapes, sizes, and types, and are made from a variety of materials. How do you select the right ones? There are several criteria to consider—your budget, your home's style, and how you want the window to perform. Think about the relative importance of ventilation and security, and how easy it should be to maintain. And decide whether you want to emphasize the window as a focal point or have it serve in a more practical manner.

Windows are either fixed or operable. The illustrations on these pages show the common varieties and will give you basic information about how they perform.

Materials

Windows are made from a variety of materials, including wood, aluminum, steel, vinyl, and fiberglass—or from a combination of these materials. In general, those that offer better weather protection cost more, but they pay off in low maintenance and energy savings.

WOOD Wood tends to be the most popular window material, particularly for the parts of a window that are seen from indoors. Wood doesn't conduct cold or allow for condensation as much as other materials do. However, wood is subject to shrinkage and swelling, so it will warp and rot over time—especially on the exterior—unless it is protected.

Wood windows typically come unfinished unless you order them otherwise. If you intend to paint them, save work by purchasing them already primed on the exterior and/or interior surfaces of the frame and sash. Or you may be able to eliminate painting altogether by buying them pre-painted in some standard colors by certain manufacturers.

CLAD-WOOD You'll find that many of today's windows are wood inside and clad on the outside with a tough, attractive exterior jacket of extruded aluminum or vinyl. The cladding, available in a few stock colors, covers both sash and frame; it will keep windows virtually maintenance-free for years. With vinyl, the color permeates the material, so scratches don't show. Aluminum will scratch, but it is tougher, available in a wider variety of colors, and easier to paint (though neither vinyl nor aluminum should require painting). Neither type will rust or rot.

ALUMINUM Aluminum windows are more durable than bare wood—also thinner, lighter, and easier to handle. They are insulated with a thermal break of extruded vinyl and sometimes also foam, which reduces heat loss and condensation. Finishes protect the aluminum from corrosion, but deteriorate in coastal areas due to the salty air.

(continued on page 180)

 TILT-TURN WINDOWS

Tilt-turn windows offer distinctive European styling with a special advantage over conventional double-hung windows: They tilt in toward the room at the top and also turn a full 180 degrees for easy cleaning. This feature also makes them excellent for where you might need an emergency exit. Look for a multipoint locking system—this adds security and helps keep the window tightly closed.

Horizontal sliders

These work well at sealing in energy. They may have one or more fixed panels and one or more panels that slide in horizontal tracks. Only half of the total window may be opened for ventilation at one time.

Double-hung

Classic in style, double-hung windows have an upper, outside sash that slides down, and a lower inside sash that slides up. Hidden springs, weights, or friction devices help lift, lower, and position the sash. With certain types, the sash can be removed, rotated, or tilted for cleaning. If only one sash slides, the window is called a vertical sliding or single-hung.

Awning

An awning window is like a horizontal, top-hinged casement—it tilts out at the bottom, offering partial ventilation, an unobstructed view, and reasonably good security. A top-opening style, typically placed low on a wall, is called a hopper window.

Casement

Hung singly or in pairs, a casement window is operated by cranks that swing the sash outward or inward. It opens fully for easy cleaning and offers excellent ventilation because it can scoop in breezes.

Jalousie

Jalousie windows are made of a number of glass slats set in metal clips, which can be opened and closed in unison. These offer good ventilation but are cold and drafty in cold climates.

Bay window

A bay window projects out from the wall and has a center window parallel to the wall flanked by two windows attached at an angle—usually opening casements or double-hungs. Box bays have the side windows at a 90-degree angle.

Bow window

A bow window projects like a bay but has more than three sections, joined to form a gentle curve. Center windows are generally fixed; side sashes are typically casement windows.

FIXED WINDOWS

Fixed windows are stationary units mounted within a frame. They're great for letting in light and exposing views, but provide no ventilation. Among the more visually interesting choices are octagonal, half-circle, and ellipse windows and a corner window that has a single pane bent at a 90-degree angle.

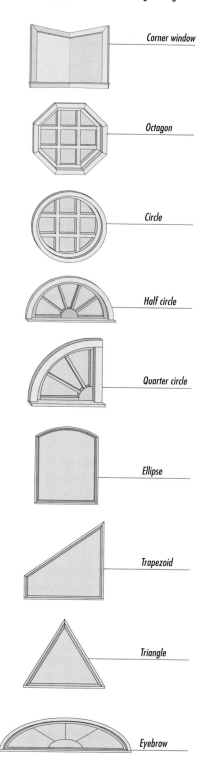

Corner window

Octagon

Circle

Half circle

Quarter circle

Ellipse

Trapezoid

Triangle

Eyebrow

179

Buying Windows

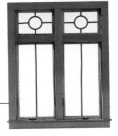

(continued from page 178)

VINYL Vinyl windows are made from rigid, impact-resistant polyvinyl chloride (PVC), with hollow spaces inside to make them resistant to heat loss and condensation. Inexpensive vinyl windows have a tendency to distort when exposed to extremes of heat and cold, making them harder to operate and allowing for air leakage. Vinyl windows can't be painted, and darker shades may fade over time.

STEEL Steel is more resistant to the elements than both aluminum and wood; however, steel windows generally are not used in homes because of their expense. If you have the budget, they are attractive, low maintenance, and will last for years.

Construction

Most wood windows come prehung in complete frames that fit into a rough opening in the wall. They are attached with nails driven through the exterior casing, or brickmold, on the outside, and through the jambs on the inside.

Vinyl or aluminum windows and some wood windows with a vinyl or aluminum cladding have a factory-installed nailing flange on the outside that you attach to the perimeter of the window's rough framing.

Window Hardware

All operable windows come equipped with hardware—the mechanisms used for opening and closing the sash, the latches, and so forth. Here is a closer look at key types:

CRANKS Casement, awning, and hopper windows utilize cranks for opening and closing. (Older types used push-bar operators.) Some manufacturers offer cranks in nonmetallic finishes (notably white), and some new types have a fold-down handle that makes them less conspicuous.

LATCHES & LOCKS Latches on the frame are used to hold the window tightly closed. On hinged windows, two are recommended on tall or wide frames. On double-hung windows, sash locks pull together the upper and lower sash to minimize drafts. Keyed sash locks can improve security.

On sliders, look for security locks to keep the operable sashes from being jimmied open.

HINGES Hinges should allow arm space between the sash and the window frame to make washing exterior glass an easy job. You can ask for special European hardware that turns a casement window into a hopper window. Unlike American casement-window hardware, the European mechanism swings into the room. Because the hardware locks tight in several places around the frame, the windows have very low air infiltration, but the inward swinging feature can interfere with draperies. See related information about tilt-turn windows on page 178.

COUNTERBALANCES On double-hung windows, the sash is counterbalanced on the sides by weights or other counterbalancing mechanisms, such as torsion screws. In some replacement windows, friction may be all that holds the sashes in place.

SLIDING MECHANISMS Most sashes of aluminum and vinyl windows are lightweight enough to slide in the sill tracks. But large, door-height sashes must be supported by rollers.

Window Orientation & Size

The view out a window is as important as how much light and ventilation the window provides. Windows connect us to the outdoors and enhance the sense of interior space. For this reason, the placement and size of your windows—and what you'll see from them—is no small consideration.

Where your windows are placed, how large they are, and what type they are have a significant effect on the amount of light and ventilation they provide.

A south-facing window lets in the most light and is desirable in all but the hottest climates; a north window provides soft, diffuse light. Because of the low angle of the sun in the morning and late afternoon, light from east- and west-facing windows can be too intense.

Windows & Doors

When gauging the placement of a window, consider not only the view but how the room is used. For example, in a kitchen, the sill should be above the level of the counter; in a living room, 10 to 14 inches from the floor so you can view the outdoors from a couch.

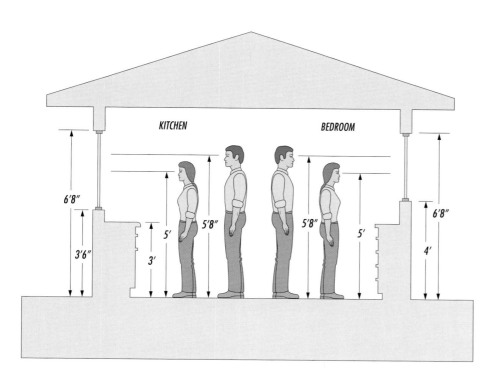

Glazing for Windows & Doors

Unfortunately, glass is not nearly as good at conserving energy as an insulated wall, so glazed doors and windows can be responsible for a major part of a home's energy loss if they're not well chosen. Storm windows and doors and window coverings can help retard heat movement, but the surest and most effective way to save energy is to utilize high-performance glazing.

Two important ratings to check when buying windows and glazed doors are the R-value and the overall U-value. An R-value measures a material's resistance to heat transfer; the higher the R-value, the better the insulating properties of the glazing. The U-value measures overall energy-efficiency. It tells you the rate at which heat flows through the entire window or door, frame and all. The lower the U-value, the more energy-efficient the window or door. An average U-value is fine for warm climates; in cold climates, a lower U-value is worth the premium you are likely to pay for it.

Insulating glazing typically has two, or sometimes three, panes of glass sealed together with either air or argon gas trapped between them to act as an insulator. Some units have a plastic film suspended between two glass panes. If the unit is properly sealed, condensation shouldn't occur between the panes; sometimes a drying agent (called a desiccant) is used in the spacer (the strip inside the panes, which helps keep them apart) as added insurance against condensation. One important reason for buying windows and doors with a strong warranty is to ensure that they will be backed if the seal fails and condensation occurs (there is no easy way to get rid of condensation in dual glazing).

You will discover that there are also a number of glass products on the market for special uses, including safety glass and stained glass. Here is a closer look at both high-performance and specialty glazing:

LOW-EMISSIVITY (OR LOW-E) GLASS Low-e glazing has a film applied to one of the glass surfaces or suspended between the panes. This coating or film allows light in but prevents some solar rays from being transmitted through the glass. A low-e coating can help keep your home cool on a hot day by blocking longer-wave radiant heat from entering, and on a cold day it can prevent the radiant interior heat from escaping through the glass. Some low-e coatings combine these two functions. Low-e coatings also block ultraviolet rays, and reduce the fading of carpets and upholstery.

TINTED GLASS Usually given either a bronze or gray cast, tinted glass reduces glare and limits the amount of light and heat from the sun (solar gain) in your home.

REFLECTIVE GLASS This type also reduces solar gain and obscures the view from outside. It is mainly used in commercial applications.

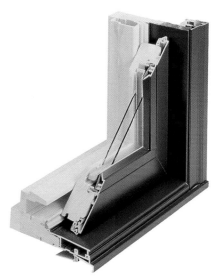

High-performance glazing
Cross-section of high-performance glazing shows two panes of glass with a space in between. In some cases, the space is filled with argon or a similar inert gas, which serves as an insulator. In addition, a low-emissivity coating deflects outside ultraviolet rays while retaining indoor radiant heat.

SAFETY GLASS Required by certain local building codes for certain situations, safety glass is always a good choice if there's any risk of a person walking through a window. Safety glass is available tempered, laminated, or wire-reinforced. Tempered glass is heat-treated during the manufacturing process and crumbles if broken rather than shattering. Laminated glass has a film of plastic that holds the glass together if broken.

STAINED GLASS Before choosing a stained-glass window, don't just consider its design and size—think about the color scheme of the room, the direction the panel will face, and the amount of outdoor view you'd like. A rectangular or curved stained-glass frame around a clear pane can focus attention on the view, while a stained-glass panel the size of the window will block out an undesirable view. Stained glass also can be lovely around doors, but check if this is permitted by your local building code, and don't use stained glass where people could walk or fall into it.

You can install small stained-glass panels in the same way you would install ordinary clear panes. Large panels need additional support for permanent installation; fit them into their own routed wood frames, or block their edges on both sides with wood strips nailed to the sill and window frame. Be sure to set the panel in glazing putty and caulk all outside joints.

Mini-blinds under glass
Double glazing contains an internal mini-blind that never needs to be dusted. The space between panes also serves as an insulator. Blinds are operated by discreet hardware located on the window frame.

Buying Doors

When shopping for new doors, you will discover a wonderful smorgasbord of options—hundreds of types and sizes from conventional wood models to steel and fiberglass composite entry systems. Armed with a basic understanding of how doors are made, decide upon whether you want an exterior entry door or an interior door—there are distinct differences between the two, as explained below. Then explore the many options within that category to find the perfect door for your needs.

Door Construction

Regardless of whether they are made from wood or another material, doors are termed either "flush" or "paneled" doors. These terms describe how a wood door is built or, in the case of nonwood doors, simply refer to the door's general style and appearance.

Paneled doors have rectangular recesses—panels—framed by horizontal rails and vertical stiles. They are sometimes called stile-and-rail doors. Superior strength and traditional looks make this type a wise choice for exterior doors and for interior doors of homes with traditional decor. Panel construction on a wood door also minimizes cracking and warping because panels have room to shift as they expand and contract with changes in moisture.

Flush doors are flat and smooth on both faces. Wood ones are covered with birch or other wood veneer that's easy to stain and varnish or paint. Nonwood doors are clad with fiberglass or steel. Flush doors may have a solid-wood or a foam-filled core, or—in the case of interior doors—they may have a "hollow core" filled with lightweight baffles, such as a honeycomb of dense cardboard. The latter type is relatively inexpensive and lightweight.

All swinging doors are attached to the jambs with two or three hinges. On exterior doors, the hinges are on the inside of the house, to prevent removal of the hinge pins by a potential intruder. The door frame consists of jambs, casing, stops, sill, and threshold, as shown in the illustration on facing page.

Glass sections of doors are called lights. A six-light door, for example, has six glass panes, separated by muntins. You can buy true divided-light doors from some companies or, if you just want the look of divided lights, snap-in muntins that do a fair job in mimicking the look but are much less expensive to buy (and they make glass easier to clean).

What we refer to as French doors are simply multiple-light, hinged doors that are paired together. Patio and sliding doors may have a single light (a full-sized glass panel) in each door or multiple lights, but they slide rather than swing. See more about sliding doors, pages 186–187.

Interior doors do not have to meet the same standards for weatherization as exterior doors. Both panel and flush doors are thinner ($1^3/_8$ inch) and lighter weight. Also, there are a variety of interior doors that can be used for specialty needs: bifold, accordion, and bypass doors for closets and storage spaces, and pocket doors that help save space by sliding into a cavity in the wall, for example.

A typical height for doors is 6 feet, 8 inches but you can buy doors up to 8 feet tall. Widths of interior doors vary from 12 inches up to 36 inches or more. Typical exterior doors range from 30 to 36 inches; a wide door for an entry is a smart choice for making it easier to move furniture indoors and out. Thickness typically is $1^3/_4$ inches for exterior doors.

Interior doors typically are hinged to swing in toward a room, with the exception of closets and other storage rooms, which are hinged to swing outward. Jambs, casing, and stops are the same as for exterior doors. Interior doors do not have a sill but some have a threshold that hides the transition between two different flooring materials.

This four-panel exterior door is mounted to the jambs with three hinges. The stops are wood strips that the door fits against when closed. The sill fits between the jambs, forming the frame bottom. The threshold, or saddle, sometimes along with weatherstripping, is fastened to the sill. Casing covers the space between wall materials and the jambs and strengthens the frame.

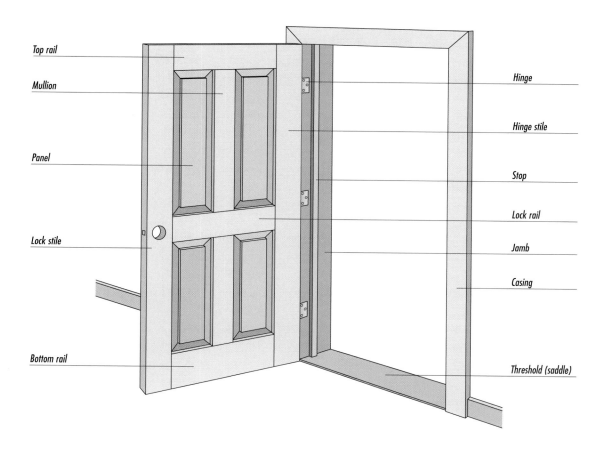

Top rail
Mullion
Panel
Lock stile
Bottom rail

Hinge
Hinge stile
Stop
Lock rail
Jamb
Casing
Threshold (saddle)

Entry Doors

You can buy an entry door singly—as a door meant to be mounted in an existing frame—or prehung in a frame. A prehung door usually comes as a complete entry system, with an integral interlocking threshold and weatherstripping encircling the door's perimeter. With an entry system, sidelights may flank the door on each side and a transom window may cap the top. Because hinges and lockset are designed as part of the system, doors tend to be very weather-tight and work extremely reliably.

WOOD ENTRY DOORS Wood has the warm, natural look and feel that most people prefer but will eventually warp, crack, and bow when exposed to the elements—so wood doors must be maintained with a durable finish. Solid wood doors tend to be more expensive than doors made from other materials. Species include oak, cherry, walnut, mahogany, maple, fir, pine, or paint-grade doors from any of several softwoods.

(continued on page 186)

Buying Doors

(continued from page 185)
Most mass-produced doors are not solid wood. Instead, they are made with an engineered-wood core that is faced with a veneer, a construction that minimizes warping and movement and makes a door more affordable to build. Be aware that veneers are easily damaged, particularly if they're thinner than about $1/16$ inch.

FIBERGLASS-COMPOSITE DOORS Where a door will be exposed to weather or particularly harsh or humid climates, fiberglass-composite doors are a smart choice. These doors realistically imitate the look of wood, thanks to a combination of molded wood grain texturing and the fact that they can be stained to match most popular woods, such as oak, cherry, and walnut. A fiberglass door's framework is usually made of wooden stiles and rails, filled with a core of foam insulation.

Fiberglass doors, like wood doors, are sold as single units or complete entry systems with appearance-grade wood jambs, a variety of glazings, oak adjustable sills, and security strike plates. Many fiberglass door entry systems are backed for as long as you own the house.

STEEL ENTRY DOORS Steel doors are extremely rugged and durable. Although some steel doors have traditional panel styling, they are not true panel doors. They have a steel or wood frame and are filled with foam insulation.

Steel doors are not as industrial-looking as they sound; most have surfaces of heavy-gauge galvanized steel that have been embossed with a wood-grain pattern. Most come factory primed with a baked-on polyester finish that may need periodic repainting. Some are given a vinyl coating for greater weather resistance. Types you can stain just like wood are given a wood-fiber coating.

BUYING TIPS When replacing an existing door, measure the door's actual width, height, and thickness. When buying a prehung door, measure the width of the existing jamb, from the inside of the exterior molding to the inside of the interior molding. Note which side the knob is on from inside the room. If the knob is on the right, the door is a "right-hand" door; if it's on the left, it is a "left-hand" door.

When buying an entry system, be sure all of the components are from the same manufacturer—not assembled by distributors from a variety of products. That way they're sure to work together effectively.

Buying Sliding Doors

Contemporary sliding or "gliding" doors have come a long way since yesteryear's aluminum sliders, infamous for their stark appearance, sweating frames, and cold glazing. Today, a new generation of high-quality models offers energy efficiency, durability, safety, and style.

Although conventional aluminum sliders maintain a popular foothold in the market, sliding doors of wood and other materials have given the genre an entirely new identity. The most popular sliders offer the warmth of wood on the inside and have a durable cladding of vinyl or aluminum on the outside. These are made just like clad-wood windows, discussed on page 178.

You can also buy all-wood sliders factory-primed or pre-painted in standard colors; some manufacturers will custom paint them for a premium. Because wood is vulnerable to moisture and sun, it must be given a durable finish.

Sliding doors also are made from fiberglass composites that won't warp or crack but resemble the look of wood; and you can buy rugged steel sliders, normally at a lower cost. Still other doors are faced on both sides with a vinyl or aluminum skin; a polyurethane foam insulation core fills the shell, offering six times the energy efficiency of wood.

Symmetrical entry features a wood entry door flanked by sidelights and crowned by an eyebrow window.

SLIDING DOOR GLAZING Of course, the largest part of a sliding glass door is glass. To make a door truly energy efficient, high-performance glazing is key. Fortunately, this is standard with most high-quality sliders. You'll find dual glazing, or—more typically—double-paned glass with low-e coating and, in some cases, argon gas filling. Low-e reduces heat transfer and protects against UV damage; argon gas filling doubles the insulation value. Some manufacturers let you specify the glazing you want when you order.

Where sun-caused fading or damage may be a serious problem, you may want to opt for glass with a solar bronze or solar gray tint to reject UV rays. In addition, some companies offer decorative stained or beveled glass with true brass caming (leading). Obscure glass is available for bathrooms or other places where privacy is a concern. Sliders are available with real or false divided lights, like other types of doors and windows.

SIZES & OPTIONS Beyond the standard 6-feet-8-inch height, sliding doors are made 6 feet 11 inches or 8 feet tall. You can also buy three- or four-door-wide configurations that run up to about 16 feet wide. And sliders are made in single-opening and double-opening styles. To extend your design options, most manufacturers provide matching rectangular and circle-head transom windows, with dimensions intended to fit above doors.

Some companies offer top-mounted insect screens that are easier to use than rolling screens. With these, dirt, leaves, and debris along the bottom glide rail are much less likely to interfere with smooth operation.

Framing for Windows & Doors

Before you add or replace a window or door, you'll have to prepare the proper rough-frame opening in the wall. To do this, you must understand how a wall is built and the various techniques needed to open it up, install the new framing members, then close it back up again. You'll find information on each of these topics in their respective sections in this book—wall framing, drywall, siding, and so forth. Here we will look at rough framing. Pay special attention to the "Walls & Ceilings" chapter for information on opening up a wall, rough framing, hanging drywall, and installing trim.

The frame you construct around a window or door opening supports not only the new window or door, but may support loads from above, including a second-story floor, ceiling, and the roof. Don't compromise your home's structure. Figure out whether your home is built with balloon framing or western framing, and whether the wall is bearing or nonbearing (see page 98). If it is a nonbearing wall, you may be able to use lighter construction than if it is bearing and you won't have to temporarily support the ceiling. If your house is balloon-framed, consult a professional for structural advice.

Bearing walls require structural headers to support the weight above them. Headers are short beams, made from lumber heavier than the studs—typically two 2 by 4s nailed together on edge with a $1/2$-inch plywood spacer, or larger material such as 4 by 6s, 4 by 8s, or even 4 by 12s. They transfer weight to the studs on each side of the opening. Nonbearing walls don't require load-bearing headers; you can usually build them from a single 2 by 4 placed flat.

Before you open the wall, check for obstructions as discussed on page 211.

TYPICAL FRAMING The illustrations on facing page show how window openings are framed. Building-code requirements for rough openings vary. For example, the illustrations show single 2 by 4s for the rough sill, but some building codes may require the use of two 2 by 4s.

MARKING THE LOCATION Mark the manufacturer's rough-opening specifications on the interior wall, using a framing square to ensure square corners. If possible, plan it so that at least one existing wall stud can serve as a king stud. (See page 103 for information on locating wall studs.) Cut through the wall covering as discussed on page 104 and pry it loose.

Using a combination square, mark the total height of the opening on the king stud or studs, marking each stud on the edge and one side. Then, from the marks you've just drawn, measure down the height of the rough opening (or the height of the unit plus $3/8$ inch), and add $1 1/2$ inches for the thickness of the rough sill. Mark the studs again.

FRAMING THE OPENING Install framing as discussed on facing page. (If you use a 2-by-12 header, place it tight against the top plate.) Using $2 1/2$-inch common nails, toenail the ends of the header to the king studs and the cripples to the header. Nail trimmer studs to king studs with $3 1/2$-inch nails. To adjust the width of the opening, toenail a doubled trimmer on one side, allowing enough shimming space for the door or window. Add spacer blocks.

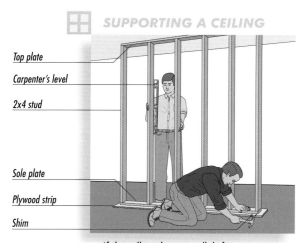

SUPPORTING A CEILING

Top plate

Carpenter's level

2x4 stud

Sole plate

Plywood strip

Shim

If the wall is a bearing wall, before removing any studs, build a temporary wall slightly wider than the width of the opening and about 4 feet away from the existing wall. Protect flooring with $1/2$-inch plywood. While a helper holds the wall plumb, drive shims between the sole plate and plywood until the plate is tight against the ceiling.

Studs to be cut

Reciprocating saw

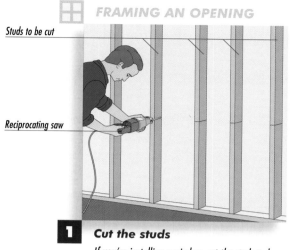

1 **Cut the studs**

If you're installing a window, cut the studs to be removed at the lines marking the bottom of the rough sill and the header's top edge. For doors, simply cut at the header's top edge and remove the studs.

Nail

Header lumber

Plywood

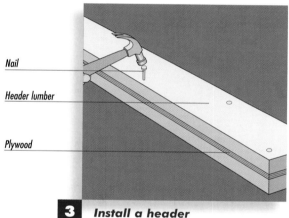

3 **Install a header**

For a bearing wall, assemble a header. With a helper, position the top of the header, crown-side up, against the upper cripple studs and nail as described in the text.

If you don't have a helper, you can prepare the header; cut trimmers to the required length; mount one trimmer and nail it to the king stud; load one end of the header onto it, and wedge the header into place with the second trimmer.

FINISHING UP On a dry day, drill holes through the wall from inside at each corner of the rough opening and stick nails through to the outside. Turn to page 192 for information on how to cut the exterior siding and how to finish installing a window.

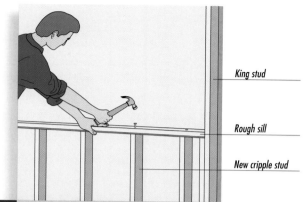

King stud

Rough sill

New cripple stud

2 **Install cripple studs**

For a window, measure the distance from the sole plate to the line marking the sill on each king stud, then cut two cripple studs to this length. Measure the distance between the king studs, then cut the rough sill to this length and nail it to each cripple stud.

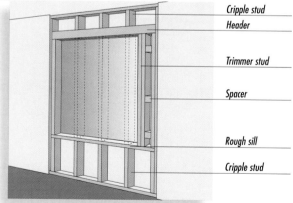

Cripple stud
Header

Trimmer stud

Spacer

Rough sill

Cripple stud

A rough opening for a window or door requires a header to carry the weight across the top and trimmer studs to support the header. A window also has a sill to form the structural base for the window, and cripple studs to support the sill.

189

Tools for Windows & Doors

Most work on windows and doors requires a host of conventional carpentry tools. Of course, you don't need all of these for every job; some repair jobs require just two or three. Depending upon the work you're tackling, be sure you also have appropriate safety equipment such as safety glasses and gloves. For many jobs, you will also need a stepladder—and you may need a pair of sawhorses to work on a door or window that isn't installed. For touch-up work, you're likely to need drywall tools (see page 101) and a variety of paintbrushes and painting tools (see pages 38–43).

CONSTRUCTION TOOLS

When installing doors and windows, you'll need a variety of basic carpentry tools, including those shown here. In addition to the electric drill, be sure you have a set of drill bits, Phillips-head screwdriver bits, and—if you intend to install a lockset or deadbolt—a hole saw. A stud finder is helpful for locating wall studs; a hand stapler fastens building paper and insulation during window and door installation.

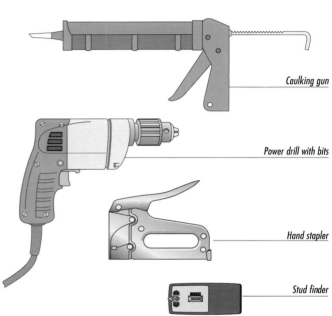

Caulking gun

Power drill with bits

Hand stapler

Stud finder

Claw hammer

Nailset

Putty knife

Adjustable wrench

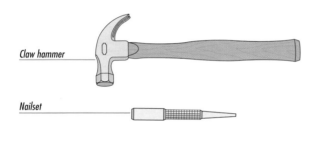

Screwdrivers

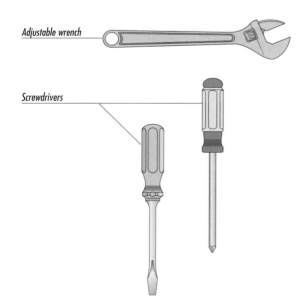

DEMOLITION TOOLS

Window and door installation often requires a bit of minor demolition work. For chipping away masonry, you'll need a cold chisel (be sure to wear safety glasses). A prybar is helpful for various tear-out jobs. A reciprocating saw makes easy work of cutting away wall materials.

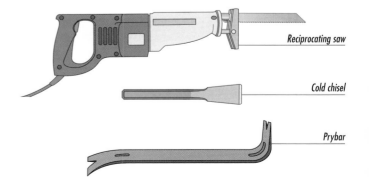

Reciprocating saw

Cold chisel

Prybar

A circular saw makes cutting wood a quick job; a handsaw allows for more controlled cutting. For other wood cutting, you'll need wood chisels in two or three sizes. A plane and perforated rasp help shave down wood—such as when you need to trim a door for a better fit. Tin snips cut metal flashing when installing windows and doors. Cutting glass requires a glass cutter. A utility knife is handy for many jobs.

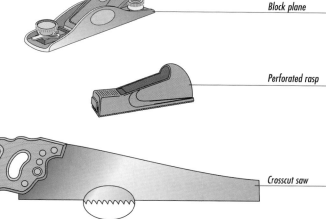

Block plane

Perforated rasp

Glass cutter

Utility knife

Tin snips

Crosscut saw

Chisel

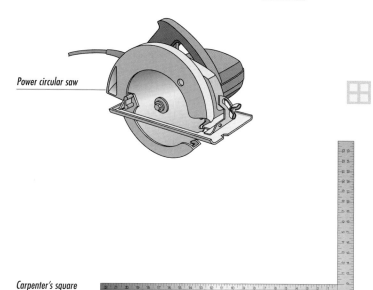

Power circular saw

MEASURING & MARKING TOOLS

The tools shown here are needed for the various layout and measuring tasks needed for installing new windows and doors. Choose a 16-foot tape measure that has markings for stud layouts marked along its blade every 16 and 24 inches.

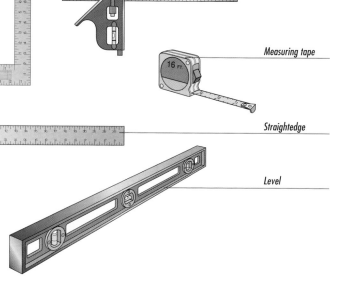

Combination square

Measuring tape

16 FT

Carpenter's square

Straightedge

Chalk line

Level

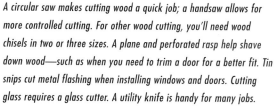

Once you have a rough opening prepared, as discussed on pages 188–189, installing a prehung window is relatively easy. The exact methods depend upon the type of window you're putting in, and they vary from one manufacturer to the next. You'll find that the instructions we offer here are generic and will be helpful, but be sure to follow the specific instructions that come with your new window.

Prehung windows are blocked and braced to prevent damage during shipping; don't remove this bracing until the window is fastened in place. After you've installed the unit, be sure the sash operates freely (for an operable window) before you install the interior trim or caulk the exterior.

Installing a Prehung Window

A prehung window comes complete with sash, frame, sill, hardware, and most of the trim (you generally have to buy the casing, stool, and apron separately). It's best to install it from the outside, though you can maneuver an operable window through the opening from the inside and lean through the window to fasten it. If you want to install the window from the inside, make sure you're safely anchored so you don't fall out.

CUTTING THE EXTERIOR OPENING After laying out where you want to put the new window from inside the room, drill holes at the corners, then drive nails through the holes. On the outside, mark the outline of the rough opening on the siding.

Using a circular saw, jigsaw, or reciprocating saw, cut through the siding and sheathing along the lines; lay the cut material aside. Make sure you have the proper saw blade—or use an old wood-cutting blade—because you

> **Don't nail vinyl and aluminum windows through the jambs—just nail the window's flange to the sheathing (over building paper or house wrap) with 1-inch roofing nails. The finished siding will butt up against the outside of the window, concealing the flange. Apply a bead of caulk around the window to weatherproof it.**

may encounter nails. For stucco, use a circular saw fitted with a masonry-cutting blade. Wear eye protection.

If necessary, assemble the mounting flanges and flashing of your window according to the manufacturer's instructions.

After holding up the window and marking its placement on the siding, remove the window and widen the cuts through the siding, but not the sheathing, to allow for the trim or flange around the outside of the frame.

MOUNTING THE WINDOW After preparing the opening and tacking the window in place from outside, as shown in Step 5 on page 194, go inside and tap shims between the window jambs and trimmer studs at the top, center, and bottom of the window (spaced about 12 inches apart) to help keep the window in position. Make sure they're not so tight that they push the jamb out of plumb. Drill pilot holes, then nail through the jamb and each set of shims into the trimmer stud, using $2\frac{1}{2}$-inch finishing nails.

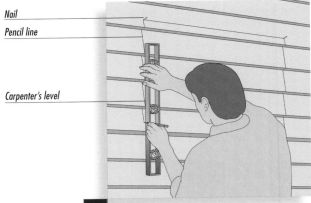

Nail
Pencil line
Carpenter's level

1   *Mark & cut the opening*

On the wall outside the new window's location, use a carpenter's level and pencil to mark the outline of the rough opening on the siding. Here you can see nails driven through at the corners from inside, used to mark the placement. Using a saw equipped with the appropriate blade, cut through the siding and sheathing along the lines.

Carpenter's level

2 **Center window in opening**
From outside the house, center and level the window in the opening and have a helper hold it in place. Then go inside and shim beneath the window unit until the window sits level. Once it's level, have the person outside mark the outline of the flange or trim on the siding. Remove the window.

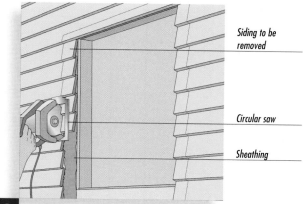

Siding to be removed

Circular saw

Sheathing

3 **Widen the cutout**
Cut along the pencil line on the siding, but don't cut the sheathing. For wood siding, finish the cuts at corners with a hammer and chisel. To finish cuts on aluminum or vinyl siding, use a utility knife or tin snips.

Inside, trim off the shims flush with the jambs. Then go back outside and finish nailing the flange or trim to the sheathing with 1½-inch roofing nails for a flange or 2½-inch galvanized casing nails for trim.

Trimming a Window

To complete your window project, you'll need to install wallboard to fill the gap around the edges of the window, as discussed on pages 108–110; fit the new pieces as close as possible to the jambs on all sides.

You'll also need to finish the inside edges of the window with molding. On a single- or double-hung window, this involves fastening a stool to the windowsill, attaching an apron to the wall underneath the sill, and fastening casings to the sides and top to cover the joints between the wall and window. Other types of windows—casement, awning, and hopper—are usually finished with casings on all four sides, though sometimes a stool and apron are used. See pages 111–113 for proper methods of trim installation.

(continued on page 194)

 USING SASH REPLACEMENT KITS

If you have old, drafty, inefficient windows, you may be able to replace them without completely tearing out the frames and preparing a new rough opening for new windows. Instead, you may be able to install a sash replacement kit in the existing window frame. These kits allow you to change an unsightly or poorly insulating sash relatively easily. You can order sizes and styles that will custom-fit most frames.

Sash replacement kits come with all necessary hardware and instructions. Basically, here is how they work:
1) You remove the old stops and the existing window from the frame, and take up all the jamb hardware.
2) Next you fasten metal brackets spaced evenly along both sides of the window, then install new jamb hardware for the replacement sash.
3) You install the new sash in the opening, according to the directions.
4) And last, you replace the existing stops by tacking them back in place.

Installing a Window

(continued from page 193)

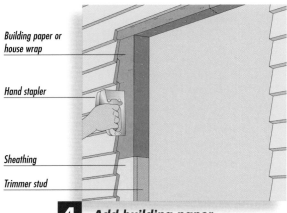

Building paper or house wrap

Hand stapler

Sheathing

Trimmer stud

4 Add building paper or house wrap

Building paper or house wrap makes the opening weather-tight. Cut building paper or house wrap into 8-inch-wide strips and slide them between the siding and the sheathing on all sides. Curl each strip around the frame, toward the interior of the house, and staple it to the sheathing and the trimmer stud. The strips should stop just before the inside edge of the opening.

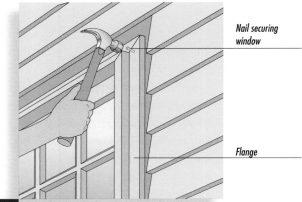

Nail securing window

Flange

5 Fasten the window

Center the window in the opening again. While your helper holds it in place, drive a temporary casing nail through the flange or trim at one of the top corners. Check that the window is level. If it is, nail through the flange or trim at the other corners. If it isn't, adjust the shims, then nail.

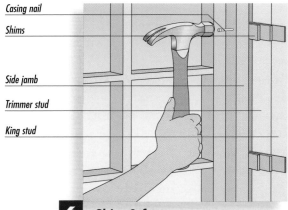

Casing nail

Shims

Side jamb

Trimmer stud

King stud

6 Shim & fasten

From inside, shim the window snugly in the opening, as described on page 192, and nail through the jamb and each set of shims into the trimmer stud with $2\frac{1}{2}$-inch finishing nails. Stuff the space between jambs and trimmer studs with insulation.

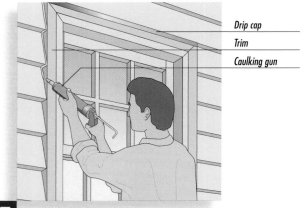

Drip cap

Trim

Caulking gun

7 Finish the outside

Finish nailing the flange or trim outside. Then, unless your roof has a pronounced overhang, install flashing, known as a drip cap, over the window. Thoroughly caulk the joints between the siding and the new window.

Installing a Bay Window

Cantilevered bay windows, box bay windows, and bow windows can be built in the same type of opening as conventional windows. The job is heavier, but in essence it is only a little more involved than installing a conventional window. Be aware that the building-code requirements for the rough sill for a bay window may be different than for a conventional window, because it must support considerably more weight. To install one of these windows higher up than the first floor, call a professional.

You can buy a bay window as a kit that includes the windows, head board, and seat board, plus various trim pieces you must assemble. Or you can buy a completely assembled unit ready to install. With the latter type, you just build the roof over the window (unless it reaches the soffit), install support brackets, and finish the inside. Some manufacturers supply a precut roof or roof framing and will also supply the support brackets or cable support system that they recommend. The installation method shown here is for a bay, but it's applicable to a bow or box window as well.

(continued on page 196)

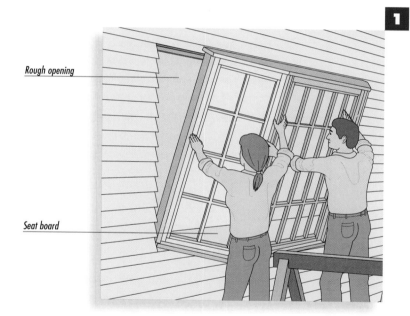

Rough opening

Seat board

1 **Place the window in the opening**
Pick up the window and rest the bottom platform on the rough sill. Then tilt the unit up so the trim around the outside butts against the sheathing. Center the jambs between the trimmer studs. While your helpers hold the window, slide sawhorses underneath to hold it.

Shim the window bottom
Use a level to determine which end of the seat board is higher. Nail that end to the rough sill. With the level positioned on the seat board, drive shims from both inside and outside between the sill and the seat board, placing the shims over each cripple stud. When the seat board is level, nail through the shims into the rough sill.

2

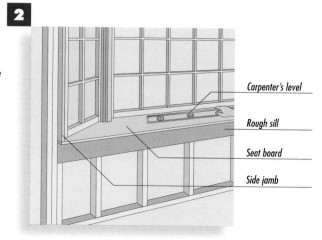

Carpenter's level

Rough sill

Seat board

Side jamb

Installing a Bay Window

(continued from page 195)
Be sure you have all the necessary materials before you start. Then prepare both the window and the opening. For information on the rough opening, see pages 188–189.

Assemble the window according to the manufacturer's instructions, and check its outside dimensions against the rough opening. It should be about $1/2$ inch shorter than the opening in both height and width. If you need to cut back the siding, follow Steps 3 and 4 on pages 193–194.

A bay window is heavy! To set it in place, you'll need helpers, one for every 3 feet of window width. You'll also need a sawhorse every 3 feet to support the window once it's in the opening.

Before starting installation, read through the following directions and study the illustrations to become familiar with the various parts and steps.

To install support brackets, toenail a cripple stud to the rough sill and the sole plate under each mullion. Position one of the support brackets under one of the mullions with the long leg against the siding; the short leg goes against the underside of the window. Use $3/8$-inch lag screws to fasten the long leg through the siding into the cripple. The other leg is fastened to the underside of the window with wood screws. Install the other bracket. For large windows, use more brackets.

Some manufacturers suggest installing brackets before the window is lifted into the rough opening; others suggest raising the window into the frame first and adding the brackets afterward. If your window requires a cable support system instead of (or in combination with) support brackets, follow the manufacturer's instructions.

POSITIONING THE WINDOW Prop the window in the rough opening and have your helpers hold it there while you go inside to get it level and plumb. Nail the highest end to the sill, about 2 inches from the jamb, then drive shims from both inside and outside between the sill and the seat

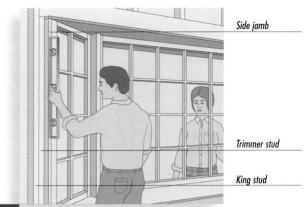

Side jamb

Trimmer stud

King stud

3   ***Shim the window sides***
Check for plumb along the jambs, both from side to side and from front to back. Drive shims between the jamb and the trimmer studs as needed, spacing them 12 inches apart. When the jambs are perfectly straight and plumb, drill pilot holes and drive finishing nails through the jambs and shims into the trimmer studs.

board, placing shims over each cripple stud, until the seat board is level. Nail through the shims to the rough sill.

While helpers move the window, drive shims between the jamb and the trimmer stud until the jamb is plumb, then nail it.

Unless your window comes with a preassembled roof, you'll have to build one; design it to reflect the style of your house. (See more about roof framing on page 320.)

Cover the top of the head board with insulation, packing it loosely inside the frame. Attach the end pieces of sheathing, then the center. You can shingle the roof of the bay to match your house or have a sheet-metal professional cover it with copper. (Some manufacturers provide a copper roof as an option.) If you shingle, you'll need to flash it as you would the main roof (see page 328).

To finish the unit, install exterior trim and caulk along it. If needed, install a skirt and bottom panel as shown in Step 7 on facing page.

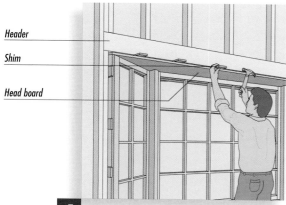

Header

Shim

Head board

4   Shim the window top

Shim the head board and header until they are both straight and level. Measure at several places between the head board and seat board; the measurements should be exactly the same. Secure the head board by driving nails through it and the shims. Fill any cavities with insulation. If the window requires cables, anchor them according to the manufacturer's instructions.

End rafter

Hip rafter

Head board

5   Build the roof

Staple plastic sheeting over the top of the window and trim the excess with a utility knife. If you're installing a roof with a prebuilt frame (see detail), position the roof frame on top of the window and fasten it to the cripple studs and the top of the window. If you're building your roof without a frame, install rafters, as shown. Cut and nail hip and end rafters at each end.

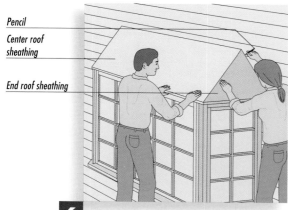

Pencil

Center roof sheathing

End roof sheathing

6   Cut siding & sheath the roof

Rest the center piece of roof sheathing against the top edge of the window and against the siding; mark where the sheathing touches the siding. Repeat with end pieces. Remove the sheathing and frame, and cut the siding along the pencil lines. Remove the siding. Then nail the sheathing to the rafters, using 2-inch nails spaced 6 inches apart.

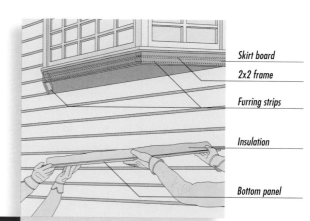

Skirt board

2x2 frame

Furring strips

Insulation

Bottom panel

7   Finish the exterior

After covering the bottom of the window with plastic sheeting, install a 2-by-2 frame near the outer edges. Nail furring strips to the skirt boards and screw the boards to the 2 by 2s. Cover the bottom panel with insulation and attach it to the furring strips.

Replacing a Broken Pane

Replacing the glass in a single-pane wooden window—especially a small one—isn't difficult. Wear heavy gloves and safety goggles. Before removing broken glass, tape newspaper to the inside of the sash to catch splinters. Pad glass shards with layers of newspaper when you're transporting it to the garbage. To bed the new glass, you can use glazing putty or glazing compound. Glazing compound is applied the same way but is easier to work with.

Don't try to replace panes of glass larger than 2 by 3 feet. These are dangerous to handle. Leave the job to a professional installer.

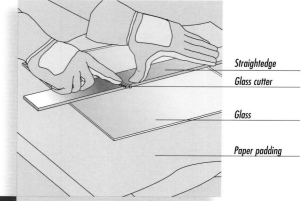

Straightedge
Glass cutter

Glass

Paper padding

2 ### Score the replacement
To determine the size of the new pane, measure the width and height of the opening, and subtract $1/8$ inch from each dimension. Measure the sash at several points in case it's out of square. Have the glass cut to size. If you must cut it yourself, place it on a carpeted bench top and score the glass deeply—only once—along a straightedge with a glass cutter. (Dip wheel in kerosene first.)

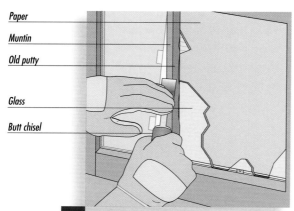

Paper

Muntin

Old putty

Glass

Butt chisel

1 ### Prepare the frame
Back the opening with newspaper. Remove large glass shards with gloved hands. Chisel out loose putty. If putty is rock hard, brush it with linseed oil and let it soak for half an hour, or gently heat it with a heat gun. Use the point of a molding scraper or a butt chisel to remove fragments. Pull out tiny metal glazier's points with long-nosed pliers. Clean and sand the wood; paint with a wood sealer.

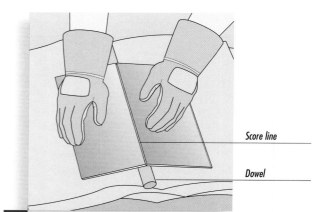

Score line

Dowel

3 ### Snap along the score
Center the score line over a small dowel and press down on both sides (or tap the underside of the score with the ball end of the glass cutter). If the break is uneven, use the notches on the cutter to nibble off jagged edges.

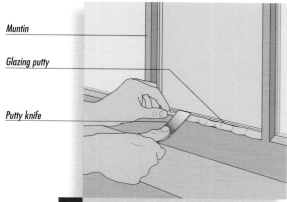

Muntin

Glazing putty

Putty knife

4 **Apply glazier's putty**

Warm putty in a pan of hot water to make it flexible. Working from outside the window, use a putty knife and your fingers to press a thin bead of glazing putty around the edges of the opening. This makes a bed for the replacement glass.

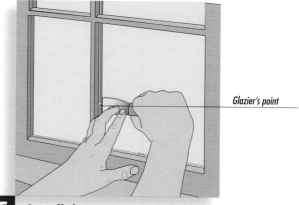

Glazier's point

5 **Install the pane**

Press the pane into place and remove excess putty. Push glazier's points into the frame with a putty knife (use two points on each side for small panes and a point every 4 inches to 6 inches for larger ones). Be careful not to push against the glass—this could crack it.

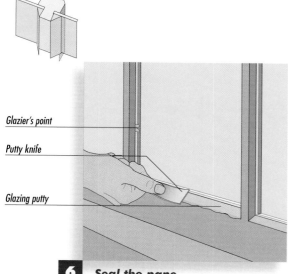

Glazier's point

Putty knife

Glazing putty

6 **Seal the pane**

Roll more putty into a rope about ¹/₄ inch thick; apply it around the outside edges. With a putty knife, smooth and bevel the putty at about a 30-degree angle, the top edge even with the inside edge of the muntin (see detail). When dry, paint to match the wood.

SEALS, GASKETS, OR MOLDINGS

To replace glass secured with rubber seals, unscrew the sash halves and remove the inside one. Brush out glass fragments, set a new pane against one sash half, replace the other half of the sash, and secure it with screws.

If the glass sits on a continuous rubber gasket (or four separate ones), remove the screws from a vertical end of the sash and pull the end away from the sash. Clean out the old glass, then pull the gasket around the new pane; slide the pane into the sash and secure the end.

To replace glass in sash with snap-out moldings, loosen one end of a piece of molding by inserting the tip of a putty knife where two ends meet. Pry gently, using the frame for leverage. Pull out the loosened strip of molding. When you've replaced the pane, push each molding piece into place with your hands. Pieces damaged during removal should be replaced.

Freeing a Stuck Sash

A simple sash or stop repair can often restore a window to good working order. If a sash is temporarily stuck because of high humidity, a change of weather may correct the problem. If a sash moves reluctantly, clean and wax the sash channels. Windows that have been painted shut can be opened.

If windows stick, chisel any dirt or large globs of paint from the channels, then sand them smooth. Coat the surfaces with paraffin so the sash moves easily.

If the sash sticks when the window is open, widen the channel. Place a wood block wider than the channel at the point that binds. Tap the block against the stop until the sash moves freely.

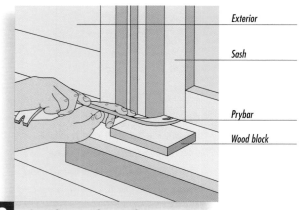

Exterior

Sash

Prybar

Wood block

2 **Gently pry the sash**
From outside, wedge a prybar between the sill and sash; work alternately at each corner so the sash moves up evenly. Protect the sill with a wood block.

FREEING A PAINT-BOUND SASH

Sash

Stop

Putty knife

Stool

1 **Break the paint seal**
Score the painted edges of the sash with a utility knife. Work a wide putty knife between the sash and frame. Tap with a mallet.

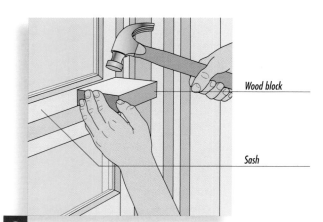

Wood block

Sash

3 **Work it up gradually**
If the window sticks partway open, place a wood block against the sash; tap with a hammer. Continue, alternating sides, until the sash is freed.

A sash that is too loose can be tightened. If the gap isn't too wide and the stop is nailed rather than screwed, you can move the stop slightly without actually removing it. Score the paint between the stop and jamb and place a cardboard shim between the stop and sash. Holding a block of wood against the stop to protect it, hammer toward the sash along the length of the stop until the paint film breaks and the stop rests against the shim. Then secure the stop with finishing nails. For wide gaps, reposition the stops.

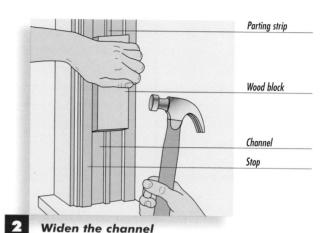

Parting strip

Wood block

Channel

Stop

2 Widen the channel

To widen the channel where stops are nailed, place a wood block wider than the channel at the point that binds. Tap the block against the stop until the sash moves.

CORRECTING A TIGHT SASH

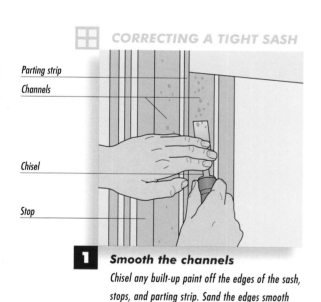

Parting strip

Channels

Chisel

Stop

1 Smooth the channels

Chisel any built-up paint off the edges of the sash, stops, and parting strip. Sand the edges smooth and apply paraffin to them.

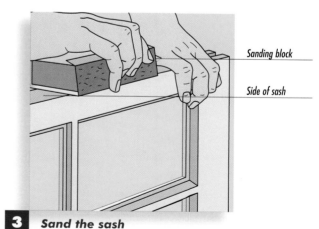

Sanding block

Side of sash

3 Sand the sash

If the sash is too wide, remove it and lightly sand each side. Check constantly for fit—sanding too much can result in a loose sash.

Window Mechanism Repairs

If a double-hung window sash refuses to remain open or closed, or if it jams in one position, repairing or replacing the balance system is the only way to fix the problem. The repair depends on the type of system: pulley and weight, spiral-lift, tension-spring, or cord. Take off any interlocking weatherstripping, then remove the sash. If just the lower sash is affected, remove only that one. If the repair involves the upper sash, remove both.

PULLEY & WEIGHT REPAIRS Pulleys and weights operate most older double-hung windows. The weights are suspended on cords or chains located behind the side jambs. If you're replacing a broken cord, it's a good idea to replace all the cords in the window at the same time, preferably with long-lasting chains or nylon ropes.

To replace a defective chain, follow the instructions for cords. Before detaching the old chain, be sure to immobilize the weights on each side by drawing up the chains until the weights touch the pulleys. Slide a nail through a link at each pulley to hold the chains in place; then detach the chains from the sash.

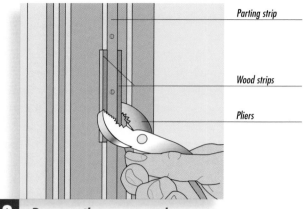

Parting strip

Wood strips

Pliers

2 **Remove the upper sash**
Pull out each parting strip with pliers (use wood strips to protect wood). Angle the upper sash out of the frame; disconnect cords.

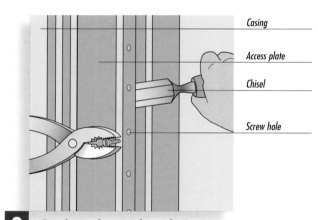

Casing

Access plate

Chisel

Screw hole

3 **Replace the cord or chain**
Remove screws to access plates, and use a chisel to remove the plates. Tape new sash cord or sash chain to the old, then feed it through the pulley. Slip a nail through the chain's other end. Untie the weights, and pull the new cords out of the openings.

▦ REPLACING CORDS OR CHAINS

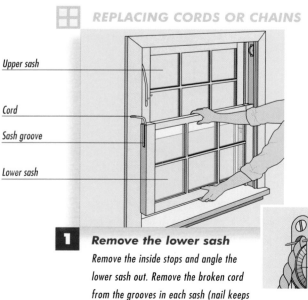

Upper sash

Cord

Sash groove

Lower sash

Nail

Pulley

1 **Remove the lower sash**
Remove the inside stops and angle the lower sash out. Remove the broken cord from the grooves in each sash (nail keeps cord from slipping through pulley).

SPIRAL-LIFT SYSTEM In a spiral-lift balance system, a spring-loaded spiral rod encased in a tube rests in a channel in the side of the stile. The top of the tube is screwed to the side jamb; the rod is attached to a mounting bracket on the bottom of the sash.

REPLACING A SPIRAL LIFT

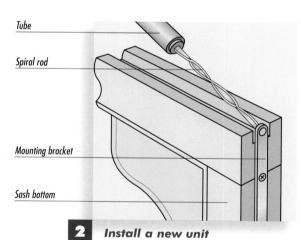

Sash channel

Tube

1 **Remove the sash**

Pry off the stop and unscrew the tube where it's fastened to the top of the side jamb. Let the spring unwind. Raise the sash 6 to 8 inches and angle it out of the frame. If the rod is attached to the bottom of the sash with a detachable hook, unhook it; support the sash in a raised position with a wood block, then unscrew and remove the mounting bracket.

Tube

Spiral rod

Mounting bracket

Sash bottom

2 **Install a new unit**

Position a new tube in the channel and screw it into the top of the side jamb. Pull the spiral rod down as far as it will go and turn it clockwise about four complete turns to tighten. Let the rod retract into the tube far enough so you can fasten the mounting bracket to the bottom of the sash. Replace the sash, adjust tension, and reposition the stop.

Adjusting the spring tension may be all that's needed to make the window operate properly. If the sash creeps up, loosen the spring by detaching the tube from the sash channel and letting the spring unwind a bit. If the sash keeps sliding down, tighten by turning the rod clockwise a few times. If this does not help, replace the unit.

TENSION-SPRING & CORD SYSTEMS In a tension-spring balance system, each window sash is operated by two balance units with spring-loaded drums inside; the units fit into the side jamb close to the top. A flexible metal tape hooks onto a bracket screwed into a groove routed in the sash.

A cord balance system, not shown here, has two spring-loaded reel units that fit into each corner of the top jamb. Nylon cords connect the units to each sash and plastic top, and side-jamb liners conceal the parts. If any component of a tension-spring or cord-balance system breaks, you'll have to remove the unit and install a new one.

REPAIRING CASEMENT, AWNING, & SLIDING WINDOWS Casement and awning windows are operated either by a sliding rod (usually found in older windows) or by a crank and gear mechanism. If a casement window resists opening or closing, look for hardened grease or paint on the sliding rod. Cleaning and lubricating the rod, channel (if any), and pivot points usually solve the problem.

REPLACING A TENSION-SPRING UNIT

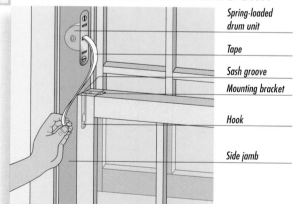

Spring-loaded drum unit

Tape

Sash groove

Mounting bracket

Hook

Side jamb

To replace a tension-spring unit, remove the stop and ease out the sash. Unhook the tape from the bracket and let it wind back slowly on the drum. Remove the screws from the drum plate and pry the unit out of the jamb pocket. Insert the new balance into the pocket and secure it with wood screws. Using long-nosed pliers, pull the tape down and hook the end onto the bracket on the sash.

Windowsill Repairs

To restore a sill that isn't badly damaged, clean out rotten wood with a chisel. Fill in any cracks or shallow holes with epoxy putty. If a crack or hole is very deep, build up the putty in layers, letting each layer dry completely. Then soak the sill with wood preservative. When dry (about 24 hours), coat it with boiled linseed oil and let it dry. Prime and repaint the sill.

A badly damaged sill can also be consolidated with liquid epoxy. Where the wood rot is deeper than 1/4 inch, drill holes to obtain deeper penetration. Apply consolidant at temperatures between 55 degrees and 75 degrees F. The next day, patch holes with epoxy putty, as above.

If you must replace a severely damaged sill, have a new one milled to match at a lumberyard or cut one yourself. Use pressure-treated lumber.

REPLACING A WINDOWSILL

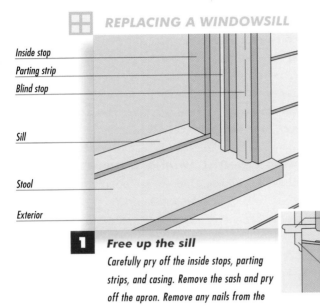

Inside stop
Parting strip
Blind stop
Sill
Stool
Exterior

SIDE VIEW
Stool
Sill
Shim
Apron

1 Free up the sill
Carefully pry off the inside stops, parting strips, and casing. Remove the sash and pry off the apron. Remove any nails from the stool and take it out in one piece.

Blind stop
Parting strip
Side jamb
Sill
Interior wall

2 Remove the sill
Measure the sill's length between the jambs. Saw the sill into three pieces; remove the center piece, then the ends. Cut off nails with a hacksaw.

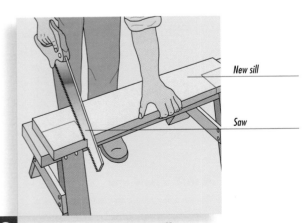

New sill
Saw

3 Cut the replacement sill
Mark the new sill to the correct length. Use the old sill's end pieces as templates, and mark notches. Cut the new sill, beveling the ends for an easier fit.

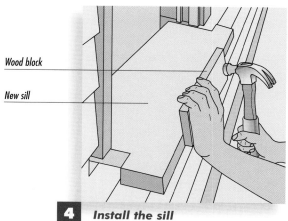

Wood block

New sill

4 **Install the sill**

Tap the sill in place, using a wood block to protect the edge. Don't force it; if it sticks, rasp or sand to the proper length.

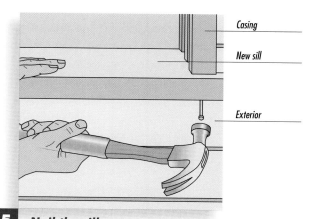

Casing

New sill

Exterior

5 **Nail the sill**

Add shims under the sill until it fits snugly. Nail it to side jambs from underneath. On the inside edge, toenail it to framing with galvanized finishing nails.

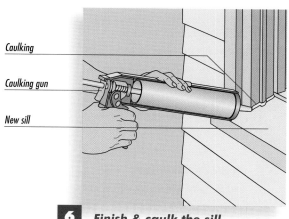

Caulking

Caulking gun

New sill

6 **Finish & caulk the sill**

Sink exposed nail heads, fill holes, and seal the wood. Caulk the sill's edges, prime and paint. Replace the stool, apron, stops, and casings.

BUILDING UP A SILL

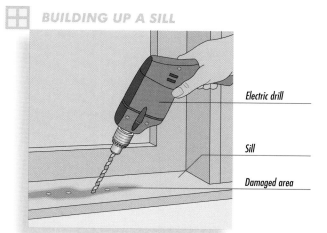

Electric drill

Sill

Damaged area

You can restore a rotted sill by drilling holes and filling them with a liquid consolidant to reinforce the wood. Then cover the sill with a putty-like mixture of resin and hardener, and then paint. Follow instructions on the kit.

Repairing Screens & Storms

To improve the view through your windows, consider replacing the screens. Sagging fiberglass screens look terrible, and rusty metal screens darken rooms. The window screens and storms in your home may be the kind you can remove, or they may be aluminum-frame combination storm and screen windows you can leave in place year-round. Chances are the frames themselves won't need attention nearly as often as the screen. The frames may be wood or metal, the screen either metal (typically aluminum) or fiberglass.

REPLACING SCREEN IN AN ALUMINUM FRAME

Spline

Putty knife

Aluminum frame

Spline channel

Old screen

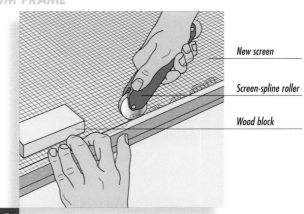

New screen

Screen-spline roller

Wood block

1 **Remove the old screen**
Pry off the splines and pull out the screen. Cut new screen the same size as the frame's outer dimensions, squaring the corners. Place the screen flush with the channel's outer edges on one end and side.

2 **Fit new screen into frame**
Bend the screen into the channel at the end of the frame, using the convex wheel of a screen-spline roller or a putty knife. Use a wood block to weight down the screen.

Convex wheel

3 **Replace the spline**
Push the spline back into the channel, using the concave wheel of the roller or a wood block and hammer. Holding the screen's edges tight, insert splines in the other end and sides.

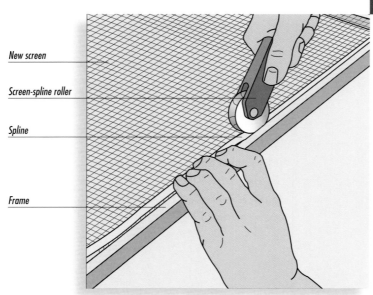

New screen

Screen-spline roller

Spline

Frame

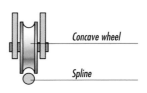

Concave wheel

Spline

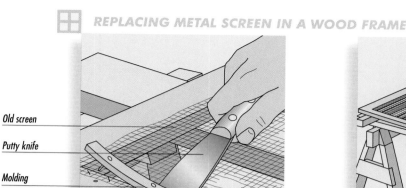

Old screen

Putty knife

Molding

Frame

Wood strip

Frame

New screen

C-clamp

Board

1 **Remove the old screen**
Pry off molding with a putty knife or chisel, working from the ends to the center. Remove old screen. Cut the new screen 2 inches larger than the opening on all sides. Use tin snips for metal. Staple the screen to one end of the frame.

2 **Fit the new screen**
Before stapling the other end, bow the frame. Place $3/4$-inch-thick strips under the ends; clamp in the middle. Staple the remaining end. This prevents sagging.

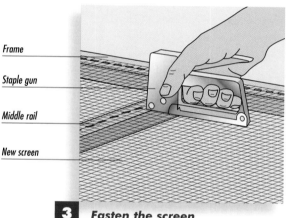

Frame

Staple gun

Middle rail

New screen

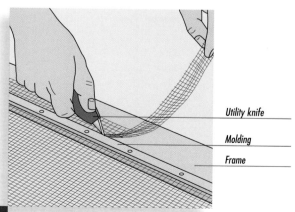

Nail

Molding

3 **Fasten the screen**
Work from the center, pulling the screen tight and stapling it. Staples should be hidden by molding. Do the middle rail last.

4 **Install the molding**
Replace any broken pieces and paint the molding before nailing it in place.

To replace fiberglass screen in a wood frame, follow the instructions for replacing metal screen, but cut the screen with the blade of a utility knife and turn the edges under $1 1/2$ inches to form a hem. To replace fiberglass screen in an aluminum frame, use a screen-spline roller to roll the screen and the spline into the channel in one operation.

Utility knife

Molding

Frame

5 **Cut off excess**
Cut away the excess screen, using the molding as a guide.

Weatherstripping Windows

Cold air entering your house in winter accounts for up to 35 percent of your heating load. Replacing ineffective weatherstripping—or adding weatherstripping where there isn't any—can cut that heat load by 20 percent.

There are many types of weatherstripping: vinyl or plastic V-shaped strips; spring-metal strips; aluminum strips with pliable gaskets; bulb-shaped vinyl; felt strips; and foam strips. Base your choice on window type, the appearance of the material, and your budget. No matter what kind of weatherstripping material you choose, the cost is relatively small compared with the energy savings.

FOR SLIDING WINDOWS Pliable vinyl or plastic V-shaped strips work best for double-hung windows; vinyl strips may even help the sliding action of older windows. These strips are usually adhesive-backed, so no tools are required. If the strips need to be nailed in place, use finishing nails and a hammer and nailset to set the heads flush.

Adhesive-backed foam strips can be applied to the frame at the closing side of horizontal sliding windows. Foam strips can also be used at the top and bottom of double-hung windows: At the top, position the tape in the channel; at the bottom, attach the tape to the underside of the rail. You can also attach weatherstripping to the bottom rail of the top sash, where the sashes meet; aluminum strips with pliable gaskets are good for this job.

FOR SWINGING WINDOWS Both V-shaped and pliable gasket weatherstripping work well on swinging windows. With V-shaped strips, the point of the V should face in the direction that the window opens, except on the hinge side, where the point of the V should be against the hinges.

Peel the covering off the adhesive, and stick the strips in place. If there is no adhesive strip, nail them in place with finishing nails, using a hammer and a nailset to set the heads flush. Attach the pliable gasket-type weatherstripping to the side of the stop with finishing nails; the window should compress the gasket when it closes.

Foam strips can also be used with swinging windows. Attach them to the inside edge of the stop moldings, so that the window presses against them when closed. On the hinged side of the window, attach the foam strip to the jamb.

Open the window fully, peel the cover off the adhesive backing of a vinyl V-shaped strip, and position the strip in the channel, with the open side of the V facing out.

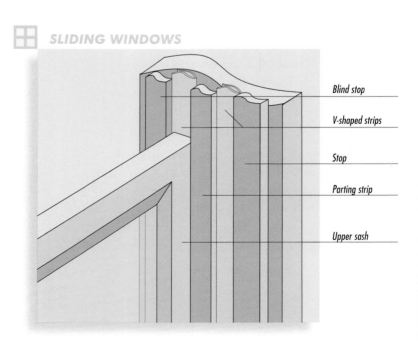

SLIDING WINDOWS

Blind stop

V-shaped strips

Stop

Parting strip

Upper sash

Vinyl V-strips

To use V-shaped strips, peel the covering off the adhesive, and attach V-shaped strips with the sharp point of the V facing out. For types that are not self-adhesive, fasten with finishing nails and set the nail heads flush.

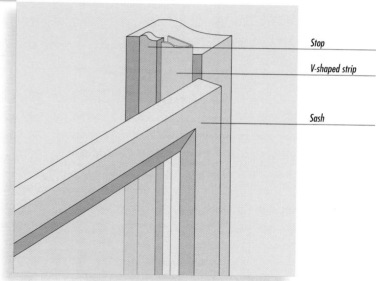

Stop

V-shaped strip

Sash

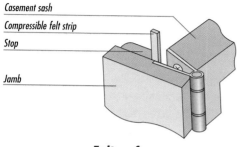

Casement sash

Compressible felt strip

Stop

Jamb

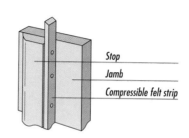

Stop

Jamb

Compressible felt strip

Felt or foam

Nail a compressible felt or foam strip (or remove the covering from the adhesive) to the stop. On the hinge side, attach it to the window frame. Set nail heads flush.

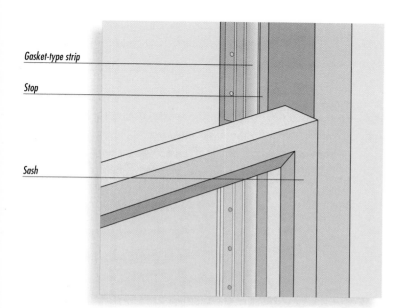

Gasket-type strip

Stop

Sash

Gaskets

On the outside of the window, gaskets should be placed snugly against the sash. Attach with adhesive backing or nail in place.

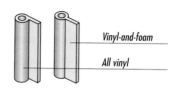

Vinyl-and-foam

All vinyl

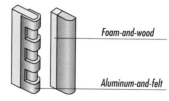

Foam-and-wood

Aluminum-and-felt

Cutting in a Doorway

Opening up a wall with a new doorway can put a whole new spin on the way traffic moves through your home, sometimes making rooms immeasurably more accessible and usable. But before you cut open a hole in a wall to add a doorway, be clear about what you might encounter.

Walls conceal a host of surprises, including wiring, pipes, and ducts that almost inevitably end up being just where you want to place the door. Investigate to discover where these or similar obstructions are located before making a final determination of where your new opening should go (see "Locating Obstructions" on facing page). If you find pipes, ducts, or extensive wiring in the way, the easiest and least expensive option may be to modify your plan for the door's location. Rerouting utilities can be quite involved—often a job for a contractor, unless you're comfortable with a variety of do-it-yourself tasks. This type of construction usually requires a permit and is regulated by local building codes.

It's relatively easy to replace a window with a door. For instance, if your breakfast room has a 6-foot-wide sliding window that overlooks the backyard, you could replace it with a 6-foot sliding door. The framing, hidden behind the drywall, is already nearly complete. To prepare, you just remove the window, the wall's surface material, and the studs below the window.

It's also fairly easy to install an interior door if the wall is not a bearing wall (see page 98). Most interior walls, called partition walls, do not carry the weight of the roof framing, though a major central wall—such as along a hallway—is likely to be bearing. The illustration on page 213 shows the installation of a door in a nonload-bearing partition wall.

Doors are sold individually or as pre-hung systems, where they are already hinged in a jamb and frame. The latter is the easiest type to install, as discussed on pages 212–213. When you buy a pre-hung door, the manufacturer should provide you with the rough opening dimensions you'll need for the structural framing. Normally, these specifications call for an opening large enough to allow an extra $1\frac{1}{2}$ inches on the top and sides around the door's frame. If the door is going into a bearing wall, the rough opening may need to be even taller to allow for a header (see more about this on pages 98–99 and 188–189).

Often it's simplest to remove the wall covering from floor to ceiling between two bordering studs (the new "king" studs) that will remain in place. On taller walls—10 feet, for example—cutting your opening slightly larger than the intended doorway may save extra drywall work later. Try to use at least one existing stud as part of the rough framing.

Drywall is easy to remove—you just cut along your outline with a saber saw and pry the cut panels off the studs. To remove plaster and lath, cut through the lath with a saber saw or reciprocating saw equipped with a blade made for the job—be sure to wear safety glasses, a dust mask, and gloves. (Be sure there are no pipes or wires inside the wall where you will be cutting.) To prevent unnecessary vibration, hold the saw's foot plate firmly against the plaster. Then use a prybar to pull down chunks of plaster and remove lath from studs.

Finally, be aware that when you remove a section of wall to install a new doorway, the floor must be repaired—there won't be any finished flooring where the wall once stood. For information on floor repairs and improvements, see "Floors & Stairs," beginning on page 128.

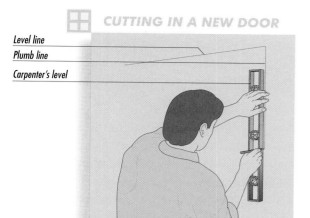

Level line
Plumb line
Carpenter's level

1 Lay out the door's location

Locate and mark all nearby wall studs. Using a carpenter's level, draw straight, level, and plumb lines to outline the rough opening's location. With a hammer, knock a small hole between studs in the area's center and look for obstructions (use a flashlight, if necessary). Then pry off the base molding and use a saber saw to cut through the drywall along the outline (don't cut the studs). Finally, pry off the drywall.

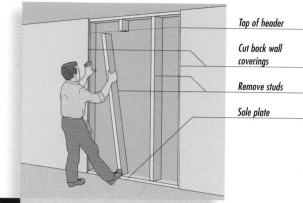

Top of header
Cut back wall coverings
Remove studs
Sole plate

2 Remove the studs

Cut the studs inside the opening to the height required for the rough opening plus a new header (bearing walls must be supported properly first). Plan to use one 2 by 4 laid flat for a header. Use a square to mark the studs on the face and one edge, then cut them with a handsaw or reciprocating saw. Pry the studs from the sole plate (bend over the nails left poking upward).

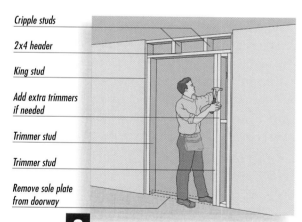

Cripple studs
2x4 header
King stud
Add extra trimmers if needed
Trimmer stud
Trimmer stud
Remove sole plate from doorway

3 Frame the new opening

Measure and cut the header and toenail it to the king studs with 2 1/2-inch nails. Nail the header to the bottoms of the cripple studs with 3 1/2-inch nails. Cut the sole plate flush with the bordering king studs, and pry it loose from the subfloor. Then cut trimmer studs; nail them to the king studs with 3-inch nails in a staggered pattern. You'll probably need to adjust the doorway's width by adding spacer blocks and an extra pair of trimmers on one side, as shown.

LOCATING OBSTRUCTIONS

On plan-view and elevation-view sketches of the wall, show the position of the nearest intersecting wall and note clues to what lies behind the wall.

From outside the house, look for any pipes coming through the roof directly above the proposed door opening. Pipes projecting above the roof indicate drainpipes in the wall directly below; you may find water pipes as well.

Check the second-story rooms above the proposed opening. Is there a radiator against the wall? If so, there may be a hot-water or steam-heating pipe in the window area. Is there a hot-air register in the wall under the proposed opening or above it on the second floor? If so, a heating duct may be in the wall. Remove the register's grille and reach into the duct to determine if it leads to the proposed door area.

On your sketches, mark the locations of receptacles, switches, and wall lights—then figure what the likely route might be for wires running between them. If you have an attic, go into it with a light, tape measure, pencil, and your sketch. (Be sure to step only on solid structural members!) Locate the top plate of the wall you propose to open. Measuring from the nearest side wall (you should be able to see the top of it), mark on your sketches the locations of any wires, pipes, or ducts coming through the top plate. If your house has a basement or crawl space, repeat the process. When you've marked all this information on your sketches, you should have a good idea of the locations of wires, pipes, and ducts hiding in the wall.

Installing a Pre-hung Door

With a factory-manufactured pre-hung door, hinges attach the door to the preassembled jambs, and the sill and jambs are braced to keep the whole assembly square until you install it. For more about the types of doors available, see pages 184–187.

Pre-hung interior doors normally have a piece of scrap trim stapled to the bottom of the door and the jambs. After carrying the door to where you intend to install it, you remove this temporary brace (you must be able to open and close the door as you place shims between the studs and jambs, drive nails to hold the jambs, and check the alignment of jambs).

When you're ordering a pre-hung door, make sure you specify the wall's overall thickness. The jambs ordered for plaster-covered walls must be wider than those for walls finished with drywall. When you fit the jamb into the rough opening, you'll see that the jamb is wider than the rough framing, and it will stick out on either side—be sure the distances are proper to allow for drywall, plaster, or sheathing and siding (in the case of an exterior door).

For information on how to prepare the rough opening, see pages 210–211.

POSITION THE DOOR PROPERLY Place the door in the rough opening, centering it in the frame and fastening it as discussed on facing page. Using a piece of drywall (or other finish material) as a spacer against the trimmer studs, slightly adjust the unit back and forth until flush with the spacer. (If the finish floor is not yet installed, raise the side jambs to the correct level with blocks; you want to avoid cutting off the bottom of a new door when possible.)

Before nailing the jambs, it's very important to make sure the door fits squarely in the opening and that the jambs are plumb, both from side to side and from front to back. Drive pairs of tapered wooden shims between the jambs and the trimmer studs (if the casing is attached to the jambs, insert shims from the open side) to adjust the unit and hold it in place until you nail it.

SECURE THE DOOR HINGE-SIDE FIRST Start by shimming the lower hinge side of the door. Nail through the jamb and shims partway (1 inch) into the stud with a $3\frac{1}{2}$-inch finishing nail; position the nail where the stop molding will cover it. Insert shims next to the upper hinge location, check the jamb for plumb, and nail partway. Again, shim, plumb, and nail halfway between the top and middle hinge positions. Repeat between the middle and bottom hinges. Check to make sure the jamb above the doorway is level. Now shim the opposite jamb at similar locations, but don't nail where you'll need to cut for the latch.

COMPLETE THE INSTALLATION Remove any bracing or blocking tacked to the unit. Close the door and check that there is the same amount of space (about $\frac{1}{16}$ to $\frac{1}{8}$ inch) between the edges of the door and the jambs. If the door sticks or is out of alignment, pull nails in the area that seems to be the problem, using a block to protect the jambs from your hammer. Adjust shims and renail. Install the lockset as discussed on pages 218–220. Drive the nails home and set the heads with a nailset. Cut the shims off flush with the jambs, using a handsaw (you can just break off short, thin pieces). Finish with door casing or other trim (see pages 111–113).

For exterior doors, nail the threshold between the jambs, shimming below it if the threshold does not rest securely on the subfloor. Finally, install the stop molding with $1\frac{1}{2}$-inch finishing nails.

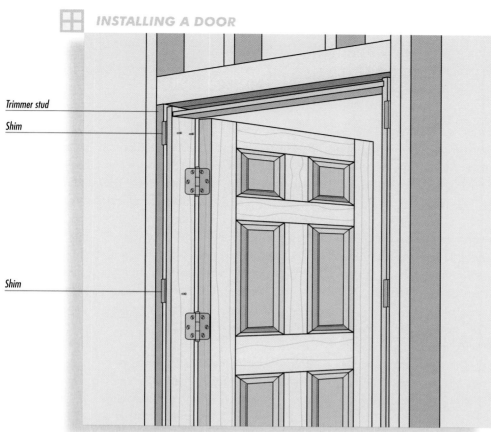

Trimmer stud

Shim

Shim

Position the pre-hung assembly in the opening and temporarily secure it in place with shims and finishing nails, as shown in the inset and discussed in the text on facing page. Adjust for plumb as necessary. After final adjustments are made, set the nail heads, cut the shims flush using a handsaw, and install the trim.

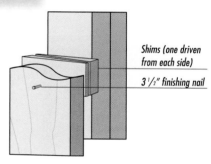

Shims (one driven from each side)

3 $\frac{1}{2}$" finishing nail

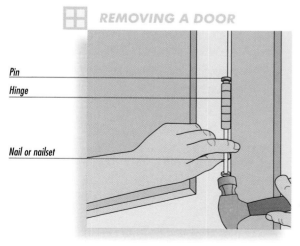

Pin

Hinge

Nail or nailset

To remove a door, close the door securely (place a wedge under it or have a helper hold the door). Using a hammer and a nail, gently tap on the bottom of the lowest hinge pin or on the underside of its head to drive it up and out of the hinge barrel. Remove the middle pin, if any; then remove the top pin. Carefully dislodge the door from its hinges. When you reinstall the door, interlock the hinge leaves, then replace the top pin first. Next replace the middle and bottom pins. Tap the pins home with a hammer only after the hinges are correctly aligned.

Installing a Patio Door

Door Improvements

Installing a sliding or French door is a wonderful way to open up your house to the yard. Not only will you gain interior light and improve the traffic flow to your yard—but the new view might inspire you to add that deck you've been dreaming about.

For information about buying doors, see pages 184–187. If you choose a French door rather than a sliding patio door, be sure there is space for it to swing open. Choose a door that is pre-assembled for relatively easy installation.

This project combines a variety of tasks that are discussed elsewhere in this book. Installation requires temporarily supporting the ceiling, opening up a wall, cutting the wall studs and rough-framing the opening to receive the new door, installing the door in the opening, then adding trim around the new door.

For information about opening up a wall, see pages 104–105. Use the principles discussed on pages 188–189 ("Framing for Windows & Doors") and pages 210–211 ("Cutting in a Doorway") to do the rough framing. Turn to pages 111–113 for a discussion of installing various types of trim.

The rough framing needed is the same for either a French or sliding door. You build the rough frame just as you would for a 5- or 6-foot-wide window, but you don't install a rough sill and cripple studs at the base—you open the wall all the way to the floor.

The process of installing the door in the rough opening is almost identical to the techniques used for installing a window (pages 192–194) and installing a pre-hung door (pages 212–213). The primary differences are that you'll be working with a particularly large (and therefore heavy) exterior door, and you'll need to properly mount the threshold to the subfloor.

Also, it's important to install metal flashing along the subfloor at the base to protect the structure from water damage. Either shape rolled aluminum flashing to fit, or measure the opening and have the flashing made up in a sheet metal shop. It should overlap the rough framing and extend 6 inches up the sides of the door.

Refer to the pages referenced as you work your way through these steps. Note: If your siding is metal or vinyl, you'll have to allow for the appropriate trims (see pages 302–305) when cutting the siding.

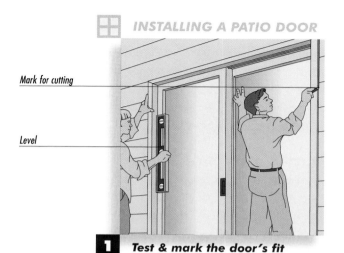

Mark for cutting

Level

1 **Test & mark the door's fit**

Have a helper assist you in test-fitting the door in the rough opening. Center it and make sure it's plumb, using a level to test along the jamb edges. If it isn't level, place shims under the side jamb to raise one end. Trace around the brick mold (outside trim) to mark the siding for cutting.

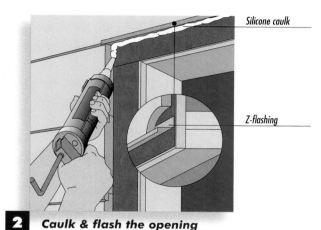

Silicone caulk

Z-flashing

2 **Caulk & flash the opening**

After cutting the siding and preparing the rough opening as discussed on pages 192–194, apply silicone caulk liberally along the subfloor where the threshold will go. Also caulk on top of the building paper at the side and top jambs where the brick mold will be installed. Tuck a piece of Z-flashing under the siding across the opening's top to shed rainwater.

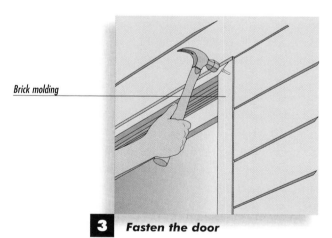

Brick molding

3 **Fasten the door**

With a helper, position, shim, and plumb the door in the center of the opening. Fasten it there using the same methods discussed on page 194 for installing a window. Outside, use $2\frac{1}{2}$-inch galvanized casing nails, spaced every 12 inches, to nail the brick molding to the framing members. Set the nail heads and fill with putty.

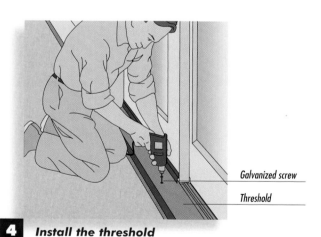

Galvanized screw

Threshold

4 **Install the threshold**

Screw the threshold to the subfloor and seal any gap with sill nosing. Drill pilot holes and fasten with $2\frac{1}{2}$-inch galvanized casing nails. Caulk the threshold with sill nosing. Also caulk around the perimeter of the brick mold, using paintable silicone caulking compound.

Installing Storm & Screen Doors

Storm doors block drafts in the winter, helping to minimize energy loss, and many have clip-in tempered glass panels that you can remove and replace with insect screen panels for the summer. In addition, storm doors protect the prime (main) door, and newer models can actually add to your home's curb appeal.

CHOICES Sturdy storm doors that don't rattle, twist, or dent are made with a solid particleboard core that has an outer aluminum skin given a baked-on finish. They are sold as pre-framed units that are easily screwed into existing doorjambs. Both storm and screen doors come in standard door widths of 30, 32, 34, and 36 inches and may be hinged on either side. (When buying one, be sure you get the right size—measure the door's opening between the door-jambs, not the size of the door.) Some are made so that the unused glass or screening panel stores inside the door. Those designed for security often have a heavy-duty aluminum or steel frame with a foam or solid wood core and tamper-proof hinges and deadbolt.

If you want to display your front door or maximize light and views, choose a storm door with a full-height glass panel. The mid-view type has a solid panel in the bottom third of the door; a high-view door has a glazed section that extends to about half the door's height.

If you know the brand of door on your home, check to see if the manufacturer provides a door kit for storms and screens. This is an especially good idea if you have a sliding or French door. The kit will match the door's design and fit properly over the threshold.

ABOUT INSTALLATION Storm doors come with full instructions and a template for mounting the hardware. Major manufacturers offer assistance by phone and instructions or troubleshooting information on the World Wide Web. There are two areas where you can make mistakes that are difficult to fix. The first can occur when cutting the vertical mounting frames—these must fit your openings. Don't cut them too short. Also, when drilling a wood-core storm door for the hardware, drill holes precisely. Manufacturers supply a template to make this job easier. Take your time and follow the instructions.

DOOR CLOSERS To automatically close the storm or screen door, install a closer—either a simple chain-linked snubber or a pneumatic or hydraulic type, as shown on facing page. The closer ensures that the door closes smoothly and protects the door from being opened too wide or with too much force. A closer also keeps the door from being jerked open by the wind.

Installing a closer is fairly simple. Before you begin, check that the door operation is smooth and that the door hardware is in good working order. If you're installing a snubber, fasten the door mounting bracket to the door's top rail and the jamb mounting bracket to the head jamb. Adjust the length of the chain as necessary. For a pneumatic closer, install the door mounting bracket on the door's top rail, mount the closer in the bracket, and fasten the jamb mounting bracket to the hinge jamb; then adjust the tension.

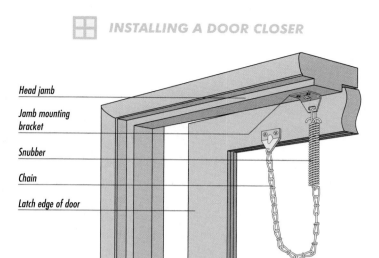

Head jamb

Jamb mounting bracket

Snubber

Chain

Latch edge of door

Snubber

This is the least expensive door-closing device. A simple chain with a coil, it can be used on aluminum- or wood-frame storms and screens. Instructions on the package should show you where and how to mount the door mounting bracket.

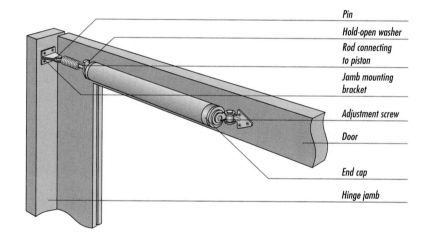

Pin

Hold-open washer

Rod connecting to piston

Jamb mounting bracket

Adjustment screw

Door

End cap

Hinge jamb

Pneumatic closer

A pneumatic closer provides a little resistance so the screen or storm door won't slam shut. The hold-open washer allows you to prop the door open when you're carrying groceries into the house. Turn the adjustment screw to reduce the tension on lightweight doors.

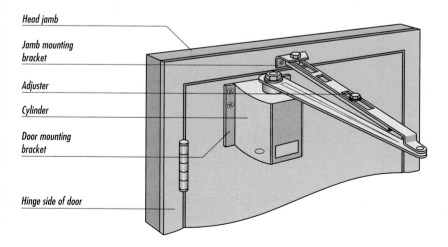

Head jamb

Jamb mounting bracket

Adjuster

Cylinder

Door mounting bracket

Hinge side of door

Hydraulic closer

To make sure an exterior door closes automatically, you can install a hydraulic closer on it. Some types fit only a right-handed or left-handed door; others can be adjusted for either type of door by inserting a screwdriver in the adjustment screw, pushing in, and turning the screw 180 degrees. A slight adjustment to the same screw changes the door's closing speed.

Installing a Lockset

When doorknobs or latches cease to work properly, replacement is often the easiest and fastest answer to the problem. And replacing door hardware can be a very effective way to dress up a door—giving it just the type of visual detail that can add character and style to a home.

Many exterior doors have a standard cylindrical lockset—the type shown on this page; it has a round body that fits into a hole drilled in the door. Some exterior doors, especially front doors, have a mortise lockset, with a squared body that slides into a deep notch in the door's edge. The latter type may have a combined latch and deadbolt mechanism. In addition, exterior doors may have a deadbolt lock or a surface-mounted rim lock (see pages 221–223). Interior doors have either a cylindrical lockset operated with a push button, or a tubular lockset, similar to a cylindrical one but simpler and less rugged.

Here we look at how to replace a lockset and how to prepare a new door to receive a lockset. If you need to drill holes to install a new lockset, be sure that you have the right size of hole saw (usually $2\frac{1}{8}$ inch for the lock hole) and spade bit (usually 1 inch for the latch hole). You'll have best results using a hole saw with an integral guide bit.

⊞ REPLACING A LOCKSET

Faceplate
Handle trim
Shank
Interior knob
Screwdriver

1   Remove the interior knob

Remove screws from the inside face. If there are none, look for a small slot in the shank. Push the tip of a small screwdriver or nail into the slot, then remove the knob and handle trim.

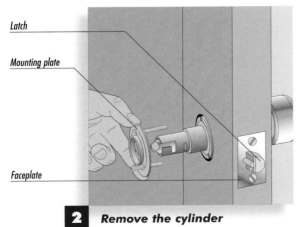

Latch
Mounting plate
Faceplate

2   Remove the cylinder

Unscrew and remove the mounting plate; slip out the knob and cylinder. Unscrew and remove the faceplate and latch assembly, then remove the strike plate from the door jamb.

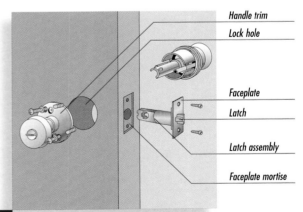

Handle trim
Lock hole
Faceplate
Latch
Latch assembly
Faceplate mortise

3   Install the new lockset

Insert and screw on the new latch assembly and faceplate. Holding the exterior knob and cylinder, slide the cylinder in and engage it with the latch assembly. Attach the mounting plate, handle trim, and knob. Screw on the new strike plate (see page 220) and make sure that the latch engages in the strike plate. (See pages 230–231 if it doesn't.)

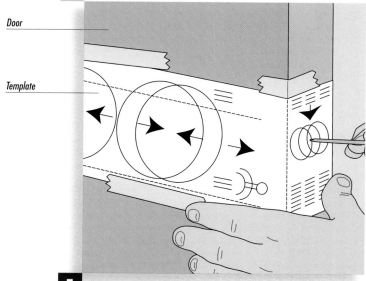

Door

Template

1 Locate the holes

A template and instructions should be included with your new lockset. Plan to place the knob 36 to 37 inches above the floor. Tape the template to the door, then use a nail or awl to mark the centers of the lock and latch holes.

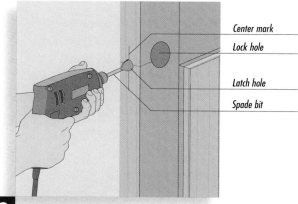

Center mark

Lock hole

Latch hole

Spade bit

2 Drill the holes

Always bore the lock hole first, using a hole saw. As soon as the guide bit on the hole saw exits the opposite side of the door, stop and continue from the other side. This will help prevent tearout when the hole saw exits. Use a spade bit to bore the latch hole, as shown. Take care to drill straight, level holes.

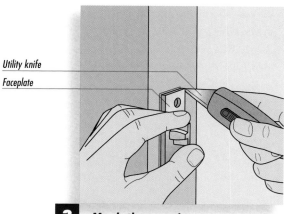

Utility knife

Faceplate

3 Mark the mortise

Insert the latch assembly. Holding it square, trace the outline of the faceplate with a sharp pencil. Then use a utility knife or awl to score the outline. Alternatively, trace around the faceplate with a utility knife, as shown.

(continued on page 220)

 BUYING TIPS: If possible, take the old lockset with you when you're buying a new one. If you can't, know:

▪ **the type of lock**
▪ **the diameter of the cylinder and latch holes**
▪ **the distance from the door's edge to the doorknob's center**
▪ **the door's thickness**
▪ **the direction in which the door swings**

219

Installing a Lockset

(continued from page 219)

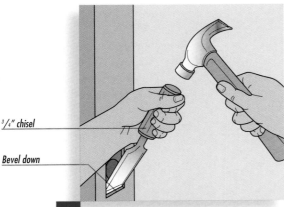

³/₄" chisel

Bevel down

4 **Cut the mortise**

With a ³/₄-inch chisel and hammer, score the two long sides; hold the chisel at a 45-degree angle, with the beveled edge toward the wood. Working from the center of the mortise, tap the chisel to the bottom, then to the top. The finished mortise should be about ³/₁₆-inch deep. Insert the latch; if necessary, shave off a little more wood.

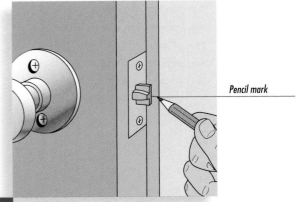

Pencil mark

5 **Locate the strike plate**

With the lockset installed and screws tightened, close the door until the latch just hits the jamb. With a pencil, mark the spot where the center of the latch contacts the jamb.

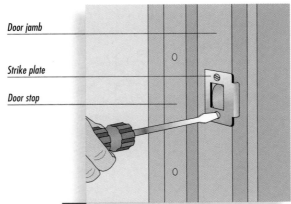

Door jamb

Strike plate

Door stop

6 **Install the strike plate**

Using the pencil mark as your guide, hold the strike plate against the jamb and trace its outline with a sharp pencil. Score the outline and chisel the mortise as described in Step 4. Note that you may have to cut the mortise all the way to the edge of the jamb. After checking the alignment, attach the strike plate to the jamb with screws.

CUSTOM-DRILLING DOORS

Lock manufacturers provide all the hardware for locksets. If you're ordering a pre-hung door and know the measurements of the lock you will be installing, you can give the template and specifications to the door manufacturer. They will bore the necessary holes for the door and jamb. This will make installing your lock much easier. If not, you'll have to drill the holes yourself.

Installing Deadbolts

Deadbolt locksets provide security on exterior doors. The deadbolt is stronger and more difficult to tamper with than a conventional lock, and the bolt's "throw" (the distance it extends) is generally longer. Replacing a deadbolt lockset is easy if you buy one similar to the lockset you are replacing.

SINGLE-CYLINDER DEADBOLTS Opened from the exterior with a key, and from inside the house by hand with a thumb turn, single-cylinder deadbolts are often keyed differently from the knob and latch set on the door.

DOUBLE-CYLINDER DEADBOLTS These locks are opened by a key on both sides. While these are the most secure on doors with windows, local building and fire codes may prohibit them because they can make it difficult to exit the building in an emergency. Check the regulations before installing one.

SURFACE-MOUNTED LOCKS Surface-mounted locks (also known as rim locks or vertical deadbolts) can be used as the only lockset on an exterior door or in conjunction with other locks for added security. They are easier to install than deadbolt locks, but they are also less visually appealing from the interior. The lock has a bolt that fits through the strike plate on the doorjamb and is controlled by either a key on the outside or a thumb turn on the inside of the door. It can improve security on secondary entry doors, such as those to basements and back porches. The rim lock has a bolt that fits through the strike plate on the doorjamb and is controlled by either a key on the outside or a thumb turn on the inside of the door.

(continued on page 222)

DEADBOLT LOCKSET

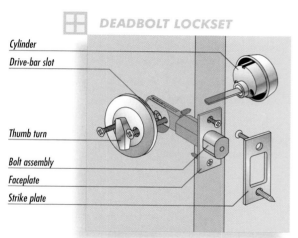

Cylinder
Drive-bar slot
Thumb turn
Bolt assembly
Faceplate
Strike plate

A single-cylinder deadbolt has a thumb turn on the inside and a keyed cylinder on the outside. With a double-cylinder deadbolt, a second keyed cylinder replaces the thumb turn.

SURFACE-MOUNTED LOCK

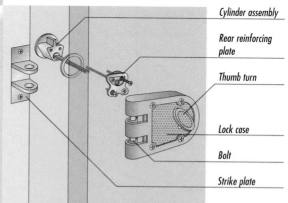

Cylinder assembly
Rear reinforcing plate
Thumb turn
Lock case
Bolt
Strike plate

A surface-mounted lockset adds security, not beauty, to a door. Use the lockset's template and package instructions to guide installation.

Installing Deadbolts

(continued from page 221)
If you are replacing a surface-mounted lock, buy a new one of the same type and size and proceed with the instructions on facing page. For a new installation, tape the template to the door as instructed by the manufacturer. Mark guide holes with a nail or awl, then drill the holes.

Door Improvements

▦ INSTALLING A DEADBOLT

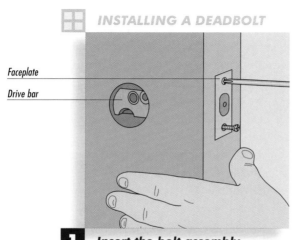

Faceplate

Drive bar

1 Insert the bolt assembly

Drill holes in the door (unless you're replacing an old deadbolt), using the manufacturer's template as a guide. Insert the bolt assembly and screw the faceplate to the edge of the door.

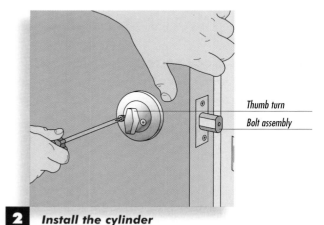

Thumb turn

Bolt assembly

2 Install the cylinder

Mount the cylinder assembly by carefully and precisely inserting the drive bar into the drive-bar slot. Attach the cylinder to the thumb turn with two mounting screws. Test the bolt to ensure that it moves in and out.

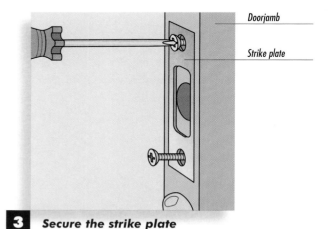

Doorjamb

Strike plate

3 Secure the strike plate

Use 3-inch screws to secure the strike plate to the doorjamb. If this is a new installation, first cut a mortise for the strike plate as explained in Step 4 on page 220. Then drill a recess hole for the bolt.

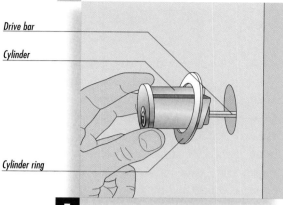

Drive bar

Cylinder

Cylinder ring

1 Install the cylinder ring

Slide the ring over the cylinder. From the outside of the door, insert the cylinder and drive bar into the hole so the keyhole is on the outside and the bar is in the horizontal position.

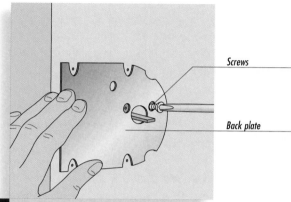

Screws

Back plate

2 Mount the back plate

Drill the necessary holes, then place the back plate ⅛ inch from the door edge on the inside. Drive screws through the plate into the screw holes in the cylinder.

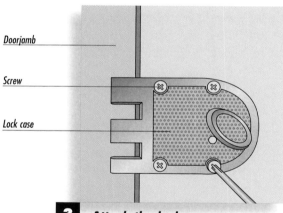

Doorjamb

Screw

Lock case

3 Attach the lock case

Place bolt in the unlocked position. Fit the drive bar into the slot on the rear side of the lock case and attach it to the inside of the door using the screws provided with the lock.

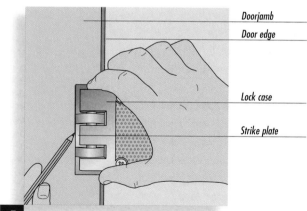

Doorjamb

Door edge

Lock case

Strike plate

4 Mount the strike plate

Hold the strike plate in position and measure and mark it when the bolt is in the locked position. Cut a mortise, if necessary, and screw the strike plate in place on the jamb.

Loose or Binding Doors

Age and continual use can cause even a well-fitted door to loosen, bind, or warp. Binding or loose doors—or doors that have latches that don't catch properly—are relatively easy to fix. On the other hand, a door that's badly warped will have to be replaced.

You don't necessarily have to remove a door to fix it. If you're working on just one hinge at a time or on the top of a door, you need only open the door partially and drive a wedge underneath the latch side to hold the door steady. But for other repairs, such as sanding or planing the side or bottom of a door, you'll need to remove it from its hinges to effectively do the repairs.

TIGHTENING A LOOSE DOOR If a door is too small for its frame, an easy solution is to install weatherstripping on the latch side of the jamb. If a loose door is causing latch problems, you may be able to adjust the strike plate. If the latch doesn't reach the strike plate, shim out the plate or add another strike plate. If the latch still won't reach, shim out the door's hinges.

Often, simply tightening loose hinges gets a sagging door back in alignment. Clean off any dirt and repair or replace any bent hinges. Tighten loose hinge screws. If they can't be tightened, remove them and repair the screw holes with glued-in wood dowels or, for lightweight doors, glued-in toothpicks. Cut the patch flush and drill new pilot holes for the screws.

ADJUSTING A WARPED DOOR To fix a slightly warped door, adjust the stop, partially shim the hinges, or add a hinge. Where there's a slight bow on the hinge side, centering a third hinge between the top and bottom ones often pulls the door back into alignment. If the bow is near the lock side and the door latches only when slammed, first try adjusting the latch. Then try removing and repositioning the stop, as for a window. If necessary, adjust the strike plate. If the top or bottom of the door does not meet the stop on the lock side, try repositioning the stop and the strike plate.

You may also have to shim the hinges to change the angle of the door's swing. You can move a door closer to the lock side of the jamb by inserting a shim under the hinge leaves. Use thin sheet brass or dense, hard-surface cardboard (such as a postcard). Double if you need thicker shims. Place a half shim under each hinge leaf either on the side of the leaf that's closest to the pin or on the opposite side (depending on the warp). Usually the other hinge is shimmed in the opposite way, on the side of the leaf farthest from the pin.

BINDING DOORS Identify the spots that bind by sliding a thin strip of cardboard or wood between the door and jambs. Look for a buildup of paint. Chisel off excess and sand. Coat the door edges and the jambs with paraffin.

If you must remove excess wood from the door edges, sand with coarse, followed by finer, sandpaper. Plane only if absolutely necessary. When sanding or planing the stiles, concentrate on the hinge side since the lock side is usually beveled to allow for a tight fit.

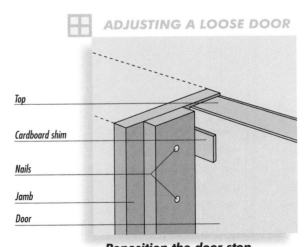

ADJUSTING A LOOSE DOOR

Top

Cardboard shim

Nails

Jamb

Door

Reposition the door stop
If a door is loose because it's warped, you can reposition the stop, spacing it slightly with a thin cardboard shim; nail the stop in place.

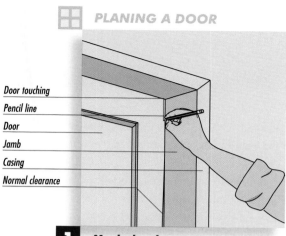

Door touching
Pencil line
Door
Jamb
Casing
Normal clearance

1 **Mark the door**

Use a pencil to carefully mark the area to be planed on both faces of the door before removing it from the hinges. Keep a close eye on your marks as you plane, supporting the door as shown below right.

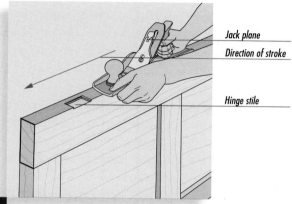

Jack plane
Direction of stroke

Hinge stile

2 **Plane the stile**

Use long strokes with the plane parallel to the stile; the blade should be wider than the thickness of the door so the cuts will be level. Cut with the grain. After you plane, deepen the hinge mortises. If you're planing the lock side, be sure to reform the bevel.

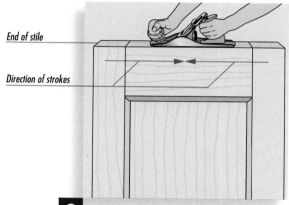

End of stile

Direction of strokes

3 **Plane the top or bottom**

Plane from each end toward the center to avoid splitting the ends of the stiles. Keep the plane flat, and stop before you reach the end of the forward stroke.

☞ **SUPPORTING A DOOR**

One way to support a door while you're working on it is to set it on edge, and pad and wedge one end into a corner of the room. A better way is to build door jacks. The door's weight will bend the plywood strips and press the 2-by-4 wood blocks against the door like a vise.

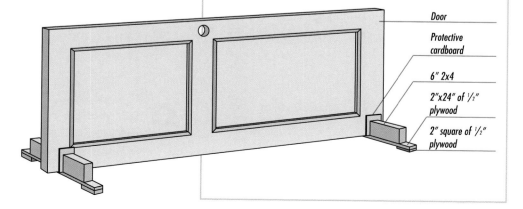

Door
Protective cardboard
6" 2x4
2"x24" of ½" plywood
2" square of ½" plywood

Replacing a Door

With new construction, installing a pre-hung door unit, as discussed on pages 212–213, is usually far easier than building a frame and hanging a door in it. But if you want to replace a door in an existing doorjamb, it's easier and less expensive to just buy a door and hang it.

Before purchasing a replacement door, remove the old door and measure the opening from top to bottom on both sides. Then measure across the opening at two or more points; check the upper corners with a steel square to make sure the opening is square. Doors, particularly hollow-core ones, have only a $1/2$-inch trim margin. You can't cut or plane them more than that or the baffles in the middle of the door will be exposed. Be sure the replacement door will fit without a lot of trimming. Double-check all measurements before cutting.

Here are a few points to keep in mind when hanging a door:

■ Sand or plane any excess wood up to $1/16$ inch on the door's top and bottom, up to $1/4$ inch on the sides. Saw off any excess that's greater; then sand.

■ Leave a $1/16$-inch clearance around the door on the top and sides. Bottom clearance should be at least $1/2$ inch more if you need to clear a rug.

■ Bevel the lock side of the door $1/8$ inch so the door will clear the jamb as it opens and closes. If the door is already beveled, install it so the beveled edge is on the lock side, not the hinge side.

■ When installing a hinge on the door itself, leave at least a $3/8$-inch margin between the edge of the door and the hinge-leaf edge.

■ If you're hanging a new door in an existing frame, use the existing hinges if possible. If you can't use them or must move them, follow the instructions for cutting a strike plate mortise on page 220.

■ Place the top hinge about 7 inches below the top of the door; the bottom hinge the same distance from the bottom.

■ Hinge mortises are recesses into which hinge leaves are fitted so they sit flush with the door or jamb surface. You'll need to cut hinge mortises if you're hanging a new door.

INSTALLING A REPLACEMENT DOOR

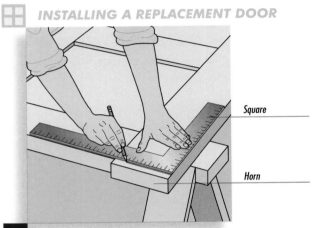

Square

Horn

1 **Prepare the door**
If the replacement door has horns, mark them and cut them off flush with a saw. If the opening isn't square, mark the door itself to fit, being careful not to exceed the door's trim margin (usually $1/2$ inch).

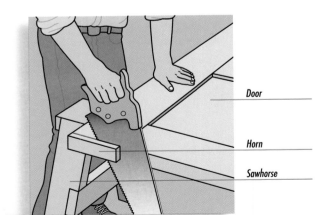

Door

Horn

Sawhorse

2 **Test, mark, & cut the door**
Place the door in the opening and shim at the top for a $1/16$-inch clearance; insert wedges under the door to hold it in place. Mark and cut the bottom, leaving a minimum $1/2$-inch clearance.

3

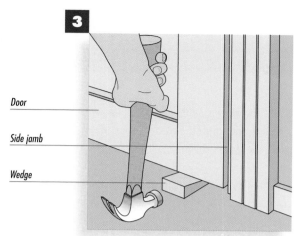

Door

Side jamb

Wedge

Trim the door

Wedge the door snugly against the lock side, maintaining the $1/16$-inch top clearance. Mark a trim line for a $1/8$-inch clearance on the hinge side, and then trim. Bevel the lock side if necessary.

4

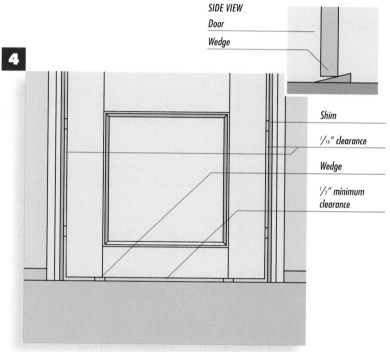

SIDE VIEW

Door

Wedge

Shim

$1/16$" clearance

Wedge

$1/2$" minimum clearance

Wedge the door in place

Hold the door in position with shims and wedges, and double-check the clearances—$1/16$ inch on top and sides, a minimum of $1/2$ inch on the bottom. Sand where needed.

5

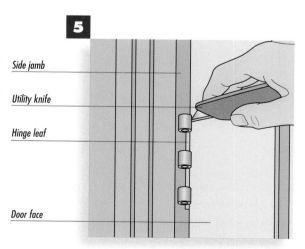

Side jamb

Utility knife

Hinge leaf

Door face

Mark hinge positions

Remove the hinge-side shims and push the door tightly against the hinge jamb. Mark the hinge locations on the door with a utility knife, using the hinge leaves on the jamb as guides. Outline the hinges, using the marks made on the door. With a wood chisel, mortise recesses for the hinge leaves.

Replacing a Threshold or Sill

A door sill forms the bottom of the frame at an exterior doorway and serves a function similar to a windowsill—it serves as a durable base that diverts water away from the door and house. The sill fits snugly under the casing and against or under the jambs, as shown on facing page.

Fastened to the sill is a threshold, which helps seal the air space under a door. Thresholds are often used in interior doorways, too, to cover a transition between different flooring materials.

Because all sills and thresholds are exposed to continual foot traffic and exterior ones are exposed to the elements, they can become worn or damaged and may need to be replaced.

TYPES Also called saddles, thresholds are made from either hardwood or metal (usually aluminum). Special types may act as weatherstripping by mating with a matching strip installed on the bottom of the door; because the pieces interlock, they prevent cold-air entry.

Other flat thresholds can be installed for wheelchair access. With these, the door's bottom edge must be weather-stripped (see pages 234–235).

ABOUT REMOVAL Remove a damaged threshold or sill very carefully so you don't damage the door frame or, in the case of a sill, any flashing underneath. If the old threshold is metal, just unscrew and remove it. Be sure your replacement is long enough, and measure carefully before cutting the new threshold to length. (For cutting an aluminum threshold, use a hacksaw or a saber saw with a metal cutting blade, and wear safety glasses.)

INSTALLATION NOTES Check that the clearance between the bottom of the door and the new threshold is about 1/8 inch. If it's less, mark the bottom of the door, using the new threshold as a guide, and sand or trim the door to fit.

Once a wooden threshold is in place, sink the nail heads or countersink screws and fill the holes. Sand smooth and coat with clear penetrating wood sealer or polyurethane.

REPLACING A THRESHOLD

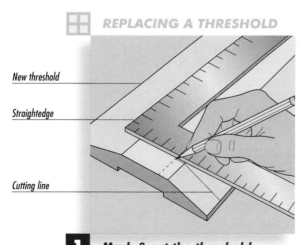

New threshold

Straightedge

Cutting line

1 **Mark & cut the threshold**
Mark the new threshold to fit between the jambs; cut, notching the ends to fit around the stops. Sand all cut edges. Caulk the underside and ends; center it under the door.

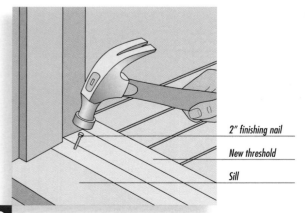

2" finishing nail

New threshold

Sill

2 **Fasten the threshold in place**
Nail the threshold to the sill with 2-inch finishing nails (predrill the holes). Countersink the nail heads and fill the holes with wood putty. Finish the threshold.

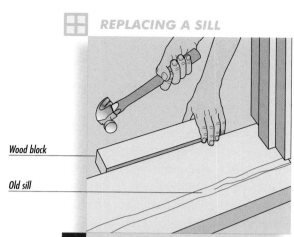

Wood block

Old sill

1 *Remove the old sill*

After removing any nails, drive out the old sill (or saw it into three pieces and remove the center, then the ends). Take care not to damage any flashing underneath.

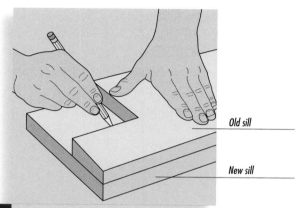

Old sill

New sill

2 *Mark & cut the new sill*

Using the old sill as a template, mark and cut the new sill to fit. If the old sill isn't in one piece, fit it together and make very accurate measurements before cutting.

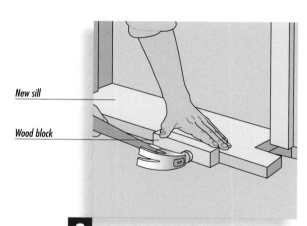

New sill

Wood block

3 *Position the new sill*

Gently tap the new sill into place, being careful not to force it. (A wood block protects the sill from dents and splitting.) Sand or trim the sill for a snug fit.

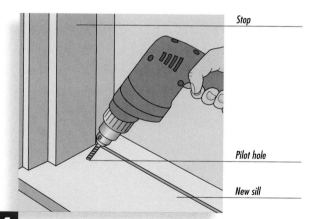

Stop

Pilot hole

New sill

4 *Fasten down the new sill*

Drill pilot holes for nails or screws after shimming the sill for fit, if necessary. Secure the sill, sink the nail or screw heads, and fill the holes with putty. Last, apply a finish.

Fixing Locksets & Knobs

Many lockset problems can be corrected before they become so serious that the lockset won't work. Problems are typically caused by a malfunctioning latch assembly or the lock mechanism. A latch problem may be the result of a poorly fitting door. The lock mechanism may not work simply because the lock is dirty or dry and needs to be lubricated with graphite (do not use any type of oil).

For serious lock problems, it's usually best to call a locksmith or to replace the lock entirely. If your problems require professional help, keep in mind that removing the lock and taking it to a locksmith is far less expensive than having the locksmith come to you. For information on how to replace a lockset, see pages 218–220.

If a door latch doesn't operate smoothly, the latch bolt on the door may not be lined up properly with the strike plate on the door jamb. Repairs range from minor latch adjustments to repositioning the door.

If the latch does not catch, close the door slowly to watch how the latch bolt meets the strike plate. The bolt may be positioned above, below, or to one side of the strike plate. (Scars on the strike plate show where it's misaligned.) It's also possible the door has shrunk and the latch no longer reaches the strike plate. Once you've figured out the problem, try one of the methods shown on this page.

ADJUSTING A STRIKE PLATE

File
Strike plate
Vise

File the strike plate

For less than a ⅛-inch misalignment of the latch bolt and strike plate, remove the strike plate and file its inside edge to enlarge the opening. (You may also need to extend the bolt mortise.)

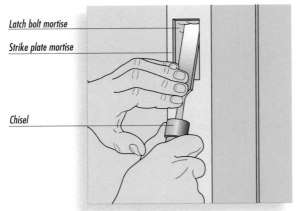

Latch bolt mortise
Strike plate mortise

Chisel

Move the strike plate

For more than a ⅛-inch misalignment, remove the strike plate and extend the mortise higher or lower. Replace the plate, fill the gap at top or bottom with drillable wood putty, and refinish.

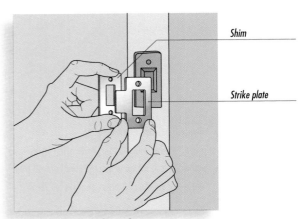

Shim

Strike plate

Shim the strike plate

If the latch doesn't reach the strike plate, shim out the plate or add another strike plate. If the latch still won't reach, shim out the door's hinges. Replace the door with a wider one, if necessary.

On mortise locksets, the doorknobs may become loose over time. To tighten them, loosen the screw on the knob's shank. If there is a knob on the other side of the door, hold it tight and turn the loose one clockwise until it fits snugly. Then tighten the screw until you feel it resting against the flat side of the spindle. The knob should turn freely. If this doesn't help, remove the knob and check the spindle; if it's worn, it must be replaced. If the whole lockset is worn, it is best to replace it entirely.

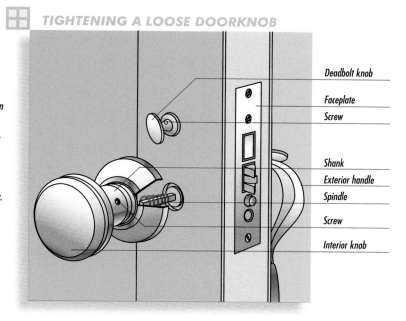

TIGHTENING A LOOSE DOORKNOB

Deadbolt knob

Faceplate

Screw

Shank

Exterior handle

Spindle

Screw

Interior knob

TROUBLESHOOTING A PROBLEM LOCKSET

PROBLEM	POSSIBLE CAUSE	REMEDIES
Latch sticks or responds slowly	Gummed up or dirty lock mechanism	Blow a pinch of powdered graphite or pencil lead into the lock mechanism or keyway
Key doesn't insert smoothly	Dirty keyway and tumbler area Foreign object in keyway	Blow a pinch of graphite or pencil lead or spray silicone spray into keyway (don't use oil) Attempt to dislodge object with thin, stiff wire
Key doesn't insert at all	Ice in keyway	Chip ice from opening; carefully heat key with a match; then insert key in lock and work it gently until ice melts
Key is broken in lock	Improperly inserted key, ill-fitting replacement key, or wrong key forced into lock	Remove broken key with thin, stiff hooked wire or with coping saw blade; if this doesn't work, remove lock cylinder and push key fragment out from other side with thin, stiff wire
Key won't turn in lock	Cylinder turned in faceplate Poorly duplicated key Damaged tumblers	Move cylinder to proper position Check key against original; replace if necessary Replace cylinder or entire lockset
Key turns but doesn't operate locking mechanism	Broken lock mechanism	Repair or replace lockset

Repairing Doors That Slide

Though hardware variations are almost unlimited, all sliding, bypass, and pocket doors operate in basically the same way. Some lightweight sliding doors, such as bypass closet doors and pocket doors (which slide into walls), are hung from the top rail. Moderately heavy doors, such as patio doors, rest on the bottom rail. Plastic guides at the top or bottom keep the doors vertical and aligned with their tracks.

Removing a sliding door for maintenance or repair is simple, but keep in mind that the door can be very heavy, especially a door with double- or triple-pane glass. If the tracks are dirty, use a vacuum cleaner with a wand attachment rather than taking the door out.

All tracks, especially the one that supports the rollers, must be kept free of foreign objects and dirt. Occasional application of a little graphite or paraffin to the track and a drop of oil to each roller bearing will help keep the operation smooth and quiet.

REMOVING SLIDING DOORS

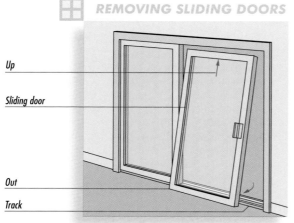

Up

Sliding door

Out

Track

Bottom-supported door

Lift a bottom-supported door straight up to clear the track; to remove it, sharply angle the lower part of the door outward. You may need a helper to hold the door since it can be heavy.

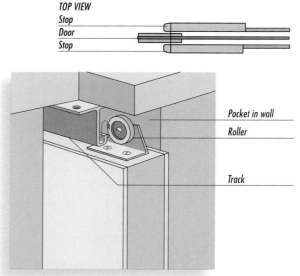

TOP VIEW
Stop
Door
Stop

Pocket in wall

Roller

Track

Pocket door

On a pocket door, remove both stops from the head jamb. Take off one side-jamb stop to allow the door to swing out. To remove the door, angle the bottom out, then carefully lift it up.

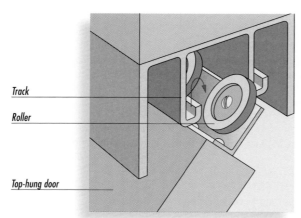

Track

Roller

Top-hung door

Top-mounted door

Lift a top-hung door straight up, and angle it to lift the rollers out of the track. (Some doors have notches on the track that you must align with the rollers before you lift the door out.)

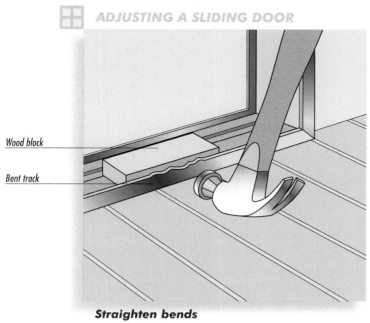

Straighten bends

Use a hammer and wood block to straighten a bent metal track. Replace a track that is badly bent or broken.

Wood block

Bent track

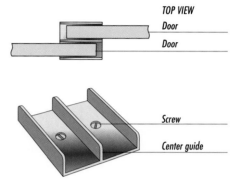

TOP VIEW
Door
Door
Screw
Center guide

Reposition the guide

Check the alignment of the guide if the door binds. Reposition the guide so the door doesn't catch on it.

Sliding doors glide on rollers that need periodic adjustment. Tighten any loosened screws in the frame or track and replace any part that's worn, broken, or missing. If a door jumps off its track, check for a dirty track, a section that's worn or bent, or a guide that's out of alignment. A door tilted in its frame usually needs roller adjustment (there should be 3/8-inch clearance between the bottom of the door and the floor or rug).

Pocket doors and bypass closet doors may warp, causing them to jam. You can compensate for a minor warp by adjusting the rollers to make the door higher or lower. You may also need to change the alignment of the door guide. If a door is badly warped, you'll need to replace it. Make sure the new door is sealed with paint or varnish on all sides and edges, including the bottom, to prevent the problem from recurring.

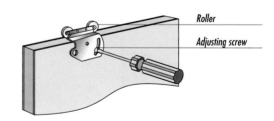

Roller

Adjusting screw

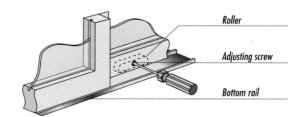

Roller

Adjusting screw

Bottom rail

Adjust the rollers

Adjust the roller height at both ends of a tilting or dragging door until the door is correctly aligned.

Weatherstripping Doors

Drafts and moisture can penetrate easily through the cracks around an unsealed door, causing discomfort and significant energy losses. Though most new doors are engineered for weathertightness, older units tend to be leaky unless they're weatherstripped. Here we will look at how to apply weatherstripping to a door. For information on weatherstripping windows, see pages 208–209.

Installing weatherstripping is usually easy: In most cases, you need only a few common household tools and the patience to align and fit the pieces properly. Just follow the instructions that come with the product. You may have to trim a door, either to make room for the weatherstripping or to get the door to fit properly. For more about trimming a door, see pages 226–227. Before installing weatherstripping, be sure to correct any problems with the way the door fits in its opening (see pages 224–225).

For sealing the bottom of a door, you can use a rain drip, door sweep, automatic sweep, or door shoe. Rain drips merely shed rain; other types block drafts and moisture. Also available are thresholds that act as weatherstripping.

Jamb weatherstripping, for sealing around a door's edges, comes in many forms. The spring-metal and cushion-vinyl types provide an efficient seal and are unobtrusive, but they tend to make a door difficult to open and close. Foam weatherstripping can be peeled off and replaced, but it is the least permanent solution. Gasket weatherstripping is efficient, though very visible. Interlocking weatherstripping for both door bottoms and jambs can be either surface mounted or recessed in the door. Both installations require precise fitting. The recessed type (not shown here) fits into grooves in the door and should be installed by a professional.

(continued on page 236)

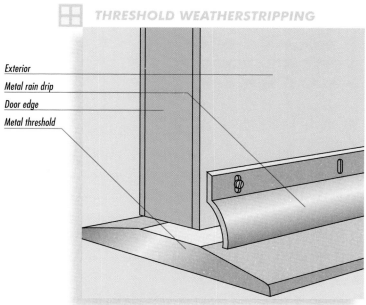

Exterior
Metal rain drip
Door edge
Metal threshold

Rain drip

A metal rain drip sheds rain, but it's the vinyl gasket beneath the door that seals the crack. Notch the rain drip at both ends to clear stops.

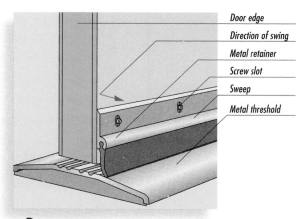

Door edge
Direction of swing
Metal retainer
Screw slot
Sweep
Metal threshold

Door sweep

A door sweep screws onto the door's bottom face; elongated screw slots allow for height adjustment. Place the sweep on the interior side of an inward-swinging door.

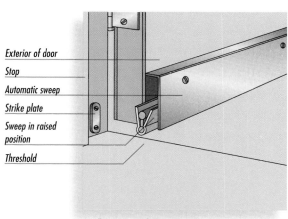

Exterior of door
Stop
Automatic sweep
Strike plate
Sweep in raised position
Threshold

Automatic sweep

This retractable sweep is spring-loaded inside a metal frame. When the door opens, the sweep lifts above the threshold. (When trimming the sweep to fit, don't cut the springs.)

(continued from page 234)

You won't know until winter whether the weatherstripping is doing its job. If you feel cold air coming through the cracks, try these remedies. Bend spring-metal or cushion-vinyl weatherstripping to increase the pressure on the door. If threshold weatherstripping has elongated screw holes, adjust the height for a better fit.

Vinyl-gasket threshold

With this type, a special threshold replaces a standard one. The door should press lightly against the gasket when closed. Bevel the door bottom $^1/_8$ inch, tapering down in the direction of the swing.

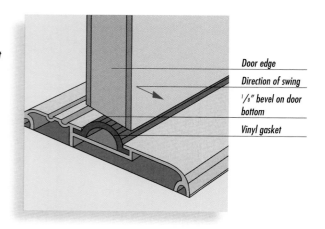

Door edge
Direction of swing
$^1/_8$" bevel on door bottom
Vinyl gasket

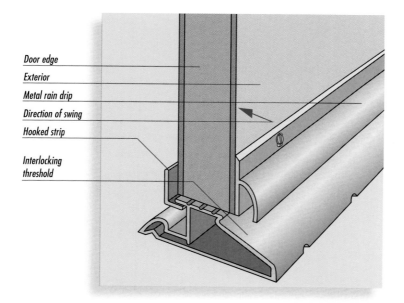

Door edge
Exterior
Metal rain drip
Direction of swing
Hooked strip
Interlocking threshold

Interlocking system

A surface-mounted interlocking threshold consists of a threshold plus a hooked strip that's mounted on the door. Allow a $^1/_8$-inch clearance between the threshold and the door bottom.

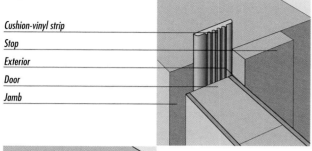

Cushion-vinyl strip
Stop
Exterior
Door
Jamb

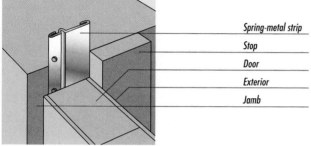

Spring-metal strip
Stop
Door
Exterior
Jamb

Spring-metal or vinyl

Spring-metal or cushion-vinyl weatherstripping is nailed to jambs around the door, starting on the hinge side. Strips butt against the stops; miter the top corners and cut the lock-side strip to fit around the strike plate.

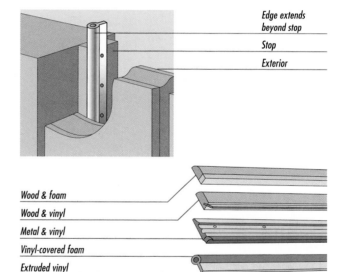

Edge extends beyond stop
Stop
Exterior

Wood & foam
Wood & vinyl
Metal & vinyl
Vinyl-covered foam
Extruded vinyl

Gasket weatherstripping

This type is nailed or screwed to the face of the stops and head jamb. Attach a top piece so it's flush with the side stops; the side pieces should butt against the top piece. (You may need to notch the top end of the side strips so they fit tightly.) The seal should be light. Be careful not to kink the strips as you attach them.

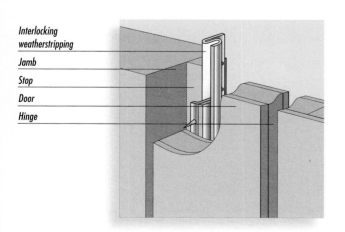

Interlocking weatherstripping
Jamb
Stop
Door
Hinge

Interlocking weatherstripping

Surface-mounted interlocking weatherstripping is nailed to both the door and the stops (follow the manufacturer's directions). Fit the top strips first; then attach the side strips to the jambs and the door edges, using small nails. Precise fitting is essential—the channels must align exactly in order for weatherstripping to be effective.

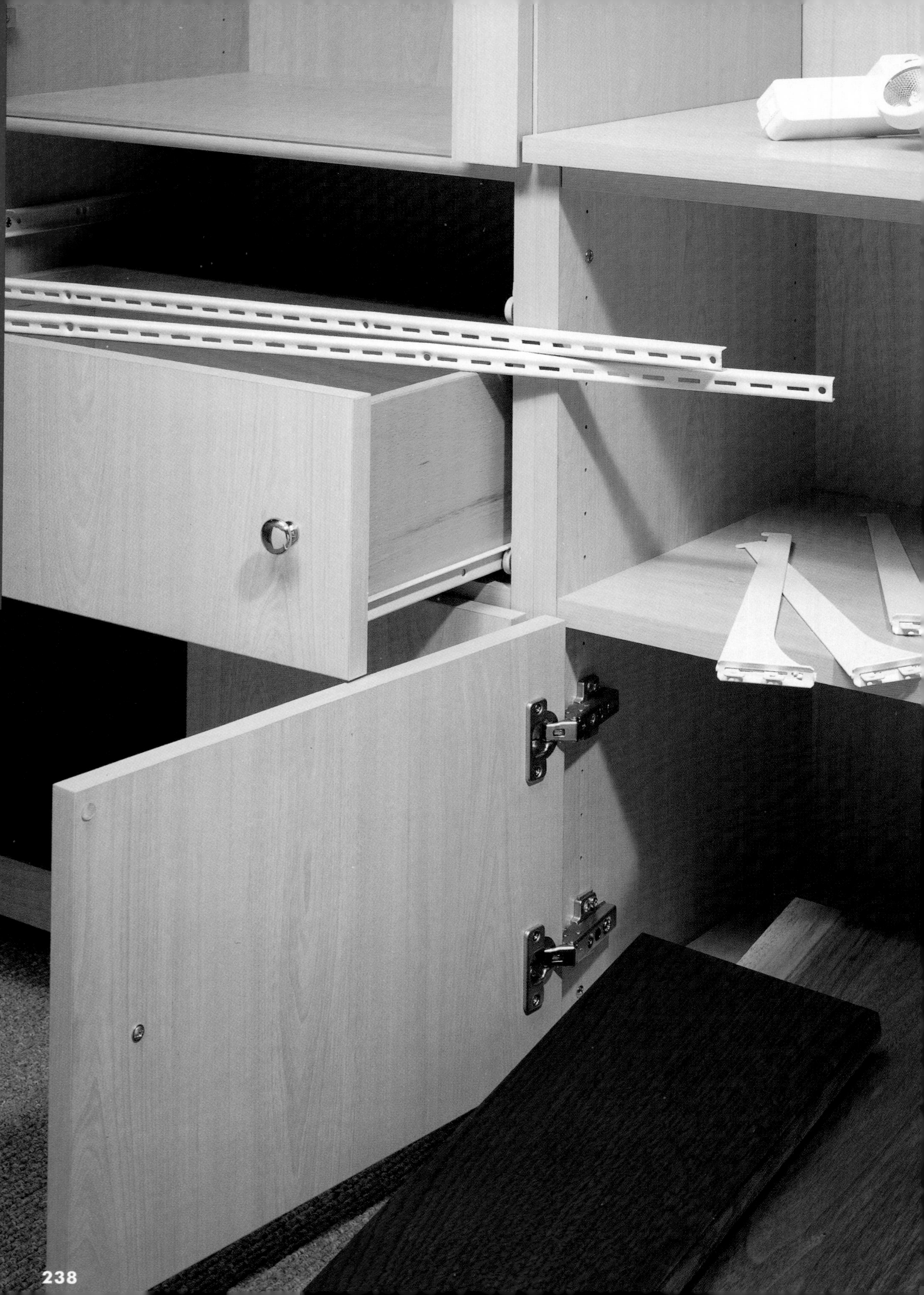

Storage

Fresh paint and fine decorating may give your house its polish, but the backbone of any comfortable, organized home is its storage. If you are like most homeowners, your most common complaint about bedroom, bathroom, kitchen, and public areas is that there's never enough closet space to store all your belongings—or at least to store them in a manner that makes them easy to find and access. Well-planned storage can be a great tonic to constant clutter. Not only does it add value to your home, it can improve your quality of life as well. Happily, today, home improvement centers abound with clever, efficient, and easy-to-install storage systems that allow you to upgrade or modernize existing storage or add whole new storage capacity. In this chapter, you will learn all you need to know about planning storage, choosing and installing cabinets, selecting proper countertop materials, installing a countertop, adding a closet, and more.

Choosing Cabinets

Cabinets are more than just functional storage systems. They are the face of your kitchen or bathroom, setting the room's style or theme. Since cabinetry is one of the largest investments you will make in your kitchen or bathroom, it pays to be well versed in cabinet terminology before you begin the design and shopping process. Traditional or European style; custom, stock, or custom-stock hybrids; wall, base, end, and corner units—these are just some of the options you will have as you put together the perfect combination to suit your needs. The following pages and accompanying illustrations offer an overview of the basic distinctions in cabinet systems to help guide you through the heady selection process.

Wall-Mounted & Base Cabinets

While materials, colors, and styles vary widely, there are basically two types of cabinets: wall cabinets that, as the term suggests, are affixed to the wall, and base cabinets that

rest on the floor. Kitchen and bath storage systems are generally composed of a mix of the two that, with other accessory pieces such as corner and end units, complete what is known in the trade as a "cabinet run." Kitchen cabinetry in particular offers a great number of specialty options, such as pullout pot and pantry shelving, lazy Susans, flip-up appliance shelves, tray holders, and built-in storage compartments for dry staples such as flour, rice, and beans. (See, for example, the illustration of cabinet types on pages 242–243.) Together with traditional two-, three-, and four-level compartments, you can combine these various cabinets to form a personalized cabinet run.

Standard wall cabinets typically come in single case, double case, and other specialty sizes. The basic wall cabinet runs 12 to 15 inches deep and 9 to 60 inches wide. The most popular heights are 15, 18, and 30 inches, but they can range from 12 to 36 inches.

TYPICAL KITCHEN CABINETS

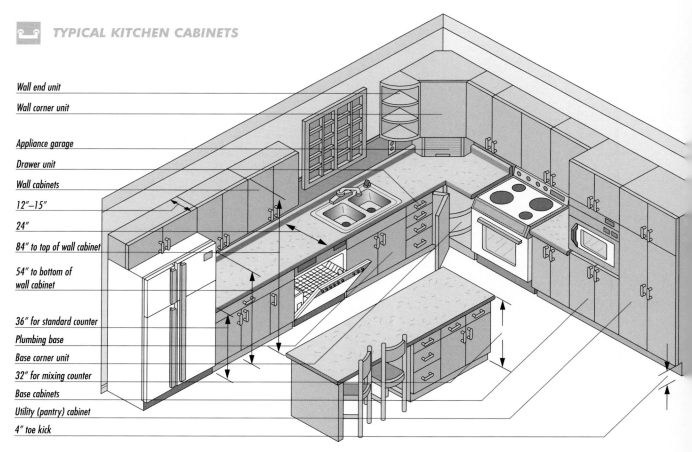

Wall end unit
Wall corner unit

Appliance garage
Drawer unit
Wall cabinets
12"–15"
24"
84" to top of wall cabinet
54" to bottom of wall cabinet

36" for standard counter
Plumbing base
Base corner unit
32" for mixing counter
Base cabinets
Utility (pantry) cabinet
4" toe kick

Storage

Standard base cabinets normally measure 34½ inches tall, figuring another 1½ inches of countertop for a total height of 36 inches. Cabinet width also varies from 9 to 60 inches, and standard depth is 24 inches. A typical base cabinet often includes a drawer above the cabinet proper and can include a pull-out cutting board.

Corner and end units join and complete cabinet runs. Corner units, either open shelving or closed door, turn the corner for a cabinet run that fills two walls. End units, which can be straight-edged or rounded, plain or outfitted with open shelving, finish the run.

Traditional or European-Style Cabinets

All cabinetry, wall or base, breaks down into two basic styles of construction: traditional faceframe cabinets and European frameless cabinets. Traditional is an older, more common American style, but the space-efficient European cabinet has swiftly caught up in popularity. The differences between the two are readily apparent.

Traditional cabinets mask the raw front edges of each box with a 1-by-2 "faceframe." Doors and drawers then fit in one of three ways: flush, partially offset with a lip, or completely overlaying the frame. Since the faceframe covers up the basic box, thinner or lower-quality wood can be used for the sides to decrease cost. The downside is space. Faceframe cabinets have smaller boxes, so drawers or slide-out accessories must be significantly smaller than the full width of the cabinet, decreasing storage capacity.

European cabinets, a product of post–World War II lumber shortages and European ingenuity, offer frameless construction. A thin trim strip covers raw edges, which butt directly against one another. Doors and drawers often fit to within ⅛ inch of each other, revealing a thin sliver of the trim. Interior components can be sized practically to the full dimensions of the box, and double boxes do not have the clumsy center post that blocks full access to the cabinets.

Another big difference: Frameless cabinets typically have a separate toe-space pedestal, or plinth, that allows you to set counter heights specifically to your liking, stack base units, or make use of space at floor level. The terms "system 32" and "32-millimeter" refer to precise columns of holes drilled on the inside faces of many frameless cabinets. These holes generally are in the same places no matter what cabinets you buy, and interchangeable components

TWO CABINET STYLES

Traditional faceframe cabinets have a wooden frame that covers the cabinet's front edges. European-style frameless cabinets eliminate the frame for a simpler, more flexible system.

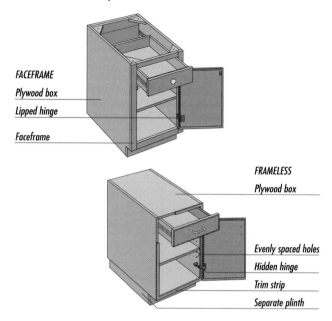

FACEFRAME
Plywood box
Lipped hinge
Faceframe

FRAMELESS
Plywood box
Evenly spaced holes
Hidden hinge
Trim strip
Separate plinth

such as door hinges, drawer guides, shelf pins, and pullout baskets just plug right into them.

Custom, Stock, or Custom-Stock

Cabinets are manufactured and sold in three different forms. It is important to understand the differences, since the type you choose will affect the cost, overall appearance, and functionalism of your kitchen.

CUSTOM If you have the resources, nothing beats having an experienced cabinetmaker come to your house, measure your kitchen, discuss your very specific needs, and return to the shop to build custom boxes, drawers, and doors. Custom cabinetmakers can match old cabinets, cope with odd configurations and other complexities, and create a truly unique look that stock or even custom-stock cannot yield. Such service comes at a price, however. Custom cabinets generally take longer to produce than stock and custom-stock. If money and time are not an issue, custom may be the way to go.

STOCK You can visit home improvement centers and buy your kitchen cabinetry off the shelf. So-called "stock" cabinetry

(continued on page 242)

Choosing Cabinets

(continued from page 241)

means the components are in stock, in set sizes, materials, and finishes. What you see is what you get. These mass-produced cabinets are the least expensive way to go, and, if this is the choice for you, it pays greatly to shop around. Some stock cabinet lines today offer an array of options in door styles and finishes and can provide a handsome look and suitable function for a reasonable price.

CUSTOM-STOCK This confused-sounding hybrid is actually one of the most popular cabinet choices today. Also called "semi-custom" or "custom modular" units, these cabinets are manufactured, but they are of a higher grade and offer more design flexibility than stock cabinets. Custom-stock cabinets come in a wide range of sizes, with many design options—in materials, door styles, finishes, and accessories—within each size. You can special order everything for these basic modules: sliding shelves, wire baskets, flour bins, appliance garages, and pullout pantries—and even replace doors with drawers. Heights, widths, and depths can be modified to fit almost any design. As with custom cabinets, "customizing" in this way requires time, so order as much ahead of your completion date as possible.

Judging Cabinet Quality

The rule of thumb for judging the quality of a cabinet is to look closely at the drawers. Budget drawer boxes may feature self-closing epoxy guides, while a premium cabinet will include solid-wood drawer boxes with dovetail joints and invisible, full-extension, under-mounted ball-bearing guides. Door hinges are also critical hardware elements. European or "invisible" hinges are the most trouble-free. Check for adjustability: Invisible hinges should be able to be reset and fine-tuned with the cabinets in place.

Premium custom cabinets are made from solid hardwood or softwood inside and out. Most cabinet boxes are made

STANDARD WALL CABINETS

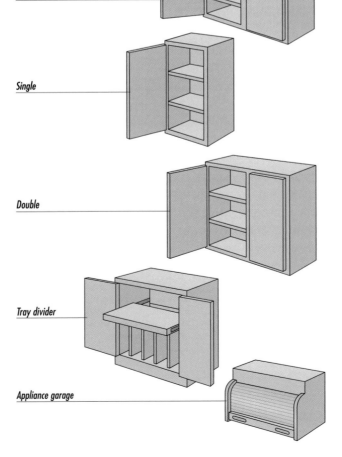

Short cabinet

Single

Double

Tray divider

Appliance garage

WALL CORNER UNITS

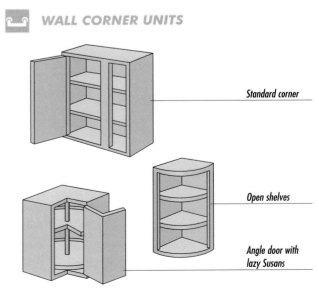

Standard corner

Open shelves

Angle door with lazy Susans

Storage

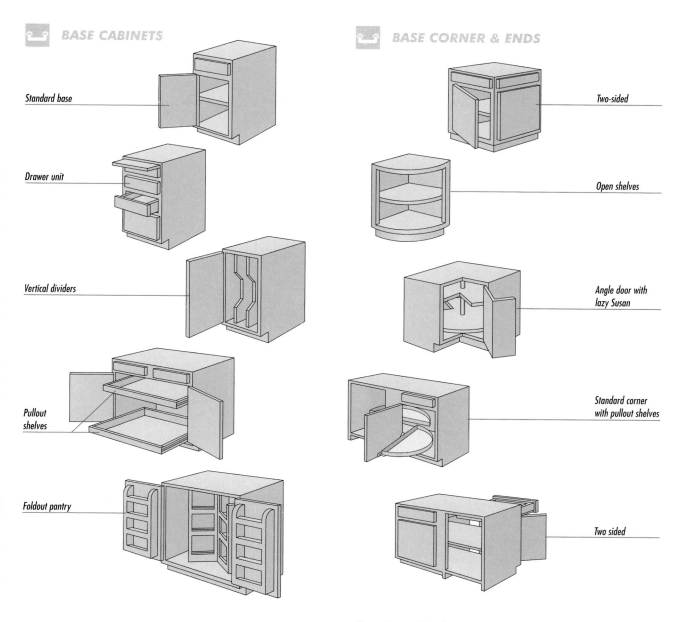

Standard base

Drawer unit

Vertical dividers

Pullout shelves

Foldout pantry

Two-sided

Open shelves

Angle door with lazy Susan

Standard corner with pullout shelves

Two sided

from sheet products such as plywood, plain or laminated particleboard, or medium-density fiberboard (MDF). Hardwood plywood is surfaced with attractive wood veneers on face and back; of course, the higher the face grade, the more you'll pay. Particleboard costs less, weighs more, and is both weaker and more prone to warping and moisture damage than plywood. Generally, particleboard cabinets are faced with either high-pressure plastic laminates or a softer material called melamine. MDF, a denser, furniture-grade particleboard, is tougher, smoother, and available with high-quality hardwood veneers. Make sure that laminate and edge banding are thick enough at the corners and edges, since peeling is death to a cabinet.

Getting Help

The good news is that there's lots of assistance out there when you shop for cabinets. Home improvement centers have design consultants that can help you plan your cabinetry needs and place your order. When you buy cabinets, some of what you're paying for is the degree of help you require with your kitchen plan. You may be offered an informational questionnaire to fill out to help you determine your needs. You will want to have a style in mind. The best piece of information to bring with you, however, is an up-to-date and accurately measured floor plan. With that in hand, designers can plot out, usually on computer, a series of kitchen cabinet options that will address all of your desires.

Choosing Countertops

As the finishing touch to cabinet storage units, countertops provide a functional work surface while helping to establish a room's decorative style. Today, an eye-popping array of countertop materials in just about every color and style imaginable awaits you. Where once wood or ceramic tile were the only choices, plastic laminate, solid surface, stone, stainless steel, glass, and even cast concrete have joined the selection pool. Some of the pricier countertops, such as stone or solid surface, are best used in kitchen areas to take full advantage of their ruggedness and stain- and heat-resistant qualities. Some of the best designs, however, employ a mix of countertop materials—solid surface for the work areas, ceramic tile backsplash and wall murals for flair, and a baker's insert of cool marble or granite for dough preparation.

Not surprisingly, countertop surface material varies greatly in price.

Plastic laminate, which offers perhaps the greatest range of styles and colors, is relatively inexpensive and can be purchased in prefabricated lengths ready for installation. Its downside is that it shows wear-and-tear faster than most other materials. Ceramic tile is a perennial favorite and, depending on the tile chosen, can be a bargain. Grout lines can stain and collect dirt, however, and need upkeep and repair. Solid surface is some of the most expensive material on the market and requires a professional installer, but those who own it sing its praises for durability and ease of cleaning.

Each of the most popular countertop materials has its advantages and disadvantages, as detailed in the accompanying chart.

 A COMPARISON OF COUNTERTOPS

MATERIAL
Plastic laminate
Synthetic marble
Ceramic tile
Solid surface
Stone
Wood
Stainless steel

Storage

ADVANTAGES	DISADVANTAGES
■ Laminate, composed of layers of paper soaked and stacked in plastic, comes in a wide range of colors, textures, and patterns. It is durable, easy to clean, water-resistant, and relatively inexpensive. ■ Ready-made molded versions are called postformed, while custom or self-rimmed countertops are built from scratch atop particleboard or plywood substrates. ■ With the proper tools, laminate is the easiest of the countertops to install.	■ It can scratch, chip, and stain, and once marred it is difficult to repair. Ready-made postformed countertops can look cheesy. ■ Conventional laminate has a dark backing that shows at the seams, while new solid-color laminates, designed to hide these lines, are somewhat brittle and more expensive. High-gloss laminates show every smudge.
■ These man-made products, collectively known as "cast polymers," include cultured marble, cultured onyx, and cultured granite. Primarily sold for bathroom use, all three are relatively easy to clean and usually include an integrated sink.	■ Cast polymers often look cheap. In addition, they aren't very durable. They tend to scratch and ding and are tough to repair. ■ Backings typically are porous. Quality varies widely. Look for Cultured Marble Institute certification for the best.
■ A kitchen and bath classic, ceramic tile comes in a multitude of colors, sizes, textures, and patterns, and a range of prices. Tile is either machine- or hand-made, with the latter popular for rustic-style design. Installed correctly, it is heatproof, and scratch- and water-resistant. Grout is also available today in a number of colors to blend in or add contrast. Since some tile is meant for floors, be sure to buy a tile rated for countertop use.	■ Some tile glazes can react adversely to acids or cleaning chemicals, so be sure to ask the dealer about care. Hand-made tiles, especially Mexican tiles formed from soft clay, are prone to chipping. ■ Light-colored grout lines stain and can be tough to keep clean, particularly as they wear down. Hand-made tiles usually take thicker grout lines, which can exacerbate the problem. Using stain-resistant epoxy grout and machine tiles that take thin grout lines can mitigate grout trouble.
■ Durable, nonporous, heat- and stain-resistant and a breeze to clean, this marble-like material is made of cast acrylic or polyester plastic with mineral fillers. It can be shaped and joined seamlessly. Sink and countertop can be fashioned in one continuous piece for a sleek look. Any blemishes and scratches can be sanded out easily.	■ Solid surface is among the most expensive countertop materials available today. Fabrication and installation are best left to the pros for good results. The material needs very firm support underneath. Add to the basic cost the high price of contrast lines, wood inlays, and other interesting edge details. Darker toned surfaces tend to show blemishes faster.
■ Few materials beat the elegance and outright beauty of natural stone countertops, particularly multihued granites and marble. Stone is heatproof, water-resistant, easy to clean, and hard as a rock—because it is rock. The countertop's cool surface is perfect for working with dough or making candy. Granite is almost impervious to stains. Stone can be purchased as cut tiles in a variety of sizes or as solid slabs. The variety of colors and internal patterning provides for intriguing looks.	■ The price. Granite especially can be worth its weight in gold, and solid stone slabs are among the most expensive countertop materials on the market. Stone tiles, however, particularly slate and limestone, are less expensive, but can be tough on delicate glassware. Stone also needs strong support. Oil, alcohol, and any acid such as lemon or wine will stain marble or at least damage its high-gloss finish. There's usually a wait time for custom-cut solid slabs, and you'd be wise to let a pro install it.
■ A wood countertop adds warmth to any kitchen. Wood is handsome, comes in shades from dark to light, is easily installed and easy on glassware and china. Maple butcherblock, the most popular and functional choice for kitchens, is sold in 24-, 30-, and 36-inch widths. ■ Installation costs are comparable to ceramic or top-of-the-line laminate.	■ Wood can scorch and scratch and may blacken when near a moisture source such as a sink. Sealers such as mineral oil and polyurethane are available, but neither is ideal. If you use mineral oil, you must coat both sides—top and bottom—of the wood slab or it will warp. If you choose polyurethane, which is a permanent protective sealant, you cannot cut on the bare counter.
■ Most city health codes require stainless steel in public food preparation places for good reason: stainless is ultra-hygienic and easy to clean. In addition, it's waterproof, heat-resistant, and very durable. ■ Countertops are available with integrated sinks. Generally, stainless is perfect for a modern look.	■ You can't cut on it or you'll ruin both the surface and your knives. Fabrication can be expensive, since you may need to have cutouts for sink and faucet holes. Typical detailing includes bends and welds for edges and backsplashes. Custom touches and high-chromium stainless add significantly to the cost.

Storage Tools

Working on cabinetry, countertops, shelving, and closets calls for quite a few conventional carpentry tools. You don't need all of the tools shown here for every storage-related project, but you'll find this is a good selection to have on hand—particularly if you'll be doing much finish carpentry work. Be sure you also have basic safety equipment, such as safety glasses.

In addition to the tools shown here, you may need electrical and plumbing tools if your work will involve moving receptacles, switches, or plumbing fixtures. And for any job that requires working with walls, you'll need some of the tools discussed on pages 100–101. If you take on tile work, you'll need a few basic tile tools, such as a notched spreader, a trowel, a rubber-backed trowel, a tile cutter, and tile nippers.

 CONSTRUCTION TOOLS

For the basic construction tasks of most work on cabinets and shelving, you'll need some—but not necessarily all—of these general construction tools.

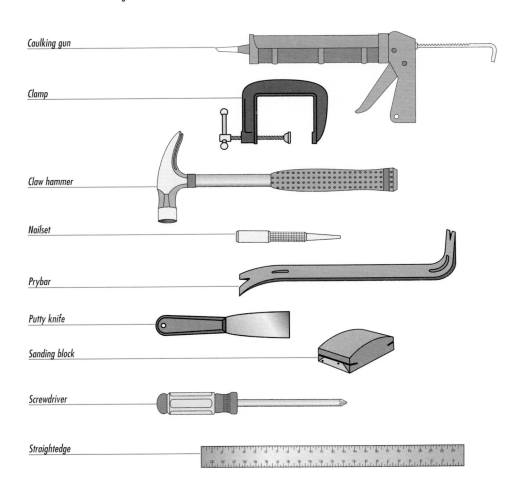

Caulking gun

Clamp

Claw hammer

Nailset

Prybar

Putty knife

Sanding block

Screwdriver

Straightedge

For layout work, you'll want to have a carpenter's square, combination square, chalk line, and measuring tape. A stud finder is helpful for locating hidden studs when you need to fasten cabinets and shelves securely to the wall. A level (or plumb bob) is necessary during installation of cabinets and shelves.

A handsaw and power circular saw will help you cut straight lines; a coping saw and saber saw will cut curves. Chisels, rasps, and planes help to remove small amounts of wood for fine fitting. A utility knife is very handy for many jobs. And you'll need a power drill with drill bits, for drilling holes, and with screwdriver tips to ease driving screws.

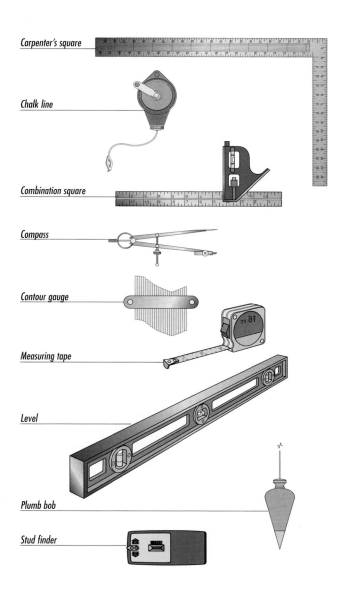

Carpenter's square

Chalk line

Combination square

Compass

Contour gauge

Measuring tape

Level

Plumb bob

Stud finder

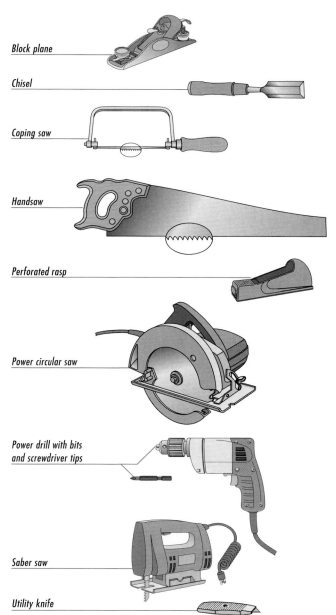

Block plane

Chisel

Coping saw

Handsaw

Perforated rasp

Power circular saw

Power drill with bits and screwdriver tips

Saber saw

Utility knife

Installing Cabinets

Installing cabinetry doesn't take a pro, but it does take an eye for precision. By starting with a clean, flat wall and carefully marking cabinet placement as you go, you will ensure a picture-perfect lineup of cabinets that open and close properly and that are securely fixed.

The key to any cabinet installation is the condition of the wall behind. The wall should be smooth, level, and clean. After washing it down and allowing it to dry, check its flatness by placing a long straightedge against it, marking bumpy or bulging areas for sanding.

Use a scribe rail (see sidebar on the facing page) to overcome major surface irregularities. Next, locate the wall studs using a stud finder or other method (see page 103). Mark with a pencil their location both above and at least 6 inches below the intended position for the cabinets.

When you hang upper cabinets, be sure to fasten them through a strong part of the cabinet—ideally, a support rail made for this. Remember that cabinets will be very heavy when full. For each cabinet, at least three screws should go into the wall studs a minimum of 1 inch deep.

For a lower cabinet, particularly a corner unit, you may want to add scribe rails along its length before you add shims.

Position the base cabinet so that either the cabinet edge is against the wall or, if using a scribe rail, the rail touches the wall. Remember to position base cabinets so they line up with upper cabinets.

INSTALLING CABINETS

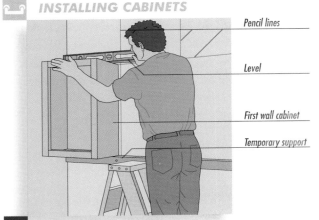

Pencil lines

Level

First wall cabinet

Temporary support

1 ***Install the first cabinet***
Draw pencil lines on the wall corresponding to the cabinet's dimensions. Screw a level temporary support rail to the wall, aligning the top edge of the rail with the line for the bottom edge of the cabinets. While a helper holds the cabinet in place, drill pilot holes through either the sturdy cabinet back or its support rail and into the wall studs. Screw the cabinets to the wall using 1³/₄-inch (or longer) screws. Check across the top for level.

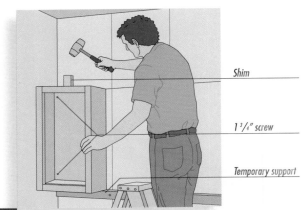

Shim

1³/₄" screw

Temporary support

2 ***Shim & fasten the cabinet***
Check the edges of the cabinet for plumb. If it is out of alignment, back off the screws and drive one or more wood shims as needed between the cabinet and the wall to correct the position. Recheck for plumb and, if the cabinet now hangs fine, refasten the screws into the wall studs.

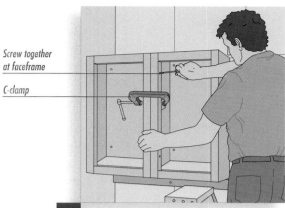

Screw together at faceframe

C-clamp

3 *Join the cabinets*

As you install each cabinet, secure it to the one beside it with a C-clamp. Make sure that each cabinet is shimmed out the same distance from the wall for plumb. Screw together adjoining cabinets. On faceframe cabinets, first drill two ¹/₈-inch pilot holes through the sides of the faceframe. With frameless cabinets, predrill bolt holes through shelf-peg holes and bolt together.

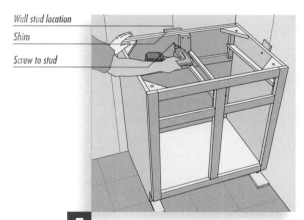

Wall stud location

Shim

Screw to stud

5 *Fasten lower cabinets*

Once the cabinet is level and plumb and the scribe rails (if any) fit securely against the wall, drive screws through the cabinet back and shims into the wall studs. Use a knife or sharp chisel to trim any excess material from the shims. Continue to add adjoining cabinets in this manner. Join base cabinets as you did the wall cabinets in Step 3.

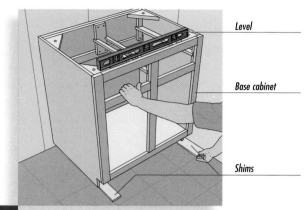

Level

Base cabinet

Shims

4 *Shim base cabinets*

Level the base cabinet by placing wood shims underneath it or, if the cabinet has legs, by adjusting leg height. Make sure that adjoining cabinets are plumb. If not, drive wood shims between the cabinet and the wall at stud positions to correct the misalignment.

USING A SCRIBE RAIL

Most walls will sport the occasional bump or hollow that can make cabinet installation troublesome. If the irregularities are significant in either size or number, you can easily compensate for a less-than-flat wall by using a scribe rail. A scribe rail is a length of wood cut and shaped to fit as a buffer between the wall and the backside of the cabinet. A scribing tool traces the wall's irregular surface onto the scribe rail to ensure a tight fit. As you mark the rail, tilt the scribing tool slightly for a precise fit. Once the rail is marked, plane the rail's edge to correspond to the marks. Scribe the rail before fastening the cabinet to the wall but after the unit is level and plumb.

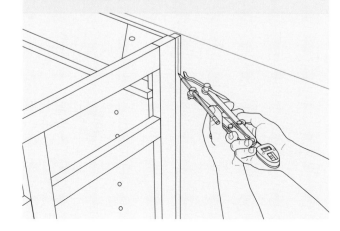

Installing a Vanity

A bathroom vanity is similar to a kitchen base cabinet, usually just shorter and not as deep. It is designed to offer storage in the bathroom and to provide a base for a countertop and sink (or lavatory). Bathroom vanities are readily available in an array of different styles and finishes at home improvement centers. They come as narrow as 12 inches and as wide as 60 inches, with the usual height of 30 inches. You can purchase a vanity with or without a countertop and sink. Installing a vanity and integrated sink-countertop, as shown on these pages, is a relatively easy task for an attentive and patient beginner. For more about installing

INSTALLING A VANITY

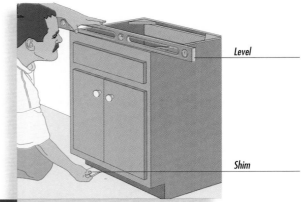

Cutout for plumbing

Pipes

Level

Shim

1 **Cut an opening**
If the back doesn't have a plumbing opening, align the unit with the plumbing lines, mark their positions, and draw a triangle around the marks. Drill a starter hole and cut the opening with a saber saw.

2 **Level the vanity**
If there is a tile baseboard, scribe the outline of the baseboard on the vanity corners and trim to the line with a coping saw. Set the vanity in place tightly against the wall. Level it from side to side and front to back using wood shims.

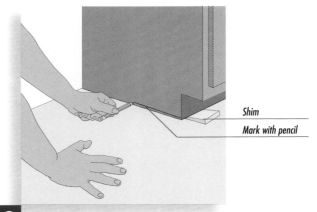

Shim

Mark with pencil

3 **Scribe the bottom**
If the floor isn't flat, scribe the vanity's bottom edge by sliding a pencil along the floor. Using a saw or sander, trim the cabinet to the line. If the back wall is crooked, you may need to scribe and plumb the back of the vanity as well.

bathroom lavatories, see pages 422–423. Countertops are discussed on pages 252–257.

You will do well to purchase a vanity with an open back ready to accommodate plumbing fixtures. If the vanity of your dreams has a solid back, you will need to cut that opening (or drill individual holes for each required plumbing opening). Remove any wood baseboard or trim along the wall the width of your vanity before installation. If the floor is irregular, you can scribe and trim it as shown in Step 3 or leave shims in place, trim them with a utility knife, and cover them with molding once installation is complete.

Before setting the sink-countertop on the cabinet, apply a bead of caulk or sealant, as specified by the countertop manufacturer, around the vanity's upper edges. Some countertops should be fastened with screws driven up through the corner blocking in the vanity.

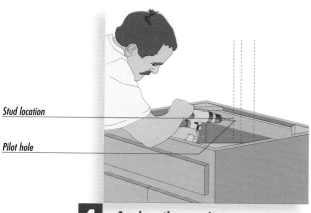

Stud location

Pilot hole

4 Anchor the vanity

Locate the studs behind the wall with an electronic stud finder, as discussed on page 103. Drive 2-inch wood screws through the vanity back brace into the studs.

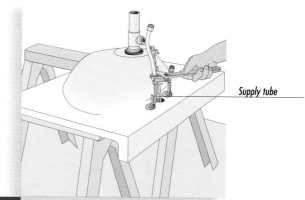

Supply tube

5 Install the hardware

Install the faucet according to the manufacturer's directions and attach new flexible supply tubes. Seat the drain flange in a ring of plumber's putty around the drain hole. Thread the gasket and locknut onto the drain tailpiece and tighten.

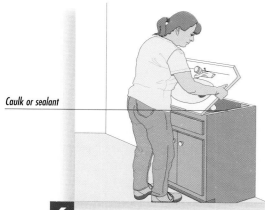

Caulk or sealant

6 Set the sink-countertop

Apply a bead of caulk or sealant, as specified by the countertop manufacturer, around the upper edges of the vanity. Center the sink-countertop over the vanity and press it firmly into place. As you press, use a slight twisting motion to ensure a good seal. Some countertops should be fastened with screws driven up through the corner blocking in the vanity.

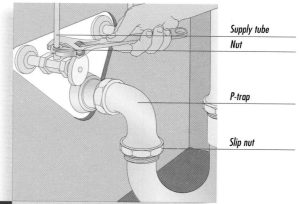

Supply tube

Nut

P-trap

Slip nut

7 Attach supply tubes & trap

Attach the supply tubes to the shutoff valves. Tighten the nuts by hand, then give a final quarter-turn with an adjustable wrench. Slide the P-trap over the sink tailpiece and attach it to the wall drainpipe. Tighten the slip nuts. Turn on the water supply, then the faucets, and check for leaks.

Tiling a Countertop

Ceramic tile as a countertop material never seems to lose its appeal. One reason is its design versatility. A tile countertop can be solid-colored and sleek, or wildly patterned, modern and sophisticated, or charmingly rustic. Installing tile requires patience and an eye for straight lines, but the results are eminently rewarding. Consider tile installation as a two-process job: the first involves laying and spacing the tile, the second grouting and sealing it.

The most common backing for ceramic tile countertops is ³/₄-inch exterior-grade plywood. It should be rigid and well supported. For the typical countertop with a width of 24 inches or less, there should be crossbraces every 36 inches. Where plywood pieces butt up against each other, leave about ¹/₈-inch space to permit expansion. Also leave about a ¹/₈-inch gap between the plywood and the back wall. Use a latex- or polymer-modified thin-set adhesive to set the tile.

PLANNING THE LAYOUT First, mark with a pencil from front to back on plywood the center point of any sink you plan to install or, if there is no sink, the midpoint of the counter. Do a test layout of edge and field tiles, starting with full tiles along the front edge and working from front to back. Allow appropriate space for cove tiles for the backsplash. If there is no backsplash, leave a ¹/₈-inch gap between the last counter tile and the wall.

Use plastic spacers for accuracy. Work from the marked center point outward so that any cut tiles will be balanced on both sides. If there is less than half a tile at the end, move the line over one-half a tile in either direction. Be careful not to tile over the edge of the sink hole, since the tile must be fully supported underneath or the weight of the sink will flip it up. Once you have laid the tiles to your satisfaction, either mark the location of key tiles on the plywood backing or set the edge trim before you remove the field tiles. If you choose the latter, mark field tile reference points on the edge trim.

SETTING EDGE TILES Since field tiles generally line up with the edge trim, set the edge trim first. If you are using cove tiles for the backsplash, set them after the edge trim pieces are in place, making sure to line up the base of the cove tiles with the edge tiles so that the grout lines run straight between the two. As frequently is the case, you may need to cut the last tiles on the ends to fit. (See pages 159–160 for instructions on marking and cutting tiles.)

SETTING SINK TRIM A self-rimming sink goes in after you have set all of the tile, but a recessed sink is installed before the field tile is set. Once you have placed the sink and caulked carefully between the sink and backing, you are ready to set the trim tile around it.

SETTING FIELD TILES After you have set all trim pieces, lay the field tiles. If you have installed a sink, work from the sink outward. If the surface has no sink, start laying field tiles from the center of the counter outward. Use spacers if the tiles do not have integral spacing lugs, checking the grout joint alignment frequently to maintain straight lines. To bed and level the tiles, place a small piece of plywood over several tiles at a time and tap gently with a mallet or hammer.

TILING THE BACKSPLASH If you used cove tiles at the bottom of the backsplash, continue setting field tiles on the wall, again working from the center outward. If you did not use cove tiles, use regular field tiles, spacing them one grout width above the counter tiles. Use bullnose tiles if there will only be one row of backsplash tiles or for the top row of tiles, unless you are tiling up to the base of a medicine cabinet or windowsill. For this last row, apply adhesive to each tile individually before setting it in place. If the wall contains electrical outlets or switches, cut the tile or tiles to fit around the outlet. Make sure to bring the outlet out flush with the tile.

PREPARING FOR GROUT As the tile sets and the adhesive cures, clean any excess adhesive from the tile faces and wall surface. Once the adhesive has dried as indicated by its

(continued on page 254)

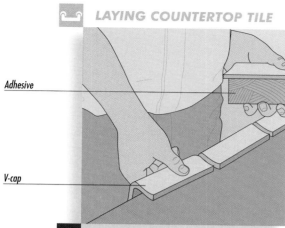

Adhesive

V-cap

1 **Set edge tiles**

Apply a thin layer of adhesive both to the back of the tile and the counter edge, raking it on with a notched trowel in a squiggle pattern. Press the first tile into place with a slight twisting motion and press firmly. Use tile spacers to maintain an even distance between successive tiles. If your edge trim consists of two pieces instead of the one-piece V-cap, set the vertical piece on the front of the counter first. Tape both pieces in place with masking tape until the adhesive sets.

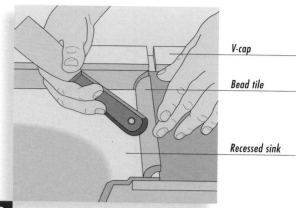

V-cap

Bead tile

Recessed sink

2 **Set sink trim**

On a recessed sink, use the midpoint marks on the backing for a starting point and work from the front of the sink to the back. Liberally spread adhesive on one trim piece at a time. Tap each carefully into place with the back of the spreader. If you are setting a bead trim, set the pieces at the sink corners first.

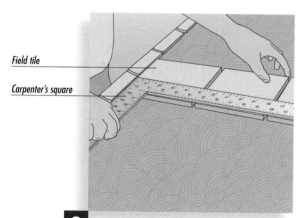

Field tile

Carpenter's square

3 **Set field tiles**

Using a notched trowel, spread adhesive over a section of counter. Lay the field tiles from front to back, placing them with a slight twisting motion. Use spacers if the tiles do not have integral spacing lugs, checking the grout joint alignment frequently to maintain straight lines. To bed and level the tiles, place a small piece of plywood over several tiles at a time and tap gently with a mallet or hammer.

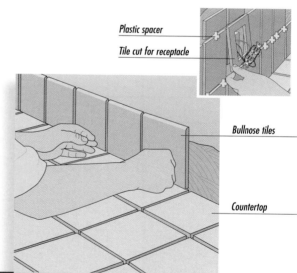

Plastic spacer

Tile cut for receptacle

Bullnose tiles

Countertop

4 **Tile the backsplash**

Spread adhesive on the wall to just shy of the desired tiling height and press the tiles in place. Also, apply adhesive to each tile individually before setting it in place. If the wall contains electrical outlets or switches, cut the tiles to fit around them (inset). Be sure to turn off the power to the device first and bring the outlet or switch out flush with the tile.

Tiling a Countertop

(continued from page 252)
instructions—24 hours is generally the minimum—you are ready to grout the tiles. Scrape any remaining adhesive out from between the tile joints.

APPLYING THE GROUT Mix the grout according to the manufacturer's instructions. Properly mixed grout should be the consistency of cookie dough. Ideally, grout should sit just below the tile surface to show the tile in relief, but be careful not to let the grout sit too low or it will be difficult to wipe away crumbs and dirt.

CLEANING UP Cleaning grout off the tiles can be tricky, since you want to remove excess grout before it dries without disturbing the grout lines as they firm up. Once the grout has dried, polish the tile with a soft, clean cloth.

Absorbent, unglazed tile should be sealed to protect it from staining. If you opt to use epoxy grout, you will not need to seal the grout lines to make them stain-resistant. Cement-based grout, however, should be sealed to protect it from stains and increase water resistance. On new tile installations, wait at least two weeks to allow the grout to cure completely before applying a sealer. Both tiles and grout should be clean and completely dry before sealing. Follow the manufacturer's instructions for applying the sealer, which usually involves spreading it on and wiping off any excess or film.

If you want to seal the grout but not the tile, you'll have to give the job more attention, since the sealer often leaves an unwanted shine on the tile. Be sure to wipe each tile clean immediately after sealer application.

GROUTING TILE

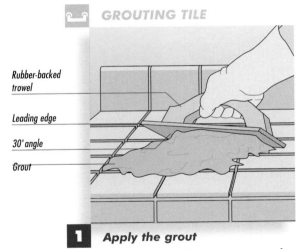

Rubber-backed trowel

Leading edge

30° angle

Grout

1 Apply the grout
Spread about a cup of grout across a section of tiles no more than 5 feet square with a rubber-backed trowel. Hold the leading edge of the trowel at about a 30-degree angle and spread the grout firmly over the tile. Work the trowel back and forth at different angles to force the grout into the joints. Fill the joints compactly so that no voids or air pockets remain.

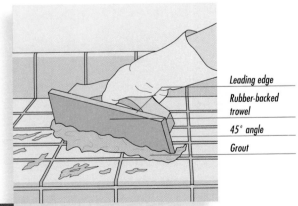

Leading edge

Rubber-backed trowel

45° angle

Grout

2 Remove the excess
After grouting the first tile section, scrape off the trowel and go over the section again to pick up the excess, holding the trowel at a 45-degree angle and working at a diagonal to the joints. Clean the trowel frequently in a bucket of water as you work.

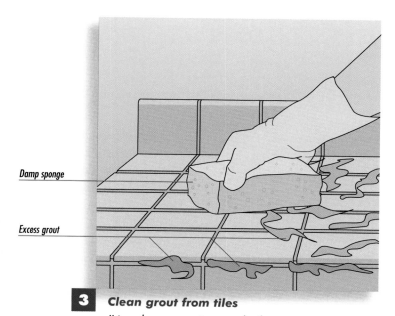

Damp sponge

Excess grout

3 **Clean grout from tiles**

Using a damp sponge, wipe across the tile at an
angle to the grout lines, rinsing the sponge
frequently in clear water. If the grout seems too
soft, move on to grout another area, then come
back to the first area. When the tiles appear to be
as clean as you can get them, let the grout dry
until a dull haze appears over the tile surface.

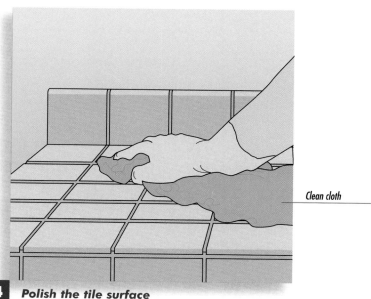

Clean cloth

4 **Polish the tile surface**

When the grout has hardened and a haze has
appeared on the tile surface, wipe the haze off
each individual tile with a soft clean cloth, again,
without disturbing the grout in the joints. If grout
has ridden up onto the tile in some spots, use the
back of an old toothbrush or a small stick wrapped
in a cloth to clean along the tile edges. When the
surface is clean, let the grout dry overnight.

Installing Laminate Counters

For an easy-to-find and easy-to-install countertop, you need look no further than prefabricated laminate. Available at most home improvement centers in lengths from 4 to 12 feet and widths from 18 to 60 inches, prefabricated laminate counters come in a variety of colors and patterns, from basic white to faux butcherblock. They have a durable, hard surface of laminate that has been applied over particleboard—you just fasten the top to your base cabinets. They're sold by the running foot and can be cut to length—the cut ends are simply capped with matching laminate end pieces.

After ordering your counters, test fit the pieces. This is the step where you're likely to discover that your walls are not perfectly flat—gaps may show up along the back of the counter. If they do, scribe and trim the back edge of the backsplash as shown on the facing page.

Before installing the pieces, apply the laminate trim pieces that finish the cut ends. Some of these trim pieces are designed to iron on, others are applied with contact cement. Follow the manufacturer's instructions.

Fit the countertop in place on top of the base cabinets and secure by driving screws through the cabinet's top or corner blocks. (Another option is to secure it with metal angle brackets.) Be sure to use short screws that won't penetrate the top of the counter.

PLANNING A COUNTERTOP

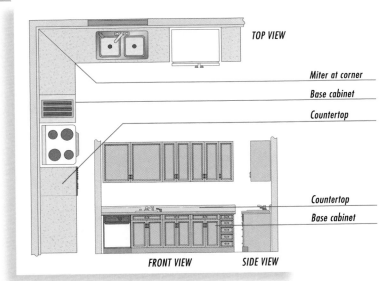

TOP VIEW

Miter at corner

Base cabinet

Countertop

Countertop

Base cabinet

FRONT VIEW   SIDE VIEW

Before ordering, plan your layout carefully. When figuring the length of pieces that meet in a corner, be sure to measure all the way to the corner for both sides. (If possible, buy pieces that have been pre-cut for corner installation; this cut must be very accurate in order to ensure a tight seam.)

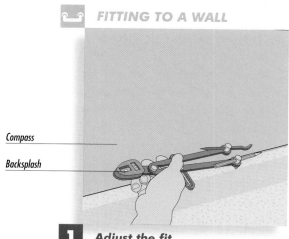

Compass

Backsplash

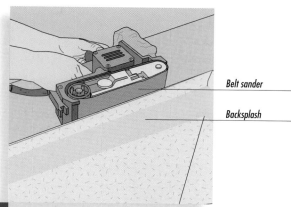

Belt sander

Backsplash

1 **Adjust the fit**

To mark the counter's backsplash to fit an irregular wall, set a compass slightly wider than the distance between the wall and the counter. Drag the scribe along the wall so that the pencil marks the top edge of the backsplash with a line that conforms to the wall.

2 **Sand high spots**

Holding the belt sander at an angle, gently sand the counter down to the scribed line—since the backsplash is usually only about $3/4$ inch thick, it should be fairly easy to shape. Angle the sander to slightly undercut the edge for a tight fit. After installation, run a bead of caulk along the gap between counter and wall.

CUTTING A SINK OPENING

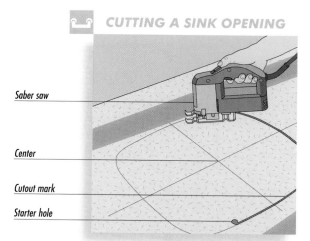

Saber saw

Center

Cutout mark

Starter hole

Follow the sink manufacturer's directions and template for marking the sink-cutout hole. Be sure to position it where you won't cut into cabinet sides or other obstacles. Drill a $1/2$-inch starter hole, then cut along the cutout mark using a saber saw with a combination blade (or a plunge router with a panel pilot bit).

Adding a Built-in Closet

The top of many a homeowner's wish list is more closet space. If you have adequate floor space and some carpentry skills, you can add a closet—in a bedroom, guestroom, den, or hallway—that will look like it's been there all along.

This project's first step is to build the closet frame and fasten it to the surrounding walls. Next, you will trim the door opening and install the doors of your choice. Then you will hang the closet rods or customize the interior with rods, shelving, drawers, and any other accessories you desire.

FRAMING THE CLOSET WALLS Plan to build the closet frame from 2 by 4s, allowing an inside depth of at least 27 inches. You can construct the frame in one of two ways: either build the walls flat on the floor and then raise them up into position, or build the walls in place. It's far easier to nail the framing members together on the floor if the room has a clear area that's large enough to do this. But, using this method, you'll have to make a slight modification in the walls' height because it isn't possible to tilt an 8-foot-tall wall up into an 8-foot-high space (as you angle it into position, it's actually about $1/4$ inch taller). You need to build the wall about $1/4$ inch less than the ceiling's height, then place shims or thin blocks between the top plate and the ceiling.

First, mark the positions of the top plate and the sole plate. On the ceiling, mark both ends of the center line of the new closet wall. Measure $1^3/4$ inches (half the width of a 2-by-4 top plate) on both sides of each mark. Snap parallel lines between corresponding marks with a chalk line to show the position of the top plate.

Next, hang a plumb bob from each end of the lines and mark these points on the floor. Snap two more chalk lines to connect the floor points, marking the sole plate's position. If the closet has a side wall return like the one shown on the facing page, lay out the top plate and sole plate the same way; use a framing square to make sure this will be perfectly perpendicular to the front wall. Cut each sole plate and top plate to the desired length.

MARKING STUD POSITIONS Lay each top plate edge-to-edge against its matching sole plate and flush at both ends.

Beginning at an end that will be attached to an existing wall, measure in $1^1/2$ inches—the thickness of a 2-by-4 stud—and draw a line across both plates with a combination square. Starting from that end, measure and draw lines at $15^1/4$ and $16^3/4$ inches. From these lines, advance 16 inches at a time, drawing new lines for stud locations until you reach the far end of both plates.

FRAMING EACH WALL Frame each wall according to the drawing on the opposite page, but note that the sole plate has been cut out where it spans the door's opening—you cut this after the wall is erected. The rough opening for the door requires a king stud and trimmer stud on each side, a header across the top, and cripple studs between the header and the top plate.

Cut the full-length studs to a length equal to the ceiling height minus $3^3/4$ inches (for the $1^1/2$-inch-thick top and sole plates and the needed $1/4$-inch clearance).

Nail short "cripple" studs into the top plate at appropriate intervals or, if you have nailed in studs across the doorway, cut these to size. Measure and cut the header and nail it to the bottoms of the cripple studs with 16-penny nails. Then toenail it to the king studs with 8-penny nails. Measure and cut two trimmer studs and nail one to each king stud with 10-penny nails in a staggered pattern. You'll probably need to adjust the width of the opening by adding a pair of trimmers on one side.

BUILDING THE WALLS Once the walls are built, lift them into place and shim between the top plate and the ceiling joists. Anchor the end studs to existing wall studs or to blocking inserted between the studs.

Lay each sole plate between the lines on the floor and nail them in place with 10-penny nails spaced every 2 feet. Do not nail the portion of the sole plate that runs across your planned closet doorway. Nail them to the header and sole plate. Cut out the sole plate, taking care not to damage any flooring beneath it, to match the width of the rough opening. Pry the sole plate away from the subflooring or flooring.

FINISHING Add wall coverings to match the room. If you're installing gypsum wallboard (see pages 108–110), tape the seams between the new and old wallboard and protect any outside corners with metal cornerbead. For information on painting, refer to the Painting chapter, which begins on page 28.

Next, hang the doors. Bifold doors move in metal tracks mounted to the bottom of the head jamb. Pivots turn in top and bottom brackets and a center guide at the top runs in the track. Sliding doors run on rollers inside metal tracks with floor guides below that maintain the doors in line. Tracks are available to fit standard 1⅜-inch interior doors. A trim strip hides the track. Most doors come with all the necessary hardware.

To install a rod inside a closet, a good option is to use pole sockets. First, screw one socket in place, then insert the rod and level it before fastening the other socket. If the rod is very long, provide additional support by fastening a hook to the top or back of the case near the middle of the rod.

BUILDING A CLOSET

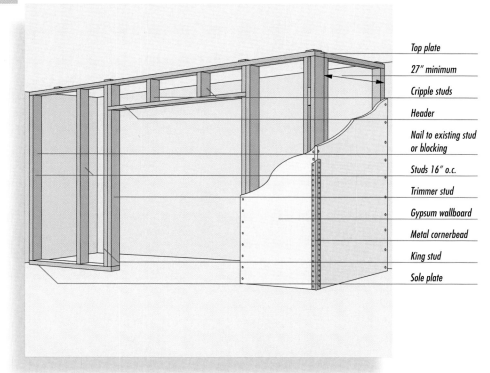

Top plate
27" minimum
Cripple studs
Header
Nail to existing stud or blocking
Studs 16" o.c.
Trimmer stud
Gypsum wallboard
Metal cornerbead
King stud
Sole plate

BIFOLD DOORS

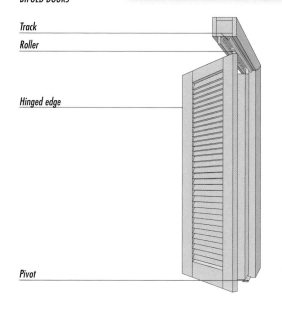

Track
Roller
Hinged edge
Pivot

SLIDING DOORS

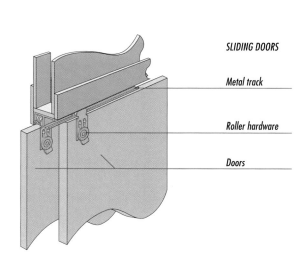

Metal track
Roller hardware
Doors

Assembling a Closet System

When it comes to storage, it isn't necessarily how many closets your home has that counts but how well-organized and efficient those closets are. Good storage means maximizing space as well as storing items in an easy-to-access fashion. Modular closet organizers featuring shelves, drawers, and rods can turn the messiest area into perfectly functional storage space. Most modular closet systems allow you to choose the various components—shelves, cabinets, drawers, tie racks, shoe racks—that you want. Some come as a prepackaged set.

FIGURING CLOSET LAYOUT

Knowing the basic dimensions of the items you would like to store will help you plan your system and choose components. Check your own clothing and other storage needs against these measurements to customize your closet system for a perfect fit.

Modular systems are sold either pre-assembled, requiring you to simply mount the components on supports and sometimes install door fronts on cabinets, or as ready-to-assemble—"RTA"—kits. Most RTA storage systems are made of melamine, plastic-laminate, or wood-veneered panels that are connected with special knockdown hardware—a combination of special cam studs and locks that fit into pre-bored holes. Assembly is simple, requiring a few basic hand tools (sometimes the tools are even included in the package).

When putting together the right system for your needs, consider both the types of items you want to store plus their general dimensions, such as the hanging length of dresses, coats, shirts, blouses, and pants.

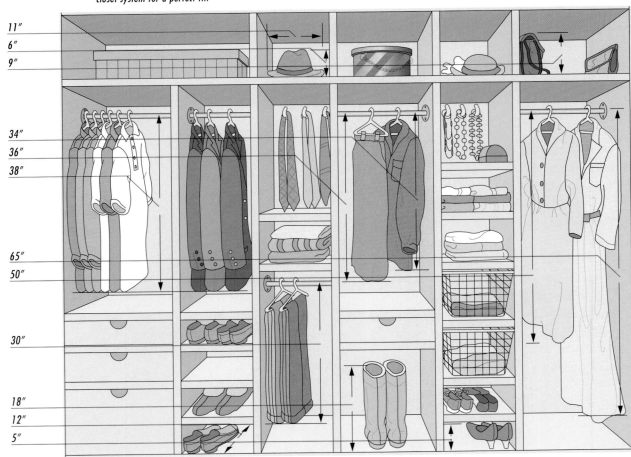

11"
6"
9"
34"
36"
38"
65"
50"
30"
18"
12"
5"

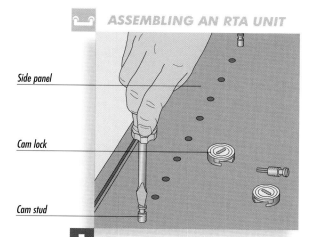

Side panel

Cam lock

Cam stud

1 Fix cam studs

Lay the unit's side panels (the uprights) flat on the floor, next to each other. Decide where each shelf and horizontal panel in the unit will be located. Screw cam studs into the holes in the side panels at those locations. Turn the studs clockwise until they are fully seated.

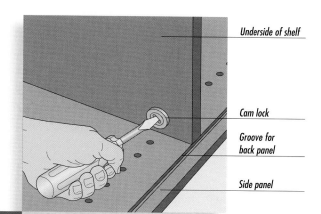

Underside of shelf

Cam lock

Groove for back panel

Side panel

2 Attach the shelves

Push the cam locks into the pre-bored holes on the bottom corners of the shelves and turn them so they are oriented to receive the cam studs. Slip the holes at the shelves' ends onto the cam studs. With a screwdriver, rotate the cam locks to secure the shelves.

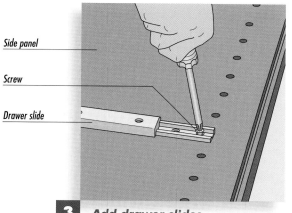

Side panel

Screw

Drawer slide

3 Add drawer slides

If your unit has drawers, screw the drawer slides to the sides of the cabinet at the appropriate heights. Then attach the slides to the drawer sides.

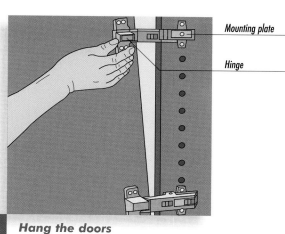

Mounting plate

Hinge

4 Hang the doors

Attach the hinges to the doors. For each hinge, screw the mounting plate, which detaches from the hinge, into the proper hole in the cabinet. Then attach the hinges to the mounting plates according to the manufacturer's instructions.

Installing Shelving

Dollar for dollar, there is no cheaper, nor more functional, storage on the market than a set of sturdy shelves. Installed in cabinets, built into wall units, or simply mounted by themselves on brackets or supports, shelves recapture lost space to support books, photos, clothing, towels, kitchenware, sporting goods, knickknacks, and just about anything else you can imagine.

Installing shelving is also perhaps the easiest project for the novice do-it-yourselfer, and the quickest way to increase your storage capacity.

 SHELF SUPPORTS

Both track-and-bracket and track-and-clip systems allow you to adjust shelf height at will. Shelf brackets, Z-brackets, and L-braces are used for fastening a shelf to a wall or case. Ledger strips are fastened along the back and sides of a case or to the sides of studs to support the shelving.

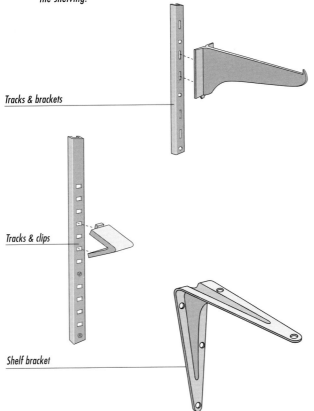

Tracks & brackets

Tracks & clips

Shelf bracket

MATERIALS Good, strong shelves can be made from a number of different materials: solid lumber such as pine or fir, plywood, particleboard, or glass. Choosing the right material for your needs depends on both the appearance and the strength you want the shelving to have. Strength is based on the load the shelf will bear and the distance it will span between supports.

Some materials can span farther than others without bowing or breaking under a given load, so match the shelf material and support span to the load. If, for example, you intend to place your television and VCR on a shelf, you will either need to use a strong material or shorten the span, or both. Glass shelving takes light loads only.

Of the solid woods, softwoods such as pine and fir are sold as boards through lumber dealers and are a good choice for relatively inexpensive shelving. You can choose from several grades. The most popular choices are Select (sometimes called Clear) and Common. Look for C-and-better Select if you want flawless, knot-free wood. Other, less expensive choices for shelving are No. 2 and No. 3 Common "knotty" pine. Whatever the grade, let your eyes be the final judge.

Hardwoods such as oak, birch, and maple also are available through hardwood lumber dealers. They are beautiful, and you pay for that beauty. Hardwoods run from expensive to very expensive depending on the rarity of the wood.

Hardwood-veneered plywood is more commonly used for shelving than is solid hardwood. Plywood is considerably less expensive, comes in wide (4-by-8-foot) sheets, and won't warp or twist as readily as will solid wood. In cabinet construction, the plywood is usually edged with hardwood veneer tape or trimmed with solid hardwood to hide its laminated core.

Laminate and melamine are a hallmark of European-style wall systems and are known for their ease of maintenance and reasonable prices. Shelves with a core of plywood are sturdier and less likely to sag than those with a core of particleboard or related medium-density fiberboard (MDF). Of the surfacing materials, plastic laminate is by far the most durable. Melamine, a surface layer of resin-impregnated paper, is very serviceable and considerably less expensive than plastic laminate. Vinyl paper-wrapped shelves (or shelves made of raw particleboard) are the lowest grade.

Plate glass with ground edges is a popular shelf material for display because it doesn't block light. Choose $1/4$-, $3/8$-, or $1/2$-inch thickness, depending on the span, and use it only for lightweight loads.

SHELF SUPPORTS Many types of brackets are available for attaching shelves to walls, including track-and-bracket systems, track-and-clip systems, shelf brackets, and more. Shelf brackets and track-and-bracket systems attach to the wall; track-and-clip systems go on the sides of cabinet walls or shelf supports.

A shelf is only as strong as the solidity of its attachment to the wall. To support heavy objects, the brackets should be fastened into a stud or masonry wall. For lightweight storage, you can fasten to wallboard or plaster. (See "Fastening to Walls & Ceilings," pages 102–103.)

MOUNTING TRACKS & BRACKETS

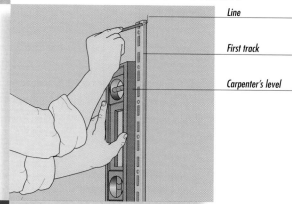

Line
First track
Carpenter's level

1 Install the first track

Cut the tracks to length with a hacksaw, making sure that the slots will align. Locate the wall studs (see page 103) and center the first track over one. Drill a pilot hole through a hole in the track and drive in a screw until almost tight. Check the track for plumb, mark a line along it on the wall, line up the track, bore pilot holes, and drive in the remaining screws.

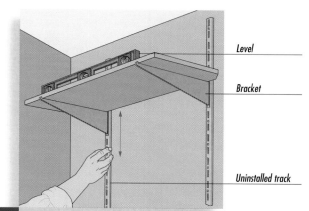

Level
Bracket
Uninstalled track

2 Install the second track & shelf

Insert a bracket in the first track and one in the matching slot of the second track. Holding the second track in position, lay a shelf across the brackets. Place a carpenter's level on the shelf, adjust the second track until level, and mark the top of the track on the wall. Check the track for plumb and screw it in place. Finally, install the brackets and shelf.

MAXIMUM SHELF SPANS

MATERIAL	SPAN
1-by-$3/4$-inch pine or fir	30 inches
2-by-$1 1/2$-inch pine or fir	48 inches
$5/4$-inch hardwood	48 inches
$3/4$-inch plywood-core veneer or laminate	36 inches
$3/4$-inch particleboard-core veneer or laminate	24 inches
$1/4$-inch plate glass (12 inches deep)	36 inches
$3/8$-inch plate glass (12 inches deep)	48 inches
$1/2$-inch plate glass (12 inches deep)	60 inches

Note: Reduce all spans for heavy loads. Glass shelves are sized for lightweight loads only.

Cabinet Repairs

Sometimes all your cabinets need to give your kitchen system a whole new lease on life is a bit of basic repair or a few minor improvements. Changing your pulls, for example, can completely alter the look of your cabinets. (Before you invest, remember to measure the distance between the screw holes in the cabinet face because you won't want to drill new holes.)

HINGES If your cabinet doors droop or shut poorly, consider repairing or changing the hinges. First, try tightening the screws. If a screw won't tighten, remove it, squirt a little white glue into the screw hole, and break off some wooden toothpicks in the hole to fill it up (wipe off any excess glue). After the glue dries, cut the toothpicks flush with the surface using a utility knife, and drive the screw into the refurbished hole (you may have to drill a small pilot hole first).

Exposed decorative hinges can also add a new design element to your cabinets. Hinges can be found at hardware and home centers in virtually every style and size. You're sure to find replacements that will both fit your cabinets and perk up their appearance.

If it seems that your cabinet doors are perpetually hanging open, you may want to switch to self-closing hinges, which do not require a separate catch to keep the door closed. Many types of hinges are available in self-closing styles.

If you have European frameless-style cabinets and the doors are out of adjustment, the chances are good that you can adjust the hinges. Most of the hinges that attach doors to these types of cabinets can be adjusted with the turn of a screw to bring the door into line. They're usually mounted directly to the interior cabinet side and are hidden when the door is closed. They also do not require a catch since they are self-closing.

DOOR HINGES

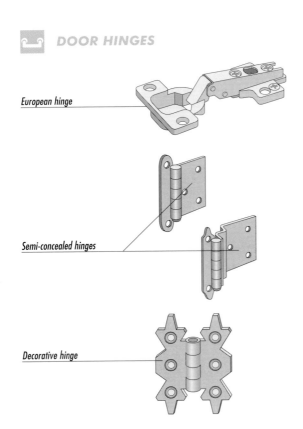

European hinge

Semi-concealed hinges

Decorative hinge

DOOR CATCHES & LATCHES

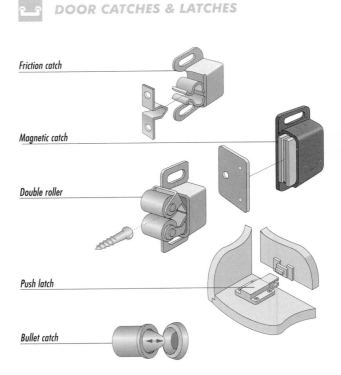

Friction catch

Magnetic catch

Double roller

Push latch

Bullet catch

CATCHES & LATCHES Hinges alone may not be adequate to keep wayward doors closed. If you think you'd like extra holding power—perhaps due to the presence of a small child or the likelihood of earthquake rattling—catches, latches, and locks may add an extra measure of security.

Magnetic catches work well in most conventional situations, since they are less dependent on strict alignment than are other types and they do not wear out. Other alternatives include friction catches, with a metal protrusion that catches or clicks into a metal opening, and double and single rollers, with spring-loaded arms that close over a strikeplate or screw.

Locks can also be used on display cabinets to keep valuables visible but safe, particularly in earthquake country.

Lock assemblies comprise a bolt, a strikeplate, and an escutcheon, which encircles the keyhole.

DRAWERS Another common, and easily accomplished, repair involves misaligned drawers, or drawers that don't close easily or well. This problem can usually be solved by re-attaching or replacing the drawer's glides. For the smoothest, most trouble-free drawer opening and closing, purchase prefabricated metal ball-bearing glide sets that attach to the drawer bottom or sides, depending on your drawer's construction and current type of glide. The manufacturer's instructions should detail proper installation.

If you want to use side glides in a faceframe cabinet, you'll need to bring the mounting surface flush with the edge of the faceframe stiles by gluing and screwing filler strips to the inside of the cabinet's sides.

 TWO TYPES OF DRAWER GLIDES

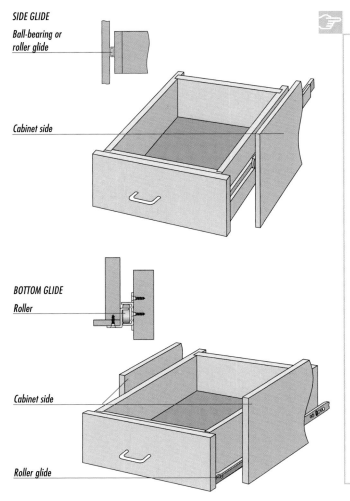

SIDE GLIDE
Ball-bearing or roller glide

Cabinet side

BOTTOM GLIDE
Roller

Cabinet side

Roller glide

 REFACING CABINETS

If your goal is to update your present kitchen, or if you're on a tight budget, a cost-effective and speedy alternative to completely replacing your cabinets is to reface them.

Refacing literally gives a face-lift to your cabinet fronts. With this process, a specialty company or cabinetmaker removes existing doors and drawer fronts and replaces them with new ones. Visible surfaces such as cabinet ends, edge banding, and faceframes are finished to match. The results often look as good as if you had replaced the entire cabinet system.

When is refacing, rather than replacing, a good idea? If the basic boxes are in good shape and you are satisfied with your current layout, this could be an attractive option. You can usually choose from a broad range of door and drawer styles, hardware, and finishes. Typically, the company's representatives will show you samples, take measurements, and return for the installation. Refacers probably won't work on cabinet interiors, so you may want to refinish or repaint them yourself before the new cabinet faces are installed. Cabinet refacers are usually listed in the Yellow Pages under "Cabinet Refinishing & Refacing," "Kitchen Cabinets & Equipment," or similar headings. In addition, many home improvement centers and lumberyards either offer these services or provide references.

Hearth

It is almost primal, our love of the hearth. In winter particularly, and with a roaring fire going, the fireplace is the gathering spot of choice, guaranteed to suffuse the room with light and warmth and its inhabitants with a cozy sense of well-being. A welcoming hearth is an asset to any room in the house and, more and more, hearths are turning up in master suites, family rooms, and kitchens, where, equipped with built-in grill racks and rotisseries, they often double as alternative cooking sources.

Along with traditional built-in fireplaces, direct-vent, zero-clearance, and a host of other fireplaces are readily available today; so are new turns on the tried-and-true wood stove. This chapter introduces you to the range of fireplace options, and the differences between a fireplace and a wood stove. You will also learn the basics of installing prefabricated fireplaces and wood stoves, as well as how to handle basic hearth repairs.

Fireplaces & Wood Stoves

One look at the dense plume of smoke coming from the chimneys of traditional fireplaces and older wood stoves clearly evidences why home fires have come under scrutiny in recent years. In certain areas, weather conditions called inversion layers trap pollutant-laden air close to the ground, resulting in thick, stifling, health-threatening smoke and gases. As a result, many regional air quality agencies now ask homeowners to limit or forgo fires.

The good news is that these concerns have spawned a new generation of fireplaces and wood stoves that burn fuel so cleanly that they are usually exempt from limitations or prohibitions. Not only do they pollute less, but they also can significantly contribute to meeting a home's heating needs. The cleanest-burning ones use natural gas or propane, though others that burn solid fuels such as firewood or compressed sawdust pellets are cleaner-burning than their predecessors. As a result, installing and upgrading fireplaces and wood stoves are popular home improvements.

Fireplace Options

When considering a fireplace, you can select from any of many possibilities, from classic masonry fireplaces to heat-efficient direct-vent models.

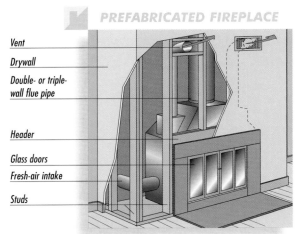

PREFABRICATED FIREPLACE

Vent
Drywall
Double- or triple-wall flue pipe

Header
Glass doors
Fresh-air intake
Studs

A zero-clearance, prefabricated fireplace can be built right into a wood-frame wall. This type is heat circulating—cool air is warmed in the air space around the firebox and then vented into the room.

MASONRY FIREPLACES A masonry fireplace has a solid firebox, leading upward to a damper, a smoke shelf, a smoke dome, and a chimney.

The mass of the firebox and chimney can weigh more than 5,000 pounds, requiring it to rest on a concrete foundation. Building a masonry fireplace within an existing home is difficult and expensive, so most masonry contractors only build on an outside wall. To economize, the ash pit may be eliminated, but the flue and hearth are safety features every fireplace needs.

Most masonry fireplaces don't supply much heat to a room. Because wood needs oxygen to burn, the fire draws air through cracks around doors and windows, displacing the warmer room air, which goes up the chimney along with flue gases. To improve heating efficiency, you can add ceramic or tempered glass doors to the front of the fireplace. These help control the amount of air being pulled into the fireplace, minimizing interior room drafts. You also may have the option of providing combustion air directly into the firebox.

PREFABRICATED FIREPLACES Factory-built prefabricated ("prefab") fireplaces come in both radiant and heat-circulating designs. Unlike masonry fireplaces, they have metal fireboxes and outer metal shells that allow them to be placed near wood framing (these are often called zero-clearance fireplaces). Sizes and corresponding heat (or Btu) output vary to accommodate different heating needs. (For wood-burning units, there is an additional special category—the masonry heater.) They are also relatively lightweight (600 to 800 pounds) compared with their masonry counterparts. Units can be fitted to existing masonry chimneys or double-wall metal flues.

One of the most appealing features of the new gas units, as well as of some pellet burners, is that the temperature and particulate level of the exhaust is low enough to allow direct venting through a wall. Doing away with the need for a chimney not only reduces cost, but also allows these units to be installed almost anywhere there is an outside wall.

For large rooms where the fireplace will be the focal point, an inside installation, with the boxed-in chase, or fireplace enclosure, jutting into the room, is preferable.

If you want to maximize space around the fireplace, an outside installation is the answer. You'll need a new foundation to support the weight of the firebox and of the double-wall flue. The firebox and flue will be surrounded by a wood-framed chase, then covered with stucco or other material to create a chimney shape.

HYBRID FIREPLACES Hybrid fireplaces replicate most of the heat-producing elements of wood stoves, including the means of controlling combustion. Similar to wood stove inserts, hybrids have large, gasketed glass doors that prevent air leaks, heat-exchange systems that allow them to burn at an efficiency level equal to that of many wood stoves, and heat ducts that vent hot air back into the room by natural convection or small fans.

Hybrids cost more than factory-built fireplaces but may lower heating bills. If you plan to retrofit a hybrid into an existing fireplace, consult the dealer to see if special supports or clearances are necessary.

FREE-STANDING FIREPLACES Free-standing fireplaces work best if they're located where heat can radiate to all parts of a room. One type of free-standing fireplace has a fire pit with exposure all around; smoke rises into a hood and then into a chimney. Another type is made from prefabricated metal, typically shaped between a cylinder and a sphere, with exposure on one side only. Because they're lightweight, you can even install them on a second floor.

Wood Stoves

As heaters, wood stoves are more economical than fireplaces. With a plentiful wood supply and proper installation, a wood stove can pay for itself in a few years, especially in areas where utility rates and the need for supplementary heat are high.

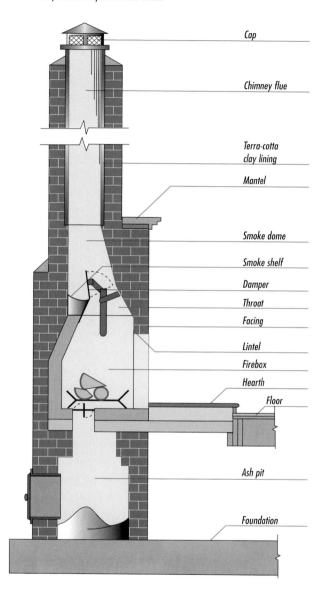

 CONVENTIONAL FIREPLACE

A conventional masonry fireplace rests on a reinforced concrete foundation. Many fireplaces today omit the ash pit below the firebox. The cap at the top of the chimney may not be required in all areas.

Cap

Chimney flue

Terra-cotta clay lining

Mantel

Smoke dome

Smoke shelf

Damper

Throat

Facing

Lintel

Firebox

Hearth

Floor

Ash pit

Foundation

Using a wood stove to heat part or all of your home is also a lifestyle decision, especially if you're used to regulating heat with a wall thermostat. Locating, buying, carrying, splitting, and stacking wood, as well as stocking and tending the fire and dumping the ashes, are chores you may find objectionable. While wood stoves require consistent care and attention, they return the investment by lending charm to a room and radiating comforting warmth.

(continued on page 270)

Fireplaces & Wood Stoves

(continued from page 269)

Although stoves come in hundreds of different interior and exterior designs, they fall into three main categories: conventional stoves, fireplace inserts, and pellet stoves.

CONVENTIONAL WOOD STOVES Conventional stoves are cast-iron or welded-steel boxes with an outside "skin" made from ceramic tile or soapstone. Inside the stove is a firebox lined with refractory brick. Stoves can have either of two heat-exchange systems—radiant or convective. In radiant-heating models, the metal box is heated by fuel combustion, and the heat is allowed to radiate into the room by passing through the walls of the stove.

Convective, or heat-circulating, wood stoves provide more even heat distribution. The firebox is encased in a vented metal shell. Cool room air is pulled into the stove through vents near floor level; then, after being heated by the firebox, the air exits through the stove's upper vents by convection—the natural tendency of warm air to rise. Some stoves use small fans to augment the movement of heated air.

Convective stoves also heat by radiation, but the outside surfaces don't heat up as quickly as those surrounding a radiant stove. This makes convective stoves slower to heat a room, but it also makes the stove much less hot—and therefore safer when children are nearby. Also, heat-circulating stoves generally don't need as much clearance from combustibles, a distinct advantage if you're adding one to a small room.

Air pollution regulations have forced wood stove manufacturers to incorporate new design features into their products. Stoves with catalytic combustors reduce emission levels for particulate matter and carbon monoxide, and have better heating efficiency than noncatalytic models.

FIREPLACE INSERTS Many fireplace inserts—wood stoves that are designed to be placed into an existing fireplace—combine elements of both radiant and convective designs. They have large radiant surfaces that face the room and circulating jackets on the other sides to capture heat that would otherwise go up the chimney.

If you already have a traditional masonry or prefabricated metal fireplace, an insert can convert it to an energy-efficient heater. You will also need to modify your chimney with a properly sized liner that will slip inside your existing flue and join directly to the insert. This assures the unit will have the proper draw and burn rate and minimizes the risk of a chimney fire caused by creosote buildup. For more about inserts, see page 282.

PELLET STOVES A relatively recent development on the market, pellet stoves are so named because they burn small pellets made from wood byproducts. Some stoves have large glass doors and ceramic logs to create the illusion of a bigger fire. Pellet stoves look like wood stoves or fireplace inserts, but their interior construction makes them unique.

A microprocessor directs the air and fuel intakes. An electric auger feeds the pellets from a hopper into the fire chamber, where blown air creates a superheated firebox. The fire burns at such a high temperature that the smoke is literally burned up, and no chimney is needed. As in a clothes dryer, the waste gases are vented outside through a duct.

The outside air intake is operated by an electric motor; another small electric fan blows the heated air from the fire chamber into the room. The electronic microprocessor controls the operation, allowing the pellet stove to be controlled by a thermostat.

Although they require periodic maintenance, much like a boiler or furnace, pellet stoves are easy to operate and can burn for up to 80 hours without having to be refueled. An additional advantage to such stoves is that the pellets come in easy-to-store plastic sacks, eliminating the need for cutting, hauling, and stacking firewood. Before deciding on this option, however, check the price and availability of pellets in your area. Also, make sure you can easily obtain parts and service.

Fireplace & Wood Stove Planning

If you've been thinking about adding a fireplace or wood stove, chances are you already know where you want it and how you want it to look. Before you make your final decision, however, consider these important points:

SIZE & SHAPE OF THE ROOM In a large rectangular space, such as a family room, most people naturally gravitate toward a source of heat. Place the firebox on a long wall if possible, to accommodate groups wanting to cozy up to the hearth. If the room is square, consider installing it in a corner to provide maximum exposure.

If space is limited, think about a flush installation—adding the fireplace or wood stove so that its depth protrudes outside the wall. You will need to make sure the clearance between your property and your neighbor's is sufficient, however. If you need to split the difference, with the fireplace partially projecting into the room, keep in mind how this will affect furniture placement and traffic flow.

STRUCTURAL LIMITATIONS Fireplace location may be determined by your home construction and property limitations. For example, a factory-built fireplace and its flue may require the building of a foundation. The weight of a flue can be as much as 8 pounds per linear foot. The firebox or stove can range from 150 to 700 pounds. An interior installation may require reinforcing floor joists. If weight is a problem, direct-vent fireplaces, which require no foundation or flue, are alternatives.

Multistory homes pose special challenges. The flue must be taller and, if it is located inside, must pass through the upstairs room. If you've decided to build a fireplace on the lower floor, think about placing another one on the upper floor. Both flues can be enclosed in the same chase for a moderate additional cost.

(continued on page 272)

CLEARANCES TO COMBUSTIBLES

Safe installation of any fuel-burning appliance, as well as accompanying flues and stovepipes, requires a distance from all combustible materials and surfaces. A combustible wall or floor is constructed of or contains a flammable material such as wood, wallboard, or vinyl. Tile is also considered a combustible material because cracks in the grouting can provide openings for embers to ignite interior walls. Solid masonry walls and floors (unpainted brick, stone, or concrete) are considered noncombustible.

The National Fire Protection Association (NFPA) recommends safety clearances and installation standards for wood stoves. These standards have been adopted by most building departments across the country and by the stove industry as a whole. Before buying a wood stove, check that it has a label with clearance and hearth requirements. The NFPA recom-

mends that wood stoves be at least 36 inches away from combustible walls and ceilings.

You can reduce clearance requirements by setting your fireplace or wood stove flush to a wall and by following fire-safe construction rules. Most stoves provide metal shields or double-wall chimney connectors, allowing them to pass building department inspections. Still, you may want to protect adjacent walls with a noncombustible material, such as 3½-inch-thick masonry, 24-gauge sheet metal, or ½-inch-thick cement board; all should be installed with spacers to maintain a 1-inch ventilated air space between the wall and the shield.

In addition to hearth clearance requirements, allow adequate clearance where the chimney connector meets the chimney by installing an insulated support assembly or an insulated pipe fitting.

Hearth

(continued from page 271)

LOCATING & ESTIMATING FOR THE FLUE One of the most important considerations when installing a fireplace or wood stove is the flue. The flue and all its connections should be set as vertical as possible because horizontal runs, bends, or offsets will restrict draft.

If you're planning to vent a wood stove into an existing fireplace or unused chimney, you have additional considerations. For the best draw, center the stove below the thimble (the opening where the stovepipe enters the flue). Never place a stove in a closet or alcove unless it has been tested and approved for that type of placement.

Make a sketch of your home's elevation, measuring the height from the foundation where your flue will be installed to the highest point of the roof. The flue must extend at least 2 feet above this and at least 12 feet above the firebox. The stove or fireplace manufacturer should provide a list of all acceptable brands of flue.

THE HEARTH Adding beauty to your home is not the only function of a hearth. Almost always made of noncombustible material, it protects the adjoining floor from sparks, runaway logs, and heat radiated from the fire. Any fireplace set into or against a wall requires a hearth that extends a code-required distance from the front opening and out to each side, depending on the size of the fireplace.

Most hearths are either flush with the floor or raised above it. Space often dictates the choice: Small rooms are better endowed with flush hearths; large rooms command raised hearths to match the scale of the space.

THE FIREPLACE MANTEL A wood- or gas-burning fireplace often calls for a mantel—a horizontal shelf above the fireplace, usually made of brick, wood, metal, or a synthetic masonry material. A mantel serves a purely decorative function. They can be custom-made from mills or carvers, or bought premanufactured.

FACING MATERIALS A time-honored choice for mantels, wood is also a popular choice for fireplace facing. Typical code requirements dictate that the wood be set back at least 6 inches from both sides of the firebox opening and 16 inches from the top. Check with your building department for local clearance requirements. Brick, marble, slate, and tile also are popular facing materials, but, like wood, their installation must meet fire-safety and other codes. Clearly, the kind of facing you choose isn't just a decorating choice, and is affected by the projection of the firebox.

The thickness of your facing material affects how you frame the wall. For example, if you're facing the surrounding wall with standard-size brick, the offset must equal the depth of the brick, plus $3/8$ inch for the wallboard or plywood skin covering the framing, plus the thickness of the mortar between brick and skin.

The duct locations for heat-circulating fireplaces also can affect the facing design. Some fireplace models take in air from the front and expel it from the sides; others in reverse.

 STANDARD HEARTH & STOVE CLEARANCES

For a fireplace, the hearth should extend at least 8 inches on each side and 16 inches from the front of the opening. For fireplaces with openings greater than 6 square feet, the hearth should extend no less than 12 inches on each side and 20 inches from the front.

For a stove, the hearth should extend at least 18 inches on all sides. Stoves with legs providing less than 2 inches of ventilated air space to the floor should be placed on a non-combustible floor. Stoves with legs providing 2 to 6 inches of ventilated air space to the floor may be placed on a combustible floor provided that the subfloor is protected with 24-gauge sheet metal and one course of hollow masonry units at least 4 inches thick.

Stoves with legs providing more than 6 inches of air space underneath the unit can be placed over combustible floors. In this situation, the subfloor must be protected with 24-gauge sheet metal and solid masonry units 2 inches thick to ensure safe clearance.

Hearth Improvement Tools

Most of the improvements discussed in this chapter deal with installing a prefabricated fireplace, wood stove, or fireplace insert. Be aware that these are comprehensive construction jobs and may involve not only a range of skills but a wide variety of tools, from those used for building a foundation to those needed for finishing a wall.

For a complete fireplace installation, you'll need most of the tools shown for walls and ceilings on pages 100–101, some flooring tools (pages 136–137), roofing tools (pages 324–325), and, in some cases, siding tools (page 290). You may also need electrical tools (pages 474–475) if your installation entails wiring, and a few plumbing tools (pages 408–409) for installing a gas hook-up. Finally, you'll need a ladder when installing a chimney.

CONSTRUCTION TOOLS

Shown here are some of the key tools necessary for installing a new prefabricated fireplace.

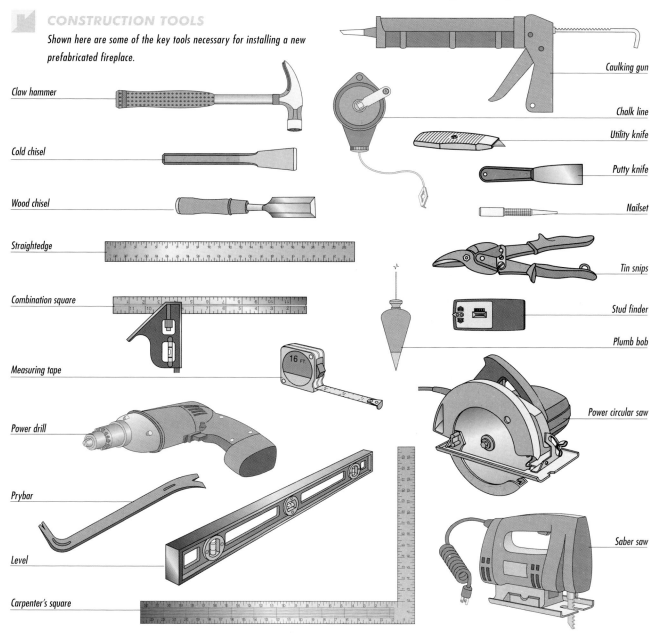

Claw hammer

Cold chisel

Wood chisel

Straightedge

Combination square

Measuring tape

Power drill

Prybar

Level

Carpenter's square

Caulking gun

Chalk line

Utility knife

Putty knife

Nailset

Tin snips

Stud finder

Plumb bob

Power circular saw

Saber saw

Installing a Prefab Fireplace

Unlike building a traditional brick fireplace, installing a factory-built fireplace requires no masonry skills. The project is straightforward unless the installation involves running a flue through an upstairs bedroom or attic. Nevertheless, this is a relatively big job that does require knowledge of basic construction techniques such as working with concrete foundations, framing walls, and more. If you're not an avid do-it-yourselfer, you're better off having your new fireplace professionally installed.

A fireplace can be installed flush in a wall as discussed on the next three pages; or boxed in at the end of a room, or in a corner, as shown below. Installing a fireplace inside the walls of your home is considerably more involved because you must provide proper support under the floor and run a flue up through the ceiling and out the roof. For this type of project, call a building contractor or professional fireplace installer.

Following are general guidelines for accomplishing an outside installation. Manufacturers provide specific guidelines for framing, depending on the product. Be sure to check those specifications and follow the directions precisely.

THE OVERALL STRATEGY The firebox and flue are installed in a chimney-like enclosure called a "chase," which is framed like a conventional wall. The chase must be supported by a foundation. It can narrow above the fireplace and be covered to resemble a masonry chimney, or it can extend in an unbroken line to the top and be covered to match the siding of the house.

Although factory-built fireplaces come in a wide range of shapes and sizes, a typical firebox opening is 28 to 42 inches wide and 16 to 24 inches high. The overall dimensions of the fireplace and the size of the room determine whether the fireplace projects fully into the room, is placed entirely outside the wall, or falls somewhere in between. Typical outside dimensions for built-in fireplaces are 38 to 52 inches wide, 23 to 26 inches front to back, and 40 to 58 inches from the bottom of the firebox to the top of the smoke dome.

Detailed dimensions may matter more than overall dimensions if your space is tight. For example, the chimney collar may fall at the center of the front-to-back axis or off to one side. The exact location of the chimney collar will affect the placement of your fireplace and its foundation.

If you're installing a heat-circulating fireplace with flexible ducting, you'll have to frame openings for inlets and/or outlets. You may want to make a trial assembly of the ducts before framing to make sure you understand the needs of the installation. Also, before you begin to frame, plan where you'll place the opening for an outside combustion air duct and where you'll plumb the gas line for a gas lighter, if you're using these optional devices.

(continued on page 276)

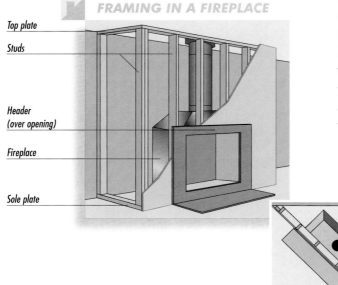

FRAMING IN A FIREPLACE

Top plate

Studs

Header (over opening)

Fireplace

Sole plate

TOP VIEW

Fireplace

Framed wall

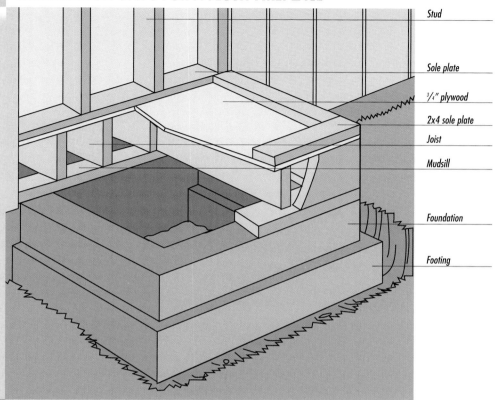

Stud

Sole plate

³/₄″ plywood

2x4 sole plate

Joist

Mudsill

Foundation

Footing

1 **Build the platform**

Pour a foundation as discussed on page 276 and cut open the wall. Then build a platform flush with the subfloor and a ³/₈-inch-thick hearth flush with the finished floor. Lap the joists for the platform at least 1 foot along existing subfloor joists and nail with at least three 3¹/₂-inch common nails on both sides, at each end of the overlap.

2

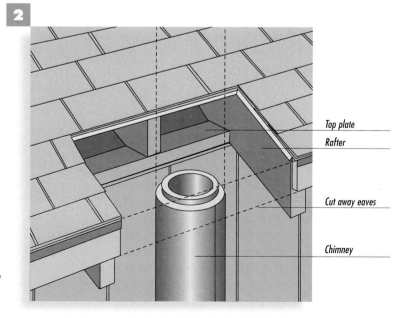

Top plate

Rafter

Cut away eaves

Chimney

Assemble the chimney

Position the fireplace, then assemble the chimney to the eaves. Hold the pipe in place with temporary plumber's tape bands until you build the framing. Cut the roof eaves' line back flush with the house wall and just wide enough to accept the framing plus its covering.

(continued on page 277)

Installing a Prefab Fireplace

(continued from page 274)
Factory-built fireplaces have stand-offs and V-shaped spacing tabs on the firebox to maintain clearances, so framing members may not be notched to fit these in. Don't be misled by the term "zero clearance," which only applies to the base, not the top or sides.

ESTABLISHING A BASE As shown on page 275, dig out the site for a continuous footing and foundation to the same depth as the house's. Build concrete forms and tie steel reinforcing bars in the footing into those in the existing foundation. Top the foundation with a mudsill that is flush with its counterpart in the main foundation.

Then cut away both interior and exterior wall surface materials to expose the wall's framing. Erect a support reaching from floor to ceiling and beyond each side of the opening to support the ceiling joists while you cut out the studs and replace them with a framed opening, as discussed on pages 188–189. Build the header from a pair of 2 by 6's on edge. If you're planning an outer hearth, trim the sole plate flush with the inside finished floor.

If you plan to change level in order to have a raised hearth, or to lower the fireplace so the firebox floor is flush with the hearth extension, consult your building department before designing a foundation and joist system. Especially in cases of lowering a firebox, you risk violating codes on minimum clearances of wood from earth and wood from firebox opening. Once the platform is complete, slide the fireplace into position, then add a sole plate around the platform perimeter.

BUILDING THE CHASE After you position the fireplace, assemble and attach the flue up to the eaves (if you're using 15-inch-diameter pipe, it won't fit between studs set 16 inches on center). Pipes of smaller diameter can be assembled after framing is complete. For more about framing techniques, see page 98.

Use 2-by-4 studs spaced 16 inches on center to build exterior walls around the perimeter. Diagonal bracing or plywood sheathing may be required by code. Secure the studs butted against the wall to the main wall's studs.

One area of some complexity is fireblocking. One fireblock is required for every 8 feet of vertical rise. These fireblocks must form a solid horizontal stop across the chase to block upward drafts, and the chimney must have a firestop spacer where it passes through the fireblock, as in inside installations. The example shown approximates the framing for a code-approved firestop, but be sure to check with your building inspector before designing your chase. The horizontal cover is usually made of $5/8$-inch plywood. It must fit snugly against the walls of the chase on all four sides, meeting firestop blocks set between the studs.

When the chase is constructed to its full height, install roof flashing and a closing, such as prefabricated sheet-metal closures available in several sizes from fireplace dealers. Then top the chimney with a cap made for it.

FINISHING THE INTERIOR Replace the interior wall covering (or repair damage), holding any combustible material back the required clearance from the fireplace.

FACING THE FIREPLACE If your facing is made of plywood, drywall, or any other combustible material, it must not cover the fireplace face frame. Instead, butt it flush against the outer edges of the frame, or, if it's to project from the face frame, set it at least 6 inches from the sides of the firebox opening and 12 inches above the top. This setback requirement also applies to mantels.

FINISHING THE HEARTH For a raised hearth, frame a platform over the finished floor, using $3/4$-inch plywood. Place a 24-gauge galvanized steel or aluminum sheet under the firebox and extend it to the end of the hearth to serve as a spark guard.

Reinforce the platform with 2-by-4 cross members centered beneath joints in the plywood. Remember that the bottom thickness of a factory-built fireplace firebox can range from 6 to 9 inches, so the opening will be noticeably higher than the hearth extension unless you set the fireplace on a separate, lower platform.

For a hearth extension approximately flush with the finished floor, cut away the floor to the desired width and length. Lay down $1/2$-inch-thick cement board and bond tile or slate to the board. A hearth laid over a finished floor will require no carpentry, but such hearths produce a toe-stubbing lip, and particularly thick ones may obstruct the inlets of a heat-circulating fireplace.

(continued from page 275)

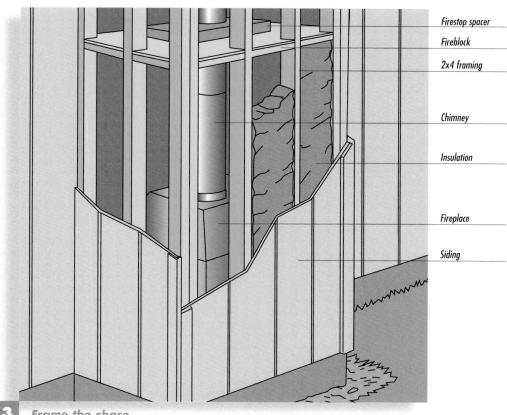

Firestop spacer
Fireblock
2x4 framing
Chimney
Insulation
Fireplace
Siding

3 *Frame the chase*

Using 2-by-4 studs spaced 16 inches on center, build exterior walls around the perimeter. At the top, install roof flashing and a closing, such as a prefabricated sheet-metal closure. Cap the chimney with a manufactured cap. Insulate the chase with unfaced batts. Sheathe or side the exterior of the chase to match the house.

Installing a Wood Stove

When you install a new wood stove (or free-standing fireplace), you don't need to excavate a foundation or build a chase unless you wish to box in the metal flue. Most can be placed directly on a hearth over an unreinforced floor because they are relatively lightweight. For these reasons, the job is considerably easier than the task of installing a new fireplace. The instructions given here are to serve as a general guide; be sure to follow the stove manufacturer's detailed directions.

One of the prime requirements for a safe stove installation is that you place the stove and stovepipe a safe distance from all combustible materials and surfaces. See more about this on page 271.

The flue can pass from the unit up through the ceiling and out the roof, or it can go out the wall and then up past the roofline. The flue for a wood stove is supported by a flue-pipe support system, attached to the wall or ceiling structure. It includes all the pieces needed to support the weight of the flue.

Chimney installation is accomplished in two parts: installing the flue itself, and then placing the stove and connecting it to the flue with the stovepipe.

CHIMNEY INSTALLATIONS

The proper method for installing a chimney depends upon the stove's location and whether or not the home has an attic and/or a second floor.

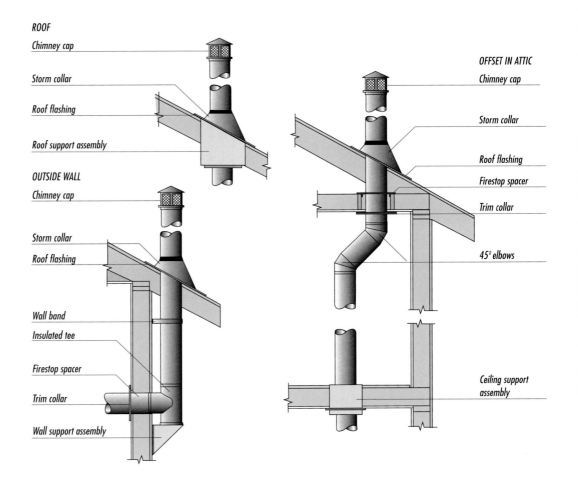

ROOF
Chimney cap
Storm collar
Roof flashing
Roof support assembly

OUTSIDE WALL
Chimney cap
Storm collar
Roof flashing
Wall band
Insulated tee
Firestop spacer
Trim collar
Wall support assembly

OFFSET IN ATTIC
Chimney cap
Storm collar
Roof flashing
Firestop spacer
Trim collar
45° elbows
Ceiling support assembly

CHOOSING THE PROPER FLUE An insulated flue must be used for wood stoves so that smoke and flue gases will remain hot enough to rise. If the flue gases cool before rising to the top, creosote will build up on the inner surfaces and the stove will not draw efficiently, resulting in "back-puffing" of smoke through the stove.

Pipes and fittings for prefabricated metal flues must be approved by Underwriters Laboratories (UL) and by local codes. Several kinds of insulated and ventilated double- and triple-wall stainless steel pipe are approved for wood stove flues. Do not use vent pipe intended for gas or oil furnaces and water heaters, even in a second-story room. These pipes are not approved for use with wood stoves and can lead to fires.

GENERAL TIPS Three things are a must for safe stove installation: proper materials, adequate clearance, and proper assembly of all components. If the chimney is not installed in strict accordance with the manufacturer's instructions, your insurance company may not pay for damages resulting from a chimney fire.

CUTTING THE HOLES If you must cut a joist as shown in Step 2 on page 280 and you don't have attic access, it definitely complicates the job. You'll have to support the ceiling from below and enlarge the ceiling opening to accommodate doubled joist headers and crosspieces. This may necessitate pulling off a broader section of ceiling material and repairing the area when you're finished. You'll also have to install the firestop spacer from below. Call a professional to handle this job unless you're comfortable with the extent of work involved.

Unless you have a beamed ceiling, you'll have to cut holes in both ceiling and roof; cut the ceiling hole first. Then, using a plumb bob, align the ceiling hole with the proposed roof hole. You may have to offset the flue pipe slightly with a pair of elbows to center the roof support assembly between the roof rafters (don't cut rafters) or to pass pipes closer to the roof ridge. This process is similar to the work involved when installing a skylight; for more detail about that, see page 334.

WALL-SUPPORTED CHIMNEY For a wall-supported chimney, the support assembly consists of an insulated tee, a firestop spacer, and a support bracket. The tee should pass completely through the wall and end a minimum of 4 inches beyond the inside wall surface. Wall-supported chimneys either penetrate the roof through the eaves or bypass it, depending on the width of the eaves. If the roof overhang is wide, cut through the roof. Otherwise, bypass it as shown on page 281.

THE HEARTH The stove must sit on a noncombustible hearth. Typically, you can lay down $1/2$-inch-thick cement board and then bond tile, brick, or other masonry to it. Then you grout the joints. Extending a masonry shield up the wall is more difficult, especially if it requires wall protection behind it. You'll need considerable experience for most of these types of installations. If your hearth or its extension is fairly complicated, get help from an experienced mason or stove installer.

CONNECTING THE STOVE Stovepipes come in diameters to fit conventional stoves. If possible, the diameter of the stovepipe should be the same size as the flue opening in the stove. Some stoves may require the use of a flue damper to control the draft; install it in the first section of the stovepipe 6 to 12 inches above the flue collar.

Assemble the pipes, crimped ends down, so creosote won't leak through the joints. Unless you have a specially made piece, you may have to trim off the crimped end of the first section so the pipe will fit the flue collar.

Support horizontal runs of pipe every 2 feet (runs should rarely be longer than that); support vertical pipe at least every 6 feet. Be sure all pipe and fittings have the required 18-inch clearance from combustible surfaces.

(continued on page 280)

Installing a Wood Stove

(continued from page 279)

If you need to cut any lengths of pipe, be careful not to bend the pipe out of shape when cutting. Slip adapters can help eliminate unnecessary cutting. Most prefabricated chimney manufacturers have flue connection kits that include enough interlocking pipe plus the necessary components to perform a single installation.

The final length of stovepipe connects to the chimney support assembly or insulated chimney fitting that is in the wall or ceiling.

TESTING THE EQUIPMENT Once your stove is connected to the chimney and the installation is complete, check the entire chimney and chimney connection, inch by inch. Make sure all joints and other components are fastened securely. Next, light a small, smoky fire in the stove, using damp leaves or newspaper, and check the chimney again for smoke leaks. Make any necessary adjustments.

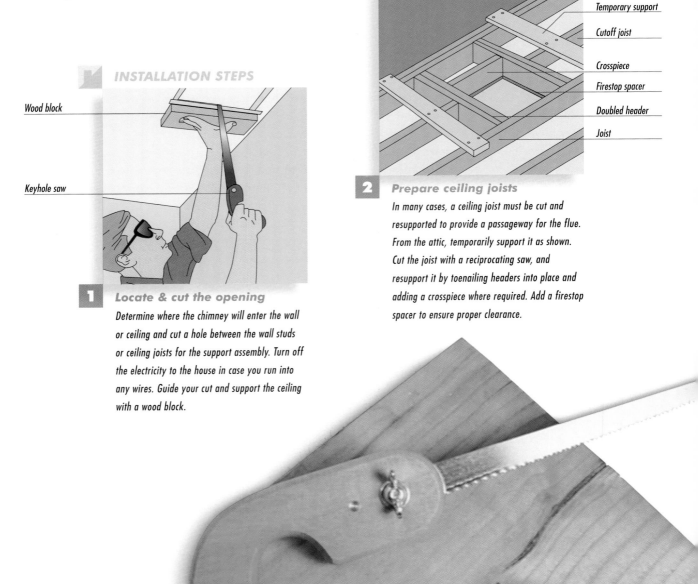

INSTALLATION STEPS

Wood block

Keyhole saw

1 Locate & cut the opening

Determine where the chimney will enter the wall or ceiling and cut a hole between the wall studs or ceiling joists for the support assembly. Turn off the electricity to the house in case you run into any wires. Guide your cut and support the ceiling with a wood block.

Temporary support

Cutoff joist

Crosspiece

Firestop spacer

Doubled header

Joist

2 Prepare ceiling joists

In many cases, a ceiling joist must be cut and resupported to provide a passageway for the flue. From the attic, temporarily support it as shown. Cut the joist with a reciprocating saw, and resupport it by toenailing headers into place and adding a crosspiece where required. Add a firestop spacer to ensure proper clearance.

Hearth Improvements

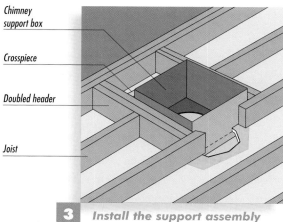

Chimney
support box

Crosspiece

Doubled header

Joist

3 **Install the support assembly**
Following the manufacturer's directions, install the
chimney support box or assembly. Typical support
assemblies are illustrated on page 278 and below.

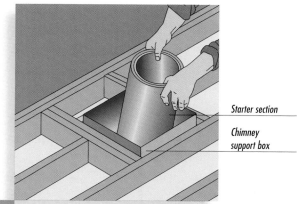

Starter section

Chimney
support box

4 **Assemble the chimney**
Before installing the chimney pipe sections,
practice fitting them together. Insulated flue pipe
sections interlock and are usually marked with an
arrow or the word "up" to orient you. Fit the
starter section into the support box and attach any
fittings by slipping them into position over the
pipe before adding more lengths.

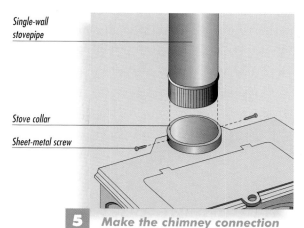

Single-wall
stovepipe

Stove collar

Sheet-metal screw

5 **Make the chimney connection**
Carefully position the stove on the hearth
prepared for it (as explained on page 279).
Use 24-gauge single-wall stovepipe (or the type
recommended by the manufacturer) to connect
the stove to the chimney opening. Don't use
aluminum or galvanized pipe. Fasten with
sheet-metal screws.

BYPASSING THE ROOF

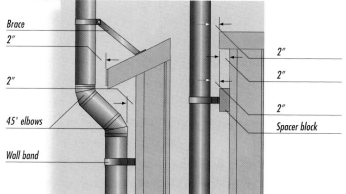

Brace
2"

2"

45° elbows

Wall band

2"

2"

2"

Spacer block

If the eaves area is narrow, use a telescoping tee
to offset the chimney or use spacer blocks nailed
to the wall to anchor the wall bands. If the roof
overhang is at least as wide as the pipe's outside
diameter, offset the chimney with two 45-degree
elbows. In either case, support and brace the
section above the eaves line.

Installing an Insert

A fireplace insert can make a traditional masonry or prefabricated metal fireplace far more energy efficient by controlling the amount of heat and room air that goes up the chimney and by radiating heat into the room. When installing an insert, you must modify your chimney by slipping a properly sized liner into it; this assures proper draw and burn rate and minimizes the risk of a chimney fire caused by creosote buildup. The problem is that many existing chimneys, especially masonry ones, have too large a flue to provide optimum efficiency for today's wood stoves. Moreover, the flues are often in poor condition.

When you buy an insert, complete installation instructions should come with it. Be sure to follow these exactly; it is very important to install an insert properly. Keep in mind that your existing hearth must meet the clearance require

ments specified by your wood stove insert manufacturer. If it doesn't, you'll have to adapt it as well. Although installing an insert and chimney liner can be a messy and awkward job for a homeowner, it is a breeze for installers who do this work every day. Consequently, it's usually well worth the extra expense to have your insert professionally installed.

Have the existing chimney thoroughly checked by a professional mason, chimney sweep, or member of your local fire department for defects and creosote buildup prior to installing the new insert. If the chimney needs repair, get an estimate from two or three masons. You may find it will cost more to repair the old chimney than to install a new one. Be sure your chimney will accommodate the size of the new insert's flue.

You can reline your existing chimney by adding a rigid or flexible stainless steel insert surrounded by nonflammable insulation or by installing a stainless steel pipe with insulation built in.

INSTALLING A FIREPLACE INSERT

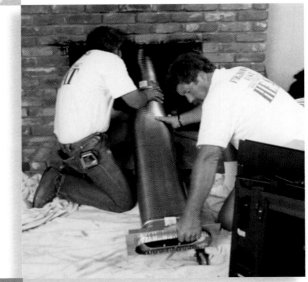

1 *Install the liner*
Properly sized liner fits inside the existing flue. Because the metal is corrugated, it can be worked up into the flue from the room below.

2 *Install the insert*
The main body of the insert slips inside the fireplace opening; then the flue is connected to the insert's top.

Fireplace & Stove Repairs

Typical problems with a fireplace or wood stove usually relate to a fireplace being overly smoky or needing to be cleaned. For more about repairing chimney flashing or the chimney itself, see pages 344–345 and 348–349.

A SMOKY FIREPLACE If a fireplace smokes up your home, it's nearly impossible to enjoy a cozy fire—and the smoke can cause considerable damage to your furnishings. If your chimney doesn't draw properly, you'll need to do a little detective work to pinpoint the cause. Nearby hills or tall trees can cause down drafts that bring smoke into the room. Adding a metal chimney cap—stationary or rotating—may be all that's needed to solve the problem.

Forced-air furnaces, kitchen fans, or doors opposite the firebox also can pull smoke from the fireplace into the room. Potential remedies are installing a draft inducer (a fan that draws hot air up and out the flue), temporarily turning the furnace fan off, or installing a solid room divider between the door and the fireplace.

If you've checked for birds' nests or other obstructions in the chimney and the problem persists, it may be due to faulty construction of the fireplace, such as the opening being too large for the flue area. The best solution is to install a firebox insert, a factory-built steel addition that slips into the existing firebox, as well as a flue liner.

REMOVING SMOKE STAINS Smoke stains on masonry can be removed with a solution of $1/2$ pound trisodium phosphate (or a nonphosphate substitute) dissolved in a gallon of water. Wear gloves and apply the solution with a natural bristle scrub brush.

Muriatic acid will often remove stubborn stains, but the acid may discolor bricks. Never use it on stone. The mixture should be 1 part acid to 10 parts water. Pour the water into a wide-mouthed jar, then add the acid. Apply with a cloth and immediately rinse off with water. Wear rubber gloves, old clothes, and eye protection.

CLEANING THE CHIMNEY Built-up soot and creosote will restrict the draft of your chimney and may cause a chimney fire that could spread to your house or nearby trees. Creosote also corrodes the flue and can reduce overall energy efficiency.

The only way to prevent this buildup from occurring is to clean the flue periodically. You may want to hire a chimney sweep to do this messy job. For information about how to do it yourself, see page 348.

 KEEP YOUR CHIMNEY CLEAN

Different woods emit varying amounts of creosote—hardwoods and properly cured woods less than softwoods or "green" wood. And airtight wood stoves and fireplace inserts produce creosote buildup much faster than open fireplaces. It's time to clean the chimney when about $1/4$ inch of creosote collects.

Siding

Attractive, well-maintained siding ensures that your house always has its best face forward. Siding that is free of cracking, peeling, or sagging clues in visitors that they are entering a well-cared-for home. On the other hand, a bedraggled exterior is a sure sign of internal trouble brewing. Rain can penetrate small cracks in siding to seep behind paint and into the wall's interior. As this process continues, the paint blisters and peels, allowing more water to penetrate the wall and escalating the problem dramatically. Before you know it, the house will sustain structural damage. Regular maintenance can spare you an almost certain large and painful repair bill later. This chapter instructs you on the ways to keep your existing siding in fine repair, as well as on ideas for improving your siding situation, including re-siding with a variety of market-ready materials.

Typical Wall Construction

If you're repairing or replacing siding, it is important to understand how exterior house walls are built. Here we look at how exterior wood-frame walls are clad with a variety of siding materials.

Wall construction varies slightly, depending upon the type of material that is applied as a siding. The various available sidings are discussed on pages 288–289, but for an overview of construction methods, this book divides those types into three categories: 1) wood and manufactured sidings, such as vinyl and aluminum; 2) stucco and related coatings; and 3) brick and masonry sidings.

Wood-frame walls are usually constructed from 2-by-6 or 2-by-4 studs. Insulation is placed between the studs, which are then covered with sheathing of wood-based panels or insulation board. Depending on the type of siding to be used, building paper or house wrap may be applied over the sheathing to provide additional weatherproofing.

Then the siding is nailed on. Or, in the case of masonry walls, a veneer of brick or stone is applied. With masonry, each course of bricks or stones is attached to the underlayment with short metal strips called ties, and the bricks or stones are mortared in place.

ANATOMY OF EXTERIOR WALLS

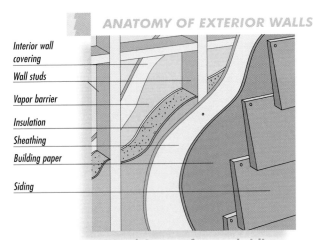

Interior wall covering
Wall studs
Vapor barrier
Insulation
Sheathing
Building paper
Siding

Wood & manufactured sidings

If walls are to be finished with wood, aluminum, steel, or vinyl siding, the sheathing is covered with building paper. The siding boards or panels are then nailed on, lapped from the bottom up to allow for water runoff.

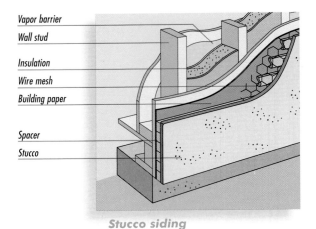

Vapor barrier
Wall stud
Insulation
Wire mesh
Building paper
Spacer
Stucco

Stucco siding

For standard stucco siding, wire mesh is nailed directly to sheathing covered with building paper (or to spacers). Stucco is applied over the wire mesh in three layers. In a contemporary variation of this time-honored method, many contractors now install stucco-like systems that use special backerboards with polymer-based coatings.

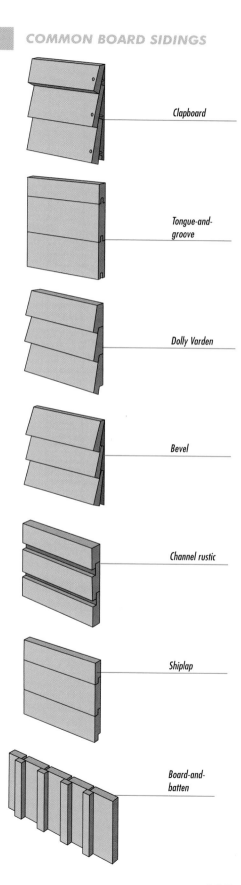
Clapboard

Tongue-and-groove

Dolly Varden

Bevel

Channel rustic

Shiplap

Board-and-batten

Vapor barrier

Insulation

Interior wall covering

Building paper

Tie

Brick

Foundation

Masonry siding

For masonry walls, a veneer of brick or stone is attached outside the building paper with short metal strips called ties. Then the bricks or stones are mortared in place. Their weight is supported by part of the foundation.

 WOOD SIDING VARIATIONS

Most wood siding patterns are milled with special overlapping or interlocking edges and in beveled or tapered profiles. The types that lock together, such as tongue-and-groove, don't allow for expansion or contraction and so are more prone to problems. Though most patterns are meant to be installed horizontally, some are milled for vertical installation. Widths run 4, 5, 6, 8, 10, and 12 inches; boards are given nominal dimensions before drying and milling, so each size actually measures about ½ inch smaller. Widths of 8 inches or narrower shrink less and don't have the same tendency to cup as wider sizes. See more about types of siding on pages 288–289.

Types of Siding

When selecting a siding material, pick one that is durable, easy to maintain, complementary to your house's architectural style, and within your budget. For a comparative look at various materials, see the chart below.

 BUYER'S GUIDE TO SIDING MATERIALS

MATERIAL	TYPES AND CHARACTERISTICS	DURABILITY
Solid boards	■ Available in many species; redwood and cedar resist decay. Milled in various patterns. ■ Nominal dimensions are 1" thick, 4"–12" wide, random lengths to 20'. Bevel patterns are slightly thinner; battens may be narrower. ■ Sold untreated, treated with water repellent, primed, painted, or stained. ■ Applied horizontally, vertically, or diagonally.	30 years to life of building, depending on maintenance.
Exterior plywood	■ Most siding species are Douglas fir, Western red cedar, redwood, and Southern pine. Face veneer determines designation. Broad range of textures. Typical pattern has grooves cut vertically to simulate solid board siding. ■ Sheets are 4' wide, 8'–10' long. Lap boards are 6"–12" wide, 16' long. Thicknesses of both are $\frac{3}{8}$"–$\frac{5}{8}$". ■ Applied vertically or horizontally.	30 years to life of building, depending on maintenance.
Hardboard and OSB	■ Available smooth or textured—rough-sawn, board, stucco, others. ■ Sheets are 4' wide, 8'–10' long. Lap boards are 6"–12" wide, 16' long, $\frac{3}{8}$"–$\frac{5}{8}$" thick. ■ Sold untreated, treated with water repellent, or opaque stained. ■ Sheets are usually applied vertically.	30 years to life of building, depending on maintenance. Prepainted finish guaranteed to 20 years.
Shingles and shakes	■ Mostly Western red cedar, some white cedar. Shingles are graded: #1 ("blue label") are best; #2 ("red label") are acceptable as underlayment when double-coursing. Also available in specialty patterns. Shakes in four shapes and textures, varied by scoring, sawing, or splitting. "Sidewall shingles" are specialty products with heavily machine-grooved surfaces. ■ Widths are random from 3"–14". Lengths are 16" (shingles only), 18", and 24". Shakes are thicker than shingles, with butts from $\frac{3}{8}$"–$\frac{3}{4}$" thick. Shingles and shakes come prebonded on 8' plywood panels. ■ Primarily sold unpainted. Also available prestained, painted, pressure-treated with fire retardant or preservative.	20 to 40 years, depending on heat, humidity, and maintenance.
Vinyl	■ Extruded from polyvinyl chloride (PVC) in white and light colors. Smooth and wood-grain textures are typical. Horizontal panels simulate lap boards. Vertical panels simulate boards with battens. ■ Standard length is 12' 6".	40 years to life of building.
Aluminum	■ Extruded panels in a wide range of factory-baked colors, textures. ■ Types and dimensions are the same as vinyl. Also sold as 12"-by-36" or 12"-by-48" panels of simulated cedar shakes.	40 years to life of building.
Steel	■ Extruded panels in a wide range of factory-baked colors, smooth and wood-grain textures. ■ Types and dimensions are the same as vinyl.	40 years to life of building.
Brick and stone veneers	■ Thin bricks or stones or cultured synthetic masonry materials from $\frac{1}{2}$"–4" thick. ■ Sold in individual units or panelized. ■ Applied over wood framing.	Life of building.
Stucco systems	■ Traditional compound made from fine sand, portland cement, hydrated lime, and water. ■ Applied wet over wire lath in two or three coats. Pigment added to final coat, or surface can be painted when dry. Newer polymers are sprayed onto foam- or fiber-cement board sheathing.	Life of building.

Siding

Wood board siding has served as the standard for many years because of its ready availability, natural appearance, and adaptability to a wide range of styles. But because scarce supplies have driven up costs of wood board siding, and wood tends to require a lot of maintenance, a number of synthetic products have been developed to imitate the appearance, but sidestep the problems, of wood.

If you decide to buy solid-wood siding, be sure to pay special attention to the wood's grade and species. There are big variations in price and appearance from one grade to another. Cedar and redwood heartwoods are preferred for their natural resistance to decay. If you're trying to stretch your budget, check out local species, which tend to be in good supply and, therefore, less expensive. Be sure to install them properly and give them a protective finish.

MAINTENANCE	INSTALLATION	MERITS AND DRAWBACKS
Before using, seal all edges with water repellent. Needs painting every 4–6 years, transparent staining every 3–5 years, or finishing with water repellent every 2 years.	Difficulty varies with pattern. Most are manageable with basic carpentry skills and tools.	■ Merits: Natural material. Many styles and patterns. Easy to handle and work. Accepts a wide variety of finishes. ■ Drawbacks: Burns. Prone to split, crack, warp, peel (if painted). Species other than cedar and redwood must be finished to protect from termites and rot.
Before using, seal all edges with water repellent, stain sealer, or exterior house paint primer. Restain or repaint every 5 years.	Sheets go up quickly. Manageable with basic carpentry skills and tools.	■ Merits: Can serve as sheathing and siding, adding great structural support to a wall. Many styles, patterns. ■ Drawbacks: Burns. May "check" (show small surface cracks). Susceptible to termite damage when in direct contact with soil, and to water rot if not properly finished.
Before using, seal all edges with water repellent, stain sealer, or exterior house paint primer. Paint or stain unprimed and preprimed hardboard within 60 days of installation; then repeat every 5 years.	Sheets go up quickly. Manageable with basic carpentry skills and tools.	■ Merits: Uniform appearance, without defects typical of wood. Many textures, designs. Accepts finishes well. ■ Drawbacks: Lacks plywood's strength. Susceptible to termite damage when in direct contact with soil, and to water rot and buckling if not properly finished. Cannot take transparent finishes.
In hot, humid climates, apply fungicide/mildew retardant every 3 years. In dry climates, preserve resiliency with oil finish every 5 years.	Time consuming because of small pieces, but manageable with basic carpentry skills and tools plus a roofer's hatchet.	■ Merits: Rustic wood appearance. Provides small measure of insulation. Easy to handle and work. Easy to repair. Adapts well to rounded walls and intricate architectural styles. ■ Drawbacks: Burns. Prone to rot, splinter, crack, and cup. May be pried loose by wind. Changes color with age unless treated.
Hose off annually.	Manageable with basic carpentry skills and tools, plus a few specialty tools.	■ Merits: Won't rot, rust, peel, or blister. Burns, but won't feed flames. Easiest synthetic to apply, repair. Resists denting. Scratches do not show. ■ Drawbacks: Light colors only. Sun may cause long-range fading. Brittle when cold.
Hose off annually. Clean surface stains with nonabrasive detergent. Refinish with paint recommended by the manufacturer.	Manageable with basic carpentry skills and tools, plus a few specialty tools.	■ Merits: Won't rot, rust, or blister. Fireproof. Impervious to termites. Lightweight and easy to handle. ■ Drawbacks: Dents, scratches easily. May corrode near saltwater.
Hose off annually. Paint scratches to prevent rust.	Best left to professionals.	■ Merits: Won't rot or blister. Fireproof. Impervious to termites. Resists denting. ■ Drawbacks: Difficult to handle, cut. Rusts if scratched.
Hose off annually.	Professionals only.	■ Merits: Fireproof, durable, and very solid. ■ Drawbacks: Needs professional installation. Expensive.
Hose off annually. If painted, repaint as required.	Professionals only.	■ Merits: Fireproof, durable, solid, and seamless. Can be any color. ■ Drawbacks: Needs professional installation. Expensive. Real stucco can crack with building movement.

Siding Tools & Equipment

For most siding installation work, you'll need quite a few carpentry tools, as well as key safety equipment such as gloves and safety glasses. You'll need at least one ladder and—particularly if you'll be working up high along walls—scaffolding (see more about ladders and scaffolding on pages 42–43).

Depending upon the work you're tackling, you'll need a few specialty tools, too. For removing shingles, a shingle ripper (see page 341) is a very helpful tool. For cutting sheet metal, you'll want tin snips. For bricks or other masonry siding, you may need a ball-peen hammer and a cold chisel, along with a hawk, a trowel, and a jointer, as shown on pages 316–317. Working with vinyl and aluminum calls for a special tool called a zipper (see page 314); a brake (see page 302) may also come in handy. For cleaning siding, you'll want the cleaning equipment discussed on pages 310–311.

 HELPFUL SIDING TOOLS

The tools shown here are the assortment you'll likely need for extensive repairs to wood siding (these as well as a few specialty tools are needed for most other types of siding).

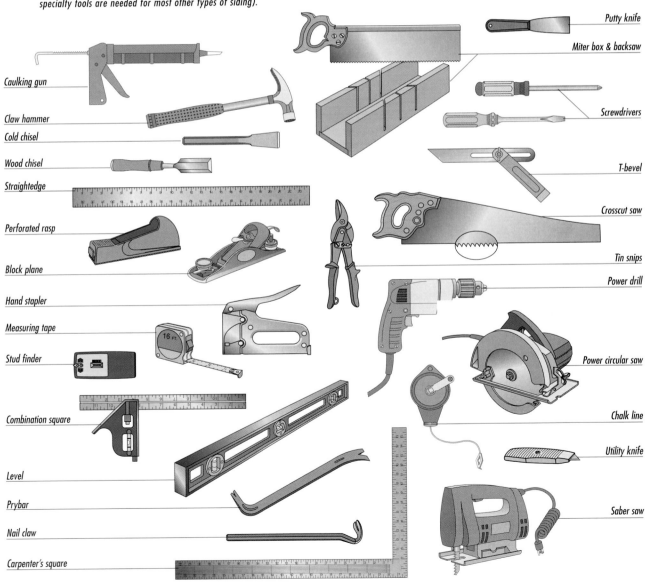

Caulking gun

Claw hammer

Cold chisel

Wood chisel

Straightedge

Perforated rasp

Block plane

Hand stapler

Measuring tape

Stud finder

Combination square

Level

Prybar

Nail claw

Carpenter's square

Putty knife

Miter box & backsaw

Screwdrivers

T-bevel

Crosscut saw

Tin snips

Power drill

Power circular saw

Chalk line

Utility knife

Saber saw

Siding

Preparing to Re-Side

Siding a house is a big job. Though you may be able to save about half the job's cost by doing the work yourself, be realistic about the work involved at the outset. You must be willing to take on the heavy labor, and you should be a careful worker who is competent with tools, adept at following instructions, and able, if necessary, to adapt instructions to the eccentricities of your house. If you live in a large house or a tall one perched on a hillside, strongly consider hiring a contractor to install siding.

ESTIMATING YOUR NEEDS Figuring the amount of siding needed to cover your house is usually just a matter of measuring exterior walls, calculating square footage, and adjusting the resulting figures for waste. Divide the surfaces to be covered into rectangles, and calculate the area by multiplying length by width (rounding measurements off to the nearest foot).

Add together all the areas you've computed. Then (except for sheet sidings, such as plywood), subtract the areas of windows, doors, chimneys, and other places the new siding will not cover. The result is approximately how many square feet of siding you'll need; add 10 percent for waste. If your house has steep angles at the gables or other architectural features that will necessitate a lot of cutting, add another 15 percent to the total amount you will need to order.

Be sure to take into account the overlap of most board sidings. You'll need about 1,240 square feet of 8-inch horizontal bevel siding, for example, to cover 1,000 square feet of wall space. Manufacturers offer charts to help estimate your needs, based on their specific patterns.

Vinyl and aluminum sidings are usually sold by the number of square feet a given amount covers. When ordering, you must also estimate how many linear feet of various trim pieces you'll need.

Plywood and hardboard sheets are sold in sizes that correlate directly with square footage. Add 10 percent for normal waste and—if your house has sharply angled walls—another 15 percent for extra cutting.

Preparing the Walls

If you're siding over an existing wall that is flat and sound, you may be able to nail new siding directly over it. By doing this, you may avoid substantial work, mess, and weather exposure. On the other hand, if the existing siding is metal, vinyl, or masonry, or is bumpy and irregular, you'll either have to strip it off or provide a nailing base of furring strips on top of it (as discussed on pages 293–294).

For siding removal, use a claw hammer and a flat prybar for prying, and a "cat's paw" and a pair of locking pliers for pulling nails. When removing most types of siding, start at the top and work your way down. If you want to avoid marring the wood, use the cat's paw on the first board and then raise nails from subsequent boards with a prybar.

To remove shingles and shakes from a wall, insert a square-bottom shovel underneath the shingles or shakes, lift them up, and pull them off. It's usually easiest to start at the top and work down the wall. Pull any remaining nails.

(continued on page 292)

ASBESTOS-CEMENT SHINGLES

Because of cancer risks associated with airborne asbestos particles, asbestos-cement shingles should only be removed by an asbestos-abatement contractor. The Environmental Protection Agency (EPA) and the Consumer Product Safety Commission (CPSA) recommend leaving inert asbestos alone unless it's friable—flaking or crumbling. For your state and local regulations, contact public health agencies. Some experts recommend leaving asbestos shingles in place and covering them over with vinyl or aluminum siding.

Preparing to Re-Side

(continued from page 291)
Removing stucco is hard work; if at all possible, apply new siding over the top. For an extensive removal job, call a demolition contractor.

Sheathing the Walls

Most new walls need sheathing to strengthen them, serve as a nailing base for siding, and/or boost insulation. Existing walls usually don't require sheathing unless you're stripping off the old siding and applying a different type that calls for sheathing. Check the siding manufacturer's directions and local codes to determine whether sheathing is required.

Sheathings are of two sorts, structural and nonstructural.

STRUCTURAL SHEATHING These are an integral part of the house's framing. They tie together wall studs, contributing shear strength and rigidity and forming a solid nailing base for siding materials. Most structural sheathings don't add much insulation value.

Common structural sheathings are plywood, oriented strand board (OSB), and waferboard. Exterior gypsum board is another type, but it is normally chosen for commercial construction.

When choosing plywood, OSB, or waferboard panels, be sure they are rated as wall sheathing, and choose an appropriate thickness. Although you can use panels as thin as $5/16$ inch for some applications, it's usually a good idea to spend a little bit more for sturdier $1/2$-inch panels. The most common panel size is 4 by 8 feet; you can get some products in 4-by-9- and 4-by-10-foot sheets.

Using 2-inch galvanized nails, fasten panels (usually horizontally) to wall studs, spacing nails 6 inches apart along the panels' edges and 12 inches apart mid-panel (or as specified by codes). Allow an expansion gap of $1/16$ inch between panel ends and $1/8$ inch between panel edges.

NONSTRUCTURAL SHEATHING These don't add significantly to a wall's strength but can greatly increase its insulation value. Rigid foam and cellulose-fiber panels may be attached directly to wall studs or masonry walls, under or over structural sheathing (depending upon nailing requirements), or, in some cases, over existing siding before re-siding. Your building materials supplier can offer advice appropriate for your particular circumstances.

The two most common types of foam board sheathing are made of polyisocyanurate or extruded polystyrene. Polyisocyanurate has higher per-inch insulation (R) values—up to R-8.7 per inch—than polystyrene, though its value decreases when it's punctured by nails. For more on R-values, see page 522.

Foam board thicknesses range from $3/8$ inch to $4 1/4$ inches. For covering existing siding, $1/2$-inch and $3/4$-inch thicknesses are commonly used. Standard panels are 2 by 8, 4 by 8, and 4 by 9 feet, though some foam can be purchased in fan-folded panels that run up to 50 feet long. Most panels have square edges meant to be butted together; some have shiplap or tongue-and-groove edges.

Foam panels come plain or with either reflective aluminum or matte facings. Which type to choose—and which side to face outward—depends upon your wall's makeup and the siding you're applying. As a rule, use foil-faced panels beneath brick, stucco, and some wood sidings. Non-foil-faced panels are generally recommended beneath aluminum, vinyl, and wood-based sidings.

Fire codes and safety may affect how nonstructural panels are applied. Despite the fact that foil facings help reduce the combustibility of nonstructural sheathing panels, these products should not be left exposed—be sure to follow manufacturer's instructions in this regard. Foam and cellulose panels can feed a fire, and foam, in particular, can give off toxic smoke if ignited.

Siding Improvements

Most foam and cellulose panels are extremely lightweight and can be cut with a utility knife. Nail the panels to wall studs with large-headed galvanized nails that are long enough to penetrate studs at least 1 inch. Space nails according to manufacturer's instructions (because these panels are not structural, 12-inch spacing is usually sufficient). Drive nails flush, being careful not to crush the panels with your final hammer blow.

Applying Building Paper

Building paper, a black felt or kraft paper impregnated with asphalt, is applied between the sheathing (or the unsheathed studs) and the siding to resist wind and water without trapping moist air. It comes in rolls 36 to 40 inches wide and long enough to cover 200 to 500 square feet (allowing for overlap).

Though some building codes require the use of building paper, it isn't always mandatory. You may want to apply it anyway if your siding will be subjected to heavy winds or to wind-driven rain or snow, or if it consists of boards or shingles that present numerous places for wind and water to penetrate.

Applying House Wrap

Air infiltration typically causes more than 20 percent of a house's heat loss. To protect against this, many builders now apply house wrap before installing siding. This spun-bonded or woven polymer material keeps water and drafts out yet breathes so it doesn't trap moisture in the walls.

It comes in 8-foot-wide rolls and is easy and quick to install. On a still day when you have a helper, start at one corner of the house and, holding the roll vertically, unroll about 6 feet of the material. Let it overlap the corner about 12 inches, and fasten it in place there with "cap nails" (roofing nails that have a plastic or metal washer-type head). Keep the material plumb and the bottom edge aligned with the foundation line. Secure the material every 12 to 18 inches along studs (most types of house wrap have stud lines marked on the fabric—just align the first one, and the others should automatically fall on subsequent studs). Lap it by about 2 inches between sheets, seal seams with special house wrap tape, and cut out window and door openings.

Attaching Furring Strips

If your present siding is masonry or is bumpy and irregular, you may need to install a base of furring strips, generally a gridwork of 1-by-3 boards or strips, placed to provide flat nailing support for the new siding at appropriate intervals. Be aware that furring out a wall or applying siding directly over the top of old siding will add to the wall's thickness, which will affect how window and doorjambs are trimmed at the surface.

Use a long, straight board or taut line to determine where it is necessary to shim furring strips in order to create a flat plane. To shim, tap wood shingles between the wall and furring strips. Check furring strips for plumb before you nail them in place and adjust if necessary.

(continued on page 294)

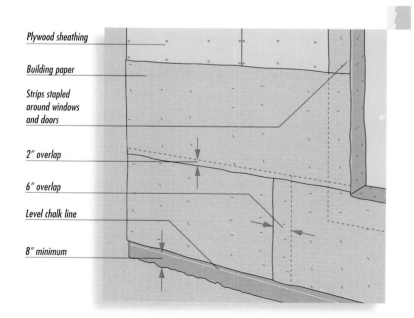

Plywood sheathing

Building paper

Strips stapled around windows and doors

2" overlap

6" overlap

Level chalk line

8" minimum

Preparing to Re-Side

(continued from page 293)
Secure the strips every 12 inches with nails long enough to penetrate studs at least 1 inch. If the existing walls are masonry, use concrete nails or masonry anchors.

Preparing Windows & Doors

Unless you strip the walls first, furring strips and new siding will add to the thickness of your walls. For both weather-proofing and appearance, it's usually necessary to build up the jambs and sills of windows and doors to compensate for the added thickness. Depending upon your particular situation, it may be easier to add jamb extensions after the new siding is applied, as shown in the illustration below. (For synthetic sidings, special add-on trim pieces are provided to handle this.)

Flashing Siding

Flashing prevents water that runs down a wall from penetrating the joints between materials. Standard galvanized and aluminum flashing is available at home-improvement centers. Types made for vinyl and metal sidings are sold by siding manufacturers. Specialty flashings and flashings made of copper are usually custom fabricated at sheet-metal shops.

ADDING A JAMB EXTENSION

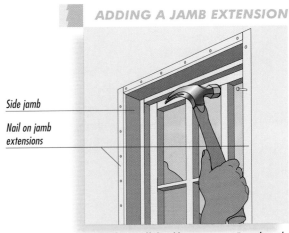

Side jamb

Nail on jamb extensions

Gently pry off the old exterior trim. Extend wood jambs by adding small wood strips to them. Cut extenders the same width as the jambs and deep enough to be flush with the siding's surface. Nail on the top piece, then the sides, and the sill last. Fill any gaps between old and new with wood putty and sand flush.

DRIP CAPS

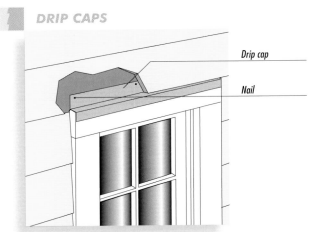

Drip cap

Nail

Before applying siding, be sure L-shaped or Z-shaped drip caps protect the tops of wood window and door frames. Cut them with tin snips. Position nails where siding will cover them.

Use galvanized nails for galvanized flashing, aluminum nails for aluminum flashing, and bronze nails for copper flashing. Combining differing metals can cause corrosive electrolysis that may weaken nails and stain siding.

Establishing a Baseline

No matter what siding you install, you'll have to align its lowest edge along the base of each wall by snapping a level chalk line no less than 8 inches above grade (ground level). When applying new siding over old, the line is usually set 1 inch below the lower edge of the existing siding.

Excavate any surrounding soil that interferes with this 8-inch clearance, sloping the grade away from the house so water won't pool by the foundation. You may find it necessary to "step" the siding—adjust the baseline up or down—to conform to a hillside or irregular grade. If you're applying horizontal siding, shingles, or shakes, work out the sizes of the required steps so they correspond with the planned exposure for each course.

If you have no helper, stretch the chalk line from a concrete nail pounded into the foundation wall (use one at each end if necessary).

Before you start nailing up siding boards, be sure to read through the information on preparing the wall, beginning on page 291. When you have the siding delivered, allow the wood to acclimate to local humidity. Store boards flat, raised above the ground on blocks or scraps. To make painting or staining the siding an easier job later, prime or prefinish it before installation, then touch up the cut ends as you work.

Be sure to plan your layout and decide how you will treat the corners (see illustrations on this page). When working out your layout, try to plan the siding boards to fit seamlessly around windows, doors, and other openings. With horizontal siding, a slight adjustment to your baseline may do the trick. If you must butt board ends together, stagger the joints.

(continued on page 296)

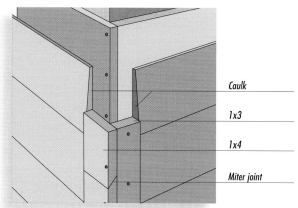

Caulk
1x3
1x4
Miter joint

Butted outside corner

A relatively easy way to handle an outside corner is to butt the siding boards against a vertical 1 by 3 and 1 by 4. When joining these vertical boards end to end, miter the joint at a 45-degree angle, with the board ends sloping toward the faces as shown to ensure proper water runoff.

HANDLING CORNERS

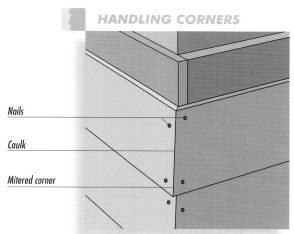

Nails
Caulk
Mitered corner

Mitered outside corner

For an outside corner, you can miter the board ends so no end grain is visible or exposed to the elements. To do this method well takes a fairly high degree of craftsmanship but, when done well, looks great.

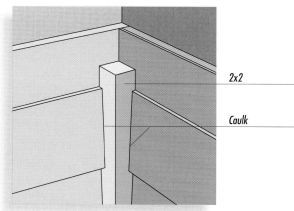

2x2
Caulk

Inside corner

At inside corners, run a length of 2 by 2 vertically and butt the siding board ends against it. Caulk along the joints.

295

Applying Lap Siding

(continued from page 295)

NAILING Nail each board individually; don't nail through overlapping parts. Use stainless steel, high-tensile-strength aluminum or hot-dipped galvanized siding or box nails to face-nail, or similar casing nails to blind-nail. Spiral or ring-shank nails offer the best holding power.

Choose nails long enough to penetrate studs at least 1¼ inches. Boards that are 6 inches wide and narrower require only one nail per bearing; wider boards require two. If boards tend to split, try blunting the nail tips with a hammer; otherwise, predrill nail holes, using a drill bit that is slightly smaller than the nails' diameter.

CUTTING Mark all 90-degree cuts using a combination square. Do the cutting with a power circular saw, a handsaw, or—if available—a table saw or radial-arm saw.

FIRST BOARD The first board goes at the bottom. Most types require a 1-by-2 starter strip beneath the board's lower edge, along the wall's base, to push the first board out so it will match the angle of the other boards.

SUCCESSIVE BOARDS To lay out horizontal board siding, you'll need a "story pole," made from a 1 by 2 that's as long as your tallest wall's height (unless that wall is more than one story). Starting at one end, mark the pole at intervals equaling the width of the siding boards, as shown in the drawing on facing page.

CORNERS & TOP OF WALLS When installing horizontal siding, determine whether the cornice will be open or closed (see page 301) before nailing the last board in place at the top of the wall. Where boards must be cut at an angle to match the roofline, figure and cut the angle as shown on facing page.

OPEN & CLOSED CORNICES Cornices (sometimes called soffits) are often left open with wood-board siding—so the boards extend to the tops of the rafters. For this method, notch board ends where they intersect rafters and caulk them thoroughly after they're in place. Trim along the top edge, between rafters, using quarter-round molding or a narrow trim board (called a "frieze board").

If you prefer a closed cornice, you can build one as shown on facing page or buy or make a special wood board called a "plowed fascia board." This board, nailed over the rafter ends or existing fascia, has a routed groove near one edge for holding soffit boards or panels, as shown in the drawing on page 301.

USING A STARTER STRIP

Second board

Wall

Sheathing

First beveled board

Starter strip

Establish the proper angle for the first board by running a 1-by-2 starter strip beneath the board's lower edge, along the wall's base.

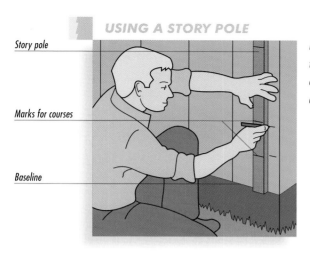

Story pole

Marks for courses

Baseline

Hold or tack the story pole flush with the baseline, then transfer the marks for each siding board to each corner and to the trim at each window and door casing.

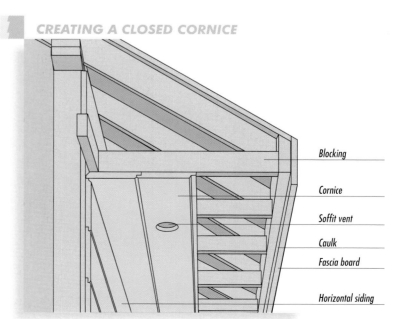

TRANSFERRING AN ANGLE

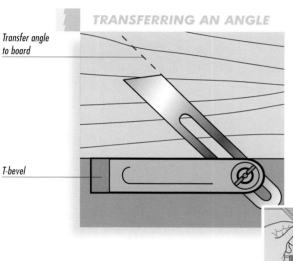

Transfer angle to board

T-bevel

To match the slope of a roofline, measure the angle with a T-bevel. Transfer the angle to each board end, then cut.

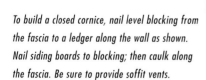

Roofline

T-bevel

To build a closed cornice, nail level blocking from the fascia to a ledger along the wall as shown. Nail siding boards to blocking; then caulk along the fascia. Be sure to provide soffit vents.

CREATING A CLOSED CORNICE

Blocking

Cornice

Soffit vent

Caulk

Fascia board

Horizontal siding

Applying Panel Siding

Plywood and hardboard siding panels are popular because their large 4-by-8-, 4-by-9-, or 4-by-10-foot sizes give quick coverage. In addition, plywood's strength can eliminate the need for bracing and sheathing on a new wall's frame (check your codes). Hardboard panels, nailed on according to the manufacturer's specifications, can also provide shear strength.

Though codes may not demand the use of building paper or house wrap beneath plywood, it's a good idea to install this extra barrier under either plywood or hardboard sidings (see page 293), particularly if the panel edges do not interlock or are not covered with battens. It's also important to brush all siding panel edges with a water sealant prior to installation.

Panels may be mounted either vertically or horizontally. Because vertical installation minimizes the number of horizontal joints, it's the preferred method. If you choose a horizontal pattern, stagger vertical end joints and nail the long, horizontal edges into fire blocks or other nailing supports. (See more about wall framing on pages 188–189.) Because hardboard is not as strong as plywood, it needs firmer backing and attachment.

Plywood and hardboard lap sidings (as opposed to panels) are installed using methods similar to those used for installing board sidings. For more information, see pages 295–297.

NAILING Fasten the panels with 2-inch or 2½-inch corrosion-resistant common or box nails, depending upon the manufacturer's recommendations for application to your nailing base. For re-siding over wood boards or sheathing, use hot-dipped galvanized ring-shank nails. Don't use finishing nails, staples, T nails, or bugle-head nails. Hardboard manufacturers sell nails with heads colored to match factory finishes on the hardboard.

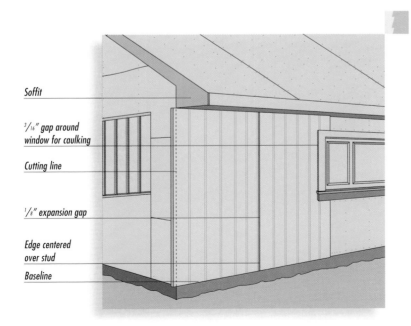

Soffit

³/₁₆″ gap around window for caulking

Cutting line

¹/₈″ expansion gap

Edge centered over stud

Baseline

INSTALLING PANEL SIDING

Tack the first sheet in place, flush with the baseline and with the inward edge perfectly plumb and centered over a wall stud. Align the second panel with the edge of the first one.

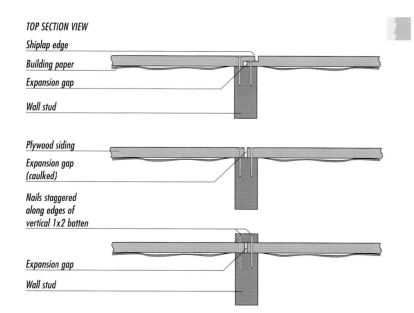

TOP SECTION VIEW

Shiplap edge
Building paper
Expansion gap
Wall stud

Plywood siding
Expansion gap (caulked)
Nails staggered along edges of vertical 1x2 batten
Expansion gap
Wall stud

■ **VERTICAL JOINTS**

The panels' vertical edges may interlock with a shiplap joint, be butted together and caulked, or may be covered with a vertical batten, such as a 1-by-2 strip.

Where a single panel isn't long enough to reach from top to bottom on a wall, two or more panels may be needed. To ensure that water is shed properly, horizontal joints should be protected with Z-flashing or a shiplap edge (the latter method is used when panels are applied horizontally).

■ **HORIZONTAL JOINTS**

SIDE SECTION VIEW

Plywood siding
Blocking or plate
Horizontal Z-flashing

Shiplap edge
Expansion gap

Blocking or plate

Nails should be long enough to penetrate studs or other backing by at least 1½ inches. For new siding nailed directly to studs, use 2-inch nails for ⅜-inch or ½-inch panels, 2½-inch nails for ⅝-inch panels. Nail every 6 inches around the perimeter of each sheet and every 12 inches along studs or furring. If hardboard panels are meant to supply shear strength where not applied over sheathing, space nails every 4 inches around the perimeter and intermediately every 8 inches along studs.

When driving in nails, be careful not to dimple the panel's surface with the last hammer blow. Don't set nailheads below the surface.

When you nail a panel, first tack it in position with nails at each corner (leave these nailheads protruding so you can pull them if necessary). Then nail from top to bottom along one edge (the edge adjoining the preceding panel). Move to the next stud or furring strip and nail along it; move on to the next support, and so on. This method prevents the panel from buckling in the center.

MEASURING FOR HEIGHT Before you begin putting up panels, you'll need to figure how long they should be; measure from the base chalk line to the soffit. If you plan to create a closed cornice, it may be simpler to install the soffit before the siding panels.

(continued on page 300)

Applying Panel Siding

(continued from page 299)
Should the distance from baseline to soffit be longer than the siding sheets, you'll need to join panels end to end, using one of the methods for horizontal joints shown on page 299.

THE FIRST SHEET Position the first sheet at an outside corner, its bottom edge flush with the baseline and the inside vertical edge centered over a stud, furring strip, or other firm backing. Use a carpenter's level to make sure vertical edges are plumb. If the corner itself isn't plumb, you'll need to trim the panel edge to align with it. Hold or tack the sheet in place, flush with the baseline, and trace along the outermost points of the existing siding or framing from top to bottom.

Take the panel down and cut along the line you traced, using a circular saw or handsaw. Nail the trimmed panel in place.

SUCCESSIVE SHEETS The next sheet butts against the first sheet, often with an overlapping shiplap vertical edge (see edge details on page 299). Leave a 1/16-inch expansion gap at all joints (in humid climates, leave 1/8 inch). Sheets must join over studs, blocking, or other sturdy backing. Be careful not to nail through both parts of the laps.

If your panel doesn't have a shiplap edge, caulk along the vertical edges and butt them loosely together, leaving about 1/16 inch for expansion. Unless there's building paper or house wrap behind each joint, you'll need to cover the joints with battens (1-by-2, 1-by-3, or 1-by-4 strips that protect seams). Horizontal seams between top and bottom edges of panels (such as on a two-story house) must be protected with metal Z-flashing or by applying panels horizontally with shiplap edges.

OBSTACLES As you install sheets, you may encounter some obstacles such as gas pipes or hose bibbs. Cut out a section with a saber saw so the sheet can be put in place. Mount and nail the sheet; then fashion a cutout to fit around the protrusion and fasten that area in place with glue and—if possible—with nails.

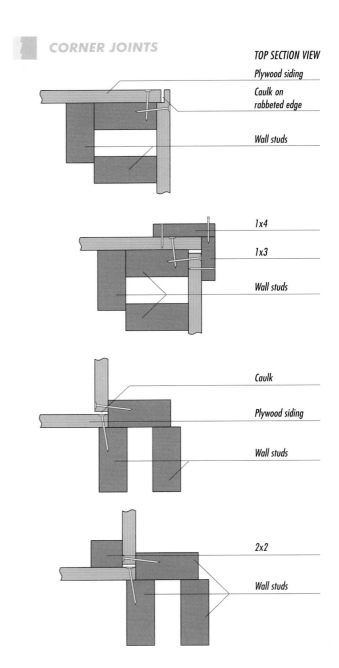

CORNER JOINTS

TOP SECTION VIEW

Plywood siding

Caulk on rabbeted edge

Wall studs

1x4

1x3

Wall studs

Caulk

Plywood siding

Wall studs

2x2

Wall studs

CORNERS Panel siding requires special corner construction to ensure a weatherproof joint. Outside corners can be rabbeted together and caulked or covered by 1-by-3 and 1-by-4 trim boards; inside corners are generally just caulked and butted together. You can also use a vertical corner trim board, such as a 2 by 2 (see above).

Siding Improvements

If the plywood panels are milled with grooves, the grooves under corner boards might let dirt and water penetrate. To prevent this, nail the vertical trim boards directly to the corner studs or existing siding, caulk along the edges, and butt the plywood against them.

WINDOW & DOOR OPENINGS When dealing with these large areas, remember the carpenter's maxim, "Measure twice, cut once." For ease of fitting, allow an extra $^3/_{16}$-inch gap around all openings. If possible, center the seams between sheets over or under the opening.

Use a carpenter's square or chalk line to lay out cuts, a circular saw for straight cutting, and a saber saw for cutting corners and curves. Since these saws cut on the upstroke, cut the sheets on the back side so you won't splinter the face. But don't forget, when laying out the lines, that the sheet will be flipped during installation.

CORNICES On panel-sided houses, cornices (or soffits) are usually closed; an open cornice requires very precisely made cuts to fit snugly around rafters. Consider running a plowed fascia board along rafter tails and a 2-by-2 block along the wall, and attaching lengths of siding along the soffit, as detailed in the drawings below.

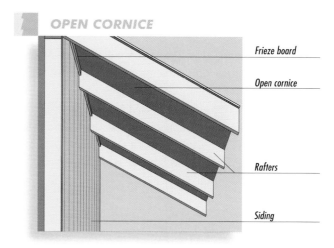

OPEN CORNICE

Frieze board

Open cornice

Rafters

Siding

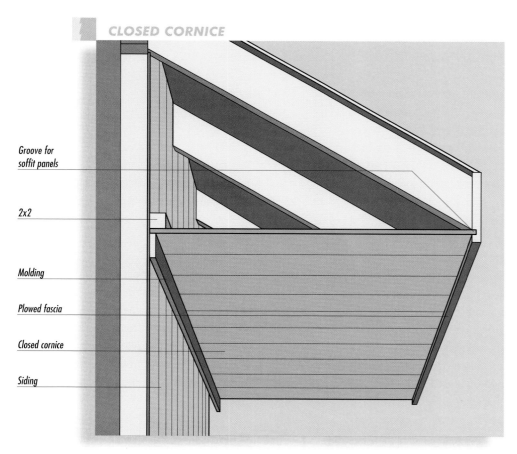

CLOSED CORNICE

Groove for soffit panels

2x2

Molding

Plowed fascia

Closed cornice

Siding

Applying Vinyl & Aluminum

Vinyl, aluminum, and steel sidings are sold as complete systems that include not only the siding panels but all necessary attachment strips, trim, and related parts and pieces. Because the materials are lightweight and easy to cut and nail, some vinyl and aluminum systems can be homeowner-installed; steel siding, however, is better left to professionals. Both vinyl and aluminum systems come in a range of panel sizes made for either horizontal or vertical installation.

General Tips

Nearly all manufacturers supply installation instructions for their products. Be sure to pick up a guide when you buy your siding. Techniques for installing vinyl and aluminum sidings are almost identical.

The backing must be smooth enough for the panels to lie flat. To be assured of such a surface, you'll need either smooth sheathing over wall studs or furring strips nailed to the butts of lap siding. A popular backing for vinyl and aluminum siding is ⅜-inch foam board insulation. See more about preparing a wall for siding on pages 291–294.

TOOLS Most of the tools required are the same needed for basic carpentry jobs. In addition, you will need tin snips or aviation shears for cutting and shaping the vinyl or aluminum. Other helpful tools for vinyl include a snap-lock punch, which can punch connecting ears on the edges of siding used along the top or finishing courses, and a nail-hole punch, which produces elongated holes for nailing cut pieces. A power circular saw equipped with a fine-toothed blade (12 to 16 teeth per inch) can greatly speed cutting; some installers recommend mounting the blade in the reverse direction (only for cutting vinyl).

NAILS & NAILING With vinyl siding, use aluminum, galvanized steel, or other corrosion-resistant nails. For aluminum siding, use only aluminum nails. The nails, with ⅛-inch shanks and heads at least ⁵⁄₁₆ inch in diameter, should be long enough to penetrate solid backing at least ¾ inch. As a rule, you can choose 1½-inch nails for general use and trim and 2-inch nails for re-siding. Longer nails may be needed for going through insulation board into studs.

The two most important things to remember when nailing either vinyl or aluminum panels are: 1) unless otherwise specified, always nail in the center of nailing slots, and 2) never drive nails in too tightly. You want to hang panels from nails, not nail them fast.

TOLERANCES These materials expand and contract significantly as they warm and cool. When cutting and attaching vinyl, figure it will expand ¼ inch per 10-foot length; aluminum will expand ¹⁄₁₆ to ⅛ inch. If you're installing these materials in cold weather, allow another ⅛ inch. These tolerances are averages—adjust them as necessary.

CUTTING A radial-arm saw or a circular saw with a fine-toothed blade (mounted in the reverse direction for vinyl) works best. Tin snips or aviation shears are better for small or irregular cuts. For bending aluminum, you can rent a brake from a tool-rental company. This allows you to bend siding so it conforms to corners and window and fascia trim. For small cuts, you can simply score a cut with a utility knife and snap off a section of the siding material by bending it back and forth. Corner posts and heavy trim are easier to cut with a hacksaw.

Handling Corners & Trim

With aluminum and vinyl systems, the trim is installed first—around the house baseline and window and door frames, and against soffit or gable edges—and panels are then fitted into it. The illustration on facing page shows the basic components of a typical system with the various corner posts and trim pieces in place.

INSTALLING POSTS Position each post by driving two nails through the top of the uppermost slots; the post should hang from the nails. Use a level to check for vertical alignment. Then fasten the posts with nails every 12 inches. If you must stack one corner post above another, trim ¼ inch from the nailing flange at the bottom end of the top post. Then mount the top post so it overlaps the lower one by about 1 inch.

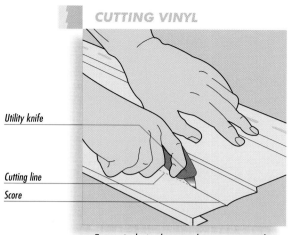

Utility knife

Cutting line

Score

To cut vinyl, simply score along your cutting line with a sharp utility knife, then bend the material back and forth.

INSTALLING STARTER STRIP OR VERTICAL BASE TRIM Install the starter strip (for horizontal siding) or vertical base trim (for vertical siding) along the base chalk line. (With aluminum siding, this strip may be the same for either direction.)

Align the upper edge of the base trim with the chalk line and nail every 6 inches. When you come to an outside corner, allow ¼ inch (vinyl) or ⅛ inch (aluminum) for expansion between the starter strip or base trim and corner post.

INSTALLING DOOR & WINDOW TRIM Your next step is to mount strips of appropriate trim around window and door openings. To reduce moisture and air flow, however, first run a bead of caulk around the openings, forming a seal. (If you intend to put vinyl covers on windowsills and casings, do that before installing accessory trim.)

When you install door and window trim, do the top first, then the sides, and finally the under-sill trim. Aluminum fittings are often folded, while vinyl is not. Aluminum J fittings around windows, for example, are often bent for a tight fit.

Along tops of doors and windows, install J-channel trim if you're using horizontal siding, vertical base trim if you're using vertical panels. Use lengths of trim that measure two channel widths longer than the top of the opening; either miter the ends or cut tabs at each end. Nail 12 inches on center.

Along the sides, use mitered trim if the top trim is mitered. When fitting side pieces, position the top nail at the top of the nailing slot, but drive remaining nails every 12 inches in the slots' centers.

(continued on page 304)

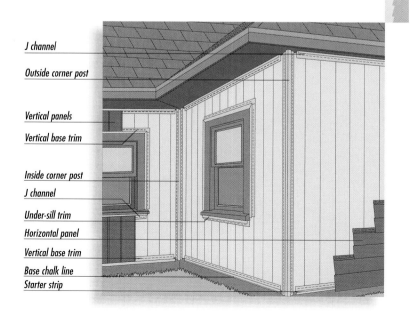

J channel

Outside corner post

Vertical panels

Vertical base trim

Inside corner post

J channel

Under-sill trim

Horizontal panel

Vertical base trim

Base chalk line

Starter strip

TYPICAL SYSTEM COMPONENTS

Install posts at inside and outside corners, allowing ¼ inch (vinyl) or ⅛ inch (aluminum) for expansion at the upper trim line and running the posts down to the base chalk line. Inside and outside corner post details are illustrated below.

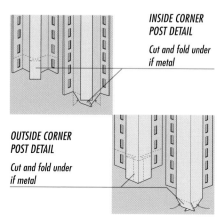

INSIDE CORNER POST DETAIL

Cut and fold under if metal

OUTSIDE CORNER POST DETAIL

Cut and fold under if metal

Applying Vinyl & Aluminum

(continued from page 303)

To avoid problems fitting horizontal panels into narrow places (between adjacent windows, for example), fasten down the trim along only one side of such areas. Trim on the other side can be fastened as panels are put in place. Under windows, install under-sill trim for horizontal siding, J-channel trim for vertical. Add furring strips where necessary to maintain the slope of siding.

INSTALLING TRIM UNDER EAVES & RAKES If you're installing horizontal siding, use F-channel trim at the soffit and at the gable rake (remove existing rake molding first). For vertical panels, use J-channel trim. Nail 12 inches on center. Add furring strips if needed.

Working with Horizontal Panels

Allowing for expansion (¼ inch for vinyl, ⅛ inch for aluminum) where the panel fits into the J channel, fit and securely lock the starter panel into the starter strip. If you are installing the insulating backerboard that comes with some sidings, drop it behind the panel, with its beveled edge down and toward the wall.

FITTING END JOINTS Where panels meet, overlap the ends 1 inch. Run overlaps away from the most obvious focal point on each wall—such as the front walk or porch—so joints will be less obtrusive. When overlapping, cut 1½ inches of the nailing flange away from the end of one panel to allow for expansion.

Some vinyl and most aluminum horizontal sidings use backer tabs at joints to make the material more stable over long spans. Slip the backer tabs, flat side out, behind the joints. Try to offset the joints at least 24 inches from one course to the next so vertical seams don't line up.

FITTING PANELS AROUND WINDOWS & DOORS You'll need a sharp knife, tin snips, or a power saw (for insulated siding) to trim panels to fit around windows and doors. Remember, though, to use either the saw or knife—never the tin snips—to cut the locking detail at the lower edge of the panel.

Measure window and door openings and cut panels to fit, allowing ¼ inch (for vinyl) or ⅛ inch (for aluminum) for expansion. Before fitting cut vinyl panels to under-sill trim, use a snap-lock punch to crimp nubs or "ears" along the trimmed edge. The ears, spaced 6 to 8 inches apart, should face outward so they can hook onto the under-sill trim.

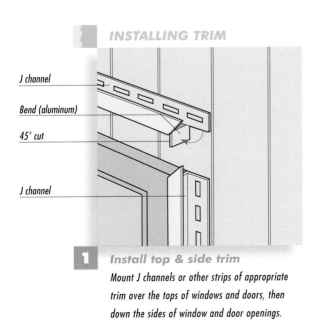

INSTALLING TRIM

J channel

Bend (aluminum)

45° cut

J channel

1 **Install top & side trim**
Mount J channels or other strips of appropriate trim over the tops of windows and doors, then down the sides of window and door openings.

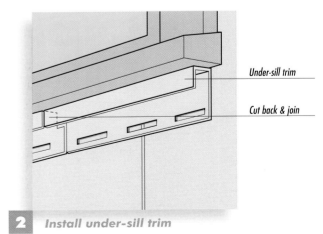

Under-sill trim

Cut back & join

2 **Install under-sill trim**
After applying J channels or vertical base trim to the tops and sides of windows and doors, install under-sill trim beneath windows.

Fascia

F channels

Soffit panels

Wall

Fit soffit panels into F channels, installed both along the wall and along the fascia.

Roof

Scrap siding

Mark angle for cutting

To mark the angled roofline on a panel for cutting, hold a piece of scrap siding in line with the roof and use it as a guide as shown here.

With aluminum siding, gutter-seal adhesive holds panels under windowsills and at soffits, especially where there is no other means of support. The gutter seal serves the same purpose as the ears crimped on vinyl.

To fit horizontal panels into narrow places, slip each panel into the trim along one side; as successive panels go into place, nail down the trim along the other side.

INSTALLING TOP PANELS AT EAVES OR GABLES Measure from the bottom of the top lock to the eaves and subtract ¼ inch (for vinyl) or ⅛ inch (for aluminum) for expansion. To determine the width of the final horizontal panel, measure in several places along the eaves.

Cut the panel, and use the snap-lock punch to crimp ears every 6 to 8 inches along its upper edge. Tuck the panel into the trim. At the gables, cut panels at an angle to fit into the J channels, F channels, or quarter-round moldings along the gable rake. Crimp ears as for window trim.

Handling Vertical Panels

Once the corner posts and trim are in, locate the center of each wall and, using a level and a straightedge, draw a line down the center. Allowing ¼ inch (for vinyl) or ⅛ inch (for aluminum) for expansion at the top, center the first panel over the line. Fasten it every 8 inches with nails positioned at the top of the nailing slots.

Working from this starter panel, install successive panels. These should be long enough to fit between the trim strips, minus ¼ inch (for vinyl) or ⅛ inch (for aluminum) for expansion. Panels should rest on the vertical base trim.

Insert each panel into the J channel along the top of the wall. Letting it rest on the vertical base trim, lock it into the previous panel.

Nails for successive panels should be positioned in the slot centers, spaced every 8 to 16 inches (depending on the manufacturer's recommendations).

When fitting vertical panels around windows and doors, follow instructions on facing page.

Before you insert the last panels into the corner posts, install J or U channels or under-sill trim in the corner post slots (manufacturers' instructions vary). You may want to raise the J channels with ⁵⁄₁₆-inch shims (for ½-inch J channels) to keep panels on the same plane. Then insert uncut panel edges into the J channel. Cut edges of flat sections should be inserted between the J channel and the post's outer flange.

Special Situations

Vinyl siding systems can include fascia trim, window trim, and other specialty parts that give a finished look. Their installation—as well as soffit panel application and the handling of transitions between horizontal and vertical panels—varies from one manufacturer to another. For details on your particular siding system, consult the manufacturer's recommendations.

Installing Shingle Siding

Wood shingles are relatively easy to use as a siding material because they are a manageable size and easy to handle—but shingling an entire house can be a very tedious job, so you'll want to set aside a large block of time if you intend to tackle it.

Shingles require a fairly flat, sturdy nailing base. You can put them over existing siding if it is relatively flat; they ride over slightly bumpy wall surfaces better than most siding materials do. Installation requires only standard carpentry tools. For more about tools, see page 290.

EXPOSURE Before applying shingles or shakes, you must determine the correct exposure for them (the amount of each shingle or shake to be exposed to the weather).

Because greater exposures are allowed on walls than on roofs, a square (the measurement by which shingles are purchased) may cover more than 100 square feet of a wall. The table below will help you determine the actual coverage you'll get with various exposures of shingles and shakes (single courses).

FIRST STEPS Assuming that you've prepared the wall as described on pages 291–294, measure the distance from the base chalk line to the soffit at both ends of the tallest wall. Compensate for any steps in the base chalk line and split any difference to figure the average distance from the soffit to the baseline. Divide that distance by the maximum exposure for your shingles or shakes. If your computation doesn't yield a whole number of courses, decrease the exposure enough to make the courses come out evenly. Also adjust the number of courses to achieve a full exposure below windows.

TYPICAL CORNER TREATMENTS

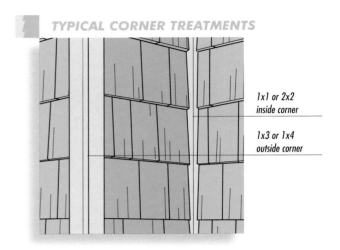

1x1 or 2x2 inside corner

1x3 or 1x4 outside corner

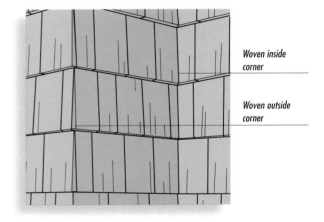

Woven inside corner

Woven outside corner

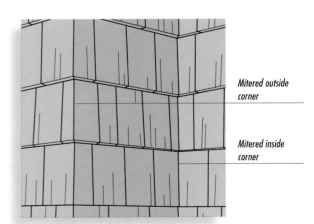

Mitered outside corner

Mitered inside corner

Shingles may be butted against trim pieces, woven, or mitered, depending upon how much work you want to tackle. The first method is easiest in most cases.

 MAXIMUM SHINGLE EXPOSURE

Shingle Lengths	Maximum Exposure
16"	7½"
18"	8½"
24"	11½"

Siding Improvements (vertical sidebar)

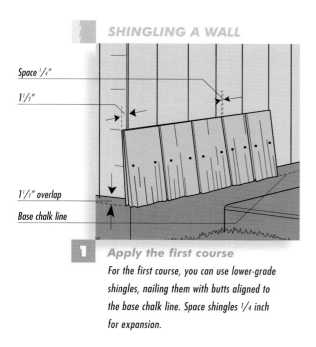

Space ¼"

1½"

1½" overlap

Base chalk line

1 *Apply the first course*

For the first course, you can use lower-grade shingles, nailing them with butts aligned to the base chalk line. Space shingles ¼ inch for expansion.

Offset joints by at least 1½"

1½" minimum

1x4 tacked to wall

2 *Continue up the wall*

As you work your way up the wall, align shingle butts along chalk lines or tack a 1 by 4 to the wall and butt the shingles against it.

Make a story pole from a 1 by 2 the length of your tallest wall's height, as shown on page 297. Starting at one end, mark the story pole at intervals equal to the established exposure. Holding or tacking the story pole flush with the baseline, transfer the marks to each corner and to the trim at each window and door casing.

NAILING Nails are concealed 1 inch above the line where the butts of the next higher course will go. Drive a nail ¾ inch in from each side and then use additional nails every 4 inches between.

Use hot-dipped galvanized box or shingling nails that are 1¼ inches long or longer. They should be long enough to penetrate sheathing or solid backing by at least 1 inch.

CORNERS Before beginning, you'll want to decide how you'll handle shingling at both inside and outside corners. Typical methods for finishing shingles at corners are shown on facing page. For outside corners, plan to bring shingles or shakes flush to a vertical 1 by 3 or 1 by 4. Or miter the corners—but prepare to spend a lot of time at it if you do. More typically, you can "weave" the corners by alternately overlapping them. Trim or plane the overlapping shingles flush. If this is how you will finish outside corners, plan to let the shingles extend beyond the corner (on the first wall) by about 1½ inches so you can trim them later.

At inside corners, plan to bring shingles and shakes flush to a 1 by 1 or 2 by 2 nailed in the corner. Or miter or weave them, being sure to flash behind with right-angle metal flashing that extends 3 inches under the shingles or shakes of each wall.

FIRST COURSES Nail on the first course of shingles, keeping the butts flush with the base chalk line. You can use low-grade shingles for the first course—they will be covered by the next course. Leave ¼ inch for expansion between shingles.

Directly over the first course, apply a second course. Offset all joints between shingles of different courses by at least 1½ inches so water will run off properly.

SUCCESSIVE COURSES Lay successive courses from the first course to the soffit. As you finish each course, snap a chalk line over it or tack on a straight 1 by 4 board with a couple of small nails as a guide for laying the next course.

OBSTACLES Shingles and shakes are easy to cut and fit around doors, windows, pipes, meters, and so forth. For curved cuts, use a coping saw or saber saw. Caulk well around edges.

CORNICES Cornices can be either open or closed. You can easily trim wood shingles or shakes to fit neatly around rafters in an open treatment. Closed cornices (see pages 296–297 and 301) are best handled by installing board siding finished to match the other trim.

Solving Siding Problems

A thorough siding inspection involves looking for obvious problems such as warped boards, missing or damaged shingles, holes in stucco, crumbling mortar, cracks, and defective paint. Don't ignore interior problems such as dry rot and termite damage; these can eventually destroy your house.

Begin with a visual inspection: The drawing on facing page shows likely trouble spots. The paragraphs that follow provide some more detailed observations.

DETERIORATED CAULKING Make a note of any caulking that has dried out, and renew the seals to prevent both moisture and pests from entering. Check the seals around windows and doors; around any plumbing, millwork, or other protrusions; and where a deck or masonry fireplace adjoins a house wall. Caulk any cracks in board siding.

DEFECTIVE PAINT If you find minor problems such as peeling, cracking, scaling, bubbling, or flaking, see pages 36–37 for painting tips. If repairs are required, do them first, then repaint or restain the siding.

MILDEW Combined heat and humidity can encourage mildew to develop on wood and painted surfaces; it may show up as a fungus-like discoloration or as whitish or moldy deposits. Mildew should be treated with an approved mildewcide.

 HOMEOWNER'S GUIDE TO BUGS

BUG	SIGNS	FAVORITE FOODS	FAVORITE PLACES
Carpet beetles	Visible beetles, holes in carpet and fabrics.	Carpets, clothing, fabric, flower pollen.	Carpets, rugs, baseboards, closets, dresser drawers. Outdoors: white or cream-colored flowers.
Carpenter ants	Ant trails, ant nests in walls, winged ants in house, tiny ant wings scattered on the ground, small piles of coarse sawdust near cracks.	Decaying wood, sweets, water.	Wall interiors, crawl spaces.
Cockroaches	Visible cockroaches scurry away when you turn on the lights.	Food, garbage, anything organic.	Warm, dark places; food cabinets; garbage.
Powder post beetles	Tiny holes pepper wood's exterior surface; wood's interior is reduced to powder.	Hardwoods such as oak, walnut, and ash; anobiid type also eats softwoods.	Unheated crawl spaces, wood trim, wood siding, framing.
Silverfish and firebrats	Ragged holes in papers, books, and some fabrics.	Paper, paste, fabric, food, garbage.	Damp places, baseboards, wall cracks, loosened wallpaper, books, papers.
Termites, drywood	Smooth galleries inside wood, tiny holes in surface, pellets piled outside or under infected wood, tiny termite wings on the ground.	Wood.	Rafters, roofs, eaves, framing.
Termites, subterranean and Formosan	Pellet-free gritty, mud-like substance inside layered galleries, mud tubes up foundation walls, swarms of winged termites, termite wings on ground.	Soft parts of wood grain.	Damp crawl spaces, foundation areas, primarily lower sections of house structure.

EFFLORESCENCE Brick or stone veneer may become covered with a white powder called efflorescence, formed when water-soluble salts are washed to the surface. In an old wall, this may be the result of a leak that should be fixed. See more about efflorescence on page 398.

DRY ROT & TERMITE DAMAGE Dry rot is a fungus that causes wood to crumble; termites destroy wood by chewing out its interior. Both can work away at wood timbers

 GETTING THE BUGS OUT

Probe the edges of wood siding with a knife and look for soft, spongy spots. Pay special attention to any area that has been near or in contact with the ground.

To check for visible traces of termites, look for the translucent ½-inch-long wings they grow and shed or the mud tubes some types build. If you find evidence of dry rot or termites, don't wait for the problem to get worse. Consult a licensed termite inspector or pest control professional. If you've caught the problem early, the solution may be relatively simple and inexpensive.

 **PROBLEM AREAS**

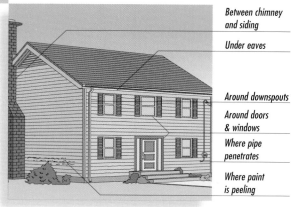

Between chimney and siding

Under eaves

Around downspouts

Around doors & windows

Where pipe penetrates

Where paint is peeling

and siding in a way that might easily escape your notice. Eliminate damp areas, fix any broken gutters (see pages 346–347), and repair any rotted wood. Be sure no parts of your house are in direct contact with the ground. Clean up and clear out areas that provide safe harbor for insects.

ACTIONS TO TAKE	NOTES
Caulk cracks; weatherstrip; frequently vacuum rugs, carpets, and upholstery. Apply powdered chlorpyrifos to suspected areas of infestation.	
Caulk cracks and openings, weatherstrip, eliminate moisture problems and decayed wood. For localized problem, apply boric acid, pyrethrum, or chlorpyrifos according to label. For extensive problems, call an exterminator.	Carpenter ants have wings during their reproductive stage.
Caulk openings, weatherstrip, eliminate moisture problems, store food in sealed containers, keep garbage outdoors, clean thoroughly. Apply boric acid according to label. Kill survivors with poisonous baits.	Cockroaches are some of the most adaptable creatures on Earth.
For localized problem, apply chlorpyrifos or other approved pesticide according to label. For extensive problems, call an exterminator.	Old house borers, a related, highly destructive variety, infest seasoned wood.
Caulk openings, weatherstrip, eliminate moisture problems, store food in sealed containers, keep garbage outdoors, clean thoroughly. Apply boric acid to infested areas according to label.	Be sure to check old books for infestation before bringing them into your home.
Eliminate moisture problems and decayed wood to prevent infestation. If you suspect infestation, call an exterminator.	These are less common than subterranean termites but more difficult to detect.
To prevent infestation, eliminate moisture problems and any wood that contacts ground. Spread polyethylene sheeting across crawl space. Remove mud tubes and treat soil along foundations with pyrethrin or other termite control. If you suspect infestation, call an exterminator.	Formosan termites produce hard, sponge-like material in galleries. Termites have wings during their reproductive stage.

Cleaning Siding

Sometimes a house that looks as if it needs a new coat of paint really only needs to be cleaned. With that in mind, cleaning is a logical first step along the road to rehabbing your home's exterior. Even if you decide to paint, cleaning is an important step because paint will not adhere properly to dirty surfaces.

One way to clean your house is to scrub it with a solution of warm water, bleach, and trisodium phosphate (TSP) or a nonphosphate substitute. TSP is a cleaning agent available in powdered form at most hardware stores. To mix the solution, follow the directions on the label. Because the solution is caustic, it is not intended for bare wood or masonry walls.

Before washing surfaces, cover plants, stone and brick walls, and patios close to the house with plastic tarps to protect them from splattering (and be sure to uncover plants as soon as you've finished washing to avoid suffocating them). Protect yourself by wearing old clothes, safety goggles, and rubber gloves.

Clean bare wood by sweeping off loose dirt with a broom, working from top to bottom. If the wood has been exposed to the elements for more than a few weeks, sand it first to remove mold and mildew.

One way to make quick work of a house-cleaning project is to rent a power washer. Power washers—high-pressure cleaning tools—are particularly useful for large jobs or for surfaces that are extremely dirty. They force water through a hand-held nozzle, allowing you to blast away dirt and loose paint. Most models have a separate reservoir for cleaning agents, which means that the same tool can be used for both cleaning and rinsing. Be sure to read the operator's manual before using a power washer.

CLEANING WITH A BRUSH

1 Wash the surface

Wash a roughly 15-foot-wide section of the surface with a brush dipped in a TSP solution. Using generous quantities of the solution, sweep the brush across the surface; hard scrubbing shouldn't be necessary.

2 Rinse off with a hose

After washing the first section with the TSP solution, rinse it thoroughly with a garden hose, starting at the top and working down. Repeat Steps 1 and 2 until all surfaces are clean. Let surfaces dry for one to two days before painting.

1 **Wash the surface**

Fill the washer with the cleaning solution
recommended by the manufacturer. Holding the
nozzle about 18 inches from the surface, squeeze
the trigger and slowly spray back and forth across
a section of the wall, working from the top down.
Repeat the process at 5- or 6-foot intervals.

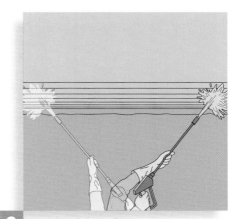

2 **Rinse the surface**

Holding the nozzle closer to the surface (about 6
to 10 inches away), rinse thoroughly with fresh
water. Once again, spray successive sections of the
wall by moving the nozzle slowly back and forth,
moving from top to bottom.

Repairing Wood Siding

In time, even the best-maintained wood siding begins to show signs of deterioration. The most common problem you are likely to come up against is rot. If the damage is limited, you can dig out the bad wood with a scraper or old screwdriver and fill in the hole with caulk or plastic wood fillers.

If the damage is spread across an entire siding panel or there is not enough wood left to hold a repair, the entire section of siding will have to be replaced.

Before you repair any damage, however, you will want to determine the cause of the problem, which is most likely moisture. Leaks in gutters or roofing are common culprits, so check them and repair any leaks before painting (see Rooftop chapter).

When the source of moisture is not obvious, look into hiring a professional. If you don't remedy the cause of the problem, the repaired surface will only disintegrate again.

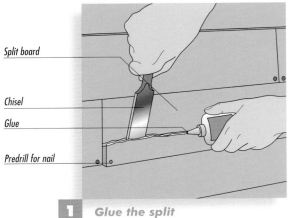

Split board

Chisel

Glue

Predrill for nail

1 **Glue the split**
A clean split or crack can be repaired by carefully prying the board apart with a chisel, then coating both edges with waterproof glue.

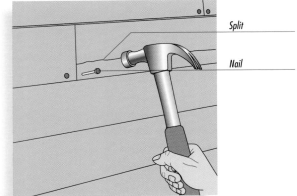

Split

Nail

2 **Fasten the board**
Push the edges of the pieces tightly together, drill pilot holes, then secure both sections of board to the sheathing with nails or screws. Fill any gaps and cover the fastener heads with wood putty, then sand and paint.

REPLACING A TONGUE-AND-GROOVE BOARD

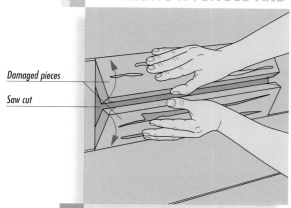

Damaged pieces
Saw cut

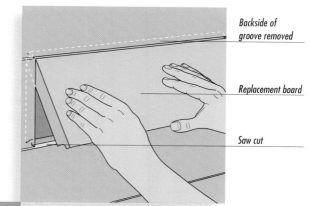

Backside of groove removed
Replacement board
Saw cut

1 Remove the board

To remove the section, cut at each end of the damage, then lengthwise, with a circular saw that has its blade depth set just shy of the siding thickness. Very carefully hold back the blade guard, then lower the moving blade into the wood to start each cut. Finish the cuts with a chisel and mallet. Cave in the board, then pull out the damaged pieces. Repair any cuts in the building paper with roofing cement.

2 Install a new board

Slide the backside of the groove on the replacement board into place and nail the board to the sheathing. Putty the nail holes and end joints, and sand.

REPLACING A PIECE OF CLAPBOARD SIDING

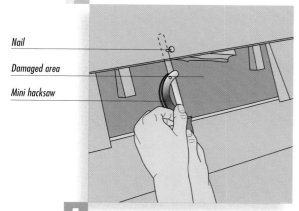

Nail
Damaged area
Mini hacksaw

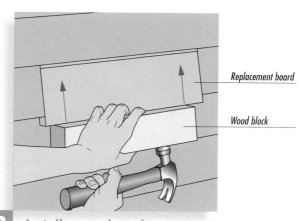

Replacement board
Wood block

1 Remove the board

Mark cutting lines on each side of the damaged area at wall stud locations. Use a backsaw to cut out the damaged piece. Pry up the damaged board, then drive small wooden wedges underneath it at each end. Finish the cuts with a compass saw or a chisel and mallet, and cut off any remaining nails with a mini hacksaw. Repair any tears in the building paper with roofing cement.

2 Install a new board

Trim a replacement board to length and drive it into position by hammering against a wood block. Nail the board's bottom edge to the sheathing. Putty the nail holes and board ends, then sand before painting.

Repairing Synthetic Siding

Siding Repairs

Both aluminum and vinyl siding panels have interlocking flanges along both edges. The panels are nailed to the sheathing through slots along one flange; the other flange interlocks with the adjacent panel. Panels may be installed vertically or horizontally. A typical horizontal installation is shown. For more about vinyl and aluminum siding, see pages 302–305.

You can successfully repair minor dents, scratches, and corrosion in aluminum siding. More extensive damage usually can't be repaired; instead, the damaged pieces of siding must be replaced, as shown on facing page.

REPAIRING ALUMINUM SIDING To remove a dent in aluminum siding, drill a hole in the center of the dent and screw in a self-tapping screw with two washers under the screw head (the screw cuts its own thread as it is driven in). Gently pull on the screw head with a pair of pliers.

Remove the screw and fill the hole with plastic aluminum filler (follow directions on the tube). When dry, sand the filler smooth and touch up with matching paint.

Conceal scratches in aluminum siding by applying metal primer over the scratch. When the primer is dry, coat with acrylic house paint.

Clean corroded areas with fine steel wool. Prime the area with rust-resistant metal primer, specifically for aluminum, and cover with acrylic house paint.

REPLACING ALUMINUM SIDING If a section of your aluminum siding is damaged beyond a simple surface repair, you can replace it by cutting out the damaged part of the panel, leaving the nailed portion in place. Use tin snips to cut the new section of siding (it should overlap the existing siding by 3 inches on each side), then install it.

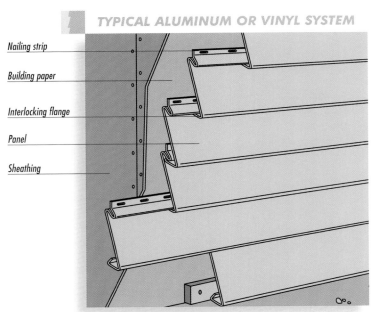

TYPICAL ALUMINUM OR VINYL SYSTEM

Nailing strip

Building paper

Interlocking flange

Panel

Sheathing

Both vinyl and aluminum siding are installed with interlocking flanges. To remove a piece, use a special tool called a "zipper" to separate the panels.

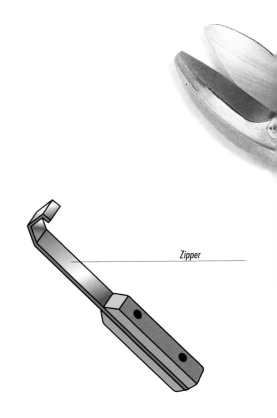

Zipper

Cut a replacement piece 2 inches longer than the section you just removed to allow for a 1-inch overlap on each end. (Cut only 1 inch longer if the damaged section ends at a corner or joint.) Snap the top edge of the new section in place and nail it with aluminum box nails long enough to penetrate 1 inch into the studs. Using the zipper, snap in the other edge.

REPLACING A SECTION

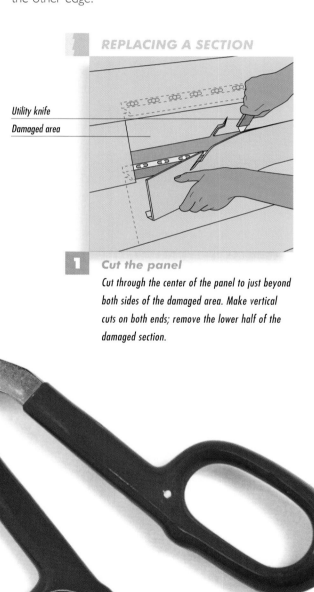

Utility knife
Damaged area

1 Cut the panel
Cut through the center of the panel to just beyond both sides of the damaged area. Make vertical cuts on both ends; remove the lower half of the damaged section.

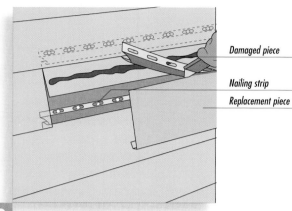

Damaged piece
Nailing strip
Replacement piece

2 Remove nailing strip
Cut the nailing strip off the replacement with a utility knife. The new piece should be 6 inches longer than the damaged section, 3 inches if one end is at a joint or corner.

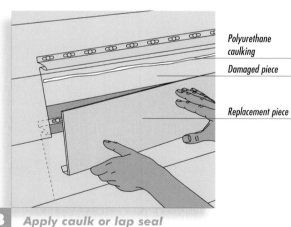

Polyurethane caulking
Damaged piece
Replacement piece

3 Apply caulk or lap seal
Generously apply polyurethane caulk or lap seal to the damaged panel. Press the new piece in place so each end overlaps existing siding by 3 inches. Hold or prop until dry.

Repairing Masonry Siding

Cracks and holes in stucco and brick siding may result from poorly applied or poor-quality material, from freeze-thaw cycles in cold-winter climates, or from movement—such as that caused by settling or earthquakes. Protect the house from moisture damage by repairing damage promptly.

STUCCO PROBLEMS Stucco walls typically consist of three layers of stucco applied over self-furring spacers and wire mesh. The final coat is either pigmented or painted and can be textured in a variety of ways.

Though cracks and holes are relatively easy to repair, it can be tricky to match both the texture and the color of the surrounding wall. If you're unsure of your abilities, you may be better off having a professional mason handle the work.

Hairline and small cracks can usually be filled with caulking compound and then painted with latex paint. For large cracks and holes up to about 6 inches wide, use stucco patching compound. Follow the instructions on the bag or can.

For larger holes, you'll need three coats of stucco—a "scratch" coat, a "brown" coat, and a final coat that is colored. You can buy it this way and texture it to match the original.

For the first and second coats buy a bag of stucco mix. Add $1/10$ part lime for easier working. Mix with enough water to make a fairly stiff paste. For the final coat purchase a stucco color coat mix in the desired color. This final coat should be flush with the surrounding wall. While it's wet, texture it to match (you'll have to experiment). For a smooth texture, draw a metal float across the surface. For other textures, daub a sponge or brush on the surface, or splatter with more stucco and smooth down high spots. To cure stucco, cover with a plastic sheet and keep it damp for about 4 days. Wait a month after curing if you need to paint.

BRICK PROBLEMS Brick-veneer siding is usually applied to a wood frame wall over building paper; the mortared joints may be "tooled," or finished, in a number of ways. Properly tooled joints are essential to ensure strong, watertight walls.

1 PATCHING STUCCO

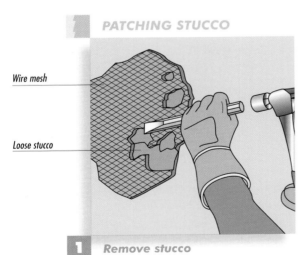

Wire mesh

Loose stucco

1 Remove stucco
Remove loose stucco from the hole with a cold chisel and ball-peen hammer; blow out the dust. Paint around the edges of the patch with a concrete bonding agent. Staple new wire mesh over any damaged mesh. Spray with water.

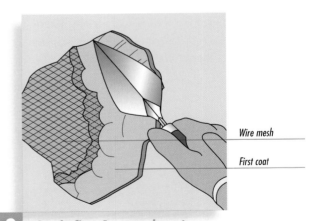

Wire mesh

First coat

2 Apply first & second coats
Apply the first coat of stucco to within $1/4$ inch of the surface using a mason's trowel (stucco should ooze behind mesh). When firm, scratch with a nail. Allow it to cure for 2 days. Apply the second coat over the dampened first coat to within $1/8$ inch of the surface. Let it cure for 2 days.

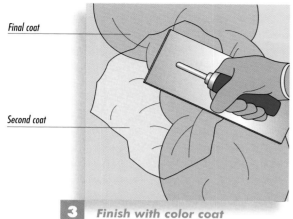

Final coat

Second coat

3 Finish with color coat

Apply the finish color coat over the dampened second coat with a metal float. Smooth it flush with the existing surface. Texture as desired; cure for 4 days covered with plastic.

To repair cracked or crumbling mortar, you'll have to remove the old mortar and "repoint" the joints (fill them with new mortar), as shown below.

Though you can make your own mortar, it's easier to use dry ready-mixed mortar (use weather-resistant type N), available at building supply stores. Prepare the mortar according to package directions.

Using a jointer, steel rod, or trowel, tool the new joints to match the existing ones. Mortar joints should be tooled when they are "thumbprint hard" (neither so soft that they smear the wall nor so hard that a metal tool leaves black marks). Keep tooled joints damp for 4 days to cure.

REPOINTING MORTAR JOINTS

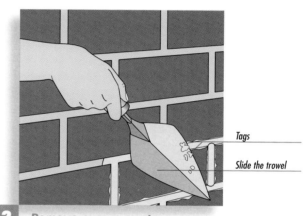

Tags

Slide the trowel

2 Remove excess mortar

Cut off the tags (excess mortar) by sliding the trowel along the wall. Finish the horizontal and vertical joints.

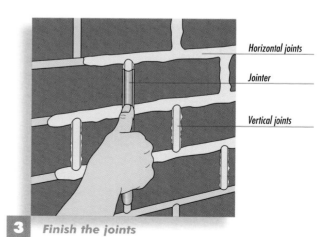

Horizontal joints

Jointer

Vertical joints

New mortar

Open joint

Hawk

1 Apply new mortar

Pack mortar into dampened (not wet) open joints, using a small trowel and a hawk. Tamp the mortar with a trowel or piece of wood.

3 Finish the joints

When the mortar is thumbprint hard, finish the joints by pressing and drawing a jointer (or other appropriate tool) along each joint.

Rooftop

The notion of shelter begins with the roof. A roof protects us from the elements, retaining heat in winter and maintaining coolness in summer in the living spaces below. It also serves as an architectural element that establishes the style of a house.

Since it is constantly exposed to sun, wind, and precipitation, the roof takes a continual pounding as the years go by—wear-and-tear that may not be obvious until a heavy rain sends a stream of water drip-drip-dripping through the ceiling. Keeping your roof in repair is essential to your peace of mind and the soundness of your home's structure.

This chapter begins with a primer on roof construction and the various roofing materials available today. You will learn how to install the common asphalt shingle roof, and how to repair different types of roofs and roof-related drainage problems. We also offer advice on installing and repairing rain gutters and downspouts, and installing skylights.

Typical Roof Construction

Understanding the structure of your roof is the first step toward diagnosing problems, initiating improvements, and making repairs. With that in mind, these two pages will give you a glimpse at how roofs are built.

A typical roof begins with a framework of rafters that supports a roof deck (sometimes called a subroof) consisting of sheathing and underlayment. The roof deck, in turn, provides a nailing base for the roof surface material.

THE ROOF DECK Though the way a roof deck is built can vary depending on the roof surface material, most decks include both sheathing and underlayment.

Sheathing, the material that provides the nailing base for the roof surface material, ranges from solid plywood to oriented strand board to open sheathing (used with wood shingles).

Sandwiched between the sheathing and the surface material is the underlayment, usually roofing felt. A heavy, fibrous black paper saturated with asphalt, roofing felt is waterproof enough to resist water penetration from outside, yet porous enough to allow moisture from inside the attic to escape.

ANATOMY OF A ROOF

Many different components work together to give a roof strength and make it weathertight.

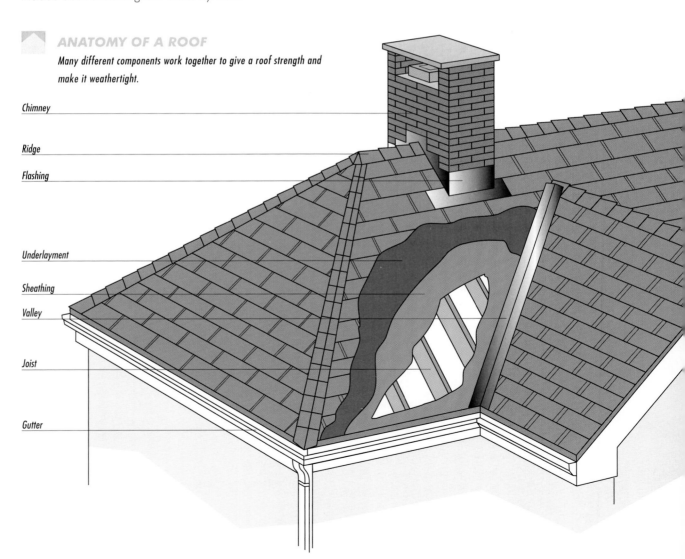

Chimney

Ridge

Flashing

Underlayment

Sheathing

Valley

Joist

Gutter

THE ROOF SURFACE The material on the roof must be able to resist wind, rain, snow, hail, and sun. A wide variety of roof surface materials is available. Key types are discussed on pages 322–323. Some may be used on nearly flat roofs, while others rely upon the slope of a pitched roof to shed water from the surface.

When dealing with a roof, you'll discover several words that may not be familiar. On pitched roofs, materials are applied in horizontal layers, called "courses," which overlap one another from the eaves to the ridge. The portion of the material exposed to the weather is called the "exposure," and the edge that is down-roof is called the "butt." Asphalt shingles, the most common roofing surface, are sometimes called "composition" or "comp" shingles and are divided into sections called "tabs."

MEASURING ROOF PITCH

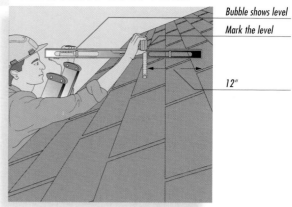

Bubble shows level

Mark the level

12"

Mark a line 12 inches from one end on a level and rest that end on the roof. Raise or lower the opposite end until the tool is level. Then measure the distance between the roof and the 12-inch mark to determine the pitch. If it's 3 inches, for example, the roof's pitch is "3-in-12."

Roof pitch is a term used to express the ratio of a roof's vertical rise in inches to each foot of run—the horizontal distance. A "3-in-12 pitch" describes a roof that rises 3 inches vertically for every 12 inches of horizontal distance.

Typically, a roof's surface is broken by angles and protrusions such as vent pipes, chimneys, and dormers. All of these require a weathertight seal, usually provided by flashing. Made from malleable metal or plastic, flashing appears as the drip edge along the eaves of a roof, the collars around ventilation and plumbing pipes, the valleys between two roof planes, and the "steps" along a chimney. Less obvious flashing also protects other breaks in the roof, such as skylights. See more about flashing on pages 328–329.

At the roof edges, gutters, discussed on pages 332–333, catch water runoff and channel it to the ground via the downspouts, which direct water away from the house and into the soil.

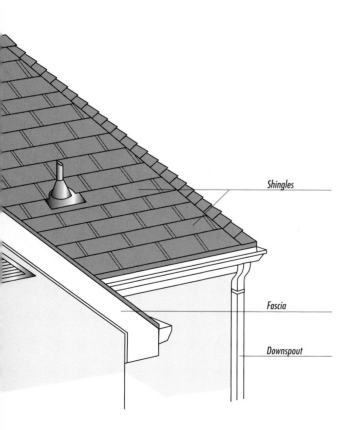

Shingles

Fascia

Downspout

Types of Roofing

Roofing varies widely in size, shape, and material. Traditional sloping roofs are usually covered with overlapping layers of asphalt shingles, wood shingles or shakes, or masonry materials such as tile, slate, or concrete. Less traditional options include aluminum and steel.

Flat or low-sloping roofs are most often surfaced with alternating layers of roofing felt and asphalt or tar, with a layer of gravel on top. These types are known as built-up, or tar-and-gravel, roofs. Some flat roofs are covered with insulating polyurethane foam or a rubber-like modified-bitumen membrane.

Your roof's pitch (see page 321) and local building codes determine the list of roofing materials that are suitable. The chart at right will help you narrow down your choices.

The Underwriters Laboratory has tested all types of roofing materials for fire resistance. Look for the UL symbol; materials are rated Class A (those with the most fire-retardant qualities), Class B, and Class C. Because of their flammable nature, materials such as untreated wood shingles or shakes receive no rating.

 COMPARATIVE GUIDE TO ROOFING

MATERIAL	POUNDS PER SQUARE FOOT
Asphalt shingles (felt base)	240–345
Asphalt shingles (fiberglass base)	220–430
Wood shingles and shakes	144–350
Tile (concrete and clay)	900–1000
Slate	900–1000
Aluminum shingles	50
Metal panels (aluminum or steel)	45–75
Asphalt roll roofing	90–180
Asphalt ("tar") and gravel	250–650
Sprayed polyurethane foam	20 for 1" thickness

It's a backbreaking job to load materials onto the roof. When ordering, ask your dealer for "rooftop delivery," that is, to deliver them directly onto the roof. Have materials delivered just before it's time to install them, and spread out the bundles to distribute the weight load.

MATERIALS

DURABILITY	FIRE RATING	MINIMUM SLOPE	CHARACTERISTICS
12–20 years, depending on sun's intensity	C	4 in 12 down to 2 in 12 with additional underlayment	Available in wide range of colors, textures, standard and premium weights; easy to apply and repair; low maintenance; economical. Less durable and fire resistant than fiberglass base shingles, though equal in cost.
15–25 years, depending on sun's intensity	A	4 in 12 down to 2 in 12 with additional underlayment	Durable and highly fire resistant; available in wide range of colors, textures, standard and premium weights; easy to apply and repair; low maintenance. Brittle when applied in temperatures below 50° F.
10–15 years, depending on slope, heat, humidity	None, untreated; C, if treated with retardant; B, with use of retardant and foil underlayment	4 in 12 down to 3 in 12 with additional underlayment	Appealing natural appearance with strong shadow lines; durable. Use #1 ("Blue Label") shingles for roofing. Flammable unless treated with retardants; treated wood expensive; time-consuming application.
50+ years	A	4 in 12 down to 3 in 12 with additional underlayment	Extremely durable; fireproof; comes in flat, curved, and ribbed shapes; moderate color range. Costly to ship; hard to install; needs strong framing to support weight; cracks easily if walked on.
50+ years	A	4 in 12	Attractive, traditional appearance; does not deteriorate; fireproof; comes in several colors. Expensive to buy and ship; hard to install; requires strong framing to support weight; may get brittle with age.
25+ years	A, B, or C	4 in 12	Light; fire resistant; resembles wood shakes; moderate range of colors. Can be damaged by heavy hail, falling branches.
20+ years	A, B, or C	1 in 12	Aluminum: lightweight; durable; maintenance-free; sheds snow. Steel: strong; durable; fire resistant; sheds snow. Contraction and expansion can cause leaks at nail holes; noisy in rain.
5–10 years (depends on water runoff at low slope)	A, B, or C	1 in 12	Economical, easy to apply, but drab appearance.
10–20 years, depending on sun's intensity	A, B, or C	1/4 in 12	Membrane roof; most waterproof of all. Must be professionally applied; built-up and single-ply; hard to locate leaks; black surfaces absorb heat (white gravel helps reflect sun's rays).
Life of building with proper maintenance	A	1/4 in 12	Continuous membrane produces watertight surface; good insulation value; lightweight; durable when maintained. Must be professionally applied; deteriorates under sunlight if not properly coated (and periodically recoated).

Roofing Tools & Equipment

Although minor repairs are relatively easy and require only a few tools, extensive roofing work can be difficult and demands a fairly complete selection of carpentry and roofing tools and equipment. For starters, you will need ladders for climbing onto the roof (see more about ladders on pages 42–43).

To look for leaks, you'll want good lighting, so if your attic isn't lit, you'll need a safety light. For removing shingles, a shingle ripper (see page 341) is a very helpful tool. A variety of tools is needed for working with sheet metal flashing and gutters, including tin snips and, in some cases, pliers or a vise. If you'll be reroofing entirely, consider renting a pneumatic roofing nailer.

HELPFUL ROOFING TOOLS

Whether you're installing asphalt or wood shingles, extensive roofing jobs call for an assortment of tear-off, layout, and installation tools.

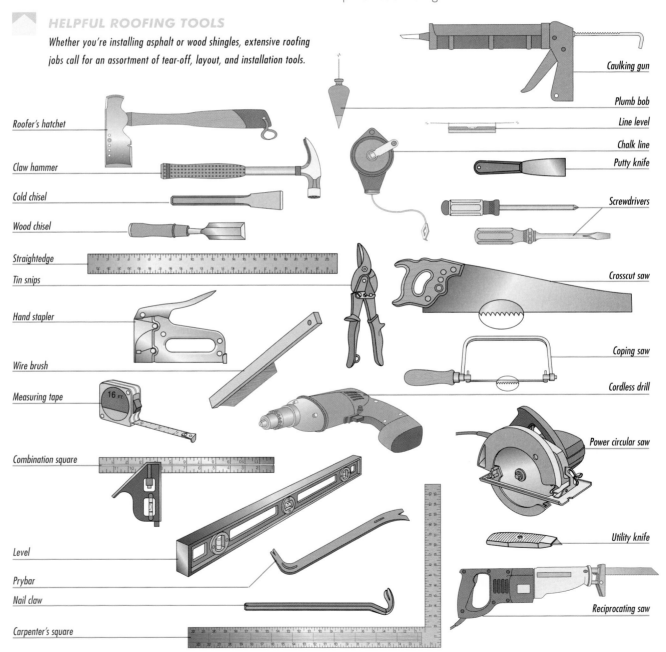

Roofer's hatchet

Claw hammer

Cold chisel

Wood chisel

Straightedge

Tin snips

Hand stapler

Wire brush

Measuring tape

Combination square

Level

Prybar

Nail claw

Carpenter's square

Caulking gun

Plumb bob

Line level

Chalk line

Putty knife

Screwdrivers

Crosscut saw

Coping saw

Cordless drill

Power circular saw

Utility knife

Reciprocating saw

For jobs such as installing a skylight, you'll need a pretty complete carpentry toolbox in addition to roofing tools, including many of the wall and ceiling tools discussed on pages 100–101 for interior trim work.

If you'll be doing any work on the chimney, you may need a ball-peen hammer and a cold chisel, along with a trowel and a few other masonry tools (see pages 316–317 for more about masonry tools).

WORKING SAFELY

Before venturing up a ladder to repair roofing, siding, windows, or gutters, it's important to know the following safety precautions.

LADDER SAFETY Ladders for long reaches range from straight wooden types to aluminum extension ladders (one that extends to 20 feet is adequate for most houses). Be sure your ladder is strong yet light enough to be handled easily. Below are some tips for using a ladder safely:

▪ Inspect your ladder for cracks and other weaknesses before you lean it against the house.

▪ Place the base of the ladder on firm, level ground at a measured distance from the side of the house.

▪ Get on and off the ladder by stepping onto the center of the rung. Use both hands to grip the ladder rails (not the rungs). Reposition the ladder if it wobbles.

▪ Keep your hips between the ladder rails. Don't lean out to reach an area; instead, reposition the ladder.

▪ Make sure that only one person stands on a ladder at a time.

▪ Install rubber safety shoes (available at home improvement centers) on the ladder feet if the ladder is to stand on a slick surface.

▪ Don't stand on the top two rungs of a ladder. If you're repairing a roof, at least two rungs of the ladder should extend above the eaves so you can step directly out onto the roof.

▪ Be sure the rung hooks of an extension ladder are locked in place and that no section is extended more than three-quarters of its length.

▪ Pull materials up a ladder with a rope and have a place to store them at the top; do not try to carry them up.

ROOF SAFETY Working on a roof requires extra caution. The surface is usually slick, sloped, and well above the ground. Following are some precautions to take when making roof repairs:

▪ Don't walk on a roof any more than is necessary or you

may cause more damage. Don't walk on tile and slate roofs at all—they're slippery and breakable.

▪ Let a professional make any repairs on a steeply pitched roof—one that slopes more than 25 degrees or rises more than 4 vertical inches for every 12 horizontal inches.

▪ Wear loose, comfortable clothing and non-slip rubber-soled shoes with good ankle support.

▪ Work on the roof only in dry, calm, warm weather. A wet roof can be treacherously slick; a sudden wind can knock you off balance.

▪ Never work on the roof when lightning threatens.

▪ Be careful not to put your weight on brittle or old roofing materials or rotted decking.

▪ Stay well away from power lines and be sure neither your body nor any equipment comes into contact with them. Keep children and pets away.

SPECIAL SAFETY EQUIPMENT The standard safety devices listed below help to distribute your weight evenly and provide for secure footing. All are available from tool rental companies. In addition, be sure to check with your local state safety office regarding the laws outlined by OSHA (Occupational Safety & Health Administration); each state has its own safety requirements for roof work.

▪ A safety harness, used in conjunction with a fall-arrest rope, is an added precaution when working on steep inclines and will keep you from sliding off the roof.

▪ A metal ladder bracket allows you to hook your ladder over the ridge.

▪ Nailed to the roof framing, a 2-by-6 plank supports you and your working materials. Use strong, straight-grained lumber no longer than 10 feet unless you support the middle with another jack. Jacks have notches in them so they can be slipped off the nails. When you're finished, set and caulk the nails to prevent leaks.

▪ An angled seat board allows you to sit on a level surface while working.

Preparing to Reroof

To offer years of trouble-free service, a roof must have a proper, sound deck—the part of a roof, consisting of sheathing and underlayment, that supports the finish roofing. Sometimes you can roof right over the old roof, using it as a deck. But if your roof doesn't meet the conditions outlined here, you will have to strip the old shingles or completely remove and replace the decking.

Your new roofing material will dictate what type of deck is best. For most materials, the manufacturer's recommendations and local codes specify the appropriate underlayment, sheathing, flashing, and so forth. In this book, we discuss how to install asphalt shingles because they are, by far, the type most commonly used on American roofs.

While preparing the deck, handle all related changes to the roof, such as adding skylights, vents, or insulation.

TEARING OFF THE OLD ROOF Removing existing roofing is a dirty, dangerous job. Though you can save money by doing this work yourself, it's often well worth the price to hire a service to strip the roof and remove the debris (look under "Demolition Contractors" in the Yellow Pages).

If you do this work, be very careful. Wear a dust mask to screen out airborne particles, and wear heavy-duty gloves. Keep your weight on top of the rafters; if you step on weakened sheathing, you could go right through.

Protect windows and doors by leaning sheets of plywood against them. To keep debris from falling onto your flower beds, wrap the upper ends of 6-mil plastic sheeting around 2 by 4s and tack these underneath the eaves, then anchor the sheeting to the ground with a board. Plan to rent a large refuse bin from your garbage-collection service for the discarded materials, and park it as close to the work site as possible.

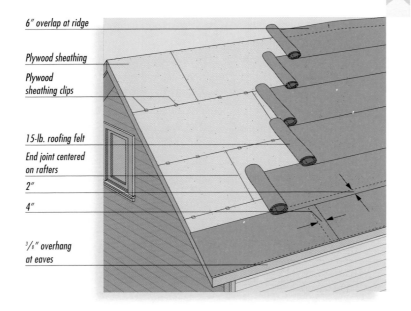

6" overlap at ridge

Plywood sheathing

Plywood sheathing clips

15-lb. roofing felt

End joint centered on rafters

2"

4"

³⁄₈" overhang at eaves

INSTALLING SHEATHING

Either ¹⁄₂-inch or ⁵⁄₈-inch plywood sheathing offers a sturdy nailing base. Stagger the panels horizontally with the ends centered on rafters. Leave a ¹⁄₁₆-inch expansion gap between adjoining panels and ¹⁄₈ inch between edges (double this in a very humid area). Space nails every 6 inches along vertical ends and every 12 inches at intermediate supports.

If there are two or three existing roofs, remove all of them, one at a time. Be careful not to damage any flashing; even if it has deteriorated and must be replaced, it's useful as a pattern for fabricating new flashing.

When the old shingles have been removed, pull nails and, if necessary, repair or install new sheathing.

SELECTING SHEATHING Every roof has either solid or open sheathing across the rafters to provide a nailing base and—in most cases—add to the roof's structural integrity. Solid sheathing materials come in two forms: panels and boards. Panels, typically 4-by-8-foot sheets of CDX-grade plywood or a pressed-wood product called oriented strand board (OSB), are preferred for most roofs because they're relatively inexpensive and fast to install.

INSTALLING PANEL SHEATHING When installing solid panel sheathing, begin at one lower corner and lay a sheet horizontally across the rafters with its inward edge centered on a rafter, as shown on facing page. Work your way across the eaves, then lay another full course with the end joints staggered by 4 feet. Leave a $1/16$-inch expansion space between the ends of adjoining panels and a $1/8$-inch gap between the long sides. In exceptionally humid climates, double this spacing. Use 2-inch nails for $1/2$-inch sheets, and $2^1/2$-inch nails for thicker sheets.

If your house has open overhangs, you may want to install starter boards before the first course of panels. Starter board material—$5/8$-inch-by-6-inch V-rustic or shiplap siding—is much more attractive to look at from under overhangs than plywood or OSB. When installing starter boards, first snap chalk lines along the eaves as guides for aligning their edges. Join the boards' ends over rafters.

You can install $3/8$-inch panel sheathing over the top of existing open sheathing, but the roof will have more structural integrity if you remove the open sheathing and start from scratch with thicker panels. It's usually necessary to support standard $1/2$-inch panels mid-span between rafters, either with blocking or with special H-clips that serve to keep panels flush. Or buy plywood panels that have interlocking V-grooved edges. Let panels extend over hips and ridges. Snap a chalk line across them flush at rakes, hips, and ridge, and cut them off in place.

APPLYING DRIP EDGES Before you install underlayment, install metal drip edges along the eaves and valley liners and flashing. After underlayment is in place, drip edges are applied along the rakes. Refer to pages 328–329 for information on drip edges and flashing.

INSTALLING UNDERLAYMENT Roofing felt, a heavy, asphalt-impregnated black paper sold in large rolls, provides a second layer of weather protection. On most roofs, strips of standard 36-inch-wide, 15-pound felt are lapped from the eaves to the ridge and are used to line valleys. If underlayment is not pre-marked, snap horizontal chalk lines before you begin, to keep it straight on the roof. Sweep off the roof deck and check for protruding nails, then prepare to roll out the underlayment. Snap the first line $33^5/8$ inches above the eaves to allow for a $3/8$-inch overhang. Then, providing for a 2-inch overlap between strips of felt, snap succeeding chalk lines at 34 inches.

Start at one end of one of the eaves and work from rake to rake. Tack the felt at its center with three roofing nails and roll a strip to the other end of the eaves. Cut it off flush at the rake. Adjust the strip up or down and smooth it out. Nail the material in place with roofing nails or staples spaced 3 to 4 feet apart along the lower half of the felt.

Repeat this process until you reach the ridge. Trim the felt with a utility knife, flush at rakes and overlapped 6 inches at valleys, hips, and ridges. Where two strips meet end to end, overlap by 4 inches. When you encounter a vent pipe, slit the felt to fit around the pipe.

DEALING WITH ICE & SNOW To protect an asphalt shingle roof against ice dams in cold climates, first apply standard underlayment to the sheathing. Then cover the eaves area—to 12 inches inside the exterior wall line—with a 36-inch-wide sheet of 90-pound mineral-surface or 50-pound smooth-surface roll roofing. Allowing a $3/8$-inch overhang along the eaves, fasten down the roll roofing at intervals of 12 to 18 inches, 6 inches from the bottom edge and 1 inch from the upper edge. At vertical joints, allow 4 inches overlap; fasten the lower lap to the roof with nails every 12 inches, and cement the ends. For more about ice dams, see page 349.

If you need more than one width of roll roofing to reach 12 inches inside the wall line, overlap horizontal courses by at least 6 inches, applying plastic roofing cement liberally where they overlap.

Flashing for a New Roof

Flashing materials made of galvanized steel, copper, or aluminum direct water away from valleys, chimneys, vent stacks, skylights, and where dormers and other walls meet the roof. Flashing is also required along eaves and rakes (the ends of a gable roof). Here's a closer look at the flashing that protects various parts of a roof:

VALLEYS Valleys require particularly sturdy flashing because they carry more water than any individual roof plane. On most roofs, metal valley flashing is installed after the roofing felt liner and before the primary underlayment and finish roofing, as shown at top left on facing page.

On some asphalt-shingle roofs, shingles are woven across the valleys, eliminating the need for metal flashing. This is generally the best way to handle valleys between roof planes of different pitches. Another fairly common technique for asphalt-shingle roofs is to flash valleys with roll roofing that's the same color as the shingles. To do this, first nail an 18-inch-wide strip along the valley, with the finished surface down; set nails 1 inch from the edges and 12 inches apart. Then roll out a 36-inch-wide strip, finished side up. Center it over the first strip and nail it down.

ROOF EDGES Drip edge flashing helps keep water from wicking back under the shingles (see top right on facing page). In climates where ice dams occur, flash the eaves with a special rubber ice-shield membrane or roll roofing. On a cedar shingle or shake roof, use 30-pound felt for this task.

VENT PIPES Before you begin to roof, be sure to have on hand vent pipe flashing for each pipe that penetrates the roof. Two types are available: sheet-metal cones that you caulk to the pipe, and self-sealing types that have rubber gaskets. Vent pipe flashing is installed when the new shingles reach the base of the vent pipe. Cut the roofing to fit around the pipe, then slide the flashing over the pipe so that its base flange lies on top of the roofing on the downslope side. Then continue roofing over the flashing, cutting the shingles to fit around it.

CHIMNEYS Chimney flashing consists of several parts as shown in the illustrations on facing page.

DORMERS Dormer walls are flashed with step flashing placed between each course of roof shingles. Ideally, the vertical flange of step flashing should be slipped under the siding. If that's not possible, caulk the flashing to the siding.

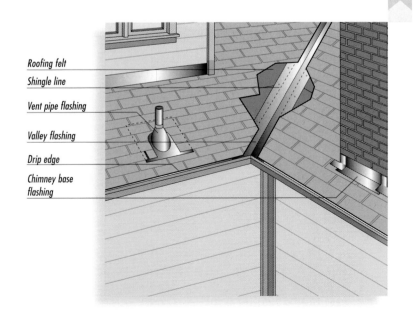

Roofing felt

Shingle line

Vent pipe flashing

Valley flashing

Drip edge

Chimney base flashing

TYPICAL ROOF FLASHING

Metal flashing helps seal out water from many critical spots on a home's roof, including valleys, around chimneys and vent pipes, beside dormer walls, and along the rakes and eaves. The roof illustrated here has an open valley made from a continuous piece of metal flashing. Note how the roof shingles are cut back from the valley centerline, leaving the flashing visible.

1"

2'

Install valley flashing

To install metal valley flashing for an asphalt-shingle roof, first roll out a length of 15-pound roofing felt cut to the length of the valley. Push it snugly into the valley, then nail it every 2 to 4 feet along the outside edges. If you need more than one length of flashing to cover the valley, start at the bottom and overlap the first piece with the second one by at least 6 inches.

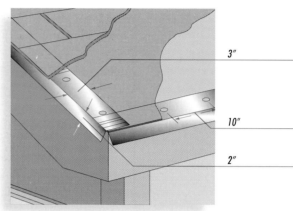

3"

10"

2"

Install drip edges

At eaves, nail preformed metal drip edge in place before applying the roofing felt. After the felt is down, nail drip edge along the rakes.

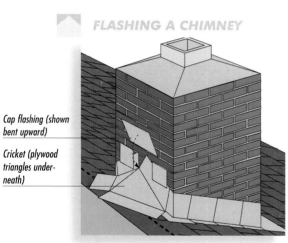

Cap flashing (shown bent upward)

Cricket (plywood triangles underneath)

Build a cricket

If the roof is particularly steep or if the chimney is more than 2 feet wide, build a "cricket" to prevent water and snow from collecting behind the chimney. Cut and install two plywood triangles to form the cricket. Then cover the plywood with a custom-bent saddle flashing. Protect the saddle with cap flashing.

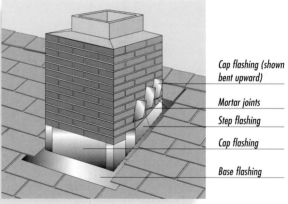

Cap flashing (shown bent upward)

Mortar joints

Step flashing

Cap flashing

Base flashing

Use cap flashing

Cap flashing extends down from above to prevent water from seeping behind flashing installed below it. It's typically used all around a chimney to protect base flashing, step flashing, and cricket. Cap flashing is usually installed in narrow slots cut into the mortar joints, but it can also be caulked to the chimney.

Applying Asphalt Shingles

Standard three-tab asphalt shingles are the easiest of all roofing materials to install. They are a manageable weight to carry and a breeze to cut and nail. In addition, the 12-by-36-inch shingles, when given a standard weather exposure of 5 inches, cover large areas very quickly. Asphalt roof shingles are also affordable, long lasting, and readily available at home centers and lumberyards. Before installation, review instructions on flashing a roof on pages 328–329.

CUTTING Cut asphalt shingles face down on a flat surface with a sharp utility knife. Hold a carpenter's square or straightedge on the cut line and score the back of the shingle with the knife. Then bend the shingle to break it on the scored line.

FASTENING Secure asphalt shingles with 12-gauge galvanized roofing nails. Use 1¼-inch-long nails for new roofs, 1½-inch nails when reroofing over an old asphalt roof.

Begin nailing the starter shingles at the rake and continue along the eaves. Allow a ½-inch overhang along the eaves and at both rakes, and ¹⁄₁₆-inch spacing between shingles. Use four nails each, nailed 3 inches above the eaves. Nail the first course over the starter course, using four nails per shingle.

When laying the successive courses, your main concern is proper alignment of the shingles—both horizontally and vertically. To horizontally align shingles that will be nailed over roofing felt, snap chalk lines; if you're reroofing without adding felt, just butt the new shingles against the old ones.

STANDARD THREE-TAB SHINGLE

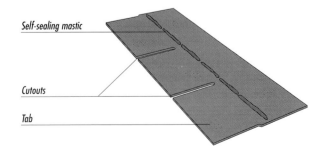

Self-sealing mastic

Cutouts

Tab

LAYING ASPHALT SHINGLES

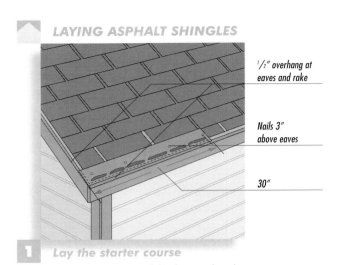

½" overhang at eaves and rake

Nails 3" above eaves

30"

1 Lay the starter course

A narrow starter course of shingles runs along the eaves to form a base for the first full course. When reroofing, cut the starter course 5 inches wide to match the exposure of the existing first course. For a new roof, cut a 9-inch-wide starter course. Trim 6 inches off the length of the first starter shingle to offset the cutouts in the starter course with the cutouts in the first full course.

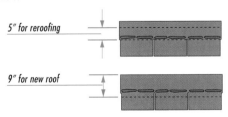

5" for reroofing

9" for new roof

When working with standard three-tab shingles, you can produce centered, diagonal, or random roof patterns by adjusting the length of the shingle that begins each course. Centered alignment creates the most uniform appearance, but is also the most difficult pattern to achieve. Diagonal alignment is a little more forgiving since the joints of four courses in a row are offset. Random alignment produces a more rustic appearance and is the easiest of the three patterns to lay: Just offset the joints of three courses in a row by at least 3 inches.

If you haven't purchased ready-made hip and ridge shingles, you can cut and bend 12-inch squares from standard shingles. Snap chalk lines along each side of the ridge and along each hip, 6 inches from the center.

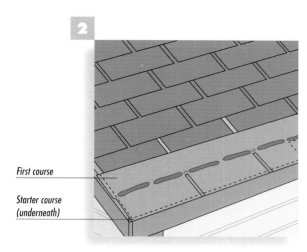

2

First course

Starter course
(underneath)

Lay the first course

On a new roof, use full-width shingles for the first course. When reroofing, use a 10-inch-wide course to cover the two 5-inch exposures of the existing first two courses. Allow the same $\frac{1}{2}$-inch overhang at the rakes and eaves and $\frac{1}{16}$ inch between shingles.

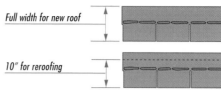

Full width for new roof

10" for reroofing

Lay successive courses

If you're using chalk lines, snap one every 10 inches from the bottom of the first course up to the ridge. Before you start the second row of shingles, also snap vertical chalk lines from the roof ridge to one end of every shingle along the first course, or every 36 inches. (This drawing shows how to stagger and align shingles—be sure to complete each course before laying the next one.)

3

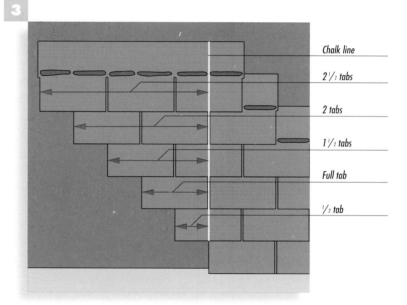

Chalk line

$2\frac{1}{2}$ tabs

2 tabs

$1\frac{1}{2}$ tabs

Full tab

$\frac{1}{2}$ tab

4

Ridge

5" exposure

Hip

Chalk line

Install hip & ridge shingles

If your roof has hips, shingle them before the ridge, beginning with a double layer of shingles at the bottom of one hip. Work toward the ridge, applying shingles with a 5-inch exposure. Align the edge of each shingle with the chalk line. To shingle the ridge, start at the end opposite the direction from which the wind most often blows. Use nails long enough to penetrate the ridge board securely (about 2 inches long).

Nail 1" in from edge

$5\frac{1}{2}$"

Installing Gutter Systems

Most gutters are installed on existing roofs, but adding new gutters when you're reroofing makes installation easier and integrates gutters into the entire roof system, making them work better.

Though wood gutters used to be very common, today they are virtually obsolete, except for their use in restoration work, because they are heavy and prone to multiple water-related problems. Contemporary gutters are made from vinyl, aluminum, galvanized steel, and, for high-end installations, stainless steel and copper made by sheet-metal fabricators.

You may be able to save labor costs by installing your own gutters, but this isn't always worth the effort. The most popular gutters today, "seamless gutters," are extruded from metal (typically aluminum with a baked-on finish) "coil" stock on site by a gutter fabricator. They tend to be secure and relatively inexpensive to have installed.

The gutter systems that you can buy at home-improvement centers and install yourself are typically made of vinyl, pre-painted steel, galvanized steel, or painted aluminum. These are known as "sectional" gutter systems. With these, you buy preformed channels from 10 to 22 feet long and any of many different components that join onto the channels, as shown in the illustration on facing page.

Standard gutter profiles are a simple "U" shape and a "K" style, which has an ogee-shaped front. The channels may be 4, 5, or 6 inches in diameter. Matching downspouts are 2-by-3-inch or 3-by-4-inch rectangular profiles, or 3- or 4-inch round (often corrugated) pipes. The larger systems are less likely to clog, so they're a good choice if you have trees overhanging your house. The appropriate size for gutters is usually figured as a factor of the roof's square area. The chart below left can help in determining size.

One typical vinyl system has elbows, connectors, and other components with silicone gaskets that form watertight seals. You simply plug together the system. Other types are glued together with PVC cement.

Gutters are attached along a house's eaves by any of several types of straps, brackets, and hangers, as shown in the illustration on facing page. Of these, bracket hangers, screwed to the fascia or rafter tails, tend to be the preferred method. But if the roof doesn't have these support members, a strap—ideally mounted beneath the shingles—is the method used.

Downspouts are connected to the gutter with a series of elbows and then secured to the house with wide straps. Plan to install one hanger for every 3 feet of gutter and three straps for each 10 feet of downspout.

Before hanging the gutter, assemble the parts on the ground (as much as possible). If your system is the type that utilizes PVC cement to glue together the parts, do not cement the downspouts to the drop outlets. Otherwise you won't be able to take them apart for cleaning.

 FIGURING GUTTER SIZE

ROOF AREA (SQ. FT.)	GUTTER DIAMETER	DOWNSPOUT DIAMETER
100–800	4"	3"
800–1,000	5"	3"
1,000–1,400	5"	4"
1,400+	6"	4"

TYPICAL GUTTER SYSTEM

A sectional gutter system is composed of many connected parts. Each drop outlet and exposed gutter end requires an end cap. If your roof has overhangs, you'll also need elbows to connect each downspout to its drop outlet.

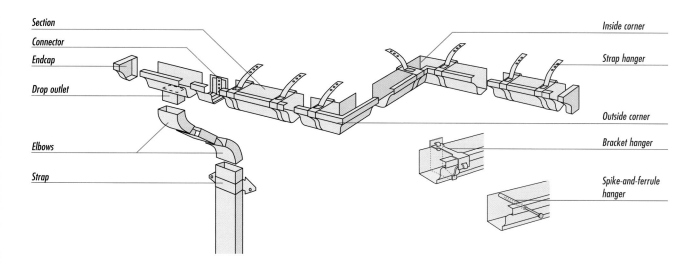

Section
Connector
Endcap
Drop outlet
Elbows
Strap

Inside corner
Strap hanger
Outside corner
Bracket hanger
Spike-and-ferrule hanger

INSTALLING A GUTTER SYSTEM

Line level

1 Determine the slope

Position a string line immediately below where the gutter will be located and tie it to nails at each end. Use a line level to level the string, then lower the string at the downspout end to achieve a drop of 1 inch per each 20 feet.

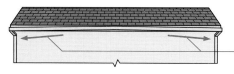

Slope toward downspouts

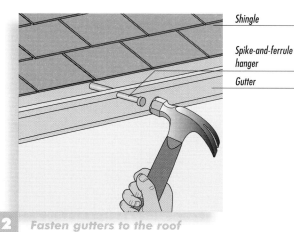

Shingle
Spike-and-ferrule hanger
Gutter

2 Fasten gutters to the roof

Align the gutter with the string. Nail or screw the first hangers at the downspout end (spike-and-ferrule is shown). Work outward from that point, fastening the gutter with one hanger every 3 feet. Secure the downspout with straps, using screws for wood siding and expanding anchors in masonry. Seal the straps with caulking compound.

Installing a Skylight

If you understand basic carpentry, installing a fairly small self-flashing skylight on an asphalt or wood-shingle roof with a moderate slope is manageable. For other situations, have the skylight installed by a professional. Be sure to find out whether a building permit is required.

LIGHT SHAFTS If your house has an attic or crawl space between the ceiling and the roof, be aware that you must install a light shaft to direct the light through the attic to the room below. In the attic, protect your head with a hard hat, and step only on ceiling joists or on boards supported by joists.

When planning your skylight's size, consider that some light will be lost in the shaft; the longer the light shaft, the larger the skylight must be to achieve the same level of lighting. Splaying the light shaft will help minimize this problem.

PLACEMENT Mark the four corners and the center of the proposed skylight opening on the ceiling. Then drive long nails through these five points. If any of them hit a ceiling joist, consider moving the proposed opening or adjusting its size to save framing work later. Ideally, two opposite sides will butt up against the facing sides of two joists.

In the attic, locate the five nails, clearing away any insulation material. Look for obstructions—wires, pipes, or heating or cooling ducts—within the area of the proposed opening. Also check the underside of the roof for any obstructions.

If the roof ridge or a major structural member crosses the opening, relocate the opening and either move the proposed ceiling opening or use an angled or splayed light shaft between the roof and the ceiling. You should never cut trusses; if you have trusses rather than rafters, install a skylight that fits between them such as one of the newer systems that utilizes a light "tube" capped on the roof by a small dome.

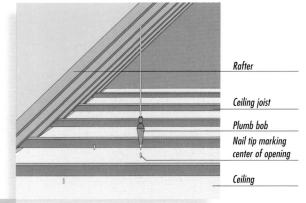

Rafter

Ceiling joist

Plumb bob

Nail tip marking center of opening

Ceiling

1 Mark the roof opening

Use a plumb bob to transfer the ceiling opening's center nail straight up to the roof. Mark the manufacturer's recommended roof-opening dimensions on the underside of the roof. Ideally, one edge will occur along a rafter to simplify framing. Drill a small hole at each corner and drive a 3 1/2-inch nail up through the holes to mark the corners on the roof's surface.

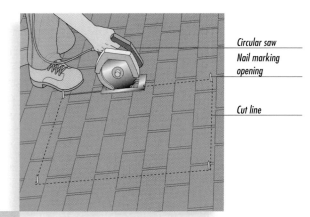

Circular saw

Nail marking opening

Cut line

2 Mark & cut the rough opening

Use a chalk line to snap cutting lines between each of the corner nails. Cut shingles with a circular saw fitted with an old carbide-tipped blade. Be sure to adjust the blade's cutting depth so it will cut through the roofing material and sheathing but not into the rafters. Carefully remove shingles and pry up the sheathing.

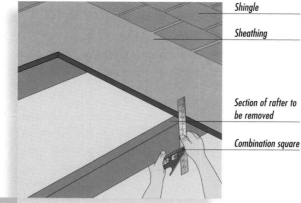

Shingle

Sheathing

Section of rafter to
be removed

Combination square

3 *Mark & cut the rafter*

*If a roof rafter is in the opening, determine the
angle to cut it, then mark the cuts, using a
combination square or adjustable T-bevel. Also
mark lines on the rafters at both sides of the
opening to indicate placement of the headers.
Support the rafters with 2 by 4s nailed between
the rafters and ceiling joists at each side of the
opening before cutting (leave these in place until
after headers are installed). Finally, cut through
the rafters along the marked lines with a
reciprocating saw—but only after you're sure the
structure is properly supported.*

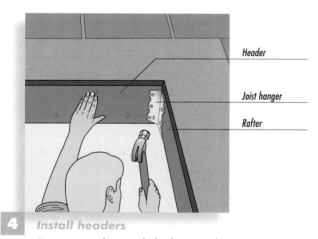

Header

Joist hanger

Rafter

4 *Install headers*

*Measure, cut, and position the headers across the
opening, as discussed at right. Nail the joist
hanger to the rafter, using framing anchor nails,
and to the header using 3 1/2-inch nails. Toenail
the header to the cut rafter with 2 1/2-inch nails.*

CUTTING For wood shingles or shakes, use a circular saw with a combination blade. For asphalt shingles, use a circular saw with an old carbide-tipped blade (wear safety glasses). (Or use a utility knife to cut through shingles, then use a circular saw with a combination blade to cut through sheathing.) For a built-up roof, buy a disposable saw blade. When using a power saw, avoid awkward positions and keep out of the line of the blade. Caution: Be alert while sawing—a blade that binds can throw you off the roof.

Adjust your saw so that the blade cuts through the roofing material and the sheathing but not into the rafters. Resting the front of the saw's base plate on the roof, align the saw blade with the chalk line, pencil line, or knife cut. Turn on the power and lower the saw until the base plate is resting on the roof. Saw slowly and steadily along the marked line until you reach a corner. Repeat for the other sides and remove the section of roof.

REMOVING THE ROOFING MATERIAL The amount of roofing material you'll have to remove depends on the type of skylight you're installing. Try not to damage the shingles, since you'll have to replace some of them when you're flashing the unit. For self-flashing skylights, remove shingles in an area about 10 inches wide on the sides and top of the rough opening, but do not remove any shingles from the bottom of the opening. Don't worry if the shingles below the opening have been cut through—they will be covered with the bottom flange of the skylight.

INSTALLING HEADERS Headers carry and distribute the loads across the span where one or more rafters (or joists) are removed. The way you build and install headers will depend upon the roof's slope and the type of skylight shaft you're building.

Measure the distance between the rafters. If your headers will be set at a 90-degree angle to the roof surface, use lumber of the same thickness and width as the rafters; cut four pieces to the length measured. Nail them together in pairs to form two doubled headers. Place two nails at the ends, then nail along the length of the header, staggering the nails about 6 inches apart. Insert each header into double joist hangers.

(continued on page 336)

Installing a Skylight

(continued from page 335)
If your headers won't sit at a 90-degree angle to the roof surface, use lumber the same size as the rafters and attach the headers at an angle, or cut the headers from larger stock, angle-ripping (beveling) each piece to the appropriate angle. To attach headers at an angle, use framing anchors instead of joist hangers.

For single headers, cut just two pieces of lumber, and use single joist hangers. Otherwise, installation is the same.

CUTTING THE CEILING Clear the area below the ceiling opening and protect furniture and floors with heavy dropcloths. Cut through drywall with a reciprocating saw, saber saw, or compass saw. Cut lath and plaster with a reciprocating saw or saber saw fitted with a coarse wood-cutting blade. When you come to a joist, cut through the wallboard but don't cut the joist. After the opening is cut, break off the wallboard and remove the fasteners.

SUPPORTING & CUTTING THE JOISTS If you have to cut one or more joists, you'll need to add sister joists to beef up the structure. But beware: Removing more than one joist can seriously compromise the ceiling's structural integrity; get advice from a professional. After supporting joists (see facing page), use a reciprocating saw to cut the joists (following instructions for cutting a rafter on page 335).

FRAMING THE SHAFT The frame for the light shaft not only provides a nailing surface for the walls of the shaft, but also joins the ceiling to the roof, giving support to both. After installing the headers as shown on page 335, measure the distance between the ceiling headers and the roof headers at every corner and at least every 16 inches in between. Cut vertical studs to the measured lengths. Unless your roof is flat and your light shaft straight, you'll need to cut one or both ends of the studs at an angle; mark the cuts with an adjustable T-bevel. Toenail the studs to the ceiling and roof headers with $2\frac{1}{2}$-inch nails. Install two studs at each corner to provide nailing for the wallboard.

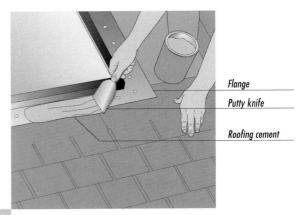

Skylight

Roofing cement

Flange

Putty knife

Roofing cement

5 *Place the skylight*

Make sure that the sheathing around the rough opening is covered with roofing felt. If needed, slide pieces under the existing felt above and trim them at the edges of the opening. With a putty knife, spread roofing cement (or recommended sealant) in a band 4 inches wide and $\frac{1}{4}$ inch thick around the rough opening. Align the skylight over the opening and press the nailing flange down onto the roofing cement. At the bottom, the flange should rest on top of the shingles.

6 *Secure skylight & replace roofing*

Fasten the skylight to the sheathing through the flange, using the type of fastener suggested by the manufacturer. Apply more roofing cement on top of the flange, covering both the screws and the edge of the flange. Press a shingle into the cement along the bottom of the skylight. Then replace the shingles at the sides and top, shingling right up to the sides of the skylight.

Rooftop Improvements

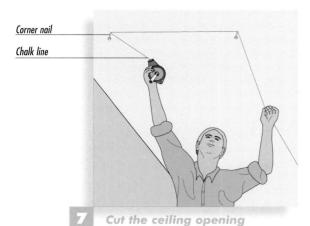

Corner nail

Chalk line

7 Cut the ceiling opening

In your attic, use a tape measure and carpenter's square to check the ceiling opening's position. Then, from below, stretch a chalk line around the corner nails and snap the line between each pair of nails to mark the opening. Clear the area below the opening, and protect the floor and the furniture with dropcloths. In the attic, clear away any insulation. Wearing a dust mask and goggles, cut the opening as discussed on page 334.

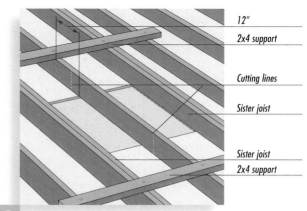

12"

2x4 support

Cutting lines

Sister joist

Sister joist

2x4 support

8 Support joists before cutting them

Cut two pieces of 2-by-4 lumber long enough to span both the opening and two joists on each side of the opening. Position the pieces at least 12 inches from the edges of the opening and fasten them with wood screws to the joists as shown.

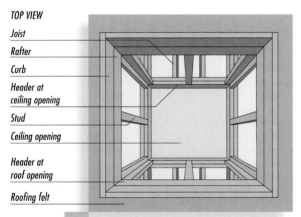

TOP VIEW

Joist

Rafter

Curb

Header at ceiling opening

Stud

Ceiling opening

Header at roof opening

Roofing felt

9 Install headers & frame shaft

To frame the ceiling opening, refer to the instructions for framing the roof opening (see page 335). Then use 2 by 4s to frame the shaft as shown, so that you have a solid nailing base for drywall at all corners and intermediate support within 16 inches of corners. Insulate between the framing members (see page 522).

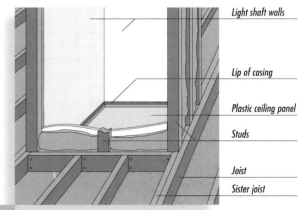

Light shaft walls

Lip of casing

Plastic ceiling panel

Studs

Joist

Sister joist

10 Drywall the shaft

Following the instructions on page 108, install drywall in the shaft area. Around the ceiling opening, apply molding that is wide enough to cover the edges of the paneling and the wallboard, as well as the joint between the wallboard and the ceiling. To help distribute light more evenly, rest a translucent polycarbonate ceiling panel on a narrow strip of molding around the inside perimeter of the shaft.

Solving Roof Leaks

It's a good idea to inspect and repair your roof in autumn, before the hard weather hits. Examine the roof again in spring to assess any winter damage. If you discover problems, make the necessary repairs, following the instructions on pages 340–343.

INSPECTING FROM INSIDE Begin an inspection in the attic, using a strong flashlight, a thin screwdriver, a knife, and a piece of chalk to examine the ridge beam, rafters, and sheathing. Look for water stains, dark-colored areas of wet wood, moisture, and soft spots that may indicate dry rot. Mark the wet spots with chalk so you can find them easily later on.

Be very careful when in the attic that you step only on ceiling joists or other surfaces that are strong enough to support you. If it's necessary to remove insulation batts to examine the sheathing, be sure to wear gloves, goggles, a respirator for protection, and loose clothing to protect against skin irritation.

Next, turn off any lights. If you see any holes above you, drive nails or poke wire through them so they'll be visible from the roof's surface. (In a wood-shingle roof, shafts of light coming in at an angle indicate separations that may shut when the shingles are wet.)

INSPECTING FROM OUTSIDE When you examine the roof from outdoors, evaluate the condition of the roof structure, surface material, flashing, eaves, and gutters.

To check the roof structure, stand back from the house and look at the lines of the ridge and rafters. The ridge line should be perfectly horizontal, and the line of the rafters, which you can assess by looking along the plane of each roof section, should be straight. If either sags, call in a contractor—your house may have a structural problem.

Next, inspect the roof's surface. Before climbing up on your roof, be sure to read the safety tips on page 325. If you're at all nervous about going up on the roof, make the inspection from a ladder, using a pair of binoculars. Don't walk on the roof any more than is absolutely necessary; you can easily cause more damage.

Inspect the flashing for corrosion and broken seals along the edges. If you have metal gutters and downspouts, look for rust spots and holes. Then examine the roof surface for signs of wear, loose or broken nails, or curled, broken, or missing shingles.

Use a knife and screwdriver to test the boards along the eaves and rakes. If you encounter damage caused by dry rot, replace the boards and finish them to match the existing areas.

Roof leaks usually appear during storms when you can't make permanent repairs. But you can take steps to temporarily divert or halt the flow of water, as shown in the illustrations on facing page.

Generally, leaks begin at a roof's most vulnerable spots—at flashing, where shingles are damaged, in valleys, or at eaves. The water may show up far from its point of origin after working its way through layers of roofing materials and down rafters to collect in a puddle in the attic or other areas of the house.

During a storm, trace the course of water to find where it's coming through the roof. If you can find a hole or leak, drive a nail or wire through the hole so you can find it later when you get up on top of the roof. Once the roof is dry enough, look for spots that indicate the source of the leak. Remember, the point where a nail or wire is poking through may not be below the actual source. For permanent repairs, see pages 340–343.

Leaks rarely appear directly below where they originate. A spreading water stain on the ceiling indicates puddling water. Drive a nail or poke a wire up through the leaking area to drain some of the water into a bucket directly below.

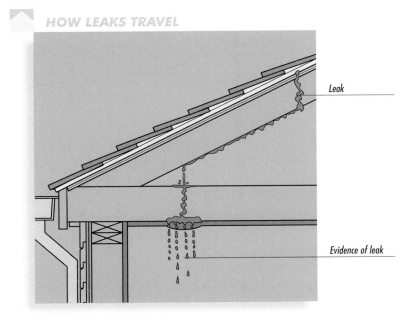

Leak

Evidence of leak

TEMPORARY REPAIRS FOR ROOF LEAKS

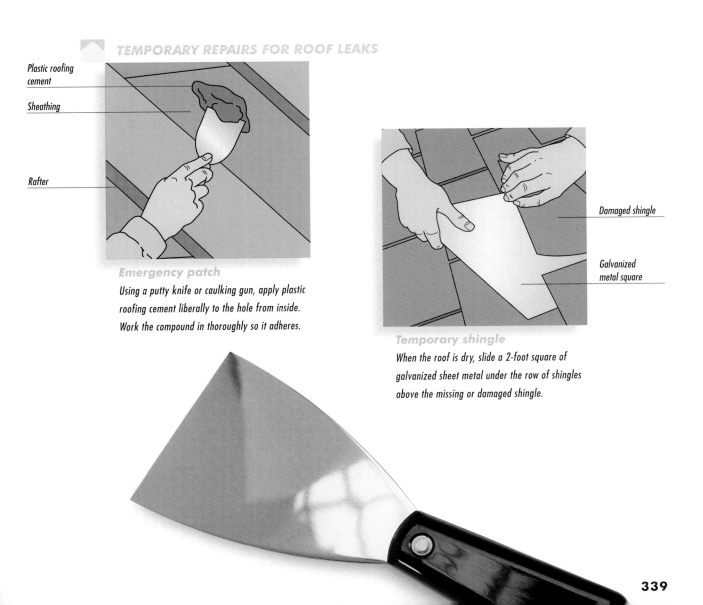

Plastic roofing cement

Sheathing

Rafter

Emergency patch

Using a putty knife or caulking gun, apply plastic roofing cement liberally to the hole from inside. Work the compound in thoroughly so it adheres.

Damaged shingle

Galvanized metal square

Temporary shingle

When the roof is dry, slide a 2-foot square of galvanized sheet metal under the row of shingles above the missing or damaged shingle.

Shingled Roof Repairs

When shingles begin to age, they can become brittle and crack, allowing water to penetrate. Some shingles can be repaired, but replacement is often the necessary remedy.

ASPHALT SHINGLES The first signs of aging are bald spots and a heavy accumulation of granules from the surface in the gutters.

Check your roof's condition on a warm day when the shingles are flexible. Remove a tiny piece of the corner from one or two shingles on each roof plane; the core of the shingle should be black. Gently bend several shingles back to see if they're flexible. If a number of shingles appear gray and bloated, if the material crumbles easily, or if you see large bare spots or damaged areas, consider replacing the roofing.

Cracked, torn, or curled shingles can be repaired, as shown at left; replace any loose or missing nails. If some of the shingles are badly worn or damaged, replace them (see below). Use shingles that remain from the original roof installation. If you don't have any leftover shingles, you'll have to buy new ones, identical in brand, color, and size, if possible (it's always a good idea to store a few extra shingles when you reroof so that you have material for repairs). Fasten the shingles with galvanized roofing nails that are long enough to penetrate all roofing layers (at least 1½ inches).

ASPHALT SHINGLE REPAIRS

Roofing cement

Nails

Repair tears, cracks, & curls

Seal a crack with roofing cement, applying the cement with a putty knife or caulking gun. For tears or curls, liberally apply roofing cement under the pieces, press them down, and secure with roofing nails if necessary. Cover nail heads with roofing cement.

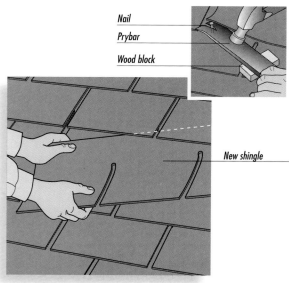

Nail

Prybar

Wood block

New shingle

Replace a shingle

Slide the new shingle into place, taking care not to damage the roofing felt (snip the top corners if the shingle sticks). Nail on the new shingle; if you can't lift the tab above it high enough to nail underneath, use a prybar as shown in the detail.

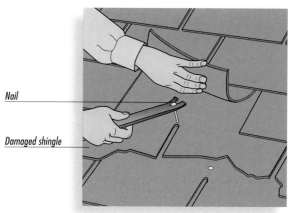

Nail

Damaged shingle

Remove a damaged shingle

Lift the shingle tab above the damaged one and, with a prybar, pry out both rows of nails holding the damaged shingle.

Don't remove a damaged shingle that's on a ridge or along a hip; instead, nail each corner in place. Then apply roofing cement to the bottom of a new shingle and place it over the defective one. Nail each corner, then cover the nail heads with roofing cement.

When you repair asphalt shingles, do the work on a warm day when the shingles are more pliable. Also, have roofing cement at room temperature so it will spread more easily.

WOOD SHINGLES & SHAKES Inspect a wood shake or shingle roof for curled, broken, or split shingles, and for any shingles that have been lifted by wind. Look also for shingles thinned by weathering and erosion, especially around areas where an attic inspection reveals pinpoints of light (page 338).

The extent of the defects you find will indicate whether you can repair or need to replace shingles or shakes. If only a few shingles or shakes are split or wind-lifted, you can repair them; those that are badly splintered or curled should be replaced. If the damage is extensive, consider having the entire roof replaced.

To remove the nails from a damaged shingle or shake you're replacing, either rent a shingle ripper to cut them or use a hacksaw blade. To use the ripper, slide it under the shingle and around a nail; then cut the shank of the nail with a hammer blow (see below).

Trim the replacements to fit the space, allowing ¼-inch clearance on each side for expansion of the wood. Use a roofer's hatchet or a saw to do the trimming.

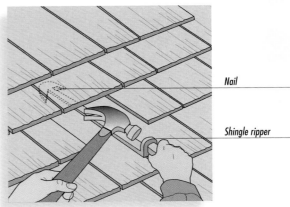

Nail

Shingle ripper

Remove a damaged shingle
After splitting and pulling out loose pieces, cut the nails securing the shingle to the roof deck, using a shingle ripper as shown (or saw nails off with a hacksaw blade). Don't damage the sheathing or underlayment.

WOOD SHINGLE REPAIRS

Roofing cement

Split shingle

Split or loose shingle
Butt the split pieces together. To fasten, drill pilot holes and nail in place with galvanized roofing nails. Cover nail heads and joint with roofing cement, using a caulking gun or putty knife.

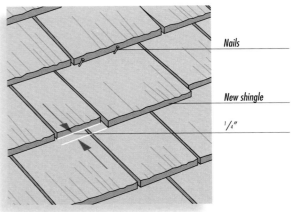

Nails

New shingle

¼"

Replace a shingle
Insert the replacement shingle so it protrudes ¼ inch below adjoining shingles; allow ¼-inch clearance on each side. Drive in two roofing nails at an angle just below the edge of the row above. Drive the edge of the new shingle even with the other shingles, using a hammer and wood block.

Built-up Roof Repairs

Homes with flat or low-sloping roofs usually have a built-up roof surface, also called a tar-and-gravel roof. A built-up roof consists of several layers of roofing felt, each coated with hot- or cold-mopped asphalt. The top layer is gravel that protects the asphalt from ultraviolet light.

Leaks in a flat roof are almost always easy to locate—they tend to be directly above the wet area on the ceiling below. Leaks may develop at flashing (see pages 344–345) or where wind has blown the gravel away. Leaks are also likely where weather and wear have caused blistered asphalt, separations between the roof surface and the drip edge, curling or split roofing felt that's exposed, and cracks or holes in the roof material.

Fill in any cracks with roofing cement. If you're repairing a blister or small hole, insert roofing cement inside the sliced blister or under the hole, cut the patch you need from a piece of asphalt shingle, and insert the patch in the hole. Cover the area with a liberal coating of roofing cement. For holes larger than a square foot or to reroof entirely, call a professional roofer.

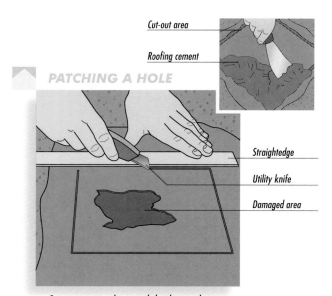

PATCHING A HOLE

Cut-out area

Roofing cement

Straightedge

Utility knife

Damaged area

Cut out a rectangle around the damaged area, remove the pieces, then cut a patch to fit the rectangle exactly. Fill the hole with roofing cement and place the patch on the cut-out area. Apply more cement, extending beyond the patch edges. Replace the gravel as cement begins to dry.

REPAIRING A BLISTER OR HOLE

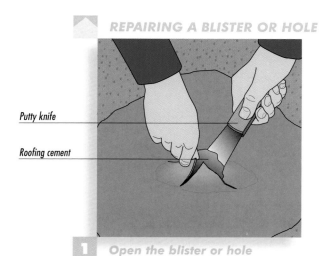

Putty knife

Roofing cement

1 Open the blister or hole

Sweep all gravel aside. Then, with a utility knife, cut into the asphalt and roofing felt until the pressure under the blister is released. Using a putty knife, work a generous amount of roofing cement inside the lacerated blister or hole and under each edge of the cut.

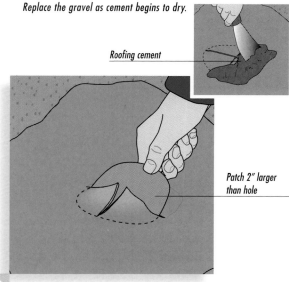

Roofing cement

Patch 2" larger than hole

2 Seal the hole

Cut a patch 4 inches larger than the slit or hole. Press it into the cement, making certain to cover as much area inside the cut as possible. Cover the blister or hole with roofing cement to seal the patch, working the cement about 2 inches beyond the edges. Replace gravel as cement begins to dry.

Tile & Metal Roof Repairs

Most masonry tile and metal roofs last as long as the house, so problems with them are usually limited to leaks, broken tiles, and dented or damaged metal shingles or panels. Though you may be able to handle small patches or replacements, it's better to hire a professional roofer for major problems—particularly with ceramic tile, rounded concrete tile, and metal panel systems.

MASONRY TILE Small holes or cracks can be patched with plastic roofing cement. If the corner or butt of a masonry tile is cracked, clean the area with a wire brush and seal the crack with plastic roofing cement. If the crack extends above the overlap of the tile below, it's best to remove and replace the tile.

If you're replacing a tile on a roof where tiles have been laid directly on decking: 1) gently pry up the appropriate tile or tiles in the course above the cracked one, 2) remove the old tile pieces, 3) spread a little roofing cement on the underside of the replacement tile, and 4) slide the new tile into position.

If you're replacing tiles that are nailed to battens, use a hammer to break up the old tile. Remove as much of it as you can. Use a prybar to lift the tile or tiles directly above the broken one, and remove nails and any remaining shards with a shingle ripper, prybar, pliers, or wire cutters. Spread a little roofing cement on the underside of the replacement tile and slide it into position, hooking it over the batten (do not nail it).

METAL SHINGLES Small holes in metal roofing can be patched like those in metal flashing (see pages 344–345). For large repairs or replacements, call a metal-roofing specialist.

If you have extra shingles that match the ones on your roof, study the method of interlock to understand what you need to do to remove and replace a shingle that's beyond repair. The chances are good that you'll need to cut the damaged shingle to remove it and modify interlocking edges to slip a new one in place. Be sure to protect underlayment beneath shingles and to seal joints with silicone caulking compound or plastic roofing cement.

REPLACING MASONRY TILE

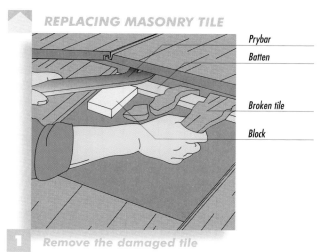

Prybar

Batten

Broken tile

Block

1 Remove the damaged tile

Carefully break the damaged tile with a hammer (wear safety glasses) and pull out the pieces. Using a prybar, carefully lift the tile directly above to remove shards of the broken one. Also pull or cut off any protruding nails.

Underside of tile hooks over batten

2 Install a replacement

Slide the replacement tile under the interlocking edge of its neighbor and push it up under the tile above, hooking it onto the batten.

Repairing Roof Flashing

Flashing protects the roof at its most vulnerable points: in the valleys, at roof and plumbing vents, around chimneys, along the eaves—anywhere water can seep through open joints into the sheathing (see page 320). As you might expect, the areas where flashing is located are the most prone to leaks. For information on where flashing is located, see page 328.

Although you'll find flashing made from plastic, roll roofing, roofing felt, and rubber, the best choice for most homes is flashing made from rust-resistant metal, such as galvanized steel, aluminum, or copper. The flashing joints may be sealed with roofing cement or caulking. Cracked or crumbling roofing cement or caulking is a major cause of leaks around flashing.

REPAIRING FLASHING Inspect flashing semiannually. Renail any loose nails and cover all exposed nail heads with roofing cement. Look carefully for holes. You can plug pinholes with spots of roofing cement.

Patch holes up to about 3/4 inch in diameter with the same material as the damaged flashing. To do this, roughen the area around the hole with a wire brush or sandpaper, then clean the surface. Cut a patch of flashing material 2 inches larger than the hole on all sides. Apply roofing cement, then press the patch in place and hold it for several minutes. Cover the patch with another generous layer of cement. If you find larger holes, strongly consider replacing the flashing.

Check the all-important seals at the flashing's edges. If the roofing cement or caulking is cracked, dried, or crumbling, reseal the joints promptly.

RENEWING FLASHING SEALS

Mortar

Caulking gun

Caulking

Cap flashing

Step flashing

Chimney flashing
Chip out the old mortar and caulking along the cap flashing. Caulk the joints between the flashing and chimney and between the cap and step flashing.

REPAINTING A FLASHING To make the flashing less conspicuous, it's often painted to match the roof. Before repainting, use a stiff brush and solvent to remove any flaking paint, rust, or corrosion from the flashing (keep solvent off asphalt shingles; it will dissolve them). Tape newspaper to the roof around the flashing. Apply a zinc-base primer, then spray on two or more light coats of rust-inhibiting metal paint.

REPLACING A FLASHING You'll need to replace any flashing that has large holes or is badly corroded. You can buy new flashing or cut it out of aluminum or copper (use the same material as the existing flashing and use the old flashing as a pattern). To install new flashing, several courses of shingles as well as the flashing itself have to be removed. If you have no roofing experience, you may want to hire a professional for this job.

 ## HOW TO REMOVE ROOFING CEMENT

Roofing cement works wonders, but when it gets all over you and the roof, it can create a mess. Fortunately, roofing cement can be removed with relative ease. Use a rag moistened with kerosene to scrub unwanted cement from both the roof and you. Promptly wash any kerosene from your skin and dispose of the rag properly.

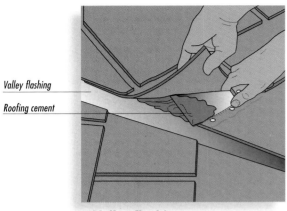

Valley flashing
Roofing cement

Valley flashing

Lift the edges of the shingles along the flashing and spread roofing cement on the flashing to about 6 inches in from the edges of the shingles.

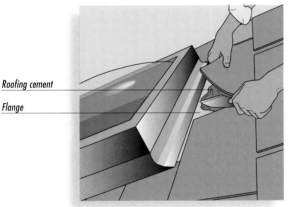

Roofing cement
Flange

Self-flashing skylight

Lift the adjacent shingles and spread roofing cement liberally on the joints between the skylight flange and roofing felt.

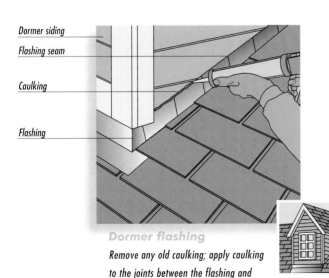

Dormer siding
Flashing seam
Caulking
Flashing

Dormer flashing

Remove any old caulking; apply caulking to the joints between the flashing and siding or shingles and between flashing seams.

Vent pipe
Caulking
Vent pipe flashing
Roofing cement
Flashing flange

Vent pipe flashing

Caulk the joint between the flashing and pipe. Lift the side and back shingles; apply roofing cement to the joints between the flange and shingles.

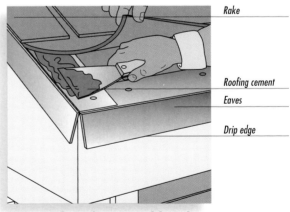

Rake
Roofing cement
Eaves
Drip edge

Drip edge along a gable rake

Lift the shingles and spread roofing cement on the top of the drip edge. Note: Do not seal the drip edge along the eaves.

Repairing Gutters

A roof sheds water, but it's the gutter and downspout system that carries the water away from the house. Most gutters and downspouts are made from galvanized steel, aluminum, or vinyl, though you may find some made from wood or copper.

Gutters are attached to the eaves of the house with strap, bracket, or, most commonly, spike-and-ferrule hangers. Downspouts are attached to the exterior walls with straps. For more about gutters, see pages 332–333.

To work effectively, gutters and downspouts must be in sound condition with watertight joints; they must slope properly and be free of leaves, twigs, and other debris. Regular maintenance is crucial to avoid flooded gutters. In fall and spring, clean out debris with a hose and scrub brush.

FIXING POOR DRAINAGE Make sure the gutters drain properly by running water through them. If drainage is slow, reposition gutters; they should slope toward the downspouts at a rate of 1 inch for every 20 linear feet. To correct low spots, adjust the hangers. Very long gutters often drain very slowly or not at all. The remedy: Raise the middle and install a downspout at each end.

REPAIRING WATER DAMAGE Test for weaknesses in gutters, downspouts, and fascia boards by probing with an awl, thin screwdriver, or pocket knife. Also look for flaking or peeling paint, rust spots, loose spikes, and leaky joints. If you find a rotted fascia board, carve out the bad spots and fill them in with an exterior-grade wood putty or simply replace the damaged section of board with a piece of well-seasoned lumber (apply a wood preservative first).

THREE GUTTER REPAIRS

Connector

Silicone sealant

Fix a leaky joint

Apply silicone sealant or butyl-rubber caulking to seal around the seams between sections on the inside and outside of the gutter.

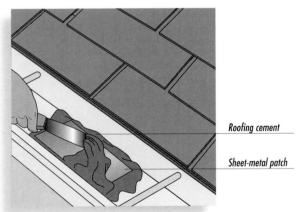

Roofing cement

Sheet-metal patch

Patch a large hole

Apply a thick, uniform layer of roofing cement to the damaged area, extending the cement 6 inches beyond each side of the hole. Then, to cover the roofing cement, cut a repair patch from a piece of aluminum, copper or galvanized metal flashing, depending on what the gutter is made of. Embed the patch in the cement, and apply another coat of cement over the top.

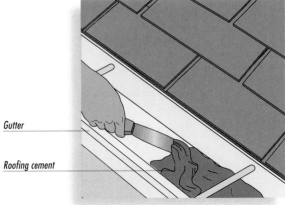

Gutter

Roofing cement

Patch a small hole

Using a putty knife, patch with a thin coat of roofing cement, spreading the cement and extending it beyond the hole in all directions.

Also tighten loose hangers and replace any that are broken. Check that downspout straps are secured to the house walls and that all elbow connections are tight. Secure loose elbows with $1/2$-inch sheet-metal screws or pop rivets. If a large section of gutter is badly damaged, replace the whole section.

FIXING LEAKS & HOLES If wood gutters leak, let them dry out thoroughly, then repaint the insides with latex house paint. You can seal pinhole leaks with dabs of roofing cement.

For metal gutters that are rusting, thoroughly wash the gutter of all dirt and debris, and wipe the damaged area dry. Then use a wire brush or coarse sandpaper to remove any paint, grease, or corrosion. Wipe the surface clean with a rag. Apply aluminum paint to the inside and rust-preventative zinc-based primer to the outside. Mend holes as shown on facing page.

UNCLOGGING GUTTERS & DOWNSPOUTS

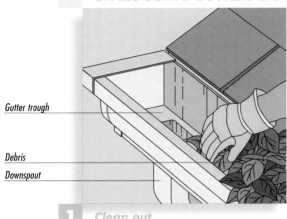

Gutter trough

Debris

Downspout

1 Clean out

Remove leaves, twigs, and other debris from gutter troughs (protect your hands with gloves). Loosen dirt with a stiff brush; hose all debris out of the system.

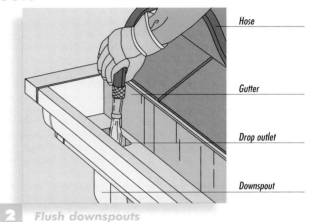

Hose

Gutter

Drop outlet

Downspout

2 Flush downspouts

Clean blocked downspouts by spraying with a garden hose turned on full force. For a stubborn clog, feed a plumber's snake into the downspout and then flush all loosened debris out with a hose.

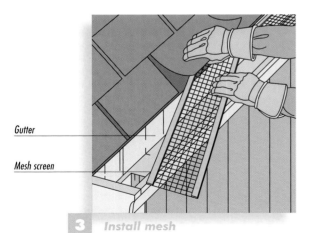

Gutter

Mesh screen

3 Install mesh

Add mesh screens or other types of leaf catchers (see box at right) to deflect leaves, twigs, and other debris over the edge of the gutter. A leaf strainer will admit water and filter out debris.

LEAF-CATCHING SYSTEMS

Keep gutters free of leaves and other debris so they won't clog and fill with water. The weight of water when they're filled can dislodge or bend them. And, over time, sheet metal gutters may rust when water pools in them.

To cut back on gutter-cleaning chores, consider a leaf-catching system. These will filter leaves and debris from the water. But buyer beware; not all types work successfully. And a demonstration won't necessarily reveal how one of these will work in reality. The best way to check out a system is to request the names and phone numbers of satisfied customers whom you can call.

Of course, even gutters protected by a leaf-catching system will need to be cleaned occasionally. Be sure you can remove the system easily (some are difficult to take off because they are screwed in place or tucked under shingles). And pay special attention to cost—some sophisticated leaf-catching systems are more expensive than the gutters themselves.

347

Chimney Repairs

A chimney that's used regularly must be cleaned and inspected at least once a year. Using a strong flashlight, check inside the chimney for soot buildup and any obstructions, such as birds' nests or leaves. Also check the flue tiles for cracks or missing mortar. On the chimney's exterior, look for crumbling mortar between bricks and at the cap, loose or missing bricks, or flashing that has corroded or pulled away from the chimney; all can cause chimney leaks.

Here we discuss cleaning the chimney and making minor repairs. If the chimney is leaning, if a number of bricks are missing, or if the flue needs repair, you should consult a professional. For more about chimneys, see the "Hearth" chapter beginning on page 266.

CLEANING THE CHIMNEY Whenever a fireplace or wood stove burns wood, creosote—a tar-like substance—rises with the smoke, cools, and collects on the flue's inner walls. Creosote corrodes the flue, reduces energy efficiency, and can ignite into a raging flue fire. To prevent this buildup, clean the flue periodically. This is a job you can do yourself, but it is extremely messy and can be quite dangerous if the top of your chimney is very high or the roof is steep. In most cases, it's money well spent to call a chimney sweep.

To sweep it yourself, you'll need a chimney brush sized and shaped for your flue (these are generally available at home-improvement centers). Choose metal wire for a masonry flue, synthetic for a metal flue. And you'll want a rope and a weight (a plastic bottle filled with water) for moving the brush inside the flue. You can rent a brush and fiberglass extension rods that fit onto it, but if you plan to do this more than once, it usually pays to buy the tools.

After making sure the fire is completely out, completely seal off the fireplace opening with a paper dropcloth and wide masking tape. Put a dropcloth on the floor and hearth, and cover nearby furniture with large dropcloths.

From the roof, remove the chimney cap or spark arrester (if there is one). Attach a quality steel chimney-sweeping brush to a long rope and a water-filled plastic bottle to the end of the brush. Pass the brush repeatedly down to the bottom of the flue and pull it up again until you no longer hear creosote dropping.

If the roof is steep, you can attach fiberglass rods to the brush and push it up from below, but this is even messier—strongly consider hiring a chimney sweep. When you're finished, replace the chimney cap or spark arrester.

Carefully remove the masking tape and paper from the mouth of the fireplace. Using a hand-held wire brush and scraper, clean the firebox and all areas you can reach. Then remove all ashes and creosote. Using a heavy-duty vacuum, not a household one, vacuum out the fireplace.

REPAIRING A CHIMNEY To repair a cracked or crumbling cap, see the illustrations on facing page. Replace mortar around chimney bricks as you would for brick veneer (see facing page). For instructions on making repairs to chimney flashing, see page 344.

ANATOMY OF A CHIMNEY

Flue
Cap

Bricks
Mortar

Shingles

Flashing

Most chimneys are built of brick and lined with fireproof flue tiles. A cap of mortar seals the top against the weather. Flashing seals the joint between the chimney and roofing.

REPAIRING A CHIMNEY

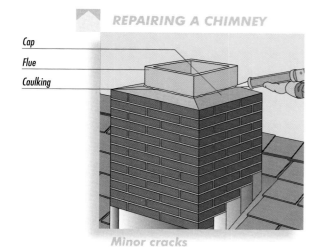

Cap

Flue

Caulking

Minor cracks

Caulk all joints and any cracks in the cap; seal the joint between the flue and the cap with caulk.

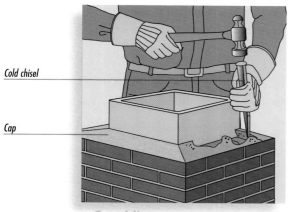

Cold chisel

Cap

Crumbling cap

Chip out the old mortar and rebuild the cap with new mortar, sloping the cap away from the flue.

 You can install mesh spark arresters to prevent sparks and embers from flying out of the chimney and starting a fire, and to discourage birds from entering. Rain guards and draft deflectors deflect flying embers, rain, and drafts. Look for these at home-improvement centers.

PREVENTING ICE DAMS

Winter storms can wreak havoc on your roof. Ice dams that form at the eaves can cause water to back up on the roof surface until it finds a place to leak under shingles. You can prevent most problems by keeping the attic cold through good insulation in the attic floor and with well-placed attic vents to draw out any heat that does escape from the house.

Ice dams typically result when snow on the roof alternately thaws and freezes during warm days and cold nights, or when heat rises up through the attic and melts snow on the roof. When this happens, the icy water flows down the roof and refreezes over the colder eaves area.

AIR SEALING Your best defense against ice dams is to seal off all the places where warm air can leak into the attic from the house. Check the attic during or just after a rainstorm. If there are no water leaks, check around all light fixtures that penetrate the attic floor and around ducts, plumbing stacks, and attic hatches. If light comes through joints or you feel a draft, use caulking or weatherstripping to seal the spaces and create a solid air barrier.

SOFFIT VENTS Your second line of defense against attic moisture, these work most efficiently when all air leakage problems are corrected. To prevent ice dams resulting from poor ventilation, install soffit vents and gable vents, making sure they are not blocked by insulation. Used together, they vent warm attic air that might otherwise melt snow on the roof and cause ice dams. Electric exhaust fans actually pull warm air from the house and cause damage; avoid them if you have a problem with ice dams.

INSULATION More insulation means a colder, less moist attic. Make sure that your insulation is distributed evenly and that there is full-depth coverage. If any of the insulation is damp, repair the source of the leak and then replace the insulation (see pages 522–523).

EAVES REINFORCEMENT For extra protection on a section of roof where ice dams often form, reinforce the eaves area by installing a sheet of roll roofing or a rubber-like membrane under the shingles so it extends 12 inches inside the wall line. (This is best done when a new roof is being installed; otherwise, you'll have to replace several courses of shingles.)

DE-ICING TAPES These tapes, insulated for safety, are clipped to the shingles in a zigzag pattern (or run along gutters and inside downspouts) and are plugged into a weatherproof electrical outlet. When they are heated, they create drainage channels for water that otherwise would back up behind an ice dam or freeze inside the gutters and downspouts.

Controlling Groundwater

Groundwater can be a very serious problem when it finds its way into your basement, floods a crawl space, or seeps through a slab floor. Not only does it ruin furnishings and stored goods, but it can damage your home's structure. If your basement, foundation, or slab becomes damp or flooded during heavy rains, cure the problem immediately.

A damp basement doesn't always mean a groundwater problem. It may be simply humid air condensing on cool surfaces. Before you can correct the condition, you'll need to determine the source of the water.

DETERMINING THE SOURCE If you can see water flowing out of a crack in a wall or floor, you know that the source is groundwater. In the absence of such obvious evidence, you'll have to make a test to determine whether the dampness is caused by groundwater or by condensation.

Cut two 12-inch squares of plastic sheeting or aluminum foil. Tape one to the inside of an outside wall and one to the basement floor (make sure the surfaces are dry). After two or three days, remove the plastic or foil and examine the side that was next to the wall or floor. If it's dry, the culprit is condensation; if it's wet, groundwater is seeping in.

REDUCING CONDENSATION Dampness may simply be the result of humidity, caused by something like an unvented dryer or high ambient moisture. When the basement air is humid, the moisture in the air may condense on cool surfaces, such as the concrete floor.

The following suggestions will help to lower the air's humidity:

- Cover exposed dirt with plastic sheets.
- Raise the temperature in the basement.
- Vent moist air from a clothes dryer to the outside.
- Install a dehumidifier in the basement area.
- Insulate cold-water pipes and basement walls.
- Improve ventilation by opening basement windows or installing an exhaust fan in the basement.

CONTROL STRATEGIES If moisture is coming from the ground, the solutions may involve more work. When water collects next to a foundation wall or when the water table (the water level under your property) is higher than your basement floor, hydrostatic pressure develops. This can force water through joints, cracks, and porous areas in concrete walls and floors and through cracked or crumbling mortar joints in masonry walls. As soil settles around a

When water collects next to a foundation wall or when the water table (the water level under your property) is higher than your basement floor, hydrostatic pressure develops. This can force water through joints, cracks, and porous areas in concrete walls and floors.

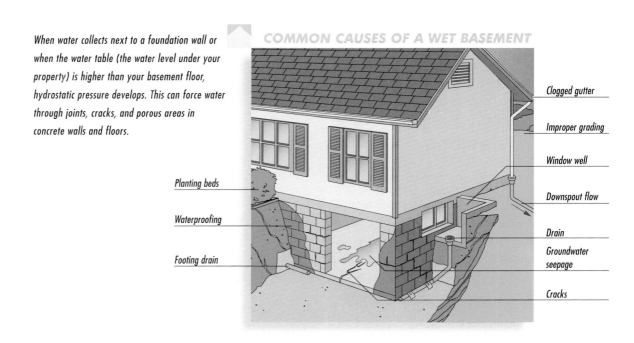

COMMON CAUSES OF A WET BASEMENT

Planting beds

Waterproofing

Footing drain

Clogged gutter

Improper grading

Window well

Downspout flow

Drain

Groundwater seepage

Cracks

house, letting water puddle near the walls, the water resistance goes down. Poor construction practices—clogged or nonexistent footing drains, poorly applied or nonexistent moistureproofing on the foundation, through-the-wall cracks, and improper grading—often cause dampness in the basement.

Correcting any of these problems is a major job that requires digging out the foundation to the bottom of the footings. Though this may well be the most permanent repair, first try the remedies that follow. If they don't work, then you'll have to contact a foundation engineer or contractor for a more lasting solution. Today the most effective waterproofing methods call for fiberglass drainage board, installed on the outside of the foundation, or exterior waterproof membranes.

 CAUTION: If you see horizontal cracks in a wall that's bowing inward; long, vertical cracks wider than ¼ inch; or a crack that's getting wider (measure it periodically), this indicates a structural problem, and you should contact a private building inspector at once.

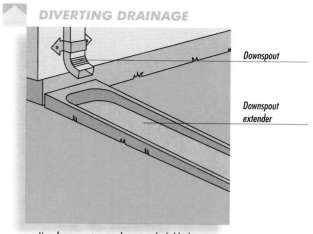

DIVERTING DRAINAGE

Downspout

Downspout extender

Use downspout extenders or splash blocks to carry drainage from downspouts away from the house. Water that is allowed to flow from your downspouts directly into the ground may end up in your crawl space or basement and can erode the soil along the house, causing settling.

EXTERIOR REMEDIES Roof and surface water collecting next to the foundation may be causing the dampness in your basement. Use the following checklist, and correct any problems you find.

■ Gutters and downspouts should be clear and should direct water away from the foundation. Clean gutters (page 347) and improve drainage at downspouts, making sure that water is carried far away from the house.

■ For proper grading around the house, the ground should drop 1 inch per foot for the first 10 feet away from the foundation walls. This is essential to ensure good surface drainage.

■ Planting beds next to the foundation should not allow water to collect or pool there.

■ Window wells around basement windows should be free of debris, have good drainage, and be properly sealed at the wall.

INTERIOR REMEDIES The following simple interior repairs may alleviate or cure your water problems:

■ Apply a concrete moisture-sealing coating to the wall. Most coatings are painted on; some are plastered on with a trowel.

■ Patch cracks in walls and floors with portland or hydraulic cement. Hydraulic cement expands and hardens quickly, even under wet conditions. Make sure that any cracks wider than ⅛ inch are undercut—chiseled out so the inside of the crack is wider than the outside (see the illustration on page 370). This will prevent water pressure from popping out the patch.

■ Chisel out a groove along the wall if water is entering through a floor/wall joint. Fill the groove with hydraulic or epoxy cement and cove (form in a concave shape) as shown on page 371.

■ Chisel out cracked mortar joints in masonry walls and fill them with hydraulic or epoxy cement. Water that comes through cracks in a concrete floor or through the joint between the basement floor and wall is caused by hydrostatic pressure. In addition to the procedures described above, remedies for the problem include installing drains under the floor, adding a sump pump, or waterproofing the exterior foundation wall by installing bentonite panels—all jobs that are best left to professionals.

■ For persistent problems, install a basement sump pit, tying it to the drain tile. The pump's drain line should deposit water far from the foundation walls. If all else fails, call a contractor to discuss excavating and waterproofing the walls.

Garage

Your garage may be something of a stepchild when it comes to home maintenance, but it pays to attend to the upkeep of this critical structure. For one thing, the garage houses your home's largest moving part—the garage door—and moving parts can stop working with time and wear.

The garage door and (if it has one) the electric opener need to be maintained, as do the slab and foundation. You may also consider upgrading your existing garage—adding a new door or electric door opener, or even a more efficient storage system for tools, sports gear, barbecuing equipment, and other odd collections that seem to migrate to the garage. This chapter discusses some key garage improvements and repairs you may want to consider.

Garage Anatomy

Though building a new garage is beyond the scope of this book—and a project you'll probably need to hire a contractor to accomplish—on these two pages, you can gain an understanding of how garages are put together so that you're equipped to handle basic improvements and repairs.

Minor improvements, such as replacing a garage door, normally don't require permits unless running new electrical wiring is necessary. If you intend to build a free-standing garage or undertake major garage improvements, you will need both a building permit and permission from the city's planning department. Be sure to check with them for height limits and minimum setbacks from property lines.

Garage Construction

Garages are built much like houses that have a slab foundation and wood frame structure. One difference is that a garage floor may be pitched very slightly toward the garage door for runoff, particularly near the opening.

The illustration below shows typical construction. Walls are normally framed with 2 by 4s, attached to a treated-lumber sole plate. Corners are braced with plywood sheathing, let-in braces, or metal straps. Insulating foam sheathing adds no structural support, but can make a garage warmer in winter and cooler in summer. Building paper or house wrap over the sheathing provides extra weather protection. Windows and doors are installed after the walls are sheathed or sided. A garage roof is often framed with trusses, but some are "stick framed" with rafters and ceiling joists of 2-by lumber. The roof is typically sheathed with plywood or oriented strand board. Flashing and roofing are applied just as on the roof of a house (see chapter on roofing, beginning on page 318).

ANATOMY OF A GARAGE

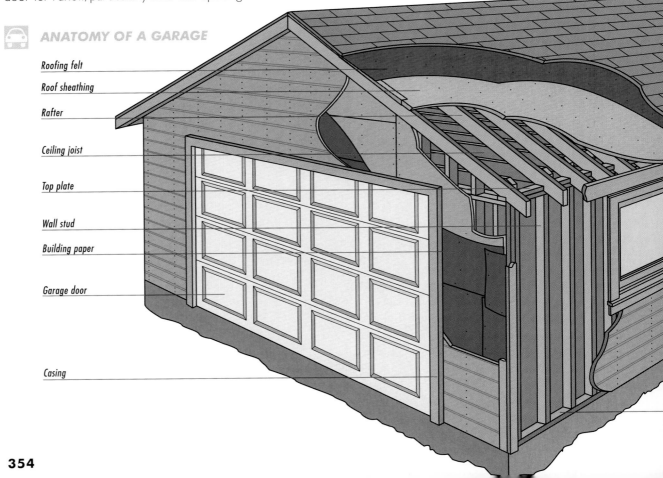

- Roofing felt
- Roof sheathing
- Rafter
- Ceiling joist
- Top plate
- Wall stud
- Building paper
- Garage door
- Casing

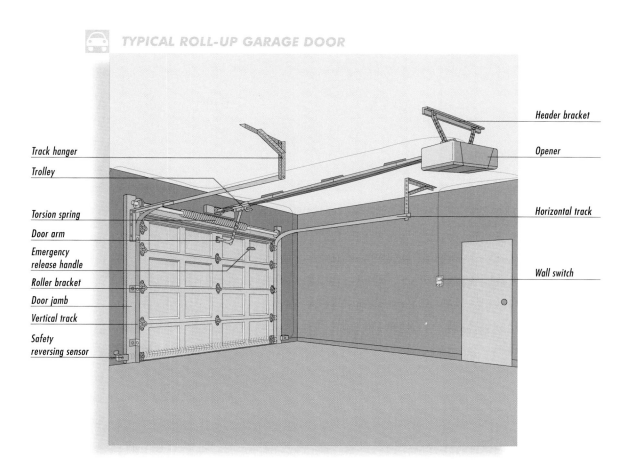

Track hanger

Trolley

Torsion spring

Door arm

Emergency
release handle

Roller bracket

Door jamb

Vertical track

Safety
reversing sensor

Header bracket

Opener

Horizontal track

Wall switch

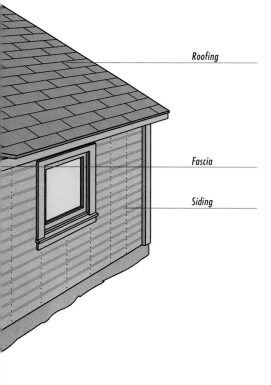

Roofing

Fascia

Siding

Treated sole plate

The Garage Door

The two main types of garage doors are tilt-ups and sectional roll-ups. A roll-up, or sectional, door is the most common type on the market. It's made up of several sections, hinged together; it moves up and down on rollers housed in channeled tracks along each side so the door can roll straight up and back. A torsion spring across the top of the door, or extension springs along the sides, help when lifting or lowering the door. Although the latter system is easier and safer to install, a torsion spring requires less regular maintenance once it's in place.

Swing-up or one-piece doors pivot on hinges and are assisted by large springs on each side. They cost 25 to 35 percent less than roll-up doors, but they offer less headroom, don't seal the garage opening as tightly or securely, and swing outward—which means you can't park the car within 2 or 3 feet of them.

Both roll-up and swing-up doors are made from a variety of materials in flush, raised-panel, and recessed-panel designs and can be purchased with options such as windows and electric openers. See more about garage doors on pages 356–357 and pages 372–373.

Buying a Garage Door

Because a garage door typically is used day after day and is normally a very visible, key element on a house, it's important for your home's garage door to work well and look good. If your garage door is shoddy or falling apart, it's probably best to replace it with one that is easy to maintain and operate, rather than repair it. See information on basic types—roll-up and sectional garage doors—on page 355 and repair information on pages 372–373.

Selecting the Right Material

You can purchase a garage door made from wood, steel, aluminum, or fiberglass. Each of these materials has certain benefits, but wood and steel are favored for a variety of reasons.

WOOD DOORS Wood is affordable and attractive, but is subject to weather damage. With changes in moisture, it expands and contracts—which can cause it to warp—so it requires periodic repainting or refinishing.

WOOD GARAGE DOOR

Dark-stained wood garage door adds a touch of elegance to this contemporary home.

A tilt-up wood door, in some cases, can be built right in the driveway by applying a skin of exterior plywood—usually ³/₈ inch thick—to a frame of Douglas fir, spruce, or a similar softwood. Or the frame and plywood can be covered with siding to match the house. Unless you're an accomplished carpenter, this job is best left in the hands of a garage door installer.

Roll-up wood door sections may have either flush sections, made by fastening a plywood panel over a wooden frame; or panel construction, where manufacturers fit several separate rectangular panels into a wooden frame. Panels meant to be painted may be made from wood, plywood, or wood-composite products (some composites come with 20-year warranties). Installed, an average-size (16-by-7-foot) paint-grade sectional door normally costs about $800 to $1,000.

Stain-quality doors have solid wood panel inserts, made from any of a variety of softwoods and hardwoods. Be aware that if these panels are made from several pieces edge-glued together, the joints between them may show when the panels are stained. Appearance-grade wood doors are the most expensive garage doors on the market, ranging from about $1,500 to $2,000 or more.

STEEL DOORS Steel garage doors are very strong, durable, and secure. And thanks to durable coatings and embossing technologies, many of the newer steel doors do a fairly successful job of imitating the look of wood. Unlike wood, steel doors won't crack, warp, or fall apart—and they have extremely durable finishes. They're often warranted for as long as you own the house (though not against fading). But steel will dent, and dents can be difficult to fix.

STEEL GARAGE DOOR

Steel garage door offers easy maintenance, durability, and security.

The best steel doors are a full 2 inches thick, are clad in 24-gauge steel, and have a core of rigid foam insulation built into a steel frame. The insulation helps keep the garage temperate inside and makes the door lightweight. Double-skin construction, where the inside of the door has a skin similar to the outside, is the best (and most attractive) construction. For an average-size steel door (16 by 7 feet), expect to pay from $750 to $1,200 installed.

ALUMINUM DOORS Aluminum garage doors are extremely lightweight and won't rust—they also have durable finishes and wood-grain embossing—but they are easily dented. They cost from $400 to $700.

FIBERGLASS DOORS Fiberglass doors are sometimes appropriate for corrosive ocean climates or where the homeowner wants plenty of daylight, because fiberglass is translucent. But fiberglass cracks and breaks fairly easily, and may yellow with age.

Garage Door Options

Most manufacturers offer window sections that provide both daylight and a decorative accent. The windows in these sections may have conventional single glazing or more energy-efficient dual glazing.

Some sectional-door manufacturers offer torsion springs as an option. These are the safest and best type for sectional doors because they distribute the door's weight more evenly and cannot break and fly off the way an extension spring can.

A favorite option is the automatic operator. The good ones have lifetime warranties, photoelectric safety devices, and frequency codes that can't be cracked by thieves.

Where to Buy Garage Doors

If you intend to install your own garage door, check out the offerings at home centers. Be sure the door you buy comes with complete, easy-to-follow instructions and (if it has extension springs) includes an extension spring containment kit for safety. If you want to buy a door and have it installed, look up "Garage Doors & Door Operating Devices" in the Yellow Pages to find companies that distribute or manufacture and install doors. Be sure to get at least three bids.

 GARAGE DOOR OPERATOR

Garage door operator makes opening and closing the door as easy as a touch of a button. For installation instructions, see pages 364–367.

Garage Improvement Tools

For the projects on the following pages, you'll need carpentry tools that go beyond the basics. For half-day projects, renting will save you money, but if you need the tool for long periods, you're better off buying. For building projects or to install a garage door, you'll want a variety of conventional carpentry tools, including a hammer, screwdrivers, power drill with bits, saw, and a long tape measure. In addition, consider some of the other helpful tools shown here.

LAYOUT TOOLS

A 4-foot level can be used to check framing and garage door track for plumb and level; a plumb bob is helpful for finding plumb where there is no vertical surface to put the level against. A line level checks level across distances, such as when hanging a garage door opener. A combination square is an important all-purpose tool, and it's helpful to have a scratch awl for accurate marking. A framing square is for checking the "square" cuts, as well as for laying out rafters and stairs.

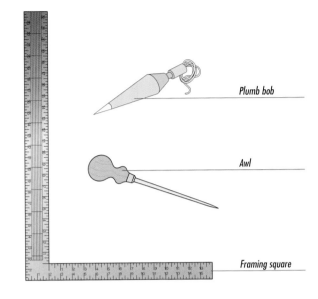

Plumb bob

Awl

Framing square

Line level

Carpenter's level

Combination square

CONCRETE-REPAIR TOOLS

For concrete and masonry repair, a 1-inch cold chisel has a hard steel edge and is used to chip out the edges of cracks. The tip of a pointed trowel is used to push masonry repair material into a crack, and the edge is used to strike off the excess.

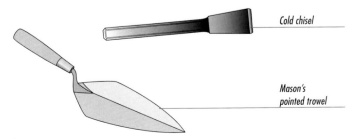

Cold chisel

Mason's pointed trowel

HELPFUL BUILDING TOOLS

A socket wrench and socket set are handy for garage door installation and related tasks. To cut the garage door track, you'll need a hacksaw. Allen wrenches may also be needed for door installation. A circular saw, equipped with a combination blade, can handle both rip and crosscuts; a 7¼-inch model is most common.

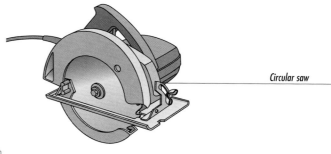

Circular saw

Allen wrench

Hacksaw

Goggles

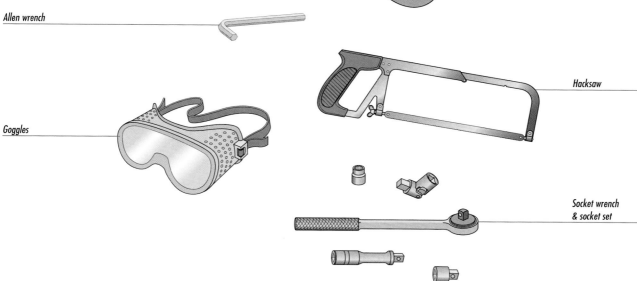

Socket wrench
& socket set

ELECTRICAL TOOLS

Some of these may be needed when installing a garage door opener: wire cutters, wire strippers for removing insulation from wire, and a circuit tester for checking whether electrical wires are live.

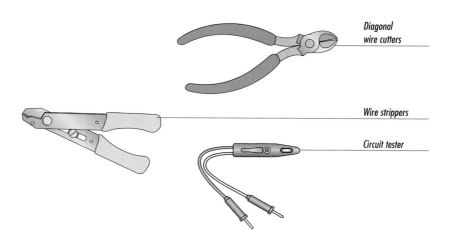

Diagonal
wire cutters

Wire strippers

Circuit tester

Installing a Garage Door

Sectional garage doors move up and down on rollers housed in channeled tracks. You can assemble the door and tracks, but once your assembly is complete, call a professional to install the torsion springs that lift the door. Torsion springs can be difficult and dangerous to install, and their installation requires special winding tools. The directions given on these pages are fairly specific for a common type of garage door—of course, techniques will vary, depending upon the product you install. Be sure to follow the manufacturer's instructions.

ASSEMBLING THE DOOR

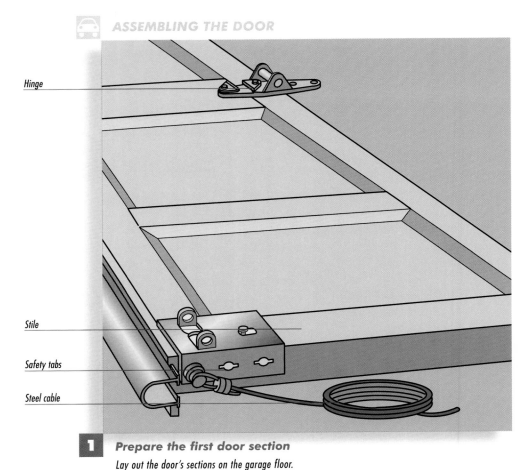

Hinge

Stile

Safety tabs

Steel cable

1 *Prepare the first door section*
Lay out the door's sections on the garage floor. Position the bottom brackets above the weatherstripping, making sure safety tabs in the bracket line up with the slots on the end stile. Secure the brackets with sheet metal screws. Hook the steel cable over the protrusions. Attach the No. 1 hinges.

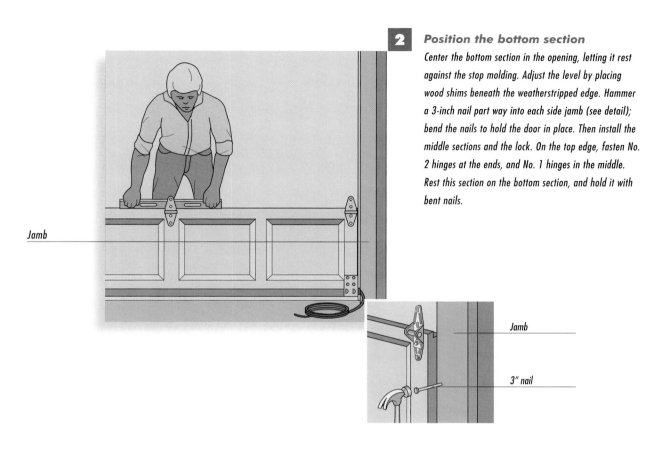

2 **Position the bottom section**

Center the bottom section in the opening, letting it rest against the stop molding. Adjust the level by placing wood shims beneath the weatherstripped edge. Hammer a 3-inch nail part way into each side jamb (see detail); bend the nails to hold the door in place. Then install the middle sections and the lock. On the top edge, fasten No. 2 hinges at the ends, and No. 1 hinges in the middle. Rest this section on the bottom section, and hold it with bent nails.

Jamb

Jamb

3" nail

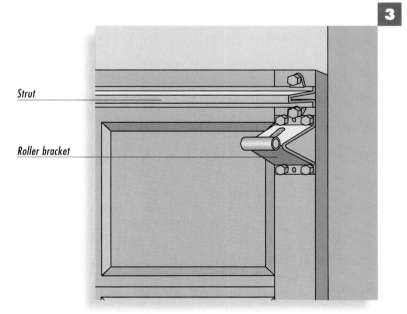

3 **Attach the top section**

Position roller brackets over the predrilled holes at the top corners. If the door requires a strut for reinforcement, attach it with strut clips. Mount the top section, hold it in place with nails, and attach hinges. Install rollers in the hinges' tube openings and in the top and bottom brackets.

Strut

Roller bracket

(continued on page 362)

Installing a Garage Door

(continued from page 361)

 ASSEMBLING THE TRACK

Install the vertical track

1

Fasten the three brackets to the straight piece, using track bolts and flange nuts. Holding the track with both hands, place it over the rollers on the door. Push the rollers all the way into the hinges. Lift the track and temporarily attach the flag bracket and track brackets to the jamb with lag screws. Tighten track bolts and nuts. Adjust the height of each track until the tops are level.

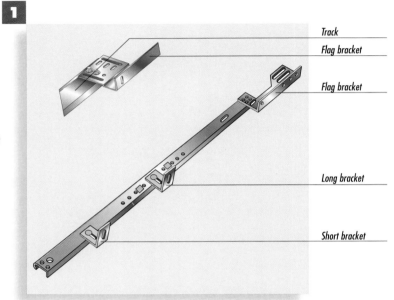

Track

Flag bracket

Flag bracket

Long bracket

Short bracket

Install the horizontal track

2

Fasten the angle piece to the horizontal track, using track bolts and flange nuts. Then position the curved bracket over the top roller, and fasten the curved end to the flag bracket. Bolt the angle piece to the flag bracket with a carriage bolt and hex nut (inset).

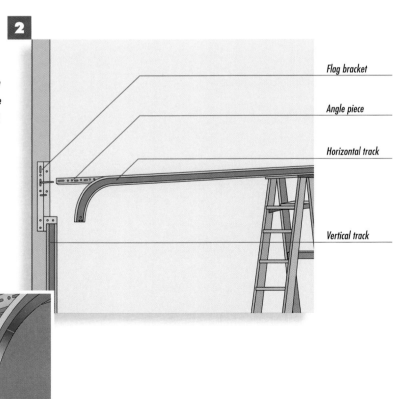

Flag bracket

Angle piece

Horizontal track

Vertical track

Carriage bolt

Top roller

Garage Improvements

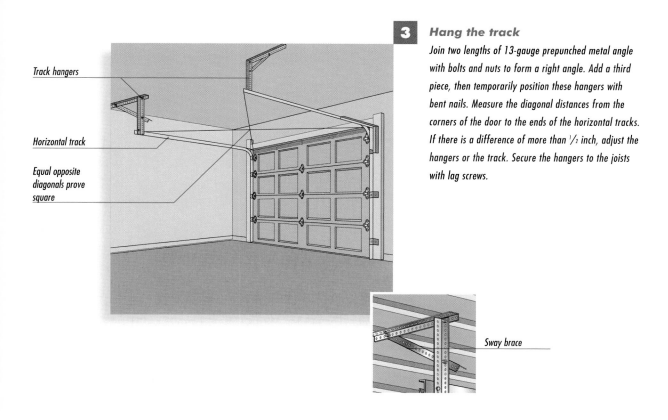

Track hangers

Horizontal track

Equal opposite
diagonals prove
square

Sway brace

3 Hang the track

*Join two lengths of 13-gauge prepunched metal angle
with bolts and nuts to form a right angle. Add a third
piece, then temporarily position these hangers with
bent nails. Measure the diagonal distances from the
corners of the door to the ends of the horizontal tracks.
If there is a difference of more than $1/2$ inch, adjust the
hangers or the track. Secure the hangers to the joists
with lag screws.*

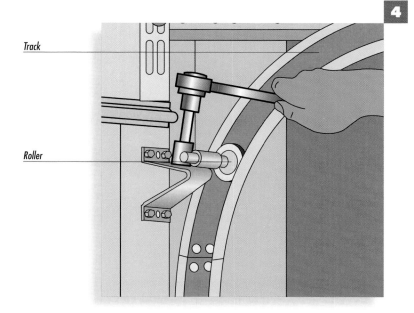

Track

Roller

4 Make final adjustments

*With a socket wrench, loosen the slide bolt on the top
bracket, then force the top of the door against the stop
molding on the door jamb. Pull the roller toward you so
that it's securely in the track's groove, then tighten the
slide bolts. Finish by assembling the lock and remove all
temporary nails from the track hangers and door jambs.
Call a professional to install torsion springs.*

Installing a Door Opener

The standard garage door opener uses a chain drive (shown below). If there is a room above the garage, consider a screw- or belt-drive model. The quieter drive mechanisms and improved controls prevent sudden stops and starts, reducing vibration. The instructions shown here are for one common type of opener; be sure to follow your manufacturer's directions.

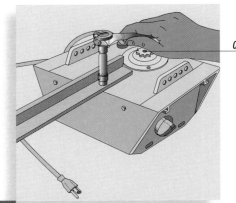

Opener sprocket

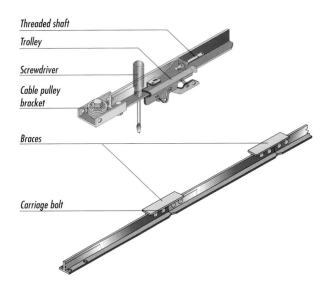

Threaded shaft

Trolley

Screwdriver

Cable pulley bracket

Braces

Carriage bolt

1 Assemble the T-rail & trolley

If the T-rail is made in sections, like the one shown, assemble it on the floor. To avoid obstructing the trolley, install nuts on the brace side of the rail. Position the cable pulley bracket on the front end of the T-rail. Fasten the bracket with hex screws, lock washers, and nuts. Next, attach the threaded shaft piece to the trolley. Position the trolley on the track and install a temporary stop in the hole near the front end of the T-rail. Slide the trolley to make sure it runs smoothly.

2 Attach the T-rail to the opener

To keep from scratching the cover of the opener, place a pad under it. Support the cable pulley bracket on a 2 by 4. Remove the screws from the top of the opener. Align the holes in the T-rail with the holes in the opener, then securely fasten the rail with the screws. Insert a hex screw into the T-rail's trolley-stop hole; attach a lock washer and nut and tighten.

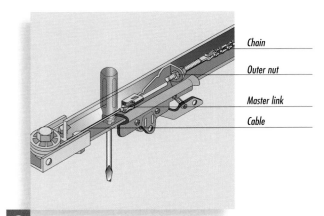

Chain

Outer nut

Master link

Cable

3 Connect the chain & cable

Attach the cable loop to the trolley with a master link. Run the cable around the pulley and back toward the sprocket on the opener. Attach the sprocket cover to the mounting plate on the opener. Tighten the chain and cable assembly by turning the outer nut on the threaded shaft clockwise.

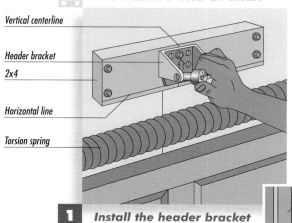

Vertical centerline

Header bracket

2x4

Horizontal line

Torsion spring

Header wall

2"

Highest travel point

Door

1 *Install the header bracket*
With the garage door closed, find its
vertical centerline and mark it above the
door on the header wall. Open the door
and draw a horizontal line 2 inches higher
than the door's highest travel point. Next, center a
2 by 4 on the wall where the vertical and
horizontal lines intersect, and fasten it to the studs
with lag screws; draw the two lines across the face
of the 2 by 4. Center the header bracket on the 2
by 4 at the vertical line, placing the bracket's
bottom edge on the horizontal line. Attach the
bracket with lag screws.

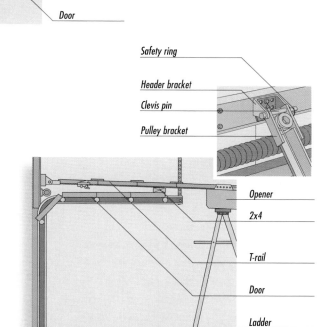

Safety ring

Header bracket

Clevis pin

Pulley bracket

Opener

2x4

T-rail

Door

Ladder

2 *Position the unit*
Lift the T-rail and align the pulley bracket with the
hole in the header bracket. To connect the two
brackets, insert a clevis pin in the hole and attach
a safety ring at the end of the pin. Place the
opener on a stepladder and open the door. Lay a 2
by 4 on the top door section underneath the T-rail.
There should be a bit of clearance between the T-
rail and the 2 by 4. Lower the opener or raise it
slightly by placing wood shims under it.

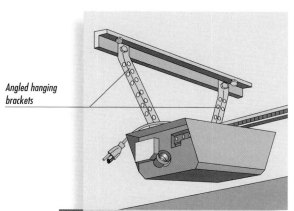

Angled hanging
brackets

3 *Hang the opener*
Directly above the opener, drill holes in a length
of angle iron, and lag screw it to the ceiling joists.
Cut two hanging brackets from perforated metal
strapping, and install them at an angle. Attach the
opener to the hanging brackets. Slide the 2 by 4
from under the T-rail.

(continued on page 366)

Installing a Door Opener

(continued from page 365)

Garage Improvements

4

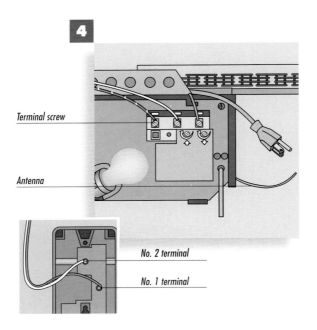

Terminal screw

Antenna

No. 2 terminal

No. 1 terminal

Connect the control

The basic wall switch (door console) is mounted inside the garage at least 5 feet above the floor. Strip ¹/₄ inch of insulation from one end of the bell wire, then connect the white wire to the No. 2 terminal screw on the back of the door control, and the white/red wire to the No. 1 terminal screw. Remove the control's cover and fasten the console to the wall. Connect the bell wire to the terminal screws on the right side of the opener panel.

Install the sensor

Assemble the mounting brackets for the sensors. Locate a stud, and position one bracket 4 to 6 inches above the floor. Use lag screws to attach the bracket. Mount the other bracket at the same height. Adjust the bracket arms so the lenses point at each other across the door. Run wires from both sensors to the opener, and strip ¹/₄ inch of insulation from the ends. Connect the white wire to the No. 2 terminal screw, and the white/red wire to the No. 3 screw.

5

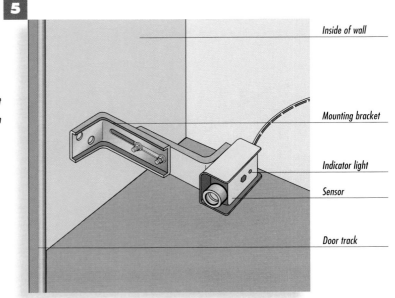

Inside of wall

Mounting bracket

Indicator light

Sensor

Door track

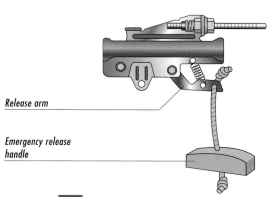

Release arm

Emergency release
handle

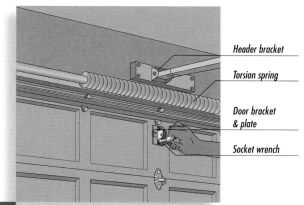

Header bracket

Torsion spring

Door bracket
& plate

Socket wrench

1 *Attach the emergency release*

Cut a 6-inch piece of rope. Thread one end through the emergency release handle, and tie a knot 1 inch from the end. Thread the other end through the trolley's release arm. The handle should hang 6 feet above the floor. Note: The handle should only be used to disengage the trolley when the door is closed.

2 *Attach the bracket to the door*

For aluminum, steel, glass, or fiberglass-panel garage doors, added horizontal and vertical reinforcement may be needed. For wood doors, use carriage bolts, lock washers, and nuts to install the door bracket and its plate. Place the door bracket 2 to 4 inches below the top edge of the door, centered below the header bracket.

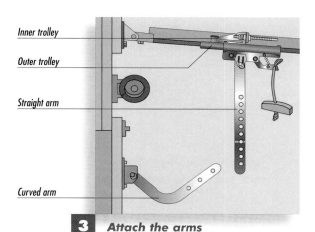

Inner trolley

Outer trolley

Straight arm

Curved arm

3 *Attach the arms*

With the door closed, pull the emergency release handle to disconnect the outer trolley from the inner trolley. Slide the outer trolley 2 inches away from the door. Using a clevis pin and safety ring, attach the straight door arm to the outer trolley section. Fasten the curved door arm to the door bracket. Then line up the holes and bring the two arms together. If the straight arm extends past the edge of the curved arm, detach it and cut it back.

ADJUSTING A DOOR OPENER

Here are a few simple adjustments you can make to keep your door operating properly and safely. Be sure to refer to your owner's manual for proper calibrations.

ADJUST THE UP/DOWN LIMITS With the door closed, press the OPEN button on the wall control panel. If the door opens at least 5 feet but not completely, turn the limit adjustment screw clockwise slightly. Similarly, if the door won't close, turn the down adjustment screw counterclockwise. If nothing is blocking the sensors yet the door reverses when closing, increase the down force.

ADJUST THE FORCE If the door doesn't open at least 5 feet, increase the up force slightly. Forces set too low cause stops in the up direction and nuisance reversals in the down direction. To adjust, press the down button on the control panel. While it's on the way down, grab the bottom. If the door doesn't reverse, or if the door reverses automatically while closing, decrease the down force. To adjust the up force, grab the door as it's opening. If the door doesn't stop, decrease the up force.

ADJUST THE SAFETY REVERSE To test the safety reverse system, close the door on a 2 by 4. If the door stops but does not reverse, increase the down limit one-quarter turn clockwise; repeat the test. The setting is fine when the door reverses on the 2 by 4.

Storage Improvements

The garage is often one of a home's key storage areas, but the space it offers is rarely used efficiently, so the garage is a prime candidate for storage improvements. You can buy modular storage system kits with components that can be mixed and matched to solve many storage problems. Or you can build your own storage solutions. The five improvements shown on these two pages may help you to reduce clutter, improve organization, and store seasonal items more conveniently.

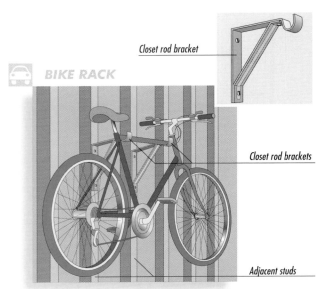

BIKE RACK

Closet rod bracket

Closet rod brackets

Adjacent studs

You can make a very simple bike rack from a pair of metal closet rod brackets screwed to adjacent studs.

T-SHAPED BIKE RACK

To hang bikes from ceiling joists, bolt notched 2 by 4s to the joists. Place the racks so the bikes won't obstruct cars.

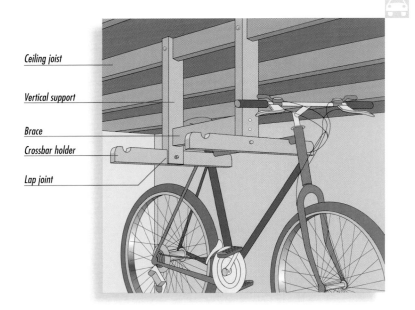

Ceiling joist

Vertical support

Brace

Crossbar holder

Lap joint

HANGING SHELVES

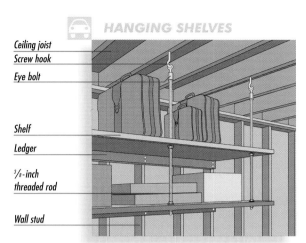

Ceiling joist
Screw hook
Eye bolt

Shelf
Ledger
3/8-inch
threaded rod
Wall stud

Sturdy shelves can be hung from ceiling joists or roof rafters, using threaded steel rods as the primary support.

SIDE VIEW
Threaded coupling
3/8-inch threaded rod
3/8-inch holes drilled through plywood
Washer and 3/8-inch hex nut

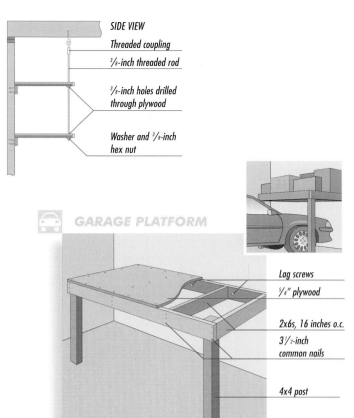

GARAGE PLATFORM

Lag screws
5/8" plywood
2x6s, 16 inches o.c.
3 1/2-inch common nails
4x4 post

Take advantage of the unused space over the hood of a car by building a simple platform. Size the pieces so posts straddle the car and the frame extends above the hood without contacting the windshield.

SPECIALTY RACKS

U-shaped racks made from 2-by-4 stock are handy for keeping storm sashes, screens, window shades, and ladders out of the way.

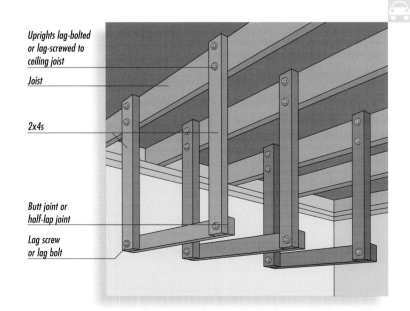

Uprights lag-bolted or lag-screwed to ceiling joist
Joist
2x4s
Butt joint or half-lap joint
Lag screw or lag bolt

Slab & Foundation Repairs

Garage floors and driveways typically are made of concrete, which is a very rugged material. Even so, concrete does crack occasionally because of settling, erosion of the soil beneath it, or extreme temperatures. It's easy to patch narrow cracks with concrete patch that can be applied with a caulking gun. Just follow the manufacturer's directions. To prevent wider cracks from becoming worse or—when patched—reappearing, you'll need to take a few more steps with a patching compound specifically made for concrete, as shown here.

If the two sides of the crack are at different levels, call a slab-jacking contractor. Slabjacking involves drilling holes in the concrete and injecting a concrete slurry beneath the slab.

PATCHING CRACKS

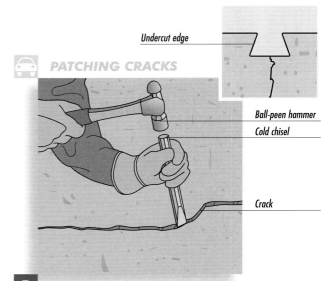

Undercut edge

Ball-peen hammer

Cold chisel

Crack

1 Widen the crack

If the crack is wider than ⅛ inch, use a cold chisel to make it even wider (wear safety glasses). This creates space for the patching material. Undercut the crack and bevel (slant) the edges as shown in the detail. Brush out all loose debris.

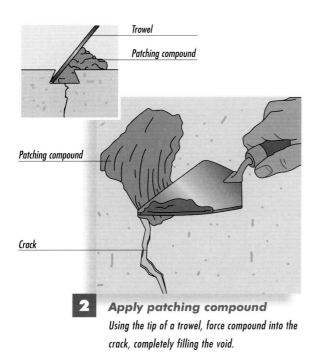

Trowel

Patching compound

Patching compound

Crack

2 Apply patching compound

Using the tip of a trowel, force compound into the crack, completely filling the void.

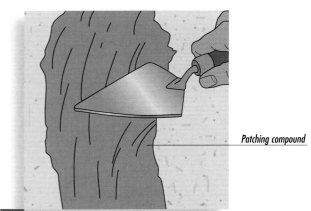

Patching compound

3 Smooth the patching compound

Using a wet trowel, smooth the patching compound after it has set. Make it flush with the rest of the slab. Keep the patch slightly damp for about a week so the concrete will cure slowly.

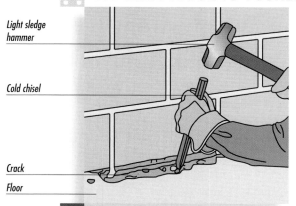

Light sledge hammer

Cold chisel

Crack

Floor

1 **Clear out the crack**

Wearing safety glasses, chip out the joint with a hammer and cold chisel. Make a groove 1 to 2 inches deep, and undercut the edges.

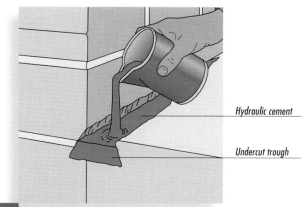

Hydraulic cement

Undercut trough

2 **Apply cement**

Pour a soupy mixture of hydraulic (or epoxy) cement from a bent coffee can to within $^1/_2$ inch of the top of the groove.

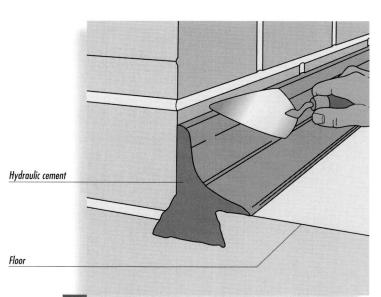

Hydraulic cement

Floor

3 **Fill the rest of the groove**

Fill the groove with a stiffer mixture of the cement, coving it several inches up the wall and along the floor.

Garage Door Repairs

When something goes wrong with a garage door, the result can be not only inconvenient but dangerous. A garage door, after all, is your home's largest moving part. With that in mind, it is important to check it yearly for problems and to maintain it properly.

Look for loose or worn hinges, springs, and hardware. Periodically clean tracks and lubricate rollers with a penetrating oil or spray. Tighten screws, bolts, and nuts on hardware, and clean and lubricate hinges. While you're at it, squirt a little graphite into the lock to keep it working right.

Inspect the springs. Look for bulges or uneven spacing. Don't try to adjust or replace the tension springs yourself—call a professional to handle this dangerous job. You can, however, safely adjust the wire tension cable.

If you're having problems with a door that has an automatic opener, disconnect the opener and try the door manually. This will tell you if the opener or the mechanics of the door are in need of repair. The door should work effortlessly before it is connected to the opener. Don't try to compensate for a bad door by adjusting the door opener; you'll just wear it out. For more information on adjusting a garage door opener, see page 367.

Prevent moisture from damaging a wood door by maintaining the door with paint or stain. A door should be finished not only on the outer surface, but on all edges—especially the bottom edge—and the inside surface as well. When the paint or stain begins to show signs of wear, re-apply. If the door and garage opening are weatherstripped, be sure the seal is in good shape. If it isn't, pry it off and nail on a replacement.

TWO TYPES OF GARAGE DOORS

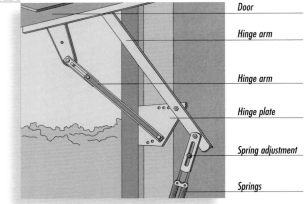

Door

Hinge arm

Hinge arm

Hinge plate

Spring adjustment

Springs

Swing-up door
A one-piece door, this pivots on hinges and usually has springs on each side to adjust the balance (only one side is shown here).

Roll-up door
A roll-up door has either two tension springs, one at each side of the door as shown, or a single spring that extends across the top of the garage door opening.

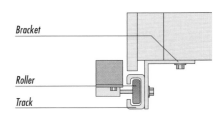

Bracket

Roller

Track

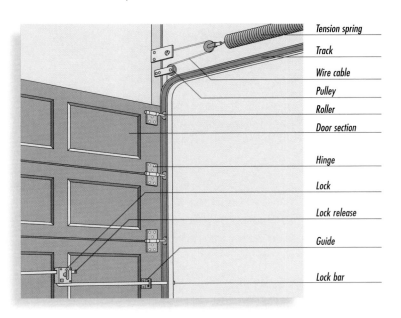

Tension spring

Track

Wire cable

Pulley

Roller

Door section

Hinge

Lock

Lock release

Guide

Lock bar

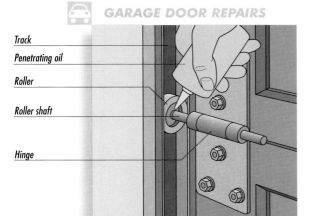

Track
Penetrating oil
Roller
Roller shaft
Hinge

When rollers bind

If some rollers bind in the tracks, tighten loose hinges and repair bent ones. Lubricate the rollers with penetrating oil. If any rollers are broken, replace them with new ones.

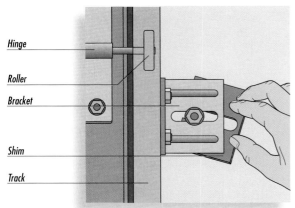

Hinge
Roller
Bracket
Shim
Track

When the door binds

Rollers are in the wrong position or set too deep when a door binds in the opening. Adjust the placement of the brackets, placing a shim behind them if necessary.

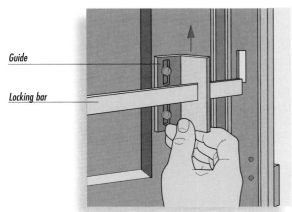

Guide
Locking bar

When the lock doesn't catch

Loosen the screws in the guide and move it up or down. Then tighten the screws.

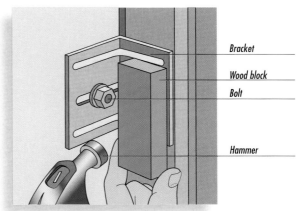

Bracket
Wood block
Bolt
Hammer

When the door drags

When a door drags in its tracks, the tracks may be out of alignment. Loosen the brackets and tap them with a wood block to realign, then tighten the bolts.

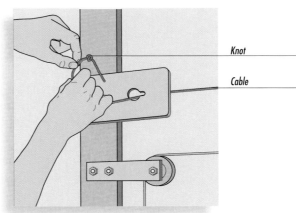

Knot
Cable

When there's no tension

Adjust the tension on a roll-up door by pulling on the wire cable to take up slack (door should be in open position and the opener disconnected). Knot the end of the cable to secure it in the slot.

Yard

Your yard is an extension of your house and as much a reflection of your home's architectural style and your taste as any other part of the house. It is common to hear landscape designers talk about the yard as an exterior "room" or series of rooms, and that's a good way to think of your outdoor space. Once you think of how you would like to use your yard, you can begin to carve up a block of unruly space into functional, and beautiful, areas. You may want, for example, a wood deck for sunbathing and entertaining, a grassy area for play, flower and vegetable beds, and a paved area for basketball and bike riding. As you plan your "rooms" you will also need to plan pathways to link the areas to one another and to the house. This chapter takes you through common yard improvements and repairs, from building a stone wall to refinishing a deck.

Yard Preparation

Building a patio, pathway, garden steps, and other types of outdoor projects requires planning and groundwork before you can begin the actual construction. For starters, good drainage is critical to protecting both your yard improvements and your home's structure. Excessive water can erode areas, pool in the yard, or—worse—collect in the basement. Proper grading, on the other hand, can ensure good drainage. Other types of preparatory work include retaining slopes and building edgings for patios and walkways.

Providing Good Drainage

The key to good drainage is to keep water flowing away from your house and other structures. Before you make changes to improve drainage, it's a good idea to contact your building department for any permits you might need. Also, make sure your runoff will eventually find its way to a sewer or storm drain and not your neighbor's property.

GRADING Horizontal surfaces such as patios should be sloped away from the house at a minimum grade of $\frac{1}{8}$ inch per foot, so that water runs off before it forms puddles.

In difficult cases, grading will require a landscape contractor. In general, though, you can take some fairly simple action of your own to deal with the majority of grading problems. This may mean nothing more than leveling humps, filling depressions, and smoothing out the ground to provide a gentle slope and a swale to carry the water away. If you need to improve grading in one specific location, such as the site for a new patio, see below.

DRAINAGE SYSTEMS Whenever you pave an area, its drainage is affected, since water tends to run off even the most porous paving.

 GRADING OVERVIEW

When properly graded, the land should slope away from structures so that runoff is directed toward the street or a swale (a low-lying stretch of land).

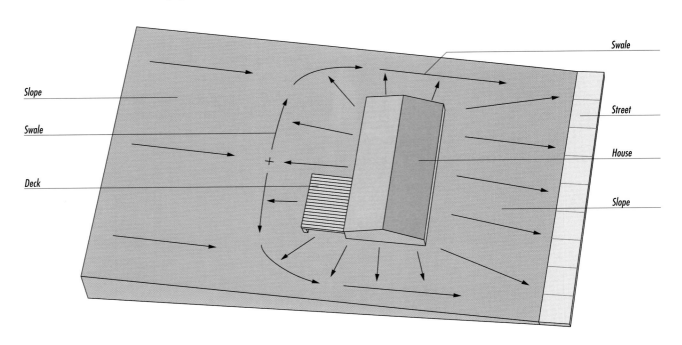

Slope

Swale

Deck

Swale

Street

House

Slope

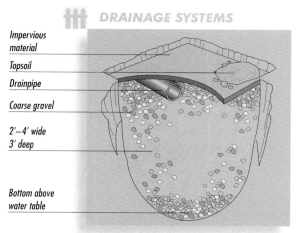

Impervious
material

Topsoil

Drainpipe

Coarse gravel

2'–4' wide
3' deep

Bottom above
water table

Dry well

Dig a hole, and trench for drainpipes to carry water
into it from other areas. Fill the well with coarse
gravel, then cover it with an impervious material,
such as roofing felt, and conceal it with topsoil.

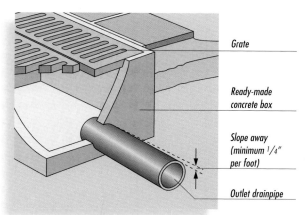

Grate

Ready-made
concrete box

Slope away
(minimum $1/4$"
per foot)

Outlet drainpipe

Surface drain box

To drain water from a low-lying area, install a
surface drain box, digging the hole for it at the
lowest point. Set a ready-made concrete drain box
into the hole, and trench for the drainpipe to carry
runoff to a storm drain or dry well.

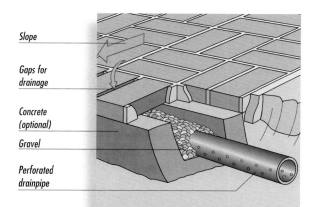

Slope

Gaps for
drainage

Concrete
(optional)

Gravel

Perforated
drainpipe

Drain trench

Perforated drainpipes drain water from under
pavings. Place pipe, perforated side down, in a
trench dug 12 inches deep (deeper in frost areas)
under the center or around the edge of the site.
The concrete trough shown is optional for this
special system, which supports spaced bricks.

Often the bed below the paving, whether it's sand or a
thicker layer of gravel, will provide adequate drainage. But
sometimes additional provisions are necessary. Shown on
this page are three different drainage systems that effectively handle runoff around a paved site. If your yard needs
one of these systems, and you plan to do the work yourself, be aware that both the surface drain box and the perforated drainpipe setup shown here require experience
placing concrete.

Retaining Walls

If your yard slopes, you may need to build a retaining wall
to hold the earth in place during times of heavy runoff.
Walls over 2 feet high require a permit in many areas, and
anything over 4 feet needs to be designed by an engineer.

It's best to build a retaining wall at the bottom of a gentle
slope and fill in behind it with soil. The hill can also be held
with a series of low, terraced walls, or with a single high
(continued on page 378)

Yard Preparation

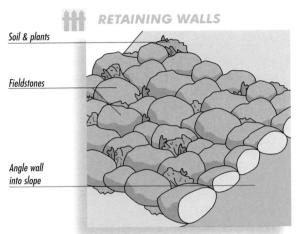

RETAINING WALLS

Soil & plants

Fieldstones

Angle wall into slope

Dry stone

A stone retaining wall can be laid without mortar and is a good choice for low, fairly stable slopes. The stones' uneven surfaces will help hold them in place. Soil-filled pockets between the rocks are ideal for colorful plantings.

(continued from page 377)
wall. Walls should rest on cut or undisturbed ground, not fill. Provide proper drainage so water doesn't build up behind the wall.

Building Edgings

Almost any patio or walkway requires some type of edging. In addition to outlining the space, edgings confine the surface materials within the desired area, an important function when working with loose materials, casting concrete, or laying brick or pavers in sand. When used to curb paved areas, edgings are usually installed after the base has been prepared but before the paving is laid. Edgings are often made of wood, but other materials can also provide the same defining and containing functions.

LUMBER EDGINGS Popular edgings are made of 2-by-4 or 2-by-6 lumber; for special emphasis, you could use 4 by 4s or 6 by 6s. Choose decay-resistant material such as pressure-treated lumber or the heartwood of cedar or redwood.

OTHER WOOD EDGINGS Heavy timbers and railroad ties make strong, showy edgings and interior dividers. In addi-

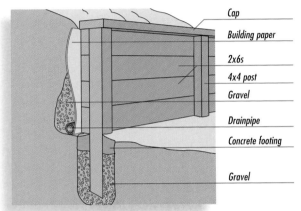

Cap

Building paper

2x6s

4x4 post

Gravel

Drainpipe

Concrete footing

Gravel

Dimension lumber

Made of decay-resistant dimension lumber (such as redwood heartwood or treated lumber) set vertically or horizontally, this wall is supported by 4-by-4 posts set in concrete. The 2-by-6 cap can provide a garden seat.

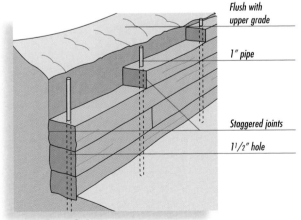

Flush with upper grade

1" pipe

Staggered joints

1½" hole

Railroad ties

Railroad ties, available from some home centers and landscape suppliers, can be stacked and strengthened with steel pipes inserted through drilled holes to provide a rugged retaining wall.

tion to rustic timbers, you can use wood posts or logs, in diameters ranging from 2 to 6 inches, to form a series of miniature pilings; set their bottoms in concrete, not in bare ground. For a more finished look, top off 4 by 4s with a horizontal 2-by-4 or 2-by-6 cap.

CURVED WOOD EDGINGS For gentle curves, use flexible redwood benderboard. Soak it in water to make it more flexible. Then work it around guide stakes set on the inside edge of the curve, nailing or screwing the board to these stakes. For an outside curve, add stakes every 3 feet or so on the outside and fasten the benderboard to them, then pull up the inside stakes.

Bend additional boards around the first board, staggering any splices, until you've built up the curved edging to the same thickness as the straight sections. Nail all layers together between stakes with 1-inch nails.

BRICK-IN-SOIL EDGINGS You can set bricks vertically, horizontally, or, for a sawtooth effect, at a uniform angle. After grading the area to be paved, dig a narrow trench around the perimeter; make it deep enough so the tops of the bricks will be flush with the finished paving. Position the bricks, then pack soil around the outside.

INVISIBLE EDGINGS An invisible edging secures paving units without any obvious support. Build temporary forms around the patio perimeter, as if for a concrete footing. Make the forms one brick-length wide in a trench deep enough to allow for a 4-inch concrete bed (deeper where the ground freezes).

Pour in concrete and, using a bladed screed, level it to one brick's thickness below the top of the forms. Place edging units in the wet concrete, butting their joints, and set them with a rubber mallet.

FLAGSTONE Before laying flagstones or other small stones, arrange them in a pleasing pattern, cutting them where necessary. Then lay the stones in 1-inch-thick mortar.

UNCUT STONE Larger rocks and boulders usually look best if they're partially buried; otherwise, prop them up with smaller rocks, then pack the area with soil and plantings. Cut formal paving units or wood decking to fit around boulders.

PREFORMED EDGINGS Manufactured plastic or aluminum edgings are easy to install. The strips secure bricks or concrete pavers below finished paving height; you then conceal them with soil or sod. Flexible sections can negotiate any tight curves.

CONCRETE EDGINGS Concrete can work like an invisible edging. Construct forms, pour the concrete, then screed it flush with the top of the forms so the edging will be even with the paved surface. Finish the concrete as desired and let it cure.

INSTALLING WOOD EDGINGS

8'

90°

10'

6'

Mason's twine

Batterboards

1 **Set up perimeter lines**
Use mason's twine and batterboards to lay out the shape of your patio or walkway as shown. Set up batterboards about 18 inches beyond the corresponding outside corners. To establish a perfectly square corner, use the 6-foot, 8-foot, and 10-foot measurements shown.

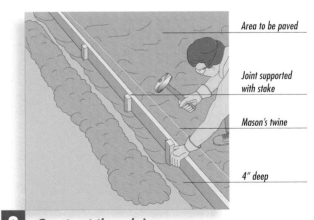

Area to be paved

Joint supported with stake

Mason's twine

4" deep

2 **Construct the edging**
Drive several 12-inch stakes made from 1 by 3s or 2 by 2s into the soil, aligning their inner faces with the mason's twine.

Yard Improvement Tools

Improvement jobs in the yard range from building stone walls to construction decks or screened-in rooms. Because of this, the variety of tools needed for these tasks ranges widely, from digging and yard preparation tools to masonry and carpentry tools. In addition to the tools shown on these two pages, you'll need basic safety equipment, such as gloves and safety glasses, as well as boots if you'll be digging. You might also need a cement mixer if you'll be pouring concrete or mixing a lot of mortar. One of these, along with wheelbarrows and similar heavy equipment, can be rented. If you're interested in cleaning a wood deck, see pages 400–401 for information on the tools you'll need.

 YARD PREPARATION TOOLS

You'll need a shovel and/or a spade for digging and a steel rake for grading areas in your yard; a wheelbarrow is also a must for moving soil from one place to another and can second as a receptacle for mixing and pouring concrete.

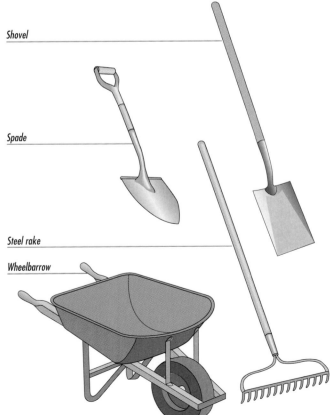

Shovel

Spade

Steel rake

Wheelbarrow

BRICK & MASONRY TOOLS

Whether you're making repairs or installing brick or masonry, you'll need many of the tools shown here. A bricklayer's hammer and brickset are used specifically for brickwork.

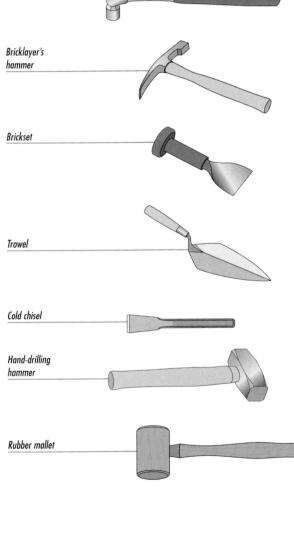

Ball-peen hammer

Bricklayer's hammer

Brickset

Trowel

Cold chisel

Hand-drilling hammer

Rubber mallet

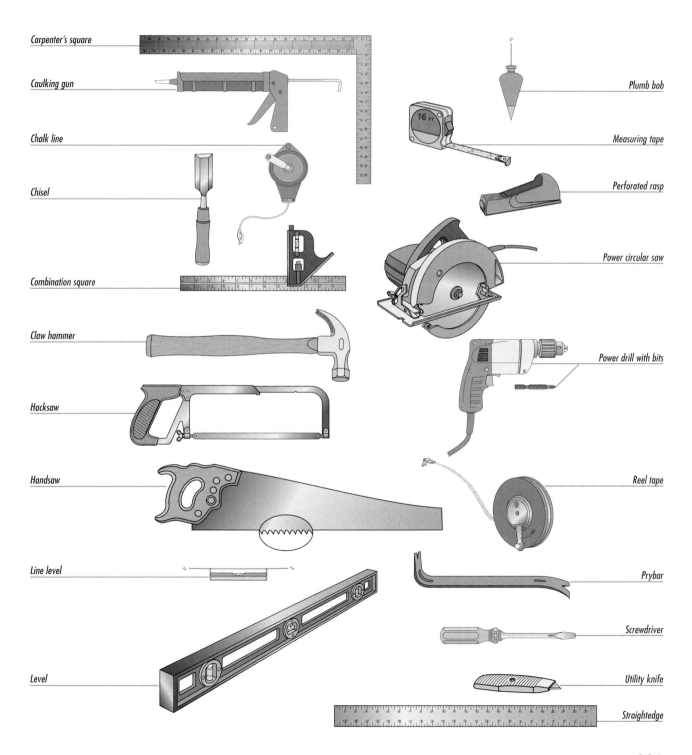

CARPENTRY TOOLS

For building decks, patio overheads, screened-in rooms, and similar wooden structures, you'll need a variety of basic tools.

Carpenter's square

Caulking gun

Chalk line

Chisel

Combination square

Claw hammer

Hacksaw

Handsaw

Line level

Level

Plumb bob

Measuring tape

Perforated rasp

Power circular saw

Power drill with bits

Reel tape

Prybar

Screwdriver

Utility knife

Straightedge

Brick-on-Sand Paving

Brick is a favorite material for garden paving and other outdoor construction because it is durable and easy to maintain, and because it blends beautifully with the garden. In addition, the small, uniform units of brick are easy to install, particularly when set in sand.

Most garden paving is done with common brick, though brick is available in an almost unlimited range of colors, sizes, and finishes. The standard modular brick is about 8 inches long by 4 inches wide by 2 3/8 inches thick. "Paver" bricks are roughly half the thickness of standard bricks, though it's best to use standard thicknesses when setting bricks in sand.

After you have graded the area and built the edgings, you're ready to start paving. Laying units in sand is explained here because it is the easiest method for do-it-yourselfers. Your first step will be placing and striking off a bed; next, you'll lay the units with the appropriate spacing; finally, you'll fill the joints to secure the units in place.

PREPARING THE BASE After grading the area to be paved and constructing edgings, you can begin to lay the sand base. Set temporary guides inside the edgings so that their top surfaces are one brick's thickness below the finished grade. If you use 2 by 4s, the sand bed will be approximately 2 inches deep. Strike off as shown in Step 1 below.

SETTING THE BRICKS OR PAVERS Working from a corner outward, place the bricks as shown in Step 2. Remove the temporary guides as you work, and use a trowel to fill in the area with sand. Strike off the area where the guide was with a short board. Use the leveled section as a guide, being careful not to disturb it.

 CUTTING BRICK

No matter how carefully you plan, some brick cutting is almost inevitable. Save your cutting for last so you can do it all at once. If you have just a few cuts to make, the best tool is the brickset. Tap the brick lightly to score a groove across all four sides before the final blow. Set the brick on flat sand and place the brickset (with the bevel facing away from the piece to be used) along the cut line. Tap the brickset sharply with a small sledgehammer. If necessary, chip away the rough edges with the brickset or a mason's hammer.

If you have a lot of cutting to do, you can rent a hydraulic brick cutter. For repeated angle cuts, a diamond-bladed tub saw is the best bet.

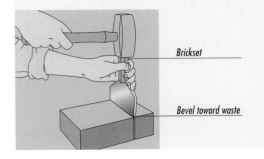

Brickset

Bevel toward waste

LAYING BRICKS IN SAND

Edging

Temporary guide

2" dampened sand bed

Strikeoff

Temporary guide

1 **Strike off the base**

Set temporary guides inside the edgings, with their top surfaces one brick's thickness below the finished grade. Shovel dampened sand between the guides and strike it off smooth, about 3 feet at a time, as shown. Tamp the sand.

Mason's line

Trowel

Dip (fill in)

2 **Set the bricks or pavers**
Using a mason's line as a guide, place the bricks or pavers, working from a corner outward. Tap them into place with a mallet or piece of wood. Check level as you go, using a carpenter's level on the edge of a 2 by 4 placed along the bricks.

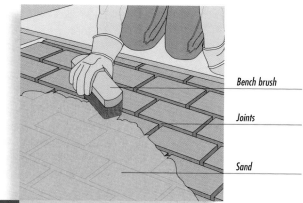

Bench brush

Joints

Sand

3 **Sand the joints**
Spread fine sand over the surface of the finished paving. Let it dry thoroughly, then sweep it into the joints, applying more sand as necessary to fill. Use a fine spray to wet the finished paving down; this helps settle the sand.

 LAYING TILE & STONE

Heavy, ³/₄-inch-thick tile can be laid in sand. Follow the directions for brick, but use a ¹/₂-inch sand base; a thicker base may allow the tiles to tilt out of position. If possible, use butted joints (tiles laid with edges touching), as these will give a little added stability.

Lay stones in a 2-inch sand bed, following the directions for brick on these pages; edgings are optional. Scoop out or fill in sand as necessary to compensate for variations in stone thickness. If you're using irregularly shaped stones, lay them out in advance, adjusting the pattern and the joint spacing as needed. Use a level as you work.

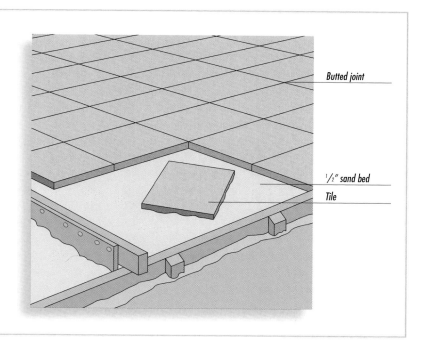

Butted joint

¹/₂" sand bed

Tile

Stone-in-Mortar Paving

Setting stone (or other masonry units such as bricks) in mortar creates a permanent, solid paving. Mortar is the "glue" that binds masonry units together, and it has several other functions: It seals out wind and water, compensates for variations in the size of masonry units, anchors metal ties and reinforcements, and provides various decorative effects, depending on how the joints are tooled, or "struck."

Stone—especially large flat stone, such as flagstone—can be laid directly on stable soil as well as in sand or mortar. But if you're going to use mortar, plan to put it on a poured concrete slab.

MIXING MORTAR Mix mortar from a 1:3 portland cement–sand mix without lime. Stone should be set in rather stiff mortar because it is relatively nonabsorbent. Consult your building supplier about the quantity of mortar you'll need. Mortar sand should be clean, sharp-edged, and free of impurities (never use beach sand). Use drinkable water for mixing mortar.

In mixing mortar, measure and mix the dry ingredients first, either in a power mixer or by hand, then add and mix in the water. The amount of water cannot be specified in advance, as it depends entirely upon the composition of the mortar and the absorption rate of the masonry units to be laid, factors that can vary according to the weather.

Ready for use, your mortar should have a smooth, uniform, buttery consistency; it should spread well and stick to vertical surfaces, yet not smear the face of your work. Add water a little at a time and mix until these requirements have been met.

Small amounts of mortar can readily be mixed by hand. You'll need a wheelbarrow or a mortar box, and a hoe. Mix the sand, cement, and lime well before adding water. Hoe

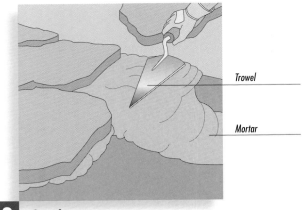

Trowel

Mortar

2 **Set the stones**
To set stones, trowel enough mortar onto the slab to make full mortar beds for one or two stones at a time.

LAYING STONES IN MORTAR

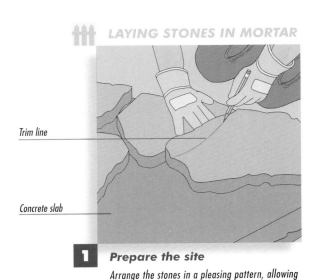

Trim line

Concrete slab

1 **Prepare the site**
Arrange the stones in a pleasing pattern, allowing approximately the same space for mortar joints throughout. Trim stones as necessary, marking them as shown.

the dry ingredients into a pile, make a hole in the top, and add some water; mix, then repeat as often as necessary to achieve the proper consistency.

For large jobs, power mixers can be rented in a variety of sizes. With the mixer running, add some water, half the sand, and all of the lime. Caution: Never put the shovel inside the mixer. Next, add all of the cement, the rest of the sand, and enough water to achieve the right consistency. The mixer should run for at least 3 or 4 minutes once all the water is added. Mix only enough to last you about 2 hours; more than that is likely to be wasted.

SETTING STONE Unless you are using sawn stone, such as slate, you'll need to vary the thickness of the setting bed to make up for variations in stone thickness, but it should be at least 1 inch thick. Keep the mortar stiff enough to support the stones. Make sure stones are clean and dry to be certain you're getting a good bond.

CUTTING STONE To trim a stone, lap it over its neighbor and mark the trim line. To cut, score the line with a brickset or stonemason's chisel, prop the edge to be cut off on a wood scrap, and strike the scored line with a brickset (or stone chisel) and a hand-drilling hammer.

CLEANING STONE Muriatic acid washes, commonly used to clean cured masonry, can be used except with limestone and marble; the acid mars these types of stone.

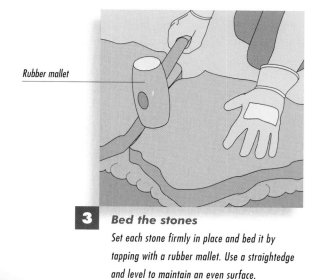

Rubber mallet

3 **Bed the stones**

Set each stone firmly in place and bed it by tapping with a rubber mallet. Use a straightedge and level to maintain an even surface.

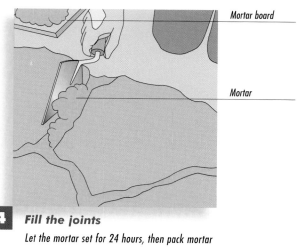

Mortar board

Mortar

4 **Fill the joints**

Let the mortar set for 24 hours, then pack mortar between the stones. Smooth the joints with a pointing trowel and clean up spills with a sponge and water.

Building a Stone Wall

Yard Improvements

More than any other masonry material, stone lends an aura of permanence to a structure.

Rubble stonework is built up without courses, designed to achieve a pleasing arrangement of different sizes. It can be laid dry, with the stones holding each other in place by weight and friction. This is usually the cheapest method for building a stone wall—sometimes it's even free, as is true of the famous New England dry stone walls built by farmers in the course of clearing their fields.

PROPER BUILDING As you work, be sure that vertical joints are staggered; there should always be an overlap with the stones above and below.

Free-standing walls are usually laid up in two rough wythes with rubble fill. Bond stones run across the wall, tying it together. You should use as many bond stones as possible—at least one for every 10 square feet of wall surface.

Most stone walls should slope inward (toward the center) on both surfaces. This tilting of the faces is called batter and helps secure the wall, since the faces lean on each other. Dry-laid walls should have 3 to 4 inches of batter for every 2 feet of rise.

The batter gauge shown in Step 2 can be made from 1 by 2s nailed together. The vertical strip should equal the height you plan to build your wall. Nail a slightly longer diagonal strip to it at one end, then nail a short piece to the ends of the two long strips. The length of this short piece should equal the amount of batter required for your wall's height (the vertical strip and short piece should be at right angles).

Plan on a battered wall no higher than it is thick at its base. Very round stones will require so much batter that the resulting dry wall may be no higher than a third of its thick-ness. The casual rubble wall shown here is not meant to be taller than 3 feet, especially in earthquake-prone regions.

Even in severe frost areas, dry walls are built in very shallow trenches without footings. Since the wall is flexible, frost heaves tend to dislodge only a few stones, which can easily be replaced.

Select your largest stones for the foundation course to spare your back and strengthen the wall. Save the flattest, broadest stones for the top.

CUTTING STONE First, always wear safety goggles. To fit an awkwardly shaped stone, you can trim by hammering at the stone with a bricklayer's hammer. If you need to cut a stone, a stone chisel or brickset will work. Score a line completely around the stone, tapping the chisel with a hand-drilling hammer. Then drive the chisel against the line to break the stone apart; try to work with the natural fissures in the stone.

BUILDING WITH STONE

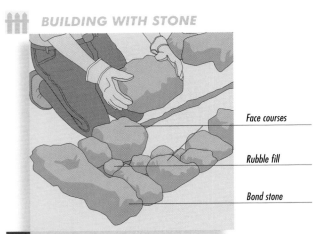

Face courses

Rubble fill

Bond stone

1 **Lay the first course**
Lay the foundation stones in a shallow trench; this will help stabilize the wall. Begin with a bond stone—a stone the width of the wall—and then start the two face courses. Try to lay stones flat, as they occur naturally. Fill the center with rubble.

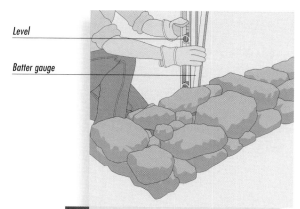

Level

Batter gauge

2 **Lay the second course**

Lay stones on top of the first course, being sure that vertical joints do not line up. Stones of each face should tilt inward toward each other. Use your batter gauge and level on sides and ends to maintain proper slope. Again, fill the center with rubble.

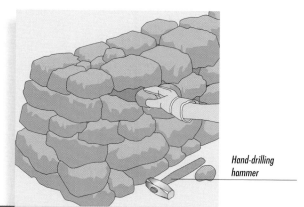

Hand-drilling hammer

3 **Add additional courses**

Continue in the same manner, maintaining an inward tilt so that gravity will hold the wall together. Place bond stones every 5 to 10 square feet. Use small stones to fill large gaps; if you tap them in with a hammer, the wall will be stronger. But don't overdo it—driving them in too far will actually weaken the structure.

4

Lay the top course

Save your flattest, broadest stones for the top. If you live in an area with freezing temperatures, consider mortaring the cap as shown in the detail; this will drain water away from the wall and help prevent frost damage.

Large, flat stone

Mortared cap

Building a Simple Deck

A simple, low-level deck can transform any unused part of your yard into a comfortable surface that's ideal for almost any outdoor activity, from sunbathing to picnicking. The deck shown here is small enough (8 feet by 12 feet) to fit in almost any yard and its construction is simple if you have basic building experience. You can adapt this plan to suit your yard; just be sure changes will meet local codes. For example, if your deck will be more than 30 inches off the ground, it may require a railing.

Before beginning, prepare the area as discussed on pages 376–379, and set up perimeter lines for the deck using batterboards as shown in Step 1 on page 379.

LOW-LEVEL DECK PLAN

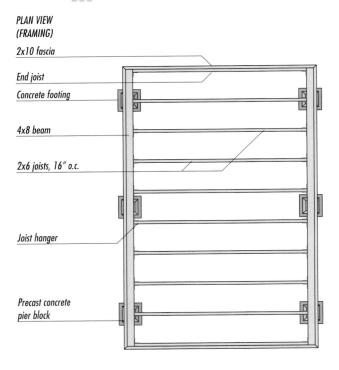

PLAN VIEW
(FRAMING)

2x10 fascia

End joist

Concrete footing

4x8 beam

2x6 joists, 16" o.c.

Joist hanger

Precast concrete
pier block

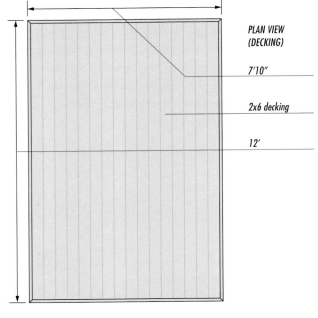

PLAN VIEW
(DECKING)

7'10"

2x6 decking

12'

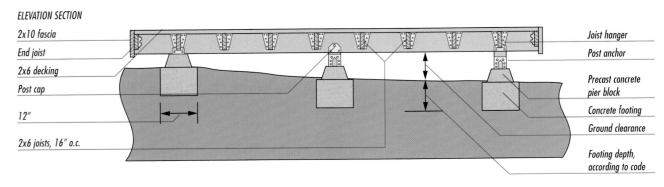

ELEVATION SECTION

2x10 fascia

End joist

2x6 decking

Post cap

12"

2x6 joists, 16" o.c.

Joist hanger

Post anchor

Precast concrete
pier block

Concrete footing

Ground clearance

Footing depth,
according to code

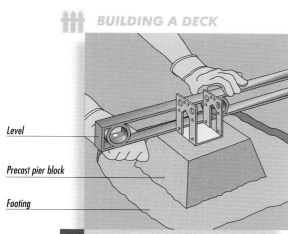

Level

Precast pier block

Footing

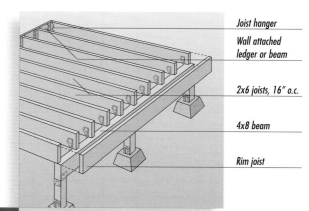

Joist hanger

Wall attached
ledger or beam

2x6 joists, 16" o.c.

4x8 beam

Rim joist

1 *Place the footings & piers*

According to the plan, cast footings to the depth and size required by local codes; the top of the footing should be about 1 inch below grade. Wait until concrete has stiffened slightly and level a pier block on each footing. Cover the exposed part of the footing with earth.

2 *Build the structure*

After footings have cured, build the structure as shown in this drawing and the deck plan. Use galvanized 3 ½-inch common nails for all nailed connections and framing anchors. Note: The left side of the drawing shows how to connect joists to a house-attached ledger or beam using joist hangers; the right side of the drawing shows how to set joists on top of a beam and connect them with a rim joist. Choose the method that suits your site.

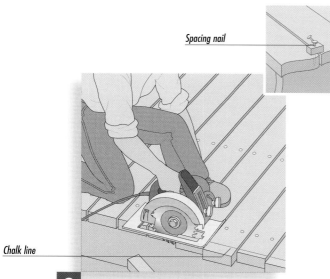

Spacing nail

Chalk line

3 *Attach & trim decking*

Fasten 2-by-6 decking perpendicular to joists with two 3 ½-inch galvanized nails (or power-drive deck screws) per board. When appearance allows, face them "crown" up (the convex, outer side of the tree's growth rings). Space them ⅛ inch (use a nail as a spacer). Allow them to run beyond the deck's edge, then snap a chalk line and trim.

💡 **Avoid splitting boards by blunting each nail's tip with a light tap of the hammer, then angling the nails slightly toward the board's center as you nail. Be careful not to crush the wood with the final hammer blow.**

Building a Patio Overhead

The steps below will give you a general idea of the building sequence for a free-standing overhead. Sizes, spans, and spacings of framing materials must be designed to meet local code requirements, so be sure to discuss your plans with local building officials. In areas with harsh winters, your structure will have to support the weight of snow and ice.

The main components of an overhead are posts, beams, rafters, and surfacing. When an overhead is attached to the house, a ledger takes the place of one beam. Roofing can take many forms.

Special connectors and fasteners strengthen the structure and make building easier. Post anchors hold posts in place. They can be set in a concrete slab just after the concrete has been placed. Post anchors can also be fastened to an existing slab with lag screws and anchor shields or to piers set outside the patio perimeter (facing page).

ASSEMBLING AN OVERHEAD

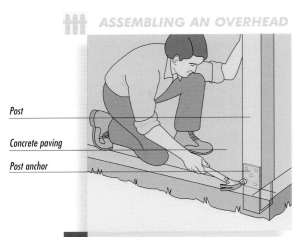

Post

Concrete paving

Post anchor

1 Set the posts
Cut posts to length and nail post/beam connectors on top. Place the posts in post anchors. Keep the posts vertical and nail the post anchors to them. (The post anchors shown must be used with a new concrete slab.)

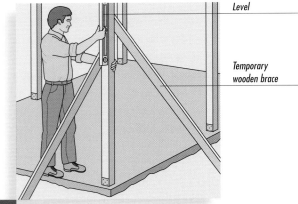

Level

Temporary wooden brace

2 Plumb the posts
Plumb each post using a carpenter's level placed on two adjacent sides. Secure the posts in position with temporary wooden braces nailed to stakes driven into the ground.

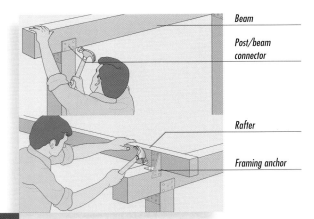

Beam

Post/beam connector

Rafter

Framing anchor

3 Attach beams & rafters
Position a beam on top of the posts that will support it. Check that the posts are vertical and the beam is level, and make adjustments as necessary. Nail the post/beam connectors to the beam. Set and space rafters on the tops of the beams and secure them with framing anchors.

Nail or bolt 1-by-4 or 1-by-6 knee braces with ends cut at 45 degrees between the beams and posts. Cut the knee braces long enough so that the beam ends are at least 2 feet from the post/beam connectors. Remove the temporary post braces.

4 **Brace the overhead**

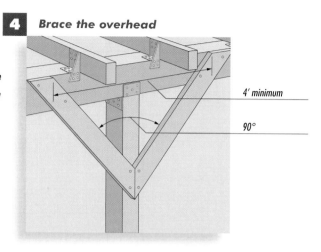

4' minimum

90°

Lath, 1x2, or 2x2

Rafter

Beam

Knee brace

Post

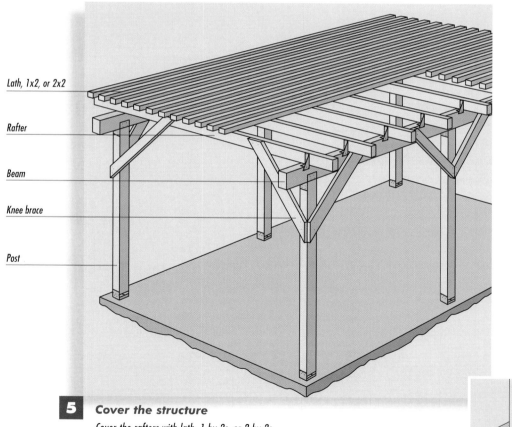

5 **Cover the structure**

Cover the rafters with lath, 1 by 2s, or 2 by 2s spaced to achieve the desired amount of shading. Or cover the roof with another material, according to your design specifications. Posts can be set in post anchors fastened to an existing patio with lag screws and anchor shields as shown in the detail.

Post

Metal post anchor

Existing slab

Anchor shield

Screening in a Porch

In some regions, bugs can take over outdoor living spaces during certain seasons. The evening hours, when mosquitoes come to life, can be downright unbearable unless some form of protection is in place. The easiest way to keep bugs at bay is to enclose a part of your outdoor space with screens.

When you're starting from scratch, installing a commercial awning or canopy with screens is probably the easiest and quickest route to a full-fledged screened room. Many manufacturers market screening attachments for their overheads, installed by one of several simple methods—spline

systems and special screen-holding tape are just a couple of ways. These create an attractive screened space in little time and at reasonable cost. And their screens are usually easy to remove.

If you already have a roof or overhead above your porch, deck, or patio, adding screens is a fairly straightforward task. The easiest method involves installing 1-by-1 stops on the support members of the overhead structure and stapling screening to the stops. You then cover the staples and screening edges with a special molding called screen bead. The one problem with this approach is that the screens will not be removable.

A second approach, shown on these pages, involves mounting screened frames in the openings. This requires more time and effort, but the structure will be much sturdier and the screens can be removed and stored in winter if necessary. For both methods, use pressure-treated lumber for sole plates laid on the deck, porch, or patio surface.

(continued on page 395)

 ANATOMY OF A SCREENED ROOM

Beneath an existing roof, openings are framed by 4-by-4 posts and 2-by-4 studs, sole plates, top plates, knee rails, and knee-rail supports. Screen surrounds consist of 2-by-4 frames and 2-by-2 stops; removable screen frames fashioned from 1 by 4s are screwed to the stops. The doorway king studs, jack studs, and header are positioned to accommodate a prefabricated screen door.

- 2x4 top plate
- 2x4 header
- 2x4 end stud
- Screening
- Commercial screen door
- 2x4 knee rail
- 2x4 king stud
- 2x4 jack stud
- 4x4 post
- Fascia board
- 1x4 screen frame
- Screen surround: 2x4 frame, 2x2 stop
- 2x4 knee-rail support
- 2x4 sole plate

Yard Improvements

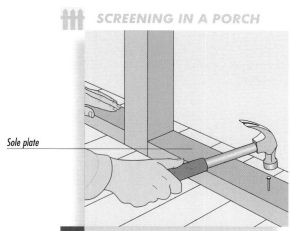

Sole plate

1 **Attach sole and top plates**

Cut the sole and top plates to length and nail or screw them to the ceiling and floor every 16 inches, if possible, to the supporting joists. Once the sole and top plates are installed, frame the door opening as shown in the large illustration on facing page.

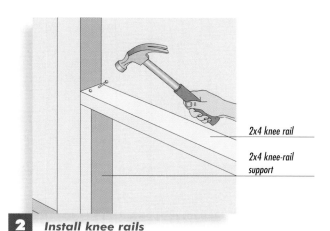

2x4 knee rail

2x4 knee-rail support

2 **Install knee rails**

Cut 2-by-4 knee rails to fit between the posts. Cut a pair of 2-by-4 knee-rail supports to hold up the ends of each board, then toenail the knee rails in place about 3 feet above the sole plates. If the distances between posts are long, fasten extra knee-rail supports midway between posts.

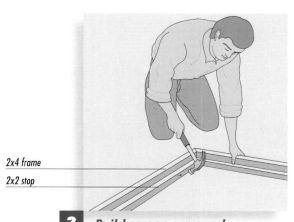

2x4 frame
2x2 stop

3 **Build screen surrounds**

Assemble frames of beveled 2 by 4s to fit in the openings formed by the support members. Attach 2-by-2 stops flush with the outside edge of the frames.

CHOOSING SCREENING

Most screening is made of aluminum or vinyl-coated fiber-glass. You'll find very little difference in the performance of these two types: Both are rustproof and stain-resistant. The biggest differences are that aluminum tends to dent easily and vinyl-coated fiberglass stretches and may tear.

Vinyl-coated fiberglass is slightly less expensive. It comes in at least three colors: aquamarine, silver-gray, and dark gray. The type made for screened rooms often has fairly large wires—.013 mil—for greater strength, and an open mesh—18 by 14 rather than 18 by 16 (this means it has 18 horizontal and 14 vertical wires in every square inch). An ultrafine 20-by-20 mesh is also available to repel even the tiniest of insects, but will also prevent a breeze from blowing through. Solar screening, which is made from vinyl-coated fiberglass, shades most sunlight but allows good visibility from inside.

Aluminum comes in black, dark gray, and bright aluminum colors in 18-by-16 mesh (18 horizontal and 16 vertical wires in every square inch). Other, more costly screen materials include bronze, copper, brass, and stainless steel.

Screening is sold in 7-, 25-, and 100-foot-long rolls, from 18 to 72 inches wide. When selecting, be aware that darker colors are the most opaque from outside and offer the best visibility from inside.

Screening in a Porch

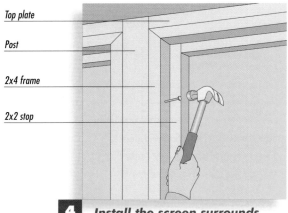

Top plate

Post

2x4 frame

2x2 stop

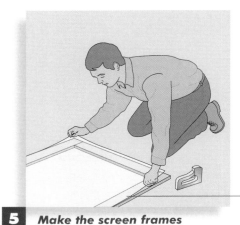

1x4 screen frame

5 **Make the screen frames**

After measuring the openings, join the frames at the corners with L-brackets. Next, cut pieces of screening slightly larger than the frame openings. Pull the screening taut and fasten it to the screen frames with rustproof staples every 2 inches. Then, trim excess screening material with scissors or a utility knife.

4 **Install the screen surrounds**

Nail the screen surrounds into place in the openings. Check the corners for square as you go, and adjust the surrounds if necessary.

6 **Secure the frames in place**

Secure the frames to the stops on the surrounds with rustproof screws (this will allow you to remove the screens easily for repair or storage).

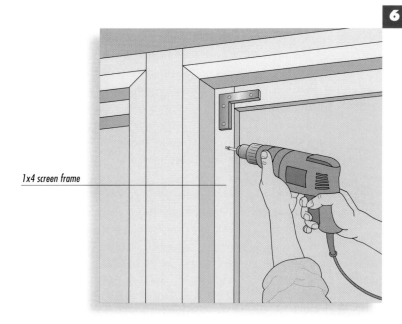

1x4 screen frame

(continued from page 392)
Remember that bugs can slip through the smallest of openings. The covering on an overhead used for a screened room will have to be impervious to bugs. Also, if you have clapboard or shingle siding, you may need to caulk gaps between the house wall and the screen framing.

The only other decision you need to make is about the screening to use. See the sidebar on page 393 for information on different screening materials.

FIRST STEPS Sole and top plates are 2-by-4 horizontal supports placed between the bottoms and tops of the posts that support your overhead or porch roof. Cut them to length and fasten them in place as shown in Step 1 on page 393. Leave an opening for a doorway 3¼ inches wider than the commercial screen door you plan to use. If the floor surface is concrete or brick, you will have to shim sole plates and fasten them with masonry anchor shields and lag screws.

BUILDING THE SCREEN FRAMES Measure the openings of the screen surrounds carefully, then assemble 1-by-4 screen frames to fit the openings.

 PROPER SLOPE FOR DRAINAGE

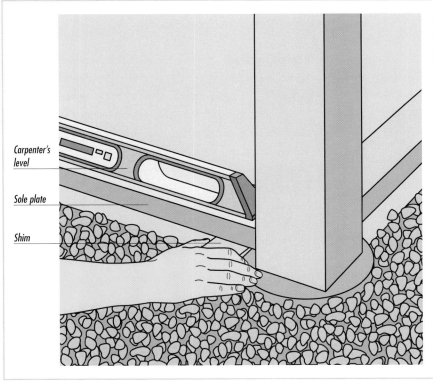

Carpenter's level

Sole plate

Shim

For proper drainage, well-built patios slope away from the house slightly. If you are screening in a patio, you will need to compensate for this slope by shimming the sole plates that run away from the house so they are perfectly level. Insert the shims to support the sole plate and check for level as shown here. Trim the shims flush with the edges of the sole plates.

On a concrete or brick patio, you will also have to use a different method to fasten the sole plates. Mark the location of the sole plates on the patio, then drill holes every 18 inches for anchor shields, leaving an opening for a doorway. Shim the sole plates, then fasten them by driving lag screws through them into the anchor shields. Seal gaps with caulk.

Masonry Repairs

Although masonry materials are fairly maintenance-free, they may require occasional cleaning, and, in spite of their durability, they can be damaged. Here we look at how to care for and repair masonry.

Most masonry can be kept clean with plain water, but you may occasionally have a problem with smears and stains that water can't cure. On these pages you will see how to clean off everything from efflorescence and mortar smears to smoke and soot.

Cracked and broken bricks and blocks, crumbling mortar joints, and chipped and broken concrete are problems that may never occur in a well-made masonry structure. But shifting earth, impacts, and freeze-thaw cycles are beyond human control, and they can damage even a good mason's work.

Cleaning Masonry

Efflorescence is a white, powdery deposit caused by water dissolving the mineral salts contained in mortar; mortar smears are an inevitable result of learning to work with masonry. Both efflorescence and mortar smears are common problems.

Many other substances can stain the surface of your project. For the most part, you can use ordinary household detergents, cleansers, and scouring powders. Some stains will require acid. Specific remedies for each type of stain, and some cautions, are given below.

Do not use acids on marble or limestone. Clean with water only, as even detergents can be harmful. Always use fiber brushes; steel brushes are too abrasive and may leave rust marks. Sometimes you can clean stone by rubbing it with a piece of the same type of rock.

EFFLORESCENCE The mineral salts that appear as efflorescence, especially on brick paving or walls, are carried to the surface by water, which then evaporates, leaving the salts behind. The deposits will disappear once all the salts have been leached out, but this may take a couple of years. If you're impatient, try brushing and scrubbing the deposits away without using water; then follow with a thorough hosing. Water tends to redissolve some of the salts, and they will reappear again later. Remove as much as you can by dry scrubbing before using water. In an extreme case, follow the directions for removing mortar smears. To prevent efflorescence from coming back, improve drainage to reduce the amount of water that reaches the masonry.

Efflorescence on brick

A white, powdery substance on brick and masonry surfaces, called efflorescence, is a naturally occurring problem that can be remedied by scrubbing surfaces and eliminating the source of water that encourages it.

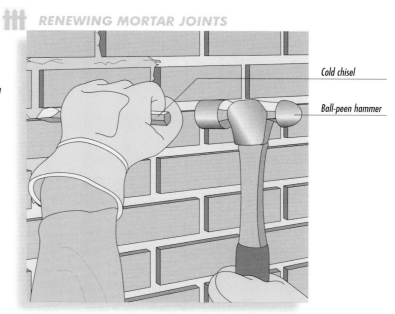

Using a narrow-blade cold chisel and a ball-peen hammer, chisel out old mortar to a depth of at least ³/₄ inch. Thoroughly brush joints out with an old paintbrush. Dampen the area with a brush or a fine spray of water. When the units are damp but not shiny wet, fill the joints completely with mortar, tamping it in well (use a small piece of wood for deep joints).

Cold chisel

Ball-peen hammer

MORTAR SMEARS Remove these with muriatic acid, available at masonry supply stores. The acid works by attacking the calcium contained in cement and lime. Use a 1:9 acid-water solution on concrete, concrete block, and dark brick. On light-colored brick, this solution may leave stains, so use a 1:14 or 1:19 solution. Do not use acid on colored concrete; it may leach out the color.

Never use acid on marble or limestone. Caution: When preparing the solution, always pour the acid slowly into the water—never the reverse. Wear eye protection, a face shield, and rubber gloves, and work in a well-ventilated area. First wet the wall, then apply the acid with a stiff brush to a small area at a time, let it stand for 3 or 4 minutes, and flush thoroughly with water.

Muriatic acid may change the color of masonry, at least slightly. You may want to treat the whole area to be sure it maintains an even color.

OIL & GREASE Before the stain has penetrated, scatter fine sawdust, cement powder, or hydrated lime over the surface. If you catch it in time, these materials will soak up much of the oil or grease and then can simply be swept up.

If the stain has penetrated, try dissolving it with a commercial degreaser or emulsifier. These are available at masonry and home supply centers and at auto suppliers; follow the manufacturer's directions. Residual stains can sometimes be lightened with household bleach, as explained below for rust. Avoid hazardous solvents such as kerosene, benzene, or gasoline; they aren't worth the risks of fire or toxic inhalation.

PAINT To clean up freshly spilled paint, wipe and scrub it up with a rag soaked in the solvent specified for the paint. For dried paint, use a commercial paint remover, following the manufacturer's instructions.

RUST Ordinary household bleach will lighten rust stains (and most others). Scrub it in, let it stand, then rinse the surface thoroughly. A stronger remedy is a pound of oxalic acid mixed into a gallon of water; follow the mixing directions for muriatic acid given for mortar smears. Brush on the acid, let it stand for 3 or 4 minutes, then hose it off. Remember that acid washes (and bleach) can affect the color of a surface. Test them in an inconspicuous area first.

SMOKE & SOOT Scrub with a household scouring powder and a stiff brush, then rinse with water.

(continued on page 398)

Masonry Repairs

(continued from page 397)

Repairing Brick & Stone

Most trouble in a mortared wall or paving develops at the mortar joints. Sometimes the shrinking of mortar without lime will cause the joints to open; mortar with lime often crumbles.

Freeze-thaw cycles worsen the problem. Water penetrates the tiniest cracks; upon freezing, it expands, enlarging the cracks and making it easier for the process to recur. Renewing the mortar joints will prevent future shrinking, crumbling, and cracking.

Settling of a mortared wall or paving can crack the joints, and sometimes the bricks, stones, or other units themselves. A heavy impact can do the same thing. This cracking calls for replacement of the mortar and possibly one or more units; in extreme cases, a whole section may need to be completely rebuilt.

You'll find directions for all these repairs in these pages. The information applies to all unit masonry walls and pavings (brick, block, adobe, and stone), even though the drawings show only brick. Stone can be repaired in the same way as other units, although it may be more difficult to remove a damaged stone and to fit a new one into the gap.

RENEWING MORTAR JOINTS Fresh mortar will not adhere to old, so when renewing mortar joints, you'll need to chisel out the cracked and crumbling old mortar to expose as much of the mortar-bearing faces of the bricks or other units as possible, as shown on page 397. Be sure to always wear eye protection.

Mix Type N mortar to a stiff consistency (for stone, mix mortar without lime—see page 384). When the units are damp but not shiny wet, use a joint filler or small pointing trowel to press mortar into the joints. You may find that a hawk will help you hold mortar close to the job.

Smooth the joints when the mortar is stiff enough. Keep the repair damp for four days to cure the mortar.

FILLING LONG CRACKS You can fix long cracks by following the directions for renewing mortar joints, but you'll probably find grouting easier, as shown on facing page. Work with a helper if possible. Fill 3 or 4 feet of crack at a time, waiting several hours between pours to let the grout set. Keep the area damp for four days to cure the grout.

REPLACING A BRICK When a brick or other unit is badly damaged, you can replace it if it isn't supporting some of the wall's weight. Check whether the unit is carrying a load by trying to move some of the broken pieces—if the pieces move, you can take the unit out and replace it with a new brick or block. If the pieces seem reluctant to move, the unit is probably carrying a load; leave it alone, or consult a professional mason before removing it.

To replace a unit, put on safety glasses and chip out the old mortar with a narrow-blade cold chisel. Work carefully so as not to disturb adjacent units. Once the mortar is out, you should be able to remove the unit. If necessary, break it up carefully with the chisel and remove the pieces. Clean up the cavity, removing all the old mortar.

Dampen the cavity and the replacement unit with a wet brush or fine spray of water, then prepare a batch of mortar with a 1:2 cement-sand mix (no lime) to the consistency of soft mud. Replace the unit as shown on the facing page. Make sure the cavity is damp but not wet. Keep the area damp for four days to cure the mortar.

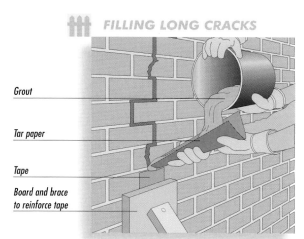

Grout

Tar paper

Tape

Board and brace
to reinforce tape

Dampen the cracked surfaces several hours before
grouting. When they are no longer shiny wet, pour
grout into cracks through a tar paper or cardboard
chute. Apply wide, waterproof, surgical adhesive
tape to dam up the grout in walls. (Hold the tape
to the wall with a board, if necessary.)

REPLACING A PAVER UNIT

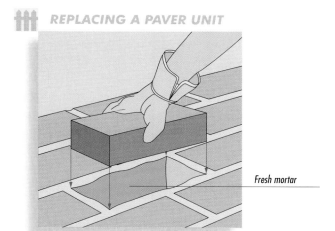

Fresh mortar

Dampen the cavity and the replacement brick with
a wet brush or fine spray of water, then prepare a
batch of mortar with a 1:2 cement-sand mix (no
lime) to the consistency of soft mud. Apply a thick
layer of mortar to the bottom and sides of the
cavity and push the brick into place, keeping it
level with the surrounding ones.

REPLACING A WALL UNIT

To replace a non-load-bearing brick, chip out all
the old mortar with a narrow-blade cold chisel
(wear safety glasses). Dampen the cavity with a
wet brush or fine spray of water. Apply mortar in
the cavity and to the top of the new brick and
push the brick into place; a small board makes
aligning it with the wall an easier job. Mortar
should squeeze out from the joints; if it doesn't,
add more. Trim off excess mortar and smooth the
joints. Keep the area damp for four days to cure
the mortar.

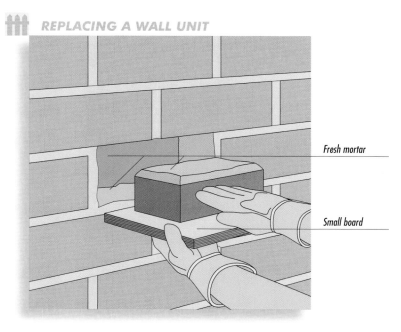

Fresh mortar

Small board

Cleaning & Refinishing a Deck

A wood deck gives a home a natural connection with the outdoors, but over time, a deck can become weathered and uninviting. Fortunately, if a deck is built of naturally decay-resistant woods such as redwood or cedar heartwood, or pressure-treated pine, most problems are purely cosmetic.

Ultraviolet radiation (UV) from the sun deteriorates the surface fibers and lignin of wood, which causes the wood to erode and gray on the surface. In dampness, moisture can stain wood and encourage surface mildew. And some woods, notably redwood and cedar, can "bleed" natural extractives that discolor the surface.

CLEANING A DECK To prevent moisture from building up between deck boards, remove debris that clogs the spaces between them. Use a powerful nozzle on a garden hose to blast out this material, then push out remaining debris with a putty knife. Mount a stiff brush on a long handle and, with a sudsy mixture of laundry detergent and water, thoroughly scrub the surface, working in small sections. Rinse periodically. Then allow the deck to dry and re-evaluate it—this may be all it takes to restore the wood's natural beauty.

For washing a large deck, consider renting a power washer that delivers 1,200 pounds per square inch (psi) of pressure or less. Be sure to equip it with a nozzle that fans an arc of about 25 to 40 degrees so you don't erode the wood. When using it, wear safety goggles, hold the nozzle about 6 inches above the deck's surface, and spray slowly in line with the wood grain, overlapping your path.

After washing the deck's surface, let it dry for several days before applying a finish.

ELIMINATING DISCOLORATION Several readily available products will remove stains and discoloration. You can buy powder and liquid concentrates that have either an oxalic acid or nonchlorine base, with or without a detergent. Bleach-based products kill mildew; acid-based materials help eliminate graying and stains.

Always follow the label directions, and wear rubber gloves, goggles, and old clothes when applying chemicals. Be sure to test any material in an inconspicuous place. Caution: Never mix detergent containing ammonia with household bleach; the resulting fumes can be highly toxic.

To test for mildew, apply a drop of undiluted liquid household bleach to a small black spot. If this eliminates the spot, mildew is the problem. In this case, clean the deck with a mild cleanser (no ammonia) and scrub with a solution of 1 part household liquid bleach to 4 parts water. Wait about 15 minutes, then rinse with water.

If the stain doesn't go away with a bleach solution, it probably isn't mildew. It may be dirt, natural wood extractives, or corrosion from hardware. If the problem is general graying, this is usually caused by wear and UV radiation.

For this, choose an oxalic acid-based deck restoration product, following the label directions. Wearing rubber gloves, safety glasses, and old clothes, apply the solution to one board at a time and scrub with a soft brush. Allow to dry, then hose off the deck with clear water.

DECK CLEANING & FINISHING TOOLS

At the very least, you'll want a bucket, hose, goggles, rubber gloves, and a sturdy scrub brush with a handle for cleaning a deck. A power washer makes cleaning a large deck much easier—and a putty knife is helpful for cleaning out the gaps between decking. Depending upon the type of finish you apply, you may want a pressure sprayer, a paint roller, and a paintbrush.

Pressure sprayer

Bucket

Scrub brush with handle

Spray gun

Hose

Paint roller

Goggles

Putty knife

Paint pad

Rubber gloves

Paintbrush

To brighten and clean an aging deck, scrub it with an oxalic acid-based deck restoration product. Be sure to follow the label directions.

FINISHING A DECK Though you can paint decks with deck paint, most people prefer to take advantage of the natural beauty of expensive decking woods by applying a clear or lightly stained finish. If you do choose to paint, be sure to apply a stain-blocking oil or alkyd primer first.

Choose finishes that soak into the wood, not heavily pigmented solid stains that provide a surface film (the latter type will show wear patterns and may peel).

The finish should be "water repellent" or "waterproof," not just "water resistant." It should offer UV protection and, if mildew is a potential problem, the finish should contain a mildewcide, which a "wood preservative" does. For a product that will offer long-term UV protection, choose a "toner"—this will last up to four years. Regular preservatives need to be reapplied once a year. Follow the label directions for proper application.

Repairing a Deck

Yard Repairs

Although a deck's surface is usually built from decay-resistant lumber, parts of the substructure are vulnerable to decay caused primarily by excessive moisture. On these pages, we look at a few common problems and typical remedies that are relatively easy to handle. For information on restoring a deck's surface, see pages 400–401.

⚎ DECK STRUCTURE REPAIRS

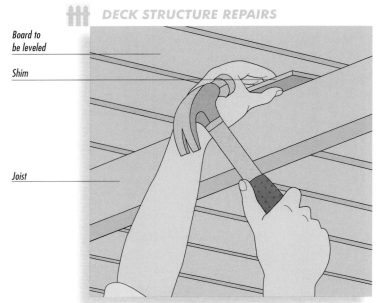

Board to be leveled

Shim

Joist

Raising a deck board

If the surface of a board is lower than its neighbors, insert shims underneath it, between the board and the joists. Break off cedar shingles to approximately the same width as the deck board, insert one from each side of the joist, and tap them together with a hammer.

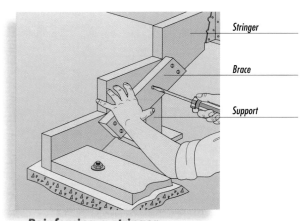

Stringer

Brace

Support

Reinforcing a stringer

If a stair stringer is weakened by cracks or splits, reinforce it. First, temporarily brace it from underneath with a short length of 2 by 4. Cut a support from a 2 by 4 or 2 by 6 that's long enough to extend about 6 inches past each side of the damaged section. Drive screws in pairs along the support's length, two at each end and spaced about 10 inches apart.

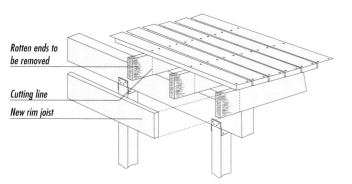

Rotten ends to be removed

Cutting line

New rim joist

Removing rotten joist ends

If the ends of cantilevered joists have rotted, carefully remove deck boards in the way, and the rim joist (if there is one). Snap a chalk line across the top of all joists along that side to establish the cutting line, far enough back to eliminate all bad wood. Mark each joist for straight, square cuts, using a combination square. Cut the joists with a power circular saw or handsaw. Treat the ends with wood preservative and, if you wish, nail on a new rim joist.

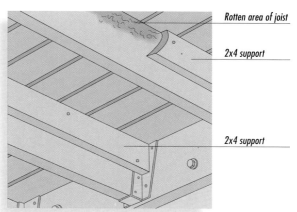

Rotten area of joist

2x4 support

2x4 support

Reinforcing a joist

To reinforce a rotten joist, first apply preservative to the rotten area. Then cut a 2 by 4 or 2 by 6 to make a support; make it long enough to extend past the rotten section about 6 inches on each end. Screw or nail the support onto the side of the joist, staggering fasteners every 10 to 12 inches.

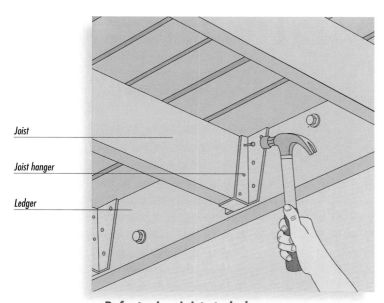

Joist

Joist hanger

Ledger

Refastening joists to ledger

If joist ends have loosened or rotted slightly where they connect to a ledger, coat the ends with preservative and slide metal joist hangers onto the ends. Force the hangers up tight and nail them to each joist and the ledger.

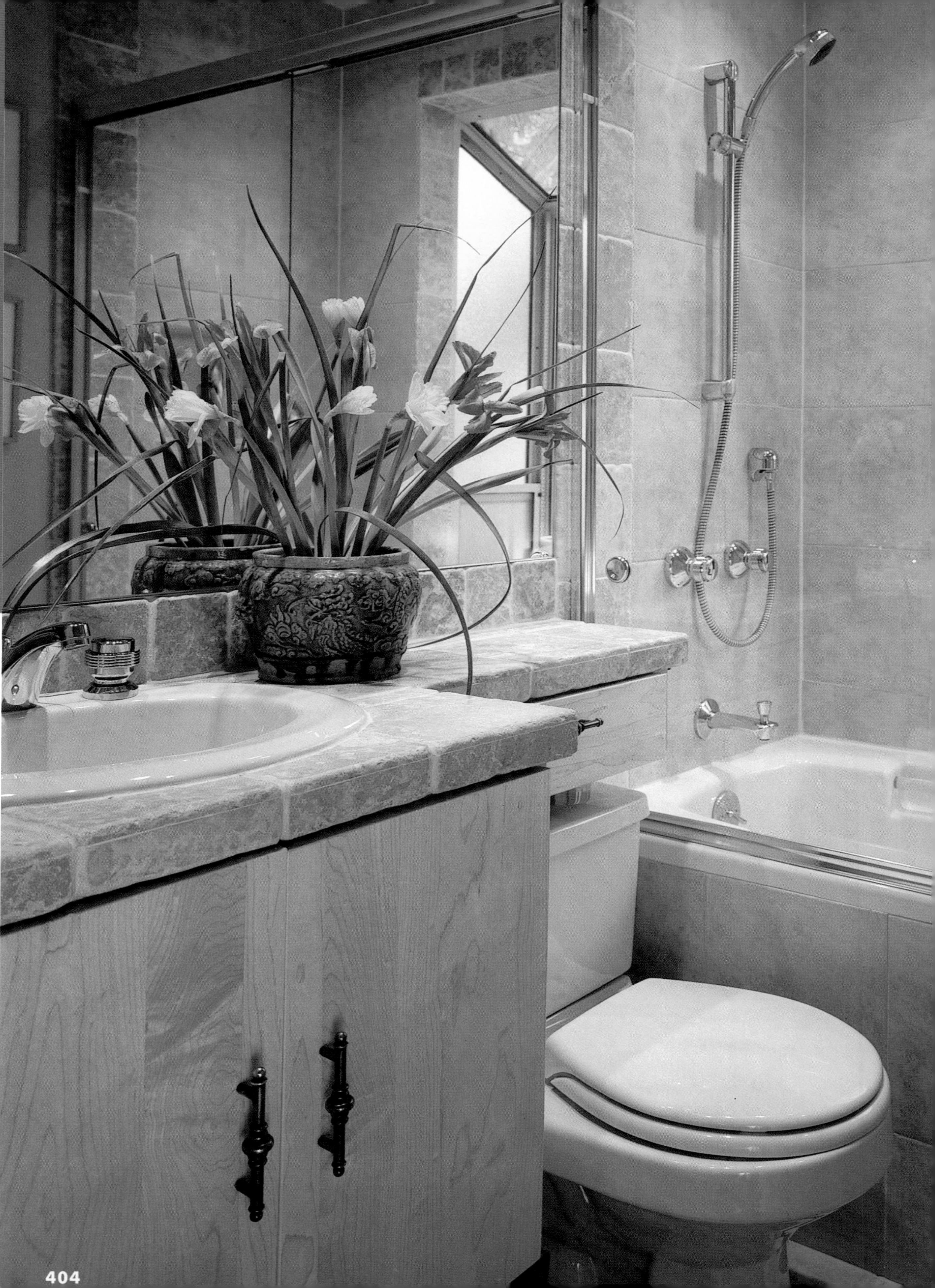

Plumbing

We tend to take plumbing for granted—until the system stops working properly. Then it becomes painfully apparent just how much we rely on this key system. Fortunately, plumbing repairs are among the most accessible for the do-it-yourselfer. And plumbing improvements such as updating fixtures or replacing water-wasting toilets can make a significant difference in the beauty and efficiency of a home.

Anatomy of Home Plumbing

You may be surprised at the simplicity of the system of pipes behind the walls and beneath the floors of your house. As shown below, your plumbing system is three separate but interdependent systems: supply, drain-waste, and vent. (The drain-waste and vent systems are interconnected, though, and are often referred to as the DWV system.) Before you begin any plumbing project, large or small, it's a good idea to become familiar with these systems. Once you understand how plumbing works, you'll find that making repairs or adding fixtures is nothing more than a series of logical connections.

Water enters your house through a main supply pipe that is connected to a water utility main or to a well on your property. Water travels through a meter or pressure tank before branching into separate lines for hot and cold water. The house shutoff valve shown below should be located near the meter or pressure tank. Close this valve to stop water from flowing anywhere in the house. Cold water may pass through a water softener or filtering system.

YOUR PLUMBING SYSTEM

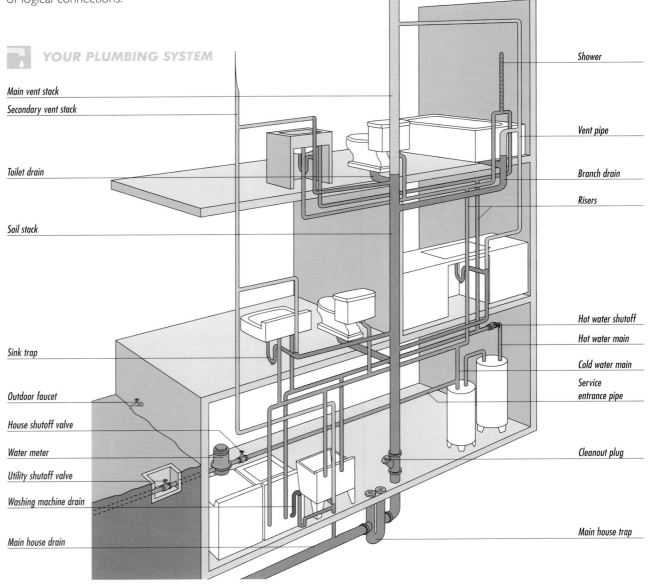

Main vent stack
Secondary vent stack
Toilet drain
Soil stack
Sink trap
Outdoor faucet
House shutoff valve
Water meter
Utility shutoff valve
Washing machine drain
Main house drain

Shower
Vent pipe
Branch drain
Risers
Hot water shutoff
Hot water main
Cold water main
Service entrance pipe
Cleanout plug
Main house trap

Supply pipes are always under pressure; if a leak occurs, water will spurt out until the water supply is shut off. This is why most homes have shutoff valves located near each fixture or appliance. By closing the valve, you can safely work on the fixture or appliance without affecting the water supply to the rest of the house.

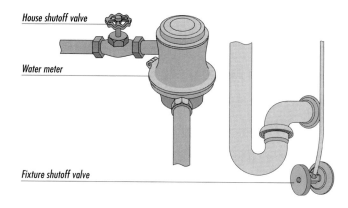

House shutoff valve

Water meter

Fixture shutoff valve

Cleanout fittings

Y-fitting with cleanout insert

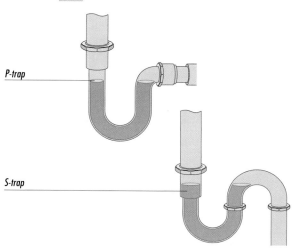

P-trap

S-trap

For most of their run, hot and cold pipes are next to each other. When they reach the fixtures or appliances, however, they separate. Pipes that run vertically from one floor to the next, usually in the walls, are called risers. Horizontal runs may be inside walls, fastened to floor joists, or buried in a concrete slab.

In older houses, the supply pipes are often composed of galvanized steel, with threaded connections. Over time, these pipes corrode and clog up, leading to leaks and reduced pressure. Newer houses more often have copper supply lines, which are easier to install and last much longer.

The drain-waste system relies on gravity, rather than pressure, to carry water and waste out of the house. Drain and waste pipes lead away from all fixtures at a precise slope. If the slope is too steep, water will run off too fast, leaving solids behind; if it's not steep enough, the drain will empty too slowly and back up into the fixtures. The normal pitch is $1/4$ inch for every horizontal foot of pipe. Cleanout fittings, such as those shown at left, provide easy access to drainpipes when clogs must be removed.

The workhorse in the drain-waste system is the soil stack, a vertical section of 3- or 4-inch-diameter pipe that carries waste away from toilets and other fixtures and connects with the main house drain. From there, the wastes flow to a sewer or septic tank.

The vent system gets rid of sewer gas and maintains atmospheric pressure inside the drain-waste system. To prevent potentially dangerous sewer gases from entering the house, each fixture should have a trap, as shown at left, which must be vented. P-traps are used in new-home construction, while S-traps can still be found in older houses.

GAS PIPING

If you plan to do any plumbing jobs and your house is supplied with gas, first learn to distinguish water supply pipes from the pipes that carry natural gas throughout the house. Gas pipes are usually black and run from the gas meter directly to an appliance or heating system. A separate shutoff valve for emergencies is required on each gas pipe. Do not try to work on gas piping yourself; call a professional.

Also, if your house is heated with a hot water or steam system, identify and avoid the heating pipes, which run from each heating outlet to the furnace or boiler. Leave repairs to an expert.

Plumbing Tools & Equipment

Plumbing improvements often require a host of tools for various aspects of the work—for example, carpentry tools for opening up walls. You probably already have many of these in your toolbox, but most jobs also require at least a few specialized tools that may be a bit less familiar. Here is a closer look at some of them and the jobs they handle. Fortunately, most of them are relatively inexpensive; the ones that aren't can usually be rented.

 PIPE SUPPORTS

When hanging and mounting pipes to framing members, use these common supports. A copper or plastic tube strap hangs copper or plastic tubing. A wire hanger can hang lightweight pipe and tubing. A pipe clamp, similar to a pipe strap but secured on one side only, is generally used for vertical pipes. Self-nailing pipe straps are used on galvanized steel pipe. Tubing hangers allow tubing to expand and contract with the flow of hot water. Plumber's tape is used for a variety of tasks.

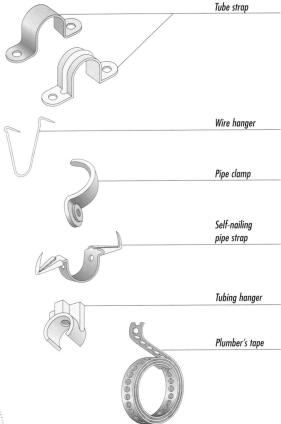

Tube strap

Wire hanger

Pipe clamp

Self-nailing pipe strap

Tubing hanger

Plumber's tape

 TOOLS FOR CLEARING CLOGS

With its funnel cup, a toilet plunger dislodges clogs by alternating pressure and suction. The flat face of a sink plunger works better for sink drains. A drain-and-trap auger, also known as a snake, is used to remove deep drain blockages. A toilet auger is designed to work down into the trap of a toilet.

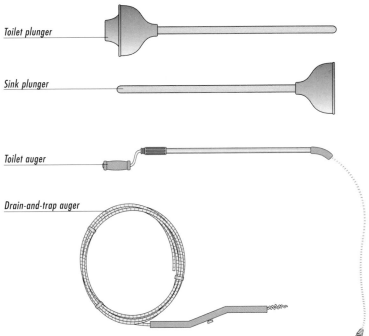

Toilet plunger

Sink plunger

Toilet auger

Drain-and-trap auger

Plumbing

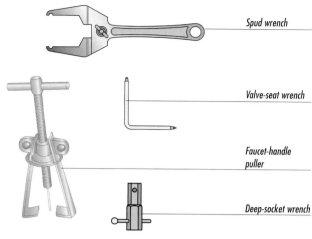

Spud wrench

Valve-seat wrench

Faucet-handle puller

Deep-socket wrench

Basin wrench

A spud wrench adjusts to fit up to 4-inch nuts, such as slip nuts on traps and tailpieces. A basin wrench gives access to nuts underneath sinks and other hard-to-reach places. A valve-seat wrench removes and replaces valve seats. If a faucet handle won't come off, get a faucet-handle puller. A deep-socket wrench is often necessary for removing recessed packing nuts on tub faucets.

Metal pipe cutter

Propane torch

Pipe wrench

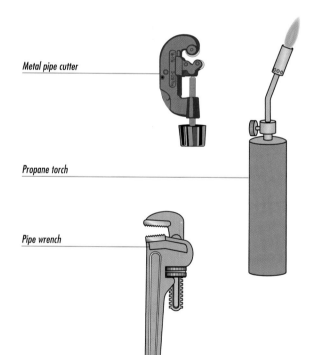

TOOLS FOR CUTTING & JOINING PIPE

You'll want a metal and/or plastic pipe cutter—which is much easier to use than a hacksaw. Pipe wrenches are necessary for gripping pipes and screwing together (or unscrewing) pipes and threaded fittings. Get two—one for holding a pipe, the other for turning the other pipe or fitting. Twelve-inch or 14-inch models will handle most chores. For soldering copper pipe, you'll need a propane torch with disposable tank.

PLUMBING SUPPLIES

You can buy plumbing supplies as you need them—or keep most of these on hand for typical plumbing repair and improvement tasks.

- Plumber's putty
- Pipe-joint compound
- Solder
- Flux
- Brush for flux
- Emery cloth
- Penetrating oil
- Plumber's grease
- Silicone grease (for rubber parts)

Working with Copper Tube

Copper tube or pipe is lightweight; fairly easy to join by sweat soldering or with flare, compression, or union fittings; resistant to corrosion; and rugged. Its smooth interior surface allows water to flow easily and doesn't allow mineral deposits to build up.

Types of Copper Pipe

Two kinds of copper tube are used in supply systems to carry fresh water: hard- and soft-temper. Another type of copper tube—corrugated supply—is used as flexible tubing to link hard or soft tube to fixtures. Large-diameter copper pipe is used in drain-waste–vent (DWV) systems.

HARD-TEMPER COPPER This is sold in lengths of 20 feet or less. Because it can't be bent without crimping, it must be cut and joined with fittings whenever a length is extended or it must change direction. It comes in three thicknesses: K (thick wall), L (medium wall), and M (thin wall); M is usually adequate for home plumbing. Nominal diameters range from $1/4$ to 1 inch and larger; actual diameters are greater. For tube-sized piping, the outside diameters are equal but the inside diameters vary; those with thicker walls are smaller on the inside.

SOFT-TEMPER COPPER This is sold in 20-, 60-, and 100-foot coils. More costly than hard-temper supply tube, soft-temper copper offers the advantage of not needing as many fittings, since it can be bent without crimping. Soft-temper copper is available in K and L thicknesses; L is adequate for above-ground plumbing. Nominal diameters range from $1/4$ to 1 inch; actual diameters are slightly greater.

COPPER DWV PIPE This is usually sold in 20-foot lengths and in nominal diameters of $1 1/2$, 2, and 3 inches. Copper DWV pipe with a nominal diameter larger than 2 inches is very expensive, so it isn't readily available.

FLEXIBLE TUBING Used for linking supply tube to fixtures, this corrugated, smooth, or chrome-plated copper comes in short lengths. It can conform to tighter curves than soft copper tube and has a nominal diameter of $3/8$ or $1/2$ inch. It often comes in kit form; follow the manufacturer's instructions.

Working with Copper Pipe

Sweat soldering is the best way to join copper pipe. Hard supply tubing can also be joined with compression fittings, soft supply tubing with compression or flare fittings. If you want to be able to take apart a run of copper tube in the future (to replace a water heater, for instance), without unsoldering or cutting the run, fit two short lengths of the pipe together with a union (see facing page).

 Caution: Before beginning any work on existing copper plumbing, be sure to turn the water off at the house shutoff valve (see page 406). Dry the pipe as much as possible. Wear safety glasses and gloves while working.

REMOVING PIPE Drain water from the pipe by closing the supply valve and opening a faucet that is lower in the system than the fitting you're removing. Cut copper pipe with a hacksaw or pipe cutter, or loosen a soldered joint with a propane torch as shown on the facing page. Brace and support the pipe to prevent sagging. Unscrew compression, flare, or union fittings.

CUTTING THE PIPE Before cutting a new length of pipe, be sure to consider the makeup distance, as shown on the facing page. You can use a hacksaw to cut copper pipe, but using a pipe cutter is much easier and makes a cleaner cut.

SOLDERING JOINTS Soldered joints, often called sweat joints, are made with standard copper fittings. You'll need a small propane torch, very fine sandpaper or emery cloth, a can of soldering flux, and some lead-free plumber's solder. See the illustrated sequence on page 412 for proper techniques.

SOLDERED FITTINGS

*Reducer
coupling (solder)*

90° elbow

T-fitting

45° elbow

FLARE FITTINGS
90° elbow (adapter)

90° elbow

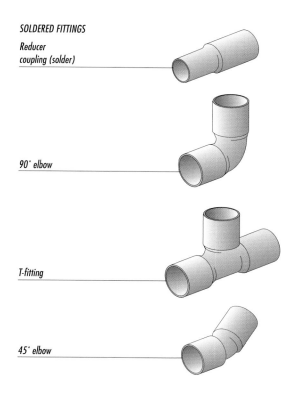

JOINING COPPER TO OTHER PIPES

Reducer fittings allow you to link pipes of different diameters; transition fittings enable you to join copper tube with plastic tube or galvanized steel pipe. If you link copper with galvanized steel, though, you must use special dielectric fittings to prevent electrolytic corrosion.

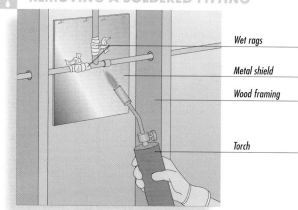

Wet rags

Metal shield

Wood framing

Torch

Drain water from the pipe as discussed on the facing page. Heat the fitting—not the pipe. Shield flammables with metal or a flame guard (keep a fire extinguisher nearby). Wet rags help cool the surrounding pipe.

MEASURING COPPER PIPE

To determine how much new tubing you need, measure the distance between fittings, then add the distance the tube will extend into the fittings ("makeup distance").

SOLDERED JOINT
Makeup distance

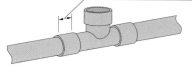

COMPRESSION JOINT
Makeup distance

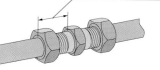

UNION JOINT
Makeup distance

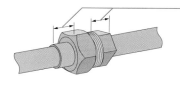

FLARED JOINT
Makeup distance

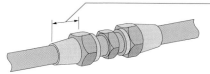

(continued on page 412)

411

Working with Copper Tube

(continued from page 411)

Use a pipe cutter designed for copper tubing. Twist the knob until the cutter wheel contacts the surface. Rotate the cutter around the pipe, tightening a little after each revolution, until the pipe snaps in two. Remove burrs from the pipe's edge using the reamer attached to the pipe cutter, or a round file.

USING A PIPE CUTTER

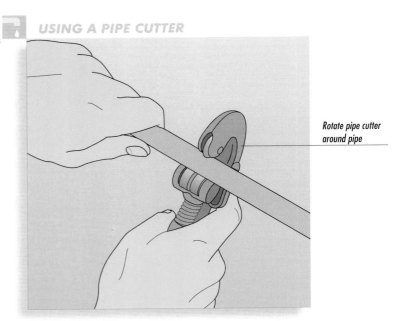

Rotate pipe cutter around pipe

SOLDERING JOINTS

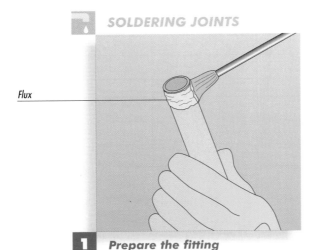

Flux

1 Prepare the fitting
Use fine sandpaper or emery cloth to polish the last inch of the outside of the pipe and inside of the fitting down to the shoulder until they are shiny. With a flux brush, apply flux to both polished surfaces. Place the fitting on the pipe. Turn the pipe or fitting back and forth to spread the flux evenly.

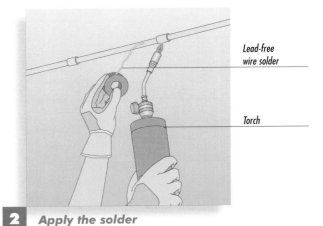

Lead-free wire solder

Torch

2 Apply the solder
With the fitting positioned on the pipe, heat the fitting evenly with the torch. Touch the solder to the joint occasionally. The instant the solder melts, remove the flame and keep the solder in contact with the joint. Capillary action will pull the solder into the joint. Remove the solder as soon as it encircles the fitting. When the joint cools, wipe off surplus flux with a damp rag.

Flared joint

A flared joint is only for soft copper tubing. Because it tends to weaken the end of the pipe, use a flared joint only if you can't solder and can't find the right compression fitting. Use a flaring tool to form the flare.

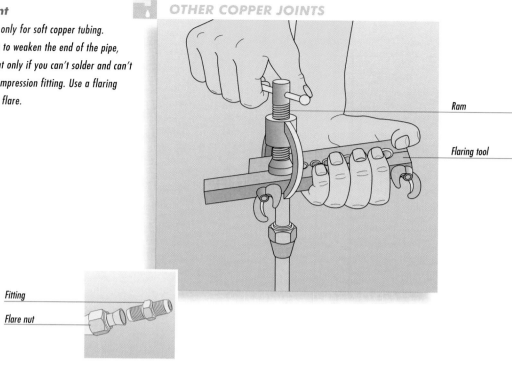

Ram

Flaring tool

Fitting

Flare nut

Broad shoulder

Compression nut

Compression ferrule

Threaded body

Compression joint

Compression fittings work equally well on hard and soft copper tubing, giving them an advantage over flared fittings when creating nonsoldered joints. A further advantage is that, unlike flare fittings, compression fittings don't require a special tool for assembly.

Union joint

Union joints are soldered joints, but you can easily disassemble them. They are available only as straight couplings and only link tubes of the same diameter. You slide on the nut, then sweat-solder the male and female shoulders. When the fittings cool, screw the nut onto the male shoulder.

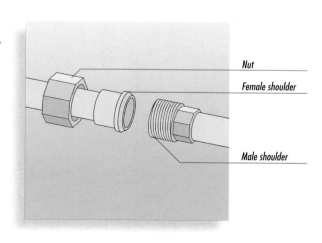

Nut

Female shoulder

Male shoulder

Working with Steel Pipe

For decades, galvanized-steel pipe was used for water supply pipes and sometimes for drain-waste–vent (DWV) pipes as well. Today, steel pipe is used primarily to route gas inside the home; old galvanized water supply pipes are routinely replaced with copper. There are occasions, however, when you may wish to use galvanized pipe for a repair.

Galvanized-steel pipe and fittings are coated with zinc to resist corrosion (uncoated "black" steel pipe is normally used for gas). Despite this additional protection, galvanized-steel pipe not only corrodes faster than cast iron or copper, but because of its rough interior surface, collects mineral deposits that, over time, impede water flow. Many fittings are available for joining galvanized steel with steel, copper, or plastic pipe.

You may prefer to replace a leaking length of galvanized-steel pipe with the same type of pipe. It often requires less equipment and expense than using copper, plastic, or cast iron. But when extending a supply system of galvanized pipe, use copper (page 410) or plastic (page 416).

Fittings are connected to pipe by means of tapered pipe threads. Galvanized-steel pipe is sold threaded on both ends. If you cut into existing galvanized pipe, to replace a section for example, you'll have to reconnect the ends with a union—a special fitting that allows you to join two threaded pipe ends. Reconnecting will require cutting threads at the pipes' ends or replacing the pipe sections with lengths that are threaded at both ends.

Threading pipe is not particularly difficult, but it requires specialized tools. Some home centers will thread pipes for you for a nominal fee—you just give them the precise measurements. Or you can rent threading tools, but this may eliminate any savings of doing the work yourself.

PIPE & FITTINGS Galvanized-steel pipe comes in nominal diameters of $1/4$ to $2 1/2$ inches and in lengths of 10 and 21 feet, or it can be custom-cut and threaded. Also available are short threaded pieces—called nipples—in $1/2$-inch increments, from $1 1/2$ to 6 inches long, and then in 1-inch increments up to 12 inches long (the diameters match the pipes).

STEEL PIPE FITTINGS

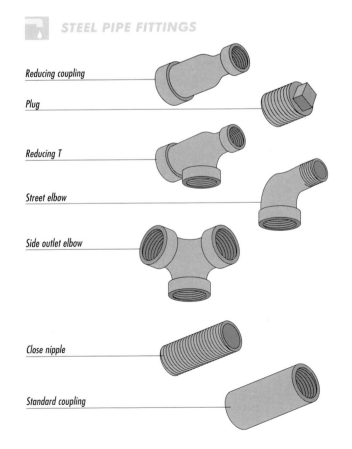

Reducing coupling
Plug
Reducing T
Street elbow
Side outlet elbow
Close nipple
Standard coupling

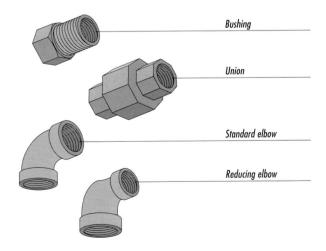

Bushing
Union
Standard elbow
Reducing elbow

MEASURING & CUTTING Galvanized pipe must be cut perfectly square so that threads can be started accurately. Use a pipe cutter with a blade designed for steel pipe, and follow the directions for cutting copper pipe given on page 412. After you have finished cutting, use the reamer in the cutter handle to remove burrs from inside the pipe. When measuring for the lengths you'll need, be sure to allow for the makeup distance as shown below.

GENERAL TIPS Loosening galvanized supply pipes requires the simultaneous use of two pipe wrenches. If there is no convenient union in the run, saw the pipe run in two. Steady the pipe with your hand or a wrench. Use a reciprocating saw or coarse-toothed hacksaw, and put a bucket underneath to catch spills. Don't let the cut pipe sag.

Support horizontal runs of new pipe every 6 to 8 feet, and vertical runs every 8 to 10 feet. When joining pipes to fittings, wrap the threads with pipe-joint compound or pipe-thread tape (see below right) to seal them against rust and make assembly and disassembly easier. Apply pipe-joint compound with the brush attached to the lid of the container, using just enough to fill the male threads.

Screw the pipe and fitting together by hand as far as you can. Finish tightening with two pipe wrenches, as shown at right, reversing the direction of the wrenches.

USING PIPE WRENCHES

Always use pipe wrenches in pairs—one to grasp the fitting, the other to grasp the pipe inserted into the fitting. Rotate only one of the wrenches. A fitting always screws on clockwise and off counterclockwise. Apply pressure toward the jaws on the wrenches as shown.

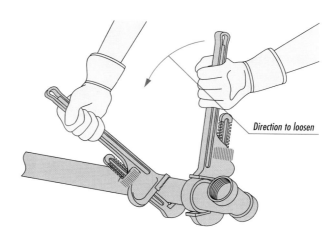

Direction to loosen

Caution: Before beginning any work on galvanized-steel plumbing, be sure to turn the water off at the house shutoff valve (see page 406) and open a faucet that is low in the system to drain the pipes. Wear safety glasses and work gloves when cutting pipe.

MEASURING PIPES

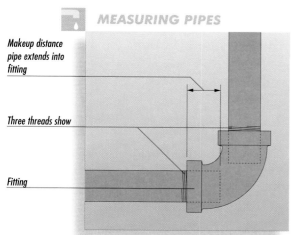

Makeup distance
pipe extends into
fitting

Three threads show

Fitting

To determine exactly how much new galvanized-steel pipe you will need, measure the distances between the new fittings, then add the makeup distances that the pipes will extend into the fittings. The distance allowed for each fitting should be less than the pipe's diameter.

USING PIPE-THREAD TAPE

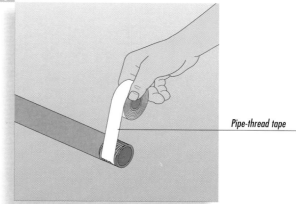

Pipe-thread tape

Before joining pipes to fittings, wrap the male threads with pipe-thread tape (or use pipe-joint compound). Wrap the threads in a clockwise direction, 1 1/2 turns. Pull the tape tight enough so that the threads show through.

Working with Plastic Pipe

Plastic pipe is lightweight, inexpensive, and easy to cut and fit. Unlike metal pipe, plastic is also self-insulating and resistant to damage from chemicals and electrolytic corrosion. In addition, plastic's smooth interior surface provides less flow resistance than metal.

Plastic pipe is used for drain-waste–vent (DWV) lines in new construction and to replace sections of old cast-iron pipe. Local plumbing codes often require you to use either ABS or PVC. ABS is black, while PVC is white or cream-colored. (Do not try to mix ABS and PVC; their fittings are not interchangeable.) Some types of plastic tubing can also be used for water supply pipes, although codes are often quite strict about this. PVC is often used for cold-water supply, while CPVC and flexible PE are frequently allowed for hot and cold water lines. Check your local code before buying any plastic pipe.

PLASTIC PIPE FITTINGS

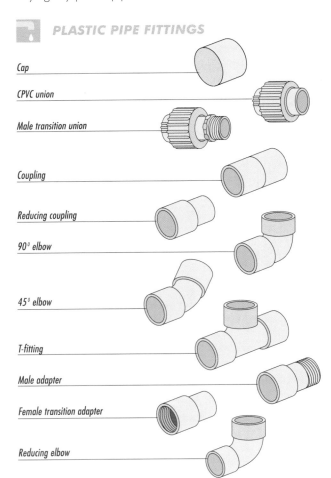

Cap

CPVC union

Male transition union

Coupling

Reducing coupling

90° elbow

45° elbow

T-fitting

Male adapter

Female transition adapter

Reducing elbow

CUTTING PLASTIC PIPE

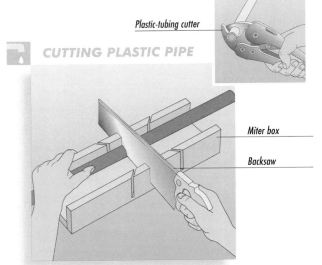

Plastic-tubing cutter

Miter box

Backsaw

You can cut plastic pipe with a variety of tools. A plastic-tubing cutter makes quick, clean cuts on pipe up to about 2 inches in diameter. You can cut any size of plastic pipe with a fine-toothed backsaw or hacksaw. To ensure square cuts, use a miter box.

MEASURING PIPE LENGTHS

First determine the face-to-face distance between new fittings, then add the distance the pipe will extend into the fittings (the makeup distance).

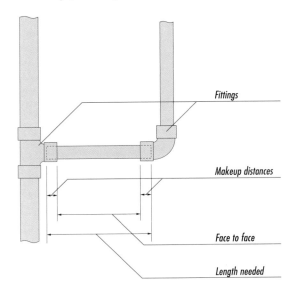

Fittings

Makeup distances

Face to face

Length needed

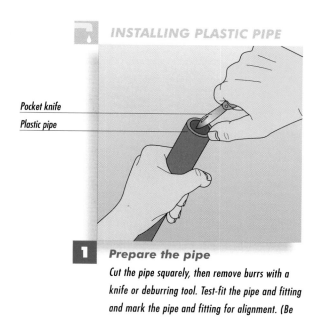

Pocket knife
Plastic pipe

1 *Prepare the pipe*

Cut the pipe squarely, then remove burrs with a knife or deburring tool. Test-fit the pipe and fitting and mark the pipe and fitting for alignment. (Be aware that the pipe will not slide into the fitting completely until the cement is applied.)

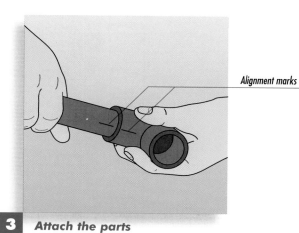

Solvent cement

2 *Apply the cement*

Using the appropriate solvent cement, spread a smooth coat onto all mating surfaces (PVC and CPVC require a special primer first). Work in a well-ventilated area, avoid breathing the fumes, and keep flammables away from the cement.

Rigid plastic pipe (PVC, CPVC, and ABS) is generally sold in lengths of 10 and 20 feet. It is lightweight and easy to work with, making it an ideal material for do-it-yourselfers. Sections are joined by a process known as "solvent welding." Special cement is spread on the mating surfaces, which become fused together once the parts are joined.

Before beginning any work on plastic pipe, be sure to turn the water off at the house shutoff valve (see page 406) and drain the pipes by opening a faucet that is low in the system. Wear safety glasses.

If you must cut already installed pipe with a saw, brace the pipe to prevent excess motion that could affect the squareness of the cut.

When hanging pipe, use plastic hangers that hold it snugly yet allow it to move with expansion and contraction. Support vertical and horizontal runs every 4 feet.

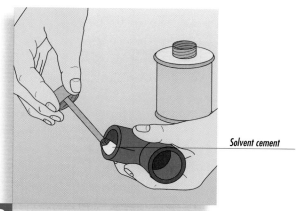

Alignment marks

3 *Attach the parts*

Immediately join the pipe and fitting with a slight twist, bringing the fitting into correct alignment. Hold for a few seconds while the cement sets. Wipe away any excess. If you make an error, cut off the fitting and replace it with another, joining it with two couplings and two short lengths of pipe.

Working with Cast-Iron Pipe

If your home was built before 1970, there's a good chance it has cast-iron piping in its drain-waste–vent (DWV) system. Cast-iron pipe is strong, resists corrosion, and is dense enough to be the quietest of all piping materials.

There are two types of fittings for cast iron: bell-and-spigot and no-hub, or hubless. Bell-and-spigot joints are usually found in older homes and might have been joined using molten lead and oakum. These materials are rarely used in residences now, as most codes no longer permit lead in DWV piping. The no-hub joint is most commonly used because it takes up little space—a 3-inch stack will fit into a 2-by-4 stud wall without extra preparation. It also can be used to modify bell-and-spigot systems.

USING A SNAP CUTTER

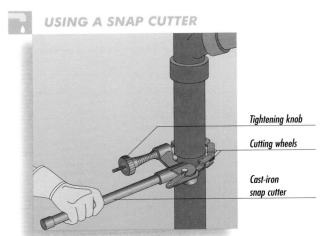

Tightening knob

Cutting wheels

Cast-iron snap cutter

A snap cutter, available at equipment rental stores, can be used to cut cast-iron pipe (or you can use a reciprocating saw with a metal-cutting blade). The snap cutter uses a ratchet action to increase pressure equally on cutting wheels that encircle the pipe, causing the pipe to snap.

CAST-IRON FITTINGS

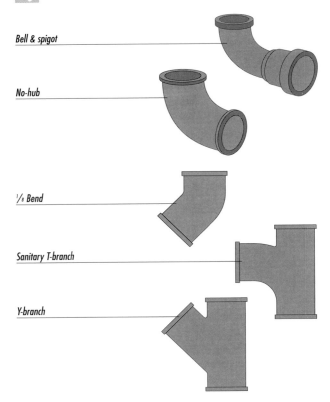

Bell & spigot

No-hub

⅛ Bend

Sanitary T-branch

Y-branch

A wide variety of fittings is available for use with both types of cast-iron pipe. Drainage fittings, unlike water-supply fittings, don't have interior shoulders, and each has a built-in fall or slope to allow for gravity.

No-hub cast-iron pipe ranges in diameter from 1½ inches to 4 inches and larger. It is usually bought in 10-foot lengths (shorter lengths are available for bell-and-spigot). Cast iron should be supported every 4 feet in horizontal runs, and within a few inches of joints. Plumber's tape, hangers, and straps are commonly used.

CUTTING THE PIPE When cutting cast-iron pipe, wear safety glasses and work gloves. Be sure to turn off the water supply and alert others in the house not to use toilets and other plumbing fixtures. Before removing pipe, securely support the section to be removed, as well as the sections of pipe on either side of it. You can use plumber's tape for this support—pull it taut and nail it to nearby joists or studs. To determine how much new no-hub pipe you need, simply measure the length of pipe that has been removed.

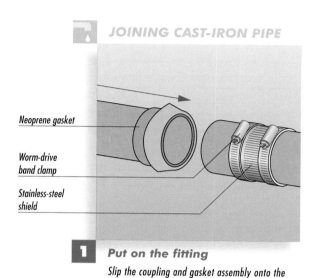

Neoprene gasket

Worm-drive
band clamp

Stainless-steel
shield

1 Put on the fitting

Slip the coupling and gasket assembly onto the end of the pipe or fitting. The gasket sleeve has a built-in stop to help you center the assembly at the joint. Move the stainless-steel shield away from the joint and fold the lip of the gasket back.

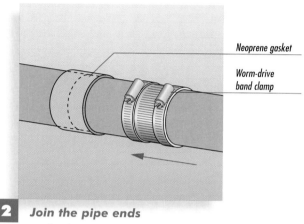

Neoprene gasket

Worm-drive
band clamp

2 Join the pipe ends

Set the edges of the pipe together. Roll the gasket lip into place. Slide the shield over the gasket.

To cut cast-iron pipe, the tool of choice for do-it-yourselfers is a reciprocating saw equipped with a metal-cutting blade. You can also use a snap cutter, as shown in the illustration on the facing page. In a pinch, you can use a hacksaw, cold chisel, and ball-peen hammer to cut the pipe. Chalk a cutting line all around the pipe, then score it to a depth of $1/16$ inch with the hacksaw. Tap all around the pipe with the hammer and chisel until it breaks.

JOINING THE PIPE To connect a no-hub fitting or pipe to existing cast-iron pipe, use a no-hub coupling (see above). The coupling consists of a neoprene gasket, a stainless-steel shield, and worm-drive band clamps for compressing the gasket around the pipe.

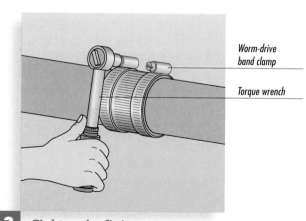

Worm-drive
band clamp

Torque wrench

3 Tighten the fitting

Use a special torque wrench to tighten the band screws. The wrench has an internal clutch that releases when the screws are as tight as necessary. A wrench preset for the torque needed may be found at an equipment-rental store.

Roughing-in Fixtures

In this section we'll look at a variety of common plumbing improvements that involve changing or installing plumbing fixtures. Of course, to install a fixture, the proper configuration of pipes must be in place—usually in the wall and/or under the floor. The first stage of preparing for fixtures is known as "roughing-in" the plumbing.

The proper rough-in for fixtures depends upon a number of factors, notably the way the fixture is made, the room's layout, and building and plumbing codes (be sure to check your local codes). When you buy a new sink, toilet, or similar fixture, rough-in templates and instructions are nearly always included with the product. Carefully read the manufacturer's directions before roughing in a fixture.

Following are directions for roughing-in two common fixture improvements: a bathroom sink and a toilet.

A bathroom sink is fairly easy to install and has little effect on a drain's efficiency, though a new sink must be vented as stipulated by your local code. You can run pipes along the surface of a wall in certain circumstances, but it's best to handle all rough-in plumbing during the framing stage of construction, when the walls are open, so pipes may be concealed. Otherwise, in most cases, you'll have to remove wall surface materials and replace them when you're finished.

A toilet is the most troublesome fixture to install in a house because it requires its own vent (2-inch minimum) and at least a 3-inch drain. If it is on a branch drain, a toilet cannot be upstream from a sink or shower.

ROUGHING-IN A BATHROOM SINK

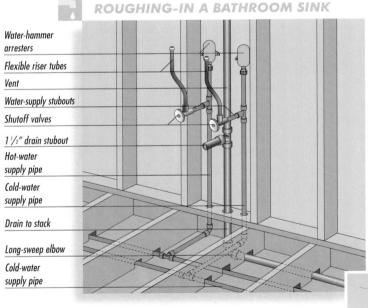

Water-hammer arresters
Flexible riser tubes
Vent
Water-supply stubouts
Shutoff valves
1 ½" drain stubout
Hot-water supply pipe
Cold-water supply pipe
Drain to stack
Long-sweep elbow
Cold-water supply pipe

In addition to vent connections, you will need ½-inch hot- and cold-water supply stubouts; shutoff valves; transition fittings, if necessary; and flexible riser tubes. You may also need water-hammer arresters on the supply pipes to prevent pipes from banging.

Centerline
Sink rim
Supply stubouts
6" to 8"
31"
4"
Drain outlet
18"

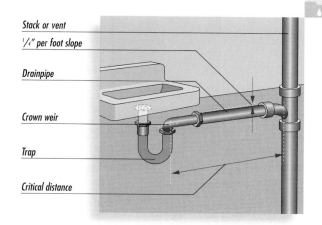

Stack or vent

¹/₄" per foot slope

Drainpipe

Crown weir

Trap

Critical distance

The maximum distance allowed from the trap to the stack or vent is called the critical distance. The drain outlet cannot be below the level of the trap's crown weir, as shown. If the fixture drain is vented properly within the critical distance, the drainpipe may run on indefinitely to the actual stack or main drain.

ROUGHING-IN A TOILET

The closet bend and toilet floor flange must be roughed in first, as shown (be sure to allow for the wall covering material's thickness when measuring the outlet's distance from framing). The floor flange must be positioned at the level of the eventual finished floor. You will also need the following piping supplies: ¹/₂-inch riser tube, a cold-water supply stubout, shutoff valve, and flexible riser tube.

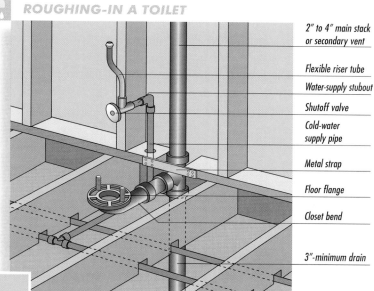

2" to 4" main stack or secondary vent

Flexible riser tube

Water-supply stubout

Shutoff valve

Cold-water supply pipe

Metal strap

Floor flange

Closet bend

3"-minimum drain

Center line

Supply stubout

12" from finished wall (typically)

Bowl outlet

Finished floor

8"

4"

FRAMING A TOILET DRAIN

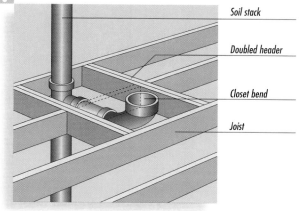

Soil stack

Doubled header

Closet bend

Joist

When installing a new toilet, you may need to cut an entire section out of a joist to accommodate the drain piping. Reinforce that section by nailing doubled headers on both sides of the cut.

421

Installing a New Sink

One great way to update a kitchen or bath, particularly if you're also redoing the cabinets or counters, is to install a new sink (actually, the proper term for a bathroom washbowl is "lavatory" or—for short—"lav"). In recent years, plumbing-fixture designers have created a wonderful smorgasbord of kitchen sinks and high-style bathroom lavatories that turn what was once a mundane fixture into a work of art.

Kitchen sinks tend to be larger and deeper than bathroom lavs, with a large drain hole located in the center of the bowl. Lavatories have a smaller drain hole and are usually made with an overflow hole that prevents water from running over the sides. Despite the differences, both types are installed in the same manner.

KITCHEN SINKS Sinks are available in single-, double-, and triple-bowl designs made from stainless or enameled steel, porcelain-coated cast iron, composites, or other durable materials. Self-rimming sinks are extremely easy to install—you simply seat the sink in a hole cut in the countertop, as shown on page 424. Recessed sinks have a lip that is covered by tile—making installation of this type a bit trickier. A third type of kitchen sink sits flush with the countertop; it has a metal sink rim that hides the gap between sink and counter. See the photographs on these pages for examples of these styles.

BATHROOM SINKS From white porcelain classics to colorful contemporaries, lavatories are made in hundreds of styles and finishes, from vitreous clay or fire clay to metal or glass—just about any material that will hold water. In addition, lavs (and kitchen sinks) are made from low-maintenance, solid-surface material that is integrated seamlessly into the countertop.

As with kitchen sinks, lavatories are categorized by their support method: the familiar pedestal, the wall-mounted, the countertop-mounted, and the popular new "consoles," which stand on legs in table-like fashion. Recessed or under-mount bowls, mounted to the underside of the counter by special clamps, are quite popular because they allow easy clean-up of the counter and sink. They can be installed in practically any type of counter: tile, wood, marble, stone, laminate, or solid surface.

Self-rimming kitchen sink offers both beauty and durable cast-iron construction.

Chrome and glass combine to create a stunning contemporary wall-mounted lav.

Self-rimming bathroom basin features a hand-painted look—just one of countless decorative styles available.

Easy cleanup and a clear, uninterrupted counter make an under-mounted sink a popular choice.

For practical bathrooms, lavatory bowls usually combine with a countertop that caps a vanity cabinet, which hides exposed plumbing and provides hidden storage. This setup also allows for plenty of counter space, often enough for two bowls with counter to spare. For more about installing vanities and basin-countertop combinations, see pages 250–253.

INSTALLATION TIPS When installing a sink in a new countertop, you'll first need to make a cutout for the sink. Nearly all sinks are sold with a template for marking this hole. You can also set the sink upside down on the countertop and trace the outline. If you do that, though, be sure that you do not cut along the traced line; instead, draw a second line about ³/₄ inch inside the existing line—this will be your cut line. Locate the cutout according to the manufacturer's directions—normally, about 1³/₄ inches from the countertop's front edge. The sink usually should be centered over a cabinet; avoid placing it directly over a cabinet side or other obstacles.

Before making the cut, find a scrap board long enough to span the cutout and attach it with a screw to the center of the cutout—this board will prevent the cutout section from falling away as you finish the cut.

When installing a cast-iron kitchen sink, you can use a bead of plumber's putty rather than adhesive to seal the edges; the weight of the sink will hold it in place. If you are installing a recessed or frame-mounted sink, attach the mounting clips or metal strip included with the unit.

METHODS OF MOUNTING SINKS

Self-rimming sinks have a molded lip that rests on the edge of the countertop cutout. Recessed or undermount sinks fit flush with the countertop or attach to the counter's underside. Frame-mounted kitchen sinks have a metal rim that hides the gap between the sink and the counter.

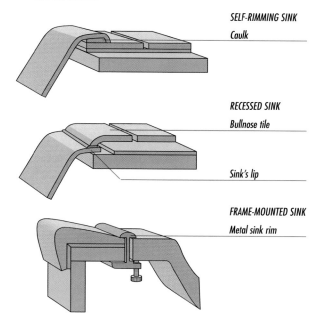

SELF-RIMMING SINK
Caulk

RECESSED SINK
Bullnose tile

Sink's lip

FRAME-MOUNTED SINK
Metal sink rim

(continued on page 424)

Installing a New Sink

(continued from page 423)

INSTALLING A SELF-RIMMING SINK

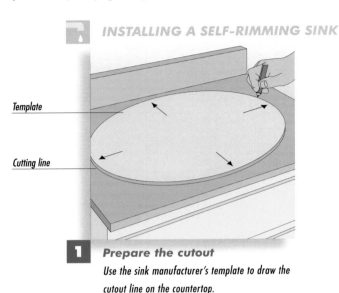

Template

Cutting line

1 **Prepare the cutout**
Use the sink manufacturer's template to draw the cutout line on the countertop.

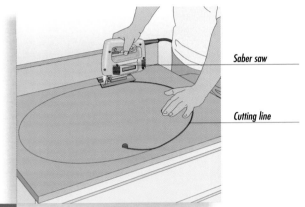

Saber saw

Cutting line

2 **Cut out the countertop**
Carefully drill a ³/₈-inch starter hole inside the cut line. Using a fine-tooth blade in a saber saw, make the cutout.

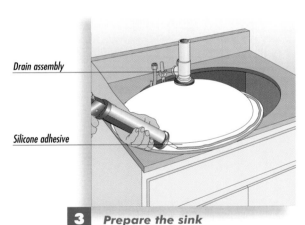

Drain assembly

Silicone adhesive

3 **Prepare the sink**
If you haven't already done so, install the faucet and drain assembly in the sink. Place the sink upside down and run a bead of silicone adhesive along the underside of the molded lip (or use the adhesive included with the new sink).

Press in place

4 **Set the sink**
Turn the sink over and, holding it by the drain hole, carefully set it in place. Make sure the sink's edge is aligned with the countertop's front edge. Press firmly around the lip to form a good seal. After the adhesive has set, apply a bead of latex caulk around the edge, then smooth it with a wet finger.

Plumbing Improvements

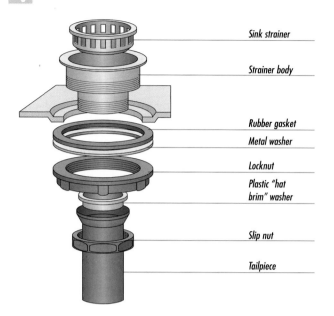
Sink strainer

Strainer body

Rubber gasket

Metal washer

Locknut

Plastic "hat brim" washer

Slip nut

Tailpiece

INSTALLING A STRAINER

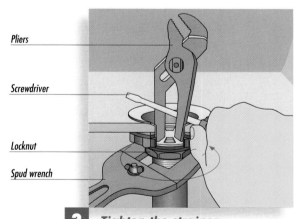

¹/₈" bead of plumber's putty

Strainer body

1 Prepare the strainer

To install a strainer, place a bead of plumber's putty around the bottom edge of the housing lip, then press the housing into the drain hole. Attach the gasket and washer, then tighten the locknut. Attach the tailpiece to the housing with the slip nut and washer.

PARTS OF A BATHROOM POP-UP

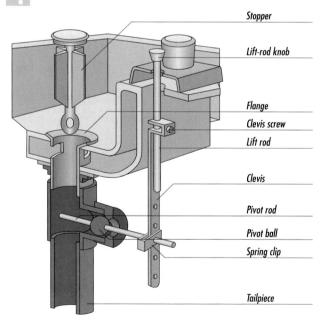

Stopper

Lift-rod knob

Flange

Clevis screw

Lift rod

Clevis

Pivot rod

Pivot ball

Spring clip

Tailpiece

Pliers

Screwdriver

Locknut

Spud wrench

2 Tighten the strainer

Have a helper hold the handles of a pair of pliers in the housing with a screwdriver to prevent it from turning while you tighten the locknut. Remove any excess plumber's putty.

(continued on page 426)

425

Installing a New Sink

(continued from page 425)

 REMOVING A WALL-HUNG SINK

Before adding a new bathroom sink, it's often necessary to remove an older wall-hung model. Most rest on a bracket attached to the wall or are bolted to the wall.

Supply tubes

Trap

1 **Disconnect the trap & supplies**

Turn off the water supplies. Place a bucket under the sink and disconnect the supply tubes. Using rib-joint pliers, disconnect the nuts on either side of the trap and remove the trap assembly.

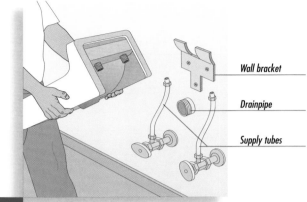

Wall bracket

Drainpipe

Supply tubes

2 **Lift off the sink**

With a utility knife, cut through any caulk or sealant around the sink's edges. Lift the sink off the wall bracket and remove the bracket. If your sink sits on angle brackets or is bolted to the wall, remove all screws or bolts before lifting the sink.

 INSTALLING A PEDESTAL SINK

Most pedestal sinks consist of a sink and the pedestal (or base). Nearly all come with installation instructions and the materials for supply and drain plumbing rough-ins.

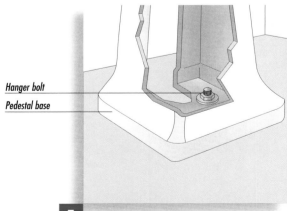

Hanger bolt
Pedestal base

1 **Mount the base**

Following the manufacturer's instructions, position and bolt the pedestal to the floor using double-ended hanger bolts.

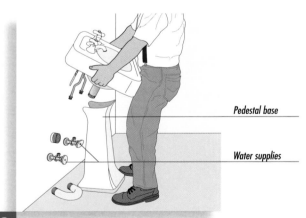

Pedestal base

Water supplies

2 **Connect the sink**

Set the sink onto the pedestal and bolt it to the wall if specified by the instructions. If the sink has a nut or rod that connects it to the pedestal, secure the device. Last, connect the water-supply tubes and the drain assembly.

Tub & Shower Improvements

Bathtub and shower improvements generally involve protecting the surrounding area from water damage by maintaining the proper seals. For example, as a bathtub is repeatedly filled and emptied, it will tend to shift under the weight, breaking the seal between the top of the tub and the wall. You can renew the seal with silicone rubber tub caulk or—for a more permanent improvement—cover the joint with bead tiles as shown below left. If the grout between the tile around your tub or shower is cracked or crumbling, replace it as discussed on pages 170–171. For information on repairing and replacing tub and shower faucets and shower heads, see pages 450–451.

SEALING AROUND A TUB

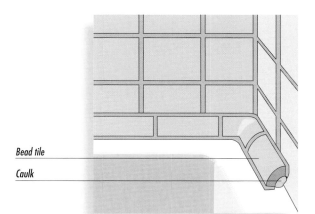

Caulk

Applying new tub caulk
First, cut away the old caulk with a utility knife. Clean and dry the area thoroughly. Apply silicone rubber tile-and-tub caulk. For most, you hold the tube at a 45-degree angle and slowly squeeze in a steady, continuous motion. Smooth with your finger and wipe off excess with a rag.

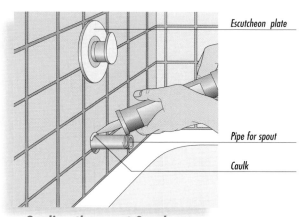

Escutcheon plate

Pipe for spout

Caulk

Sealing the spout & valve
To prevent water from running behind the valve's escutcheon plate and the spout, seal the area behind them with silicone rubber caulk.

Bead tile

Caulk

Applying edging tiles
If you find that the caulked bathtub-wall joint opens repeatedly, apply bead edging (quarter-round) tiles that match or accent the existing tile, using rubber caulk as an adhesive. Be sure to first cut away old caulk and clean and dry the area.

PREVENT SCALDING SHOWERS

If the water in your shower turns scalding hot when a toilet is flushed elsewhere in the house, you can eliminate the hazard and the discomfort of fluctuating water temperatures by installing a pressure-balance shower valve.

Compensating for changes in water pressure that occur when water is drawn to another fixture (such as a toilet or washing machine), a pressure-balance valve keeps shower and tub water temperature constant. And, if the cold-water supply stops for some reason, it will protect you by reducing water flow to a trickle.

The difficulty of installation depends upon the situation. You (or a plumber) may be able to replace a conventional single-handle valve by removing the cover plate. But replacing a two-handle valve may require removing tile or cutting into the wall (manufacturers sell special plates designed to cover the cut-away area).

Installing a New Faucet

New deck-mounted faucets are available in a wide variety of styles and configurations. For the most part, however, they are installed as shown below. Choose a faucet with inlet shanks spaced to fit the holes in the sink. If possible, take the old faucet along when you buy the replacement. Also, measure the diameter of the supply pipes. Choose a new faucet that comes with clear instructions and is made by a well-known company that has repair kits and replacement parts available.

Some faucets come with the copper or plastic tubing for the water supply already attached. Plain copper flexible tubing is most often used where it will be concealed by a cabinet. If the tubing will be in plain view, or the existing tubes are damaged, you might want to buy replacements.

Before doing any work on a faucet, turn off the water at the fixture shutoff valves or the house shutoff. Have a bucket ready to catch water left in the supply tubes.

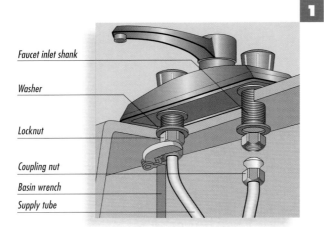

Faucet inlet shank

Washer

Locknut

Coupling nut

Basin wrench

Supply tube

1

Remove the old faucet
Use a basin wrench to remove the nuts that connect the supply tubes to the faucet inlet shanks. Loosen the locknuts on both shanks and remove the locknuts and the washers. Lift out the faucet.

Remove other parts
If you are working on a bathroom sink with a pop-up assembly, remove the stopper (see page 455). On a kitchen sink with a spray hose attachment, use an adjustable or basin wrench to loosen the nut connecting the hose to the hose nipple under the faucet body.

2

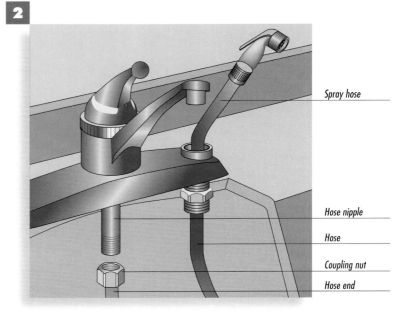

Spray hose

Hose nipple

Hose

Coupling nut

Hose end

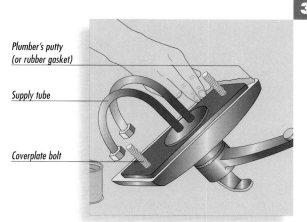

Plumber's putty
(or rubber gasket)

Supply tube

Coverplate bolt

3 **Prepare the new faucet**

Clean the surface where the new faucet will sit. Most faucets have a gasket that goes on the bottom; if yours does not, apply plumber's putty around the edges before setting the faucet in place.

Install the new faucet **4**

If your faucet comes with attached tubes, as shown, straighten the tubes enough to feed them through the middle sink hole. Press the faucet onto the sink and securely bolt it in place. If your sink has a spray hose, attach it next. For a faucet like that shown in Step 1, screw the washers and locknuts onto the faucet inlet shanks by hand; tighten further with a basin wrench.

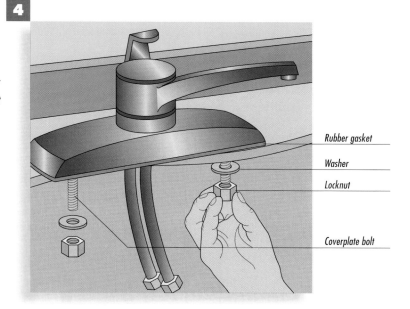

Rubber gasket

Washer

Locknut

Coverplate bolt

5 **Connect the supply tubes**

Connect the supply tubes, gently bending them to meet the shutoff valves. Join the supply tubes to the shutoff valves, using compression nuts or flared fittings. Turn on the water and check for leaks.

Supply tube

Compression nut

Shutoff valve

Installing a Toilet

If your toilet has seen better days, you'll be glad to know that replacing it is a one-afternoon project that you can tackle yourself. Installing a toilet in a new location is more of a challenge because of the need to extend supply pipes and drainpipes. You may want to have a professional run the pipes to the desired spot, then do the installation yourself.

When shopping for a toilet, you'll find there are many choices. The two-piece type illustrated here is the most common. Most toilets are ready to install, with the flush mechanism already in place. With the toilet you will get the necessary gaskets, washers, and hardware for fitting the tank to the bowl, but you may need to buy hold-down bolts and a wax gasket. Also, buy a can of plumber's putty to secure the toilet base to the floor and the caps to the hold-down bolts. Finally, if the old toilet didn't have a shut-off valve, it's a good idea to install one now.

Before starting, turn off the water at the shutoff valve or the house shutoff valve. Flush the toilet to empty the bowl and tank, and sponge out any water that remains.

The hold-down bolts that fasten a toilet to the floor may be corroded to the point where you can't remove the nuts. If this is the case, soak them with penetrating oil or cut the bolts off with a hacksaw. When you reinstall the tank on the bowl and bolt the bowl to the floor, be careful not to overtighten—this could crack the porcelain.

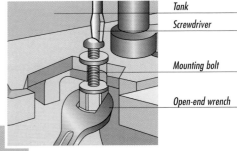

Tank
Screwdriver
Mounting bolt
Open-end wrench

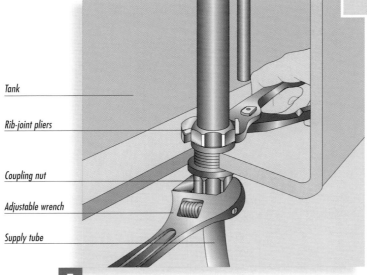

Tank
Rib-joint pliers
Coupling nut
Adjustable wrench
Supply tube

1 **Remove the old tank**
Unfasten the coupling nut on the supply tube at the bottom of the tank. If the supply tube is kinked or corroded, replace it with a new one. Then unbolt the empty tank, using a screwdriver to hold the mounting bolt inside the tank while unfastening its nut with a wrench from below (see detail).

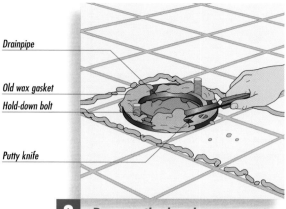

Drainpipe

Old wax gasket

Hold-down bolt

Putty knife

2 Remove the bowl

Pry the caps off the hold-down bolts and remove the nuts with an adjustable wrench. Gently rock the bowl from side to side to break the seal between the bowl and the floor, then lift the bowl straight up, tilting it forward slightly to avoid spilling any remaining water. Stuff a rag in the drainpipe. Clean the wax gasket remains from the floor flange and replace the old hold-down bolts if necessary. (If the floor flange is cracked or broken, replace it, too.)

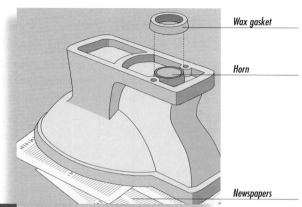

Wax gasket

Horn

Newspapers

3 Install the wax gasket

Turn the new bowl upside-down on a cushioned surface. Place a new wax gasket over the horn on the bottom of the bowl, with the tapered side facing away from the bowl. If you use a wax gasket with a plastic collar, install it with the collar away from the bowl. (First make sure that the collar will fit into the floor flange.)

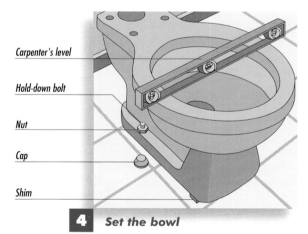

Carpenter's level

Hold-down bolt

Nut

Cap

Shim

4 Set the bowl

Remove the rag from the drainpipe. Gently lower the bowl into place atop the flange, using the bolts as guides. Press down firmly while twisting and rocking. Checking with a level, straighten the bowl; use plastic shims if necessary. Hand-tighten the washers and nuts onto the bolts.

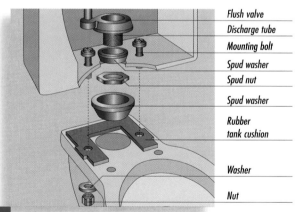

Flush valve

Discharge tube

Mounting bolt

Spud washer

Spud nut

Spud washer

Rubber tank cushion

Washer

Nut

5 Attach the tank

Assemble the flush valve and tighten the spud nut. Place the rubber tank cushion on the bowl. Position the tank over the bowl and tighten the nuts and washers onto the mounting bolts. Snug up the hold-down nuts, but don't overtighten. Fill the caps with plumber's putty and place them over the bolt ends. Hook up the supply tubes and turn on the water.

Replacing a Water Heater

For many homeowners, replacing an old water heater is a simpler job than they imagine, especially if the new unit is similar to the old one. If you want to change from electric to gas or vice versa, however, it would be wise to let a professional do the job.

Most homes can be serviced by a 30- to 50-gallon model. Compare the recovery rates on the units you look at; water heaters with faster recovery rates will heat the water faster (gas heaters have faster rates than electric and, in most parts of the country, are far less expensive to operate). The drawing on page 465 shows the typical parts of a gas water heater.

Before starting work on a water heater, shut off the water and fuel or power supply. If there is no floor drain beneath the valve, connect a hose to the drain valve near the base of the tank and run it to a nearby drain or outdoors.

If your home is in an earthquake zone, you will need to install straps around the new water heater (check with your local building department for exact details).

If the new tank is a different height than the old one, use flexible pipe connectors for the water inlet and outlet; they will bend as needed to make the hookup. If the pipes are not threaded, replace them with threaded nipples and secure the connectors to them with an adjustable wrench. Install a new temperature and pressure-relief valve on the new tank.

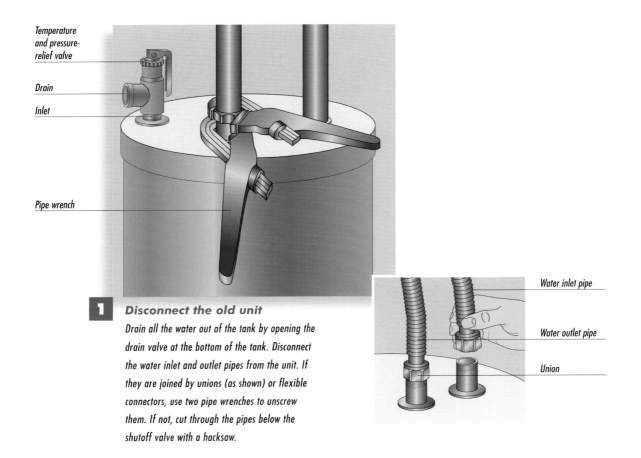

Temperature and pressure-relief valve

Drain

Inlet

Pipe wrench

1 *Disconnect the old unit*
Drain all the water out of the tank by opening the drain valve at the bottom of the tank. Disconnect the water inlet and outlet pipes from the unit. If they are joined by unions (as shown) or flexible connectors, use two pipe wrenches to unscrew them. If not, cut through the pipes below the shutoff valve with a hacksaw.

Water inlet pipe

Water outlet pipe

Union

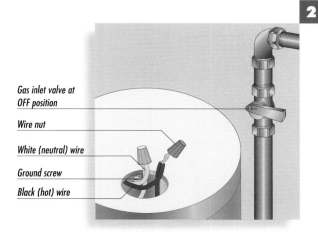

Gas inlet valve at OFF position

Wire nut

White (neutral) wire

Ground screw

Black (hot) wire

2 *Detach the power or fuel line*

Shut off the power to an electric water heater at the two circuit breakers that protect it and test exposed wiring with a neon tester. When you are sure the power is off, remove the electrical cable from the heater. (Call an electrician for this work unless you are confident that you can do it safely.) For a gas unit, shut off the fuel and use two pipe wrenches to disconnect the union between the fuel supply pipe and the inlet valve. Also unscrew and remove the flue hat from the flue pipe.

Install & plumb the new unit **3**

Remove the old water heater and set the new one in place. Check that the unit is plumb and level; shim if necessary. Fasten the sections of a gas heater's vent pipe together with sheet metal screws driven through the overlaps at every joint. Be sure to follow the manufacturer's instructions when installing the unit.

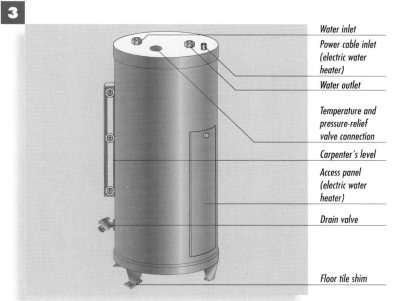

Water inlet

Power cable inlet (electric water heater)

Water outlet

Temperature and pressure-relief valve connection

Carpenter's level

Access panel (electric water heater)

Drain valve

Floor tile shim

4 *Activate the water heater*

With all the connections made, open the water inlet valve to the heater. When the tank is filled with water, bleed the supply pipes by opening the hot-water faucets to allow air to flow out of the pipes. Test the temperature and pressure-relief valve by squeezing the lever. Open the gas inlet valve and light the pilot. Check all connections for leaks; brush soapy water onto them and watch for bubbles.

Gas line

Gas inlet valve

Soapy water (bubbles indicate leaks)

Connecting a Washing Machine

If you are installing a washing machine in a new location, you will need to run both hot- and cold-water supply pipes to the connection point. In addition, each supply pipe needs a shutoff valve and, if necessary, a water-hammer arrester (see page 439 for more about this). Install the latter according to the manufacturer's instructions.

First, locate and drain the nearest hot- and cold-water pipes. Supply pipes for an automatic washer are usually ½ inch in diameter. Check your local code and also the manufacturer's instructions before you install supply pipes. Extend the pipes to the desired point just above the washer and install a T-fitting at the end of each pipe (leave enough space above the washing machine for shutoff valves). Install either two hose-bibb valves or a single-lever valve. (Many codes require that a washing machine's inlet be connected through a backflow-prevention device.)

If there is a sink, the drain hose is designed to hook over the edge of the laundry tub. If there is no sink or laundry tub nearby, you will need to drain the washer into a standpipe—a 2-inch-diameter pipe with a built-in trap that taps into the nearest drainpipe. The standpipe should be between 18 inches and 30 inches above the trap (some codes allow a range of 18 to 42 inches). The trap itself should be 6 to 18 inches above the floor. Standpipes are available with built-in traps or they can be assembled from standard drainpipe and fittings.

 ## THE SHUTOFF VALVE

The shutoff valves shut off the water supply to your washing machine—something you should do before disconnecting a hose. But the shutoff valves can also protect your washing machine and perhaps prevent a flooded house if you close them whenever the machine is not in use. (This is one reason why single-lever valves are particularly popular.) This relieves the constant pressure on the hoses and the water inlet valve in the machine. Should a hose begin leaking with the shutoff valves open, water will flood the floor until the valves are closed. This won't happen if you get in the habit of closing the valves when you finish running the machine.

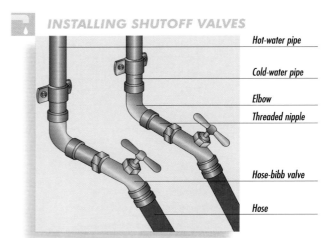

INSTALLING SHUTOFF VALVES

Hot-water pipe

Cold-water pipe

Elbow

Threaded nipple

Hose-bibb valve

Hose

Hose-bibb shutoff valve
To install, add elbows at the end of the supply pipes and attach threaded nipples, then hose bibbs to accept the machine hoses.

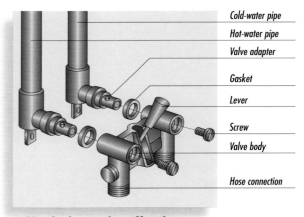

Cold-water pipe

Hot-water pipe

Valve adapter

Gasket

Lever

Screw

Valve body

Hose connection

Single-lever shutoff valve
This turns off both hot and cold water simultaneously. It can replace existing valves with little or no modification. Unscrew the valve adapters from the single-lever unit and attach one to the end of each supply tube. Slide the gaskets and valve body onto the valve adapters. Insert and tighten the attachment screws, then thread on the washer hoses.

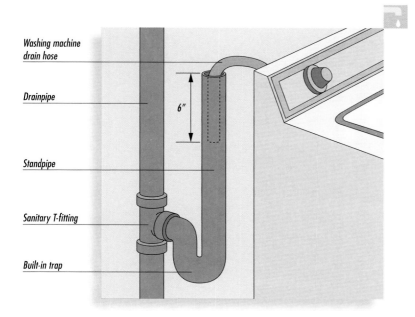

Washing machine drain hose

Drainpipe

6"

Standpipe

Sanitary T-fitting

Built-in trap

ATTACHING THE STANDPIPE

To install a standpipe, cut into a drainpipe and install a sanitary-T fitting. Attach the standpipe to the fitting and push the washing machine's drain hose about 6 inches down into the standpipe—be sure the hose won't be forced out of the pipe by the water pressure.

 TROUBLESHOOTING A WASHING MACHINE

PROBLEM	POSSIBLE CAUSE	REMEDIES
Washer won't fill	Blocked water inlet screens	Clean or replace water inlet screens
	Defective temperature selector	Replace temperature selector
	Defective water inlet valve	Test/replace water inlet valve
Washer won't agitate	Loose or broken drive belt	Tighten or replace belt
	Defective agitator solenoid	Replace agitator solenoid
	Defective water level switch, timer, drive motor, or gearbox	Test/replace individual part
Washer won't spin	Clothes jammed between basket and tub	Remove basket to access clothing
	Loose or broken drive belt	Tighten or replace belt
	Defective lid safety switch, timer, or spin solenoid	Replace individual part
	Defective clutch	Replace clutch
Washer won't drain	Jammed or defective drain pump	Clear jam or replace clutch
	Kinked drain hose	Replace drain hose
Washer leaks	Loose or broken hoses	Tighten clamps or couplings, or replace hoses
	Defective basket gasket	Replace gasket
Excessive vibration	Machine isn't level	Adjust leveling feet
	Loose basket or worn basket support	Tighten basket hold-down nut, or replace support
	Unbalanced load	Reposition clothes

Connecting a Dishwasher

If your dishwasher is cycling toward its last wash, take heart in the fact that replacing it is a relatively easy job, and you're likely to be happier with the features of one of today's models. New dishwashers tend to use less water and less energy than older ones, and they operate much more quietly and with a greater range of control. For example, dishwashers are available with built-in preheating elements that independently heat the water to 160 degrees F so that you can keep your water heater set at a lower temperature.

A built-in dishwasher needs an electrical receptacle for power, a hot-water supply pipe connection, a drainpipe fitting, and—in most cases—an air-gap venting hookup. Always turn off the power to the dishwasher's circuit before working on the appliance or its wiring. Even with the power turned off, make sure you don't touch any bare wire ends with your hands or with tools; handle them by the insulation only. Test all exposed wires with a neon tester to be sure the circuit is dead before proceeding.

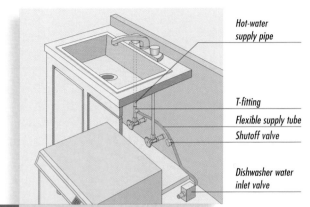

Hot-water supply pipe

T-fitting
Flexible supply tube
Shutoff valve

Dishwasher water inlet valve

1 Attach the supply line
Shut off the water supply and drain the hot-water supply pipe. Cut into the pipe and install a T-fitting or a special three-way valve to isolate the water supply to the dishwasher. Run a flexible supply tube from the T-fitting to the water inlet valve for the dishwasher. Always install a shutoff valve in the dishwasher supply pipe.

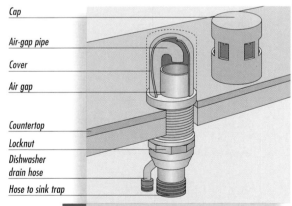

Cap

Air-gap pipe

Cover

Air gap

Countertop

Locknut

Dishwasher drain hose

Hose to sink trap

2 Set up the drainage
Most codes require you to connect an air gap to the dishwasher's drain hose to prevent contamination of the potable water system. To install the air gap, first bore a hole into the countertop using an electric drill with a hole saw installed. Insert the air gap through the hole, secure it, and connect it to the dishwasher drain hose and sink trap or disposer following the manufacturer's instructions.

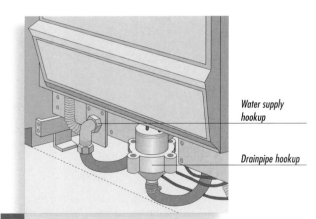

Water supply hookup

Drainpipe hookup

3 Complete the installation
Slide the dishwasher into place and make the supply and drain hookups. Level the dishwasher by adjusting the height of its legs. Anchor the unit to the underside of the counter with screws provided. Restore water pressure; check for leaks.

Installing a Garbage Disposer

Before you install a garbage disposer, check the codes in your area for any restrictions. Installation takes only a few hours, and the work isn't very difficult. Most units fit the standard drain outlets of kitchen sinks and are mounted somewhat like a sink strainer. However, like all plumbing products, garbage disposers vary from brand to brand.

Plumbing a disposer means altering the sink trap to fit the unit. Some models have direct wiring that should be connected by a licensed electrician. Other plug-in disposers require a 120-volt grounded GFCI-protected outlet under the sink (see page 483).

Always be cautious—water and watts don't mix. If you're replacing a disposer, turn off the electricity to that circuit and unplug the unit or disconnect the wiring before removing it. Don't touch bare wire ends with hands or tools; handle them by the insulation only. Test exposed wires with a neon tester to be certain the circuit is dead. Follow the detailed installation instructions that come with your disposer. Below are the typical steps to follow.

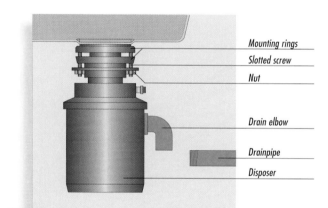

Mounting rings
Slotted screw
Nut
Drain elbow
Drainpipe
Disposer

Sink
Sink flange
Plumber's putty
Gasket
Mounting ring
Snap ring
Mounting ring
Slotted screw
Flange neck

1 Attach the mounting assembly

Disconnect the tailpiece and trap from the sink strainer; disassemble the strainer and lift it out. Clean around the opening. Place a rim of plumber's putty around the sink opening and seat the flange in it. From below, slip the gasket, mounting rings, and snap ring onto the neck of the sink flange. Tighten the slotted screws in the mounting rings. Remove any excess putty.

2 Fasten the unit

Attach the drain elbow to the unit, following the manufacturer's instructions. Align the flange holes with the slotted screws in the mounting rings. Align the drain elbow with the drainpipe. Tighten the nuts securely on the slotted screws.

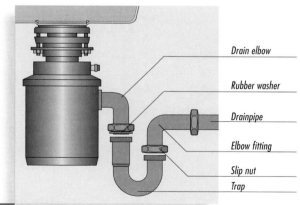

Drain elbow
Rubber washer
Drainpipe
Elbow fitting
Slip nut
Trap

3 Hook up the drain

Fit a slip nut and washer onto the drain elbow, then attach the trap. Add an elbow fitting to the other end of the trap, and connect it to the drainpipe. Run water through the disposer to test for leaks.

Repairing Pipes

Plumbing pipes can function without problems for decades. When a problem does develop, however, you want to be able to react quickly. A higher-than-normal water bill might give you the first indication of a leaking pipe. Or you might hear the sound of running water even when all the fixtures in your home are turned off. A faucet that refuses to run is the first sign of frozen pipes. Pipe noises range from loud banging to high-pitched squeaking.

If a leak is major, turn off the water immediately at the fixture or house shutoff valve. The best long-term solution is to replace the pipe, but simple temporary solutions are shown below.

If pipes bang when the water at a faucet or an appliance is turned off quickly, the problem is water hammer—the noise of rushing water hitting a dead end at the faucet or appliance. Water systems often have short sections of pipe rising above faucets or appliances, called air chambers, that allow a cushioned stop. Air chambers have a tendency to fill completely with water, losing their effectiveness as cushions. See facing page for tips on solving water hammer.

THREE PIPE FIXES

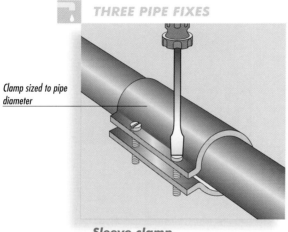

Clamp sized to pipe diameter

Sleeve clamp

Sleeve clamps should stop most leaks for months or even longer; it's a good idea to keep one on hand for emergencies. They are usually sold with a built-in clamp.

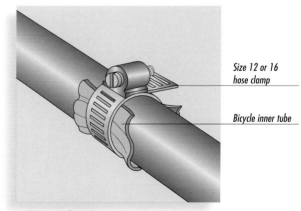

Size 12 or 16 hose clamp

Bicycle inner tube

Hose clamp

An adjustable hose clamp (size 12 or 16) can stop a pinhole leak on a normal pipe. Use a piece of rubber, such as from a bicycle inner tube, or electrician's rubber tape with the clamp.

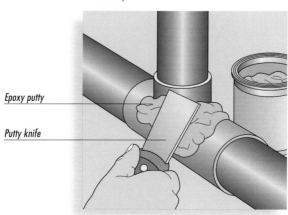

Epoxy putty

Putty knife

Epoxy putty

Epoxy putty will often stop leaks around joints where clamps won't, but it doesn't hold as long. The pipe must be clean and dry for the putty to adhere; turn off the water supply to the leak to let the area dry.

THAWING FROZEN PIPES

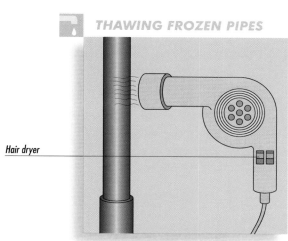

Hair dryer

If a pipe freezes, first shut off the main water supply and open the faucet nearest the frozen pipe. Place rags around the frozen section of pipe and, working from the faucet back toward the iced-up area, use a kettle to pour hot water over the rags. Or, if water isn't puddled in the area, plug a hair dryer into a GFCI outlet and train hot air from the dryer on the pipe. Avoid any contact with water when using the electrical appliance.

QUIETING NOISY PIPES

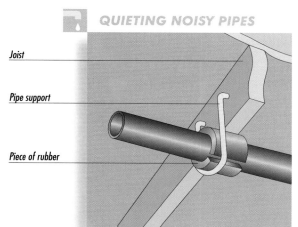

Joist

Pipe support

Piece of rubber

Pipes may rattle or bang if they're poorly anchored, so look for a section that is loose from its supports. Slit a piece of old hose or cut a patch of rubber and insert it in the hanger or strap as a cushion. For masonry walls, attach a block of wood to the wall with lag screws and masonry anchors, then secure the pipe to it with a pipe strap. Install enough hangers to support the entire pipe run. But allow the pipe, especially a plastic pipe, room for expansion due to temperature changes.

STOPPING WATER HAMMER

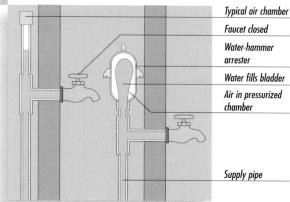

Typical air chamber

Faucet closed

Water-hammer arrester

Water fills bladder

Air in pressurized chamber

Supply pipe

To restore air chambers in pipes, close the shutoff valve below the fixture that makes a banging sound, then close the house shutoff valve. Open the highest and lowest faucets in the house to drain all water. Close the faucets and reopen the shutoff valves. You can install special water-hammer arresters like the one shown (above) on hot- and cold-water lines near the fixtures, following the manufacturer's instructions.

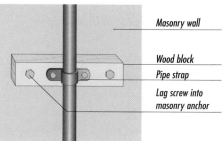

Masonry wall

Wood block

Pipe strap

Lag screw into masonry anchor

Fixing Sprayers & Aerators

Many kitchen sink sprayers have a spray head attached to a hose, which is connected to a diverter valve in the faucet body. When you squeeze the spray-head handle, the diverter valve reroutes water from the faucet to the spray-head hose. Here we look at one type of diverter valve and how to solve clogs and problems with sprayers and aerators.

Diverter valves with compression faucets (pages 442–443) are easy to disassemble and clean, as shown on facing page. Those on other types of faucets vary. If cleaning the diverter doesn't improve the sprayer's performance, replace the diverter valve.

 ## UNCLOGGING THE AERATOR

Unscrew the aerator from the end of the spray head (or spout). Disassemble the parts, keeping them in order to simplify reassembly. Clean the screens and disc with an old toothbrush and soapy water; use a pin or toothpick to open any clogged holes in the disc. Remove hard-water scale by soaking parts in vinegar or lime remover. Flush the parts with water, then reassemble.

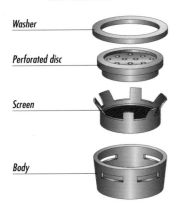

Washer

Perforated disc

Screen

Body

 ## TYPICAL DIVERTER COMPONENTS

If water flow is sluggish, make sure the hose isn't kinked; then clean the aerator in the spray nozzle. If that doesn't help, you'll have to clean the diverter valve or replace it. If the spray head leaks, remove it from the hose and replace the washer. For a leak at the faucet end of the hose, tighten the hose coupling. If the hose itself leaks, replace it.

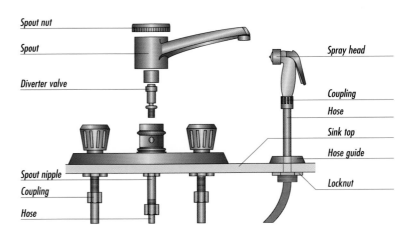

Spout nut
Spout
Diverter valve
Spout nipple
Coupling
Hose

Spray head
Coupling
Hose
Sink top
Hose guide
Locknut

INSPECTING THE HOSE

If the hose leaks where it attaches under the sink, undo the fitting from the tip of the hose by first removing the retainer clip. Undo the coupling nut under the sink using rib-joint pliers or a basin wrench—the hose might thread directly onto the base of the faucet without a coupling nut. Once the nut is detached, inspect the length of hose for kinks or cracks. If you find defects, replace the hose with a new one of the same diameter— nylon-reinforced vinyl is a durable choice.

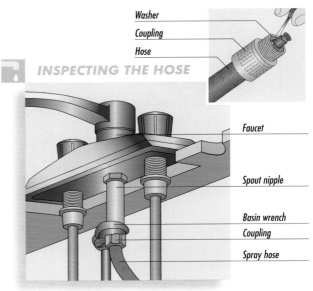

Washer
Coupling
Hose

Faucet
Spout nipple
Basin wrench
Coupling
Spray hose

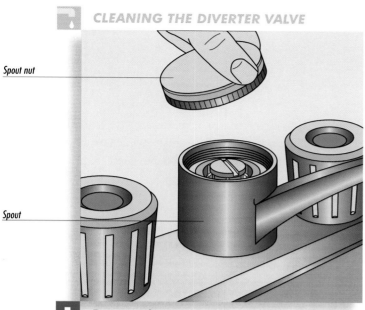

Spout nut

Spout

1 **Remove the spout**

To get at the diverter, you will need to take off the faucet spout. Some spouts simply unscrew; for others, you may need to take apart the handle.

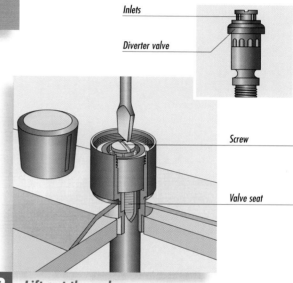

Inlets

Diverter valve

Screw

Valve seat

2 **Lift out the valve**

Once you have access to the inside of the faucet body, loosen the screw on top of the diverter valve just enough to lift the valve from the seat.

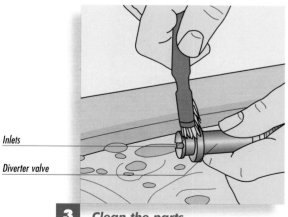

Inlets

Diverter valve

3 **Clean the parts**

Take the valve apart; clean inlets and surfaces with an old toothbrush and water (or soak the valve in white vinegar).

Fixing Compression Faucets

If your faucet has separate hot- and cold-water handles that come to a spongy stop, it's a compression faucet. In this faucet, a rubber seat washer is secured to the stem, which has very coarse threads on the outside. When you turn the handle to shut off the faucet, the stem is screwed down, compressing the washer against the valve seat in the faucet body. The stem is secured by a packing nut, which compresses the packing (which can be twine, a washer, or an O-ring) and prevents water leaks at the stem.

If water leaks around the handle, tighten the packing nut. If that doesn't solve the problem, replace the packing as shown in Step 2 on facing page.

If the faucet leaks from the spout, either a washer is defective or a valve seat is badly worn or corroded. To find out which side needs work, turn off the shutoff valves one at a time to see which one stops the drip. Then you'll need to take off the handle, remove the stem, and either replace the washer or replace the valve seat as shown in Steps 3 and 4. Check the washer first. If it isn't the problem, a damaged valve seat could be causing the leak by preventing the seat washer from fitting properly.

On most compression faucets the valve seat is replaceable. You'll need a valve-seat wrench—or the correct size of Allen wrench—to make the exchange. If the valve seat is built into the faucet, it can be dressed, or smoothed, with an inexpensive tool called a valve-seat dresser. The dressing stone can be turned by hand or with a variable-speed drill. This can be a tricky and time-consuming job, though—you may want to let a plumber handle it.

Before you reassemble the faucet, lubricate the stem threads with silicone grease. If the threads are worn or stripped, consider replacing the stem.

Before doing any work, turn off the water at the fixture shutoff valves or at the main shutoff valve. Open the faucet to drain the pipes.

COMPRESSION-FAUCET PARTS

Compression faucets are relatively easy to disassemble. Problems are usually caused by faulty washers or packing.

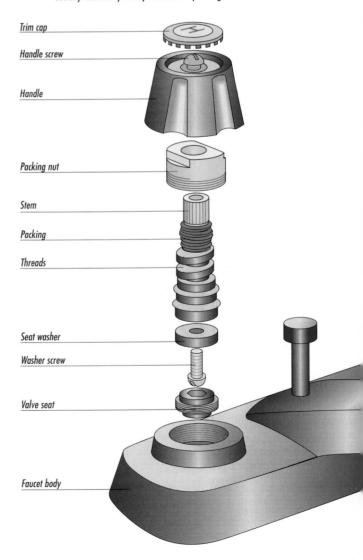

Trim cap

Handle screw

Handle

Packing nut

Stem

Packing

Threads

Seat washer

Washer screw

Valve seat

Faucet body

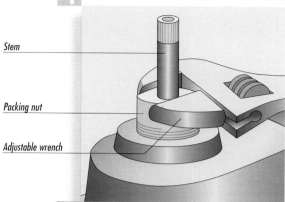

Stem

Packing nut

Adjustable wrench

1 **Disassemble the faucet**

Use a blunt knife or screwdriver to pry off the trim cap. Unscrew the handle screw and pull or pry the handle straight up off its stem. (If the handle won't budge, you may need to borrow or buy a faucet-handle puller.) Tighten the packing nut one-quarter turn with an adjustable wrench. Reassemble the handle enough to turn the water back on. If the leak persists, go on to Step 2.

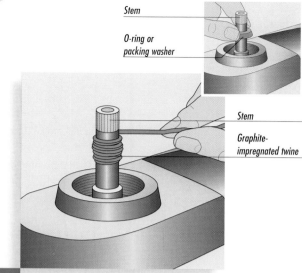

Stem

O-ring or packing washer

Stem

Graphite-impregnated twine

2 **Replace the packing**

Whatever the type, replace packing with a duplicate. Remove or scrape off the old O-ring, packing washer, or graphite-impregnated twine. Roll on a new duplicate O-ring (lubricated with silicone grease), or push on an exact replacement washer, or rewrap new twine clockwise—five or six times—around the faucet stem. Lubricate the packing nut's threads with silicone grease, then tighten on the packing nut and replace the handle.

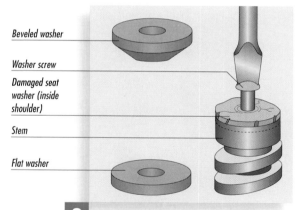

Beveled washer

Washer screw

Damaged seat washer (inside shoulder)

Stem

Flat washer

3 **Replace the seat washer**

To stop a spout leak, remove the handle and use it to turn the stem beyond its fully open position; then remove the stem. If the washer at the bottom of the stem is cracked, grooved, or marred, carefully remove the screw and replace the washer with a new, identical one. If the washer is beveled, face the beveled edge toward the screw head. If the screw appears worn, replace it as well.

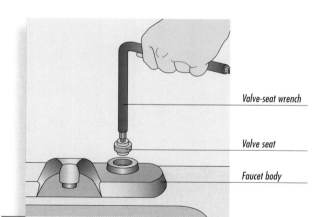

Valve-seat wrench

Valve seat

Faucet body

4 **Replace the valve seat**

Insert a valve-seat wrench into the faucet body and turn it counterclockwise to remove the seat. Lubricate the threads before installing the new seat. If it isn't removable, dress the seat as discussed on facing page. Turn the water on and off a few times to test the effectiveness of your repair.

Fixing Disc Faucets

The core of a disc faucet is a ceramic disc assembly, sometimes called a cylinder. Openings in the disc line up with inlet holes to allow the flow of water. The disc assembly itself seldom wears out, but leaks can develop when the rubber seals begin to age. On a single-handle disc faucet, three seals control the flow of hot, cold, and mixed water.

Two-handle disc faucets operate on the same principle, except that they have a single rubber or plastic seal and a small spring on each side. If this type of faucet is leaking from the handle, you should replace the inexpensive stem-unit assembly. If the faucet is dripping from the spout, remove the seal and spring using long-nose pliers and replace them with identical parts. When reassembling, be sure to align the lugs in the assembly with slots in the base of the faucet.

 TWO-HANDLE DISC FAUCET

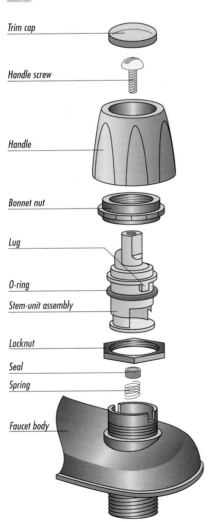

Trim cap

Handle screw

Handle

Bonnet nut

Lug

O-ring

Stem-unit assembly

Locknut

Seal

Spring

Faucet body

 SINGLE-HANDLE DISC FAUCET

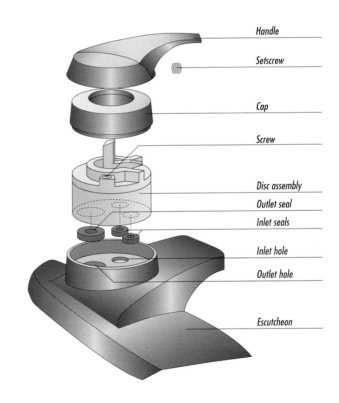

Handle

Setscrew

Cap

Screw

Disc assembly

Outlet seal

Inlet seals

Inlet hole

Outlet hole

Escutcheon

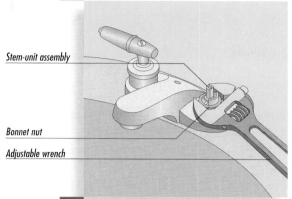

Stem-unit assembly

Bonnet nut

Adjustable wrench

1 Disassemble the faucet

Pop off the trim cap, if there is one, using a blunt knife or screwdriver. Undo the handle screw and pull off the handle. Use an adjustable wrench to remove the bonnet nut.

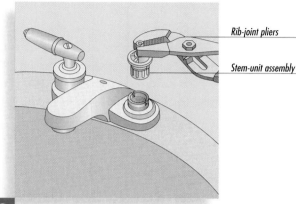

Rib-joint pliers

Stem-unit assembly

2 Replace worn parts

If the faucet is leaking from around the handle, the O-ring or stem-unit assembly needs replacing. Pull out the stem-unit assembly. If the O-ring is worn, replace it with an exact duplicate; lubricate the new ring with silicone grease before rolling it on. If the O-rings are in good condition, replace the stem-unit assembly.

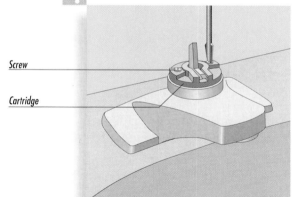

Screw

Cartridge

1 Remove the disc assembly

To repair a dripping spout or a leak at the base, remove the setscrew under the faucet handle and lift off the handle and decorative escutcheon. Then remove the disc assembly by loosening the two screws that hold the disc assembly to the faucet body.

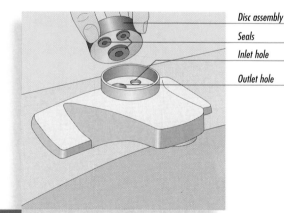

Disc assembly

Seals

Inlet hole

Outlet hole

2 Replace the seals

Under the disc assembly you'll find a set of three inlet seals. Take each one out, using the tip of a small screwdriver. Clean the disc assembly and inlet holes, and rinse out any debris with clear water. Install new seals. Reassemble the faucet, making sure to align the inlet holes of the disc assembly with those in the base of the faucet.

Fixing Rotating-Ball Faucets

Some single-lever faucets have an inner mechanism that controls the flow of water with a slotted metal ball that sits atop two spring-loaded rubber seals. Water flows when the openings in the rotating ball align with hot- and cold-water inlets in the faucet body.

If the handle leaks, tighten the adjusting ring or replace the cam washer above the ball. If the spout drips, the inlet seals or springs may be worn and need replacing. If the leak is under the spout, you must replace the O-rings or the ball.

 ROTATING-BALL FAUCET PARTS

Slots in a metal ball align with water inlets to let water flow. Problems are generally caused by failing seals.

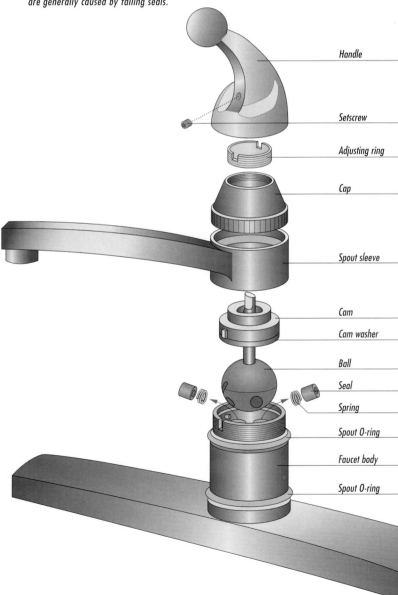

Handle

Setscrew

Adjusting ring

Cap

Spout sleeve

Cam

Cam washer

Ball

Seal

Spring

Spout O-ring

Faucet body

Spout O-ring

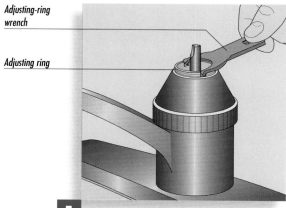

Adjusting-ring
wrench

Adjusting ring

1 **Tighten the adjusting ring**

Remove the faucet handle by loosening the
setscrew with an Allen wrench. Tighten the
adjusting ring with the special wrench, as shown,
or a kitchen knife. Put the handle back on. If this
doesn't solve the problem, move on to Step 2.

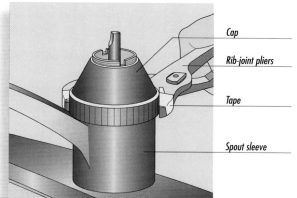

Cap

Rib-joint pliers

Tape

Spout sleeve

2 **Disassemble the faucet**

Loosen the setscrew with an Allen wrench and
remove the handle. Use tape-wrapped pliers to
unscrew the cap. Lift out the ball-and-cam
assembly. Underneath are two inlet seals on
springs. Remove the spout sleeve to expose the
faucet body.

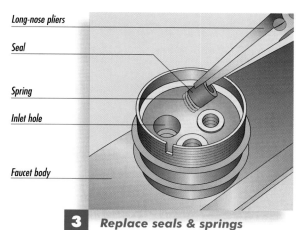

Long-nose pliers

Seal

Spring

Inlet hole

Faucet body

3 **Replace seals & springs**

Use long-nose pliers to lift out the old parts. With
a stiff brush or pocketknife, remove any buildup
in the inlet holes. If new spout O-rings are needed,
apply a thin coat of silicone grease to them to stop
leaks at the base of the faucet. Install a new
spring and seal.

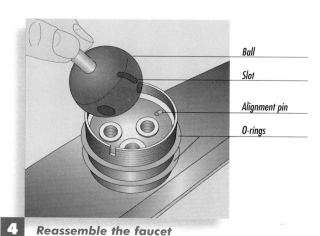

Ball

Slot

Alignment pin

O-rings

4 **Reassemble the faucet**

Before reassembling the faucet, check the ball; if
it's corroded, replace it. To reinstall the ball-and-
cam assembly, line up the slot in the ball with the
metal alignment pin in the faucet body. Also be
sure to fit the lug on the cam into the notch in the
faucet body.

Fixing Cartridge Faucets

Washerless cartridge faucets have a series of holes in the stem-and-cartridge assembly that align to control the mixture and flow of water. Problems with this type of faucet usually occur because the O-rings or the cartridge itself must be replaced. If the faucet becomes hard to move, lubricating the cartridge O-rings should cure the problem.

CARTRIDGE FAUCET PARTS

Cartridge faucets rarely fail, but when they do, you often must replace the entire cartridge.

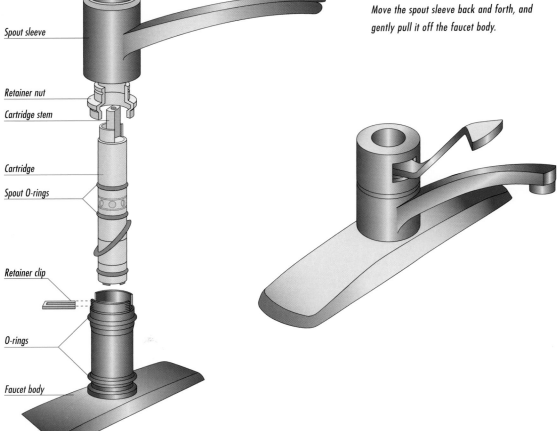

Handle
Trim cap
Handle screw
Cap
Spout sleeve
Retainer nut
Cartridge stem
Cartridge
Spout O-rings
Retainer clip
O-rings
Faucet body

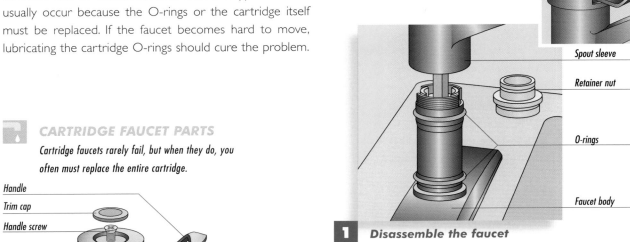

Handle screw
Cap
Spout sleeve
Retainer nut
O-rings
Faucet body

1 **Disassemble the faucet**

Remove the handle screw with a screwdriver; lift off the cap and handle. Remove the retainer nut. Move the spout sleeve back and forth, and gently pull it off the faucet body.

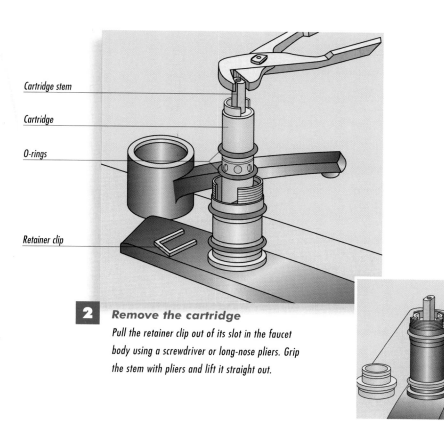

Cartridge stem

Cartridge

O-rings

Retainer clip

2 **Remove the cartridge**

Pull the retainer clip out of its slot in the faucet body using a screwdriver or long-nose pliers. Grip the stem with pliers and lift it straight out.

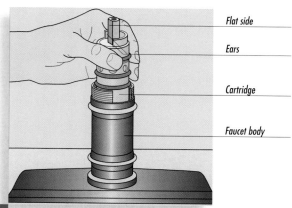

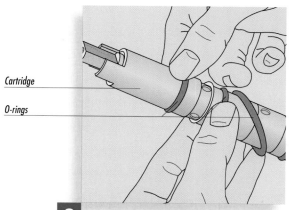

Cartridge

O-rings

3 **Change the O-rings**

Examine the O-rings on the cartridge and replace them if they show signs of wear. Apply silicone grease to the new O-rings before installing them. If the O-rings are in good shape, the cartridge should be replaced. Take the old one to the plumbing supply store and buy an exact duplicate.

Flat side

Ears

Cartridge

Faucet body

4 **Replace the cartridge**

Push the cartridge into the faucet body. Cartridges vary; one common type has two flat sides, one of which must face front—otherwise, your hot- and cold-water supply will be reversed. Fit the retainer clip snugly back into its slot. Reassemble the faucet.

Tub & Shower Fixes

Plumbing Repairs

Like sink faucets, tub and shower faucets can be either compression- or cartridge-style ("washerless"). Either way, water is directed from the faucet to the tub or shower head by a diverter valve; some, as shown below, have built-in diverter valves, while others have a knob on the tub spout. This latter type is easy to replace—you just grip the old spout with a tape-wrapped pipe wrench and turn it counterclockwise to remove it, then hand-tighten the new spout into place.

Before taking apart a tub faucet, turn off the water at the house shutoff valve (see pages 406–407) and open a faucet that is lower than the level of the tub faucet to drain the pipes. Also review the instructions on sink faucets, which are similar to tub faucets.

COMPRESSION TUB FAUCET

Compression tub faucets are repaired much like compression sink faucets (see pages 442–443). Most leaks can be fixed by replacing the washer and seat valve.

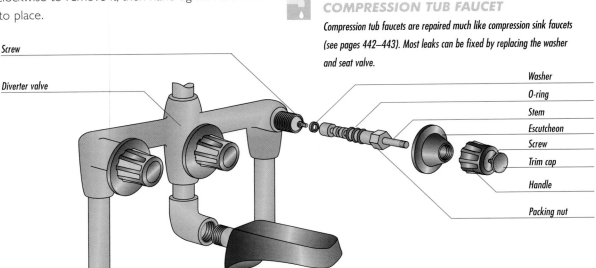

Screw
Diverter valve
Washer
O-ring
Stem
Escutcheon
Screw
Trim cap
Handle
Packing nut

CARTRIDGE TUB FAUCET

The cartridge tub faucet shown here is repaired almost the same way as a cartridge-style sink faucet (see pages 448–449). You remove the stop tube and retainer clip to access the cartridge.

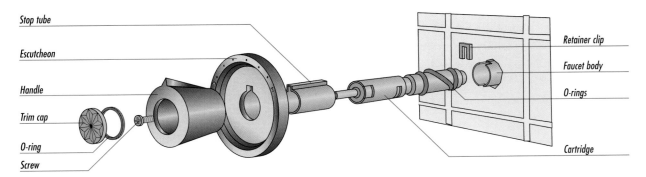

Stop tube
Escutcheon
Handle
Trim cap
O-ring
Screw
Retainer clip
Faucet body
O-rings
Cartridge

Pry off the cap, unscrew the handle, and remove the escutcheon. To access the packing nut in a compression faucet, gently chip away the wall's surface, if necessary, with a ball-peen hammer and small cold chisel (wear safety glasses) and then grip the nut with a deep socket wrench. Replace the faucet with a similar one, following the manufacturer's instructions.

REPLACING A TUB FAUCET

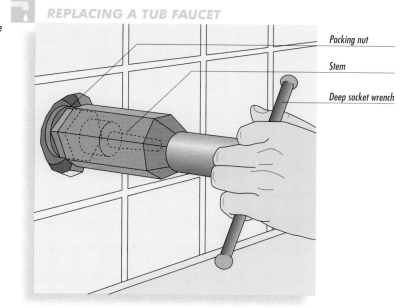

Packing nut

Stem

Deep socket wrench

REPAIRING A SHOWER HEAD

A shower head simply screws onto the shower arm stubout. Before you decide to replace a leaking or water-wasting shower head, tighten all connections with rib-joint pliers (wrap the jaws with duct tape to avoid damaging the finish). If that doesn't stop the leak, replace the washer between the shower head and the swivel ball. If sluggish water flow is the problem, remove the center screw and scrub the faceplate and screen with vinegar, using a toothbrush.

Shower arm stubout

Collar

Adjusting ring

Swivel ball

Washer

Shower head

Outlet hole

Faceplate

Screw

Shower head

Faceplate & screen

Screw

SMALL EXPENSE, BIG SAVINGS

In most homes, more money is spent heating water than on any other energy cost except home heating and cooling. Finding inexpensive ways to reduce your need for hot water can produce big savings. Low-flow shower heads and flow restrictors can reduce water flow to less than 2 1/2 gallons per minute, compared with 5 to 8 gallons per minute of older models, while still delivering satisfactory showers. They are easy to install and pay for themselves very quickly in both reduced energy bills and water savings.

Opening Clogged Drains

Dealing with clogged sinks, tubs, showers, and toilets is one of life's unpleasant necessities. The ideal is to prevent clogs entirely. At least be alert to the warning signs of a sluggish drain—it's easier to clear a drain that's slowing down than one that's stopped completely. Usually a clog will be close to the fixture. You can determine this by checking the other drains in your home. If only one fixture is blocked, you are probably dealing with a clog in the trap or drainpipe of that fixture.

If more than one drain won't clear, something is stuck farther along in a branch drain, the main drain, or the soil stack, causing all the fixtures above the clog to stop up. If there is a blockage in the vent stack, wastes drain slowly and odors from the pipes become noticeable in the house.

PREVENTING CLOGGED DRAINS A kitchen sink usually clogs because of a buildup of grease and food particles that get caught in it. To keep the problem to a minimum, don't pour grease down the drain. Another villain is coffee grounds—throw them out instead of washing them down. Kitchen drains can be kept cleared of grease by pouring a gallon of boiling water down them monthly. (If you have plastic drainpipes, use hot—not boiling—water.)

Hair and soap scum are usually at fault in bathroom drains. Clean out strainers and pop-ups regularly. Some strainers are held in place by screws. Instructions for servicing the pop-up are shown on page 455. A solution of equal parts baking soda and vinegar can help prevent soap and hair clogs. Pour some down the drain every month or so, let it fizz, then flush with hot water.

CLEARING THE MAIN DRAIN If a clog is too deep in the pipes to get at from a fixture, you can clean out the soil stack from below by working on a branch cleanout, the main cleanout, or the house trap. Cleaning the soil stack from below means working with raw sewage; have rubber gloves, pails, mops, and rags on hand. Once finished, clean and disinfect all tools and materials.

First try a hand-operated drain-and-trap auger. If you're trying to clear the clog by working through a cleanout, you can use a balloon bag attached to a hose nozzle instead. If neither of these methods does the job, you can choose to rent a power auger or to call a plumber or professional drain-cleaning firm.

OPENING A CLEANOUT

Soil stack
Pipe wrench
Main cleanout
Main drain

The main cleanout is usually a Y-shaped fitting located near the bottom of the soil stack where the main drain leaves the house, usually in a basement or crawl space or on an outside wall near a toilet. In newer buildings there are usually branch cleanouts; try reaching the clog from one of them first. Put on rubber gloves and have a pail and some newspapers to catch the waste water. Slowly remove the plug with a pipe wrench. Try to remove the clog with an auger, as described on page 456. If this doesn't work, you can try a balloon bag (see facing page).

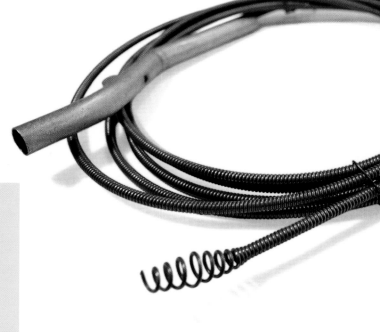

USING A BALLOON BAG

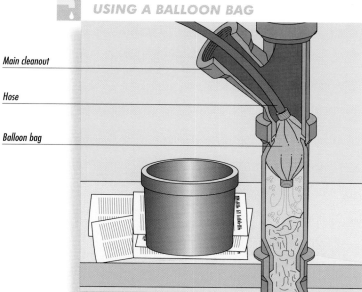

Main cleanout

Hose

Balloon bag

Buy a balloon bag, or bladder, that matches the diameter of your drain. Attach the bag to a garden hose, and then proceed as directed by the manufacturer. The balloon bag works by expanding in the drain and then shooting a stream of water into the pipe.

USING CHEMICAL CLEANERS

There are many chemical drain cleaners on the market. They are hazardous, however, and can cause injury to eyes and skin. Chemical cleaners are most successful at clearing a partially clogged drain, but they frequently cause more problems than they fix. If plunging and augering don't work, though, you may want to try a chemical cleaner before calling the plumber. Read and follow the instructions on the label. Match the cleaner with the material you're trying to dissolve (alkalis, usually containing lye, cut grease; acids dissolve soap and hair). Work in a well-ventilated room and wear rubber gloves and goggles. Don't mix chemicals; combining an acid and an alkali cleaner is potentially dangerous. Don't look down the drain after pouring in a chemical; the solution frequently boils up and gives off toxic fumes. Never plunge if you've recently used a chemical.

SNAKING THE HOUSE TRAP

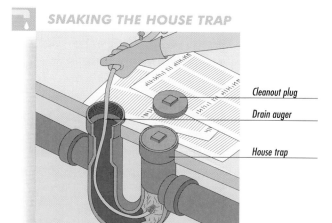

Cleanout plug

Drain auger

House trap

Carefully unscrew the cleanout plug from the main house trap; if sewage begins to seep out as you loosen it, retighten it and call a plumber—sewage may be backed up into the main drain. Otherwise, work an auger down through the drain.

Unclogging Sinks

A dose of scalding water is often effective against grease buildups. To check if a small object has slipped down the drain, remove and clean the pop-up assembly, strainer, or trap. If these simple measures fail, try the sink plunger. If the plunger also fails, you'll need to use an auger.

If your sink has a garbage disposer and the disposer drain-pipe clogs, disassemble the trap and thread an auger into the drainpipe. If both basins of a double sink with a garbage disposer clog, snake down from the one without a dispos-er. If only the basin with the disposer is clogged, you'll have to remove the trap to dislodge the blockage. If an auger through the sink drainpipe doesn't succeed, turn your attention to the main drain (see page 452).

To auger a drain, insert the auger down through the drain and operate it as shown on the facing page. If that doesn't clear the clog, put the auger in through the trap cleanout or remove the trap entirely so the auger can reach through the drainpipe to clear a clog that's farther down the drain.

USING A PLUNGER

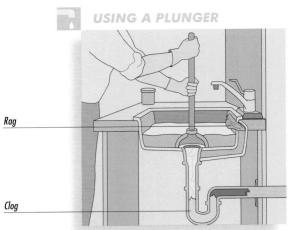

Rag

Clog

Choose a plunger with a suction cup large enough to cover the drain opening completely. Fill the clogged fixture with enough water to cover several inches of the plunger cup. Then use a wet cloth to block off all other outlets (the overflow vent, the second drain in a double sink, adjacent fixtures) between the drain and the clog. Insert the plunger into the water at an angle so that little air remains trapped under it. Holding the plunger upright, use 15 to 20 forceful strokes. Repeat if necessary.

CLEANING THE TRAP

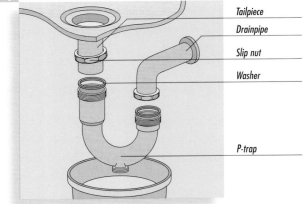

Tailpiece

Drainpipe

Slip nut

Washer

P-trap

If your trap has a cleanout plug, remove it with an adjustable wrench. Place a bucket beneath the trap to catch escaping water. If the trap is clogged, try to remove the obstruction with a piece of wire. If that doesn't work, loosen the slip nuts that attach the trap to the tailpiece and drainpipe; use a wrench or rib-joint pliers with taped jaws to protect the finish. Remove and flush out the trap, then reassemble it.

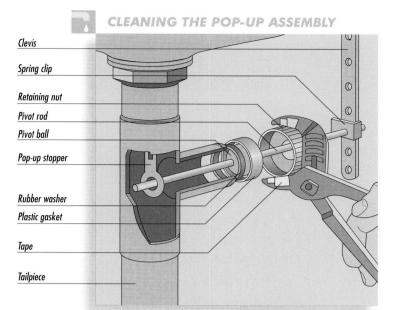

Clevis

Spring clip

Retaining nut

Pivot rod

Pivot ball

Pop-up stopper

Rubber washer

Plastic gasket

Tape

Tailpiece

Remove the stopper; some can be lifted straight out, others must be twisted first. To remove the type shown in the illustration, first undo the retaining nut and pull out the pivot rod. Clean the stopper and pivot rod of any hair or debris. Replace the assembly.

USING AN AUGER

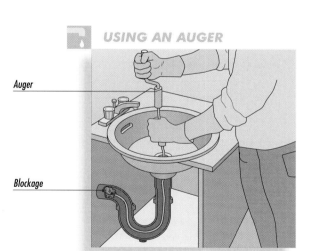

Auger

Blockage

Augering through the drain

Remove the pop-up stopper and the sink strainer. Insert the auger into the drain opening and twist it down through the trap until you reach the clog.

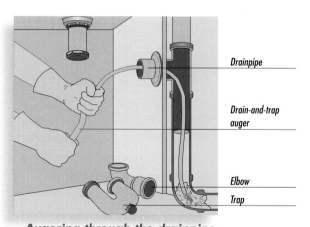

Drainpipe

Drain-and-trap auger

Elbow

Trap

Augering through the drainpipe

Remove the trap as shown on the facing page. Pull the trap downward and spill its contents into a pail. Insert the auger into the drainpipe at the wall. Feed it as far as it will go, turning clockwise until it hits the clog. Clean out the trap before reinstalling it.

Unclogging Tubs & Showers

To help prevent clogs in tubs and showers, install a hair trap. One type sits in the drain; another requires replacing the pop-up. When a tub or shower drain does clog up, first see whether other fixtures are affected. If they are, work on the main drain. If only the tub or shower is plugged, work on it. Begin by plunging (see page 454), then remove the strainer or pop-up and clean it. If this doesn't work, use an auger (see box below right) or a balloon bag (page 453).

CLEARING A DRUM TRAP

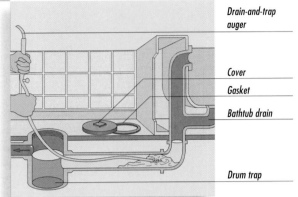

Drain-and-trap auger

Cover

Gasket

Bathtub drain

Drum trap

Instead of a P-trap, bathtubs in older houses may have a drum trap. To clear a clog, bail all water from the tub and slowly unscrew the drum trap cover with an adjustable wrench. Watch for any water welling up around the threads. Remove the cover and rubber gasket on the trap and clean any debris from the trap. If it's still clogged, work the auger through the lower pipe toward the tub and then, if necessary, in the opposite direction.

CLEARING A TUB P-TRAP

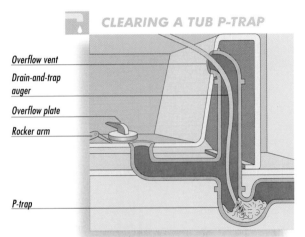

Overflow vent

Drain-and-trap auger

Overflow plate

Rocker arm

P-trap

Remove the stopper and attached rocker arm. Unscrew and remove the overflow plate and pull out the assembly. Feed the auger down through the overflow pipe and into the P-trap (as discussed in the box at right). If this doesn't clear the drain, remove the trap or its cleanout plug from below (if accessible) or through an access panel; have a pail ready to catch water. Then insert the auger toward the main drain.

USING AN AUGER

Feed the auger (also called a snake) into the drain, trap, or pipe until it stops. If there is a movable handgrip, position it about 6 inches above the opening and tighten the thumbscrew. Rotate the handle clockwise to break the blockage. As the cable works its way into the pipe, loosen the thumbscrew, slide the handgrip back, push more cable into the pipe, tighten again, and repeat. If there is no handgrip, push and twist the cable until it hits the clog.

The first time the auger stops, it probably has hit a turn in the piping rather than the clog. Guiding the auger past a sharp turn takes patience and effort; keep pushing it forward, turning it clockwise as you do. Once the head of the auger hooks the blockage, pull the auger back a short distance to free some material from the clog, then push the rest on through.

After breaking up the clog, pull the auger out slowly and have a pail ready to catch any gunk that is brought out. Flush the drain with hot water.

For a distant or particularly difficult clog, you can rent a power auger at an equipment rental supply, or call a drain-clearing company.

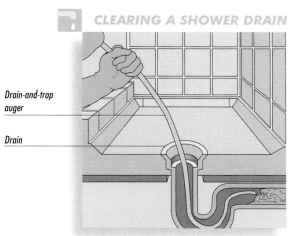

Drain-and-trap auger

Drain

Hose

Rags

Drain

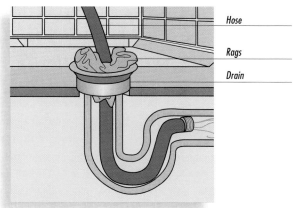

Use an auger

Unscrew and remove the strainer if your auger can't be threaded through it. Probe the auger down the drain and through the trap until it hits the clog.

Use a garden hose

Attach the hose to a faucet with a threaded adapter or run it to an outside hose bibb. Push the hose deep into the drain trap and pack wet rags tightly into the opening around it. Hold the hose in the drain and turn the hose water alternately on full force, then abruptly off. Alternatively, use the hose with a balloon bag as shown on page 453. Note: Never leave a hose in a drain; a sudden drop in water pressure could siphon raw sewage back into the fresh water supply.

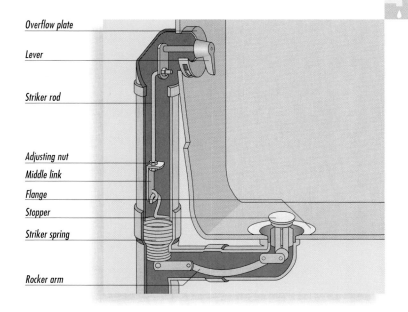

Overflow plate

Lever

Striker rod

Adjusting nut

Middle link

Flange

Stopper

Striker spring

Rocker arm

SERVICING A TUB POP-UP

Remove the stopper and rocker arm by pulling the stopper straight up. Unscrew and remove the tub's overflow plate and pull the entire assembly out through the overflow. Clean the parts of any hair or debris. If the stopper needs adjustment, loosen the adjusting nuts and slide the middle link up or down, as needed. If the tub has a strainer and internal plunger that blocks the back of the drain to stop the flow of water, the same adjustments to the lift mechanism apply.

Unclogging a Toilet

Plumbing Improvements

The most common cause of a clogged toilet is an obstruction in the trap. To remove it, use a plunger; if that doesn't clear the clog, try using a toilet auger. If neither method succeeds, try using an auger or balloon bag in the nearest cleanout (see page 453).

If the toilet bowl is filled to the brim, do not flush the toilet again. You can usually prevent an overflow by immediately removing the tank lid and pushing the stopper or flapper into the flush valve, which prevents any more water from filling the bowl. Next, reach under the toilet and turn off the supply valve (these two steps are shown opposite).

USING A PLUNGER

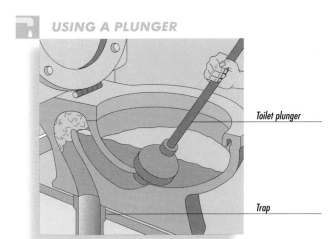

Toilet plunger

Trap

A toilet plunger has a special fold-out flange that fits snugly into the trap. To loosen a clog, pump the plunger up and down at least a dozen times, then pull it away sharply on the last stroke. The alternating pressure and suction should pull the obstruction back through the trap into the bowl. If it merely pushes the obstruction a little deeper into the drain, you will need to use a toilet auger.

USING A TOILET AUGER

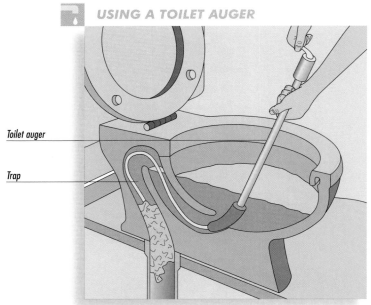

Toilet auger

Trap

A toilet auger, also called a closet auger, will reach down into the toilet trap. It has a curved tip that starts the auger with a minimum of mess and a protective housing to keep the bowl from being scratched. Feed the auger into the trap, turning the handle clockwise as you go. Once you snag the clog, continue turning the handle as you pull it out.

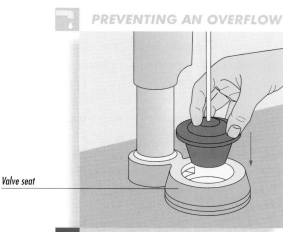

Valve seat

1 Plug the valve seat

If your toilet is about to overflow, remove the tank lid and push the flapper or stopper into the flush valve to stop the flow of water into the bowl.

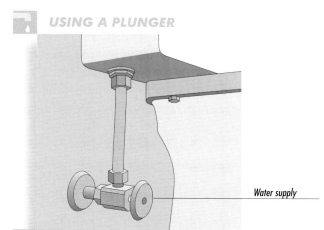

Water supply

2 Turn off the water supply

To keep the tank from refilling, turn off the water-supply valve beneath the toilet by turning it clockwise. Then plunge the toilet or use a toilet auger as shown on the facing page.

UNDERSTANDING A SEPTIC SYSTEM

A good septic tank system doesn't require a great deal of maintenance or call for many special precautions. But the maintenance it does require is crucial, since a properly functioning septic system is much less likely to clog. You should have a diagram of your septic tank's layout, showing the location of the tank, pipes, access holes, and drainage field.

Chemicals, chemical cleaners, and thick paper products should never be disposed of through the system. Chemicals may destroy the bacteria necessary to attack and disintegrate solid wastes in the tank. Paper products can clog the main drain, making the system useless.

Have your septic system checked once a year by a professional. The tank should be pumped whenever necessary, but it's best to have it done in the spring if you live in a cold climate. If you have the tank pumped in the fall, it may become loaded with solid waste that can't be broken down through the winter, when bacterial action slows.

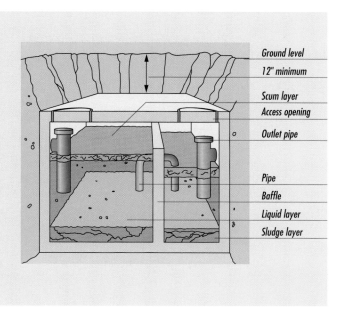

Ground level
12" minimum
Scum layer
Access opening
Outlet pipe
Pipe
Baffle
Liquid layer
Sludge layer

Repairing Toilets

The workings of a flush toilet remain a mystery to most people until something goes awry. Fortunately, what may appear to be complex is, in fact, quite simple. Basically, there are two assemblies concealed under the lid: an inlet valve assembly, which regulates the filling of the tank, and a flush valve assembly, which controls the flow of water from the tank to the bowl. The toilet bowl includes a built-in trap. For a basic explanation of how your toilet works, see the box on the facing page.

A common cause of a continuously running toilet is a defective seal between the stopper and the valve seat. To check, remove the lid and flush the toilet. Watch the stopper; it should fall straight down onto the seat. If it doesn't, make sure that the guide rod or chain is centered over the flush valve. See how to adjust this on page 463. If your toilet is clogged, see page 458.

If your toilet is whining or whistling, the inlet valve assembly may be to blame. If the inlet valve is faulty, you may be able to just replace the washers or seal, or you may need to replace the whole assembly, which isn't difficult to do. You can replace a ballcock style with a similar model, but you may be happier with a new float-cup assembly, shown on the facing page; this type is inexpensive, easy to install and adjust, and is nearly trouble-free. Be sure any replacement assembly is designed to prevent backflow from the tank into the water supply.

The water level in the tank should reach within $3/4$ inch of the top of the overflow tube. If a waterline is printed or stamped inside the tank, use it as a guide. See how to adjust this level on the facing page.

THE INNER WORKINGS OF A TOILET

The conventional ballcock-type inlet valve, shown here, utilizes a float arm and ball.

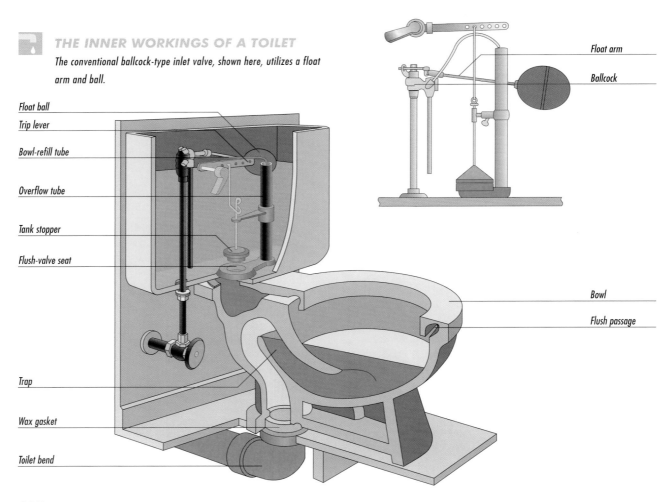

Float ball
Trip lever
Bowl-refill tube
Overflow tube
Tank stopper
Flush-valve seat
Trap
Wax gasket
Toilet bend

Float arm
Ballcock

Bowl
Flush passage

For most toilet repairs, you will need to shut off the water and empty the tank. You can shut off the water at the fixture shutoff or at the house shutoff valve. Then, flush the toilet, holding the handle down, to empty the tank completely. Finally, sponge out any water that is left.

ADJUSTING THE WATER LEVEL

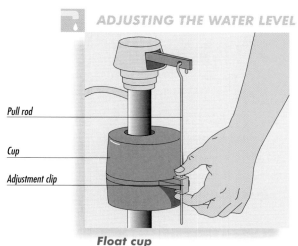

Pull rod

Cup

Adjustment clip

Float cup
Squeeze the adjustment clip on the pull rod and move the cup up or down.

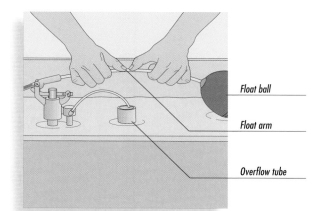

Float ball

Float arm

Overflow tube

Float arm & ball
Bend the float arm up to raise the level in the tank or down to lower the level. Be sure to use both hands and work carefully to avoid straining the assembly. The float ball sometimes develops cracks or holes and fills with water. If this happens, unscrew the ball and replace it, or replace the inlet valve with a float-cup model.

(continued on page 462)

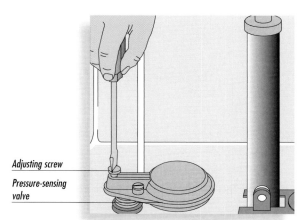

Adjusting screw

Pressure-sensing valve

Pressure-sensing valve
Turn the adjusting screw clockwise to raise the water level, counterclockwise to lower it. One turn should change the level by about 1 inch.

HOW A TOILET WORKS

Here's the chain of events that occurs when someone presses the flush handle on a toilet: The trip lever raises the lift-rod wires or chain connected to the tank stopper. As the stopper goes up, water rushes through the flush-valve seat and down into the bowl via the flush passages. The water in the bowl yields to gravity and is siphoned out the built-in toilet trap to the drainpipe.

Once the tank empties, the stopper drops into the flush-valve seat. The float ball or cup trips the inlet valve assembly to let fresh water into the tank through the tank fill tube. While the tank is filling, the bowl refill tube routes some water into the top of the overflow tube to replenish water in the bowl; this water seals the trap. As the water level in the tank rises, the float ball or cup rises until it gets high enough to shut off the flow of water, completing the process. If the water flowing into the tank fails to shut off, the overflow tube carries the excess water down into the bowl.

Repairing Toilets

Plumbing Repairs

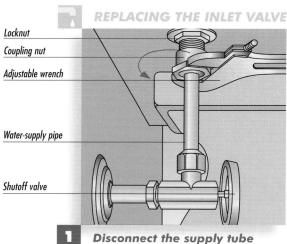

REPLACING THE INLET VALVE

Locknut
Coupling nut
Adjustable wrench
Water-supply pipe
Shutoff valve

1 **Disconnect the supply tube**

Shut off the water and flush the tank, holding the handle down to empty as much water as possible. Sponge out any remaining water. With an adjustable wrench, unfasten the coupling nut that connects the riser tube to the underside of the tank. Remove the washer (replace it if it is worn), then the float ball and arm inside the tank.

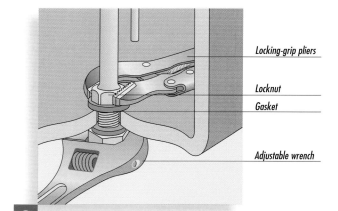

Locking-grip pliers
Locknut
Gasket
Adjustable wrench

2 **Remove the assembly**

Use a wrench to unfasten the locknut that holds the inlet valve assembly to the tank. Hold on to the base of the assembly inside the tank with locking-grip pliers and lift out the old assembly.

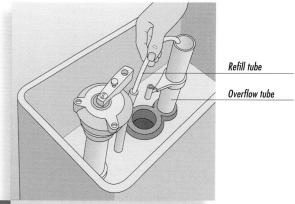

Refill tube
Overflow tube

3 **Install the new valve**

Assemble and adjust the new valve according to the manufacturer's directions, then install it in the tank hole. Tighten the locknut while pushing down. Make sure that the float cup or ball does not touch the tank. Install the refill tube so that water runs straight down the overflow pipe. Finish assembly, connect the supply tube, and turn on the water.

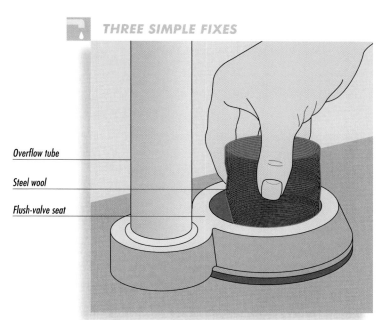

Overflow tube

Steel wool

Flush-valve seat

Repair the stopper & valve seat

If your toilet is running and the stopper doesn't fall straight down onto the seat, make sure that the guide rod or chain is centered over the flush valve. Inspect the valve seat for corrosion or mineral buildup; gently scour with fine steel wool, as shown. If the stopper is soft, encrusted, or out of shape, replace it. If the water still runs after the stopper and valve seat have been serviced, replace the flush-valve assembly.

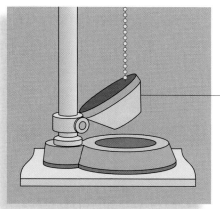

Flapper-type stopper

Replace the stopper

If the stopper needs replacing, install a flapper style with a chain, as shown. Unhook the old lift wires from the trip lever, unscrew the guide rod, then lift out the guide rod and wires. Slip the new flapper down over the collar of the overflow tube and fasten the chain to the trip lever. Adjust the chain so it is a little slack when the stopper is in place on the flush valve.

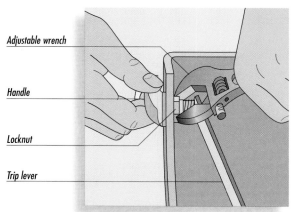

Adjustable wrench

Handle

Locknut

Trip lever

Fix the handle

A loose handle or trip lever can cause an inadequate or erratic flush cycle. Tighten the locknut that attaches the assembly to the tank. Note, however, that this locknut tightens counterclockwise. Generally, the handle and trip lever are one unit; if tightening the locknut doesn't solve the problem, replace the entire unit.

Fixing a Water Heater

When a hot water faucet is turned on, heated water is drawn from the top of the tank and replaced by cold water that is carried to the bottom via the dip tube. When water temperature drops, a thermostat activates the heat source—a burner in a gas heater, heating elements in an electric unit.

A gas heater has a flue running up the center and out the top to vent gases. An electric heater produces no gases and therefore needs no venting. In both types, a special anode attracts corrosion that might otherwise attack the tank's walls.

On a gas water heater, knowing how to light the pilot is very important. Directions vary, so follow the instructions on the tank. A gas heater has a thermocouple, which senses whether or not the pilot is on and shuts off the gas if the pilot light goes out.

Twice a year, inspect the flue assembly to be sure it's properly aligned and its joints are sealed. Then check the flue by placing your hand near the draft diverter (with the burner on); air flowing out indicates an obstruction, which should be removed immediately.

 Caution: If you smell a slight odor of natural gas near a gas water heater, turn off the gas inlet valve and ventilate the area. If the odor is strong or if it persists, leave the house immediately and call the gas company.

When an electric heater has problems, suspect the heating elements, their thermostats, and the high-temperature cutoff. The two heating elements are controlled by thermostats that, along with the high-temperature cutoff, are concealed behind an access panel on the side of the water heater (after removing the panel, insulation may also need to be cut away for access). If the high-temperature cutoff has tripped due to water that's too hot, the solution may be as easy as pushing the reset button. High voltage and inaccessibility warrant a service call to have the thermostats adjusted, the high-temperature cutoff reset, or any of these components replaced.

ROUTINE MAINTENANCE To reduce sediment accumulation, open the drain valve every six months and let the water run into a bucket until it looks clear.

At least once a year, test the temperature-pressure relief valve, which guards against hazardous pressure buildup. Lift or depress the handle; water should drain from the overflow pipe. If it doesn't, shut off water to the heater, open a hot water faucet in the house, and replace the valve.

ADJUSTING WATER TEMPERATURE Water heaters are often set to heat water to 150 or 160 degrees F. By lowering the setting to about 120 degrees F, you can save substantially on your fuel bills without affecting laundry or bathing. Dishwashers require higher temperatures to clean properly, but most models today are equipped with their own water-heating device.

DRAINING AND FLUSHING A TANK Turn off the gas or power, close the cold water valve, and attach a hose to the drain valve to route water into a drain or to the outdoors. Open the drain valve and open one hot water faucet to let in air. When all water has drained, turn the cold water valve on and off until the water from the drain looks clear. Then close the drain valve and the hot water faucet, open the cold water valve, and turn the power back on.

GAS WATER HEATER

Beneath the sealed tank of a gas water heater, a gas burner heats the water. Because it produces combustion gases, a gas water heater requires a flue to vent the fumes.

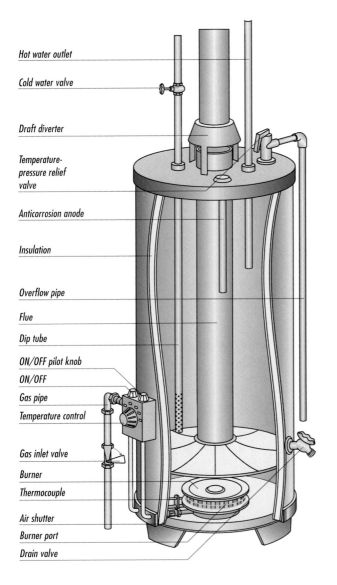

Hot water outlet

Cold water valve

Draft diverter

Temperature-pressure relief valve

Anticorrosion anode

Insulation

Overflow pipe

Flue

Dip tube

ON/OFF pilot knob

ON/OFF

Gas pipe

Temperature control

Gas inlet valve

Burner

Thermocouple

Air shutter

Burner port

Drain valve

ELECTRIC WATER HEATER

Electric resistance heating elements get hot to produce heat inside the tank of an electric water heater. Thermostats automatically regulate when the elements go on and off.

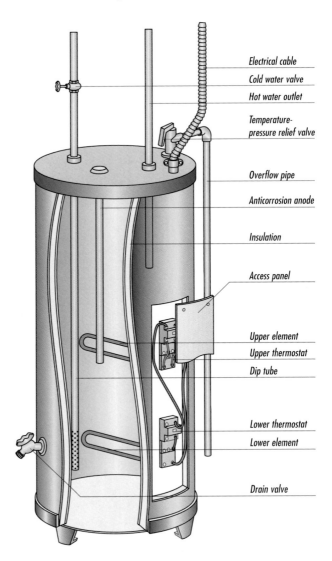

Electrical cable

Cold water valve

Hot water outlet

Temperature-pressure relief valve

Overflow pipe

Anticorrosion anode

Insulation

Access panel

Upper element

Upper thermostat

Dip tube

Lower thermostat

Lower element

Drain valve

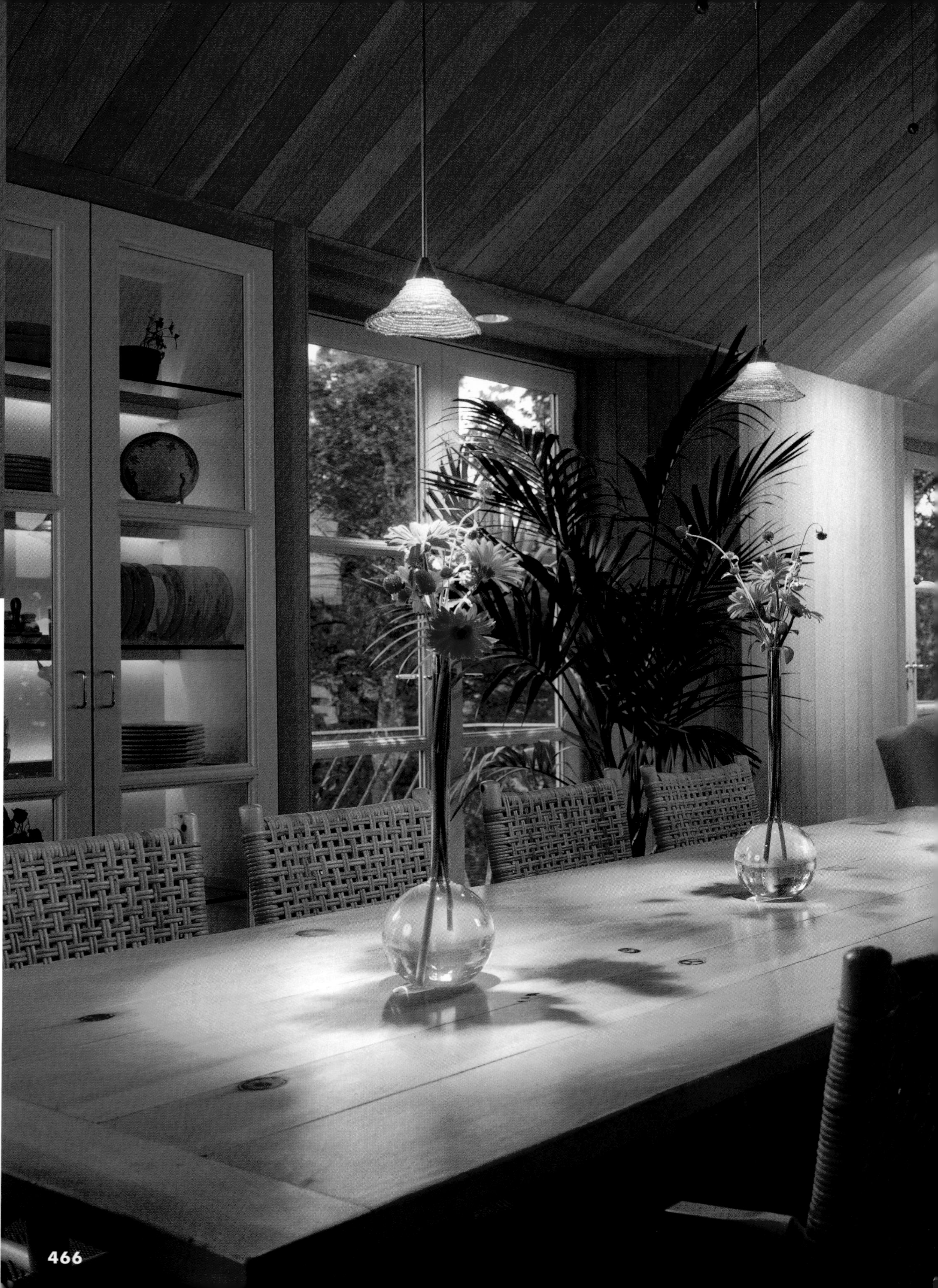

Electrical

A home's electrical system is its nerve center. Power in our homes lights our rooms and yards; runs our appliances, heating, air conditioning, and alarm systems; and drives our increasingly demanding computer systems. Indeed, many older homes today are not wired to adequately serve our technology needs. Often, improvements can require additional electrical wiring.

Electrical work, either improvements or repairs, can be intimidating for many do-it-yourselfers rightfully concerned about the risks of injury and fire from a botched job. Doing your own electrical work is relatively safe, and not that difficult, if you take the time to understand the basics of electricity and you use recommended precautions. This chapter provides that education, and guides you safely through some common electrical improvements and repairs.

Anatomy of Home Wiring

Electrical

Electricity provides us with comfort and conveniences that we often take for granted—until something goes wrong. Fortunately for the do-it-yourselfer, electrical wiring is usually simple and logical and there is considerable standardization in home electrical systems. Here we look at typical systems and how electricity energizes your home. You'll find more about current, codes, and electrical practices on the pages that follow.

ELECTRICAL DISTRIBUTION As shown in the illustration on the facing page, electricity passes through a meter before it enters the service panel. Owned, installed, and serviced by

the utility company, the meter is the final step in the installation of a complete wiring system. Once in place, the meter measures the electrical energy consumed in kilowatt-hours. The service panel usually houses the main disconnect (the main fuses or main circuit breaker), which shuts off power to the entire electrical system, and the fuses or circuit breakers, which protect the individual circuits in the home. Inside the service panel, electricity is routed to branch circuits that carry power to the different parts of the house. Typically, each cable contains three conductors. Two hot conductors (identified by red, black, or any other color except white, gray, or green insulation) go

TYPICAL HOME ELECTRICAL SYSTEMS

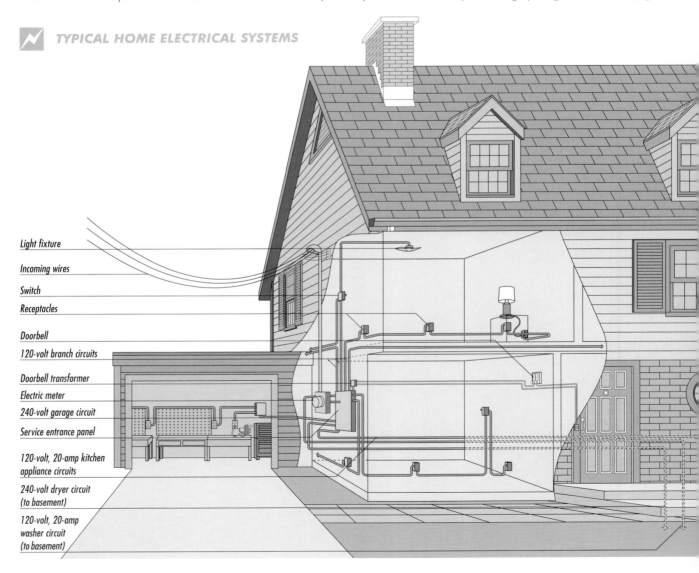

Light fixture

Incoming wires

Switch

Receptacles

Doorbell

120-volt branch circuits

Doorbell transformer

Electric meter

240-volt garage circuit

Service entrance panel

120-volt, 20-amp kitchen appliance circuits

240-volt dryer circuit (to basement)

120-volt, 20-amp washer circuit (to basement)

Electricity runs from the utility company lines, through the meter, and into the service panel. Once inside the service panel it is divided into branch circuits that transmit power to the different parts of the house.

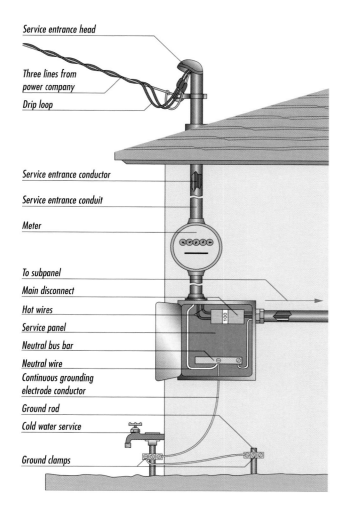

Service entrance head

Three lines from power company

Drip loop

Service entrance conductor

Service entrance conduit

Meter

To subpanel

Main disconnect

Hot wires

Service panel

Neutral bus bar

Neutral wire

Continuous grounding electrode conductor

Ground rod

Cold water service

Ground clamps

to the main disconnect. The neutral conductor (color-coded white or gray) goes directly to a device called the neutral bus bar.

There is one other important wire associated with your service panel—the grounding electrode conductor. The continuous conductor connects the neutral bus bar to the metal water supply pipe entering your home (a grounding jumper wire is used to bypass the water meter) and to a metal ground rod driven into the earth. This safety feature provides excess current with an uninterrupted metal pathway into the ground.

(continued on page 470)

WIRING GLOSSARY

AMPERE (OR AMP): The measurement used for the amount of current that flows through the wire or device. It is based on the number of electrons flowing past a given point per second.

BRANCH CIRCUIT: Any one of many separate circuits distributing electricity throughout a house.

CIRCUIT: Two or more wires providing a path for electrical current to flow from the source through some device using electricity, and back to the source.

CURRENT: The movement or flow of electrons through a conductor; measured in amperes.

GROUND: Any conducting body, such as a metal cold water pipe or a metal rod driven solidly into the earth, that provides electrical current with a path to the ground.

GROUNDING WIRE: Conductor that grounds a metal component but does not carry current during normal operation.

HOT WIRE: Ungrounded conductor carrying electrical current forward from the source. Usually identified by black or red insulation, but may be any color other than white, gray, or green.

KILOWATT-HOUR (KWH): Unit used for metering and selling electricity. One kilowatt-hour equals 1,000 watts used for one hour (or any equivalent, such as 500 watts used for two hours).

NEUTRAL WIRE: Grounded conductor that completes a circuit by providing a return path to the source. Except for a few switching situations, neutral wires must never be interrupted by a fuse, circuit breaker, or switch. Always identified by white or gray insulation.

PIGTAIL SPLICE: A connection of three or more wires.

VOLT (V): Unit of measurement for electrical pressure.

WATT (W): Unit of measurement for electrical power. One watt of power equals one volt of pressure times one ampere of current. Many electrical devices are rated in watts according to the power they use.

Anatomy of Home Wiring

(continued from page 469)

CURRENT & CIRCUITS Today, most homes have what's called three-wire service. The utility company connects three wires—two "hot" and one neutral—through a meter to your service panel. These wires branch off through the house to provide both 120-volt and 240-volt capabilities. One hot wire and the neutral wire combine to supply 120 volts, the level that is used for most household applications, such as lights and small appliances. Both hot wires and the neutral wire can form a 120/240-volt circuit.

Any electrical system is rated for the maximum amount of current (measured in amperes) it can carry. This rating, determined by the size of the service entrance equipment, is called the "service rating." Today the minimum service rating of most new homes is 100 amps. Depending on the age of your home, your service rating could be as low as 30 amps or as high as 400 amps. The best way to find out your service rating is to look at the main service panel. The service rating will usually be stamped on the main fuses or circuit breaker.

 BASIC ELECTRICAL CIRCUITS

Throughout a house, electrical current flows to appliances, switches, and receptacles through hot wires, and flows back to the service panel through neutral wires. Any deviation from this normal path is dangerous.

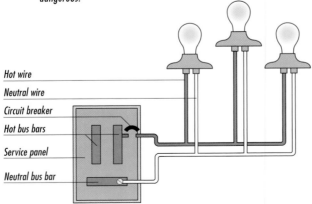

Hot wire
Neutral wire
Circuit breaker
Hot bus bars
Service panel
Neutral bus bar

 **THE IMPORTANCE OF GROUNDING**

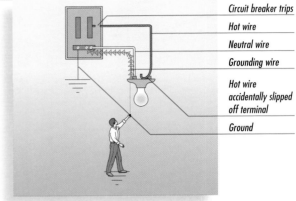

Circuit breaker trips
Hot wire
Neutral wire
Grounding wire
Hot wire accidentally slipped off terminal
Ground

Properly grounded

A grounding wire carries current from a faulty fixture back to the distribution center, preventing short circuit and shock.

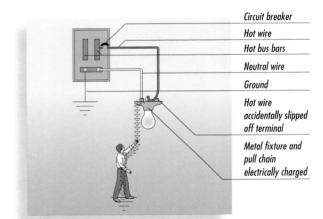

Circuit breaker
Hot wire
Hot bus bars
Neutral wire
Ground
Hot wire accidentally slipped off terminal
Metal fixture and pull chain electrically charged

Not grounded

Without a grounding wire, the body of a faulty light fixture is live, exposing you to shock if you touch it.

The National Electrical Code requires that every circuit in new construction have a grounding system. A grounding system incorporates special wires that divert any leaking current or dangerous voltage levels safely into the earth.

Electrical

MAPPING YOUR CIRCUITS

Using numbers and electrical symbols, you can make up a good working drawing of your electrical system. Such a drawing or map can save you much time, whether you plan to wire a new home, alter existing wiring, or troubleshoot a problem. Keep a copy of your map near the main service panel. The following is a circuit map of a typical two-bedroom house. Note that the dashed lines indicate which switch controls which fixture; they do not show wire routes.

1. Range (240 volt)
2. Dryer (240 volt)
3. Kitchen and dining room (20 amp)
4. Kitchen and dining room (20 amp)
5. Washer (20 amp)
6. Dishwasher (20 amp)
7. Bath and hall (15 amp)
8. Bedroom #1 (15 amp)
9. Bedroom #2 (15 amp)
10. Living room (15 amp)
11. Living room (15 amp)
12. Garage (20 amp)

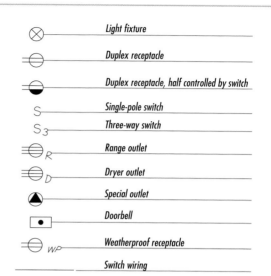

⊗	Light fixture
⊖	Duplex receptacle
⊖	Duplex receptacle, half controlled by switch
S	Single-pole switch
S₃	Three-way switch
⊜ R	Range outlet
⊜ D	Dryer outlet
▲	Special outlet
▪	Doorbell
⊖ WP	Weatherproof receptacle
	Switch wiring

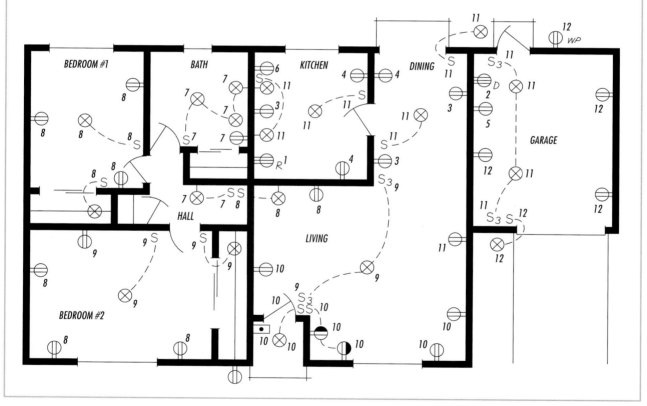

Codes & Safety

Working with electricity is one of the riskiest activities you can undertake as a do-it-yourselfer. Unless it is handled properly, electricity can cause dangerous, even deadly, shocks and fires. Take the time to understand and respect the potential hazards of electricity; once you do, you will be able to safely handle home electrical projects like those presented in this book.

The most important rule for all do-it-yourself electricians is never to work on any electrically "live" circuit, fixture, or appliance. Before starting any work, disconnect (or "kill") the circuit at its source in the service panel, as shown on the facing page. Before beginning any work, test the circuit with a neon tester, as explained on page 475.

In the United States, the rules and procedures for electrical wiring are spelled out in the National Electrical Code (NEC). Cities, counties, and states are allowed to amend the NEC—and many do. The electrical code exists to ensure that all wiring is done safely and competently.

Before beginning any major electrical work of your own, check with your local building department to see which, if any, permits and inspections may be required. They can also inform you of any restrictions that exist on the kinds of electrical wiring a homeowner may do.

The grounding system is another safeguard in an electrical system, as discussed on page 470. Grounding assures that all metal parts of a tool, fixture, appliance, or other electrical device with which you might come into contact are maintained at zero voltage. During normal conditions, the grounding system does nothing, but in the event of a malfunction, it can save your life. See more about grounding boxes on the facing page.

 SAFEGUARDS IN THE SYSTEM

Fuses and circuit breakers guard electrical systems from damage caused by too much current. Whenever wiring is forced to carry more current than it can handle safely—usually because of too many appliances on one circuit or a problem within the system—a circuit breaker will trip or a fuse will blow, immediately shutting off the flow of current. Power can be restored in a circuit breaker by flipping the switch to OFF, then back to the ON position. A blown fuse, however, must be replaced.

 If a circuit breaker trips, flip it to OFF before flipping it to the ON position.

FUSES

CIRCUIT BREAKERS

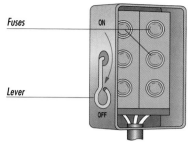

Fuses

Lever

Fuse box with lever

If the circuits are protected by fuses, removing the appropriate fuse will disconnect the circuit from incoming service. To disconnect the entire electrical system, push the lever to OFF.

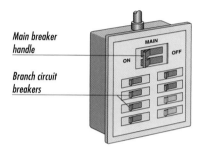

Main breaker handle

Branch circuit breakers

Circuit breakers

If the circuits are protected by circuit breakers, disconnect a circuit by switching its breaker to the OFF position. To shut off the entire electrical system, turn the main breaker switch to OFF.

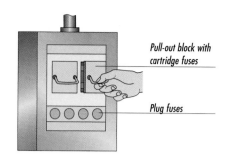

Pull-out block with cartridge fuses

Plug fuses

Fuse box with pull-out blocks

To shut off single circuits, remove plug fuses. To disconnect multiple circuits or power to the entire electrical system, remove the fuse blocks that contain cartridge fuses.

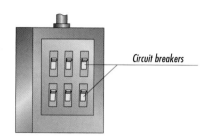

Circuit breakers

Circuit breakers in a subpanel

Shut off individual circuits by switching the disconnects to the OFF position.

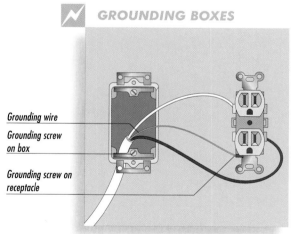

Grounding wire

Grounding screw on box

Grounding screw on receptacle

Grounding nonmetal boxes

To ground a receptacle at the end of a circuit, attach the grounding wire to the grounding screw. To ground a switch or receptacle in the middle of a circuit, attach a grounding jumper to the grounding screw, then join it with a wire nut to the grounding wires from cables entering the box.

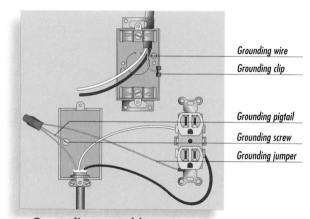

Grounding wire

Grounding clip

Grounding pigtail

Grounding screw

Grounding jumper

Grounding metal boxes

When only one cable enters a box, attach the device's grounding screw wire to the grounding screw in the back or use a grounding clip. If more than one cable enters the box or it has a grounding terminal, make a grounding jumper using a short piece of wire. Twist together the grounding wires and the jumper wire and secure them.

Electrical Tools

In addition to some basic carpentry tools that may be needed for rough electrical work, electrical improvements and repairs do require specialized tools, as well as certain testing devices, shown on the facing page, to ensure that both you and the electrical device are working safely. The most common tools in the electrical toolkit are shown here. These include a variety of pliers-like tools for cutting, stripping, and bending wire; wire strippers and cable rippers for removing wire and cable insulation; fish tape, which is indispensable for routing wires and cables behind walls; and screwdrivers for fastening screw terminals and grounding screws within boxes.

Any time you work with electrical systems, your best friends are three basic diagnostic tools. The neon tester features a neon bulb that glows when the tester probes touch wire ends, screw terminals, and receptacle slots to tell you they are hot or live. A receptacle analyzer, which plugs into a receptacle, has three diagnostic lights that indicate whether there is power to the receptacle, whether it is grounded properly, and whether the wiring is correct. A continuity tester transmits a low-voltage current through a circuit to establish if a circuit is broken or open.

 WIRING TOOLS

Lineman's pliers combine serrated jaws designed to twist wires with cutters to snip through wire. Long-nose pliers cut wire and are particularly handy for forming hooks at bare wire ends. Diagonal-cutting pliers, or "dikes," are used for wires. Wire strippers remove insulation from wires of various gauges and also attach crimp connectors to wire ends. Standard tip and Phillips-head screwdrivers fit screws on electrical devices.

 SPECIALTY TOOLS

Routing cable behind walls and through ceilings requires a fish tape (these come in 25-foot and 50-foot lengths). A neon tester works for checking receptacles and wires for power (see page 505); a receptacle analyzer diagnoses a receptacle's circuit. A continuity tester determines whether or not a circuit is complete.

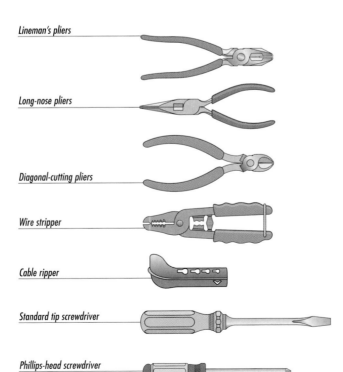

Lineman's pliers

Long-nose pliers

Diagonal-cutting pliers

Wire stripper

Cable ripper

Standard tip screwdriver

Phillips-head screwdriver

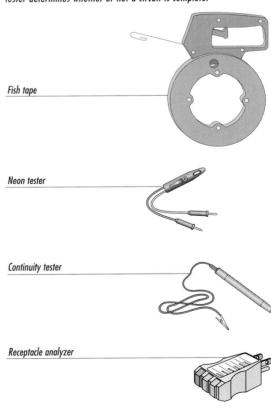

Fish tape

Neon tester

Continuity tester

Receptacle analyzer

Electrical

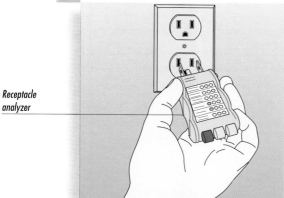
Receptacle
analyzer

Plug the receptacle analyzer into the receptacle
you are testing. Check the diagnostic chart on the
analyzer for lights indicating whether or not the
receptacle is receiving power, is grounded, and the
wiring is sound.

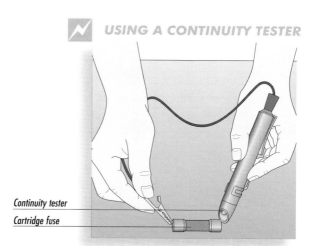
Continuity tester

Cartridge fuse

This battery-powered tester sends a small electrical
current through an electrical device, such as a
cartridge fuse, switch, socket, or wire, to
determine if its path is undamaged. If the tester
lights (or buzzes), the device is sound. To test a
cartridge fuse, first remove the fuse from the fuse
block. Touch the tester and/or probes to each end
of the fuse. If the fuse is good, the tester will light
(or buzz).

GROUND-FAULT CIRCUIT INTERRUPTERS (GFCIs)

A ground-fault circuit interrupter (also called GFCI or GFI)
is a special disconnect device that, according to electrical
codes, must be used in bathrooms, kitchens, and outdoors.
These should also be used in garages and wet areas, where
the danger of shock is great. Whenever the amounts of
incoming and outgoing current are unequal, indicating current leakage, a GFCI opens the circuit instantly, cutting off
the power.

There are two types of GFCIs. The GFCI breaker is installed in the service panel; it monitors the amount of current going to and coming from an entire circuit. A GFCI
receptacle monitors the flow of electricity to that receptacle, as well as to all devices installed in the circuit from that
point onward (called "downstream"). You can use either type
where code requires a GFCI.

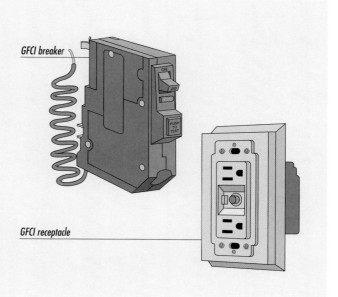

GFCI breaker

GFCI receptacle

Working with Cable & Wire

Electrical

Electrical cable consists of two or more wires contained in the same protective outer sheathing. A single conductor is an individual wire, usually sheathed with an insulating material (the grounding wire may be bare). Before connecting a cable to a device or joining it to another cable, cut open and remove the outer sheath, cut away all the separation materials, and strip the insulation from the ends of the individual conductors.

Cable is identified by the size and number of conductors it contains. For example, a cable with two #14 wires (one white and one black) and a grounding wire (green or bare) is called a "14-2 with ground." Nonmetallic sheathed cable is used in most residential wiring and comes in two types: NM (nonmetallic) and UF (underground feeder). Type AC metal-clad cable and nonflexible and flexible conduit, although more difficult and expensive to install than NM cable, are other options for indoor wiring projects; if your local code requires conduit, it's best to consult a professional.

⚡ WIRING WITH CABLE

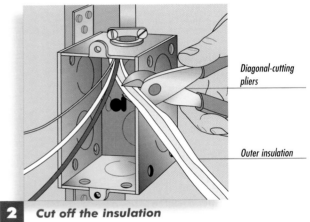

Cable ripper

Cable

1 Slice through the sheathing
Slide a cable ripper up the cable to the top of the box. Press the handles and pull. Bend the cable back to crack the score and then peel open the outer sheathing.

Diagonal-cutting pliers

Outer insulation

2 Cut off the insulation
Separate the wires from the insulation. Using a pair of diagonal-cutting pliers, cut off the opened outer sheathing and all separation materials.

⚡ SCREWING ON A WIRE NUT

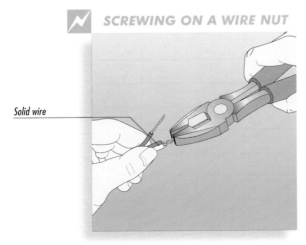

Solid wire

Strip off about 1 inch of insulation from the ends of wires you wish to join. Twist the bare ends together and snip off any excess so the bare portion is about ¾ inch long. Then screw on the wire nut, turning clockwise until tight and until no bare wire is exposed. Buy wire nuts sized for the number and size of wires being joined.

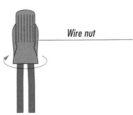

Wire nut

3

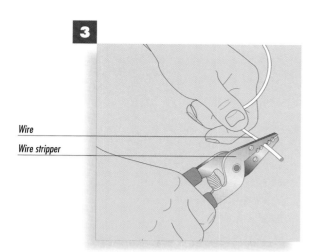

Wire

Wire stripper

Remove the insulation

Using a wire stripper, insert the wire into the matching slot. Holding the wire firmly in your hand, position the stripper on the wire at an angle and press the handles together. Rock the stripper back and forth until the insulation is severed and can be pulled off the wire.

Form a hook

Strip about ¹/₂ inch to ³/₄ inch of insulation off the wire end. Using long-nose pliers, form a loop in the bare wire. Starting near the insulation, bend the wire at a right angle and make progressive bends, moving the pliers toward the wire end until a loop is formed.

4

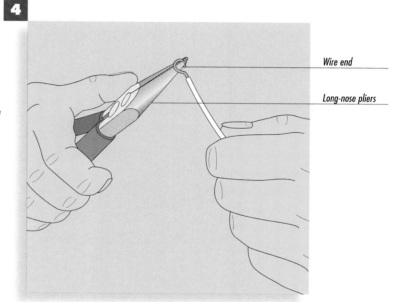

Wire end

Long-nose pliers

5

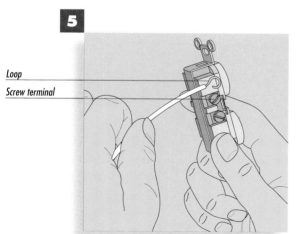

Loop

Screw terminal

Make the connection

Hook the wire clockwise around the screw terminal. As you tighten the screw, the loop on the wire will close. (If you hook the wire counterclockwise, tightening the screw will open the loop.)

Routing Cable

In new construction, all basic wiring is done before the walls, ceilings, and floors are covered. Extending a circuit in a finished house, however, is a more complicated process. You have to find ways to route cable behind existing walls, above ceilings, and under floors. It is wise to familiarize yourself with your house's construction so that you can find the most direct route from the power source to the locations for the new devices. Attic floors and basement ceilings are often easy to access, while "fishing" cable through walls and between floors may take some time. Gypsum wallboard (drywall) can be cut and replaced easily, but plaster and ceramic tile are best left alone.

 ATTACHING CABLE

In exposed (new) wiring, cable must be stapled or supported with straps within every 54 inches and within 12 inches of each metal box and 8 inches of each nonmetallic box. When using cable staples and clamps, as shown, be careful that you don't staple through or smash the cable. Cable staples and supports are not required when cable is fished behind walls, floors, and ceilings in concealed (old) work. However, the cable must be clamped to the box itself.

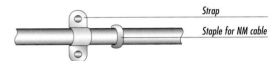

Strap

Staple for NM cable

RUNNING CABLE THROUGH WALLS & CEILINGS

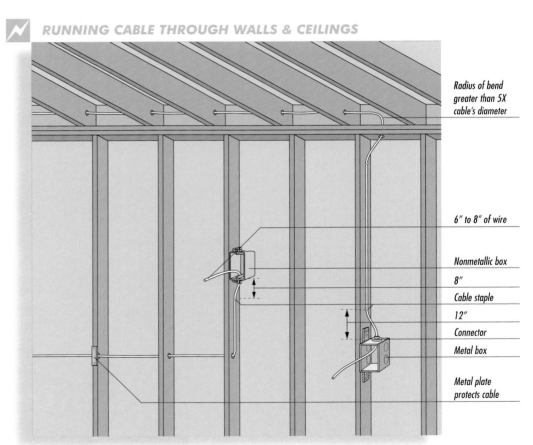

Radius of bend greater than 5X cable's diameter

6" to 8" of wire

Nonmetallic box

8"

Cable staple

12"

Connector

Metal box

Metal plate protects cable

This illustration shows a typical route for running cable through walls and ceilings. To avoid nailing through the cable once the walls and ceilings are installed, run the cable through holes drilled 1¹/₄ inches from the edge of wall studs or drilled through the center of the joists.

Electrical Improvements

RUNNING CABLE THROUGH THE BASEMENT

When running standard NM cable under the floor at an angle to floor joists, you can run it through holes bored in the joists, fasten it to the sides of beams or joists, or fasten it to a running board. Only cable that is 8 gauge or larger can be fastened directly to the bottoms of the joists.

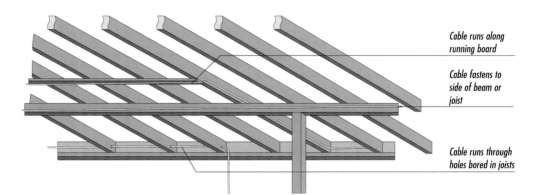

Cable runs along running board

Cable fastens to side of beam or joist

Cable runs through holes bored in joists

RUNNING CABLE THROUGH THE ATTIC

Accessibility dictates how cable runs in an attic. If a permanent staircase or ladder leads to the attic, use guard strips to protect cable that runs at an angle to the joists. In an attic reached through a crawl hole with no permanent stairs or ladder, protect the cable within 6 feet of the hole with guard strips. Otherwise, cable can usually lie on top of the ceiling joists.

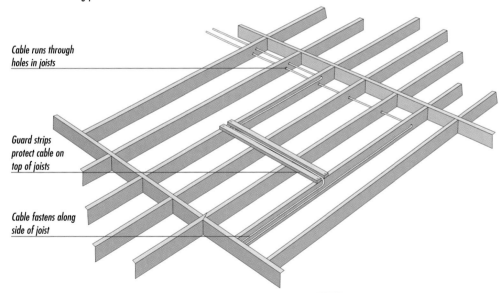

Cable runs through holes in joists

Guard strips protect cable on top of joists

Cable fastens along side of joist

DON'T MESS WITH TRUSSES

Prefabricated trusses are being used with increasing frequency to frame roofs. If you need to run cable across trusses, never drill holes or cut into them. Cutting a truss can weaken it, and it can void the manufacturer's warranty. Always use running boards across the tops, and staple the cable to the board.

Fishing Cable & Mounting Boxes

When the structural framing of new construction is exposed, installing electrical wiring is relatively easy. But what do you do when you need to run wiring inside existing walls, ceilings, or floors? Shown here are basic techniques for fishing wire and mounting electrical boxes.

The easiest way to route electrical power to the location is to draw it from an existing receptacle or nonswitched light box. Start by selecting an existing box, and decide on the locations of the new devices (be sure the circuit can handle the additional electrical load). Shut off the power to the existing box before opening it up or making any connections.

Use fish tape to pull cable through walls and framing members; some jobs require two fish tapes. For short distances, you may be able to use a piece of stiff wire with a hook formed at the end.

In new construction, electrical boxes are usually nailed to studs. In remodeling work, however, cut-in (or "old work") boxes are attached to the finished wall between two studs.

You can install cut-in boxes as shown on the facing page. Outline the box on the wall; then, in wood or gypsum wallboard, drill a starter hole. Cut the opening with a keyhole saw or jigsaw. Test fit the box. Adjust the ears so the box is flush with the finished wall. Open a knockout for each cable and pull the cable into the box. If you have plaster and lath walls, cutting holes is trickier. You may have the best luck by placing masking tape over the outline, then drilling a series of holes along the outline. Attach the box with screws driven through the ears into the wood lath.

FISHING CABLE THROUGH A WALL

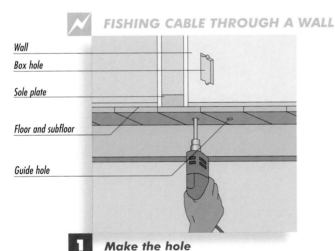

Wall
Box hole
Sole plate
Floor and subfloor
Guide hole

1 **Make the hole**
Cut the hole for the box, then drill a small guide hole in the ceiling or floor in front of the box hole. From above or below, use a spade bit to drill next to the guide hole through the sole plate or top plates. Feed fish tape through the hole, into the wall cavity, and out the box hole. If you can't, go to the next step.

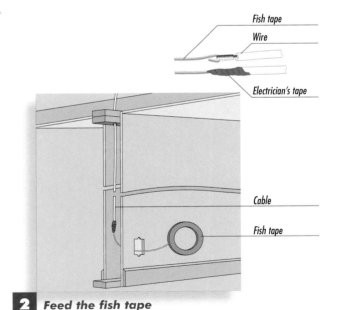

Fish tape
Wire
Electrician's tape
Cable
Fish tape

2 **Feed the fish tape**
Using a helper, run one fish tape through the drilled hole and another through the box hole. Wiggle the tape until the two hooked ends catch. Pull the tape through the box hole. Attach cable to the fish tape, then wrap electrician's tape around the connection (detail) and pull the cable through the wall.

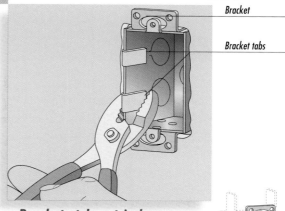

Bracket

Bracket tabs

Bracket-style cut-in box

Put the brackets in the wall, one on either side of the box. Pull the tabs snugly against the back side of the wall (detail). Bend the tabs over the sides of the box and secure them.

CABLING BEHIND BASEBOARDS

Box hole

Fish tape

Access hole

Cable

To run wire horizontally through a wall, remove the baseboard with a prybar, drill access holes, then cut a channel to connect the access holes. Fish the wire into the box holes as discussed on the facing page. Pull the cable through, leaving about 8 inches extending out of the first box hole. Secure the cable to the studs and protect it with metal plates. When you reinstall the baseboard, take care not to nail where the cable is located.

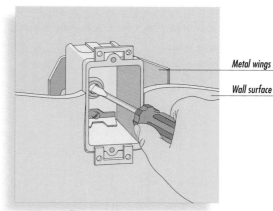

Metal wings

Wall surface

Winged cut-in box

Push the box into the wall, then tighten the screw at the back of the box to pull the wings into the back side of the wall. Take care: You can't remove this box, so make sure cables are in place and the box fits the hole before mounting.

INSTALLING A CEILING BOX

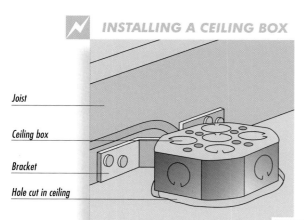

Joist

Ceiling box

Bracket

Hole cut in ceiling

If you have access from above, you can attach the box to ceiling joists with a flange-style metal box. Otherwise, use a ceiling box with an attached bar hanger, cut away a strip of ceiling, fasten the strip to joists, then repair the ceiling (see chapter on Walls & Ceilings).

Ceiling box

Offset hanger bar

Wiring Receptacles

Grounded duplex receptacles consist of an upper and lower outlet with three slots. The larger (neutral) slot accepts the wide prong of a three-prong plug; the smaller (hot) slot is for the narrow prong, and the U-shaped grounding slot is for the grounding prong. A 20-amp receptacle differs in appearance from a 15-amp receptacle in that it has a vertical slot coming off the neutral slot (the wide one).

Duplex receptacles have three different colors of screw terminals. The brass-colored screws on one side of the receptacle are hot terminals; the white- or silver-colored screws on the opposite side are neutral terminals, and the green screw is the grounding terminal.

Receptacles are rated for a specific amperage and voltage. This information is stamped clearly on the front of the receptacle. Be sure you buy what you need. To eliminate the possibility of plugging a 120-volt appliance into a 240-volt receptacle, higher-voltage circuits use special receptacles and matching attachment plugs.

Ground-fault circuit interrupter (GFCI) receptacles (see page 475) are special outlets for use in wet areas, such as bathrooms and kitchens. See the facing page for information on how to install one.

 CONVENTIONAL DUPLEX RECEPTACLE

When wiring a standard duplex receptacle, be sure to connect the black (hot) wire to the brass terminal side and the white (neutral) wire to the silver terminal side. Connect the grounding wire to the green grounding terminal.

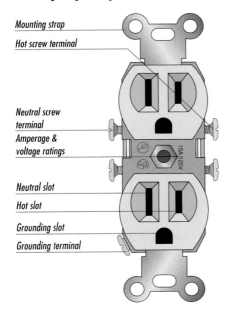

Mounting strap
Hot screw terminal
Neutral screw terminal
Amperage & voltage ratings
Neutral slot
Hot slot
Grounding slot
Grounding terminal

 PARALLEL RECEPTACLES

From source

Two-wire cable with ground

These two receptacles are wired parallel to each other in the same circuit. The receptacle on the left is in the middle of the circuit (two cables enter the box), while the one on the right is at the end of the circuit (one cable enters the box). Both the upper and lower outlets of each receptacle are always hot.

RECEPTACLES BEHIND SWITCHES

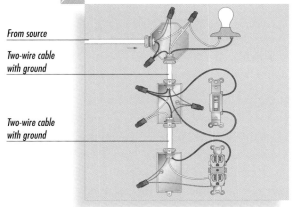

From source

Two-wire cable
with ground

Two-wire cable
with ground

In this example, a switch is wired ahead of the
receptacle in the circuit (two cables enter the
switch box). The switch controls a light. The
receptacle is at the end of the circuit (one cable
enters the box). Both the upper and lower outlets
of the receptacle are always hot.

SPLIT-CIRCUIT RECEPTACLES

Break-off fin
removed

White wire
painted black

From source

You can wire a receptacle so that one outlet is
always hot and the other is controlled by a switch.
This allows you to plug a lamp into the switch-
controlled outlet, which can be turned on when
you enter the room. In this example, the bottom
outlet is always hot, while the upper outlet is
turned on and off by the switch.

INSTALLING A GFCI

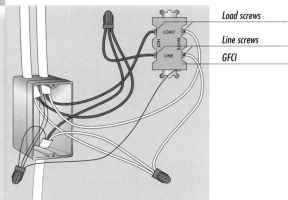

Load screws

Line screws

GFCI

To wire a GFCI receptacle for single-location
protection, connect the hot and neutral wires to
the terminal screws marked LINE. To wire it for
multiple-location protection, as shown, connect the
incoming power to the screws marked LINE and
the wires continuing farther down the line to the
LOAD screws. Connect the grounding wire or
jumper to the green grounding screw. Push the
GFCI into the box, attach the faceplate, and
restore power. Test the GFCI as recommended by
the manufacturer.

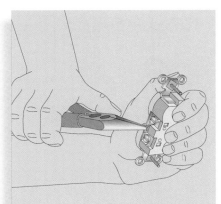

 **To make the outlets operate
independently, use pliers or a
screwdriver to remove the break-
off fin that connects them.**

Wiring Switches

When you need to buy a new switch, be sure to look for the appropriate type. Switches are stamped with their maximum voltage (V) and amperage (A) ratings. Standard wall switches are rated 15A and 120V or 125V. Switches and receptacles are available in several grades. "Residential" or "contractor" grade is the least expensive and most commonly available. Many electricians prefer to use "spec" or "commercial" grade switches, which cost a little more but are much more durable.

 CHOOSING THE RIGHT SWITCH

Though single-pole and three-way switches look somewhat alike, two features distinguish them. A single-pole switch has two terminals for wire connections and the words ON and OFF embossed on the toggle. A three-way switch has three terminals and no ON and OFF indicators.

SINGLE-POLE VS. THREE-WAY SWITCHES Single-pole switches are the most common. They control fixtures or receptacles from one location only. Three-way switches provide two separate switching locations for a single fixture, such as at the top and bottom of stairs. Four-way switches provide three switching points for a single location. Dimmer switches allow you to control a light fixture's brightness.

Before working on a switch, turn off the power to the circuit supplying it. Test the switch's wires or terminals with a neon tester to be sure they are safe to handle.

(continued on page 486)

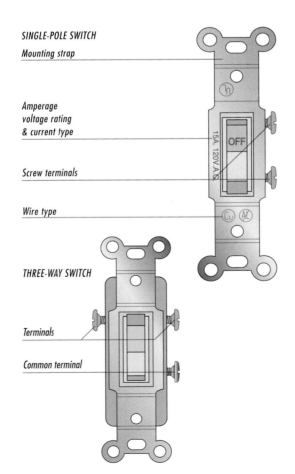

SINGLE-POLE SWITCH

Mounting strap

Amperage voltage rating & current type

15A 120V AC OFF

Screw terminals

Wire type

Cu AL

THREE-WAY SWITCH

Terminals

Common terminal

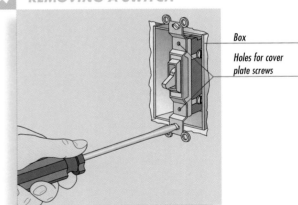 **REMOVING A SWITCH**

Box

Holes for cover plate screws

After turning off the switch's circuit, remove the faceplate and loosen the switch's mounting screws. Gently pull the switch outward, but don't touch the terminal screws or wires. Use a neon tester to confirm that power is shut off. Turn the terminal screws counterclockwise far enough to release the wires. If the wires are stuck into the push-in terminals on the back, push a small screwdriver into the release slots and pull them free.

Electrical Improvements

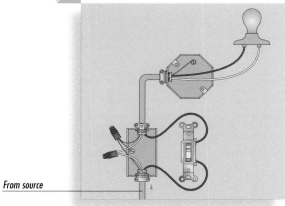

From source

Switch at middle of circuit

With this configuration, power goes through a single-pole switch located in the middle of a circuit (two or more cables enter the switch box). The switch controls a light at the end of the circuit.

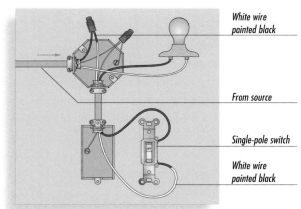

White wire painted black

From source

Single-pole switch

White wire painted black

Light at end of circuit

Use this wiring diagram to guide you when the circuit ends at a light fixture controlled by a single-pole switch.

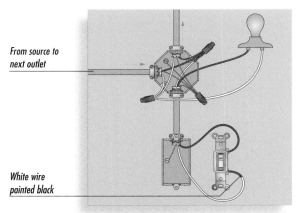

From source to next outlet

White wire painted black

Light at middle of circuit

When the light is in the middle of a circuit (two or more cables enter the fixture box), the switch controls the light in the middle of the circuit run. Note that both wires connected to the switch are hot, and that the hot wire has been marked with black tape or paint.

 ## WHICH WIRE IS HOT?

White wires are usually—but not always—neutral wires. White wires can be hot, so you should always assume a white wire is hot until you test it. When two wires enter the electrical box you are working on, it isn't always apparent which of the wires carries the electrical load. To find the hot wire, touch one probe of a neon tester to the grounding wire or grounded metal box and the other probe to the other wires, one at a time. The tester will light when the second probe touches the hot wire.

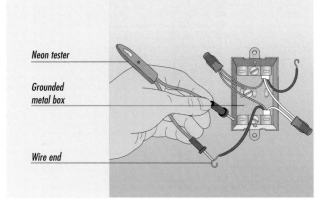

Neon tester

Grounded metal box

Wire end

Wiring Switches

(continued from page 484)
INSTALLING DIMMER SWITCHES A dimmer switch allows you to control the amount of brightness from a light. You can replace a standard single-pole switch with a comparable dimmer switch easily. Different styles of dimmers are available. Most are controlled by a rotating dial or a sliding mechanism. Most compact fluorescent light bulbs cannot be used in a fixture controlled by a conventional dimmer. As with all electrical work, remember to shut off power before you begin working with the wiring.

WIRING A THREE-WAY SWITCH If you want to be able to turn a light on and off at two locations, such as at the top and bottom of a staircase or at both ends of a hallway, consider installing a pair of three-way switches, using one of the methods shown on the facing page.

INSTALLING A DIMMER

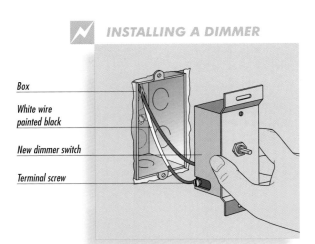

Box

White wire painted black

New dimmer switch

Terminal screw

Dimmer with terminal screws

For a dimmer switch with terminal screws on the side, loop the circuit wires clockwise around the terminal screws. Tighten the screws and carefully push the switch back into the box.

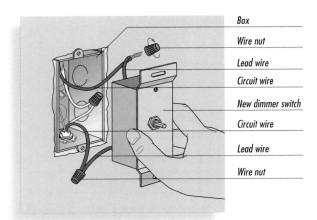

Box

Wire nut

Lead wire

Circuit wire

New dimmer switch

Circuit wire

Lead wire

Wire nut

Dimmer with lead wires

For a dimmer with lead wires, connect the circuit wires to the dimmer's lead wires with wire nuts. Carefully push the switch back into the box.

Electrical Improvements

Three-way switch at middle of circuit

To wire a pair of three-way switches, run the hot wire from the source to the common terminal of one switch; run the hot wire from the light to the common terminal of the other switch. Then wire the four remaining terminals by running two hot wires between the two terminals on one switch and the two terminals on the other switch. In this example, the light in the middle of the circuit is controlled by a pair of three-way switches.

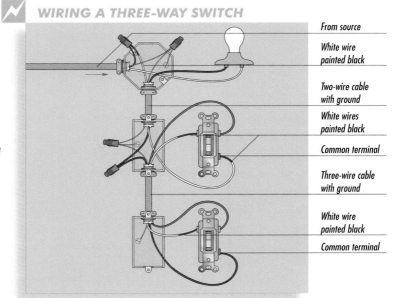

From source

White wire painted black

Two-wire cable with ground

White wires painted black

Common terminal

Three-wire cable with ground

White wire painted black

Common terminal

Light at the end of a three-way circuit

Power goes through a pair of three-way switches to a light at the end of the circuit. Caution: Check the location of the marked common terminal; if it is different from this example, connect the black (hot) wire that runs between the switches to the common terminal on each switch.

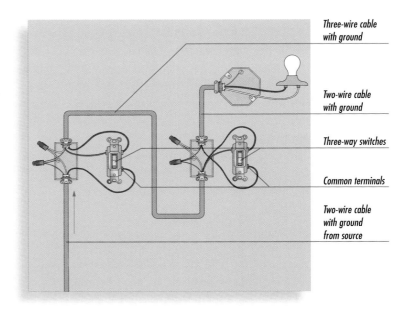

Three-wire cable with ground

Two-wire cable with ground

Three-way switches

Common terminals

Two-wire cable with ground from source

White wires painted black

Three-wire cables with ground

Three-way switches

Common terminals

Two-wire cable with ground from source

Light between two a three-way switches

Shown is how to wire a light between a pair of three-way switches. Caution: Check the location of the common terminal on the switch (it will be marked); if it isn't, connect the black (hot) wire that runs between the switches to the common terminal on each switch.

Adding New Circuits

Electrical Improvements

When you are upgrading your electrical service or installing a new appliance, or when an existing circuit can't handle a new load, adding a circuit is often necessary. Make sure that the new circuit will be within the service rating for the whole house; if you are unsure of this, ask an electrician to calculate the total house load and tell you how many new circuits can be added. Also note that all new 120-volt branch circuits must have a grounding wire and must comply with present code requirements.

Planning is the crucial first step in wiring a new circuit. The first step is to draw a diagram showing the location of each proposed switch, receptacle, light fixture, and major appliance. Refer back to the symbols shown in "Mapping Your Circuits" on page 471 to make this easier. The next step is to design the circuit. When doing this, keep in mind that it is unwise to have a single circuit supplying the lights for an entire section or floor of a house. Try to plan each circuit so one area of the home won't be left in the dark in the event that the circuit fails.

All new circuits must conform with the requirements of the National Electrical Code (NEC) and with any additional local requirements. The following minimum requirements of the NEC cover many of the most important areas of the house, but this list is not exhaustive. Always check with your local building department or a qualified electrician before proceeding with any work.

KITCHENS

- Must have at least two 20-amp small-appliance circuits.
- No light fixtures can be connected to these circuits.
- Small-appliance circuits must be spaced no more than 4 feet apart.
- All countertop receptacles must be GFCI protected.
- An island or peninsula requires at least one outlet.
- Dishwashers and garbage disposals usually require their own circuits.
- An electric range requires at least a 40-amp circuit (50-amp is even better).

☞ CIRCUIT CAPACITY

Be careful not to overload a circuit by exceeding its amperage rating. To determine its electrical load, list all the fixtures and appliances that are on that circuit and add up their wattage ratings. Look for a small plate like the one shown below affixed to the back or bottom of appliances; wattage ratings for lighting fixtures are located on a sticker near the socket. To calculate the wattage, use the formula volts x amperes = watts. In this example: 120v x 21 amps = 252 watts.

Insulation

Wallboard

Cut-in bracing

Interior wall stud

Voltage rating
Testing agency's mark
Safety remarks

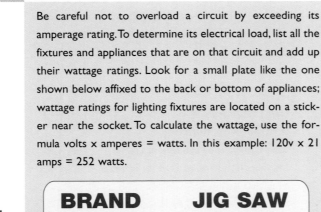

BRAND   JIG SAW
MADE IN U.S.A.   MODEL 1234-56
120V 60Hz. 2.1 A   SER. NO A-1234

WARNING
DO NOT EXPOSE
TO RAIN OR USE
IN DAMP LOCATIONS

LAUNDRY

■ The washing machine requires a separate 20-amp circuit.

■ An electric dryer requires at least a 30-amp circuit.

BATHROOM

■ Must have its own 20-amp GFCI-protected receptacle circuit.

■ Must have lighting controlled by a switch, which cannot be on the receptacle circuit.

CLOSET

■ Uncovered incandescent lights are not allowed.

■ Covered incandescent lights must be at least 12 inches from stored items.

■ Recessed incandescent lights and surface-mounted fluorescent lights must be at least 6 inches from stored items.

ATTACHED GARAGE

■ Must have at least one lighting outlet and one GFCI receptacle.

■ All receptacles must be GFCI protected.

 ## PLANNING NEW WIRING ROUTES

Wood frame homes are not all built the same way, but most have 2-by-4 stud walls, 2-by-8 (or larger) floor joists, and 2-by-6 (or larger) ceiling joists. These wooden structural members are normally spaced 16 inches apart from center to center. In some new homes, however, the spacing is 24 inches, and in some roughly built older homes it's somewhat random. The illustration below shows the skeleton of a typical wood frame house. (See more about house framing on page 98.) It is much easier to run the wiring for a new circuit before the walls, ceilings, and floors are finished. It is best to run the wire for a new circuit in the most direct route possible from the service panel. By understanding your house's inner structure, you will be able to plan the best routes and run the wiring in the most efficient manner. Use the illustration below, along with those on pages 478–479 that discuss "Routing Wire," to prepare the best plan.

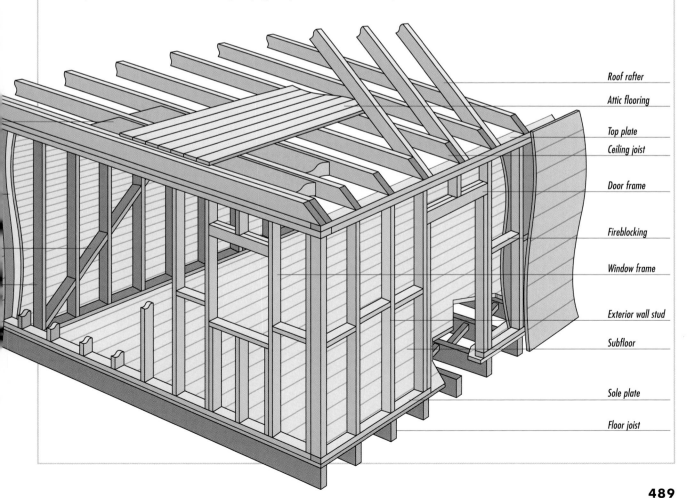

Roof rafter

Attic flooring

Top plate

Ceiling joist

Door frame

Fireblocking

Window frame

Exterior wall stud

Subfloor

Sole plate

Floor joist

Extending Phone Wiring

Extending your telephone wiring is safe, easy and—in the case of most homes built more than a few years ago—often necessary for the sorts of telephone-related devices and services that have become commonplace in recent years. The only major limitation on your work is distance: Jacks should be installed no more than 200 feet from the point where the wiring enters your home.

Before you begin stringing wire, sketch a floor plan of your home, showing the location of each existing jack and where you want to put the new ones. This will help you choose the shortest routes for the new wires and the simplest installation.

You can extend wiring from existing jacks or from a junction box located where the wiring enters your home. Or, you can combine methods, if that will produce the shortest runs of wire. Your options are to route your wires along the baseboards, through the walls, or inside them. Since telephone station wire is thin, it is relatively easy to conceal. And, because the electric current it carries is small, you do not need to take some of the usual precautions that are essential when working with electrical wiring.

Telephone Terminology

When it comes time to purchase materials or ask for advice at your home center, it helps to know the language of telephone wiring. It's simple:

HANDSET CORDS These wires, which connect telephone handsets to phones or fax machines, cannot be used to connect a phone to a jack, because the plugs and wiring pattern are different from those of line cord.

LINE CORD This wire connects jacks to telephones, fax machines, computer modems, and other devices. It is a flat cord with four colored conductors: red, green, yellow, and black. Line cord is available in many lengths, and adapters

can be used to link two cords together. However, if you need to place a telephone more than 25 feet from an existing jack, it is better to install a new jack by running station wire from the old jack.

STATION WIRE Used for permanent installations, station wire may have four, six, or eight conductors, each color-coded. Maintain the continuity of the color coding throughout your installation. Choose a special weatherproof form for outdoors.

PHONE JACKS The devices you plug the line cords into are phone jacks; they come in several types. A flush-mounted jack, installed in an interior wall, gives a flush, clean appearance. A dual-outlet jack can handle two-line phones or a phone and separate fax or modem. A phone-mount jack provides wall mounting for a telephone. Surface-mounted jacks are easy to install on the baseboard or wall. An out-

TELEPHONE WIRE & CORDS

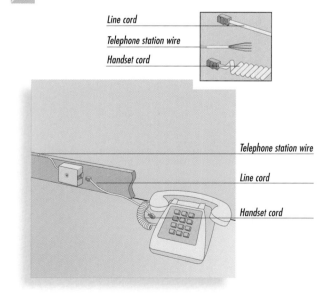

Line cord
Telephone station wire
Handset cord

Telephone station wire
Line cord
Handset cord

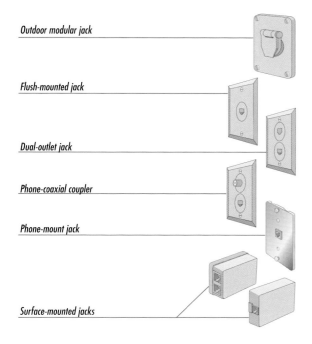

Outdoor modular jack

Flush-mounted jack

Dual-outlet jack

Phone-coaxial coupler

Phone-mount jack

Surface-mounted jacks

baseboards and trim or staple them. Special staples for station wire are available wherever the wire is sold.

WIRE SAFELY Water and heat will destroy telephone wiring. Run your wiring well away from water pipes, damp areas, heating ducts, and chimney flues, to name a few trouble spots. If you cannot avoid a wet area, run ordinary station wire through a conduit or use the special cable made for underground and outdoor uses.

Do not run wires where they will be easily worn or broken, such as through window or door openings. Never route a loose or unprotected wire across traffic routes.

For safety and to avoid interference, keep your wiring at least several inches away from electric wires and outlets. Never install jacks where they would allow someone to use the wired telephone near water, such as a bathtub, kitchen sink, or swimming pool, or while in contact with a grounded appliance, such as a refrigerator or kitchen range. Avoid steam or hot water pipes and hot-air ducts.

Routing Wire
To conceal wiring, you normally will need to run it through or inside the walls. Page 492 shows methods to make this job an easy one.

THROUGH WALLS Drilling through a wall is often the easiest way to route wire from room to room. In homes with typical gypsum wallboard walls, this is usually a simple job. First find a suitable location for the wire extension. Avoid the wall studs by knocking on the wall until you hear a hollow sound.

INSIDE WALLS Sometimes the best path for a phone line is through a wall. Usually, you'll be running the wire through one wall into the attic or basement, and from there into the wall of another room.

Drill a hole in the wall at the point where the phone wire will enter or leave it. If the wire will pass through the attic, go there and find the top plate of the wall you need. Then, using a long bit at least ½ inch in diameter, drill through the

door modular jack protects wiring from the elements. A phone-coaxial coupler provides one location for separately wired telephone and TV antenna or cable connectors.

Installation Tips
Here are a few tips that will help you safely and easily achieve a professional-looking job.

CONCEAL WIRES Naturally, you want your telephone wiring to be inconspicuous. When possible, run your wires inside cabinets or closets or beneath shelving. You can also use the voids behind paneling and trim. One natural hiding place is where carpeting meets the wall. Sometimes you can simply tuck in the wire with your fingers; other times you may have to gently remove the shoe moldings or lift the carpet by removing tacks or raising a tack strip.

When you can't hide a wire, you can run it along the baseboard, around the edges of door and window frames, under a chair rail, or in the bottoms of any joints between two surfaces.

SECURE WIRES Don't leave wires loose for more than about 16 inches. Secure them with clips that slip under

(continued on page 492)

Extending Phone Wiring

(continued from page 491)

top plate directly above the hole you made in the room below. Drop a weighted string down through the top plate. From downstairs, use a stiff, hooked wire to snag the string and pull it through the hole. Tie the string and station wire together, wrap tape around the knot to prevent it from snagging inside the wall, and pull the wire up into the attic.

When running the wire into the next wall, use the string to pull the wire down from the attic.

If you are running telephone wire through the basement, drill up through the bottom plate of the wall, push the telephone wire up, and use a hooked wire to snag it and pull it into the room. Sometimes the best way to run a wire from the floor above into the basement is to drill through the floor or diagonally through the baseboard and push the phone wire down into the basement. This will avoid the difficulty of fishing a wire out of the wall.

Installing Modular Jacks

The methods you use for installing jacks will depend upon the type of jacks you've chosen. Surface-mounted jacks are easy to install, as shown on the facing page. If you're installing a flush-mounted jack, position it between studs away from the electrical wiring, but at the same height as the electrical receptacles. When installing an outdoor jack, make sure that it is at least 16 inches above the ground.

ROUTING THROUGH WALLS

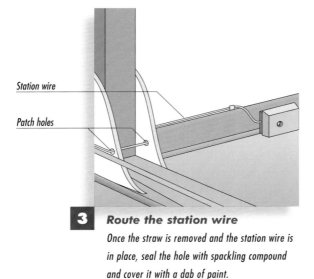

Wall stud
Wallboard
¹/₄″ drill bit

1 Drill through the wall

Use a ¹/₄-inch drill bit at least 5 inches long to drill through the wallboard just above the baseboard.

Station wire
Patch holes

3 Route the station wire

Once the straw is removed and the station wire is in place, seal the hole with spackling compound and cover it with a dab of paint.

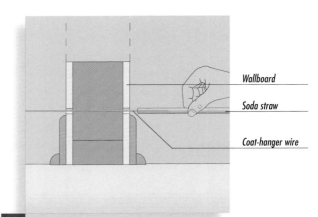

Wallboard
Soda straw
Coat-hanger wire

2 Push a straw through the hole

To feed the wire through the wall, push a soda straw through the hole, then insert the wire. If you have difficulty, insert a length of coat-hanger wire through the wall first and slip the straw over the wire. Remove the coat hanger before pushing the telephone wire through.

Electrical Improvements

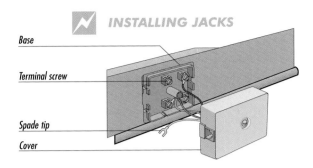

Base
Terminal screw
Spade tip
Cover

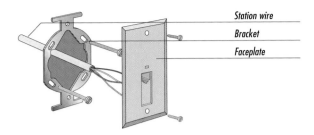

Station wire
Bracket
Faceplate

Surface-mounted jacks

Remove 2 inches of the station wire's jacket, strip the wire ends, and connect them to the terminal screws according to color designations stamped on the base. Insert the spade tips of the wires, tighten the screws, and put the cover back in place.

Flush-mounted jacks

Trace the bracket's outline on the wall. Use a compass saw to cut a hole within the circular portion of outline, then screw the bracket to the wall. Remove 3 inches of the station wire's outer jacket, strip the wire ends, and insert them into their matching color-coded slots. Bend the wire ends upward, tighten the terminal screws, and mount the faceplate.

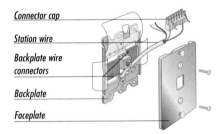

Connector cap
Station wire
Backplate wire connectors
Backplate
Faceplate

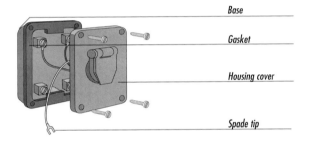

Base
Gasket
Housing cover
Spade tip

Phone-mounted jack

Screw the backplate to the wall. Remove 3 inches of the station wire's jacket. Fit the red wire into the slot on the far right side of the connector cap, extending the wire $1/4$ inch then bending it down until it slips into the groove. Repeat with the other wires. Fold back the clear plastic flaps to expose the connectors. Matching wire colors, slip the cap onto the bottom of a connector. Repeat with the other connector cap, then screw on the faceplate.

Outdoor jacks

Mount the base with the grommet hole at the bottom. Strip about 5 inches of the wire's jacket off. Hold the wires together and insert them through the grommet until about $1/4$ inch of wire jacket is inside the box. Match and connect the color-coded wires on each of the four terminals.

 ## TESTING & TROUBLESHOOTING PHONES

The simplest way to test your wiring installation is to try it out with a telephone. First make sure the phone is working by plugging it into a jack and dialing a number. (If possible, use the first jack where the phone wiring enters your home.)

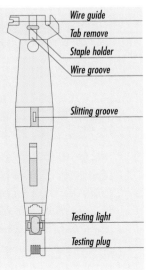

Wire guide
Tab remove
Staple holder
Wire groove
Slitting groove
Testing light
Testing plug

DIAL-TONE TEST Plug in the telephone, lift the handset, and listen for a dial tone. If you hear nothing, there is a bad contact or a wrong connection. Open the jack and check to be sure that wire color-codings match and that the wires are connected firmly to the terminals.

TIP/RING POLARITY TEST If you hear a dial tone, dial a number. If you continue to hear the dial tone during and after dialing, the red and green wires are reversed. Open the jack and switch the connections. If you have two lines and the same problem occurs on the second line, the yellow and black wires should be reversed. A telephone line tester (such as the one shown here) can make these tests without the need for an extra working telephone. Simply plug it into a modular jack and, following the directions supplied, let the lights tell you about the integrity of the circuit.

Installing Outdoor Wiring

Electrical Improvements

Because outdoor wiring must survive the elements, materials are stronger and more corrosion resistant than those used for indoor wiring. Also, everything must fit exactly, so heavy-duty gaskets are often used to seal boxes, thus preventing water from entering them. Shown on these pages are many of the devices you will need for outdoor wiring projects. In addition, any new outside receptacle must be protected with a GFCI (see page 483).

Extending a circuit to the outside of your house requires the same procedures as extending a circuit indoors (see page 478). You can tap into existing switch, lighting, or receptacle outlet boxes that are in the middle or at the end of a circuit run.

 DRIPTIGHT SUBPANEL

Usually made of sheet metal and then painted, driptight fixtures often have shrouds or shields that deflect rain. The typical unit shown is not waterproof and must be mounted where downpours, or even a steady watering from sprinklers, cannot reach it.

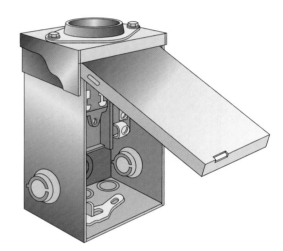

 OUTDOOR CONDUIT & TUBING

Rigid nonmetallic conduit (PVC)

Rigid nonmetallic conduit (PVC schedule 40) requires a separate grounding wire. It must be buried at least 18 inches deep unless it is covered with a concrete cap. One advantage of rigid nonmetallic conduit is that it does not corrode.

Electrical metallic tubing (EMT)

Standard electrical metallic tubing (EMT), also known as thinwall conduit, is not recommended for underground burial. Used with watertight couplings and connectors, however, EMT is a good choice in exposed locations to protect the conductors from abuse; EMT is a good choice in these situations. Coated EMT is also available and can be buried.

Rigid metallic conduit (RMC)

Rigid metallic conduit will corrode and eventually disintegrate in certain types of soils, but one advantage of this type of conduit is that it may be directly buried only 6 inches deep. In addition, unless it's used to feed a swimming pool, it doesn't require a separate grounding wire.

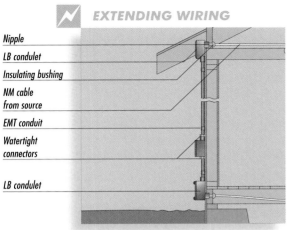

Nipple
LB condulet
Insulating bushing
NM cable from source
EMT conduit
Watertight connectors
LB condulet

From the attic

One option for extending a circuit is to tap into a junction box in the attic and run cable outside through an LB condulet to a new device.

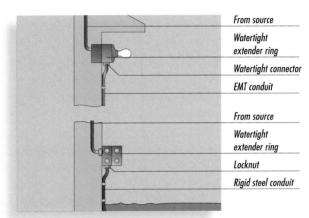

From source
Watertight extender ring
Watertight connector
EMT conduit

From source
Watertight extender ring
Locknut
Rigid steel conduit

From a porch light

A watertight extender ring can be added to an existing receptacle or a porch light. It allows room in the box to wire the new cable, which is run through the conduit to the new device.

 WATERTIGHT SWITCH BOX

Fixtures designed to withstand temporary immersion or sprinkling are watertight. Made of cast aluminum, zinc-dipped iron, or bronze, these fixtures have threaded entries. All covers for watertight boxes are sealed with gaskets; many of them are equipped with an exterior lever that enables you to operate the switch without opening the cover.

BACK-TO-BACK WIRING

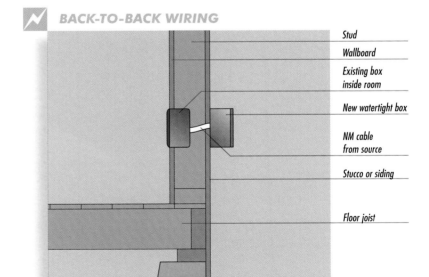

Stud
Wallboard
Existing box inside room
New watertight box
NM cable from source
Stucco or siding
Floor joist

The easiest way to install a new watertight receptacle box is to connect it back-to-back with an existing interior room box with type NM cable, run through the cavity between wall studs.

Replacing a Ceiling Fixture

Ceiling fixtures come in countless sizes and styles. They're connected directly to your home's wiring through a recessed ceiling box, which is hidden by the fixture or by a decorative canopy. The replacement procedure is basically the same for all types of fixtures. Simply detach the old fixture and undo the wiring connections, then make new ones and attach the new fixture, as shown on the facing page. Wiring connections may be made with wire nuts. Before you work on any fixture, shut off the power to the entire circuit and test that it's off (see page 475).

You may have to buy mounting hardware to hang the new fixture. If the ceiling box has a metallic stud, the fixture may be attached to it with a nipple and hickey, a reducing nut, or a strap. If there isn't a stud in the right location, the strap may be attached to the ceiling box ears. Fixtures heavier than 10 pounds should be hung from a box with a stud and nailed to the ceiling joists. Note: If the fixture is heavy, have a helper hold it, or hang it from the box with a hook made from a wire coat hanger.

 PARTS OF A CEILING FIXTURE

Ceiling box
Fixture grounding wire
Strap
Black (hot) wires
Hickey
White (neutral) wires
Fixture body
Socket
Screw
Glass shade

Strap
Fixture grounding wire
Black (hot) wires
White (neutral) wires
Fixture
Cap nut
Light bulb

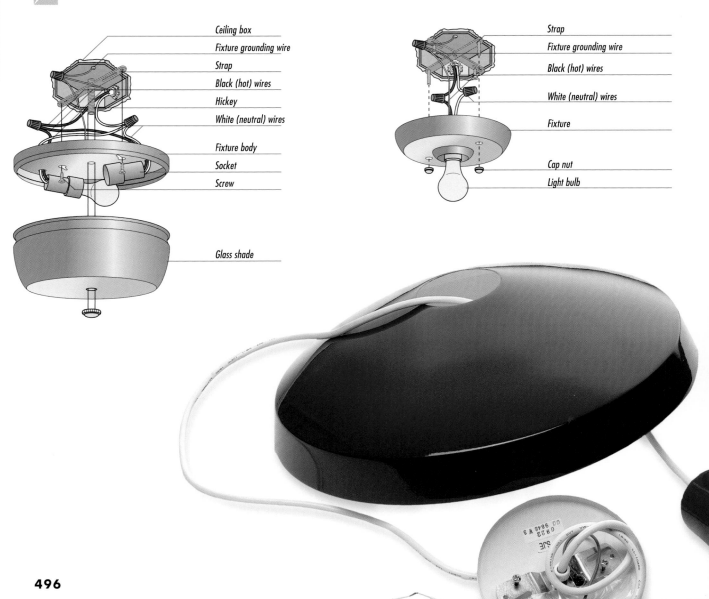

1 **Attach mounting hardware**

Most fixtures attach to a grounding bar that's first screwed to the electrical box in the ceiling. Fasten mounting bolts loosely to the bar.

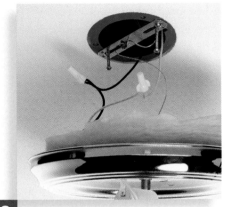

2 **Make the connections**

Splice the black fixture wire to the circuit hot wire, and the white fixture wire to the incoming neutral wire. If the fixture has a grounding wire, secure it to the grounding screw on the grounding bar. Connect the new fixture. Strip $1/2$ inch of insulation off the new wires. Wrap the bare ends around the circuit wires, then screw on wire nuts. Connect the grounding wires.

3 **Secure the canopy**

Carefully fold the wires into the housing box, then secure the canopy to the box. This fixture has keyhole slots that slip over the mounting bolts. Push the canopy into place, then tighten the bolts.

4 **Add the trim**

Screw in the light bulb or bulbs, then add the diffusing globe atop the bulbs. This globe slips over the long center hickey and is held in place by a threaded end piece.

Replacing a Light Switch

When you're buying a replacement switch, read the information stamped on the new switch; the new one should have the same amp and voltage ratings as the old. If your home's wiring is aluminum, be sure to buy a compatible replacement switch. Also be sure to buy the right kind of switch. A single-pole switch controls a fixture from only one location. A three-way switch controls the same light fixture from two different locations, such as at the top and bottom of stairs. A three-way switch has three terminals, and sometimes a grounding terminal as well. It does not have markings for ON and OFF. Instructions for replacing both kinds of switches are shown below.

Before removing a switch, turn off the power to the circuit controlling the switch. Test the switch to see that it is not functioning. Remove the screws securing the faceplate and set the faceplate aside. Loosen the screws holding the switch to the box. Gently pull the switch out of the box, taking care not to touch the terminal screws or wires. Use a neon tester (see page 505) to confirm that the electrical power is shut off.

REPLACING A THREE-WAY SWITCH

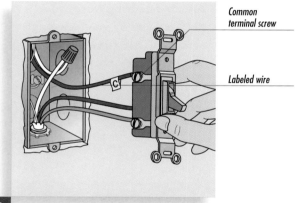

Common terminal screw

Labeled wire

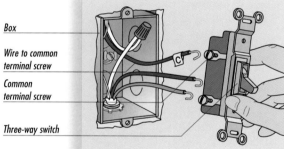

Box

Wire to common terminal screw

Common terminal screw

Three-way switch

1 Remove the switch

After turning off the power to the switch's circuit, remove the faceplate. Check the wires with a neon tester to be sure they are not hot, and remove the switch. Turn the terminal screws counterclockwise just far enough to allow you to release the wires. Label the wire to the common terminal screw (black or copper) with tape. If the switch is backwired (the wires are stuck in the push-in terminals on the back), free the wires by pushing a small screwdriver into the release slots.

2 Attach the new switch

Join the two neutral (white) wires and screw on a wire nut. Make a grounding connection by bonding the two grounding wires with a compression sleeve or wire nut. If the box is metal, also attach a grounding jumper to the grounding screw in the back of the box. Attach the labeled wire to the common terminal screw (black or copper) of the new switch. Loop the ends of the two hot (black) wires around the terminal screws on the switch, and tighten. Secure the switch as shown in Step 3 on the facing page.

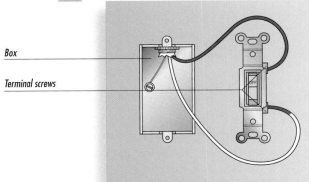

Box

Terminal screws

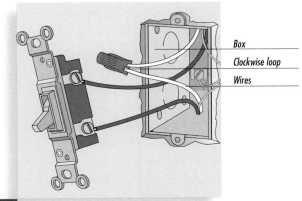

Box

Clockwise loop

Wires

1 Remove the old switch

After turning off the power to the switch's circuit, remove the switch (see facing page) and turn the terminal screws counterclockwise just far enough to allow you to release the wires from the terminals. If the wires are stuck into terminals in the back of the switch, push a small screwdriver into the release slots and pull the wires free.

2 Attach the new switch

Join the two neutral (white) wires together, twist them, and screw on a wire nut. Bond the two grounding wires with a compression sleeve or wire nut and, if the box is metal, also attach a grounding jumper to the grounding screw in the back of the box. Loop the ends of the two hot (black) wires around the terminal screws on the switch and tighten with a screwdriver.

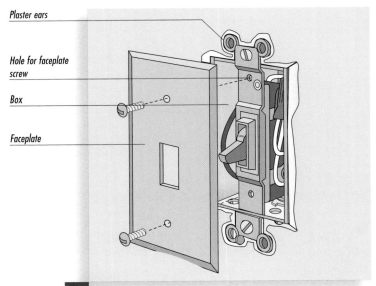

Plaster ears

Hole for faceplate screw

Box

Faceplate

3 Secure the switch

Push the wires and the new switch into the box (be sure it's right side up). Screw the mounting strap on the switch to the box; if necessary, adjust the screws in the mounting slots until the switch is straight. If the switch isn't flush with the wall surface, remove the plaster ears from the mounting strap and use them as shims to bring the switch forward. Finally, screw on the faceplate.

Installing Track Lighting

Track light systems are remarkably versatile, providing a very flexible solution to a myriad of lighting tasks. They are often used to solve such difficult problems as highlighting a work of art while providing overall room lighting. They can also be mounted on walls as well as ceilings and extended as far as needed, so long as the lights you mount do not exceed the system's rated capacity. Many different types of tracks are available, and you can get scores of different fixtures to fit each style of track.

It's a simple job to replace a conventional ceiling fixture with a track light system. Not all track systems are identical, so you should read the manufacturer's installation instructions carefully. Some connectors are held in place by a fixture box saddle to conceal the box and connections, others by the track itself. Still others attach to an adapter plate that screws to the box.

A plug-in connector lets you mount a track light without having to "hard wire" it into the electrical system. You just plug a connector into the track and run the cord to an electrical outlet. In lieu of plugging and unplugging the light, plug-ins can also be controlled using snap switches attached to the cord, like those used for some lamps. Mount the connector flush against the wall or ceiling, hold up the first length of track, join the end to the connector, and secure the track to the ceiling or wall using mounting screws or toggle bolts. Then add any additional lengths of track to the first one.

 TRACK LIGHTING FITTINGS

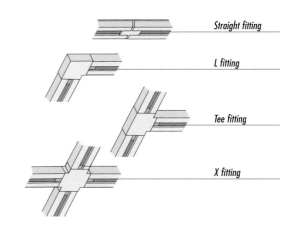

Straight fitting

L fitting

Tee fitting

X fitting

 TRACK LIGHTING FIXTURES

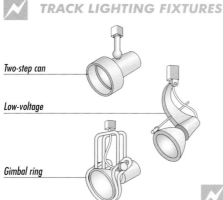

Two-step can

Low-voltage

Gimbal ring

 PRIMARY COMPONENTS OF A TRACK LIGHT

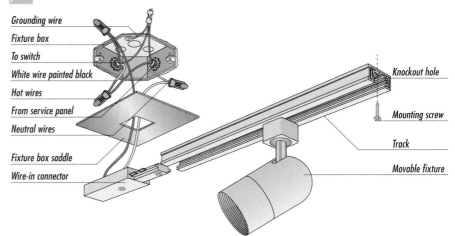

Grounding wire

Fixture box

To switch

White wire painted black

Hot wires

From service panel

Neutral wires

Fixture box saddle

Wire-in connector

Knockout hole

Mounting screw

Track

Movable fixture

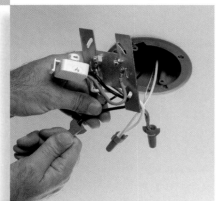

1 **Wire the track connector**

Fixtures vary, but with most, your first step is to splice the connector's black wire to the circuit hot wire, the white wire to the cable's neutral wire, and the green or bare wire to the circuit grounding wire.

2 **Fix connector to box & track**

Screw the adapter plate to the housing box; then, while holding the track in position, attach the connector by twisting it onto the track. Note: Methods may vary, depending upon the type of system and the exact pieces.

3 **Fasten the track to the ceiling**

When possible, drive screws through the track's mounting slots and into ceiling joists. If joists don't align with the fixture, secure the fixture to the ceiling material using toggle bolts.

4 **Add the fixtures**

Finally, position fixtures along the track where you want them; twist them into place like the track connector in Step #2. Add any remaining fixture trim that remains—for example, this design includes a saddle that covers both box and track connector.

Installing Recessed Lights

Recessed lights offer light without the intrusion of an obvious fixture. They can be fitted with any number of trims that aim the light exactly where you want it. Use recessed lights over sinks and countertops to spread task lighting over the work surfaces, or in stairways and entries for added visibility. Low-voltage downlights create wonderful accent lighting. You can replace an old surface-mounted fixture with a new recessed light, or you can run a series of lights in an entirely new location.

Today, recessed downlights are usually prewired and grounded to their own housing box; however, older-style downlights may require wiring into a junction box attached to a ceiling joist.

Many recessed lights produce a lot of heat, so you must either buy an IC-rated fixture for direct contact or plan to remove insulation within 3 inches of the fixture (see illustrations at right). You'll also need clearance above the unit (special low-clearance downlights are available for tight spaces). Make sure that no combustible materials are within 1/2 inch of the fixture, with the exception of joists or other blocking used for support.

If you have access from above, choose a standard new-work downlight; most of these fixtures simply fasten to ceiling joists with adjustable hanger bars. Fixture trim is added once the ceiling is in place and textured and/or painted.

When you don't have access from above the ceiling, use an old-work fixture, which can be installed from below. Before wiring one of these fixtures, you'll need to cut a hole for the housing in the ceiling between two joists. If there is no crawl space above the joists, locate the joists—and any obstructing wires or pipes—from below. Make sure to shut off the power to the circuit before working on it and to any circuits that may be wired behind the ceiling before drilling exploratory holes.

 CHOOSING THE RIGHT HOUSING

Insulated ceiling (IC) fixtures can be completely covered with insulation, making them ideal for use in ceilings below the attic. Non-IC fixtures require clearance for air circulation.

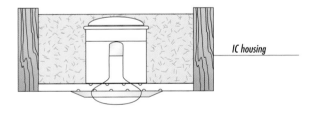

IC housing

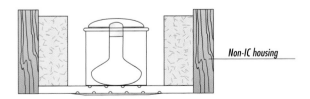

Non-IC housing

 FIXTURE TRIM

Many models of fixture trims are available. Be sure to keep the fixtures away from walls and curtains, and don't install more lights on one electrical circuit than it can handle.

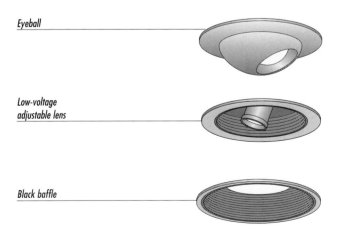

Eyeball

Low-voltage
adjustable lens

Black baffle

New-work downlights with adjustable hanger bars are easy to install from above. Simply nail the ends of the bars to joists on either side, then make wiring connections inside the unit's junction box. Replace the cover plate on the box. Once the ceiling material is in place, clip the fixture trim or baffle into place from below.

1 **Make the connections**

To install this fixture, first cut an access hole in the existing ceiling (most fixtures come with paper templates), then splice the fixture wires to the incoming circuit wires—black to black, white to white, and green or bare fixture wire to the circuit's grounding wire. Replace the cover plate on the box.

2 **Slip the fixture into position**

Thread the fixture, junction box first, into the ceiling. Attachment methods vary; this fixture has spring clips that, when locked into place, grab the ceiling material from above.

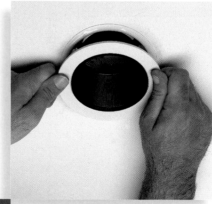

3 **Add the trim**

With the fixture secured to the ceiling, add the light bulb and baffle, diffusing panel, or other trim. The baffle shown clips onto the fixture, controlling light spread and masking the ceiling hole's rough edges.

 USING AN EXISTING BOX

You can use an existing electrical box when replacing an old light fixture with one or more recessed fixtures. With the power off, disconnect the fixture wires from the other wires entering the box and remove the fixture. Run new electrical cable from the existing box to the access hole for the recessed light. Use wire nuts to connect like-colored wires in the old box. Place a cover plate over the box, but keep it accessible for future repairs.

Diagnosing Electrical Problems

An electrical problem typically becomes evident when you turn on a lamp or appliance and it won't work. When that happens, the source of the problem may be the device itself, faulty wiring connections, or overload, or short in the circuit. Unfortunately, distinguishing between an overloaded circuit and a short circuit can be difficult. A circuit becomes overloaded when there are more lamps and appliances on it than it can safely handle. When all the lamps and appliances on the circuit are turned on at the same time, the wiring becomes overheated, causing the circuit breaker to trip or the fuse to blow. A short circuit occurs when a bare hot wire touches a bare neutral wire or a bare grounding wire (or some other ground). The flow of extra current trips a circuit breaker or blows a fuse.

RESETTING A CIRCUIT BREAKER

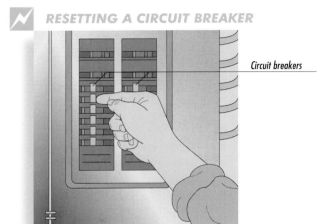

Circuit breakers

Locate the breaker that has a toggle in the OFF position. Push the toggle farther toward the OFF position before returning it to the ON position (this may require some force). If the breaker trips again, diagnose the problem by following the steps on the facing page.

Good fuse (top view)

Blown fuse (top view)

Edison-base fuse

REPLACING A BLOWN FUSE

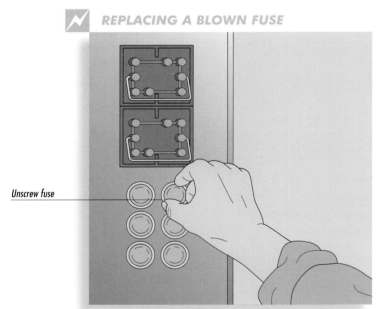

Unscrew fuse

In the service panel, locate the blown fuse. Grasp the fuse by its insulated rim (or use a fuse puller like the one at right) and unscrew it. Screw in a new fuse with the same amperage rating as the old one. If the fuse blows again, follow the steps on the facing page. Note that you may be able to get a clue as to the source of the problem by examining the blown fuse: an overload melts the bridge, while a short circuit blackens the glass.

Checking a receptacle

To see if a receptacle is dead, insert the probes of a neon tester into the slots (or use a circuit tester). Be sure to hold the tester probes by their insulation—not the metal ends. If the tester lights up, the circuit is still hot.

Checking a switch

Remove the switch's cover and unscrew the switch from its box, taking care not to touch the bare wires or metal terminal screws. Holding the probes of a neon tester by their insulation, touch one probe to a hot wire or terminal and the other to a neutral wire or terminal, grounding conductor, or grounded metal box (it must be grounded). The tester will light up if the circuit is live.

TRACING A SHORT CIRCUIT

When a fuse blows or a circuit breaker trips, the cause is often easy to spot. Look for black smudge marks on switch or receptacle cover plates, or for frayed or damaged cords or damaged plugs on lamps and appliances connected to the dead circuit. Replace a damaged cord or plug, then replace the fuse or reset the breaker. If the circuit goes dead after an appliance has been in use for a short time, you probably have an overloaded circuit. Move some of the lamps and appliances to another circuit and replace the fuse or reset the circuit breaker for the first circuit.

If you find none of these signs of trouble, you'll have to trace your way through the circuit following the steps below. If following these steps doesn't solve the problem, your wiring is faulty. Call an electrician to correct the problem.

■ Turn off all wall switches and unplug every lamp and appliance on the dead circuit. Reset the tripped breaker or install a new fuse.

■ If the circuit goes dead right away, the problem may be a short circuit in a switch or receptacle. With the circuit dead, remove each cover plate and inspect the device and its wiring. Look and smell for charred wire insulation, a wire shorted against the metal box, or a device that's defective. Replace faulty wiring.

■ If the breaker doesn't trip or the new fuse doesn't blow right away, turn on each wall switch, one by one, checking each time to see if the circuit breaker has tripped or the fuse has blown.

■ If turning on a wall switch causes the breaker to trip or a fuse to blow, there's a short circuit in a light fixture or receptacle controlled by that switch, or there's a short circuit in the switch wiring. With the circuit dead, inspect the fixture, receptacle, and switch for charred wire insulation or faulty connections. Replace a faulty switch, fixture, or wiring.

■ If turning on a wall switch doesn't trip the breaker or blow a fuse, the trouble is in the lamps or appliances. Test them by plugging them in one at a time. If the circuit does not go dead, the circuit was overloaded. Move some of the devices to another circuit. If the circuit goes dead just after you plug in a device, you've found the offender.

■ If the circuit goes dead as soon as you plug in the device, replace the plug or cord.

■ If the circuit goes dead as soon as you turn on the device, repair or replace the switch on the device.

Repairing a Doorbell

A doorbell is a real convenience when it works. But when it doesn't, it leaves your guests wondering. Fortunately, most problems with doorbells are relatively easy to fix.

DOORBELL BASICS The fundamental parts of a typical doorbell system are:

■ The push button, which completes the electrical circuit, causing the doorbell to ring

■ The bell, buzzer, or chime, which sounds when it receives electrical current

■ The transformer, which steps down the voltage from the regular 120-volt circuit to low-voltage (typically 12 volts)

■ The wiring, which carries electrical current through both the 120-volt system and the low-voltage system

The drawing below shows how a one-button doorbell system is wired. When your doorbell doesn't ring or, worse, rings constantly, the problem may lie in one of the parts or in the wires that connect them. The first place to look is at the source of power. Make sure a circuit breaker hasn't tripped or a fuse hasn't blown. Once you're certain that the 120-volt side of the transformer is getting power, shut off the power and tighten all wire connections. Then turn the power back on and check the low-voltage side.

If a doorbell won't stop ringing, turn off the power to the transformer. Remove the button from the door frame and disconnect one of the two wires connected to it. Turn the power back on. If the bell does not ring when you turn on the power, replace the button. If the bell rings, then the problem is a short between the two wires.

BASIC DOORBELL COMPONENTS

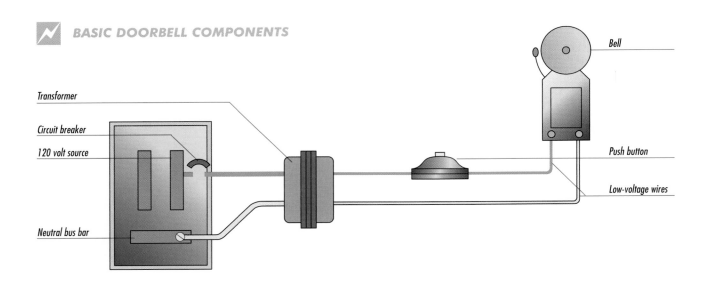

Transformer

Circuit breaker

120 volt source

Neutral bus bar

Bell

Push button

Low-voltage wires

TESTING THE TRANSFORMER The best and safest way to test whether the transformer is functioning properly is to use a volt-ohm meter. If the transformer is working correctly, the meter reading should match the secondary voltage (usually 12 volts) marked on the transformer or bell. Set the voltage range on the meter to 120 volts AC and measure the voltage between the two low-voltage terminals on the transformer. If the meter reads significantly higher than the correct secondary voltage, the transformer is defective and should be replaced. If the reading is close to the correct secondary voltage, test again by setting the voltage range on the meter to a lower value. If the new reading doesn't agree with the voltage marked on the transformer or bell, replace the transformer.

TESTING THE BELL, BUZZER, OR CHIME Have a helper ring the doorbell while you listen to the bell (or chime). If it hums or buzzes, it may be gummed up with dirt. (For example, the striker shaft on a chime mechanism can get stuck because of corrosion, dirt, or excessive grease.) Check the mechanism and clean if needed. Use fine-grade sandpaper to remove corrosion from any contacts. If it still hums or buzzes after cleaning, replace it. If it did not make any noise at all when the button was pushed, disconnect the bell, buzzer, or chime and, using new wire, hook it up directly to the transformer. If it works, inspect the old wiring. If it doesn't sound, replace it.

REPAIRING THE WIRING Examine the wiring for breaks or frayed insulation that may be causing the wires to short out. Repair any breaks and wrap the repairs with electrician's tape.

REPLACING A DOORBELL If you are unable to find the source of the problem, or if the doorbell seems hopelessly silenced, consider replacing it with a new wireless doorbell. Wireless systems are inexpensive and easy to install.

 Work safely! To diagnose most doorbell problems, you'll need to have the power source connected. But if you're going to work on the transformer or the wires in the junction box, shut off the power to the circuit and test to be sure it's off. (Remember that the input side of the transformer is high voltage—120 volts.)

 **DOORBELL REPAIRS**

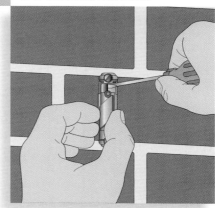

Check the contacts
Remove the doorbell cover (or unscrew the unit) and examine the contacts. If the contacts are flat, use a small screwdriver to pry them up slightly.

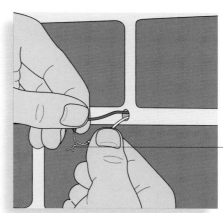

Low-voltage wires

Touch the wires together
When the doorbell won't ring, remove the push button from the wall to expose the wires. Disconnect the two wires connected to the button and short them by touching their bare ends together. If the bell rings, replace the push button. If it doesn't ring, the bell or chime mechanism or the wiring is at fault.

Comfort Systems

You want your home to stay cozy in winter and cool in the heat of summer—in other words, you want your home to be comfortable throughout the year.

Comfort is the primary responsibility of your heating, cooling, and ventilation systems. When the basic appliances are working effectively with thermostats, insulation, and a weather-tight outer shell, the system provides a consistent level of comfort.

As most homeowners know, however, comfort doesn't exactly come cheap these days, nor are our energy resources unlimited. This chapter focuses on improvements and repairs that can raise the level of comfort in your home while lowering the cost of providing it.

The Basics of Comfort

Whether or not a house feels comfortable inside depends upon a number of systems, notably heating, ventilation, and cooling. In the construction trade, these comfort systems are grouped together and given the acronym "HVAC," and the tradesperson who works on them is called an "HVAC contractor." Houses may be heated by radiant warmth from steam, hot water, or hot air, and they may be cooled by air conditioning, an air cooler, or fans. This chapter explains how each of the major heating and cooling systems works, improvements you can make to boost comfort and energy efficiency in your house, and how you can make routine repairs.

The illustration below shows the HVAC systems in a house outfitted with forced hot-air heating. A basement furnace heats cold air drawn from the rooms above, then returns it via ducts and registers. An attic fan exhausts hot air through one side, allowing cooler air to enter through vents in the other side.

The comfort systems in your home maintain the temperature, humidity, and air quality at levels that keep your environment pleasant and healthful.

A HOME'S COMFORT SYSTEMS

Attic vent

Attic fan

Warm-air registers

Warm-air supply duct

Filter

Blower

Furnace or heat source

Heating & Cooling Systems

Heating systems are distinguished largely by the type of fuel they consume and the means through which they distribute the heat throughout the house.

Different types of fuel can be used to supply heat to a house. Cost, convenience, local preferences, and the age of the house are all factors that help determine which type you use. When remodeling a house or replacing an aging heating system, it is often worthwhile to convert to a new, less expensive fuel. Following are the major alternatives:

- **Natural gas**
- **Fuel oil**
- **Liquefied petroleum gas ("LPG" or propane)**
- **Electricity**
- **Wood and coal**

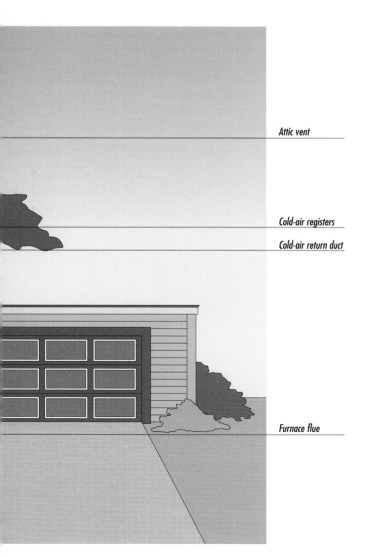

Attic vent

Cold-air registers

Cold-air return duct

Furnace flue

When you think of the type of heating system your house has, the first thing that comes to mind is the means by which the heat is delivered throughout the house. Here's a look at the major distribution systems:

FORCED AIR This is the most common type of heating. A furnace heats the air, which is then blown through supply ducts that run throughout the house. Separate return ducts pull cool air out of the rooms and back to the furnace, where it is heated. One of the biggest advantages of forced-air systems is that the same system of ducts can be used to distribute cool air from a central air conditioner.

HOT WATER Water is heated in a boiler, then circulated through pipes to radiators or convectors and returned to the boiler. Radiators are often found in older homes, while baseboard convectors are more common in new homes and remodeling projects. Hot-water systems can be zoned; that is, separate parts of the house (such as upstairs and downstairs) can be heated separately, with each zone controlled by its own thermostat.

HEAT PUMP Popular in areas with mild winters, heat pumps are primarily air conditioners that can also supply heat. An outdoor coil absorbs heat, which is carried to an indoor coil. The warm or cool air is then blown through ducts throughout the house.

STEAM Steam heating looks much like a hot-water system, with a boiler and radiators. The difference is that vapor, rather than water, is sent through the piping system. The steam condenses when it contacts the cooler radiators, causing it to flow back to the boiler. It is found mostly in old houses and large buildings.

RADIANT HEAT Most often identified by the fact that heat is distributed in the floor, radiant heat is usually delivered by hot-water tubing, electric cables, or heat-transfer plates. Radiant heat is comfortable and popular because it provides warmth without stirring up dust and allergens.

SPACE HEATING & COOLING When you need to heat or cool only a small space or for only a brief period each year, space units are often the best answer. Many types of electric space heaters are available. Heat can also be supplied by small gas- or wood-fired units. Room air conditioners are mounted in a window and can bring refreshment to just about any part of the house. Ceiling fans and portable fans can also cool off an individual room.

Heating Systems

Producing heat at the flick of a finger, modern heating systems operate cleanly and efficiently, and they tend to last a long time. Still, any heating system can break down, especially if it does not receive regular care and maintenance.

Most houses have some form of central heating, usually powered by a furnace or boiler. The most common systems are shown below and on the facing page. Although central heating systems should be checked and serviced regularly by a trained professional, you can perform many small repairs and some routine maintenance yourself. Note that the illustrations here are of typical installations; obviously, yours may differ.

FORCED-AIR HEATING Low installation cost, fast heat delivery, and reliability make forced-air heating systems the most popular heating choice. They are versatile, too, because the same ducts that deliver hot air in winter can carry air-conditioned air in the summer. Forced-air furnaces are fueled by electricity, fuel oil, or gas.

Much of the routine maintenance on a furnace can be performed by the homeowner, as discussed on pages 526–531. You can change or clean the filter, clean and service the blower, and service the burner.

STEAM HEATING A hallmark of many older homes, steam heat begins in a boiler fueled by gas, oil, or electricity. Some maintenance can be handled by a homeowner; other jobs should be performed by a professional. You can check the water and pressure levels in the boiler regularly, keep the radiators clean, service the burner (see pages 528–533), and keep the thermostat clean.

HOT-WATER HEATING With hot-water heating, a boiler heats water and delivers it to convectors, radiators, or tubing where the heat is given off in the room. With routine maintenance, a modern hot-water heating system will give you years of trouble-free performance. To service the burner and thermostat, refer to page 532 for troubleshooting tips and consult your owner's manual.

THREE CENTRAL HEATING SYSTEMS

Hot-air register with dampers

Cold-air return

Return duct

Flue

Furnace

Burner

Filter

Motor

Motor pulley

Damper

Duct

Hot-air plenum

Fan & limit control

Gas valve

Blower

Blower pulley

Belt

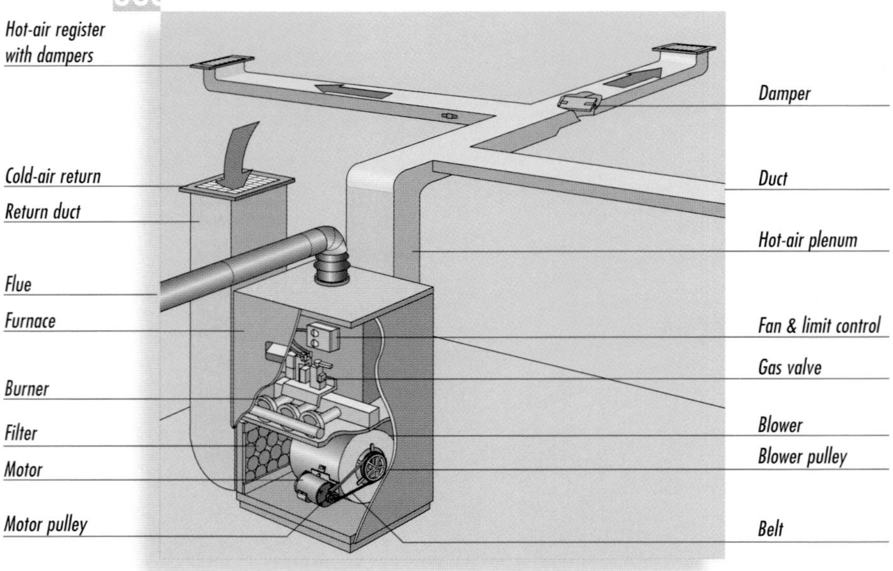

Forced-air heating

With forced-air heating, a blower pulls air from the rooms into the cold-air return duct, through a replaceable filter, and into the furnace. There the air is heated. It then flows back to the rooms through the supply ducts and registers.

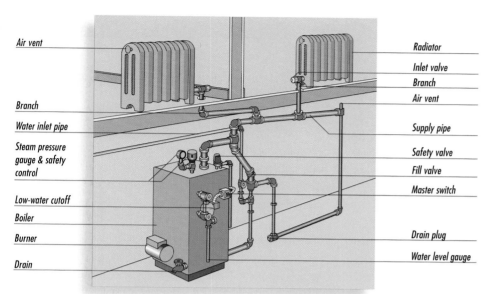

Air vent

Branch

Water inlet pipe

Steam pressure
gauge & safety
control

Low-water cutoff

Boiler

Burner

Drain

Radiator

Inlet valve

Branch

Air vent

Supply pipe

Safety valve

Fill valve

Master switch

Drain plug

Water level gauge

Steam heating system

With steam heating, a boiler turns water into
steam, which rises through pipes to radiators or
convectors. There the steam gives up its heat and
condenses into water, which returns to the boiler.

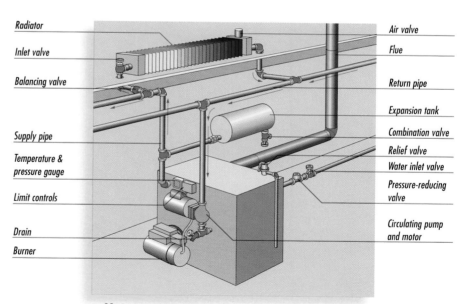

Radiator

Inlet valve

Balancing valve

Supply pipe

Temperature &
pressure gauge

Limit controls

Drain

Burner

Air valve

Flue

Return pipe

Expansion tank

Combination valve

Relief valve

Water inlet valve

Pressure-reducing
valve

Circulating pump
and motor

Hot-water system

With this system, water heated by a boiler travels
through pipes to convectors, radiators, or in-the-
floor tubing. It gives off some of its heat and
returns to the boiler. In older homes, water moves
by gravity; newer systems employ a circulating
pump. An expansion tank containing air and water
keeps the heated water at the proper pressure.

Cooling Systems

Air conditioners are a blessing in hot climates. Not only do they cool the air, but many dehumidify and filter it as well. The two most common types of air-conditioning systems for the home are evaporative and refrigerated. Both can cool just a single room or an entire house; most types are controlled by a thermostat.

Although evaporative air conditioners, also called swamp coolers, work well in dry desert regions, refrigerated units are the only practical way to cool air in all other climates. Included in the category of refrigerated units are both room air conditioners, fitted into a wall or window; and central air conditioning. Another type of refrigerated system, a heat pump, cools and heats a house.

Central air conditioning costs more to install than individual room units, but it is generally more efficient, quieter, and less costly in the long run. In a house without forced-air heat, a central air conditioner can be a single unit installed next to the house or a split unit, with the condenser and compressor outdoors and the evaporator and blower inside. For a house heated with forced air, the most economical installation is a split system (shown below).

The energy cost of most air-conditioning systems is high, so it's important that your system be properly maintained and, if necessary, professionally serviced. Maintenance and troubleshooting tips for air conditioners are provided on pages 534–535. The best source of thorough information for care and maintenance is your owner's manual.

CENTRAL AIR CONDITIONER

A home with forced-air heating is likely to have a split system, where the compressor and condenser fan are located in an outdoor unit, and the evaporator is mounted on top of the furnace's air-handling unit.

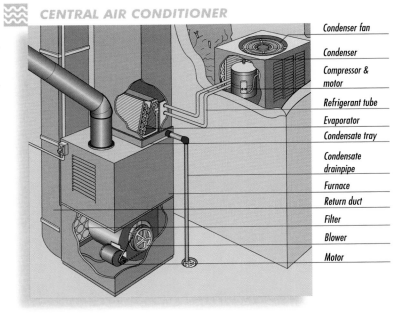

Condenser fan

Condenser

Compressor & motor

Refrigerant tube

Evaporator

Condensate tray

Condensate drainpipe

Furnace

Return duct

Filter

Blower

Motor

ALTERNATIVE COOLING METHODS

There are other ways of staying cool in warm weather without having to pay the high price of air conditioning.

■ Ceiling fans (see pages 520–521), portable fans, and whole-house fans can replace or supplement an air conditioner.

■ Keep shades and curtains closed during the hottest part of the day to prevent the sun from heating up the house.

■ Plant trees and shrubs to shade the house and channel cool breezes toward it.

■ Use insulation and weatherstripping to keep hot air (as well as cold air in winter) out of the house.

ROOM AIR CONDITIONER

A room air conditioner mounts in a window or wall and projects outside the house. A blower pulls warm room air through a filter protected by a large inlet front grill and pushes cool, dehumidified air into the room. Water condenses on the evaporator coils and drains outside, and a fan blows outside air around the condenser coils to dissipate heat.

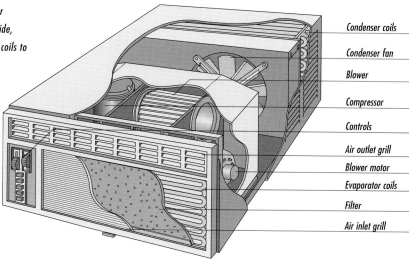

Condenser coils

Condenser fan

Blower

Compressor

Controls

Air outlet grill

Blower motor

Evaporator coils

Filter

Air inlet grill

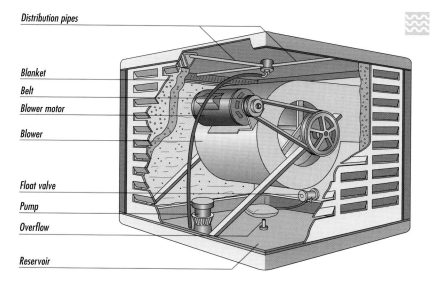

Distribution pipes

Blanket

Belt

Blower motor

Blower

Float valve

Pump

Overflow

Reservoir

EVAPORATIVE AIR COOLER

In hot, dry areas, evaporative air conditioners can cool a home efficiently. Mounted in full sun on the roof or beside the house, the unit utilizes evaporation for cooling by spraying water on porous, absorbent blankets and blowing air through them.

HOW A HEAT PUMP WORKS

A heat pump is a refrigerated air-conditioning system in which the airflow is instantly reversible. During warm weather, the pump draws heat from the air inside the house, cooling it and transferring the heat to the outside or to a large solar mass. During cool weather, the flow is reversed; heat extracted from the outside air or from a large solar mass heats the air inside the house. Once the thermostat is set at the desired temperature, the heat pump automatically heats or cools your house as required. Where temperatures below 0 degrees F are common, some other supplemental heat source is required; because this supplemental source is normally electrical, it can be very costly to operate.

Comfort Improvements

While many new houses are constructed with energy efficiency and maximum comfort in mind, most older homes can benefit from a few improvements to boost the energy performance and comfort they offer. This section offers advice on making the kinds of improvements that you can handle yourself.

Comfort inside a home is a factor of temperature, humidity, and more. It also encompasses aspects of the interior environment that can't be seen or felt. This is the subject of the relatively new concept of "indoor air quality."

INDOOR AIR QUALITY Our homes are not always as safe and secure as we think. One of the consequences of the movement toward tightly sealed, energy-efficient houses has been that some newer houses are now more polluted than older, energy-wasting houses. That's because many pollutants are now trapped inside the house along with the climate-controlled air. Also, ongoing research has found that some substances once used in household products and construction materials can pose serious health risks. Fortunately, there are steps you can take to ensure that the air quality inside your house is safe for everyone, as discussed in the box below and the chart on facing page.

TIME TO REPLACE? Replacing your furnace, boiler, or central air conditioner can be one of the most expensive improvements you will make on your house. Sometimes the choice is obvious: When an old clunker just won't work anymore, you have to get rid of it. Often, however, the decision is less clear-cut. Perhaps the old system continues to operate just fine but wastes energy.

Here are tips to help you make an informed decision:

▪ When the old unit can't keep the house at a consistently comfortable temperature, first see if you can tighten up the house. By insulating and sealing, you may find that you have made the house sufficiently energy efficient without having to spend the extra money for a new system.

▪ If you decide that you do need to replace your existing system and you live in an old house that has been recently insulated and weatherized, you may be in for a pleasant surprise. Because your house has become more energy efficient, you may be able to buy a smaller (and thus less expensive) unit than you currently have, saving money on the initial cost and the long-term costs of operation.

CAUTION: CARBON MONOXIDE

Carbon monoxide (CO) is an odorless, tasteless gas that is emitted by fireplaces, furnaces, gas appliances, water heaters, and other combustion appliances. Under normal circumstances, carbon monoxide is carried safely out of the house by vents and chimneys. But members of your household can be exposed to dangerous levels of carbon monoxide when a chimney becomes clogged or a vent pipe becomes disconnected.

Protect your family from this deadly gas by regularly inspecting all fuel-burning equipment and venting systems in your home. For added protection, install at least one carbon monoxide detector. For recommendations, check with the American Lung Association, your local health department, and consumer magazines.

Don't automatically assume that you would benefit from the most energy-efficient heating or cooling system on the market. In moderate climates, you may not.

UNDERSTANDING "PAYBACK" "Payback" refers to the amount of time required to recover the costs of home improvements. Thinking in terms of payback is helpful in making decisions about what to replace, and when.

For example, suppose you estimate that you could save $150 a year in energy costs by insulating your attic. If it costs you $600 to do the work—or have it done for you—the payback will amount to four years ($150 × 4 years = $600). After four years—and for as long as you own your house beyond that period—you will benefit from the improvement.

On the other hand, if you find that it would cost $4,000 to install a new, high-efficiency heating system that would save you only $200 a year, the payback of 20 years might not look nearly as promising. In this case, you might find that it would be more cost effective to insulate the walls or replace the windows.

Much like those yellow "Energy Guide" labels on new appliances, payback depends on too many factors to be anything more than an educated guess. But it's still useful for comparing the advantages and disadvantages of various home improvements.

HOME ENVIRONMENT HAZARDS

SUBSTANCE	WHAT IS IT?	WHERE IS IT?	WHAT TO DO ABOUT IT
Asbestos	A mineral fiber that, when inhaled, can cause cancer and other health problems.	Widely used in household products and construction materials before the 1970s. Used in insulation around pipes and heating ducts, room insulation, paint, adhesives, siding, flooring, and many other materials.	Only poses a health risk if particles are airborne. Loose or cracked material containing asbestos can often be wrapped tightly or coated to enclose the fibers. Some materials may have to be removed by a specialist. An asbestos inspector, certified by the EPA, can inspect your house and suggest remedies.
Radon	An odorless, colorless, tasteless gas that is released from the soil. Breathing high amounts over a long period may cause cancer.	Occurs naturally in nearly all soils, but in widely varying amounts from one region to another. The gas can seep into houses through crawl spaces and small openings in the foundation or slab. Can be found in old as well as new houses.	Test your house. Contact the EPA or local health department for information on testing devices. Small charcoal-canister tests are quick and inexpensive. If high levels of radon are found, seal cracks in the basement or foundation, place a plastic barrier over the ground in a crawl space, and improve ventilation in the house. If these measures are unsuccessful, contact a professional.
Lead	A metallic element that can cause damage to the brain, liver, and kidneys. Children are particularly susceptible to lead poisoning. Poses a risk when it flakes or burns.	Used in many household products for many years. Especially prevalent in old paint and solder once used for joining copper pipes.	Lead can be detected in old paint using test kits. It can be detected in water through standard water tests. Contact the local health department for recommendations.

Thermostats

A thermostat is a type of switch that is turned on by a temperature-sensitive device that, in turn, activates a boiler, furnace, electric heater, air conditioner, or other heating or cooling device. Low-voltage and millivolt thermostats are the most common types.

Residential thermostats are either electromechanical or electronic. Electromechanical ones typically sense the temperature with a bimetal coil; as the two metals expand and contract at different rates, they move. The coil's movement causes contact points to open or close, switching the low-voltage control circuit (and the appliance) off or on. (Older thermostats have a mercury-type contact enclosed in an airtight glass tube.)

Electronic thermostats sense temperature changes with an electronic element and circuitry, then turn heating or cooling equipment off and on accordingly. Like small computers, they can be programmed to automatically align room temperatures with your needs at various times of the day. As a result, they are very convenient and energy-efficient.

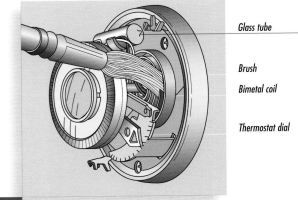

Glass tube

Brush

Bimetal coil

Thermostat dial

2 *Clean the coil*
To clean the heat sensor's bimetal coil (or element), remove the cover and gently brush the coil with a soft brush; blow the thermostat clean of debris.

CLEANING A THERMOSTAT

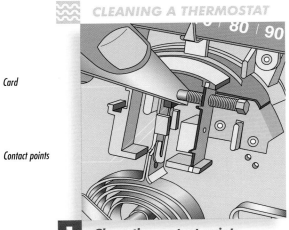

Card

Contact points

1 *Clean the contact points*
If your thermostat has exposed contact points, turn the thermostat up until the points close. Otherwise, remove the cover and wiggle a strip of thin card or heavy paper between the points. Blow clean.

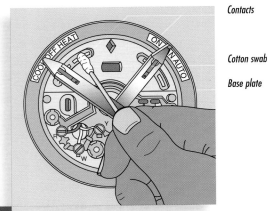

Contacts

Cotton swab

Base plate

3 *Clean the switch contacts*
If your thermostat has switch contacts, remove the cover and clean the contacts with a cotton swab moistened with alcohol.

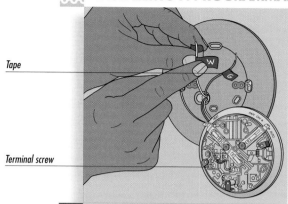

Tape

Terminal screw

1 Remove old thermostat

After shutting off the power to the circuit, remove the cover and detach the wires from their lettered terminals. Flag and label each wire to ensure you hook them up to the correct terminal and so they do not slide back into the hole.

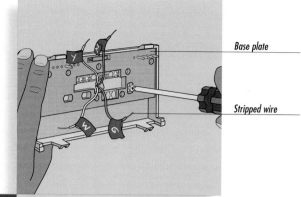

Base plate

Stripped wire

2 Wire new base in place

Attach the new base plate to the wall with screws, checking to ensure that it is level. Strip the wire ends, if needed, or scrape them clean; wrap the ends clockwise around the terminal screws and tighten the screws.

Both thermostats work with most types of heating and cooling systems (they may have wires that you connect differently depending upon the type of system). A system that provides multiple stages of heating and cooling—such as a dual-speed air conditioner or a heat pump—requires a thermostat that is designed to handle this.

Thermostats for heating or air-conditioning systems rarely break down. The only maintenance required is an occasional light cleaning. Don't attempt to make a major repair on a defective thermostat; instead, replace the entire unit. In most cases, you can remove an old bimetal coil thermostat and replace it with a new programmable model in less than 30 minutes.

When buying an electronic thermostat, choose one that will maintain a narrow "comfort window" and that can be programmed to anticipate at what point the furnace must turn off to avoid wasting residual heat in the system or overshooting the desired room temperature. Also, buy one that is easy to program.

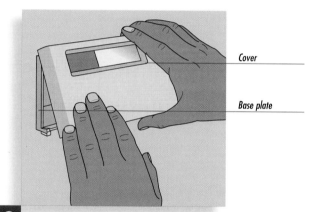

Cover

Base plate

3 Attach the cover

Mount the thermostat cover on the base plate following manufacturer's instructions. Program the thermostat as instructed by the manufacturer.

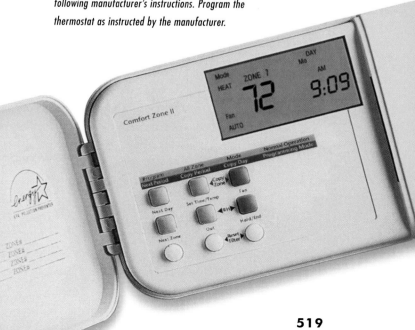

Installing a Ceiling Fan

During warm weather a ceiling fan can help cool a room, and in the winter, it can circulate warm air that rises naturally, reducing your electrical bill and increasing comfort. Ceiling fans are easy to install, and because many models include a light fixture, you can enjoy the benefits of the fan's breeze without giving up room light.

Ceiling fans are available in a variety of styles, sizes, shapes, colors, and levels of quality. Better models have heavy motors that run longer and quieter and produce a better breeze than low-cost units. Most fans have components similar to those shown in Step 1 on facing page.

SIZING THE FAN Match the size of the ceiling fan you buy with the size of the room. The table below gives general guidelines for rooms with 8-foot ceilings. For a typical 12-by-10-foot room (120 square feet), for example, a 42-inch fan would be appropriate.

ROOM SIZE	FAN DIAMETER
Up to 64 sq. ft.	36 in.
Up to 144 sq. ft.	42 in.
Up to 225 sq. ft.	44 in.
Up to 400 sq. ft.	52 in.

PROVIDING ADEQUATE SUPPORT The easiest approach to putting up a new ceiling fan is to replace an old light fixture with one, and utilize the existing wiring. Unless your house is very new, however, the electrical ceiling box that houses the wiring connections in the ceiling must be changed before you can hang a ceiling fan from it, in order to provide adequate support.

Ceiling fans must be attached to a ceiling box that is labeled as approved for ceiling (or "paddle") fans or, if they are heavier than 35 pounds, to a special J-hook screwed into ceiling joists. Always follow manufacturer's instructions.

Turn off the power to the box, then determine how you'll be able to secure it. A ceiling box with an attached flange or bracket usually can be nailed to a ceiling joist. If the joists are not located where you want to hang the fan, you can nail or screw a 2-by-4 or 2-by-6 brace between joists from the attic, then screw an approved shallow ceiling box to the brace. Once the ceiling box is in place, secure the electrical cable to the box with a cable clamp or connector.

A ceiling fan that weighs more than 35 pounds cannot be supported by a ceiling box alone. Instead, it must be supported by a J-hook attached firmly to the framing or to a special hanger bracket supplied by the manufacturer.

WIRING THE FAN Each style of fan is mounted somewhat differently; be sure to follow the manufacturer's instructions. Always work with the circuit's power turned off. On most models you first insert the downrod into the canopy, then feed the wires from the motor through the downrod and canopy. Tighten the screw or screws securing the fan to the downrod.

Then, standing on a stepladder, feed the wires from the ceiling box through the ceiling plate and attach the plate to the box. Most ceiling plates have a hook for supporting the fan during installation. If yours doesn't, make one from a clothes hanger.

Ceiling fans with attached lights can have several differently colored wires in them. Check the manufacturer's instructions for proper identification. Typically, the black and white wires from the circuit attach to the black and white wires from the fan. Bare grounding wires and green wires should be joined. Other wires should be connected as instructed. Use wire nuts to secure the connections and cover all exposed wiring. Attach the canopy to the ceiling plate and tighten the screws. Then, if the fan includes a light, wire it as specified. Last, turn the power back on and test both the fan and the light.

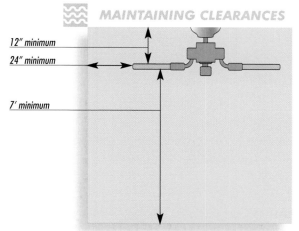

12" minimum

24" minimum

7' minimum

Ceiling fans work best in rooms with ceilings at least 8 feet high. For adequate air movement, the blades should be at least 12 inches from the ceiling and 24 inches from any wall. Any moving blades less than 7 feet high can be hit inadvertently by a raised arm. For rooms with low ceilings, you can buy fans that mount closer to the ceiling.

EXPANDABLE HANGER BARS

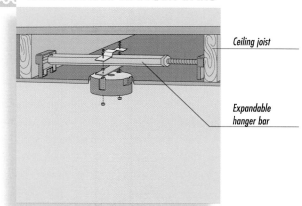

Ceiling joist

Expandable hanger bar

An expandable hanger bar approved for fans can make the mounting process easy. Slip the bar through the ceiling hole and lower it until the legs rest on the ceiling. Turn the bar by hand until the ends contact the joists, then use an adjustable wrench to force the teeth snugly into the joists. Attach the box to the bar with the supplied hardware.

Canopy-mounting screw

Ceiling-plate hook

Wire nut

INSTALLING A FAN

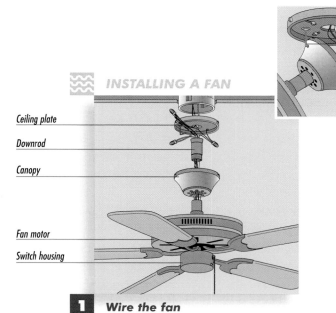

Ceiling plate

Downrod

Canopy

Fan motor

Switch housing

1 **Wire the fan**

Following the manufacturer's instructions, feed the wires from the ceiling box through the assembly and attach the fan's wires as specified, securing the connections with wire nuts. Join bare grounding wires and green wires. Attach the canopy to the ceiling plate and tighten the screws.

Switch housing

Wire nut

2 **Wire the light**

If your fan has a light fixture, connect it to the bottom of the switch housing, following the manufacturer's instructions. Attach the fan blades and test the fan and light.

Insulating

More than half of the energy used in the average American home goes toward heating and cooling. If your house isn't properly sealed and insulated, you may well be paying a significant amount to heat or cool the great outdoors.

In cold climates, warm indoor air looks for ways to move toward cooler spaces. Insulation slows that movement, allowing you to stay warm and comfortable. In summer, the warm outdoor air tries to find a way into your air-conditioned rooms; once again, insulation holds the heat at bay.

"R-value" measures the effectiveness of insulation products. The higher the R-value, the more effective the insulation.

Types of Insulation

A wide variety of insulation products comes in an equally varied array of shapes and forms. Following is a look at the main types:

FIBERGLASS Fiberglass batts and blankets are widely available and relatively easy for a homeowner to install. Both batts (precut strips) and blankets (rolls) come in standard widths so that they can fit neatly between framing in walls and ceilings. Buy fiberglass in the thickness necessary to achieve the desired R-value. Some installation tips are illustrated on facing page.

CELLULOSE Cellulose is the most common type of loose-fill insulation. It comes in bags and is usually blown into walls or attics using special equipment. Building suppliers and home centers often rent or loan blowing equipment when you buy the insulation. Dense-pack cellulose, which is blown in at a high density, both insulates and seals a wall or ceiling against air leakage. Other types of loose-fill insulation include fiberglass and rock wool.

RIGID INSULATION Rigid insulation is made from fiberglass or plastic foam that has been compressed into a board-like form. Plastic foam board is most often used under the siding in exterior walls and on foundations. It offers a high R-value with minimal thickness, making it ideal for tight quarters.

SPRAY FOAMS Spray foams are used to insulate walls and ceilings, usually by a contractor in new construction. Homeowners are familiar with foam products available in small cans that can be used to seal small, hard-to-reach places, such as around plumbing penetrations or sill plates.

Installing Fiberglass Batts

Fiberglass batts can be installed by just about anyone, but you should be aware that there is a right way and a wrong way to do the job. The right way, which really doesn't take much more time, will provide you with the protection you paid for; the wrong way can be a waste of money. When working with fiberglass batts, fill the space completely and guide—don't force—the batts into place.

RECOMMENDED MINIMUM R-VALUES

CLIMATE	WALLS & FLOORS	CEILINGS W/ ATTICS
Mild	R-11	R-19
Moderate	R-19	R-30
Cold	R-19	R-38 to R-49

BEWARE OF VAPOR

If you insulate without considering a vapor retardant, your home may wind up with moisture damage. When warm, moist air contacts cold air, it condenses. A vapor retardant blocks the moisture from passing into the wall or ceiling, thus minimizing condensation. There are several types of vapor retardants (often called, misleadingly, vapor barriers). Faced batts of fiberglass insulation have a protective layer with flanges that are stapled to studs and joists. Alternately, you can use regular, unfaced batts, and then cover them with plastic sheets, which should be overlapped at least 3 inches. As a general rule, install the vapor retardant on the warm-in-winter side of the framing.

The batts should fit snugly against all surfaces in the wall or ceiling cavity. But to assure the maximum R-value, the batts should not be compressed or crushed. Buy batts that are the right size to fit between studs or joists. When you have to contend with wires, pipes, and other components of the electrical and plumbing systems, you need to master some special techniques, as described below.

SPECIAL SITUATIONS

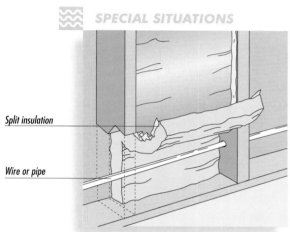

Split insulation

Wire or pipe

Pipes & wires

Don't shove the whole batt behind a run of wiring or pipes; instead, peel the batt in half just far enough so that the wire or pipe can pass through the middle. You can use this same approach for vertical wire or pipe runs as well.

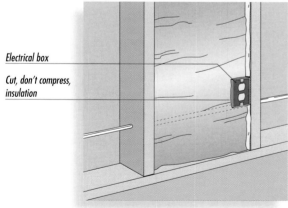

Electrical box

Cut, don't compress, insulation

Electrical boxes

Prevent compression around electrical boxes by cutting the batt to fit snugly all around the box. This is easiest if you first set the batt in the bay, then slice around the box to achieve a good fit. Be sure that insulation remains behind the box.

Cut insulation on a scrap sheet of plywood or an unfinished subfloor. With a little practice and a confident stroke, you can cut straight across a batt without the aid of a straightedge (though it's helpful to use a board as a guide for cutting insulation in the long direction). It's usually easiest to cut with the vapor retardant facing up. Use a utility knife with a sharp blade, and change blades frequently.

When using material with a vapor retardant, always place the retardant on the warm-in-winter side (in toward the room). When insulating walls, staple the vapor retardant's flange to the inner faces of studs to allow for a 1-inch air space between the insulation and the backside of the wall surface material.

In bays containing plumbing supply and drainpipes or ductwork, there often just isn't enough room for batt insulation to be effective. Here it is useful to use rigid foam board, cut to fit the bay exactly, installed between the obstruction and the outside wall. Use spray foam to seal the edges.

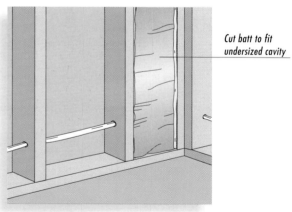

Cut batt to fit undersized cavity

Narrow bays

All houses have some bays that are narrower than the others. Your insulation will be much more effective if you cut the batt to fit snugly in the bay.

 To protect yourself from irritants when working with insulation, wear cotton gloves, plastic goggles, and a paper dust mask. It's also a good idea to wear long sleeves and a cap.

Ventilation

After spending time and money insulating and sealing your home, the idea of introducing ventilation to pump air in and out can seem downright foolish. But in truth, a properly ventilated house is more comfortable—and certainly more healthful—than a poorly ventilated house. Homes built before the days of energy consciousness leaked a significant amount of air, so they didn't require ventilation: The air was fresh but the energy was wasted. In a newer, tighter house, you can have both energy efficiency and healthful air if you plan for just enough ventilation to remove pollutants and moisture without wasting heated or cooled indoor air.

INSTALLING A BATHROOM FAN The principal job of a bathroom fan is to carry warm, humid air out of the house, lowering overall humidity. In addition, fans are useful for removing odors. If you have a bathroom that doesn't have a fan—particularly a full bathroom with a shower or tub—installing a new fan is a sensible improvement.

Before buying a fan, determine the size of the room. For a room with conventional 8-foot ceilings, you can quickly determine the square footage by multiplying the width times the length, then multiplying that result by 1.1. The final figure tells you the minimum size, measured in cubic feet per minute (CFM), of fan to buy. For a 5-by-8-foot room, the formula would be $5 \times 8 \times 1.1 = 44$ CFM.

Also take the fan's noise into consideration; in most cases, it's well worth a few extra dollars to get a quiet fan. Fan noise is rated in sones—the lower the sone rating, the quieter the fan.

When installing a fan that requires ducts to vent the vapors out through an attic or similar space, be sure to keep the duct as straight and short as possible. All fans are sold with installation instructions; be sure to follow the manufacturer's recommendations.

Ducting to the roof or eaves
Ceiling fan may ventilate through ductwork out the roof or soffit.

Roof cap
Ceiling joist
Fan
Duct

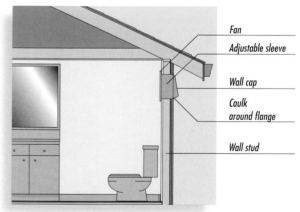

Venting through the wall
Wall fan on outside wall, installed between wall studs, ventilates directly to the outside.

Fan
Adjustable sleeve
Wall cap
Caulk around flange
Wall stud

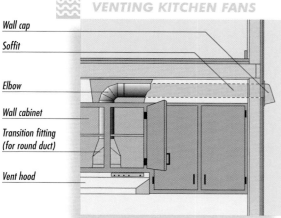

Wall cap
Soffit

Elbow

Wall cabinet

Transition fitting
(for round duct)

Vent hood

Through the wall

A kitchen fan's exhaust duct may run horizontally in the space between wall cabinets and the ceiling or behind a soffit and out the wall.

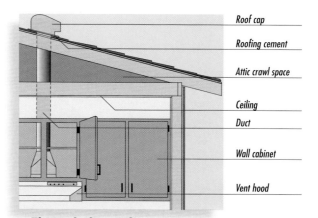

Roof cap

Roofing cement

Attic crawl space

Ceiling

Duct

Wall cabinet

Vent hood

Through the roof

A vent hood's duct may take the direct route up through the cabinet and ceiling, through the attic, and out the roof.

VENTING THE KITCHEN Kitchen vents must be able to remove moisture, smoke, grease, heat, and odors. That job is handled most effectively by a range hood installed directly over the range or cooktop. Like bathroom vents, kitchen vents are rated at the speed with which they can move air, measured in cubic feet per minute (CFM). An average 30-inch-wide hood should be rated for a minimum of 100 CFM, although 200 CFM would provide even better service. Most vent hoods produce between 3 and 8 sones; the lower the number, the quieter the fan will be.

As shown on this page, ducts for range hoods can be run straight up through the ceiling or horizontally through a wall. Downdraft cooktops installed in kitchen islands require a duct run beneath the floor.

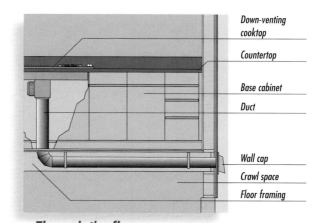

Down-venting cooktop

Countertop

Base cabinet

Duct

Wall cap

Crawl space

Floor framing

Through the floor

A down-venting unit vents a cooktop in an island or peninsula. The duct exits beneath the floor and out through a nearby wall.

Comfort Repairs

Maintenance is critical for a forced-air system to perform well and last a long time; be sure to keep yours well tuned, in accordance with the instructions in the owner's manual. Although all systems should be inspected and tuned by a trained professional every year, you can handle routine maintenance yourself.

For maximum efficiency, clean the system and inspect the burner and thermostat (pages 518–519 and 528–531). A system that's working inefficiently can be adjusted, as explained on this page and facing page. For other problems, see the chart on facing page. Caution: Turn off the switch supplying power to the furnace before beginning any work.

CARING FOR THE SYSTEM To ensure trouble-free operation, service the system as follows:

■ Clean or replace the filter every month during the heating season.

■ Brush and vacuum heat exchanger surfaces annually (see owner's manual for instructions).

■ Clean the blower blades at the start of each heating season; add a few drops of motor oil to each oil cup if your blower is equipped with them.

■ Check and adjust both belt alignment and belt tension (see illustrations below) if your furnace has a belt-driven blower. To replace a belt that is worn or otherwise damaged, first loosen the motor adjustment bolt, then remove the old belt and attach a new one.

THREE BLOWER ADJUSTMENTS

Blower
Blower pulley
Mounting bolt
Straightedge
Motor pulley
Motor

Check the pulley alignment
Place a straightedge against the pulley faces. If they're not aligned, loosen the mounting bolts and adjust the motor pulley.

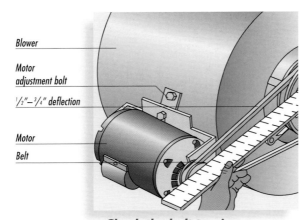

Blower
Motor adjustment bolt
$1/2"–3/4"$ deflection
Motor
Belt

Check the belt tension
Push the belt—it should deflect $1/2$ to $3/4$ inch. If it doesn't, turn the adjustment bolt and move the motor away to tighten the belt, closer to loosen it.

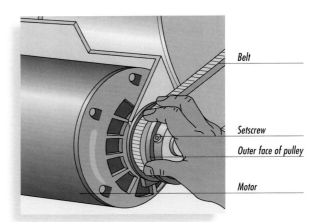

Belt
Setscrew
Outer face of pulley
Motor

Adjust the blower's speed
To speed up the blower and increase airflow, loosen the setscrew and turn the outer pulley face clockwise; turn it counterclockwise to slow down the blower.

■ Examine the ducts annually for leaks; seal any leaks with duct tape.

BALANCING THE HEAT If some rooms are too hot or too cold, try adjusting the dampers in the registers and, if your system has them, the dampers in the warm-air ducts.

On a typical cold day, leave the thermostat at one setting and let the system run for three hours to stabilize the temperature. Open the dampers wide in the coldest rooms. Then adjust the dampers, room by room, until temperatures are balanced. Wait half an hour or so after each adjustment before rechecking or readjusting.

In a home that is hard to heat, achieve maximum comfort by adjusting the blower so that it runs constantly at a lower level throughout the day. To do this, adjust the motor pulley of a belt-driven motor (see facing page) or, for a direct-drive blower, change the electrical connections (see owner's manual) for a slow blower speed that produces a 100 degree F temperature rise through the furnace while the furnace is firing.

SETTING THE FAN CONTROL If you're chilled by a blast of cool air when the blower turns on, try adjusting the fan control (see drawing at right). Caution: If your furnace has a combination fan and limit control, do not touch the pointer on the limit control side. This pointer turns off the furnace if the maximum allowable air temperature is exceeded.

As the blower turns on, hold your hand in front of the warm-air register farthest from the furnace. Your hand should feel neither cooler nor warmer. If it feels cooler, uncover the control and move the fan control's ON pointer a few degrees higher. Adjust as needed. To increase fuel efficiency, check the air just before the blower shuts off. If your hand feels warmer, move the OFF pointer a few degrees lower.

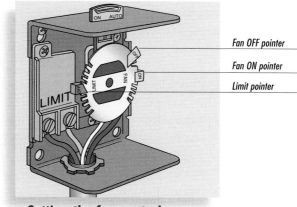

Fan OFF pointer
Fan ON pointer
Limit pointer

Setting the fan control
*To adjust the temperature of the air coming out of the registers, move the **ON** pointer to set the temperature at which the blower turns on, the **OFF** pointer to set the temperature at which it turns off.*

TROUBLESHOOTING A FORCED-AIR SYSTEM

PROBLEM	POSSIBLE CAUSE	REMEDIES
No heat No power	Defective thermostat	Check furnace switch and circuit breaker or fuse Clean or replace thermostat
Insufficient heat	Clogged filter Leaking ducts Slow blower Loose blower belt	Clean or replace filter Seal leaks with duct tape Adjust blower speed Tighten belt
Blower doesn't operate	Broken belt Fan control too high Defective blower motor	Replace belt Adjust fan control Repair or replace motor
Noisy blower	Insufficient lubrication Loose or worn blower belt	Add oil (see owner's manual) Tighten or replace belt
Blower cycles too rapidly	Fan control differential too low Blower operating too fast	Adjust fan control Adjust blower speed

Maintaining Gas Burners

Gas furnaces, water heaters, dryers, and ranges all operate in a similar manner. When the thermostat (or control) calls for heat, the burner's automatic gas valve opens, allowing gas to flow into a manifold and then into Venturi tubes, where it mixes with air. When the air-gas mixture emerges from the burner ports, the pilot ignites it and heat is created. A thermocouple adjacent to the pilot closes the gas valve if the pilot isn't working.

Whether they are fueled by natural, manufactured, or bottled or liquefied petroleum gas, gas burners are generally reliable and require little routine maintenance. Problems you may encounter are discussed below and on the facing page.

Always turn off the gas and the electricity to the unit before making any type of repairs. If in doubt about the proper procedures to take, call your gas utility—depending upon your locale, they may send out a service person free of charge.

LIGHTING A GAS PILOT Use the manual control knob on the automatic gas valve to turn off the gas to the main burner and pilot. Allow at least 5 minutes for accumulated gas to dissipate before proceeding. Use extreme caution—and take more time—if your fuel is bottled gas; it doesn't dissipate readily.

Set the thermostat well below room temperature. Turn the manual control knob to PILOT and light the pilot, holding the knob there for a minute. Release the knob and turn it to ON. If the pilot doesn't stay on, adjust the pilot (see facing page) or call the gas company. (Remember to reset the thermostat when the pilot is relit.)

CLEANING THE PILOT ORIFICE If you have trouble lighting the pilot, the orifice may be plugged. To clean it, first shut off the gas supply by turning the gas inlet valve handle so it's at a right angle to the pipe. Next, disconnect the thermocouple tube and the pilot gas line from the automatic gas valve. Then remove the bracket holding the pilot and the thermocouple.

TYPICAL GAS BURNER

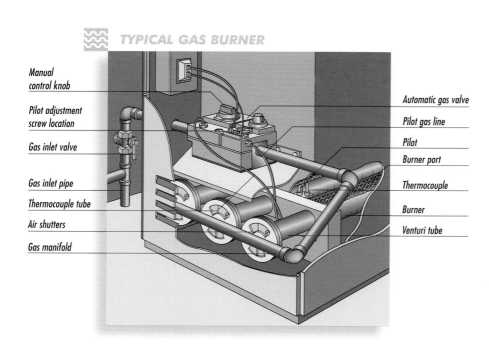

- Manual control knob
- Pilot adjustment screw location
- Gas inlet valve
- Gas inlet pipe
- Thermocouple tube
- Air shutters
- Gas manifold
- Automatic gas valve
- Pilot gas line
- Pilot
- Burner port
- Thermocouple
- Burner
- Venturi tube

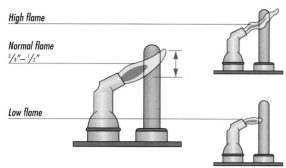

Adjusting the pilot

The pilot flame should be blue and should cover the thermocouple. Turn the thermostat down and turn off power to the system. Turn the pilot adjustment screw (often under a cover screw) clockwise to reduce the flame, counterclockwise to increase it. Reset thermostat when done.

Blow out the orifice (you can blow through a flexible vinyl tube). Reattach the bracket, pilot gas line, and thermocouple tube. Turn on the gas and relight the pilot.

CLEANING THE BURNERS Clogged gas burners and ports heat inefficiently. Clean them at the start of the heating season. To reach the ports, shut off the gas inlet valve and remove the bracket holding the pilot and thermocouple. Remove any screws or nuts holding the burners and maneuver them carefully out of the combustion chamber.

Scour the burners with a stiff wire brush; clean the burner ports with stiff wire that's slightly smaller than the diameter of the openings. Reassemble the burners in the combustion chamber, replacing any screws or nuts that secured the burners. Then mount the bracket holding the pilot and thermocouple. Turn on the gas and relight the pilot (see drawing at right). Be sure to adjust the air-gas ratio, as explained below.

ADJUSTING THE BURNERS For maximum efficiency, burners fueled with natural gas should burn with a bright blue flame that has a soft blue-green interior and no yellow tip. (Check with your gas company for the correct colors for other types of gas.)

To correct the air–natural gas ratio, you'll need to adjust the air shutters. Turn up the thermostat so the burners light, and loosen the lock screws. Slowly open each shutter until the flames are bright blue, then close the shutters gradually until yellow tips appear. Slowly reopen the shutters until the yellow tips just disappear; tighten the screws.

REPLACING A THERMOCOUPLE

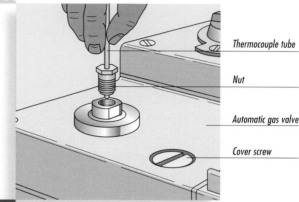

Thermocouple tube

Nut

Automatic gas valve

Cover screw

1 Unscrew the thermocouple

To replace the thermocouple, turn the manual control knob to OFF, then unscrew the nut that secures the thermocouple tube to the automatic gas valve.

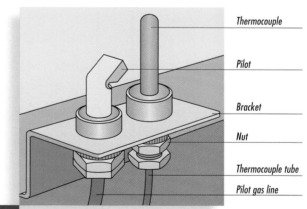

Thermocouple

Pilot

Bracket

Nut

Thermocouple tube

Pilot gas line

2 Replace the thermocouple

Unscrew the nut holding the thermocouple to the bracket; remove the thermocouple and tube. Attach the new unit to the bracket and gas valve; relight the pilot light.

Maintaining Oil Burners

There are several types of oil burners, but the high-pressure or gun type is the most common. Most oil burners run for years with few problems. For greatest efficiency, call in a professional every year to service your burner. Check the burner regularly during the heating season and clean it as needed.

HOW OIL BURNERS WORK When the thermostat demands heat, the burner motor turns on, pumping filtered fuel oil under pressure through a nozzle, forming a mist. The burner's blower forces air through the draft tube, where it mixes with the oil mist. As the mixture enters the combustion chamber, it's ignited by a high-voltage spark between two electrodes located at the end of the draft tube. If the oil fails to ignite, the burner is turned off by a flame sensor in the burner itself or by a heat sensor that is situated on the stack control attached to the flue. This mechanism prevents the boiler or furnace from being flooded by oil.

SERVICING YOUR BURNER Every year have a professional inspect and clean your burner, as well as check for efficiency. To keep repair and fuel bills low, inspect and clean the burner several times between service calls. Lubricate the motor and blower bearings by pouring oil in the oil cups if the motor and blower are equipped with them. Clean the blower, oil strainer, and sensors and, when necessary, replace the filter and gasket (see below and facing page). Be sure to turn off the power to the burner before you begin any work.

CLEANING THE SENSORS

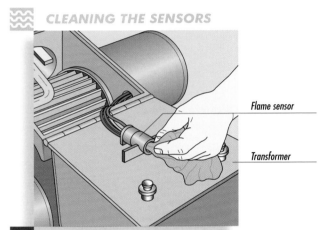

Flame sensor

Transformer

1 Clean the flame sensor
Lift the blower cover and clean the flame sensor with a soft cloth. If your flame sensor is located at the end of the draft tube, leave this task to a professional.

HIGH-PRESSURE OIL BURNER

Combustion chamber

Transformer

Draft tube

Mounting bolts

Blower

Motor

Oil inlet line

Filter

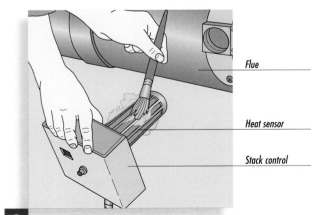

Flue

Heat sensor

Stack control

2 Clean the heat sensor
Clean the heat sensor on the stack control with hot, soapy water and a brush after removing the control from the flue; dry and replace the control.

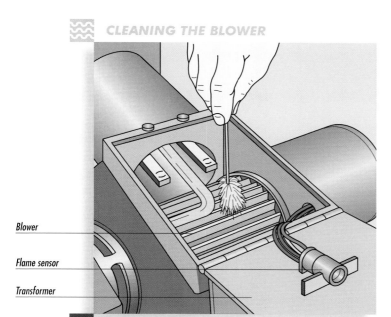

Blower

Flame sensor

Transformer

1 **Clean the blades**

Turn off the power to the heating system. Remove the cover (the transformer may be attached to the cover). Clean the blower blades with a small brush.

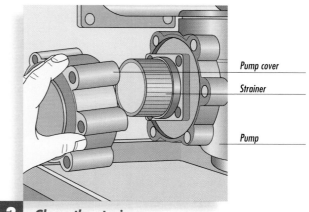

Pump cover

Strainer

Pump

2 **Clean the strainer**

To reach the strainer, unscrew the pump cover. Remove the strainer and clean it in mineral spirits or kerosene.

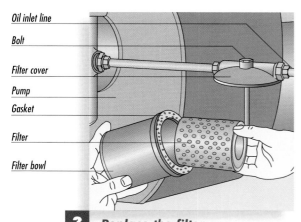

Oil inlet line

Bolt

Filter cover

Pump

Gasket

Filter

Filter bowl

3 **Replace the filter**

Shut off the valve between the filter and tank. Unscrew the bowl from the cover and change the filter and gasket.

 Caution: Be very careful when using mineral spirits or kerosene near the burner—both are highly flammable.

Maintaining a Boiler

In both hot-water and steam heating systems, water heated in a boiler travels through a network of pipes to the radiators, convectors, or runs of tubing that deliver heat to rooms. With regular maintenance and inspection, especially during the heating season, you can correct simple problems with a boiler or components of the delivery system. For serious problems, call a service professional.

Two gauges are typically mounted on a boiler: one for water temperature and another for pressure or altitude. Adjusting the temperature is a job for a professional. You can make adjustments to the pressure gauge by changing the water level.

 MAINTAINING A STEAM SYSTEM

To keep a steam heating system in good working condition, periodically check the safety valve, steam pressure gauge, and water level gauge, as explained below. Also, regularly inspect the burner and thermostat. See page 513 for an illustration of a steam heating system.

SAFETY VALVE Located on top of the boiler, the safety valve allows steam to escape if the pressure in the boiler exceeds safe levels. Test the valve every month during the heating season by depressing the handle (stand clear of the valve pipe); if steam doesn't come out, have the valve replaced.

STEAM PRESSURE GAUGE Tap the gauge lightly to make sure it's not stuck and check it to see that the pressure of the steam in the boiler is within normal bounds—typically 2 to 10 pounds per square inch (psi). If not, shut off the boiler and call for service.

WATER LEVEL GAUGE Once a month, open the valves at each end of the sight glass in the gauge—the water level should be in the middle of the glass. (Be sure to close the valves after checking.) If water is not visible, shut off the boiler and let it cool. Then add water by opening the fill valve on the water inlet pipe—unless your system has an automatic water fill valve. In that case, call for service.

To remove the sight glass for cleaning or replacement, shut off the valves and undo the collar nuts at each end of the glass. Install new gaskets when you reassemble the unit.

CHECKING GAUGES & RELIEF VALVE The pressure gauge, illustrated at right, provides a check on the water level. The fixed pointer, set when the system was installed, is a reference point for water level. The moving pointer indicates current water level and should align with the fixed one when the water is cold. If the moving pointer reads higher, drain some water from the expansion tank (far right). If it's lower and the system doesn't have a pressure-reducing valve, add water through the water inlet valve until the pointers are aligned.

A pressure gauge that reads high or a tank that feels hot indicates there's too little air in the expansion tank. Draining some of the water from the tank will restore the proper air–water ratio. You can do the job yourself, unless you have a diaphragm tank; in that case, you will have to call for professional service.

This valve releases excess pressure. Once a month, lift the valve lever; if no water flows from the valve, replace it.

Unless your system has zone controls that automatically control water temperature in specific areas, you may need to balance your system to compensate for overly cold or overly warm rooms. Turn the system on and let room temperatures stabilize before you start.

BLEEDING THE SYSTEM Convectors and radiators will not heat properly if air is trapped inside. If your units don't have automatic air valves, you'll need to bleed the air from them at the beginning of each heating season, whenever you add water to the heating system, or if a convector or radiator remains cold when it shouldn't.

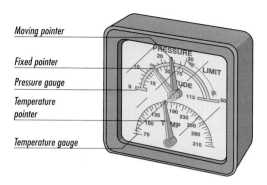

Check the gauges

In a system equipped with a pressure-reducing valve, water level should be maintained automatically. If draining the expansion tank doesn't work or if the water level is too low, it's best to consult a professional.

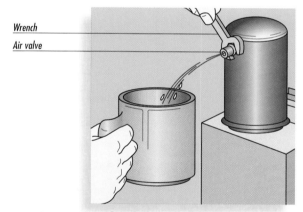

Bleed the convectors

Depending on the type of valve, use a wrench, screwdriver, or special key to open the valve. When water spurts out, close the valve. CAUTION: Water may be hot.

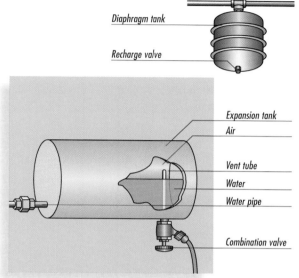

Drain the expansion tank

To drain the tank, turn off the power and the water to the boiler; let the water in the tank cool. Attach a hose to the combination valve and open it. Let water flow out until the pointers on the pressure gauge coincide. Close the valve, and then restore power and water.

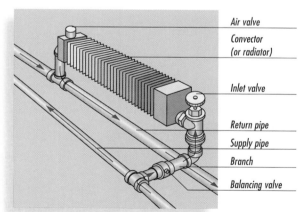

Balance the system

To adjust a convector or radiator, gradually open or close the balancing valve on that branch or the inlet valve on the affected convector or radiator. Be patient—it may take several days of adjustments to bring the system into balance.

Maintaining Air Conditioners

Central air conditioners function most efficiently when the area around the outside unit is kept clean. Keep nearby bushes trimmed and clear away leaves from the grills. Cover the unit during snow season. Clean the filter on the indoor unit every month during the cooling season; replace the filter as necessary. Check that the condensate drain is clear. Vacuum the condenser coil and fins on the outdoor unit at least once a year; be careful not to damage or deform the fins. Don't run an air conditioner when the outside temperature is below 60 degrees F—otherwise the coils could frost up and restrict airflow.

Room air conditioners generally require little maintenance. During the cooling season, clean the filter and condenser coils every month (see below and facing page); replace the filter as necessary. Turn off the unit before you begin working on it. To clean the filter on a room air conditioner, first remove it. On some models the filter may slide out from the top or side.

For problems with the operation of your air-conditioning system, see the chart on the facing page and refer to your owner's manual. Be sure to disconnect the power to the unit before working on it. Call in a professional to repair the refrigeration system if necessary.

Clean the filter

On most units you must first remove the front grill, which may be held in place by spring clips or tabs along the top edge. If the filter is foam or metal, wash it in soapy water and let dry. Replace a disposable filter. Before replacing the filter, vacuum the evaporator coil and fins located behind the filter.

MAINTAINING A ROOM AIR CONDITIONER

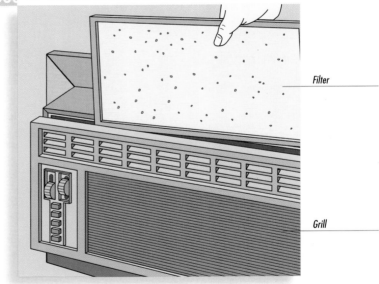

Filter

Grill

CARING FOR AN EVAPORATIVE COOLER

With conscientious maintenance, you can expect few problems with an evaporative cooler. At the beginning of each cooling season, and more often if you see a mineral buildup from evaporated water, thoroughly clean the unit, oil the pump and blower, and replace the blankets. Also, check and adjust the blower belt; if it's cracked or worn, replace it as for a belt in a furnace (see page 526).

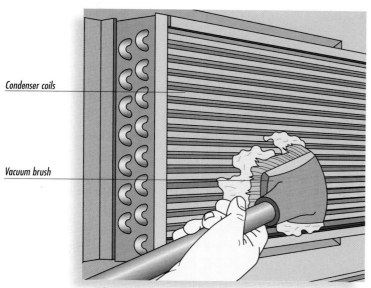

Condenser coils

Vacuum brush

Clean the condenser coils
With the unit unplugged, slide the air conditioner out of its casing. Carefully set it on a table or the floor. Brush and vacuum the coils, then reassemble the unit.

 CARING FOR A HEAT PUMP

Keep the outdoor portion of a heat pump free of snow and debris. Occasionally check the blower and filter in the air-handling unit indoors, and replace the filter monthly during periods of heavy use.

 TROUBLESHOOTING AN AIR CONDITIONER

PROBLEM	POSSIBLE CAUSE	REMEDIES
Air conditioner doesn't work	No power	Check circuit breaker or fuse
	Defective room unit power cord	Replace cord
Air conditioner doesn't cool sufficiently	Thermostat set to heat	Reset to cold
	Insufficient airflow	Clean or replace filter, and clean evaporator and condenser coils
	Defective thermostat	Clean or replace thermostat
	Defective compressor	Call a professional
	Dirty or bent evaporator or condenser fins	Clean or straighten fins
	Frost on evaporator coils	Don't operate in temperatures below 60°F
Air conditioner is excessively noisy	Dirty or bent fan blades	Clean or straighten fan blades
	Loose blower motor	Tighten mounting bolts
	Insufficient lubrication in motor	Place oil in oil cups, if any

Resources

For information about a full range of home improvement products and services, contact:

Lowe's Companies, Inc.
Customer Service
Box 1111
North Wilkesboro, NC 28656
1-336-658-7100
www.lowes.com

In addition to Lowe's, contact the following companies for product information:

Alcoa Bldg. Products
800-962-6973
www.alcoahomes.com
Vinyl & aluminum siding

American Olean
888-AOT-TILE
www.aotile.com
Tile

American Standard
800-752-6292
www.us.amstd.com
Plumbing fixtures

American Woodmark
800-388-2483
www.americanwoodmark.com
Cabinets

Amerimax Home Products
800-347-2586
www.amerimax.com
Gutters

APA-The Engineered Wood Association
253-565-6600
www.apawood.org
Wood products information

Armstrong World Industries
800-233-3823
www.armstrong.com
Flooring

Avonite
800-428-6648
www.avonite.com
Countertops

Broan Mfg. Co.
800-445-6057
www.broan.com
Ventilation products, appliances

Bruce Hardwood Floors
800-722-4647
www.brucehardwoodfloors.com
Flooring

Bryant Heating and Cooling Systems
800-428-4326
www.bryant.com
Heating & cooling equipment

Carrier Corp.
800-4-CARRIER
www.carrier.com
Heating & cooling equipment

CertainTeed Roofing
800-233-8990
www.certainteed.com
Insulation

Chicago Faucets
847-803-5000
www.chicagofaucets.com
Faucets

Delta Faucet Co.
800-345-DELTA
www.deltafaucet.com
Faucets

Elkay Mfg. Co.
630-574-8484
www.elkay.com
Plumbing fixtures

Ellison Windows & Doors
336-764-6400
www.ellisonwindow.com
Windows, doors

Flood Co.
800-356-6346
www.floodco.com
Deck & siding care products

Focal Point Architectural Products
800-662-5550
www.focalpointap.com
Exterior detailing

Formica Corp.
800-FORMICA
www.formica.com
Countertops, flooring

Fypon
800-537-5349
www.fypon.com
Decorative moldings

GAF Materials Corporation
800-ROOF-411
www.gaf.com
Roofing

The Genie Co.
800-995-1111
www.geniecompany.com
Garage doors

Grohe America
630-582-7711
www.groheamerica.com
Faucets

Hansgrohe
800-334-0455
www.hansgrohe.com
Faucets

Harbor Breeze
877-HBREEZE
www.harborbreezefans.com
Ceiling fans

Holmes Garage Door
800-998-3667
www.holmes-hally.com
Garage doors

Hunter Fans
901-744-1200
www.hunterfans.com
Ceiling fans

Jado Bathroom & Hardware
800-227-2734
www.jado.com
Plumbing fixtures

Jotul USA
207-797-5912
www.hearth.com/jotul
Wood stoves

Kobalt Tools
888-3KOBALT
www.kobalttools.com
Tools

Kohler Co.
800-4-KOHLER
www.kohlerco.com
Plumbing fixtures, faucets

Kolbe & Kolbe Millwork Co.
715-842-5666
www.kolbe-kolbe.com
Doors, millwork

KraftMaid Cabinetry
440-632-5333
www.kraftmaid.com
Cabinets

Larson Manufacturing Company
800-352-3360
www.larsondoors.com
Storm doors

Marley Mouldings
800-368-3117
www.marleymouldings.com
Millwork

Martin Fireplaces
800-227-5248
www.martinindustries.com
Fireplaces

Master Lock Co.
414-444-2800
www.masterlock.com
Locksets

Merillat Industries
800-575-8763
www.merillat.com
Cabinets

The Millworks, Inc.
970-259-5915
Molding

NAPCO Siding
800-786-2726
www.napcobuildingmaterials.com
Siding

Olympic Paints and Stains
800-235-5020
www.ppgaf.com
Finishes

Orac Deor by Outwater
800-835-4400
www.outwater.com
Millwork

Owens Corning
1-800-GET PINK
www.owenscorning.com
Insulation & roofing

Peerless Faucet Co.
317-848-1812
Faucets

Pella Corporation
800-84-PELLA
www.pella.com
Windows, doors

Phifer Wire Products
800-633-5955
www.phifer.com
Screening

Porcher
800-359-3261
Plumbing fixtures

Probilt Doors
800-251-9894
www.probilt.com
Patio doors

Quikrete
800-776-6034
www.quikrete.com
Concrete mixes

Raynor Garage Doors
800-4-RAYNOR
www.raynor.com
Garage doors

Regent Lighting Corp.
800-334-6871
www.regentlighting.com
Lighting

Reliabilt Doors
877-RB-DOOR1
www.reliabilt.com
Steel doors

Reliant Building Products
888-253-8439
972-919-1000
Patio doors, windows

Resources

Robern
800-877-2376
www.robern.com
Bath fixtures

Schlage Lock Co.
800-847-1864
www.schlagelock.com
Locksets

Solatube Intl.
800-966-SOLA
www.solatube.com
Skylights

StarMark
800-594-9444
www.starmarkcabinetry.com
Cabinets

Sterling Plumbing Group
800-STERLING
www.sterlingplumbing.com
Plumbing fixtures, faucets

Sun-Tek Skylights
800-334-5854
www.sun-tek.com
Skylights

Superior Fireplace Co.
800-731-8101
www.superiorfireplace.com
Fireplaces

Survivor Technologies, Inc.
800-926-8133
www.survivorwindow.com
Vinyl windows

The Trane Co.
608-787-2000
www.trane.com
Heating & cooling equipment

Tubular Skylight
800-315-TUBE
www.tubular-skylight.com
Skylights

USG Interiors
800-USG4YOU
www.usg.com
Building products

Valspar Corp.
800-845-9061
www.valspar.com
Paint

Vantage Products Corp.
800-334-2238
www.vantageproducts.com
Shutters

Velux-America
800-888-3589
www.velux.com
Skylights, windows

Viking Industries
800-275-9464
Interior doors

Wayne Dalton Corp.
800-827-DOOR
www.waynedalton.com
Garage doors

WeatherShield Windows & Doors
800-477-6808
www.weathershield.com
Windows, doors

Wellborn Cabinet
800-762-4475
www.wellborncabinet.com
Cabinets

Wenco Windows
800-458-9128
www.doors-windows.com
Windows, doors

Wilsonart Intl.
800-433-3222
www.wilsonart.com
Countertops, flooring

Wooster Brush
800-392-7246
www.woosterbrush.com
Paint applicators

York Intl. Corp. Unitary Prods.
717-771-6819
www.york.com
Heating & cooling equipment

Look for these fine Lowe's exclusive brands.

Doors, Windows, & Lumber
Reliabilt Doors
Top Choice Lumber

Electrical & Plumbing
Envirotemp Water Heaters
Harbor Breeze Ceiling Fans
Portfolio Lighting

Garden Products
No Pest
Sta-Green

Hardware
Phillips II Wood Screws

Home Décor
Alexander Julian
Basic Blindz
Designables
Laura Ashley

Kitchen Cabinets
Cross Creek by Kraftmaid
Shenandoah by American Woodmark

Paint
American Tradition
Laura Ashley
Olympic
One & Only
Sealzall
Severe Weather
12-Year Enterprise

Tools & Outdoor Power Equipment
Kobalt Tools
Taskforce
Troybilt

Credits

PHOTOGRAPHY

Akzo Nobel Coatings, Inc., 400.

Alcoa Building Products, Inc., 284.

APA-The Engineered Wood Association, 326.

American Wood Council, 295.

Andersen Windows, 176, 178 (bottom), 180, 183 (bottom right), 214.

Armstrong World Industries, Inc., 154.

Atkinson, Scott, 262.

Barta, Patrick (Patrick Barta Photography), 28.

Broan Manufacturing, 524, 525.

Bryant Heating and Cooling Systems, 514.

Burr, Bruce (Burr Photography for Hometips.com) 35 (top), 44, 45, 46 (bottom), 50, 51, 52 (top).

Carrier Corporation, 519.

CertainTeed Corporation, 288.

Christiansen, Glenn, 244 (stainless steel).

Clopay Building Products, 352, 357 (top).

Commercial Gutter Systems, 332.

Congoleum Corporation, 132 (bottom).

Crandall & Crandall, 56.

Darley, Mark, 10 (bottom).

Delta Faucet Company, 446.

Elk Premium Roofing, 318.

Ennis, Phillip, 46 (top).

The Genie Company, 354, 357 (bottom).

Grohe America, 450.

Harvey, Philip, 1, 12, 14, 59, 60 (top), 66 (top), 73, 96, 114, 128, 133, 183 (top), 184, 234, 238 244 (wood, plastic, stone), 261, 404, 420, 466.

Hurni, Jean-Claude, 10 (top), 64 (top), 356, 382, 386.

ICI Canada, Inc., 36, 37 (photos #8, #10, #11, #12), 396.

Jensen, Michael, 266.

Kohler Company, 422 (top, bottom left), 423, 430.

Livingston, David Duncan, 11.

Lowe's Companies, Inc., 500, 520, 528.

Marley, Stephen, 244 (marble).

Marvin Windows and Doors, 52 (bottom).

McCrae, Colin, 178 (top).

McDowell, Jack, 132 (top), 306.

O'Hara, Stephen (for Hometips.com), 16, 35 (bottom), 47, 49, 55, 62 (bottom), 65 (bottom), 67 (bottom), 81, 86, 87, 90, 95, 105, 108, 116, 152 (bottom), 154 (bottom), 171, 173, 221, 280, 283, 297, 311, 312, 315, 339, 371, 384, 441, 453, 455, 477, 485, 508, 516, 523, 534, 535.

Peerless Faucet Company, 428.

Pella Windows & Doors, 187.

Phifer Wire Products, 392.

Plate, Norman A., 226, 282, 374.

Rice, Kenneth, 37 (photos #7, #9).

Robbins Hardwood Flooring, 142.

Robern, 422 (bottom right).

Rutherford, Mark, 486, 496, 501, 503, 504, 507.

Southern Living, Inc. (©1989), 298.

Thibaut Wallcoverings & Fabrics, 72, 74, 92.

Vanden Brink, Brian (Brian Vanden Brink, Photographer) 8.

Vandervort, Don (Hometips.com) 18, 322.

Velux-Canada, Inc., 334.

Whiteley, Peter, 374.

Widstrand, Russ, 248.

Wolman Woodworx, 401.

Wong, Marcy, 10 (bottom inset).

Wyatt, Tom, 60 (all except top), 61, 62 (all steps), 63 (all steps), 64, 65 (all steps), 66 (all steps) 67 (all steps), 68, 69, 70 (all steps), 244 (ceramic tile, solid surfacing).

Zinsser/Bondex, 32, 78, 166.

DESIGN

10 (bottom): Architect: Marcy Li Wong.

11: Design: Osburn Design.

28: Architect: Bob Hull, The Miller/Hull Partnership.

46 (top): Design: Frog Hollow Interiors.

59: Peggy Del Rosario.

60 (top): Design: Osburn Design.

66 (top): Design: Tina Martinez.

70 (top): Design: Osburn Design; Decorative painting: Iris Potter.

114: Design: Sherry Faure of Faure Design and Lila Levinson of Accent on Design.

128: Architect: Morimoto Architects.

266: Architect: Bob Hull, The Miller/Hull Partnership.

298: Architect: Tony Unruh.

404: Architect: Backen, Arragoni & Ross; Design: Cia Foreman; Lighting design: Melinda Morrison.

466: Architect: Backen, Arragoni & Ross.

Index

Index

Index